OBSCURE RELIGIOUS CULTS

OBSCURE RELIGIOUS CULTS

AS BACKGROUND OF BENGALI LITERATURE

SHASHI BHUSHAN DASGUPTA

GYAN

Published by

GYAN

Gyan Publishing House
5, Ansari Road
Daryaganj, New Delhi-110002
Phone: 011-47034999, 9811692060
E-mail: books@gyanbooks.com

Distribution Network
gyanbooks.com
India, USA, Canada, UK, Australia

ISBN: 978-93-7316-606-3 (PB)

First Published, 1946

2nd Impression 2025

Printed at: Gyan Press, Delhi.

OBSCURE RELIGIOUS CULTS
Author: SHASHI BHUSHAN DASGUPTA

OBSCURE
RELIGIOUS CULTS

OBSCURE RELIGIOUS CULTS

BY

SHASHIBHUSAN DASGUPTA, M.A., PH.D.

Ramtanu Lahiri Professor and Head of the Department of Modern Indian Languages, University of Calcutta

FIRMA K. L. MUKHOPADHYAY

6/1A Banchharam Akrur Lane

Calcutta-12

TO

DR. SYAMAPRASAD MOOKERJEE

AS A TOKEN OF RESPECT AND ADMIRATION

CONTENTS

PAGES

CHAPTER V

THE VAIṢṆAVA SAHJIYĀ CULT

CHAPTER VI

A NON-SECTARIAN APPROACH TO THE DOCTRINES OF THE SAHAJIYĀS

CHAPTER VII

THE BĀULS OF BENGAL

PAGES

PART III

THE NĀTH CULT

CHAPTER VIII

LEGENDS AND HISTORY

CHAPTER IX

RELIGION OF THE NĀTH SIDDHAS

PART IV

THE DHARMA CULT AND BENGALI LITERATURE

CHAPTER X

PAGES

CHAPTER XI

CHAPTER XII

APPENDIX (B)

APPENDIX (C)

APPENDIX (D)

ABBREVIATIONS

B.N.	... Bibliotheque Nationale, Paris
B.S.P.	... Bengal Sāhitya-Pariṣat
B.S.P.P.	... Bengal Sāhitya-Pariṣat-Patrika
C.L.B.	... Central Library, Baroda
C.U.	... Calcutta University
Dhm.	... Dharma-maṅgala
G.O.S.	... Gaekwad's Oriental Series
J.A.S.B.	... Journal of the Asiatic Society of Bengal
J.D.L.	... Journal of the Department of Letters, Calcutta University
J.R.A.S.	... Journal of the Royal Asiatic Society
A.S.B.	... Asiatic Society of Bengal
Sj. S.	... Sahajiyā Sāhitya (ed. by Mr. M. Bose)

PREFACE TO THE FIRST EDITION

THE book represents the thesis of the author which was submitted by him in 1940 for the Degree of Doctor of Philosophy from the University of Calcutta. The book was written in 1939 and submitted to the Calcutta University Press for publication in 1941. A considerable portion of it was printed by the year 1942 and then the work of printing was indefinitely postponed for scarcity of paper caused by the Second World War. This will explain the long interval between the submission of the book to the press and the actual publication of it.

The aim of the present work is an expository study of the obscure religious cults that inspired Bengali literature in the old and the medieval times. Religion has always been one of the main motives of literature. It has been so in all countries and particularly in India which is pre-eminently a land of religion. As a matter of fact, the history of the modern Indian literatures is so intimately related with the history of some of the most important religious movements flourishing in this country that an intimate acquaintance with those religious movements seems indispensable for a thorough study of the vernacular literature.

But it is no use treading the beaten track. Some of the religious schools have already been discussed by scholars; some again are very simple so far as their theological standpoint is concerned. The mere introduction of a Pantheon in literature cannot be the subject of serious study unless the Pantheon in question admits of fruitful theological speculation. Instead of gleaning in the already harvested field or discussing the obvious, the writer has limited his scope by selecting the more obscure cults, which are noteworthy by nature and have inspired a considerable amount of literature, but the true nature of which has not yet been thoroughly discussed and clearly determined.

The Buddhist Sahajiyā cult has been the main source of inspiration of Bengali literature in the earliest period. By the discovery and publication of the songs and Dohās of the

Buddhist Sahajiyās, Mm. H. P. Śāstrī had, no doubt, done a memorable service not only to Bengali literature but to modern Indo-Aryan vernacular literatures as a whole; but the task of making a thorough study of the songs and Dohās in the light of the cults inspiring them had been left out by him. Dr. M. Shahidullah's *Les Chants Mystiques de Kānha et de Saraha* and Dr. N. C. Chaudhuri's *Dākārṇava* dwell more upon the linguistic than the literary and philosophical aspects of the Dohās. Dr. P. C. Bagchi, M.A., Dr. ès Lettres (Paris), in his occasional papers and articles, no doubt emphasises the doctrinal aspect of the Sahajiyās; but no comprehensive and critical study of the cult offering a consistent and connected interpretation of the songs and Dohās has yet been undertaken.

Similar is the case with the Vaiṣṇava Sahajiyā movement of Bengal. Mr. M. M. Bose, in his work *Post-Caitanya Sahajiyā Cult*, has, indeed, supplied us with valuable information regarding the literature of the Vaiṣṇava Sahajiyās and some of the doctrines and practices preached therein; but the *raison d'être* of the whole school and the process of evolution of this love religion from the ideology and methodology of the earlier Tāntric and Yogic sects remain unexplained.

The songs and Dohās of the Buddhist Sahajiyās have important bearing in spirit as well as in form and language on the songs and Dohās of many of the medieval saints, who flourished abundantly in many parts of India, and who, for reasons to be discussed later on, were mostly Sahajiyās in a wider sense. In a chapter on the Bāul-songs of Bengal the writer has dealt with the question of the relation between the earlier and the mediaeval Sahajiyās. He has also tried to show how on the spirit of a section of the Bāuls, who have stressed the conception of the 'Man of the heart,' Sūfī-istic Islam acted conjointly with the Upaniṣadic spirit ingrained in the different Sahajiyā movements as also with the Vaiṣṇavite spirit of love. In an appendix he has dealt at some length with the religious tenets of the non-Bengalee medieval saints of India in relation to those of the earlier Sahajiyās.

The nature and history of the Nāth cult, which has inspired a considerable amount of literature in Bengal as also in many other parts of India, is still shrouded in the mist of myths and legends. The stray articles found on the subject seem to be inadequate. Dr. Mohan Singh's work, *Gorakhnāth and Mediaeval Hindu Mysticism*, is hardly a sufficient exposition of the mystic religion of the sect. The recent work of Mr. Briggs, *Gorakhnāth and the Kānphaṭa Yogīs*, is a commendable accumulation of facts and traditions. But the distinctive feature of Nāthism remains hitherto unexplained. Hence there is ample scope for serious study in the practically unexplored field of Nāthism.

The Dharma cult of Bengal also invites attention. The cult is not theologically complex,—but it is queerly composite. Different conceptions of godhead have been confusedly amalgamated in the evolution of the Supreme Lord of this Dharma cult. The present writer has in this thesis passed over the simple practices, which are mainly aboriginal, but has centred his attention on analysing its composite nature.

The theory of cosmogony and cosmology, which is substantially the same in description in all the vernaculars notwithstanding small deviations of details, also demands serious attention. The tentative suggestions made by different scholars here and there about the nature and significance of this theory seem to be inadequate. The present writer has given a short exposition of the different versions of the theory as found in different types of vernacular literature, analysed ideas composing the main theory, and tried to trace their sources, Vedic, Purāṇic, Tāntric or otherwise.

The above, it is hoped, will give the reader an idea about the exact scope of the present work. To put it more briefly, the aim of the present work is a thorough study of the Buddhist Sahajiyā cult, the Vaiṣṇava Sahajiyā cult, the Bāul sect of Bengal and other mediaeval sects of India who may be called Sahajiyā in a general sense, the Nāth cult, the Dharma cult, and the cosmogonical and cosmological theories to be found in the Bengali literature of different periods. The author has thought it convenient not to distract the interest in the main contention by the occasional introduction of a mass of details, texts and stories; but as these informations cannot be altogether neglected without making the work defective, they have been included in the appendices.

In the following pages attempt has been made to make the study as thorough as possible from the religious and cultural points of view. This, it is hoped, will bring to the notice of the reader the obscure side-issues of Indian theological thought and esoteric religious practices. Whether congenial to our modern taste or not, the fact remains that these religious sects enjoyed, and some of them have still been enjoying, widespread popularity among the masses of India; it is for this reason that a critical study of these minor religious sects cannot be neglected in the history of Indian religious thought. It may easily be seen that the religious sects, with whom the present writer is dealing, represent mainly the religious views and practices of the masses of the country as opposed to the intelligentsia belonging to the higher classes. But to understand fully the civilisation and culture of a country as a whole we cannot do without a proper study of the mass-mind.

It may be added in this connection that in conducting the study the writer has tried throughout to be guided by the scientific spirit of a truth-seeker, neither defending the theories and practices of the schools, nor passing any personal judgment on them in respect of their merits. His main aim has been the correct exposition of the schools on textual basis, and the criticisms that are added are applied only to review the position from different angles of vision. The question of abuses and aberrations, which are to be found in a greater or lesser degree in the history of almost all the religious systems of the world, has been deliberately neglected; for it is the rationale of a cult or system and not its abuses and aberrations that have academic value.

The materials for the work are gathered from both published and unpublished sources. A good number of manuscripts of texts and commentaries has been utilised in the study of the Buddhist Sahajiyā cult; some of these texts are preserved in the University Library of Cambridge, some in the Bibliothèque Nationale of Paris, and some in the Central Library of Baroda,—and all these manuscripts were available to the writer in rotograph through the courtesy of Professor S. N. Dasgupta, M.A., Ph.D. (Cal.), Ph.D. (Cantab.), D.Lit. (Rome), the Indian Philosopher of international fame.

The indebtedness of the writer to Professor Dasgupta knows no bounds. The indebtedness is not only for the manuscripts which Professor Dasgupta was kind enough to procure for the writer but also for his ungrudging help and guidance which may be regarded as a rare boon to any student of Indian philosophy and literature. The rest of the manuscripts of Buddhistic texts are preserved in the Royal Asiatic Society of Bengal and the authorities of the institution deserve cordial thanks of the writer for giving him every facility to utilise them. As for the Bengali manuscripts, the author has consulted them in the Manuscript Library of the University of Calcutta and in the Vaṅgīya Sāhitya Pariṣat, Calcutta. The texts preserved in both the institutions being generally common, the manuscripts of the University Library have been referred to. The author records his deep sense of gratitude also to the authorities of these two institutions. The sources, whether published or unpublished, from which materials have been gathered, have been indicated everywhere in the form of foot-notes. To make his position clear and convincing, the author has sometimes quoted copiously in foot-notes, particularly when the sources are unpublished.

A few words must be added in connection with the method of transcription. In transcribing Sanskrit the commonly accepted device of diacritical marks has been adopted. The language of the Dohās being unanimously accepted to be Western Apabhraṃśa, the propriety of the use of 'j' to the exclusion of 'y' and the use of 's' to the exclusion of 'ś' or 'ṣ' cannot be questioned. But difficulty arises in the choice between 'b' and 'v'. With the advice of Dr. S. K. Chatterji, M.A., D.Lit., the writer has used 'v' all along in the transcription of the Dohās and 'b' initially and 'v' medially and finally in the transcription of Bengali songs. Another point to be noticed is that the phonology of modern Bengali, as also of many other modern Indo-Aryan vernaculars, seldom allows the retention of final vowels, and the medial vowel also drops when the word is composed of more than two syllables; but the dropping is never indicated in orthography. The writer has dropped the medial and final vowels in orthography, where they are dropped in actual pronunciation. The principle of transcription has often been adopted in transcribing the proper names, but rigorous consistency could not be maintained in this matter, as many of the Indian names have already been naturalised in English. Corruptions and mistakes in the spelling of old and middle Bengali texts have never been interfered with. For typographical difficulties nasalisation of vowels had to be indicated by the addition of 'ṃ' with the vowels. The writer begs to draw the attention of the reader to another important point. He has found many mistakes and corruptions in the reading of the manuscripts, both Sanskrit and Bengali. These also have not been freely handled unless the mistake or the corruption has been apparent.

In fine, the writer acknowledges his debt to Professor Rai K. N. Mitra, M.A., Bahadur, late Ramtanu Lahiri Professor of Bengali, Calcutta University, under whom he had the privilege of working as the Ramtanu Lahiri Research Assistant of the Calcutta University for about four years, and under whose affectionate care the present work was prepared. The writer records his deep sense of gratitude towards his examiners, particularly to Mahāmahopādhyaya Gopināth Kavirāj, M.A., of Benares, in whom the author has discovered a prodigy of Oriental Learning. His valuable suggestions on various topics have substantially helped the writer in revising some of the chapters of his book. In Dr. Syamaprasad Mookerjee, M.A., D.Litt., Barrister-at-Law, President, Post-Graduate Council of Teaching in Arts, University of Calcutta, the writer found a never-failing source of inspiration. In spite of the multifarious duties he has to attend to in the wider sphere of his life, he remains a true patron of learning, and the author deems it a privilege to have the name of the great man associated with his book.

S. B. Dasgupta

PREFACE TO THE SECOND EDITION

As it will appear from the preface to the first edition, the present book had been written in 1939; its publication by the University of Calcutta was delayed till 1946 because of the scarcity of paper caused by the World War II. The book was out of print by 1951; pre-occupations of the author were again responsible for the delay in handing the manuscript of the second edition over to the press after making necessary revision. Enthusiasm on the part of Firma K. L. Mukhopadhyay, the publishers of the present edition, was an active encouragement for the author.

A number of important books have been written and published during the last twenty years on the topics dealt with by the author in the present book. Some of these books present more facts and a more detailed study of some of the aspects. So far as the Buddhist Sahajiyā Cult is concerned the book, *Studies in the Tantras*, by Dr. P. C. Bagchi, M.A., Dr. ès. Lettres (Calcutta, 1939) throws sufficient light on some of the technical points. The *Doha-kośa* of Saraha-pāda critically edited with the help of Tibetan translation by Pandit Rāhul Sāṃkṛtyāyana is a scholarly textual study. The book (in Hindi) contains a Hindi translation of all the *Dohās* as also a good introduction dealing with the doctrines of the Buddhist Sahajiyās. So far as textual study in the field of Tāntric Buddhism is concerned the critical studies of the important Buddhist Tantric text, the *Hevajra-tantra*, by Mr. D. L. Snellgrove, Lecturer in Tibetan, School of Oriental and African Studies, London, (in two volumes, London, 1959) deserves respectful mention. The book *An Introduction To Tāntric Buddhism* by the present author (first published in Calcutta in 1950 and reprinted in Calcutta in 1958) presents an exposition of the Tāntric background of the Buddhist Sahajiyā cult. *Yuganaddha: or The Tantric View of Life* by Herbert V. Guenther (Banaras, 1952) is a commendable attempt at understanding the deeper implications of the principle of *Yuganaddha* or union or non-duality, much too spoken of by the esoteric Buddhists. *Siddha-sāhitya* (in Hindi, Allahabad, 1955) by Dr. Dharmavir Bharati, M.A., D.Phil. is interesting in understanding the inter-relation between the various Siddha Cults including the later ramifications.

So far as the Bāul sect is concerned, two books, one *Bāṃlār Bāul O Bāul Gān* (in Bengali, Calcutta, 1957) by Dr. Upendranath Bhattacharya, M.A., D.Phil., and the other *Bāṃlār Bāul* (in Bengali, Calcutta, 1954) by Pandit Kṣiti-mohan Sen, are commendable studies from different angles of view. On the Nāth cult there has been an attempt at a comprehensive study by Dr. Kalyani Mallick, M.A., Ph.D., in her book *Nāthasampradāyer Itihās, Darśan O Sādhana-praṇālī* (in Bengali, Calcutta 1950). *Gorakh-bāni*, an anthology of old Hindi songs ascribed to Gorakh-nāth, collected, critically edited and scholarly annotated by Dr. P. D. Barthwal, M.A., D.Litt., brought into light a large quantity of fresh materials for a study of the doctrines and practices of the Nāth Siddhas. Professor Hazari Prasad Dvivedi's book on *Nātha-sampradāya* (in Hindi, Allahabad, 1955) is also a commendable book on the subject. With regard to the Dharma cult of Bengal the long chapters devoted to the study of the Bengali Dharma-maṅgals in the book, *Bāṃlā Maṅgal-Kāvyer Itihās*, (in Bengali, Calcutta, third edition 1958) by Dr. Asutosh Bhattacharya, M.A., Ph.D., contains a study of the history of the cult as also a study of the ritualistic details.

It has been gratifying to the author to find that though the new publications throw new light on different points and supply new information they do not assail the views held and explained in his book. They have, therefore, been referred to in the contexts where they will be of profit and interest to the reader. The author has himself undoubtedly profited by them in making revision here and there.

The author expresses his gratitude to all scholars, Indian and foreign, who have encouraged him by their long reviews in respectable journals and periodicals and also by sending their opinion in personal letters. Such reviews and opinions are the best reward that a humble worker in the field can expect. He again counts on such sympathetic understanding in bringing out this revised second edition of the book. Mr. Nirodeprasad Nath, M.A., a pupil of the author, has helped him in preparing the index.

S. B. DASGUPTA

INTRODUCTION

THE origin and growth of the modern Indian literatures (we mean the modern Indo-Aryan literatures) are closely associated with the origin and growth of some religious sects, which began to stir the life of the people from about the tenth century onwards. Up till the advent of the nineteenth century with a new outlook on life and literature, none of the Indo-Aryan literatures seem to have had the capacity to stand erect without the prop of some religious view, and this again seems to be particularly the case with Bengali. We have no type of literature in Bengali even corresponding to the *Rāsau* literature (literature based on the annals of heroic episodes) of Hindi, and poets like Cānd Bardāi or Bhūṣaṇ and Lāl are almost unknown in old and medieval Bengali. In our old and medieval[1] literature man's glory is seldom depicted in its own grandeur and eulogised independently of divine glory. The versions of the *Rāmāyaṇa* and the *Mahābhārata* that we have in our literature possess a vein more religious than human; the heroes and heroines of the various Maṅgala-Kāvyas are depicted more as toys in the hands of the gods and goddesses than as dignified figures glowing with the heroic grandeur of their personality. Lāusen of the Dharma-maṅgalas is a mere agent of the Dharma-ṭhākura, Kālaketu of the Caṇḍī-maṅgalas is originally a god, being the son of Indra, and is dragged down from heaven on earth only to glorify the almighty power of goddess Caṇḍī and to establish her worship on earth. The human interest of the life-long struggle of Cānd Sadāgar of the Manasā-maṅgalas has been minimised by the undercurrent of the religious tone—by the fact that it really represents the struggle of decaying Śaivism of Bengal against the growth and spread of Śāktaism represented by the Manasā cult. During the long period, beginning with the Caryā-padas of the tenth, eleventh or twelfth century, the only type of literature that may be said to be free from the

[1] The word 'medieval' will mean throughout our discussions as belonging to the middle period of the Modern Indo-Aryan literatures, *i.e.* belonging to the period roughly between the thirteenth and the eighteenth century A.D.

influence of religion, is the ballad literature of Bengal dealing purely and simply with the diversified life of rural Bengal and pastoral love-episodes.[1]

Apart from the general relation of literature with religion and apart from the fact that Bengal is a province of India, which is specially noted as a land of religion and philosophy, there seems to be some historical reason for such predominance of religion in Bengali literature. Deep unrest is sometimes caused by social and political vicissitudes of a nation and the common man finds himself face to face with the stern realities which may help the growth and development of his personality. It is through the continual struggle for existence, fight against the adverse circumstances, conflict with the external powers that a nation becomes conscious of her real worth and learns to hold in high esteem the glories of terrestrial life. The paucity of such noteworthy social or political events happening in the life of Bengal may account for the fact that the history of Bengali literature during its old and medieval period is practically the same as the history of the different religious movements that flourished in the province for about a decade of centuries.[2] Even in the nineteenth century the general practice was to borrow stories either from the *Rāmāyaṇa* and the *Mahābhārata* or from the annals of the Rājputs, Sikhs and Mārhāṭṭās to introduce heroic grandeur in the epics, novels and dramas.

There is a striking uniformity in the historical development of the different literatures of the modern Indo-Aryan vernaculars. The reason behind this fact is that the literary history of almost all the vernaculars is moulded essentially by the religious movements in the different parts of India,

[1] It should be noted that the authenticity of many of the East Bengal ballads, as compiled by Dr. D. C. Sen, D.Litt., in collaboration with Candra Kumar De and some other assistants and published by the University of Calcutta, has been questioned. We have no scope here to enter into the details of the controversy; but our considered opinion on the point is that though the ballads may not belong to a hoary past (as Dr. Sen holds), and though there may be some handling of the verses at the time of collection and compilation, at least the skeleton of some of these verses surely belongs to the seventeenth and the eighteenth centuries and some go even earlier.

[2] Of course, in the *Caitanya-bhāgavata* of Vṛndāvan-dās we find reference to the songs of Yogi-pāl, Bhogi-pāl (*cf. yogīpāl bhogīpāl mahīpāl gīta* I *ihā śunite sav lok ānandita* II). Some are of opinion that these songs deal with the life and glory of the Pāla Kings,—but we cannot say anything about them as long as the songs are not discovered.

which, during the old and the medieval periods were strikingly similar.

Bengali, along with other modern Indo-Aryan languages, grew up with the tenets of some minor religious sects, which rose mostly outside the circle of the upper-class people and were characterised by a general tendency of protest against current orthodox religious systems. These religious movements were sponsored by people who had no aristocracy of blood or advantage of culture and education; they rose mostly from among the ranks and preached their doctrines among the masses in their own tongue. The modern Indo-Aryan literatures, as we have indicated in the preface, are, therefore, essentially mass-literature and the religions preached through them represent the mass-religions of India. But this religious zeal of the masses has been responsible for the copious growth of the vernacular literature in spite of the derision and opposition of the elite, who sometimes threatened these revolutionaries with curses of hell.

The history of Bengali language and literature, so far as it has been explored, begins with the religious doctrines and practices of the Sahajiyā Buddhists. Sahajiyā Buddhism is a particular development of a phase of later Buddhism, widely known as Tāntric Buddhism. Investigation reveals that during the reign of the Pāla dynasty Buddhism in various Tāntric forms gained popularity in Bengal and many Tāntric texts and commentaries were written in the different Buddhist monasteries that were established in Bengal. The authors of the Sahajiyā Buddhistic songs were mostly inhabitants of Bengal or adjoining areas.[1]

But though an offshoot of popular Buddhism, the real origin of the Buddhist Sahajiyā cult is not to be traced exclusively or even mainly in any of the theories and practices of Buddhism proper either in its Hīnayāna or Mahāyāna aspect. The real origin of the cult lies more outside Buddhism than inside it. The Buddhist Sahajiyā cult, notwithstanding the Buddhistic tone and colour which it assumes, is essentially an esoteric yogic cult. Side by side with the commonly known theological speculations and religious practices there has been flowing in India an important

[1] *Vide infra*, Ch. I.

religious undercurrent of esoteric yogic practices from a pretty old time; these esoteric practices, when associated with the theological speculations of the Śaivas and the Śāktas, have given rise to Śaiva and Śākta Tāntricism; when associated with the Buddhistic speculations, have given rise to the composite religious system of Buddhist Tāntricism; and again, when associated with the speculations of Bengal Vaiṣṇavism the same esoteric practices have been responsible for the growth of the esoteric Vaiṣṇavite cult, known as the the Vaiṣṇava Sahajiyā movement.

It will not be out of place to give here just an idea of the speculations and practices, round which grew all the esoteric schools either within Hinduism or Buddhism. All kinds of esoteric Sādhanā (*i.e.*, religious endeavours) of India have a common background. In all the esoteric schools the absolute reality is conceived of possessing in its nature the potency of two aspects or attributes. These two aspects or attributes are, again, conceived as the negative and the positive, the static and the dynamic, rest (*nivṛtti*) and activity (*pravṛtti*),—the principle of pure consciousness and the principle of activity;—one represents subjectivity and the other objectivity; and, again, the one is conceived as the enjoyer and the other as the enjoyed. In the absolute Being these two aspects lie unified together in a state of absolute non-duality; but in the process of becoming or phenomenalisation there comes separation and duality. This process of change or becoming through a state of duality is bondage and suffering,—and the final escape from it is liberation. The secret of all esoteric Sādhanā is to destroy all principles of dualism and to attain the final state of non-duality. This ultimate state of non-duality is variously called in the different esoteric systems as the state of *Advaya*, *Maithuna*, *Yuganaddha*, *Yāmala*, *Sama-rasa*, *Yugala*, or the *Sahaja-samādhi*, or simply the final state of Samādhi.

In Hindu Tāntricism these two aspects of the absolute reality have been conceived as the Śiva and the Śakti, or the primordial male and the female. Again, one of the fundamental tenets of all the esoteric schools is to hold that the human body is the epitome of the universe, all 'truth' (*tattva*) is contained within the body. Consistent with this view it has been held that Śiva resides in the Sahasrāra (the lotus of thousand petals situated in the cerebrum region) as the principle of pure consciousness and Śakti as the principle of world-force resides in the other pole of the Mulādhāra-cakra in the form of the coiled serpent. Now, the Sādhanā consists in raising the coiled force from the one pole to the other and to unite her there with Śiva,—and this union of the Śiva and the Śakti produces the state of the absolute. Thus the principles of Śiva-Śakti or the male and the female are contained within the person of every man and woman.

Again it has been held that the principles of the male and the female are contained within the body of a man in the right and the left respectively,—the right half being the masculine part and the left half the feminine part. This will explain the conception of Mahādeva or Śiva as *Ardhanārīśvara* or the half-female and half-male deity, and in the sculptural or pictorial representation of the *Ardhanārīśvara* the deity is always depicted as having the left half as the female and the right half as the male.[1] Thus, there are principles of masculinity and femininity contained in every man and woman,—a man is a man because of the predominance in him of the principle of masculinity, whereas a woman is a woman because of the predominance of the principle of femininity in her. Now as the left and the right represent two aspects of the absolute reality, the two important nerves in the left and the right, *viz.*, Iḍā and Piṅgalā, and the two courses of the vital wind, Prāṇa and Apāna, associated with the two nerves, are also associated with these two aspects of the ultimate reality. From this theory follows the Sādhanā of controlling the courses of the vital wind in the two nerves and of making them flow together through the middle nerve Suṣumnā. Thus the union of the right and the left through the union of the two courses of the vital wind within the middle nerve Suṣumnā, is the vital part of the Sādhanā of Haṭha-yoga, and the state that

[1] It may be pointed out that in the Sahajiyā school of Vaiṣṇavism also Rādhā and Kṛṣṇa are said to reside in the left and the right respectively; Rādhā is often said to reside in the left eye and Kṛṣṇa in the right. *Cf. bāme rādhā dāhine kṛṣṇa dekha rasik jan* । . . . .*dui netre birājamān* । *rādhā-kuṇḍa dui netra hay* । *sajal nayan dvāre bhāve preme āsvāday* ॥
Sahaja-tattva of Rādhāvallabh Dās, *Vaṅga-sāhitya-paricay*, Vol. II, p. 1658.

is attainable through such a process is the state of final non-duality.

Again it has been held, particularly in the Tāntric and the Sahajiyā schools, that the division of the creatures of the world into the male and the female has an ontological reason behind it. The male and the female represent in the visible world the division which is present in the nature of the absolute as Śiva and Śakti, and the perfect union of the Śiva and the Śakti is the highest reality. Within the physical body of man and woman reside the ontological principles of Śiva and Śakti[1]; therefore to realise the absolute truth, or in other words, to obtain the highest spiritual experience, man and woman must first of all realise themselves as manifestation of Śiva and Śakti and unite together physically, mentally and spiritually, and the supreme bliss that proceeds from such union is the highest religious gain. Such a view is the *raison d'être* of all the esoteric Sādhanā which are carried on by the male and the female together.

As a school of esoteric yoga the Buddhist Sahajiyā school is fundamentally based on the speculations explained above. The Absolute is the Sahaja—it is the ultimate reality behind the self and the not-self. The realisation of this Sahaja in and through the self and the not-self is the ultimate aim of the Sahajiyās. Now, in Sahajiyā Buddhism Śūnyatā (void) and Karuṇā (compassion), transformed as the Prajñā and the Upāya, are held to be the two primary attributes of the ultimate reality which is Sahaja. As two aspects of the ultimate reality Prajñā and Upāya are conceived in the Buddhist Tantras and in Sahajiyā Buddhism just as Śakti and Śiva of the Hindu Tāntric school. Prajñā and Upāya thus represent the principles of dualism and the unification of the two in a supreme non-dual state is the final aim of the Buddhist Sahajiyās. The practical yogic method for the realisation of the Sahaja is, therefore, fundamentally based on the principle of the union of Prajñā and Upāya. The union of Prajñā means, in the first place, the union of the female and the male, who are considered to be the manifestations of Prajñā and Upāya respectively. Again, we have seen that the two important nerves in the left and

[1] *Vide infra*, Ch. V.

the right also represent the principles of Prajñā and Upāya in the microcosm of the human body; therefore the union of the two implies the perfect control over these two nerves and the vital process associated with them and to make them function unitedly through the middle nerve which represents the principle of non-duality. The yogic practice involving this physical and physiological union of the Prajñā and the Upāya will lead the yogin to the inner union of the Prajñā and the Upāya. Upāya as the Lord (called Vajrasattva, or the principle of immutable adamantine existence) resides in the highest pole of the cerebrum region and Prajñā as the world-force[1] resides in the lowest pole (which is the plexus in the navel according to the esoteric Buddhists); the inner union consists in the raising of the Goddess from the navel region and in making her unite with the Lord of the cerebrum region.

In the Vaiṣṇava Sahajiyā school the two aspects of Sahaja or the absolute reality are explained as the eternal enjoyer and the enjoyed, as Kṛṣṇa and Rādhā; and it is further held that all men and women are physical manifestations of the ontological principles of Kṛṣṇa and Rādhā. When men and women can, therefore, realise themselves as the manifestations of Kṛṣṇa and Rādhā through a process of attribution (*Āropa*), the love of any human couple becomes transformed into the divine love that is eternally flowing on between Kṛṣṇa and Rādhā; when the union of a human couple thus becomes the union of Kṛṣṇa and Rādhā, the highest spiritual realisation dawns in the state of union or *Yugala*. The element of love is the innovation of the Vaiṣṇava Sahajiyā school; but this element of love is essentially based on the element of yoga in the form of physical and psychological discipline.

In the Nāth cult, which seems to be synchronous with the Buddhist Sahajiyā movement (though the origin of the cult may be much earlier), the two aspects of the absolute

[1] We may notice here a great anomaly. In Tāntric Buddhism the Lord as Upāya always represents the principle of phenomenalism and the consort Prajñā is generally depicted as the principle of rest or void; but in the conception of the world-force, we shall see later on, the order was reversed and Prajñā or Nairātmā herself, as associated with the principle of defilement, was conceived as the Śakti or the world-force.

reality are represented by the Sun and the Moon, where the Sun represents the principle of destruction (*kālāgni*) through the process of change and decay,—and the Moon represents the principle of immutability. The final aim of the Nāth Siddhas is the attainment of a non-dual state through the attainment of immortality in a perfect or divine body. This non-dual state of immortality can be attained only through the union or rather the commingling of the Sun and the Moon. In its speculations on the attainment of an immutable and divine body through psycho-chemical process of Haṭha-yoga involving the theory of the Sun and the Moon, the Nāth cult seems to be akin to the Rasāyana school of Indian thought, the main difference being that the medical and chemical science of the Rāsayana school became transformed into a psycho-chemical yogic science with the Nāth Siddhas.

It may, however, be noted in this connection that though the culture of the body (*kāya-sādhana*) through processes of Haṭha-yoga for the attainment of physical perfection, was of paramount importance in the Nāth cult, it was more or less common to all the esoteric schools including the school of Vaiṣṇava Sahajiyā which laid emphasis on love. The realisation of Sahaja either of the nature of 'supreme bliss' (*Māha-sukha*) as is understood by the Buddhist Sahajiyās, or of the nature of 'supreme love' (as is conceived by the Vaiṣṇava Sahajiyās), presupposes the strength of the physical organism to stand such a supreme realisation. It is for this reason that we shall find that all the esoteric schools spoke of the culture of body through some Haṭha-yogic practice.

Thus it is clear from the above that all the esoteric schools of India are fundamentally based on the speculation on the two aspects in which the ultimate reality functions and manifests itself,—and that the religious creed is based on the final aim of the attainment of a state of non-duality. It is to be noticed that this idea of unity of the esoteric systems implies no process of negation; it, on the other hand, implies a process of supreme position through a regressive process of transformation and transubstantiation. It is for this reason that all the schools of Tantra speak of the final state as a state where enjoyment and liberation have become one and the same. The process of *Āropa* which makes the ultimate union possible is not peculiar to the Vaiṣṇava Sahajiyās only,—it is a process common to all the Tāntric and Sahajiyā schools, either Hindu or Buddhist. We shall see later on that this process of *Āropa* implies no negation; it implies a change of perspective where the physical existence is not denied, but replaced by a permanent spiritual existence, where the gulf between the physical and the ontological is bridged over in an absolute existence. The Tāntric Buddhists have also repeatedly emphasised that the final state is not a state of *Nirvāṇa* as it is not also a state of *Bhava* (existence); but neither the *Bhava* nor the *Nirvāṇa* is denied it,—it is a state where *Bhava* and *Nirvāṇa* become united together in the realisation of the absolute.

Closely associated with the religious literature of the different Sahajiyā movements of Bengal is the literature of the Bāuls. The Bāuls as a religious sect are characterised by their peculiarly unconventional manners and customs in social as well as religious life. From this point of view the followers of the Vaiṣṇava Sahajiyā school and religious people much akin to such an order bear the general name of Bāul. But the Bāul songs, which are composed by illiterate masses from both the Hindu and the Muslim communities, and which are familiar to us with the theory of the 'Man of the heart' and man's love towards him, have a distinctive feature of their own. This 'Man of the heart' is the Divine in man and stands as the eternal Beloved in relation to the human personality, who is the crazy lover. Such songs of the Bāuls and similar songs of the medieval saints of Northern, Central and Upper India, represent the spirit of Sūfī-ism against the background of Indian thoughts.

The Dharma cult of Bengal and of some parts of Orissa is, as we have said in the preface, a local cult having no element of esoterism in it; as a religion it consists of extremely popular rites and ceremonies. The literature belonging to the cult embodies the infiltration and transformation of various religious ideas in the untrained mind of the masses. The cosmogonical and cosmological theories also represent popular jumbling of various older ideas received through various sources.

As all the above-mentioned obscure religious cults will come directly within the purview of our present study, we need not enter into any further details here. It will not be out of place, we think, to add here a brief outline of the other religious movements which have been strong factors in the evolution of Bengali literature as a whole and which will not directly come within the province of our present study because of the reasons adduced in the preface.

The devotional movement in Bengal, as is the case in other provinces also, has given great impetus to our literature, and the beautiful literary fragments, which are extant, can be found abundantly in the love-lyrics of the Vaiṣṇava poets. Caṇḍī-dās, Govinda-dās, Jñāna-dās, among the host of Vaiṣṇava poets, undoubtedly deserve world-wide recognition as first-rate poets. Though we have a fair amount of Rāmāyaṇic literature in Bengali and though a deep religious vein runs through many of them, the Rāma cult could not gain sufficient ground as a religious faith in Bengal, it being pushed to the corner by the Kṛṣṇa cult. The Vaiṣṇava movement of Bengal, in the line of the Kṛṣṇa cult, grew along with the traditions of the Purāṇas like the *Bhāgavata-purāṇa*, *Viṣṇu-purāṇa*, *Brahma-vaivarta-purāṇa*, etc., and there was perhaps, through the life of Caitanya and some renowned Gosvāmīs, some influence also of the devotional movement of the South.[1] The first literary record of Bengal Vaiṣṇavism is to be found in the famous lyrical poem the *Gīta-govinda* of Jaya-deva. After him Caṇḍī-dās and Vidyāpati (who, though a Maithili poet, was more popular in Bengal than in his native province) sang the immortal songs of the eternal love of Rādhā-Kṛṣṇa, and were precursors, as some scholars are disposd to think, of Śrī-Caitanya, who flourished about a century later and brought with him a devotional movement, which for a long time overflooded Bengal and some of the neighbouring provinces. Vaiṣṇavite apostles like Mādhavendra-purī, Advaitācārya Śrīvāsa and others, of course, flourished just before the advent of Caitanya,—but the advent of Caitanya was some-

[1] See an article, *Bhakti-dharmer Vivartan*, by the present writer in the *Bhārata-varṣa*, Caitra, B.S., 1343. See also an article, *Prem-dharma*, by K. N. Mitra, *Udayan*, B.S., 1341, Agrahāyaṇa.

thing like a fruition of all their devotional penances, and it was an event which was really epoch-making in the religion and literature of Bengal. Caitanya, as he is interpreted by his followers, embodies in him the quintessence of both Rādhā and Kṛṣṇa, and is both the realiser and the realised in the same personality.

Through his life and teachings Caitanya preached a doctrine of divine love, which was philosophically systematised and theologically codified by the six Gosvāmīs of Vṛndāvana, *viz.*, Rūpa, Sanātana, Raghunāth Dās, Raghunāth Bhaṭṭa, Gopāla Bhaṭṭa and Jīva Gosvāmī. The philosophical and theological system known as Gauḍīya Vaiṣṇavism (*i.e.*, the Vaiṣṇavism of Bengal) is really the contribution of these six Gosvāmīs, who were all religious apostles inspired by the life and teachings of Caitanya. Pre-Caitanya Vaiṣṇavism of Bengal generally flourished with the legends of Kṛṣṇa and his dalliances with the cowherd girls of Vṛndāvana and particularly with Rādhā; but in Post-Caitanya Vaiṣṇavism the divinity of Caitanya as the synthesis of the two aspects of the same reality as the lover and the beloved was recognised and emphasised, and as a result thereof Post-Caitanya Vaiṣṇava literature laid the same stress, if not more, on the life and teachings of Caitanya as on the legends of Rādhā and Kṛṣṇa.

The other two important cults that have influenced Bengali literature almost from the beginning are the Śaiva and the Śākta cults. So far as the religious history of Bengal is concerned, of the two, Śaivism seems to be the older and the Śākta cults, which are more often indigenous than Purāṇic, sprang up later in strong opposition to the former. In our literary records we find the Śākta cults often at daggers drawn with the cults that centred round the male deities. In this conflict with the other systems, particularly with the Śākta systems, Śaivism, the religion centring round the most indifferent and inactive god, had to give way and the Śākta cults gradually gained ground. This conflict seems to have resolved itself in another way in a synthetic transformation in the Rādhā-Kṛṣṇa cult of Bengal.

If we take a bird's eye view of the religious history of Bengal as a whole it will appear that among the Hindu deities Śiva enjoyed wide popularity in the early and medieval period. In the preliminary chapter of some of the Dharma-maṅgalas, which belong to the seventeenth and the eighteenth century, we find salutation to all the male and female deities of Bengal and also an enumeration of the localities where they were popular.[1] A general consideration of these lists of the gods and goddesses of Bengal will reveal the extent of the popularity that Lord Śiva enjoyed in Bengal even up to the eighteenth century. It is also to be noticed that though in the Dharma-maṅgala literature we find Dharma-ṭhākura identified more with Kṛṣṇa and Rāma, yet in religious practice the Dharma cult has got itself amalgamated more with Śaivism. It will also appear from a perusal of the different kinds of Bengali Maṅgala-kāvyas (which are practically propaganda literature belonging to the different religious schools) that the different Śākta cults of Bengal presuppose a Śaivite background, against which they thrived, though their origin might have been earlier.

Śiva of Bengal, at least as found depicted in Bengali literature, is not exactly the same Śiva with whom we are acquainted in the Brahminical literature, particularly in the Purāṇas. The indigenous elements of Bengalee life and culture have supplied flesh and blood to his Brahminic skeleton and made him into a typical Bengalee Śiva of the period between the tenth and the fourteenth century really represents much of the Lord Supreme of Tāntric Buddhism as indiscriminately mixed up with the ancient Lord of India. Śiva of the later period, as depicted in relation to his troublesome family, composed of two sons, two daughters and a wife, represents, through his wild mode of life and unscrupulous activities, a vivid picture of some of the aspects of the social life of medieval Bengal. In almost all the literatures belonging to this religious school, human interest of the family-life of Śiva far outweighs the interest of his divine nature, and in this indigenous character of Śiva the Purāṇic elements have been set here and there with

[1] See *Dharma Vandanā*, MS, preserved in the Bengali Manuscript Library of the Calcutta University, No. 2470. Also see the first chapter of the *Dharma-maṅgalas* by Māṇik Gāṅguli, Rām-dās Ādak and others.

the avowed purpose of giving it a Purāṇic colouring. The literature of the Śaivite cult consists chiefly of the *Śivāyanas*, which deal with the peculiar life and activities of lord Śiva, particularly in relation to his family. Like the Śaivite devotional lyrics of the South or even like the few songs on Hara-Gaurī (*i.e.*, Śiva and his wife) composed by Vidyāpati of Mithilā, we have no Śaivite devotional lyric in Bengali. A large portion of fragmentary literature concerning Śiva is, however, to be culled from the Maṅgala-kāvyas belonging to the Dharma cult and particularly to the Caṇḍī and the Manasā cults.

The Śākta cults of Bengal represent a particularly distinctive feature of the religious life of Bengal and the extent of literature which flourished under the direct influence of those cults is also fairly large. We do not know of any such Śākta influence in the religion and literature of any other province of India excepting Malabar. The Śākta literature of Bengal generally belongs to the type of Maṅgala literature, which, as we have said, is the literature of religious propaganda. Among the Sākta cults, the more important are the cults of Caṇḍī (or Kālī or Kālikā), the consort of Lord Śiva, and the cult of Manasā, the serpent goddess. We have also Maṅgala-kāvyas belonging to the cult of goddess Śītalā (the goddess of the direful small pox), Kamalā or Lakṣmī (the goddess of wealth), Ṣaṣṭhī (the goddess believed to be in charge of the welfare of children) and others, but the literature belonging to such cults is comparatively negligible both in quality and in quantity.

The Maṅgala literature of Bengal is a continuation in vernacular of the religious literature in Sanskrit, generally known as the Purāṇic literature. The Sanskrit Pūraṇas are sometimes infused with a spirit of propaganda on behalf of some half-indigenous and half-traditional religious cult and there is the spirit of glorifying some of the gods and goddesses with the help of a huge network of stories which bear testimony to their irresistible divine power and thus make them acceptable to the Brahminical people. The same spirit is found in the Maṅgala-kāvyas of Bengal, which launched vigorous and continuous propaganda on behalf of some god or goddess in question with reference to various episodes where he or she had the supreme power to save the devotee from all sorts of dangers and difficulties and to bring destruction to all who opposed his or her supremacy. These gods and goddesses of the Maṅgala-kāvyas, in spite of their Purāṇic garb, are often indigenous in nature. Naturally, therefore, when the worship of these gods and goddesses began to be introduced in the society at large their divinity was questioned and the move for the introduction of their worship was strongly resisted by different sections of people. The followers of these gods and goddesses had, therefore, to justify, in keen competition with their rivals, the divinity of the deity in question and the legitimacy of his or her claim for worship on earth; and this will explain the origin of our Maṅgala literature. But it is to be observed that, after once this literary form could gain sufficient currency and popularity, it became ere long more or less a literary convention. It cannot be said with a sufficient degree of certainty that Mukunda-rām, the greatest among the poets of the Caṇḍī-maṅgalas, was a devotee of Caṇḍī or that Bhārata-candra, practically the last and most secular of the poets of the Maṅgala literature, was a sincere devotee of Annadā. Religious garb was rather a device in medieval literature to make literature acceptable to the masses, who were prompted to listen to these literary works more with a religious fervour than with a literary taste.

Maṅgala literature may be said to have its origin in the fourteenth century, but it developed in the sixteenth and seventeenth centuries, after which the old literary convention fell into disuse and literature began to flourish with a new spirit and form. Up till the last quarter of the eighteenth century, Śākta literature consisted exclusively of the different Maṅgala-kāvyas; but by the last quarter of the eighteenth century a new type of Śākta literature flourished in the form of fine devotional lyrics mainly on Śyāmā or Kālī (popularly known as *Śyāmā-saṅgīt* or songs on Śyāmā, the universal Mother of dark-blue colour) and sometimes also on Umā, or Gaurī, the daughter of the mountain Himalaya, and the young wife of the old, wild and indifferent husband Śiva. Rāmprasād Sen of the eighteenth century, the greatest devotee of the Mother, a devotee of the most unassuming and non-sectarian type, may be taken to be the representative poet of this school. About a century later Rāma-kṛṣṇa Parama-haṃsa of Dakṣiṇeśvara, through his most devoted life and his sweet and simple teachings, gave a new impetus to this cult, and the literature of the Rāma-kṛṣṇa cult should never go unnoticed in the history of our literature. Śrī Aurabindo of Pondicherry again gave a new orientation to the Mother cult and inspired occasional lyrics on the line.

In surveying the general trends of the religious history of Bengal in particular relation to the history of Bengali literature, we cannot neglect the influence which the great religion of Islam exerted on the religion and literature of Bengal. The Mahomedans first came to the land as a conquering nation; but after they had settled here and became natives of the land and succeeded in making a large number of converts, their religious thoughts and ideas began to influence those of their neighbours; and at the same time the thoughts and ideas of their neighbours also began to affect and modify theirs in their turn. Some sort of a compromise between the religious ideas and practices of popular Islam and popular Hinduism evolved in the rank and file of the two communities through a slow and gradual process of cultural reciprocation. Islam of Bengal is rather Sūfī-istic Islam and the influence of this Sūfī-ism on the Indian religious movements is best exhibited in the songs of the Bāuls. Besides these, the divinities like Satya-pīr, Māṇik-pīr, Gāji and others of popular Islam represent the continuity of the process of a happy admixture of elements both from Islam and Hinduism. About the influence of Islam on the Dharma cult we shall have detailed discussion in our study of the Dharma cult.

The popular religious ceremonies of women-folk, particularly of the maidens, have also supplied us with nice pieces of folk literature. The ceremonies, of which there are a good number of varieties, are generally known as the *Vratas* (vows) and are accompanied by the recitation of rhymed or unrhymed verses (generally known as the *Vrata-kathā*) which contain fine touches of rural poetry. In the performance of these ceremonies there is always an element of art,—either the art of poetry or the art of painting. These *Vratas* are still adding a subconscious aesthetic pleasure to the conscious religious sentiment of the women-folk of Bengal.

The nineteenth century dawned with a new ideal of life, religion and literature. The spirit, form and technique of the old and medieval literature, flourishing up to the end of the eighteenth century, grew hopelessly monotonous and roused a subconscious feeling of dissatisfaction in the mind of the people and also an inward demand for a change; and a change was inevitable in the course of nature. The most important factor, that intensified this demand for a change and accelerated its speed, was the influence of Western thoughts and ideals on our political, cultural and religious life. From the beginning of the seventeenth century Bengalees began to come in contact with the European merchants, and clergy and as time went on, the contact began to be more and more intensified. This began to bring about a slow and gradual change in our general outlook. This was much more accelerated by the consolidation of British power in Bengal, and the political conquest soon brought with it a cultural conquest. Through the propaganda of the European clergies, whose principal business was to point out the illogicality, absurdity and immorality of the mythological Hindu faith, and through the easy accessibility of the theological and philosophical works embodying the spirit of the Western religion and culture, there actually dawned a great change in the mental horizon of the Bengalees. Western education and culture roused a spirit of revolution in the mind of youths and the revolution found expression first through the life and activities of Rājā Rām Mohan Roy, who by the first quarter of the nineteenth century had, at the very prime of his youth, the courage of standing against the prevalent religious beliefs of the Hindus, which he called superstitious and mythological. His call for revolution was responded to instantaneously by a section of the educated Bengalees and he did succeed in establishing a new religous school which was fundamentally based on Upaniṣadic monism, supplemented by cognate thoughts of Islam and Charistianity. This newly reformed religion soon developed into the religious school known as Brāhmoism, which broke asunder the barriers of the caste-system and the orthodox canons of the Hindu Smṛtis (canonical texts) and stood against all formalities in life and religion. Through the life and activities of Maharṣi Devendranāth Tagore, Brahmānanda Keśav Chandra Sen, Vijay-kṛṣṇa Gosvāmī and a host of other staunch followers of this new faith this religion soon gained a strong footing among an educated and cultured section of the Bengalees and it cannot be gainsaid that this new faith of rationalism has been exerting a reformative influence on orthodox Hinduism for more than a century, and that it exerted an appreciable influence also on the literature of the nineteenth century.

Among the important literary figures of the last half of the nineteenth century Bankim Chandra Chatterjee had a religious conception of his own, and the importance of this conception in the history of our literature lies in the fact that many of his novels and essays distinctly presuppose this religious background. Bankim Chandra was essentially a Hindu,—but he was a staunch rationalist at the same time, and this rationalism of Bankim was to a great extent roused in him through his intimate contact with the thoughts and ideas of the European scientists and philosophers of the eighteenth and nineteenth centuries. Though Bankim Chandra had a fair acquaintance with the leading philosophical views of Europe, the two systems that exerted the greatest influence on the formation of his new religious faith are the Positivism of Comte and the Utilitarianism of Mill. Bankim Chandra's religion is fundamentally based on Positivism and Utilitarianism; but he thought that Hinduism, as represented by the most popular scripture, the *Gītā* (the Divine Song), ascribed to the authorship of Lord Śrī-Kṛṣṇa, can very well be reconciled with the principles of Positivism and Utilitarianism. He, therefore, interpreted the ideals of the *Gītā* in the light of Positivism and Utilitarianism and tried to construct a new system of thought by a synthesis of the ideas from the East and the West. How far Bankim Chandra succeeded in amalgamating the religious views of the East and the West and how far his new system was placed on a sound basis is a matter of controversy;

but what concerns us here is that not only his essays but many of his novels also were infused with this new ideal of religion,—characterised by a distinct humanitarian tone, much too in keeping with the general tone of the time.

It has sometimes been said that the religious attitude and the aesthetic attitude coincide in their ultimate nature. There is no antagonism or even a relation of contrariety between truth and beauty; on the other hand truth, beauty and goodness are sometimes viewed as the three attributes of the ultimate reality. This relation of truth with beauty, or of religion with art, has best been illustrated in the art-creation of Rabindranath Tagore. There are many songs among the poetical works of Tagore, which keep us in a fix as to whether we should eulogise them as masterpieces of art or as the best expression of religious experiences. Tagore made no distinction between his aesthetic vision and his spiritual realisation, and he has repeatedly declared that as essentially a poet he could never make any distinction between the poet in him and the spiritual aspirant. As a matter of fact, rarely have we seen another poet sink so deep in the unfathomable mysteries of nature, life and mind and come out with the priceless gems of his intuitional realisation, and at the same time give them the best artistic expression.

Tagore sings of an infinite supreme Being underlying the whole cosmic process of finite creation. The world-process is an eternal process of self-realisation through self-manifestation of that supreme Being. The Infinite is becoming self-conscious through the eternal art-creation of all finitude,—and the truth of the Finite lies in the ideal of unity which it finds in the deeper relatedness with the Infinite. The Finite and the Infinite have embraced each other in the personality of man and the religion of man, which consists of his realisation of the ultimate truth in him, lies in the perfect evolution of his personality or the extension of it into infinity through the increase of knowledge, love and disinterested activities. There is an ideal unity underlying the diversity of the world-process, and the world of inanimate objects is evolving with the same rhythm with which the biological, the psychological and the spiritual processes of man are moving; and the world-process as a whole is moving towards an ideal end—the ideal of perfection, which is to be attained by the realisation of our deeper relatedness with the Infinite Being. In speaking of a vision of his childhood Tagore says in his work, *The Religion of Man*, "The rhythmic picture of the tremulous leaves beaten by the rain opened before my mind the world which does not merely carry information, but a harmony with my being. The unmeaning fragments lost their individual isolation and my mind revelled in the unity of a vision. In a similar manner, on that morning in the village the facts of my life suddenly appeared to me in a luminous unity of truth. All things that had seemed like vagrant waves were revealed to my mind in relation to a boundless sea. I felt sure that some Being who comprehended me and my world was seeking his best expression in all my experiences, uniting them to an ever-widening individuality which is a spiritual work of art." When this ever-widening individuality of personality approximates infinity, we realise the divinity in man and that is the ideal realisation of truth.

This conception of religion propagated by Tagore, both through speculative essays and through his art-creations, much akin though it may be to the Hegelian and the neo-Hegelian thoughts in striking points, is, however, fundamentally based on the teachings of the Upaniṣads, which were ingrained in the heart of poet Tagore from the early days of his childhood. On the Upaniṣadic canvas the Vaiṣṇava love poets and the mystic Bāuls of Bengal and other mystic poets of upper and northern India, *viz.*, Kabīr, Dādū, Rajjab and others have supplied colour and tone of different shades. But this background and the other probable influences do in no way minimise the individual contribution of Tagore, and it has to be admitted that Tagore, as the seer of truth, has realised something new and given something substantial to the religious thought and literature of the world.

The world has changed a good deal in this twentieth century of ours. Through the materialistic and positivistic tendencies of centuries we have now learnt to care more for our material life than for anything higher and spiritual.

The advancement of positive sciences, the growing keenness in the struggle for existence,—the sternly acute problems of the grossly real life have turned the mind of the general mass away from the problems of the supra-mental reality. This life of flesh and blood, the apparently repulsive naked truths of the mysterious sphere, commonly known as the mind, the earthy weal and woe with which we are beset in our ordinary daily life,—the mute pangs of the lowly humanity—the injustice of the powerful, the suffering of the weak—inequity of the social machine, crashing of the innocent heart,—triumph of the bourgeoisie and the cry of the proletariat—these are the things that are engaging our whole attention,—and these are the things which we think and feel, and the mysteries of which we try to give expression to. The influence of the Continental literature and the closer contact of our life with the rapidly progressive life of the rising powers of the world around are rousing in us almost a craze for realism, and history must have its course.

PART I

THE BUDDHIST SAHAJIYĀ CULT

CHAPTER I

GROWTH OF THE BUDDHIST SAHAJIYĀ CULT

(i) *General Information About The Available Literature*

THE earliest available literature in Bengali language consists of a number of fifty songs[1] composed by different Siddhācāryas (*i.e.*, preceptors who have attained perfection) belonging to the Buddhist Sahajiyā cult. These poems which are popularly known as the 'Caryā-padas' (literally, verses on practices) were first published by MM. H. P. Śāstrī under the caption of *Caryā-carya-viniścayaḥ*, this being the title found in the Nepalese manuscript. MM. Vidhuśekhara Bhaṭṭācārya, however, suggested that the correct caption should be—*Āścarya-caryā-caya*—(a collection of verses on mystic practices), which is found in the commentary of Munidatta on the opening verse.[2] Dr. P. C. Bagchi has suggested another improvement on the title which is *Caryā-ścarya-viniścaya*.[3]

Though doubt has been cast from some quarters as to whether the linguistic character of the Caryā-padas is genuine Bengali,[4] Dr. S. K. Chatterji, after a thorough examination of the linguistic character of these songs, has emphatically expressed his opinion that "the language of the Caryās is the genuine vernacular of Bengal at its basis."

[1] These songs were first discovered by the late Mahāmahopādhyāya Haraprasāda Śāstrī in the Darbar Library of Nepal in 1907. They were edited by MM Śāstrī and published about ten years later under the auspices of the Vaṅgīya Sāhitya Pariṣad under the general caption of "*Bauddha-Gān-O-Dohā*." In the edition of MM Śāstrī three songs, *viz.*, the twenty fourth, twenty-fifth and the fiftieth songs are missing. Dr. P. C. Bagchi, M.A., Dr. es Lettres (Paris), has fortunately been able to discover from Tan-jur the Tibetan translation of all the fifty songs. (*Vide Materials for Critical Edition of the Old Bengali Caryāpadas*, Part I, reprinted from the J. D. L., Vol. XXX.)

[2] *Vide* the note of MM. Bhaṭṭācārya in the *Indian Historical Quarterly*, 1928, Vol. IV, No. 2.

[3] *Vide*, *Some Aspects of Buddhist Mysticism in the Caryāpadas* in the *Calcutta Oriental Journal*, Vol. I.

[4] Mr. B. C. Majumdar, M.A., emphasised the Oḍiyā nature of the Caryāpadas (see *History of Bengali Language*, by B. C. Majumdar, Lecture XIII, also a series of articles contributed by him in the Bengali monthly *Vaṅga-vāṇī*). Again Mr. Jayaswal, following R. Sāṁkṛtyāyana, refers to the language of the Caryā-padas as old Bihārī in his presidential address to the seventh All-India Oriental Conference held in Baroda.

Inspite of sporadic intrusions of a few Maithili and Oḍiyā forms, and also of the influence of Śaurasenī Apabhraṃśa, the essential linguistic nature of these songs cannot but be admitted to be Bengali.[1] Apart from the general consideration of phonology and morphology the use of some idioms, phrases and proverbs peculiar to Bengali unmistakably points to the Bengali character of the language. The language of the Dohās, which are published with the songs, is admittedly Western Apabhraṃśa. Many names will be found common between the authors of the Western Apabhraṃśa Dohās and those of the Bengali songs. The mere commonness of names in the list of authors does not, however, establish the identity of these authors, and we have no other positive evidence to be sure that the authors of the Dohās and those of the Caryā-padas, where common names are to be found, are identical. But a comparison of the Dohās with the Caryā-padas will reveal the fact that in their religious attitude, in theories and practices and in the manner of literary representation, in imagery, phraseology and vocabulary they present a striking similarity, which warrants the belief that the authors of the Dohās and the Caryās, where common names are found, might have been identical; —we must at least admit that both the Dohās and the Caryās represent the same school of thought and they belong to the same literary school. The anomaly as to why the poets, composing songs in Bengali, should have composed songs also in Śaurasenī Apabhraṃśa on the same subject may be explained by referring to the prominence and popularity that Western Apabhraṃśa enjoyed during the period between the ninth century and the twelfth through the prestige of North Indian Rajput princes, in whose courts dialects akin to the later form of Śaurasenī were used, and whose bards spread and popularised such dialects in almost

[1] The peculiar Bengali nature of the songs will be evident if we consider the peculiar forms of the language, *e.g.*, the genitive in "era, -ara," dative in "-re," locative in "-ta;" post-positional words like "mājha," "antara," "sāṅga;" past and future bases in "-il-, -ib-" and not "al-, -ab-" of Bihāri; present participle in "-anta," conjunctive indeclinable in "-iā," conjunctive conditional in "-ite;" passive in "-ia-," which is presrved as a relic in Middle Bengali; substantive roots "āch" and "thāk," and not "thik" of Maithili or "thā" of Oḍiyā. *See* Dr. S. K. Chatterji, *The Origin and Development of the Bengali Language*, Vol. I, p. 112.

all parts of Aryan India, from Gujrat and Western Punjab to Bengal.[1]

Leaving aside the purely linguistic question, if we discuss the nature of these Dohās and songs from the religious, cultural and literary points of view, we shall find that they belong to no particular province of India, but may be regarded as representative of the earliest stage of Indo-Aryan vernacular religious poetry inasmuch as their influence in thought and presentation on a considerable portion of the medieval vernacular literatures of Western, Northern and Eastern India is palpable.

Later investigation in the field of Buddhist Sahajiyā cult and literature show that these Buddhist Sahajiyā Dohā and Caryā songs were popular in a wide area of the Indian soil during a period ranging roughly from the eighth to the twelfth century A.D. The number of the songs and Dohās was not certainly limited to what was discovered and published by MM. H. P. Śāstrī. Dr. P. C. Bagchi discovered and published more Dohās composed by Saraha-pāda and Kānha-pāda and also a number of Dohās composed by Tillo-pāda.[2] Pandit Rāhula Sāṁkṛtyāyana has discovered and published many more Dohās of Saraha-pāda; he has also published the Tibetan translation (giving a Hindi translation side by side) of a good number of Dohās of Saraha-pāda the originals of which are still missing.[3] In the appendix of his book Pandit Sāṁkṛtyāyana has published some fifteen Caryā-pādas by Vinayaśrī and a few Caryā-songs by others also. None of these songs are included in the collection of MM. H. P. Śāstrī except the last one ascribed to Kānha-pāda. Curiously enough, this last song is just a collection of some lines with slightly different readings from some of the songs of Kānha-pāda published by MM. Śāstrī. It may be noted that Munidatta in his Sanskrit commentary on the Caryā-songs has quoted fragments from a few Caryā-songs which are not yet discovered. All these lead us to think that the number of

1 Dr. S. K. Chatterji, *The Origin and Development of the Bengali Language*, p. 113.

2 *Vide*, Dr. P. C. Bagchi, *Dohākoṣa*, Part I, Calcutta, 1938 (Calcutta Sanskrit Series).

3 *Dohā-kośa* (with Hindi translation), Patna, 1957.

Dohās and Caryā-songs composed by the Buddhist Siddhācāryas had been in all probability much larger than what we have as yet been able to discover, and that these Dohās and songs obtained popular currency in a wide area so as to be mixed up and distorted.

The fact of the popularity of the Dohās and Caryā-songs over a wide area will be evident also from the influence of these Dohās and songs over the regional literatures of India during the medieval period. On the influence of the Dohās and songs on medieval Bengali literature we shall have occasion to discuss in detail in some of the chapters that will follow. In the appendix A of the book we shall see how some of the Dohās and songs composed by Kabir, the medieval Hindi poet, bear striking similarity in spirit and diction with some of the Dohās and songs of the Buddhist Siddhācāryas. It will be interesting to note that a song by Śavarapāda, collected in the edition of MM. Śāstrī (song No. 28), gives us a nice pen-picture of the crude way of the conjugal life of a couple of the hilly Śavara tribe; a striking resemblance to this song will be found in some of the songs of Vidyāpati, the well known Maithili poet, where the conjugal life of Śiva and Pārvatī are depicted.[1] Folk songs of a similar type are still found in the rural areas of Mithila. A Hindi folk song bears striking resemblance with a Caryā-song which presents us with a nice description of the sad plight of an unfortunate couple of the deer and the doe surrounded unawares by a band of shouting hunters.[2] Again the metre of the Caryā-songs with its varieties in *Pādākulaka-Pajjhaṭikā-Paddhaḍī-Caupaī* had its ramifications in medieval Bengali and Hindi poetry. Some of these were popular with the poet Jayadeva of the twelfth century in

[1] *Vide*, *Vidyāpati*, ed. by K. M. Mitra and B. B. Majumdar, Calcutta, 1953, Song Nos. 785-89.

[2] Caryā-song No. 8, MM. Śāstrī's edition. The Hindi song is—

maiṁ ṭhāḍhī ṭhāḍhī araj karāṁ., mere ab ke prān bacāo ‖
hiranā hiranī cuṁge jaṁgal meṁ vyādhe lāī phāṁs,
kuṁd phāṁd ke hiranī nikalī hiran ke lag gaī phāṁs ‖
maiṁ ṭhādhī ṭhādhī etc.
tab hiranī hiranā se boli, sun hirane meri bāt,
tum to phaṁs gaye jāl meṁ ab merā kaun havāl ‖
maiṁ ṭhādhī ṭhādhī etc.

Collected by Dr. Satyendra, M.A., Ph.D., D.Lit. of the Arga University.

his well known poetical work *Gita-govinda*. *Pādākulaka* of the Caryā-songs is probably responsible for the most popular Bengali metre *Payāra* and some of the Caryā-songs themselves supply us with clear indication of the line of change. Investigation in the field of Indian music also supply us with important data with regard to the wide-spread popularity of the Caryā-songs. Various references to this Caryā as a type of song are available in the treatises on Indian music in Sanskrit from the twelfth to the seventeenth century A.D.[1] This type of songs is described as songs dealing with religious mysticism and generally sung by a class of Yogins. As the treatises, where references to this type of Caryā songs are found, were written in different parts of India including the South and the West we can be sure of the currency of this type of religious songs over a wide area and that also for a period covering about six centuries.

Investigation reveals that many of the authors of these Dohās and Caryā-padas, besides a good number of writers of Buddhist Tāntric texts and commentaries, belong to the province of Bengal or to the close neighbourhood of Bengal.[2] Though with the insufficient data that are available about the authors of the Dohās and the Caryā-padas it is not possible to ascertain the exact time when these Siddhācāryas flourished and composed the Dohās and songs, we have reasons to believe that they flourished during the reign of the Pāla kings of Bengal, which extended from the eighth to the twelfth century A.D. Among the Siddhācāryas Lui-pā is generally taken to be the first. Lui-pā and Dīpaṅkara Śrī-jñāna conjointly wrote a book named *Abhisamaya-vibhaṅga*. Śrī-jñāna was born in 980 A.D. and went to Tibet in 1042 A.D.[3]; he preached religion in Tibet for long fourteen years and died in 1056 A.D. So it may be supposed that *Abhisamaya-vibhaṅga* was written sometime by the first quarter

[1] For these references see an article on *Caryāgīti* by Rajyeśvara Mitra in the Bengali journal *Viśva-Bhāratī Patrikā*, Vol. XVI, No. 1. See also Madan Mohan Kumar, *Bāṅglā-Sāhityer Ālocanā* (in Bengali), Calcutta, 1960, pp. 223-33.

[2] *Vide* an article on *Buddhist Tantric Literature of Bengal*, by Dr. S. K. De in the *New Indian Antiuqary*, Vol. 1, No. 1. *Vide* also, introduction in the *Bauddha-Gān-o-Dohā*, by MM. H. P. Śāstrī.

[3] *Vide* an article by Mr. N. N. Dasgupta the *Vaṅgīya-Sāhitya-Pariṣat Patrikā* B.S. 1333, No. 2.

of the eleventh century. Lui-pā was senior to Śrī-jñāna, and therefore, he may reasonably be supposed to have flourished sometime in the second half of the tenth century.[1] Again, we find in the colophon of the commentary on the *Hevajra-tantra*, called the *Hevajra-pañjikā* or the *Yoga-ratna-mālā*, preserved in manuscript in the University Library, Cambridge,[2] that the commentary was made or rather finished by Paṇḍitācārya Śrī-kānha-pāda in the thirty-ninth year of the reign of Govinda-pāla, who flourished in the twelfth century A.D. (1199 A.D.). Dr. S. K. Chatterji thinks it possible to identify this Paṇḍitācārya Kānha-pāda with the Kānha-pāda of the Caryā-padas and thus to place Kānha-pāda of the Caryā-padas in the second half of the twelth century.[3] Thus it is generally held that these poets of the Caryā-padas and of the Dohās flourished sometime between the tenth and twelfth centuries A.D. But Pandit

[1] The Presidential address of MM H. P. Śāstrī in the Vaṅgīya Sāhitya-Pariṣad in B.S. 1329.

[2] See *Bāṅgālāra Itihāsa* (in Bengali) by Rākhāldās Bandyopādhyāy, p. 318. The colophon of the manuscript referred to here in this book of Mr. Banerjee is taken from a brief notice of the MS. in Bendall's *Catalogue of Buddhist-Sanskrit Manuscripts in the University Library of Cambridge*. The MS. is, however available to the present writer in rotograph (MS. Add. 1699). There is also a copy of the MS. preserved in the A. S. B. (No. 10745), but the colophon is missing there.

[3] The evidence on the strength of which Dr. Chatterji tries to establish the identity of the author of the commentary *Hevajra-pañjikā* with the author of the Caryā-padas and that of the *Dohā-koṣa* does not seem to be convincing. In the edition of the *Caryā-padas* published by MM. Śāstrī the last couplet of the song No. 36 reads as follows:—

sāthi kariva jālandhari pātrai ।
pākhi na rāhaa mori paṇḍiā cāde ॥

The reading is evidently corrupted. The correct reading should, however, be

sākhi kariva jālandhari pāe ।
pākhi na cāhai (*or cahaa*) *mori pāṇḍiācāe* ॥

which means,— "I shall make Jalandhari-pā (reputed to be the preceptor of Kānha-pā) bear witness for me; I do not find the scholastic preceptors (*paṇḍitācārya*) standing by my side (*i.e.*, holding the same view with me)." Dr. Chatterji, however, interprets the lines in the following manner:

"I shall call to witness my Guru Jālandhari-pāda: my Paṇḍitācārya (*i.e.* myself who am a great scholar) does not look at me." (*The Origin and Development* etc., 122). With this interpretation of the couplet Dr. Chatterji thinks that the word "*paṇḍitācārya*" referred to here can very well be a reference by Kānha to himself. But the interpretation of Dr. Chatterji cannot be accepted without much twisting of the construction of the couplet, and the meaning derived thereby does not conform to the meaning that the commentary on the lines and the Tibetan translation yield. Pandit R. Sāṁkṛtyāyana gives the reading of the line like this :

sākhi karahu guru jālandhari bāja ।
mohe na bujhai paṇḍia ā(*ja*) ॥ *Dohā-koṡa*, p. 369.

This reading also goes to show that the word *paṇḍia* here does not refer to Kānha-pāda himself.

R. Sāṁkṛtyāyana holds that Saraha-pāda, and not Lui-pāda, was the earliest of these Siddhācāryas of the Buddhist Sahajiyā cult. He has his support from a number of earlier scholars also. Saraha-pāda had his disciple in Śavara-pāda and Lui-pāda was in his turn the disciple in Śavara-pāda; Lui-pāda was therefore the third in the chronology of preceptors. Saraha-pāda was the pupil of Haribhadra who again was the disciple of the well known Buddhist scholar and writer Śāntarakṣita. Haribhadra was a contemporary of King Dharma-pāla of the Pāla dynasty who ruled from 770 to 815 A.D.[1] Saraha-pāda must therefore had flourished some time in the eighth century A.D. Pandit Sāṁkṛtyāyana therefore holds that the Buddhist Dohās and songs were composed within a period extending from the eighth century to the twelfth century A.D. Pandit Saṁkṛtyāyana also gives a chart showing the chronology of the disciples[2]; if this chronology is to be given any credit, it corroborates the view that various religious Dohās and Caryā-songs were composed by a good number of poets during the period extending from the eighth to the twelfth century A.D.

(ii) *History of Buddhism in Bengal*

As already hinted, the Caryā-padas embody the religious tenets of Sahajiyā Buddhism, which was a later offshoot of Tāntric Buddhism. It will not be out of place here to say a few words about the nature and extent of the growth and spread of Buddhism in Bengal at the time of and before the rise of these Siddhācāryas. In all probability Bengal was outside the empire of Aśoka and Buddhism could have no access to this province during his reign in the third century B.C. Mention is made of various centres of Theravāda Buddhism in India from which representative monks went to Ceylon to attend the ceremony of the consecration of the Mahā-stūpa erected by King Duṭṭhagāmaṇī in the second century B.C.; but though in the list of the centres we find mention of many places closely adjacent to Bengal, we find no mention of Bengal. Traces of Buddhism as a religious faith in Bengal are, however, found from the

[1] *Dohā-koṣa*, pp. 12-13.
[2] *Ibid*, p. 21.

time of the Gupta emperors. The Chinese pilgrim, Fa-Hien, visited India during the reign of Chandragupta II. Fa-Hien stayed in Tāmralipti (modern Tamluk in Midnapore) for two years, copying Sūtras and painting images. He noticed the existence of twenty-four Saṅghārāmas in the city, which were all residential seats for the Buddhist monks. It was also noticed by the pilgrim that Buddhism at that time began to command reverence with the public in general. After Fa-Hien another renowned Chinese pilgrim, Hiuen Tsang, came to India during the seventh century A.D. in the reign of Harṣavardhana and visited Bengal. He found ten Buddhist monasteries with more than 1,000 monks residing in them in Tāmralipti, twenty Saṅghārāmas with some 3,000 priests who studied both the Little and the Great Vehicle in Puṇḍravardhana, thirty or so Saṅghārāmas with about 2,000 priests, all of the Sthavira school in Samataṭa, and ten Saṅghārāmas or so with about 2,000 priests studying the Little Vehicle of the Samataṭīya school in Karṇasuvarṇa. He also spoke of two most notable colleges, rather universities, of his time, one at Puṇḍravardhana and the other at Karṇasuvarṇa, both renowned as great seats of learning for the Eastern Buddhist scholars. I-tsing, another Chinese pilgrim, speaks of the University of Bhā-rā-hā in Tāmralipti and gives a vivid picture of its inner life, organisation, discipline, splendour and fame. While speaking of the four tracts of Bengal referred to by Hiuen Tsang, I-tsing referred to the great reverence of people in general for the Buddhist faith and for the monastic life of the Bhikṣus (monks living on alms). He also found an Aśoka tope and the vestiges of the four past Buddhas.

A renowned Buddhist teacher of Bengal of the pre-Pāla age was Śīlabhadra of Samataṭa. He was at first a disciple of Ācārya Dharmapāla of Nālandā and gradually became the head of that great Buddhist University. He was a friend as well as a preceptor of Hiuen Tsang who had deep reverence for the monk. Buddhabhadra, the nephew and disciple of Śīlabhadra, was also a devout Buddhist, and both the uncle and the nephew were reputed as great devotees and profound scholars. Buddhabhadra has been described as a specialist in Yogācāra Buddhism, and tradition says that he derived his inspiration from Avalokiteśvara, Maitreya and Mañjuśrī.

One thing to be noticed in this connection is that the evidence of the Chinese pilgrims or of the epigraphical and archaeological records does not help us much in ascertaining the nature of Buddhism that was current in Bengal before the Pālas. We find mention of Mahāyāna Buddhism as well as of Hīnayāna. It seems, however, that in the historical evolution of Buddhism, Mahāyāna, with its more liberal policy and generous ideal of the final goal, could capture the mind of the public much more than Hīnayāna with its strict monasticism and ethical rigorism, and as a result Mahāyāna was fast gaining in popularity. During the time of the Pālas, however, a tendency towards esoterism was manifest and Buddhism very soon underwent another great change from Mahāyāna to Vajrayāna.

Coming to the time of the Pālas, who were professed Buddhists, we find many Buddhist monasteries established in different parts of Bengal mainly through the patronage of these Pāla kings. The great Vihāra of Nālandā was enriched and repaired and some new land-grants were made to it by the Pālas, and it was made the meeting place of all sorts of Buddhist scholars from countries within and without India. On the evidence of Tāranātha we know that Gopāla I founded the Odantapurī or Uddaṇḍapura Mahāvihāra, while according to the *Pag-Sam-Jon-Zang* he was the founder of the monastery of Nālandā. Dharmapāla, the son of Gopāla, who himself bore the epithet of Vikramaśīladeva, founded the monastery of Vikramaśīla which for some time rivalled the glory of Nālandā. An inscribed clay-seal discovered in Pāhāḍapura bears testimony to the fact that the Mahāvihāra of Somapura in North Bengal also was erected by Dharmapāla. Close to this important monastery was situated, in the eleventh century A.D., a temple of Khasarpaṇa Avalokiteśvara, in which was permanently deposited a manuscript of the Prajñā-pāramitā in a casket artistically executed by Vipulaśrīmitra. On four sides of this big temple were built four alms-houses wherein images of the Goddess Tārā were installed. Another big temple of Tārā was built in Somapura to 'dispel entirely the eight great dreads of the people.' This monastery of Somapura and also the Vikramaśīla monastery were probably brought to perfection by Devapāla, son of Dharmapāla. The Bstan-hgyur refers to another Vihāra of Vikramapurī, which was most probably situated in Vikramapura of East Bengal. Kumāra Candra, called Ācārya Avadhūta, wrote a Tāntric commentary in this monastery of Vikramapurī. Another Vihāra which was already in existence in Bengal during the time of Dharmapāla was the Traikuṭaka Vihāra, where Ācārya Haribhadra wrote his famous commentary on the *Aṣṭa-sāhasrikā-prajñā-pāramitā*. Prajñā-varman, called Ācārya, and his preceptor, Bodhivarman, are said to have hailed from Kāpaṭya of Bengal, which was either a monastery itself or a place having a monastery. There was probably another monastery in Devīkot in North Bengal to which Advayavajra, the great Tāntric Buddhist scholar, as also Mekhalā, a nun, are said to have belonged. The *Pag-Som-Jon-Zang* mentions the Paṇḍita Vihāra of Chittagong, which was a great centre of Tāntric learning and culture, and with this Vihāra Tili-pā as Tilo-pā or Tailapāda is said to have been associated. Taila-pāda had a disciple of the name of the Nāḍa-pāda, who again is said to have been the preceptor of the renowned Bengali Buddhist missionary who went to Tibet and preached Buddhism there for full fourteen years. Nāḍa-pā was the author of the commentary on the *Vajrapāda-sāra-saṁgraha*, which is said to have been composed by Śākyabhikṣu Yaśobhadra of Kāśmīra at the demand of Vinaya-śrī-mitra and others belonging to the grand Vihāra of Kanakastūpa in the city of Paṭṭikeraka. This city of Paṭṭikeraka, frequently found in the ballads on King Gopīcānd or Govinda Candra as the city of Pāṭi-kāra, has convincingly been identified with the *paragaṇā* of Pāṭi-kārā, conterminous with Meherkul in the district of Tippera.[1]

In connection with the Buddhism of the Pāla period mention must be made here of Atīśa Dīpaṅkara, the great Buddhist scholar of Bengal. Of his life and activities in India and in Tibet we now know much, which need not be reproduced here.

[1] Mr. N. N. Dasgupta, M.A., *Buddhist Vihāras of Bengal*, *Indian Culture*, Vol. 1, No. 2.

The grand Vihāra of Jagaddala, founded by the last great Pāla king, Rāmapāla, speaks of the last glory of Buddhism in Bengal. The king installed in this Vihāra images of Avalokiteśvara and Mahā Tārā. This great monastery was situated in a part of Rāmāvatī, the new metropolis founded by Rāmapāla at the confluence of the Ganges and the Karatoyā. Bibhūticandra and Dānaśīla were the two most reputed scholars of Jagaddala. Besides, Mokṣakaragupta of the same Vihāra was a good logician and composed in three chapters the *Tarka-bhāṣā*. Śubhakaragupta, who lived there for some time, wrote a commentary on the Tāntric text *Siddhaikavīra-tantra*. Dharmakara of the same monastery translated the *Samvaravyākhyā* of Kṛṣṇa. Buddhists from Tibet flocked here to have Sanskrit texts translated into Tibetan.[1]

In the brief survey made above it must have been noticed that a good number of Tāntric scholars of Buddhism flourished during the period of the Pālas, and many of the authors of the Dohās and Caryās probably flourished during this time. The art and iconography of the same period will bear testimony to the fact that by this time Mahāyāna began to be eclipsed by Vajrayāna Buddhism. The icons of various Buddhist gods and goddesses of the period and also the representation of some of the gods (including the Lord Supreme as Hevajra or Heruka or Vajreśvara or Vajrasattva, as he was variously called in esoteric Buddhism) with their respective female consorts in a state of union (*yuganaddha*) will indicate the introduction of the female element in the Buddhist religion of the time.

With this brief survey of the history of Buddhism in Bengal before and at the time of the advent of the Buddhist Siddhācāryas of the Sahajiyā sect, let us now turn our attention directly to the religious background of the Bengali Caryā-padas, which embody the religious doctrines and practices of the Sahajiyā Buddhists. This will naturally lead us to the question of the nature, origin and development of Tāntric Buddhism as a whole, of which Sahaja-yāna is a later offshoot. The question of the inter-relation among

[1] *Ibid.*

the various schools of Tāntric Buddhism, *viz.*, Vajra-yāna, Kālacakra-yāna and Sahaja-yāna, has also to be discussed in this connection.

(iii) *Origin and Development of Tāntric Buddhism*

The phase of later Buddhism, widely and roughly known as Tāntric Buddhism, may be said to be a popular development of Mahāyāna Buddhism through a gradual process of centuries having its fullest sway during the period between the eighth and twelfth centuries A.D. Mahāyāna or the 'Great Vehicle,' as contrasted with the ethico-religious rigorism of Hīnayāna, or the 'Little Vehicle,' was a religion of progress and liberalism. In the *Mahāyāna-sūtrā-laṅkāra* of Asaṅga Hīnayāna has been characterised as a very narrow system of religion,—narrow in its aim of self-liberation, narrow teachings to realise that aim, narrow method applied for this realisation, insufficiency of equipment and the shortness of time within which final liberation is guaranteed.[1] On the other hand, the Mahāyāna school represents the religion of the dissenters and the protestants and was always characterised by a broadness of outlook and deep sympathy for the suffering beings of the whole universe.

After the death of Buddha there arose a great controversy among his followers as to the correct interpretation of the sayings of the master as well as about the rules of discipline indispensable for a monk. To settle these controversies great councils were held. It is said that in the second council held in Vesāli the controversy finally ended in a split among the Buddhists, and the dissenters convened another great assembly (*Mahāsaṅgha*) to have a separate school of their own and they were known as the Mahāsāṅghika. In this way, as time passed, the controversy between these radicalists and the orthodox elders (*thera*) began to be more and more uncompromising and the points of dissension were also gradually increasing in number. This controversy between the elders and the radicalists finally resulted in the growth of the two separate schools within the province of Buddhism itself, the canonical tenets of the elders being

[1] *Mahāyāna-sūtrā-laṅkāra*, Ch. 1, Verse 10. Lévi's edition.

styled as Hīnayāna and the tenets of the radicalists as Mahāhyāna.

Among the radical changes in thought and outlook that we find in Mahāyāna, as contrasted with Hīnayāna, the most important is the change in the conception of the final goal. Whereas the *summum bonum* of Hīnayāna is to attain Arhathood or final liberation of the self from the whirl of existence through strict ethical discipline and the processes of '*Jhāna*' (Sk. *dhyāna*, meditation), the final aim of Mahāyāna was to attain Buddhahood in and through different stages of Bodhisattvahood, which is a state of perfect knowledge about the void-nature of the self and the not-self mixed up with an emotion of universal compassion for the redemption of all the suffering beings. The conception of Bodhisattvahood, very important as it is in Mahāyāna Buddhism as well as in all forms of Tāntric Buddhism, requires some elaboration. The belief of the followers of Mahāyāna is that every man, nay, every being of the world, is a potential Buddha; he has within him all the potency of becoming the perfectly enlightened one (*Samyak-sambuddha*), which latent possibility can be made patent only through the attainment of perfect knowledge, associated with universal compassion, which prompts one to utilise that knowledge in missionary activities for the uplift of all beings. The ideal of missionary life was consequently preferred to the ideal of the attainment of final extinction (*nirvāṇa*). Bodhisattvahood means the attainment of the Bodhi-mind (*Bodhi-citta*), which is defined as a unified state of vacuity (*Śūnyatā*) and universal compassion (*Karuṇā*).[1]

The other noteworthy departure in Mahāyāna was the development of the docetic conception of the three Kāyas (bodies) of the Buddha. The Hīnayānists conceived the Buddha only as a historical personage in the life and activities of Śākyamuni; but with the Mahāyānists the Buddha is no particular historical personage, he is but the ulimate principle as the totality of things and beings in an unqualified state of all-existence. This ultimate principle has three aspects, known as the three Kāyas of the Buddha, *viz.*, the

[1] *śūnyatā-karuṇā-bhinnaṁ bodhi-cittam iti smṛtam* ||
Śrī-guhya-samāja-tantra (G.O.S.), p. 153.

Dharma-kāya (*i.e.*, primordial element, or the 'thatness' underlying all that exists), the Sambhoga-kāya (the body of bliss, or the effulgent body in the form of the Bodhisattvas) and the Nirmāṇa-kāya (*i.e.*, the body of transformation, or the historical personage of Buddha).[1] With these fundamental changes in outlook and a predominance of philosophical thought and the culture of the supreme virtues (*pāramitā*) Mahāyāna Buddhism flowed on side by side with Hīnayāna for centuries. But as, on the one hand, this freedom of thought, broadness of outlook and spirit of liberalism liberated Buddhism from the walls of narrow scholasticism and raised it from the selfish hankering of personal liberation to the sublimity of a religion for suffering humanity, it, on the other hand, contained the germs of indiscipline and the revelry of wild thoughts which reduced Buddhism to a body of unintelligible mutterings and a system of practices which are unconventional. It should be observed that the pledge of Mahāyāna was the redemption of suffering humanity as a whole, nay, the liberation of all beings. With this end in view the apostles of Mahāyāna had to make their religion catholic enough to make it acceptable even to the most ordinary people of the society. In other words, Mahāyāna, as a religion for all people, had to make provision within its fold for people of widely different tastes and intellectual calibre. It is for this reason that heterogeneous elements of faith and religious practices began first to creep in and then to rush into the province of Buddhism. For ordinary people religion consists in the belief in innumerable gods and goddesses, in time-honoured customs, muttering of mystic formulas, and in the paraphernalia of rites, ceremonies and practices; when through the zeal of liberating all the beings from the bondage of existence Mahāyāna began to be too much popularised, all these popular religious elements of heterogeneous nature began to be incorporated into Buddhism. Though the general custom is to style this composite religious system of heterogeneous faiths and practices as Tāntric Buddhism, the *raison d'être* of Tāntric Buddhism is not to be sought in this popular phase of the religion. It seems that with the purpose of attaining

1 *Vide infra.*

the final state of Buddhahood a new school developed within the province of Buddhism itself with a more forward policy. This forward school introduced elements like the Mantras and the Dhāranīs into the province of this religion. It is for this reason that in the *Tattva-ratnāvalī* collected in the *Advaya-vajra-saṁgraha*[1] we find Mahāyāna sub-divided into two schools, *viz.*, Pāramitā-naya and Mantra-naya. The principles of Mantra-naya are said to be very deep and subtle and inaccessible to ordinary men; and though the ultimate purpose of the Mantra-śāstra is the same as that of other Śāstras, it is said to be distinctly superior to them because of the fact that it is free from delusions and is accessible only to people with a higher intellectual calibre.[2] This Mantra-naya or Mantra-yāna seems to be the introductory stage of Tāntric Buddhism, from which all other offshoots, like Vajra-yāna, Kālacakra-yāna, Sahaja-yāna, etc., arose in later times. In the *Laghu-kāla-cakra-tantrarāja-ṭīkā*, entitled *Vimala-prabhā*[3] we find that the doctrines of the Pāramitā-naya are written wholly in Sanskrit, while those of the Mantra-naya are explained in Sanskrit, Prakrit, Apabhraṃśa and even in non-Sanskritic languages like those of the Śavaras and others.

Tradition holds Asaṅga, the great exponent of the Yogācāra school, to be responsible for the introduction of Tāntricism in Buddhism; he again, in his turn, is believed to have been initiated into this mystic cult by Maitreya in the Tuṣita-heaven. Others, on the other hand, hold that Nāgārjuna, the renowned exponent of the Mādhyamika school, was the real founder of the esoteric school, and that he, in his turn, received the doctrines from the Celestial Buddha Vairocana through the divine Bodhisattva Vajra-sattva in the "iron tower" in South India.

Apart from these traditions, some scholars are disposed to think that in the *Mahāyāna-sūtrā-laṅkāra* of Asaṅga there are clear references to the sexo-yogic practice of the Tāntric Buddhists. In the *Sūtrā-laṅkāra* the word *parāvṛtti* occurs several times in connection with acts which constitute the

1 Edited by MM. H. P. Śāstrī, G. O. S., No. XL.
2 *Tattva-ratnāvalī* in *Advaya-varja-saṁgraha*, p. 21.
3 MS., A. S. B., No. 4727.

supreme greatness of the Buddha. One of these verses runs thus, "In the *parāvṛtti* of sexual union supreme greatness is obtained, (namely) in the enjoyment of Buddha-happiness and in looking without impure thoughts at a wife."[1] Sylvain Lévi in translating this verse suggests that "*parāvṛtti* of sexual act" alludes to "the mystic couples of Buddhas and Bodhisattvas which have so much importance in Tāntricism." But Winternitz in his notes on the "Guhyasamāja Tantra and the Age of Tantra"[2] doubts this interpretation of Lévi and suggests that *parāvṛtti* means nothing but "turning aside, discard." The phrase *maithunasya parāvṛtti* may really refer to the Tāntric sexo-yogic practice through which there is the enjoyment of bliss similar to that arising from the sexual act,—and the significance of this mystic union and the consequent enjoyment of blissful union is given in the *Sūtrā-laṅkāra* itself.[3] If this interpretation of the word *parāvṛtti* in the present context be accepted, it may be inferred that the Tāntric ideas were already prevalent in Mahāyāna Buddhism in the time of Asaṅga (4th-5th centuries A.D.), and the tradition of Tāntricism being introduced in Buddhism by Asaṅga himself becomes to a great extent significant.

Some scholars are again of the opinion that the Tāntric elements were introduced into Buddhism by Lord Buddha himself as a mere provision for the laities whose intellectual calibre and moral equipment would not allow them to follow the path chalked out by him. Thus Dr. B. Bhaṭṭācārya says,—"Though Buddha was antagonistic to all sorts of sacrifices, necromancy, sorcery or magic, he is credited nevertheless with having given instructions concerning Mudrās, Maṇḍalas and Tantras, etc., so that, by virtue of these, prosperity in this world could be attained by his less advanced disciples, who seemed to care more for this world than for the Nirvāṇa preached by him. India in Buddha's time was so steeped in superstitions that any religion which dared forbid all kinds of magic, sorcery and

[1] *maithunasya parāvṛttau vibhutvaṁ labhyate param |*
buddha-saukhya-vihāre' tha dārā' saṁkleśa-darśane ||

[2] *Indian Historical Quarterly*, IX. 1.

[3] *Studies in the Tantras*, Dr. P. C. Bagchi, p. 92.

necromancy could hardly hope to withstand popular opposition. A clever organiser as Buddha was, he did not fail to notice the importance of incorporating magical practices in his religion to make it popular from all points of view and attract more adherents thereby."[1] As a conclusive evidence of this inference Dr. Bhaṭṭācārya refers to Buddha's belief in the four "*iddhis*" (*ṛddhi*) or miraculous power obtained by the advanced disciples and also to a verse in the *Tattva-saṁgraha* of Śāntarakṣita and its commentary by Kamalaśīla, where Buddha himself is said to have prescribed Mantra, Mudrā, Maṇḍala, etc., for his lay disciples. But the mere belief in the "*ṛddhi*" is no convincing proof of Buddha's sanction of Tāntricism, and the evidence of Śāntarakṣita and Kamalaśīla (which too is extremely insufficient by itself) cannot be credited much on the ground that they flourished about fourteen hundred years after the advent of Buddha. Of course, we find occasional references to Tāntric practices including the sex-element even in the time of Buddha,[2] but we find no conclusive evidence in any early record of Buddha's sanction to Tāntricism as the mere policy of a clever organiser.

Without entering into any controversy on the point we may say that it will perhaps be wrong to suppose that Tāntricism was introduced into Buddhism at any particular time by any particular man. Belief in Mantra or in the mysterious power in the sound of a particular syllable or a string of such syllables is a social heritage with the Indian masses from the hoary past. Such a belief in various forms is to be occasionally found in early Buddhism also. Worship of the *Stūpa*, reverence for the mystic Bodhimaṇḍala, or the circle round the famous tree beneath which Buddha attained his *Bodhi* (perfect knowledge) were popular features also of early Buddhism. The postures and gestures of Buddha were also held mystically significant. These are elements in early Buddhism which no doubt paved the path for the vigorous propagation of the Mantra,

[1] *An introduction to Buddhist Esoterism*, by Dr. B. Bhaṭṭācārya, p. 48. See also the introduction to the *Sādhana-mālā* (Vol. II), by Dr. Bhaṭṭācārya, pp. xvi-xvii.

[2] *Dīgha-nikāya*, *Brahma-jāla-sutta*; *Kathāvatthu*, XVII, 6, 7, 8, 9, 10, XXIII. 2; *Majjhima-nikāya*, Pali Text-book Society's Edition, 1, p. 305.

Mudrā (posture and gestures) and Maṇḍala (mystic diagram) elements in Tāntric Buddhism.

A popular tendency is manifest among some of the scholars to determine the priority either of the Hindu Tantras or of the Buddhist Tantras. We have pointed out in the Introduction and we shall have other occasions to repeat, that Tāntricism with its heterogeneous nature is neither exclusively Hindu, nor exclusively Buddhist in origin. It is an ancient religious cult of India manifesting itself sometimes as Hindu being associated with Hindu theology, thoughts and ideas and sometimes as Buddhist in association with later Buddhist theology, thoughts and ideas. In view of this fact it will not be sound to say, as has sometimes actually been said, that the Hindu Tantras are later in origin and are derived from the Buddhist Tantras. We have seen that Asaṅga has traditionally been held to be the propagator of Tāntricism in Buddhism; but the tradition of the existence of a vast array of Āgamas during the days of Asaṅga or even in earlier times cannot altogether be brushed aside. These ancient Āgamic texts seem to be the source of all Tāntric texts. That an extensive Tāntric literature existed in the days of Somānanda and Utpala is well-known. Internal evidences show that most of these works, even as they were then known, were very old. Abhinava Gupta's (10 A.D.) work *Tantrā-loka* is based on many ancient Āgamas, which were accessible to him personally. A study of the Buddhist Tantras and Hindu Tantras will show that there are numerous points of contact implying thereby that they had a common cultural background in the past.

Apart from the theological doctrines, which differ in details from one another, the fundamentals of the Hindu and the Buddhist Tantras are the same. It is only the colour and tone that are sometimes different. As we shall have occasions to refer to these points of similarity later on we do not propose to illustrate them here.

The Mantra-element seems to have been introduced in Mahāyāna Buddhism first in the form of the Dhāraṇī, which literally means that by which something is sustained or kept up (*dhāryate anayā iti*), *i.e.*, the mystic syllables that have got the capacity of keeping up the religious life of a man. In the *Bodhisattva-bhūmi* of Vasubandhu we find a discourse on the nature of the Dhāraṇīs and a philosophical explanation for the adoption of these unmeaning Mantras for the realisation of the ultimate truth.

According to the *Bodhisattva-bhūmi* the Dhāraṇīs of the Bodhisattva are of four kinds, *viz.*, Dharma-dhāraṇī, Artha-dhāraṇī, Mantra-dhāraṇī and the Dhāraṇī for the attainment of the transcendental merit of forbearance belonging to the Bodhisattva (*Bodhisattva-kṣānti-lābhāya ca dhāraṇī*). The Dharma-dhāraṇī is composed of that kind of Mantras through the hearing of which (even though they are not explained in any Śāstra or by any preacher) the follower attains memory (*smṛti*), perfect knowledge (*prajñā*) and spiritual strength (*bala*). Artha-dhāraṇī is that type of Mantras through the mystic power of which the correct significance (*artha*) of the Dharmas (which significance is never explained in any Śāstra or by any preacher) is revealed to the follower in a spontaneous way. The Mantra-dhāraṇī enables a man to attain perfection. The Dhāraṇī for the attainment of forbearance (*kṣānti*) is the Mantra through which the ultimate nature of the Dharmas is revealed to the reciter; through the realisation of the ultimate immutable nature of the Dharmas the follower attains generosity of heart which produces in him the merit of forbearance.[1]

In this connection, however, Vasubandhu gives a philosophical explanation of how the ultimate immutable nature of the Dharmas can be realised through the Mantras of unmeaning syllables, such as "*iṭi miṭi kiṭi bhikṣāṁti padāni svāhā*." He says that these syllables, *viz.*, "*iṭi miṭi kiṭi*, etc.," have got no meaning whatsoever,—and the follower through concentration should realise the truth that these Mantras can have no meaning at all,—this unmeaningness is their real meaning. Through this absolute negation of all possible meanings to the Mantra, the real meaning of the Mantra as pure void is intuitively revealed to a man. Thus this realisation of the meaning of the Mantras (as pure negation) helps the man to realise in pure intuition the nature of the Dharmas as essenceless. But through this negation of all

1 *Bodhisattva-bhūmi*, Ed. by Unrai Wogihara (Tokyo), pp. 272-74.

meanings to the Mantras a unique transcendental, immutable meaning is revealed to the heart of the Sādhaka; this immutable nature is the real nature of all things.[1]

Closely associated with this Mantra-element is the Mudrā element, which in Buddhism in general is but the different signs made by the particular position of the hands and the fingers.[2] This Mudrā-element, however, with the Mantra-element and some other esoteric practices has a deeper sinificance in the Yogic Sādhanā of the Tāntrics, and as the Mantra-element contains all the secrecy of the potency of sound, the Mudrā element contains all the secrecy of touch as associated with the potency of the physiological system. With Mantra and Mudrā the element of Maṇḍala or describing of mystic circles was also introduced.

But once the portals of Buddhism were flung open to let in elements of esoterism, all the traditional beliefs in gods, demi-gods, demons and ghosts, magic, charms and sorcery with all their details rushed in and quickly changed the whole ethico-religious outlook of Buddhism. To these again were added elements of Yoga,—Haṭha-yoga, Laya-yoga, Mantra-yoga and Rāja-yoga. All these elements made for the growth of the elaborate system of Tāntric Buddhism.

[1] *sa eṣāṁ mantra-padānāṁ evaṁ samyak pratipanna evam-artham svayaṁ evā'śrutvā kutaścit pratipadyati. tad yathā nāsty eṣāṁ mantra-padānāṁ kācid artha-pariniṣpattiḥ, nirarthā evaite, ayam eva caiṣāṁ artho yad uta nirarthatā...... sa teṣāṁ mantra-padānāṁ arthaṁ samyak pratividhya tenaivā'rthā-nusāreṇa sarva-dharmāṇam apy arthaṁ samyak pratividhyati svayam evā'śrutvā parataḥ | ....yā punar eṣāṁ nirabhilāpya-svabhāvatā. ayam eṣāṁ svabhāvārthaḥ.*

Bodhisattva-bhūmi. p. 273.

[2] It should be noted here that the word Mudrā in the Tantric and the Yogic literature has got different meanings. In the Tantras it often means the woman to be selected in the secret practice: in Haṭha-yoga it refers to practices including control of limbs, muscles, nerves and the vital breath-process. We have again different descriptions of four types of Mudrās associated with both processes of Yoga and meditation which are again associated with four types of realisation of bliss (*vide Catur-mudrā* of the *Advaya-vajra-saṁgraha*, G. O. S., XL.). In the University Library of Cambridge there is a manuscript with the colophon "*Śrī-mac-chākyarāja-sarva-durgati-pariśodhana-mukhā-khyāna-prathamā-diyoga-nāma samādhi* (MS. Cambridge, Add. No. 1278, available to the present writer in rotograph) with as many as one hundred and fifty-eight coloured illustrations of the different kinds of Mudrās. Of these some seem to be purely postures of the hands and fingers, some on the other hand illustrate the different manners of holding the thunderbolt (*vajra*), lotus, bell, sword, conch-shell, bunch of flowers, garlands, etc. Others again illustrate the manner of offering flowers, water, incense, lamp and other materials of worship. Some again illustrate the different manners of playing on the different musical instruments. All these are done with the aim of obtaining final purification and final deliverance from the miseries of life.

It is to be noticed that in the earlier phase of Tāntric Buddhism emphasis was laid generally on the elements of Mantra, Mudrā, Maṇḍala, Abhiṣeka (initiation and the ceremonies associated with it), etc.; but gradually the sexo-yogic practice also began to be referred to. In course of evolution, however, the sexo-yogic practice came to be held as the most important esoteric practice for the attainment of the final state of supreme bliss, all the other practices and ceremonies being held as preparatory accessories. The six kinds of ritual intended for the good or evil of anybody (*Abhicāra*) and the five accessories of wine (*madya*), meat (*māṁsa*), fish (*matsya*), woman (?) (*mudrā*) and sexual intercourse (*maithuna*) gradually made their way into Buddhism.[1]

This composite system of Tāntricism with the introduction of the sexo-yogic practice came to be known by the general name of Vajra-yāna or the Adamantine path.[2] Kazi Dawa-samdup in his introduction to the *Śrī-cakra-sambhāra-tantra* divides this Vajra-yāna into further parts, *viz.*, Kriyā-tantra-yāna, Caryā-tantra-yāna and Yoga-tantra-yāna; the last is again sub-divided into Mahāyoga-tantra-yāna, Anuttara-yoga-tantra-yāna and Atiyoga-tantra-yāna. The general custom, however, is to divide Vajra-yāna into four classes *viz.*, Kriyā-tantra, Caryā-tantra, Yoga-tantra, and Anuttara-tantra. The first two classes are called 'lower Tantras' inasmuch as they are concerned with the rites, ceremonies, worship of gods and goddesses and other practices; and the latter schools are known as 'higher Tantras' inasmuch as they describe yogic processes for the realisation of the ultimate truth and also contain discussions on the nature of the ultimate reality[3].

[1] We do not, however, find any direct mention of the *Pañca-ma-kāras* in the Buddhist Tantras; but we find sporadic mention of wine, fish, meat, etc. and much of Mudrā and sexual intercourse. We also find frequent reference to the *Pañca-kāma-guṇa* or five objects of desire through the enjoyment of which perfection can be attained.

[2] The original name Mantra-yāna is also often found used in a general sense for later Buddhist Tāntric schools. *Cf. Hevajra-pañjikā*, MS. (Cambridge Add. No. 1699), p. 45(B); *Advaya-vajra-saṁgraha*, p. 54 (G.O.S.); commentary on the *Dohākoṣa* of Kānha-pāda, verse No. 12.

[3] In this connection compare also four divisions in the arrangement of the Vaiṣṇava-tantras (found in the *Padma-tantra*), *viz.*, Jñāna-pāda, Yoga-pāda, Kriyā-pāda and Caryā-pāda. (See J.R.A.S., 1901, p. 900.)

There is still another customary way of dividing Tāntric Buddhism into three schools, *viz.*, Vajra-yāna, Kāla-cakra-yāna and Sahaja-yāna.[1] This division seems to us erroneous inasmuch as Kāla-cakra-yāna and Sahaja-yāna seem to us to be schools within Vajra-yāna. MM. H. P. Śāstrī speaks of Nāthism as another school of Tāntric Buddhism.[2] As we shall devote separate chapters to the problems regarding the nature, origin and growth of Nāthism[3] we do not propose to discuss at this stage the question of its relation to Tāntric Buddhism. The problem of Kāla-cakra-yāna, however, appears to us perplexing. About its nature Waddell says in his *Lamaism*,—— "In the tenth century A.D., the Tāntric phase developed in Northern India, Kasmir and Nepal into monstrous and polydemonist doctrine, the Kāla-cakra, with its demonical Buddhas, which incorporated the Mantrayāna practices, and called itself the Vajrayāna, or the 'Thunderbolt-vehicle,' and its followers were named Vajra-carya, or, 'followers of the Thunderbolt.'"[4] In another place he says—"The extreme development of the Tāntric phase was reached with the Kāla-cakra, which, although unworthy of being considered as a philosophy, must be referred to here as a doctrinal basis. It is merely a course of Tāntric development of the Adi-Buddha theory combined with puerile mysticism of Mantrayāna, and it attempts to explain creation and the secret powers of nature by the union of the *Kali*, not only with the Dhyani Buddhas, but even with Adi-Buddha himself."[5] The account and interpretation given by Mr. Waddell seem to us to be based on confused ideas about Tibetan Buddhism. We have not yet been able to discover the reason behind the general tendency of associating the name Kāla-cakra-yāna with the terrible aspect of Tāntric Buddhism. MM. H. P. Śāstrī, however, says on this point, "What is Kāla-cakra-yāna? The word Kāla means time,—death and destruction. Kāla-cakra is the wheel

[1] See the introduction to *Sādhana-mālā*, Vol. II, by Dr. B. Bhaṭṭācārya.

[2] See the introduction by MM. H. P. Śāstrī to *Modern Buddhism and its Followers in Orissa* of Mr. N. Vasu.

[3] *Vide infra.*

[4] *Lamaism*, by Waddell, p. 15.

[5] *Ibid.*

of destruction, and Kāla-cakra-yāna means the vehicle for protection against the wheel of destruction."[1] But this explanation of MM. Śāstrī is not confirmed by any textual evidence.

The traditional view concerning the origin of *Śrī-kāla-cakra-mūla-tantra*, which is recorded in the *Abhiniśramaṇa Sūtra*[2] is that it was delivered by the Buddha at Śrī Dhanya Kaṭaka. Regarding this system Csoma de Koros says that it was introduced in India from Śambhala at about 965 A.D.

We have at our disposal a text of the *Śrī-kāla-cakra-tantra*[3] a study of which does not substantiate the statement that Kāla-cakra-yāna is that school of Tāntric Buddhism, which introduced demonic Buddhas in it,—at least, it is not the main characteristic by which the school should be recognised. In the text at our disposal the Lord has explained how the universe with all its objects and localities are situated in the body and how time in all its divisions and sub-divisions (*viz.*, day, night, fortnight, month, year, etc.) is within the body in the processes of the vital wind (*prāṇa-vāyu*). In the text Sahaja has been explained and also the details of the sexo-yogic practice for the attainment of the Sahaja. The only thing that strikes the reader is the stress laid on the control of the vital winds (*prāṇa* and *apāna*) and the results attained thereby. A study of the commentary on the text (*Laghu-kāla-cakra-tantra-rāja-ṭīkā*, entitled *Vimala-prabhā*) also reveals no fundamental difference between the tenets of Vajra-yāna Buddhism and those of Kāla-cakra-yāna. The stress on yoga seems, however, to be the special feature, if there be any at all, of Kāla-cakra-yāna.

It is interesting to note here that similar doctrines of *Kāla-cakra* are elaborately described and explained in a fairly old text like the *Tantrā-loka* of Abhinava Gupta. The sixth chapter of the *Tantrā-loka* (which is a fairly big chapter) is devoted to the exposition of the doctrine of Kāla (time) and the process of keeping oneself above the influence of the whirl of time. Time (Kāla) in all its phases (day and night, fortnight, month, year, etc.) has been explained

[1] *Modern Buddhism*, etc., Introduction, p. 8.
[2] *Pag Sam Jon Zang.*, p. 37.
[3] MS. Cambridge Add., 1364.

here mainly with reference to the functions of the vital wind (mainly *prāṇa* and *apāna*) spread through the whole nervous system and the process of controlling time is to control the vital wind in the nerves through yogic practices.

(iv) *Mode of Transformation of the Main Ideas of Mahāyāna to those of Tāntric Buddhism*

Before we pass on to the fundamental characteristics of Sahaja-yāna, on which the Caryā-padas are based, we deem it necessary here to make a very short survey of the mode of transformation of some of the philosophical ideas of Mahāyāna Buddhism into those of Tāntric Buddhism. Tāntricism seems to be a religious under-current, originally independent of any abstruse metaphysical speculation, flowing on from an obscure point of time in the religious history of India. With these practices and yogic processes, which characterise Tāntricism as a whole, different philosophical, or rather theological, systems got closely associated in different times, and the association of the practices with the fundamental ideas of Mahāyāna Buddhism will explain the origin and development of Tāntric Buddhism. Being associated with the Tāntric system the fundamental ideas of Buddhism underwent a great change; or it may also be that the transformation of the fundamental ideas by lay people, who were indiscriminately admitted into the school of Mahāyāna, facilitated the association of Buddhism with Tāntricism. There seems to have been a mutual interaction between the cause and the effect in either case.

In this mode of transformation the most important point is the transformation of the idea of Śūnyatā (vacuity) into the idea of Vajra, or the thunderbolt. The Śūnyatā-nature of the world is its ultimate immutable nature, as immutable as the thunderbolt, and so it is called the Vajra. It has been said in the *Advaya-vajra-saṁgraha*,—"Śūnyatā, which is firm, substantial, indivisible, impenetrable, incapable of being burnt and imperishable, is called the Vajra."[1] This trans-

[1] *dṛḍhaṁ sāram asauśīryam acchedyā-bhedya-lakṣaṇam |*
adāhi avināśi ca śūnyatā vajram ucyate ||
Advaya-vajra-saṁgraha (G.O.S.), p. 37.
Cf. also, *abhedyaṁ vajram ity uktam*—*Hevajra-tantra*, MS. (A.S.B., No. 11377), p. 2 (A).

formation of Śūnyatā to Vajra will explain the title Vajra-yāna and in Vajra-yāna all the gods, goddesses, articles for worship, yogic practices and elaborate rituals have been marked with Vajra to specialise them from their originally accepted nature. The supreme deity of Vajra-yāna is the Vajra-sattva (*vajra*=*śūnyatā*=vacuity; *sattva*=quintessence), who is of the nature of pure consciousness (*vijñapti-mātratā* of the Vijñāna-vādin Buddhists) as associated with Śūnyatā in the form of the absence of subjectivity and objectivity.[1] All the other gods of Vajra-yāna are generally marked by a miniature figure of the Vajra-sattva in the crest. This Vajra-sattva as the Lord Supreme has been described by and invoked with various attributes in all the Tantras belonging to Vajra-yāna.

The Vajra-sattva is often found in the Buddhist Tantras conceived exactly in the manner of the Upaniṣadic Brahman. It is the Self in man,—it is the ultimate substance behind the world of phenomena. It is often spoken of as the ultimate reality in the form of the Bodhi-citta. The Mahāyānic idea of Bodhi-citta also underwent a change beyond recognition in esoteric Buddhism. Originally it was conceived as the mental state in which there is nothing but a strong resolution for the attainment of perfect wisdom (*bodhi*) combined with a strong emotion of universal compassion. Thus Bodhi-citta presupposes two elements in the Citta, *viz.*, Śūnyatā (*i.e.*, the knowledge of the nature of things as pure void) and Karuṇā (universal compassion). This Bodhi-citta, with the elements of Śūnyatā and Karuṇā in it, marches, after it is produced, upwards through ten stages and in the final stage of *Dharmamegha* it attains perfection. In the practice of Vajra-yāna particularly in Sahaja-yāna (where Śūnyatā and Karuṇā, the two elements to be united together for the production of the Bodhi-citta, were identified with the female and the male or Prajñā and Upāya) Bodhi-citta is conceived as the extremely blissful state of mind produced through the sexo-yogic practice. In yogic practices the union of the seed and the ovum is also known

śūnyatā vajram ity uktam—*Jvālāvalī-vajra-mālā-tantra* MS. (B. N. Paris, Sans. No. 47), p. 1 (B).

[1] *Advaya-vajra-saṁgraha* (G.O.S.), p. 24.

as Bodhi-citta and it has been held that in the process of production this Bodhi-citta acquires the nature of the five elements, *viz.*, earth, water, fire, air and ether and thus it stands as the ultimate substance of the universe.[1]

Closely related to the history of the transformation of the idea of Bodhi-citta is the history of the transformation of the ideas of Śūnyatā and Karuṇā into the ideas of the female and the male. In Mahāyāna texts we find that Śūnyatā is Prajñā, *i.e.*, perfect knowledge of the void-nature of the self and the Dharmas. Karuṇā or universal compassion is called the Upāya, *i.e.*, the means or the expedience for the attainment of the Bodhi-citta. These two terms, Prajñā and Upāya, are found already used by the Tathatāvādin Aśvaghoṣa as well as by Nāgārjuna, the exponent of the Mādhyamika school.[2] Upāya is generally explained in the Mahāyānic texts like the *Saddharma-puṇḍarīka*[3] and the *Bodhisattva-bhūmi*[4] as missionary works which are prompted by universal compassion for the suffering beings. This Prajñā as perfect wisdom was conceived as absolutely passive, the negative aspect of the reality and the primordial source of all entities; whereas Upāya, because of its dynamic nature, began to be conceived as the positive and the active aspect of the reality. Upāya brings into existence in the phenomenal world all the entities, the possibility of which lie in the Prajñā or the void. Unlike the Sāṁkhya system and the popular Vedāntic thoughts, the negative or passive or the unqualified aspect of the reality as perfect knowledge was conceived as the female in the Buddhist school,—and the positive or active principle was conceived as the male. When thus the idea of the male and the female could once creep into Buddhism the whole outlook began to change, and the production of Bodhi-citta through the unification of void-knowledge and universal compassion was trans-

[1] *Dohākoṣa* of Kānha-pāda. Dohā No. 7. See also *Hevajra-tantra*, MS. (A.S.B., No. 11317), pp 37(B)-38(A); also *Sampuṭikā* MS. (A. S. B., No. 4854), pp. 47(B)-48(A).

[2] See Aśvaghoṣa's *Mahā-yāna-śraddhotpāda-sūtra* translated as the *Awakening of Faith in Mahāyāna* by Suzuki, pp. 66, 99. *Cf.* also *Mādhyamika-vṛtti* of Nāgārjuna, La Vallee Poussin's edition, p. 2.

[3] *Saddharma-puṇḍarīka*, Ch. II, Bibliotheca Buddhica publication, pp. 28-58.

[4] The *Bodhisattva-bhūmi* is but the fifteenth section of the *Yogācāra-bhūmi* of Vasubandhu. Edited by Unrai Wogihara, Tokyo, pp. 261-72.

formed into the production of great bliss through the yogic union of the female and the male.

We shall see later on that with this identification of Prajñā and Upāya with the female and the male the idea of Śakti and Śiva was established in the Buddhist Tantras,—and through this transformation of Prajñā and Upāya to the female and the male the sexo-yogic practice could be associated with Mahāyāna philosophy. Again, consistently with the theory of all the Tantras that the human organism is but an epitome of the universe and that all truth is within this body, the Tāntric Buddhists had to locate all the philosophical truths within this physical organism,—and in that attempt Prajñā and Upāya have been identified with the two important nerves in the left and the right of the Spinal Chord, and these nerves are known in yoga-literature in general as Iḍā and Piṅgalā, the moon and the sun, the left and the right, vowels and consonants, etc.[1] The middle nerve, corresponding to the Suṣumnā of the Hindu Tantras, is called the Avadhūtikā through which Bodhi-citta passes in its upward march from the Nirmāṇa-cakra (*cf.* the Nirmāṇa-kāya of Buddha), which is situated in the region of the navel, first to Dharma-cakra (*cf.* Dharma-kāya) in the heart and then to Sambhoga-cakra (*cf.* Sambhoga-kāya) in the neck and thence it passes to the lotus in the head producing supreme bliss.

In this connection we should take notice of the import of the concept of Advaya (non-duality) and Yuganaddha (principle of union) as we find them in esoteric Buddhism. Originally the word Yuganaddha implies the synthesis of all duality in an absolute principle of unity. This principle of Yuganaddha or union is very clearly explained in the fifth chapter (*Yuganaddha-krama*) of the *Pañca-krama*. It is said there that Yuganaddha is a state of unity reached through the purging off of the two notions of the world-process (*saṃsāra*) an absolute cessation (*nivṛtti*), through the realisation of the ultimate nature of both the phenomenal (*saṃkleśa*) and the absolute (*vyavadāna*), through the synthesis of thought-constructions of all corporeal existence with the notion of the formless. It is the unification of the

[1] *See Infra.*

Grāhya (perceivable) with the Grāhaka (perceiver), of the temporal with the eternal, of Prajñā (perfect knowledge) with Karuṇā (universal compassion).[1] To enter into the final abode or the 'thatness' (*tathatā*) in body, speech and mind and thence to come down again and to turn to the world of miseries,—to know the nature of Samvṛti (the provisional truth) and the Paramārtha (the ultimate truth) and then to unite them together—this is what is called the immutable state of Yuganaddha.[2] In the *Yuganaddha-prakāśa* of *Advaya-vajra-saṁgraha* we find that the nature of the union of Śūnyatā and Karuṇā is incomprehensible; they remain always in union.[3] In the *Prema-pañcaka* of the same text Śūnyatā has been spoken of as the wife and Karuṇā, which is the manifestation of Śūnyatā, has been spoken of as the husband and the relation between them is that of conjugal love, which is but natural (*sahajaṁ prema*). So inseparable are they in their deep love that Śūnyatā without her husband, manifestation, would have been dead and Karuṇā (or *Kṛpā*) without Śūnyatā would have always suffered bondage. In the *Sādhana-mālā* it has been said that the one body of the ultimate nature which is the unity of both Śunyatā and Karuṇā is called the neuter (*napuṁsaka*) or as Yuganaddha.[4]

This principle of Yuganaddha is the same as the principle of non-duality (*advaya*). The principle of conjugal union (*maithuna* or *kāma-kalā* as it is called in the *Kāma-kalā-vilāsa*) of the Śaiva and Śākta Tantras originally refers to the same principle.[5] There also the designations of the

1 *saṁsāro nivṛttiś ceti kalpanā-dvaya-varjanāt |*
ekībhāvo bhaved yatra yuganaddhaṁ tad ucyate ||
saṁkleśaṁ vyavadānañca jñātvā tu paramārthataḥ |
ekībhāvaṁ tu yo vetti sa vetti yuganaddhakam ||
sākāra-bhāva-saṁkalpaṁ nirākaratva-kalpanām |
ekīkṛtya cared yogī sa vetti yuganaddhakam ||
grāhyañ ca grāhakañ caiva dvidhā-buddhir na vidyate |
abhinnatā bhaved yatra tad āha yuganaddhakam ||
śāśvata-ccheda-buddhiṁ tu yaḥ prahāya pravartate |
yuganaddha-kramākhyaṁ vai tattvaṁ vetti sa paṇḍitaḥ ||
prajñā-karuṇayor aikyaṁ jñā(naṁ) yatra pravartate |
yuganaddha iti khyātaḥ kramo'yaṁ buddha-gocaraḥ ||
Pañca-krama, MS. (B. N. Paris, Sans. 65), p. 31 (B) *et seq.*

2 *Ibid.*

3 *Advaya-vajra-saṁgraha*, (G. O. S.) p. 49.

4 *Sādhana-mālā* (G.O.S.), Vol. 11, p. 505.

5 See *Kāma-kalā-vilāsa* (Kāśmīra Series of Texts and Studies, No. XII), verses 2, 5, 7 and the commentary on verse No. 7.

male and the female or of the seed and the ovum were used originally to explain the two aspects of the absolute reality, static and dynamic, negative and positive; and their union refers to the unity in the ultimate truth. But though this analogy of the male and the female or of the seed and the ovum has often been declared to be merely a mode of expression,[1] yet in practice it has, more often than not, been taken as real in both the Hindu and the Buddhist Tantras. We have seen that the two cardinal principles of Śunyatā and Karuṇā or Prajñā and Upāya were transformed in Vajra-yāna to the female and the male, and this will explain the representation of the Tāntric Buddhist gods and goddesses in a state of union. Closely associated with the idea of Advaya and Yuganaddha is the idea of Sama-rasa or the sameness or oneness of emotion. In a deeper sense Sama-rasa means the realisation of the oneness of the universe amidst all its diversities,—it is the realisation of one truth as the flow of a unique emotion of all-pervading bliss. In the *Hevajra-tantra* it has been said that in the Sahaja or the ultimate state there is the cognition of neither Prajñā nor of Upāya,—there is no sense of duality of difference anywhere; in such a state everything,—whether the lowest, or the middle or the best—should be realised as the same.[2] The self should be realised as neither something static, nor something dynamic; through the transcendental meditation on the underlying oneness of the cosmic principle everything should be viewed as of the same character and function.[3] All the entities come out of transcendental knowledge of the form of Sama-rasa,—they are all equal and non-dual in nature.[4] When through the yogic process

[1] See *Gandharva-tantra* quoted in the article, *General Introduction to Tantra Philosophy*, by Dr. S. N. Dasgupta in his *Philosophical Essays*.

[2] *hīna-madhyo-tkṛṣṭāny eva anyāni yāni tāni ca* |
sarve tāni samānī'ti draṣṭavyaṁ tattva-bhāvataḥ ||
Hevajra-tantra, MS., p. 22(B).

[3] *sthira-calaṁ yāni tānī'ti sarve tānī'ti naivā'ham* |
samāni tulya-ceṣṭāni sama-rasais tattva-bhāvanaiḥ ||
Ibid., MS., p. 22(B)-23(A).

See also *Ibid.*, p. 23(B), 24(A), 27(A). All the verses found on this point in the *Hevajra-tantra* are found with slight deviations in readings also in the *Sampuṭikā*, MS. (A.S.B. No. 4854), pp. 12(A)-13(B).

[4] *advayā-kāraṁ sarvan tu dvayam etanna vidyate* |
samaṁ sama-rasā-kāram acintya-jñāna-sambhūtam ||
Acintyā-dvaya-kramo-padeśa of Kuddāla-pāda, MS. (C.L.B. No. 13124), p. 108(B).

one enters into the state of supreme bliss (*Mahā-sukha*), the whole world becomes of the form of unique emotion in the nature of Mahā-sukha, and through this unique emotion of bliss the whole world as static and dynamic becomes one.[1] This Sama-rasa has been extensively used in many of the Buddhist as well as Hindu Tāntric texts to signify the union of Prajñā and Upāya, or of the Śakti and the Śiva, or rather to signify the intense bliss that is derived from the sexo-yogic practice, which, in its highest intensity, has got the capacity of producing an absolute homogeneity in the psychical states and processes.

The other important innovation in Tāntric Buddhism is the idea of Mahā-sukha (supreme bliss) which evolved from the idea of Nirvāṇa in earlier Buddhism. Etymologically the word Nirvāṇa may mean either the final stoppage to a flow,—*i.e.*, complete cessation of the cycle of birth and death;—or it may mean 'blowing out' as in the case of a lamp;—or the eternal tranquillity resulting from the cessation of all the Vāsanā (root-instincts) and Saṁskāras (deep impressions). In either case, from the idea of complete cessation and perfect tranquillity developed the idea of perfect peace in Nirvāṇa. There is, of course, a lot of controversy over the question whether Nirvāṇa is any positive state at all; without entering into the philosophical subtleties involved in the question, we may say that in popular belief as represented through the popular Pāli literature Nirvāṇa was conceived as something positive.[2] Though in Pāli literature Nirvāṇa is often described as something unspeakable, yet in course of poetic description we find it described as supreme (*paraṃ*) tranquil (*santa*), pure (*visuddha*), excellent (*panita*), calm (*santi*), immutable (*akkhara*), eternal (*dhruva*), true (*sacca*), infinite (*ananta*), unborn (*ajāta*), uncreated (*asaṁkhata, akata*), all alone (*kevala*), and all good (*siva*). It is, as Rhys Davids puts it,[3]—"the harbour of refuge, the cool cave, the island amidst the floods, the place of bliss, emancipation, liberation, safety, tranquillity, the home of ease, the calm, the end of suffering, the medicine for all evil, the unshaken,

1 *Vyakta-bhāvā-nugata-tattva-siddhi*, MS. (C.L.B. No. 13124), p. 89(A).

2 See the discourse on Nirvāṇa in the *Milinda-pañho*, edited by Trenckner, pp. 315-26.

3 *A Dictionary of Pāli Language*. See the word *nibbāṇa*.

the ambrosia, the immaterial, the imperishable, the abiding, the further shore, the unending, the bliss of effort, the supreme joy, the ineffable, the holy city, etc." Nirvāṇa is spoken of in many popular Pāli texts as not only something positive, but as a state of infinite bliss.[1] In the Vijñāna-vāda school of Mahāyāna Buddhism pure consciousness as bereft of the notions of the knower and the knowable has been spoken of as the 'element of Nirvāṇa' (*nirvāṇa-dhātu*); and this pure consciousness (*vijñapti-mātratā*) has been described in the *Vijñapti-mātrāta-siddhi* of Vasubandhu as "the immutable element which is beyond the reach of all mentation; it is all good, permanent, perfect bliss,—it is liberation, the substance itself."[2]

This positive aspect of Nirvāṇa as supreme bliss or Mahā-sukha was emphasised in Tāntric Buddhism and in later times Nirvāṇa and Mahā-sukha were held to be identical. Nirvāṇa is described frequently in the Tantras as incessant bliss (*satata-sukhamaya*),[3] the place of both enjoyment and liberation, changeless supreme bliss, the seed (*bīja*) of all substance (*vastu*), the ultimate state of those who have attained perfection, the highest place of the Buddhas, called the Sukhāvatī.[4]

Gradually the idea of Mahā-sukha began to acquire a cosmological and ontological significance in the various schools of Tāntric Buddhism. As Mahāyāna Buddhism often speaks of Nirvāṇa as the ultimate reality—as the Dharma-kāya, which is neither existence nor extinction,—so also the Mahā-

[1] *santīti nibbāṇaṁ ñatvā*, etc. *Sutta-nipāta*, 933.
nibbāṇaṁ paramaṁ sukhaṁ. *Majjhima-nikāya*, (1.508), *Cf.* also *Dhamma-pada*, verses (203-04).
Cf. also *odhunitvā malaṁ sabbaṁ patvā nibbāṇa-sampadaṁ* |
muccati sabba-dukkhehi sa hoti sabba-sampado ||
Aṅguttara, IV. 239.
pattā te acala-ṭṭhānaṁ yathā gatvā na socare |
Vimāna-vatthu, 51.
nibbāṇa- ṭhāne vimuttā te pattā te acalaṁ sukhaṁ |
Therī-gāthā, 350.
santi-maggam eva bruhaya nibbāṇaṁ sugatena desitaṁ |
Dhamma-pada, 285.
See the word *nibbāṇa* in *A Dictionary of Pāli Language*, by Rhys Davids, and the *Pāli Dictionary* by Childers.

[2] *sa evā'nasravo dhātur acintyaḥ kuśalo dhruvaḥ* |
sukho vimukti-kāyo' sau dharmā-khyo' yaṁ mahāmuneḥ ||
Triṁśikā, verse 30.

[3] *Pañca-krama*, MS., p. 31(B).

[4] *Guhya-siddhi* of Padma-vajra. MS. (C.L.B. No. 13124), pp. 13(A)-13(B).

sukha is variously described in the Buddhist Tantras as the ultimate reality transcending, or rather absorbing within it, both existence (*bhava*) and extinction (*nirvāṇa*). It is described as something which has neither beginning nor middle nor end; it is neither existence nor annihilation, neither the self nor the not-self.[1] The Mahā-sukha is the Lord Vajra-sattva of the nature of the unity of Prajñā and Upāya; it is the non-dual quintessence of all the entities.[2] It is the Bodhi-citta or perfect enlightenment combined with compassion.[3] In the *Hevajra-tantra* it has been said that Sukha or bliss is the ultimate reality, it is the Dharma-kāya, it is the Lord Buddha Himself. Sukha is black, it is yellow, it is red, it is white, it is green, it is blue, it is the whole universe; it is Prajñā, it is Upāya, it itself is the union; it is existence, it is non-existence, it is the Lord Vajra-sattva.[4]

When Nirvāṇa was thus identified with a state of supreme bliss, the attainment of an absolute state of supreme bliss was accepted to be the *summum bonum* of life by all the Tāntric Buddhists.[5] For the realisation of such a state of supreme bliss they adopted a course of sexo-yogic practice. This conception of Mahā-sukha is the central point round which all the esoteric practices of the Tāntric Buddhists grew and developed.

After this brief account of the general characteristics of Vajra-yāna Buddhism or Tāntric Buddhism in general, and after indicating the mode of transformation of the cardinal principles of Mahāyāna into the esoteric doctrines of Vajra-yāna, let us now concentrate our attention on the study of the old Bengali Caryā-songs and the cognate Dohās, which explain the special features of the Sahajiyā school of Buddhism.

[1] *āi ṇa anta ṇa majhu ṇa ṇau bhava ṇau nibbāṇa* |
ehu so parama mahā-sukha ṇau para ṇau appāṇa ||
Quoted in the *Hevajra-tantra*, MS., p. 61(A).

[2] *Mahā-sukha-prakāśa* of the *Advaya-vajra-saṁgraha* (G.O.S.), p. 50.

[3] See *Advaya-samatā-vijaya*, quoted in the *Jñāna-siddhi* (G.O.S.), Ch. XV, verse 40.
Cf. jina-śrīherukaḥ | *tasya hṛdayam akṣara-bodhi-cittam* | *tasya hṛdayaṁ mahāsukham* etc. *Marma-kalikā-tantra*, MS., p. 29(B).

[4] *Hevajra-tantra*, MS., p. 35 (B). *Cf.* also *Sampuṭikā*, MS., p. 48(B).

[5] In this connection see *Hevajra-tantra*, MS, p. 36(A).
Also *Guhya-siddhi*, MS., p. 10(B).
Vyakta-bhāvānugata-tattva-siddhi, MS., p. 86(A).

CHAPTER II

THE GENERAL PHILOSOPHICAL STANDPOINT OF THE CARYĀ-PADAS

THE general philosophical standpoint of the Caryā-padas, as that of Tāntric Buddhist literature in general, represents unsystematised notions of Mahāyāna philosophy including the negativistic tendency of the Mādhyamikas and the positivistic tendency of Aśvaghoṣa and of the Vijñānavāda school led by Maitreya, Asaṅga and Vasubandhu. The influence of monistic thought is not also negligible.[1] In many places the Buddhist Tantras, Dohās and songs have frankly accepted the monistic standpoint of the Upaniṣads and the highest reality, either in the form of the Vajra-sattva or the Bodhi-citta or the Mahā-sukha or the Sahaja, has been conceived exactly in the line of the Upaniṣadic Brahman. It may be observed in this connection that scholars have often discovered something behind the nothingness (*śūnyatā*) even of Nāgārjuna, who has described the reality as neither existent, nor non-existent, nor a combination of both, nor the absence of both; it is but what transcends the four logical categories (*catuṣkoṭi*). Again, it may be pointed out that the Abhūta-parikalpa (the increate) or the Vijñapti-mātratā (pure consciousness) of the Vijñānavādin Buddhists approximates the Vedāntic conception of the Brahman in a striking manner. Of course, subtle points of difference there are, but they can very easily be, and have often actually been, missed by the untrained mind of ordinary thinkers. It is for this reason that the Mahāyānic ideas have frequently been confused or blended with the Vedāntic ideas; and we shall see that there is practically no difference between the Vedāntic idea of the reality and the idea of the Sahaja as conceived by the Sahajiyās. Kānha-pāda says

[1] For a detailed discussion on the philosophical position of the different schools of Mahāyāna Buddhism and its relation to the Vedāntic thoughts, and also for a detailed study of the philosophical standpoint of Tāntric Buddhist literature in general reference may be made here to the study of the subject in the work *An Introduction to Tāntric Buddhism* by the present writer.

in a song that it will be a gross mistake to think that everything ends with the decay of this body. "My Citta," says the poet, "is perfect in vacuity; don't be sorry at the disappearance of the *skandhas* or the five elements. Say, how it can be that Kānha is no more,—for he is throbbing for ever pervading the whole universe. Only foolish people are sad at the sight of the decay of the perceivable;—can the flow of waves dry up the whole sea? Foolish people do not see people who are existent (in their subtle Sahaja form) as they do not find the cream that remains pervading the milk. Here, in this world, entities neither come nor go, yogin Kānha reveals in these thoughts."[1]

The dominating philosophical note of the Caryā-songs is, however, of an inherent idealistic vein as associated with the various theories of illusion. As this idealism, associated with the theories of illusion, is common to the Mādhyamika and Vijñāna-vāda Buddhism as well as to Vedānta, we shall find a mixture of the philosophical views of these schools in the songs of the Buddhist Sahajiyā poets.

The first song of the Caryā-padas begins with the assertion that our mind (*citta*) is solely responsible for the creation of the illusory world. "In the unsteady mind"—says Lui-pā in one of his songs,—"enters Time,"[2] *i.e.*, the disturbed mind is the cause of all our spatio-temporal experiences and the disturbance of the mind is due to the defiling principle of nature (*prakṛty-ābhāsa-doṣa-vaśāt cāñcalyatayā*, etc.—comm.).

[1] *bhaṇa kaise kāhnu nāhi* |
pharai anudina tailoe pamāi ||
mūḍhā diṭha nāṭha dekhi kāara |
bhāga-taraṅga ki soṣai sāara ||
mūḍhā acchante loa na pekhai |
dudha māñjheṁ laḍa acchante na dekhai || *etc.*

Song No. 42.

As for the reading of the Caryā-padas the writer has generally accepted the readings suggested by Dr. P. C. Bagchi with the help of the Tibetan translation (J.D.L., Vol. XXX); but he has often differed from Dr. Bagchi, and the point's of difference with reasons and the suggested improvements have appeared in an article of the writer in the Bengali Monthly *Śrī-bhāratī*, (Vol. 1, No. 7). Dr. Bagchi's readings have, therefore, been accepted with the improvements suggested therein.

[2] *cāñcala cīe paiṭho kāla* || *Ibid.*, Song No. 1.

This line has been explained in the commentary in an esoteric sense. *Vide, Infra.*

The notion of difference proceeds from the notion of existence (*bhava*). It is said, "They are three, they are three—the three are held different;—Kānhu says,—all (differences) are limitations due to the notion of existence."[1] The world of our experiences is only provisional (*saṁvṛti-satya*) and the provisional nature of the world is revealed to us when we see that every thing that comes also invariably goes,—there is nothing permanent; all is an eternal flux of coming and going. It is said,—"Whatever came also went away; in this (rotation of) coming and going Kānhu has become convinced (of the unsubstantial nature of the fleeting world)."[2] But everything is pure in the ultimate nature. Neither existence nor non-existence is impure in the least; all beings, produced in the six ways (*ṣaḍ-gatikā*), are pure by their ultimate nature.[3] The empirical world is like a dramatic device (*naḍapeḍā,* Skt. *naṭa-peṭikā*=basket for holding dress, etc. for the performance of drama) with nothing real in it,—it is merely an artifice of the mind. By pure knowledge the mind must first be tranquillised and when it becomes perfectly controlled all the forces of the illusory world are subdued.[4] In that ultimate stage external objects of smell, touch, etc., remain as they were, but the perceptual knowledge of the whole world appears to be just like the perception of objects in a waking dream, *i.e.*, the whole universal process seems to be a great dream, though we remain with our outward eyes open.[5] In one song of Bhusuka-pāda, the mind (*citta*) has been compared to a fickle rat and it is said to be closely associated with the vital wind. It is said,—"Dark is the night and the play of the rat begins."[6] The dark night is the darkness of ignorance in which the function of constructive imagination goes on. It is further said,—"Kill, O Yogin, this rat of the vital wind,

1 *te tini te tini tini ho bhinnā* |
bhaṇai kāhnu bhava-paricchinnā || *Ibid.*, Song No. 7
2 *je je āilā te te gelā* |
avanā-gavaṇe kāhnu bimana bhailā || *Ibid.*
3 *chaḍagai saala sahāve sūdha* |
bhāvābhāva balāga na chudha || *Ibid*, Song. No. 9.
4 *matiem ṭhākuraka parinivitā* |
avaśa kariā bhava-bala jitā || *ibid*, Song No. 12.
5 *gandha parasa rasa jaisoṁ taisoṁ* |
niṁda bihune suinā jaisoṁ || *Ibid.*, Song No. 13.
6 *nisi andhārī musāra cārā* | *ibid.*, Song No. 21.

whereby you will escape coming and going. The rat causes existence and makes holes; this fickle rat remains inactive only when skilful devices are employed. This rat is Time or death itself (*i.e.*, the fickle mind constructs all temporal existence),—but in it there is no colour. When it rises to the void it moves there and drinks nectar. The rat remains restless (as long as it is not pacified by the instructions of the preceptor); pacify it through the instructions of the wise preceptor. Bhusuka says,—when the activities of the rat will be destroyed, all bondage will also be destroyed."

In another song of Bhusuka-pāda the mind has been compared to a deer. The song goes thus:—"Near whom and with whom am I living and in what way!—a clamour is rising around from all the four quarters. The deer has become the enemy of all because of its own flesh. I see, the hunters do not leave Bhusuka (who is like unto the fickle deer) even for a moment. The deer does not touch the grass nor does it drink water; the abode of the doe is not known to the deer. The doe says to the deer, hearest me, thou deer, leave this forest and become mad. While running in haste the hoofs of the deer are not seen,—Bhusuka says,—it does not enter into the heart of the ignorant."[1]

Here the deer represents the mind; due to the principles of defilement it is always surrounded by the hunters who are the miseries of life. As the deer is the enemy of all because of its own flesh, so also the *citta* itself is the cause of all its miseries; for, it itself constructs the world of miseries through its own activities. But when the deer *citta* is troubled thus amidst the miseries of life, then comes the doe or the goddess Nairātmā (essencelessness or perfect vacuity) to its help and she takes it away from this world beset on all sides with the hunters.

It has been said in another song,—"Going on constructing for himself (the notions of) existence and extinction, for nothing does man bring him under bondage.

[1] *Ibid.*, Song No. 6. It may be noted in this connection that the story of the deer and the doe is very popular in old and medieval folk-songs of the vernacular literatures. The saying that the deer is enemy to the world because of its own flesh is to be frequently met with in old and medieval vernacular literatures. The Siddhācārya has here made use of the popular imagery to explain the religious theory. We have already referred to a Hindi folk song which bears striking similarity with this song. See Supra.

We, the supralogical Yogins (*acinta yoi*), do not know how birth, death and existence come at all to be. Death is exactly the same as birth,—there is no distinction between being and dying. Let them, who are here afraid of birth and death, care for (the practice and ceremonies of) *rasa* and *rasāyana*.[1] Those who generally roam about (in the temples of) gods and goddesses become neither free from decrepitude, nor do they become immortal. It is not known whether there is *karma* due to birth, or there is birth due to *karma*; Saraha, however, says,—unthinkable is that abode."[2] Due to the beginningless root-instincts (*vāsanā*) man falsely constructs the notions of existence and extinction and thus himself puts the fetters of bondage on him. When the *citta* becomes tranquillised there is no birth—no death,—no bondage—no liberation,—so all the differences between all theses and anti-theses vanish at once.

In another place Lui-pāda says,—"Existence does not come, neither is there non-existence;—who does understand the truth in this way? Incomprehensible indeed is the nature of pure consciousness,—says Lui; in the three elements it sports but it itself is not known. How can the Āgamas and the Vedas explain that, whose colour, sign and form are not known? By speaking of what, should I give an exposition of truth? Just like the moon in water it is neither real nor unreal. How should it be thought of?—says Lui,—I

1 This evidently refers to the practice of the Rasāyana-school of yogins who tried to escape death through a yogic process akin to the process of Rasāyana (see *infra*). We may incidentally notice another practice held in the temple of the lamas of Tibet. It has been said:—"Another service, known by the Mongolian name Tuiurgnikji has for object the preparation of the lustral water (rasāyana). It includes prayer, absolution of sins, a recital of all the ablutions made by Sakya-muni, and finally thanksgiving. Between the first and the second part of the rite is performed the preparation of the holy water. One of the priest's assistants raises a mirror so that it reflects one of the statues of the divinities; another takes the *vessel* (*kuje*, Mongolian) filled with water and pours it upon the mirror. The water which flows off and is believed to have caught the image of the divinity is collected in a special dish (k'ris-gc'os—Tibetan) held by a third acolyte, while a fourth wipes the mirror with a silken napkin (Qadaq Mong.). Fifteen libations are made in this way and at the end of the ceremony the lustral water is poured off into a bum-pa and set on the sacrificial altar. Thereafter it is used for the aspersion of offerings and washing the mouths of the 'Lamas', while among the laity it serves the same purpose as does holy water among Catholics." Introduction by J. Deniker to the *Gods of Northern Buddhism*—by Alice Getty, p. xi.

2 Song No. 22.

do not see any magnitude or locality of what I am now (*i.e. mahā-sukha*)."[1] Here also the phenomenal world is described as neither existent, as we do not find any reality anywhere by analysing it,—nor is it non-existent, as non-existence itself is unreal (*asad-rūpatvāt*); it is not real as it has no ultimate nature (*paramārtha-satya*) neither is it unreal as it has got its provisional truth (*saṁvṛti-satya*);—it is just like the moon in the water. The ultimate truth, however, can never be explained,—for, there is no knower, no knowable—no knowledge in it,[2] the *citta* being perfectly tranquil there. It has been said,—'When one practises yoga with one's mind fixed in pure wisdom, none can ascertain where the *citta* goes and where it remains.[3] It has also been said by Āryadeva,—"When the mind, the senses and the vital wind are all destroyed, I do not know where the self goes and enters. . . . As the moon manifests itself as the rays (so also the *citta* manifests itself in the various illusory constructions, *i.e., vikalpa*); but as the moon having set, all the rays vanish, so also when the *citta* is destroyed all its modes and modifications vanish."[4] It is again said,—"The moon having set, all her rays vanish indeed; exactly in the same way, when the *citta* is merged in the Sahaja-bliss, all the impurities of

[1] *bhāva na hoi abhāva ṇa jāi* |
aisa saṁbohem ko patiāi ||
lui bhaṇai baḍha dulakkha biṇāṇā |
tia dhāe bilasai uha lāge ṇā ||
jāhera bāṇa- cihna rūva ṇa jāṇī |
so kaise āgama beem bakhāṇī ||
kāhere kisa bhaṇi mai divi piricchā |
udaka cānda jima sāca na micchā ||
lui bhaṇai mai bhāvai kīsa |
jā lai acchama tāhera ūha na disa || Song No. 29.

[2] *bhāvya-bhāvaka-bhāvanā-bhāvena kiṁ bhāvyam* |
Ibid., Com., p. 46.

[3] *cittaṁ niścitya bodhena abhyāsaṁ kurute yadā* |
tadā cittaṁ na paśyāmi kva gataṁ kva sthitaṁ bhavet ||
Quoted in the Com., p. 46.

[4] *jahi maṇa india pavaṇa ho ṇaṭhā* |
na jānami apā kahiṁ gai paiṭhā ||

. . . . . .

cāndare cānda-kānti jima paḍibhāsaa |
cia vikaraṇe tahi ṭali paisaa || Song No. 31.

false constructions are destroyed."[1] Bhāde-pāda says in one of his songs,—"Uptil now I was absorbed in self-illusion,—but now I realise the truth through the instruction of my good preceptor. Now my great *citta* is not,—it has fallen down into the ocean of the void. I behold the ten quarters all void,—without the *citta* there is neither any merit nor any demerit. The wise preceptor has explained to me all the illusions and I have destroyed them all in the void. Says Bhāde,—Taking that which is indivisible (*i.e.*, non-dual), I have devoured the great mind."[2] The active mind brings in the question of morality; but when it is destroyed there is neither any morality nor immorality,—merit and demerit are all provisional.[3] In another song of Saraha-pāda we find,—"O my mind, to drive away the impurities in the dream of ignorance the sayings of the preceptor are around you,—where shalt thou hide thyself and how? Curious indeed is the nature of illusion, through which the self and the not-self are seen; in this water-bubble of the world, the self is void itself in the Sahaja."[4]

In a song of Bhusuka-pāda the non-essential nature of the world and its illusory nature as mere subjective construction have been very nicely explained. It is said,—"Increate is the world from the beginning,—it is through illusion that it appears thus (in this form); but does a serpent actually bite the man who startles at the sight of the rope-snake? O wonderful yogin,—don't stain your hands with salt,—if you understand the world to be of this nature, your Vāsanās will be eradicated. It is like a mirage in the desert,—it is like an imaginary city of the Gandharvas,—it is just like the reflection in the mirror,—it is just like the water becoming condensed and solidified by the whirl of wind and thus

1 *astaṁgate candramasī'va nūnaṁ*
nirendavaḥ saṁharaṇaṁ prayānti |
cittaṁ hi tadvat sahaje nilīne
naśyanty amī sarva-vikalpa-doṣāḥ ||
Quoted in the Com., p. 49. (Śāstri's edition).

2 *eta kāla hāmu acchile sva-moheṁ*, etc. Song No. 35.

3 *Cf. Mādhyamika-vṛtti*. Ch. 1.

4 *suiṇe ho avidāra are nia-mana tohore dose* |
guru-baaṇa bihāreṁ re thākiva tai ghuṇḍa kaise || . . .
adabhua bhava moha re disai para appaṇā |
e jaga jala-bimvākāre sahajeṁ suṇa apaṇā ||
Song No. 39.

becoming (solid like) stone: It is just like the son of a barren woman—sporting and playing various games,—it is like oil coming out of sand,—like the horns of the hare—like the flower in the sky. Rāuta says, or Bhusuka says,—Everything is of this nature, if you be a fool, ask your true preceptor for (the solution of) your doubts taking shelter at his feet."[1] The world is as increate as the locks of hair (gossamer) seen flying in the sky by a man with defective eyes,—it is a product of constructive imaginations, which are in their turn produced by the three-fold impurities of the *citta*.[2] It has been said,—'I am as much a product of the mind as magic or dreams are.'[3] As water solidifies itself into hard stones through the whirl of wind,[4] so also through the disturbance of Vāsanā voidness itself turns into all existence.[5]

Bhusuka-pāda says in another song,—"The great tree of Sahaja is shining in the three worlds; everything being of the nature of void, what will bind what? As water mixing with water makes no difference, so also, the jewel of mind enters the sky in unity of emotion. Where there is no self, how can there be any not-self? What is increate from the beginning can have neither birth, nor death nor any kind of existence. Bhusuka says, or Rāuta says,—this is the nature of all;—nothing goes or comes,—there is neither existence nor non-existence there (in Saha-

[1] *āie anuanāeṁ jaga re bhaṁtieṁ so paḍihāi* ।
rāja-sāpa dekhi jo camakai yāre kiṁ taṁ boḍo khāi ||
akaṭa joiā re mā kara hātha lohṇā ।
āisa sabhāveṁ jai jaga bujhasi tuṭai bāsanā torā ||
maru-marici-gandhanaari-dāpaṇa-pativimvu jaisā ।
bātāvatteṁ so diḍha bhaiā apeṁ pāthara jaisā ||
bāndhi-suā jima keli karai khelai bahu-biha kheḍā ।
bāluā-teleṁ sasara-siṁge ākaśa phuliā ||
rāutu bhaṇāi kaṭa bhusuku bhaṇai kaṭa saala aisa sahāva ।
jai to mūḍhā acchasi bhāntī pucchatu sadguru pāva ||
Ibid., Song No. 41.

[2] *keśoṇḍukaṁ yathā'kāśe dṛśyate taimirikair janaiḥ* ।
tathā'lokādi-doṣeṇa bhāvo bālair vikalpyate ||
Verse of Ācārya Nidattaka, quoted in the Com. *Ibid.*, p. 63.

[3] *yathā māyā yathā svapnaṁ tathā'smi*, etc.
Quoted in the Com. *Ibid.*, p. 64.

[4] *yathā bātā-vartena nīram api prastaraṁ bhūtam* etc.—Com.

[5] *śūnyataiva bhaved bhāvo vāsanā-vāsitā satī* ।
vātā-varte dṛḍhibhūtā āpa eva ghano-palāḥ ||
Quoted in the Com. *Ibid.*, p. 64.

ja)."[1] Kaṅkaṇa-pāda says in a song,—"When the void (*i.e.*, the three-fold void of impurities) will merge itself in the void, (*i.e.*, the fourth or the perfect void)[2] the ultimate nature of all the objects will come within realisation. . . . The *bindu* and the *nāda* do not enter the heart and by seeing one (*viz.*, vacuity) the other (*viz.*, mind) is destroyed. . . . All clamour, says Kaṅkaṇa, merges into the roaring of Tathatā (thatness)."[3] The *bindu* may be explained as the principle of subjectivity; the principle of objectivity is the *nāda*.[4] This conception of the Śūnyatā as the negation of the knower and the knowable is the same as is found in the doctrine of the Vijñāna-vādins. In another song of Kānha-pāda the mind has been compared to a tree of which the five branches represent the five senses, and hopes and passions are the innumerable leaves and fruits. Kānha says,—"Cut the tree down with the axe of the great preceptor's instructions so that the tree may not shoot forth any more. The tree grows up in the water of good and evil and the wise cut it down with the instructions of the preceptor. Those fools who do not know how to cut the tree and to split it, go astray and have to accept existence (and bondage with it). The tree is of the (defiled) void, and the axe is of the perfect-void,—cut the tree down, so that no root or branch be left."[5] Our mind becomes deeply entangled in the notion of existence and all the impurities associated with it, and the notion of good and

[1] *sahaja mahā-taru phariae tiloe* |
khasama-sabhāve re bāṇata kā koe ||
jima jale pāṇiā ṭaliyā bheḍa na jāa |
tima maṇa-raaṇā re sama-rase gaaṇa samāa |
jāsu nāhi appā tāsu parelā kāhi ||
āi-aṇuaṇāre jāma-maraṇa-bhava nāhi |
bhusuku bhaṇai kaṭa rāutu bhaṇai kaṭa saala eha sahāva ||
jāi na āvai re ṇa tahiṁ bhāvābhāva ||
Ibid., Song No. 43.

[2] For threefold void of impurities and the fourth void see *infra*.

[3] *sune suna miliā javeṁ* |
saala dhāma uiā taveṁ ||

. . .

bindu-ṇāda ṇa hie paiṭhā |
āṇa cāhante āṇa biṇaṭhā ||

. . .

bhaṇai kaṅkaṇa kalaala sādeṁ |
sarva bicchorila tathatā-nādeṁ ||
Ibid., Song No. 44.

[4] Com. *Ibid.* p. 68.

[5] *maṇa taru pāñca indi tasu sāhā*, etc.
Ibid., Song No. 45.

evil acts as the dynamic principle of disturbance behind the realm of the mind. In destroying this mind we should not try only to suppress the modes and modifications of the mind (compared to the branches of the tree), but the roots of the tree, *i.e.*, the Vāsanās should also be eradicated. Jayanandi-pāda says in another song that as we perceive in dream or in the mirror objects which have no reality in them, so also is the illusion of this world. When the mind is free from this illusion, all coming and going are stopped. At that stage none can be burnt, none can be wetted, none can be cut into pieces.[1] But alas,—in spite of all these, in spite of seeing this, foolish people firmly bind themselves to illusion;—they perceive it—yet they bind themselves to this self-created false world. It is indeed astonishing that people would discard milk and take poison.[2]

But the wise Kambalāmbara-pāda says in a song,—"I have filled my boat of compassion with gold (of void) and have left silver (of all false appearances) with the world.[3] Kāmali (Kambalāmbara-pāda) is steering on towards the sky (void), —if once birth can be totally annihilated how can it recur again? I have (says Kambala) pulled the peg up and torn the rope of the boat,—and Kāmali is steering forward seeking at every step the instructions of the wise preceptor."[4] Here the peg symbolises the impure principles of the active mind (*ābhāsa-doṣāṇi*—com.) and the rope is made of the thread of book-knowledge (*vidyā-sūtram*—com). Thus, to proceed forward with the heart full of universal compassion, the Yogin must first uproot all the principles of

[1] *Ibid.*, Song No. 46.

[2] *āścaryam etaddhi manuṣya-loke kṣīraṁ parityajya viṣaṁ pivanti* ı
Quoted in the Com. *Ibid.*, p. 71.

[3] There is a beautiful pun on the word *sona* and *rūpā* here. *Sona* may be derived from the Sanskrit word *svarṇa* or *suvarṇa* (gold) or from the word *śūunya* (*cf. sona*, verse 49), and *śūnya* may here be very happily compared to gold. Again *rūpā* may be derived form the Sanskrit word *raupya* (silver) and it may also be associated with the word *rūpa* (form) and silver may also be compared to the illusory form when gold is compared to the void.

[4] *sone bharitī karuṇā nāvī* ı
rūpā thoi mahike ṭhāvī ॥ (*nāhika ṭhāvi—Bagchi*)
bāhatu kāmali gaana uvesem̐ ı
gelī jāma bāhuḍai kaisem̐ ॥
khuṇṭi upāḍī melili kācchi ı
bāhatu kāmali sadguru pucchi ॥
Ibid., Song No. 8 (1-6).

defilement in his mind and tear off the rope of scriptural knowledge. It has been declared by Saraha,—"The body is the boat, a pure mind is the oar—with the instruction of the wise preceptor take the helm (rightly). Make the mind quiet and then direct the boat on,—by no other means can one reach the other shore."[1]

The Caryā-padas, following the Tāntric texts, ofien speak of four gradations in the doctrine of Śunyatā. In the *Pañca-krama* of Nāgārjuna-pāda the four gradations have been arranged in the following manner :—the first is the Śūnya, the second Ati-śūnya, the third Mahā-śūnya and the fourth or the final is the Sarva-śūnya,—and these are all different according to their cause and effect.[2] The first stage Śūnya has been explained as light (*āloka*)[3]; it is knowledge (*prajñā*), and the mind (*citta*) remains active in it,—it is relative (*para-tantra*) by nature.[4] In this state there are as many as thirtythree impure functions (*doṣa*) of the mind; these are sorrow, fear, hunger, thirst, feeling (*vedanā*), sympathy, self-analysis (*pratyavekṣā*), kindness, affectionateness, fickleness, doubt, jealousy etc.[5] This mental state of Śūnya has also been called the woman (*strī*) and it has been said that of all illusions the illusion of the woman is the greatest.[6] It is also called the left (*vāma*), the lotus in the lunar circle,—and the first vowel. The second stage, *viz.*, Ati-śūnya is said to be the manifestation of light (*ālakā-bhāsa*), which shines like moon-rays and proceeds from the

[1] *kāa ṇāvaḍi khāṇṭi maṇa keḍuāla |*
sadguru-vaaṇe dhara patavāla ||
cīa thira kari dharahure nāhī |
āna upāye pāra na jāi ||
Ibid., Song. No. 38 (1-4).

[2] *śūnyañ ca ati-śūnyañ ca mahā-nśūyaṁ tṛtīyakam |*
caturthaṁ sarva-śūnyañ ca phala-hetu-prabhedataḥ ||
Pañca-krama. MS., p. 20 (A).

[3] *Cf. projño-tpanna ālokaḥ prādurbhūtaḥ |*
Lalita-vistara, Ed. by Dr. S. Lefmam, pp. 417-18.

[4] *ālokaṁ śūnyaṁ prajñā ca cittaṁ ca para-tantrakam |* MS., p. 20.

In the commentary (*Pañca-krama-ṭippanī* by Paṇḍita-purohita-rakṣita-pāda, MS. B. N. Sans. No. 65, 66) *śūnya-prajñā* has been explained as light (*śūnya-prajñā āloka iti yāvat*) MS., p. 43 (B).

[5] *Pañca-krama*. MS., p. 20(B),

[6] *strī-saṁjñā ca tathā proktā mandā-kārās tathaiva ca ||*
Ibid., MS., p. 20 (A)

Also, *sarveṣāṁ eva māyānāṁ strī-māyaiva viśiṣyate ||*
Ibid., MS., p. 21 (A).

former (*i.e.*, *āloka-jñāna*). It is called the Upāya and is of the nature of constructive imagination (*parikalpita*). It is also called the right (*dakṣiṇa*), the solar circle (*sūrya-maṇḍala*) and the thunderbolt (*vajra*). Forty mental functions of defilement, such as passion, contentment, joy, pleasure, wonder, patience, valour, pride, energy, greed, etc., are associated with this state. The third stage, *viz.*, Mahā-śūnya proceeds from the union of Prajñā and Upāya or *āloka* and *ālokābhāsa*, or Śūnya and Ati-śūnya,—and it is called the intuition of light (*āloko-palabdhi*) and is of the absolute nature (*pariniṣpanna*); and yet it is called ignorance (*avidyā*) and is associated with seven impure mental functions of defilement, *viz.*, forgetfulness, illusion, stupor, laziness, etc. Thus *āloka*, *ālokā-bhāsa* and *āloko-palabdhi*—these are the three stages of the *citta* from which there follow the principles of impurities, numbering hundred and sixty in all.[1] They function throughout the whole day and night with the flow of the vital wind, which has been said to be the medium (*vāhana*) through which the impurities of nature function.[2] It has been said, wherever there is the function of the bio-motor force or the vital wind, nature with all its impurities is also brought along with it, and so long as there is the function of this bio-motor force or the vital wind, the principles of impurity will not cease to function.

The fourth stage, *viz.*, Sarva-śūnya (all-void or perfect void) is free from the three-fold impurities mentioned above, and is self-illuminant. It is absolute purity obtained by transcending the principles of defilement. It is the purified knowledge, the ultimate truth, the supreme omniscience. It is a state which can be said to be neither without beginning, nor with beginning,—neither without middle nor with middle, neither without end nor with end. It is beyond the categories of either being or non-being, merit or demerit, or even a combination or the absence of both.[3]

[1] The total number of the principles of defilement (*prakṛti-doṣa*) are really eighty; (thirty-three in the first state of Śūnya, seven in the second and forty in the third state); but the number is doubled taking into consideration both day and night.

[2] *etāḥ prakṛtayaḥ sūkṣmāḥ śataṁ ṣaṣṭhy-uttaraṁ divā* |
rātrau cāpi pravartante vāyu-vāhana-hetunā ||
Pañca-krama, MS., pp. 21(A)—21(B).

[3] *Ibid.*, MS., p. 30(A).

This theory of the four Śūnyas, as expounded in the *Pañca-krama* of Nāgārjuna-pāda seems to be the reminiscence of a similar doctrine of Śūnyas expounded in some Hindu and Buddhist texts. An exposition of the theory of seven Śūnyas is found in the old Tāntric text *Svacchanda*, a theory which found its echo in many of the subsequent texts of the Śaiva and Śākta literature. The *Svacchanda* contends that there are seven kinds of Śūnya, of which the first six are impure and contain the seeds of phenomenalism,[1] whereas the seventh is the Supreme Reality itself, which is Pure Being and Consciousness and is free from all the *Vikalpas*. The doctrine of sixteen or eighteen Śūnyas as enumerated by Asaṅga or Diṅnāga (in the *Madhyānta-bibhāga* or the *Aṣṭa-sāhasrikā-piṇḍārtha*) and also by the Nātha writers is also of a similar character.

The theory of the four Śūnyas was accepted both in the Dohās and the Caryā-padas. In a Dohā of Kṛṣṇācārya it has been said that in the abode of Mahā-sukha there are four stalks and four leaves.[2] Here the four leaves are the four Śūnyas, and the four stalks are the four sources.[3] Sarva-śūnya is said to be the effulgent principle,—there is no higher truth than this.[4] It is the abode of Avadhūtī (*i.e.*, the damsel of the nature of perfect bliss), it is the abode of the Jinas.[5]

In the Caryā-padas and their commentary we find occasional reference to this theory of the four Śūnyas and the impurities of nature (*prakṛti-doṣa*), which are the cause of the cycle of birth and death and all the resulting sufferings, and they have always been prescribed to be eradicated. There

[1] *ūrddhva-sūnyam adhaḥ-sūnyaṁ madhya-śūnyaṁ tṛtīyakam |*
sūnya-trayaṁ calaṁ hy etad adho madhya ūrddhvataḥ ||
caturthaṁ vyāni-sūnyaṁ samanāyāṁ ca pañcamam |
unmanāyāṁ tathā ṣaṣṭhaṁ ṣaḍ ete sāmayāḥ sthitāḥ ||
Ch. IV, verses (289-290)
(Kashmir Series of Texts and Studies, No. XXVIII).

[2] *patta-cauṭṭha cau-mūṇāla ṭhia mahāsuha vāse |*
Verse No. 5, Dr. Bagchi's edition in the J. D. L. Vol. XXVIII. 1935

[3] *śūnyā-tiśūnya-mahāśūnya-sarvaśūnyaṁ iti catuḥ-śūnya-svarūpeṇa patra-catuṣṭayam, catur ādi-svarūpeṇa catur mṛṇāla-saṁsthitāḥ*, etc., Com.

[4] *sarva-śūnyaṁ prabhāsvaram ato nānyac chūnyaṁ tattvam astī'ty arthaḥ* Com.
This commentary on the *Dohākoṣa* of Kāhna-pāda is, however, different from the commentary discovered and published by MM. Śāstrī. It is found in a MS (B. N. Sans. No. 47, available in rotograph)., p. 43(A).

[5] *Ibid.*, MS., p. 57(A).

is a song of Dheṇḍhaṇa-pāda, which may be literally translated thus,—"On a lofty height is situated my house; no neighbour have I. There is no rice in the earthen pot,—(guests) come every day..... The bull has given birth, but the cow is barren. The milk-pot is being filled with milk thrice in the day."[1] The esoteric significance of the lines (in light of the commentary) is that when all the hundred and sixty impurities of nature pertaining to the body, word and mind all vanish away in the Mahā-sukha-cakra[2] (which is compared to the house on the height), the neighbours, *viz.*, the sun and the moon are gone;[3] *i.e.*, with the destruction of the *prakṛti-doṣas* all the functions of the sun and the moon are also destroyed.[4] The mind with the three principles of impurity (*ābhāsa-traya*), compared, to the bull, gives rise to the notion of the external world, but barren is the non-essential void (compared to the cow).[5] The Yogin always tries to destroy all these impurities (*piṭa-pīṭhakam*, *ābhāsa-doṣam*).[6] In another place Dārika-pāda says,—'Dārika revels on the other side of the sky;[7] and this sky (*gaana*=*gagana*) has been explained in the commentary as the three-fold void or light discussed above.[8] The final stage is the other side of the three-fold Śūnya. In one song of Kānha-pāda it is said,—"On the arm of the void I strike with the 'thatness' and I plunder the whole storage of attachment and take away (all it contains)".[9] The image may be explained thus:—The

[1] *ṭālata mora ghara nāhi paḍivesī* |
hāḍīta bhāta nāhi niti āvesī ||

. . .

balada biāela gaviā bāṁjhe |
piṭā duhiāi e tinā sāṁjhe ||
Song No. 33.

[2] *asadrūpaṁ kāya-vāk-cittasya ṣaṣṭhy-uttara-śata-prakṛti-doṣaṁ yasm(i)n samaye mahā-sukha-cakre layaṁ gataṁ tad eva mama gṛham.*, etc.
Ibid. Com., p. 51.

[3] *Cf.* Com. *pārśvastha-candra-sūryau.*

[4] *Candra-sūrya* may here imply subjectivity and objectivity,—or, the two nerves in the left and the right; about this we shall have detailed discussion later on.

[5] *balada ityādi—balaṁ mānasād deha-vigrahaṁ dadātī'ti baladas tad eva bodhi-citta(m) ābhāsa-traya-prastutam.* Com. p. 52, (Śāstrī's edition).

[6] *dohanam iti niḥsvabhāvī-karaṇaṁ kriyate sandhyā-trayam iti ahaḥ-niśaṁ yogīn-dreṇe'ti* *Ibid.*, Com. p. 52.

[7] *bilasai dārika gaanata pārimakuleṁ* *Ibid.*, Song. No. 34.

[8] *gaganam iti ālokādi-śūnya-trayaṁ boddhavyam* | *Ibid.*, Com. p. 53.

[9] *suna bāha tathatā pahārī* |
moha-bhaṇḍāra lai saalā ahārī || *Ibid.*, Song. No. 36.

whole storage of attachment was in possession of the three-fold Śūnya; the arms of this threefold Śūnya are struck with the perfect-void (*sarva-śūnya*) which is 'thatness', and the Śūnya is thereby undone; then the whole storage of illusory attachment is plundered and all that it contained is taken possession of. In the commentary this three-fold Śūnya has been explained as the storage of the Vāsanās,[1] which are responsible for the illusory world. In another song of Kānha-pāda it is said,—'Split up the two; O lord, you are also dead.'[2] According to the commentary the two refers to the first two principles of impure knowledge (*ābhāsa-dvayam*), *i.e.*, Śūnya and Ati-śūnya; the lord (*ṭhākura*) represents the third stage of Mahā-śūnya or the ignorant mind (*avidyā-citta*). After splitting up or destroying the two principles of the defiled void, the third or the *avidyā-citta* is also to be killed. It is further said in the same song,—"First I took the *vaḍiā* and killed it by a dash and then taking the great elephant destroyed the five."[3] Here the esoteric doctrine is explained in terms of the game of chess. The *vaḍiā* in the game represents the infantry, but here it represents the hundred and sixty kinds of impurities.[4] First the impurities must be shaken off and then raising the mind (*gaavara—gaja-vara—citta-gajendra*) the five Skandhas are destroyed. Again in a song of Śavara-pāda we find that he has awkened the Nairātmā damsel by destroying Śūnya, Ati-śūnya and also the adjoining house (*i.e.*, Mahā-śūnya) by the stroke of the fourth Śūnya of his heart,[5] and by the side of

[1] *suna ity ādi śūnyam iti* | *āloko-palabdhi-sandhyā-jñānena vāsanā-gāraṁ bod-dhavyam* | *Ibid*, Com. p. 56.

[2] Dr. Shahidullah, however is disposed to explain *mādesi re ṭhākura* as 'don't give the lord anything' (*mā* don't, *desi* give) (*Cf.* his pamphlet, Dacca Sāhitya-Pariṣad-granthāvalī, No. 10); but *mādesi* may also be explained with reference to the Prakrita form *madesi* (√ *mṛ*) and the latter derivation gives a more suitable meaning. Dr. Shahidullah in his *Les Chants Mystiques de Kānha et de Saraha* (p. 113) takes the reading as—*phiṭau duāra dekhi re ṭhākura* (La porte est overte. Oh! Jai vu le seigneur. *Ibid.*, p. 119). Dr. P. C. Bagchi takes the reading as—*phiṭau duā maresire ṭhākura*. (*Materials for*, etc. Dr. Bagchi, p. 119).

[3] *pahileṁ toḍiā baḍiā māriu* |
gaavareṁ tolia pāñcajanā ghāliu ||
Song No. 12.

[4] *vaḍiketi sandhyā-bhāṣayā-ṣaṣṭhy-uttara-śata-prakṛtayaḥ*, etc.
Ibid., Com. p. 23.

[5] *gaaṇata gaaṇata tailā bāḍī heñce kurāḍī*
kaṇṭhe nairāmaṇi bāli jāgante upāḍī ||
Ibid., Song No. 50.

the adjoining house (*i.e.*, Mahā-śūnya) shines another house lit with moon-rays, and when all the mass of darkness is driven away—the sky shines with lustre.[1] This last house is the Sarva-śūnya (all-void).

As we have seen, Mahāyāna Buddhism do not recognise Śūnyatā or the knowledge of the essencelessness of the world to be the highest truth,—the highest truth is a state where Śūnyatā and Karuṇā are united together. This element of Karuṇā or compassion is emphasised in all the Buddhist Tantras, and all the esoteric practices including the sexo-yogic practice are professed to be undertaken with the avowed intention of liberating the whole world. This emphasis on the element of Karuṇā side by side with the theory of Śūnyatā is found also in the Caryā-padas. We have seen that Kambalāmbara-pāda filled his boat of Karuṇā with the gold of vacuity.[2] In the song where Kānha-pāda explains the esoteric doctrine by the metaphor of the chess-game, compassion is made the play-board.[3] In another song he says that he has realised his body (*i.e.*, existence) in a non-dual state of compassion and vacuity.[4] The commentary on the Caryās explains that all the Caryā-songs were composed by the Siddhācāryas only for the uplift and ultimate deliverance of the beings.

The philosophical notions found in the Caryā-songs are of a general Buddhistic nature; but the Caryā-songs as a whole represent a special school of religious thought with distinctive features of its own. Let us concentrate our attention on the study of the special features of the school of religious thought, to which the Caryā-songs belong, *viz.*, the school of Sahajiyā Buddhism.

1 *tailā bāḍira pāsem̐ra johnā bāḍī uelā* ।
phiṭelī andhāri re ākāśa phuliā ॥
Ibid., Song No. 50.

2 Song No. 8.

3 *karuṇā pihāḍī khelahum̐ naa-bala* । Song No. 12.

4 *nia deha karuṇā suname herī* ॥ Song No. 13.

Chapter III

THE GENERAL RELIGIOUS OUTLOOK OF THE SAHAJIYĀS

(i) *Salient features of the religion preached in the Buddhist Dohās and Songs*

(A) The Spirit of Protest and Criticism

THE poets of the Sahajiyā school laid their whole emphasis on their protest against the formalities of life and religion and this made them distinct in their religious attitude from the Vajra-yānists or the general school of Tāntric Buddhism. Truth is something which can never be found through mere austere practices of discipline; neither can it be realised through much reading, philosophising, fasting, bathing, constructing images and painting the gods and goddesses; it is only to be intuited within in the most unconventional way through initiation in the *Tattva* (secret truth) and the practice of yoga. This process of yoga is the most natural process for a man; for in the nature of man hunger and sex are recognised by all to be the most primitive and fundamental propensities; and all religions would prescribe strict rules for their suppression; but that is a way, said these Yogins, which is absolutely unnatural. The continual suppression of natural propensities only makes a man morbid and neurotic, but never helps him in realising the truth. The Sahajiyās would never prescribe any unnatural strain on human nature, but would take human nature itself as the best help for realising the truth. It is for this reason that this path has always been described as the easiest and most natural. It will be totally wrong to suppose that the question of moral discipline was in any way less emphasised in the sahajiyā school (barring the cases of abuses and aberrations) than in the other schools of religion; but the difference of the view-point of the Sahajiyās from that of other schools lies in the fact that while the other schools recommend the total annihilation of the sexual impulse, the Sahajiyās would recommend the transformation and sublimation of them. The question of annihilation is regarded by the Sahajiyās as unnatural and impossible, and therefore, the wisest way is the way of transformation and sublimation.[1]

Thus the name Sahaja-yāna is doubly significant: it is Sahaja-yāna because its aim is to realise the ultimate innate nature (*Sahaja*) of the self as well as of the Dharmas, and it is Sahaja-yāna also because of the fact that instead of suppressing and thereby inflicting undue strain on the human nature it makes man realise the truth in the most natural way,—*i.e.*, by following the path along which the human nature itself leads him. In the *Sampuṭikā* it has been said that this supreme process of yoga is eternal,—it originates from our sex-passions; our sex-passions are part and parcel of our nature and our nature is never transgressible,—it is, therefore, wise to transform these sex-passions in the yogic process for realising the truth.[2] What is natural is the easiest and thus Sahaja, from its primary meaning of being natural, acquires this secondary meaning of being easy, straight or plain. In a song Śānti-pāda says that truth is purely of a self-intuited nature, there cannot be any speculation as to its transcendental nature;—those who have trodden the straight path have been able to reach the other shore.[3] Śānti-pāda warns the foolish beginners against missing this straight path (*uju-vāṭa*),—it is called by him the royal road (*rāja-patha*) for attaining perfection. Again Saraha-pāda says in a song,—"O Yogins, do not leave off this straight and easy path and follow the crooked and curved path;—*bodhi* lies near you,—do not go to Laṅkā (Ceylon) in search of it. Do not take the glass (*dāpaṇa*) to see the bracelets in your hands,—realise your own pure *citta* for yourself (and within yourself).[4] If the Sahaja or the Bodhi-citta can once be realised, everything is attained,—and so there remains no more necessity for the muttering of the

[1] For further discussion on the point see *infra*.

[2] *Cf. asau hi bhagavān yogaḥ sthira-śāśvata paramaḥ* |
manmathataḥ pratyutpannaḥ (sadā caiva) svabhāvo duratikramaḥ ||
Sampuṭikā, MS. p.7 (B).

[3] *saa samveaṇa sarua viārem alakkha-lakkha na jāi* |
je je ujuvāṭe gelā anāvāṭā bhailā soi || Song No. 15.

[4] *uju re uju chāḍi mā lehu re baṅka* |
niaḍi bohi mā jāhu re lāṅka ||

mantras, or of penances, fire-sacrifices, Maṇḍala (circle) or the other rites in the Maṇḍala; the Sahaja or the Bodhi-citta in the form of Mahā-sukha is the Mantra, penance, sacrifice, circle (*maṇḍala*) and everything belonging to the circle.[1]

(B) Aversion to recondite scholarship

Thus we see that the Sahajiyās were averse to the elaborate formalities of religion and concentrated their whole attention on the attainment of the blissful ultimate nature as the highest truth, for which they took help of the natural propensities of man. Deepest was their hatred towards those recondite scholars who would try to know the truth through discursive reason. Tillo-pāda (and also Saraha-pāda) says that the truth which can fully be realised only by the self, can never be known by the scholars,—for, what comes within the scope of our mind, can never be the absolute truth.[2] Kānha-pāda also says that the scholars who generally depend on their reason and scholarship, are indifferent to (or rather ignorant of) the true path of religion.[3] Saraha says,—Those who go on reciting and explaining, cannot know the truth, it is not only unknown, but also unknowable to them.[4] Those who do not drink eagerly (to their heart's content) the nectar of the instructions of the Guru, die of thirst like fools deceived by the mirage of the desert.[5] Scholars explain the scriptures, but do not know of the Buddha who is residing in their own body; by such scholarship they can never escape the cycle of coming and going,—yet those

hāthera kāṅkaṇa mā leu dāpaṇa |
apaṇe apā bujhatu niamaṇa ||
Song No. 32.

1 *na mantra-jāpo na tapo na homo na maṇḍaleyaṁ na ca maṇḍalañ ca |*
sa mantra-jāpaḥ sa tapaḥ sa homaḥ sa maṇḍaleyaṁ tan maṇḍalañ ca ||
Hevajra-tantra MS. p. 30(A).

2 *saa-saṁveaṇa tatta-phala tilapāa bhaṇanti |*
(jo maṇa-goara paiṭṭhai so paramattha ṇa honti ||)
Dohākoṣa, Dr. P. C. Bagchi's Edition, No. 9.

3 *yo mana-goara so udāsa ||*
Song No. 7.

4 *are putto vojjhu rasa-rasaṇa susaṇṭhia avejja |*
vakkhāṇa paḍhantehi jagahi ṇa jāṇiu sojjha ||
Dohākoṣa of Saraha-pāda, Dr. P. C. Bagchi's Edition.

5 *Ibid.*, p. 27.

shameless creatures think themselves to be Pundits.[1] Saraha regrets that the whole world is disturbed in its course of progress by mere thought-constructions of discursive reason,—by the mere functions of the *citta*,—but the *acitta* which transcends the function of the mind is not sung by any one.[2] The world is rather sick of scholarship,—none is illiterate here,—but Saraha says, all scholarship will be upset when one will attain that state which transcends all letters (*i.e.* scholarship).[3] People pride themselves that the secret of the great truth has long been in their keeping,—but Kānha says that even out of crores of people rarely does one become absorbed in perfectly pure truth.[4] They read the Āgamas, the Vedas and the Purāṇas and are always proud of their knowledge,—but they are like bees hovering round the ripe marmelos fruits.[5] As the bees outside go on humming at the mere smell of the marmelos fruit but can never break into the hard kernel and have the taste of the fruits —so also is the case with all the scholars who boast of their knowledge of the truth; they can have only a very faint smell of the truth from outside, but can never break into it and have a direct realisation of it. Sahaja is something supreme, declares Kānha to all,—but the Pundits read and hear the scriptures and the Āgamas, and know absolutely nothing.

(C) Scathing Criticism of the Formalities of Life and Religion

The formal rules and regulations of religion were also severely criticised by the Sahajiyās. The most penetrating and scathing criticism was made by Saraha-pāda in his *Dohākoṣa*. His first revolt is against the orthodox system of

1 *paṇḍia saala sattha vakkhāṇai* ।
dehahiṁ buddha vasanta ṇa jāṇai ||
avaṇā-gamaṇa ṇa teṇa vikhaṇḍia ।
tovi ṇilajja bhaṇai hauṁ paṇḍia || *Ibid.*

2 *Ibid.*

3 *akkhara-vāḍhā saala jagu ṇāhi ṇirakkhara koi* ।
tāva se akkhara gholiā jāva ṇirakkhara hoi ||
Ibid.

4 *loaha gavva samuvvahai hauṁ paramatthe pavīṇa* ।
koḍiha majjheṁ ekku jai hoi ṇirañjana līṇa ||
Dohā No. 1.

5 *āgama-vea-purāṇeṁ paṇḍiā māṇa vahanti* ।
pakka siriphale alia jima vāheria bhamanti ||

the fourfold division of colours (*caturvarṇa*) placing the Brahmins at the top. Saraha says that the Brahmins as a caste cannot reasonably be recognised to be the highest of men,—for the saying that they dropped from the mouth of Brahmā is a myth invented by a section of clever and cunning people; if, on the other hand, a man becomes Brahmin by religious initiations (*saṁskāra*), then even the lowest of men may be a Brahmin. If a man becomes a Brahmin by reciting the Vedas, let the people of the lower classes also recite the Vedas and they will also become Brahmins; and they also do read the Vedas, for, they read grammar which contains many words of the Vedas. The Brahmins take earth, water, *kuśa* grass and recite Mantras and perform fire-sacrifices in their houses,—in vain do they offer ghee to the fire, for thereby their eyes will only be affected with intense smoke.[1] They become holders of singlefold or of three-fold sacred threads,—but this is of no avail unless truth is realised. Deceived is the whole world by false illusion,—none does know the all-excelling truth where both religion and non-religion become one. The devotees of the Lord (*Iśvara*), again, anoint the whole body with ashes, wear matted hair on the head, sit within the house and light lamps and ring bells seated in a corner; they take a yogic posture (*āsana*) with their eyes fixed; they whisper (religious doctrines) into the ears (of credulous people) and deceive them thereby.[2] The widows, the *Muṇḍīs* (women taking the vow of fasting for the whole month)[3] and others taking different vows, get themselves initiated by these devotees who do it only in greed of money (*dakṣiṇā*). Against the Jaina Kṣapaṇaka-yogins it is said that they keep long nails, put on a pale air, become naked and shave the head; but by all these they merely lead themselves astray and

[1] *kajje virahia huavaha homeṁ* ।
akkhi uhāvia kaḍueṁ dhumeṁ ॥
Dohākoṣa of Saraha-pāda Dr. P. C. Bagchi's Edition.

[2] *airiehiṁ uddulia cchāre* ।
sīsasu vāhia e jaḍabhāreṁ ॥
gharahī vaisī dīvā jālī ।
koṇahiṁ vaisī ghaṇḍā cālī ॥
akkhi ṇivesī āsaṇa vandhī ।
kaṇṇehiṁ khusukhusāi jaṇa dhandhī ॥

[3] *muṇḍīti māsiko-pavāsikīyā*—Com.

never attain perfection. "If only the naked attain liberation, the dog and the fox would also attain it; if liberation is attained by tearing off of hairs, the hips of young women would also attain it; if liberation can be attained by merely putting on the feathers of the peacock, then the peacock and the deer should themselves attain liberation; if the eating of grass ensure liberation, why should not elephants and horses be liberated?"[1] The Cellas, the Bhikṣus and the Sthaviras (*i.e.*, the elders)[2] take the vow of *pravrajyā* (*i.e.*, renouncing the world and going away in search of truth); some of them are lost in explaining the Sūtras, some again in strenuous thinking and reading. Others again rush into the Mahāyāna fold,—but none of them get at the ultimate truth. The Lord (Buddha) has prescribed ways according to the capacities of his disciples, but can one attain liberation only by meditation?[3] What will one do with lamps, offerings, Mantras and services,—what is the good of going to holy places or to the hermitage?—can liberation be attained only by bathing in holy waters? Tear off all these irrational ties of superstition, drive away all doubt,—no *mokṣa* (liberation) can be compared with Sahaja,—and all kinds of liberation are included in Sahaja. Sahaja is what is read, what is gauged, what is explained in the scriptures and the Purāṇas. Saraha says, "The world is bound to existence by all kinds of nonsense,—the childish Yogins like the Tīrthikas and others can never find out their own nature; they lead the life of *Pravrajyā* without knowing the truth at all. One has no need of Tantra or Mantra, or of the images or the Dhāraṇīs—all these are causes of confusion. In vain does one try to attain Mokṣa by meditation,[4] —by meditation one will only be entangled in snares. Through self-conceit the truth is never perceived,—but

[1] *jai ṇaggā via hoi mutti tā suṇaha siālaha* |
lomupāḍaṇeṁ atthi siddhi ta juvai niamvaha ||
picchīgahaṇe diṭṭha mokkha (tā moraha camaraha) |
uccheṁ bhoaṇeṁ hoi jāṇa tā kariha turaṅgaha ||
Ibid.

[2] The commentary explains *cella* as *daśa-śikṣā-padī*, *bhikṣu* as *koṭi-śikṣā-padī* and *sthavira* as *daśa-varṣo-papannaḥ*.

[3] *mokkha ki labbhai jjhāṇa-(pa)viṭṭho* | *Ibid.*

[4] This *jhāna* (*i.e.*, *dhyāna*) seems to refer to the system of meditation as prescribed in the scholastic texts like the *Visuddhi-magga*, etc.

the blame is often put wrongly on the *yānas* (*i.e.*, the ways or schools for attaining *bodhi*). All are hypnotised by the system of the *jhānas* (meditation), but none cares to realise his own self.[1] This is the truth which Saraha preaches,—never does he care for any Tantra or Mantra.[2]

Lui-pā says in a song,—"Of what consequence are all the processes of meditation? In spite of them you have to die in weal and woe. Take leave of all the elaborate practices of Yogic *bandha* (control) and false hope for the deceptive supernatural gifts, and accept the side of Śūnyatā to be your own."[3] "Of what use are Mantras, Tantras and the explanation of the different kinds of meditation?"[4] Kānha-pāda says in another place that the Sahaja Ḍombī[5] sells the loom (*tanti*) and bamboo-baskets[6] (as is the general custom with the women of the Ḍoma classes). The word (*tanti*) which is derived from the Sanskrit word (*tantrī*) suggests the net-work of the false mental construction which, again, can very well be compared to the loom, the only business of which is to weave; and the basket, referred to here, is symbolical of the superstitious mental complexes. Kānha-pāda explains elsewhere that conventional practices and the outward garment do not really make a man a Kāpālika Yogin. A real Kāpālika is he who shakes off all conventionalism and realises the great bliss of the nature of the Bodhi-citta (*kaṁ mahā-sukhaṁ saṁvṛti-bodhi-cittaṁ pālayatī'ti kāpālikaḥ*—com). The Yogin Kānha says that his nerves are fully under his control and the *ḍamaru* of the spontaneous sound[7] is rising tremendously. Kānha, the Kāpālika Yogin,

1 *ahimāṇa-dosem ṇa lakkhiu tattva* |
teṇa dūsai saala jāṇu so datta ||
jhānem mohia saala vi loa |
nia svahāva ṇau lakkhai koa ||
Saraha's *Dohākoṣa*

2 *evā maṇe muṇi sarahem gāhiu* |
tanta manta ṇau ekkavi cāhiu ||
Ibid.

3 Song No. 1.

4 *kinto mante kinto tante kinto re jhāṇa-bakhāne* |
Song No. 34.

5 The conception of the Ḍombī or Sahaja-damsel wil be explained later on.

6 *tānti bikaṇaya ḍomvī avara nā cāmgeḍā* |
Song No. 10.

7 The text has *anahā ḍamaru*. The word *anahā* refers to the *anāhata* (literally, unobstructed; spontaneous) sound. It is held in the texts on Yoga that when all the senses are shut up and the nerves controlled and the breath suspended

is engaged in his yogic practices and is roaming about in the city of his body in a non-dual form.[1] The *āli* and the *kāli*,[2] *i.e.*, the principles of all kinds of duality are made the bell and the anklets; and the sun and the moon (*i.e.*, Upāya and Prajñā) have been made the ear-rings.[3] The poet has burnt into ashes all his passions, hatred and false attachment and is rubbing his body with the ashes therefrom; he is wearing the pearl-necklace of final salvation. Again, for his Tāntric Sādhanā, which requires a female companion, the poet has the Sahaja-damsel as his female consort. The Yogin says that he has killed the mother-in-law of breath (*sāsu*),[4] and done away with the sister-in-law (*naṇanda*) of his consort, which is the senses,[5] and has also put to death his mother (*māa*) of illusion (*māyā*),[6] and thus Kānha has become a real Kāpālika.[7]

It is interesting to note here that the Jaina Apabhraśṁa Dohās which seem historically to synchronise with the Buddhist songs and Dohās, are also strikingly similar in spirit as well as in form to the Buddhist songs and Dohās. The spirit is well exemplified in the collection of Dohās called *Pāhuḍa-dohā* of Muni Rāma-siṁha (1000 A.D.).[8] There

through a yogic process there arises a spontaneous sound within, which is known as the *anāhata-dhvani*. For this theory of sound see *An Introduction To Tāntric Buddhism* by the present writer. Beating of the drums is one of the customs of many sects of Yogins and ascetics.

[1] To roam about in different localities, generally in forests, lonely outskirits of villages and in cremation grounds is a custom with the Kāpālika Yogins.

[2] For a detailed discussion on the meaning of the pair of words *āli* and *kāli* see *infra* and also *An introduction To Tāntric Buddhism* by the present writer.

[3] Some sects of Yogins bear bells, anklets, ear-rings and such other ornaments.

[4] There is a pun on the word *sāsu* here which may be associated with both Sk. *śvaśru* (the mother-in-law) and with Sk. *śvāsa* (breath).

[5] Again there is a pun on the word *naṇanda* which may mean the sister-in-law of a woman, or it may mean that which gives pleasure, *i.e.*, the senses.

[6] The word used is *māa* which may be associated with both the words *mātā* (mother) and *māyā* (illusion).

[7] *nāḍi śakti diḍha dharia khaṭṭe* |
anahā ḍamaru bājai vīranāde ||
kāhna kapālī yogī paiṭho acāre |
deha naarī biharai ekākāreṁ ||
āli kāli ghaṇṭā neura caraṇe |
ravi-śaśi kuṇḍala kiu ābharaṇe ||
rāga deṣa moha lāia chāra |
parama mokha lavae muttāhāra ||
māria śāsu naṇanda ghare śāli |
māa māria kāhna bhaia kavālī || Song No. 11

[8] "As verse from this work are quoted by Hemacandra who wrote about 1000 A.D., and as it quotes verses from *Sāvaya-dhamma-dohā* which was composed

it is said,—"O the Pundit of Pundits, you are leaving aside the grains of corn and gathering husk instead. You are satisfied with the scriptures and their meaning, but O ye foolish people—you know nothing about the ultimate meaning of the world. Those who are proud of their knowledge of bombastic words do not know the *raison d'être* of things and like a Ḍoma of a very low origin is always at the mercy of others. O fools, what is the utility of reading much? A single flame of real knowledge is sufficient to burn within a moment all virtue and vice. Everyone is impatiently eager to be a perfect man,—but perfection can be attained only through the purity of heart.[1] Much has been read, but foolishness has not been removed,—only the throat has been parched into the bargain. Read a single letter through which alone you may be able to go to the city of supreme goodness.[2] Caught up in the meshes of the six systems of philosophy the mind finds no way of getting rid of illusion. The one God is divided in six ways in the six systems, and hence none atttains Mokṣa or liberation through them.[3] What can one do with the letters which will shortly die with the times? That is, O fool, called Mokṣa by which a man becomes changeless (*anakkharu*).[4] What good can the reading of books render to a man whose mind is not pure? Even the hunter, when hunting a deer bows his head down before the deer (for throwing his arrow). (The idea is that actions have no objective value in the religious sphere,—the value is always subjective). You are getting emaciated by reading books of many kinds,—but even now you have no access to the mystery of coming and going"[5]

About going on pilgrimage or wandering in forests and on mountains it is said,—"Prevent this elephant of the mind from going to the mountain of Vindhya,—for it will trample under feet the forest of Śīla (*i.e.*, good conduct

about 933 A.D. the present work may be taken to have been produced about 1000 A.D." Preface to the *Pāhuḍa-dohā* by the editor of the text, Hiralal Jain. Ambādāsa Gavare Digambara Jaina Granthamālā, No. 3.

1 *Pāhuḍa-dohā*, verses (85-88).

2 *Ibid.*, verse 97.

3 *Ibid.*, verse 116.

4 *kiṁ kijjai bahu akkharahaṁ je kāliṁ khau jaṁti* I
jema aṇakkharu saṁtu muni tava vaḍha mokkhu kahaṁti || *Ibid.*, verse 124.

5 *Ibid.*, verses 146, 173.

discipline) and once more fall into the pitfall of the world. There are stone-images in the temples, water in the sacred places and poetry in the books; all these will but be fuel to the fire (of decay). Of no avail is travelling from one sacred place to another; for the body may be cleansed with water, but what about the mind? When the body is being washed with water, the mind is being made dirty with the filth of sin, which cannot be washed away with water.[1] What may penances do when there is impurity within? Hold fast your mind to the Nirañjana (the Stainless One) and only threby will the stains of the mind be blotted out. Liberation can be attained only if the mind, stained with worldliness, be fixed on Nirañjana,—the Mantras and the Tantras are of no use.[2] The Jinas say,—'Worship and worship;' but if the self residing within one's own body be once realised in its ultimate nature, who else remains to be worshipped?''[3]

Again, it is said about people who are particular about their religious garb.—"The snake shakes off its slough, but its poison is not destroyed thereby. Putting on of religious dress can never remove the internal desire for worldly enjoyment. O, you, the head of all the shaven-headed,—you have indeed got your head shaven,—but you have not got your heart free from worldly desires;—he who has shaven his heart, *i.e.*, has made his heart free from desires, has indeed done away with this world of bondage."[4]

The above will give us an idea of the spirit of Indian literature during the proto-vernacular period and the earliest period of the vernaculars. This spirit of heterodoxy and criticism that characterises the Buddhist and the Jaina songs and Dohās is a very noteworthy phenomenon in the history of the vernacular literatures of India; for, here we find the inception of a new type of literature, which grew abundantly in many parts of India during the medieval period, and the type is not extinct even in modern times. This type of literature is generally known as Sahajiyā or the *Maramiyā*

[1] *Pāhuḍa-dohā*, Verses 155, 161-163, 178.
[2] *Ibid.*, Verses 61, 62, 206.
[3] *vaṁdahu vaṁdahu jiṇu bhaṇai ko vaṁdau hali itthu* |
ṇiyadehāhaṁ vasaṁtayahaṁ jai jāṇiu paramatthu || *Ibid.*, Verse 41.
[4] *Ibid.*, Verses, 15, 135. Also *Cf.* Verse 154.

school of literature.[1] The Vaiṣṇava Sahajiyās of Bengal and the host of village poets roughly known under the general name of Bāul belong directly to the same school of thought;[2] the Santa-poets of Northern and Upper India and the other devotional lyrists, the mystics of Mārāṭhā, and even the Śikh and Sūfī poets belong to the same school of heterodoxy and criticism.[3] Thus we see that this type of literature has a continued history in the vernaculars from the earliest period down to the modern times. As we are now dealing elaborately with the early Sahajiyās and shall also deal later on with different types of medieval Sahajiyā literature we think it necessary here to discuss in detail the possible sources of the critical spirit of the various Sahajiyā schools. The utility and relevancy of such an elaborate discussion on the point will be clearer, we hope, when the different medieval Sahajiyā schools will be studied in the succeeding chapters and also in the appendix.

(D) Possible Sources of the Spirit of Criticism of the Sahajiyās

An analysis of and scrutiny into the nature of the spirit of these different Sahajiyā schools of vernacular poetry will reveal that much of their heterodoxy and criticism is a thing of heritage; the ideas found in the vernaculars are but infiltrations from the older ideas found in the different lines of criticism in the history of Indian religious thought, and these infiltrated ideas have been variously emphasised by the vernacular poets so as to give them a new colour and tone. Older lines of criticism of different kinds have got blended in the critical and revolutionary spirt of the vernacular poetry. To make a critical study of it, it is necessary therefore to make a general survey of the different lines of heterodoxy that have moulded the religious history of India in the different periods of its evolution.

The earliest trace of heterodoxy and criticism in the history

1 The popular vernacular word *maramiyā* comes from the Skt. word *marma*, which means the vital part or the very core of anything. The *Maramiyā* school is thus the school that deals with the vital part or the inner truth of religion to the exclusion of the formalities and outward shows.

2 *Vide infra.* Chs. V., VII.

3 *Vide infra.* Appendix (A).

of Indian religious thought is to be found in the Āraṇyakas and the Upaniṣads. In its practical aspect the religion of the Saṁhitās and the Brāhmaṇas was pre-eminently sacrificial with innumerable accessories of chants, ceremonies and rituals. Though the sacrifices were generally made to some particular god or gods they were nothing of the kind of an attempt at establishing any sort of personal contact between the god or gods in question and the sacrificer. The desired effect of the sacrifice does not depend on the will of the god to whom the sacrifice is offered,—it depends absolutely on the rigorous correctitude of the sacrificial method in all the minutest details. But when we pass on from the Saṁhitās and the Brāhmaṇas to the Āraṇyakas and the Upaniṣads we find a remarkable change in the fundamental religious spirit. In the hymns and ritualistic and sacrificial net-work of the Saṁhitās we do not find any unified idea of the Brahman or the Supreme Being, though, however, we often find a tendency towards monotheism. In some of the Brāhmaṇas we first have, in a rudimentary form, the conception of the Brahman as the ultimate principle and the highest reality and the conception was established in the Āraṇyakas and the Upaniṣads. With the establishment of the conception of the Brahman the religion of the Āraṇyakas and the Upaniṣads was no longer the objective and deterministic religion of ritualism and sacrifice,—all these are made subordinate to the final end of self-realisation or Brahma-realisation. In the Āraṇyakas and the Upaniṣads ritualism and sacrifice began to be replaced by meditation, and the spirit of sacrifice sometimes began to have a philosophic interpretation.[1] When we find Maitreyī, wife of the famous seer Yājñavalkya, exclaiming,—"What shall I do with that, which will not make me immortal?"[2]—we discover the key-note of the Upaniṣadic thought, a hankering, not after any mundane happiness and prosperity,—nor after

[1] Thus the *Bṛhad-āraṇyaka* begins with a new conception of the horse of the Horse-sacrifice. There it is said that dawn is the head of the horse, the sun is his eye, wind his breath, heaven the back and the intermediate space between heaven and earth the belly; the quarters are the sides, the seasons the limbs, the stars the bones and the sky his flesh. To mediate on such a horse and to realise the truth of this horse is the real meaning of the Horse-sacrifice.

[2] *Ibid.*, (2.4).

any enjoyment of bliss in heaven,—but after the realisation of the self which is of the nature of the Brahman. It has been said that those who know the self or the Brahman and seek for truth reach the region of the Brahman wherefrom they never turn back; but those who acquire better regions through sacrifice or gift or penances roam about from this region to that and constantly suffer under the whirl of coming and going.[1] It is neither by the making of sacrifices, nor by hearing and memorising the Vedas that one can realise the Brahman or the supreme truth, it is only through the absolute purification of heart— through the removal of the veil of ignorance that one can realise the self or the ultimate truth. Thus we see that the whole emphasis of the Upaniṣads is on the subjective side of religion, which seems to be conspicuous by its absence in the Saṁhitās and the Brāhmaṇas. The Upaniṣads discourage much reading, erudition and discursive reason and also sacrifices, ritual and worship of the gods;—they on the other hand emphasise absolute purification of heart; for, it is in the absolutely purified and mirror-like heart that the supreme truth reflects itself in its illuminating and blissful effulgence.

In the post-Upaniṣadic period a free spirit of religion, leaning mainly to the subjective side, characterises the early epic literature of India, particularly the *Mahābhārata*. There are stories in the *Mahābhārata*, where the teachings of true religion are being received from people belonging to the lowest class of the social order. In the *Anuśāsanika-parva* of the *Mahābhārata*,[2] where Bhīṣma is explaining to Yudhiṣṭhira the really sacred places of pilgrimage, we find that the mind with the transparent water of purity and truth, when associated with the lake of patience, is the best of all places of pilgrimage. He whose body is washed with water, cannot be said to be the really cleansed one; he, who has controlled all his senses, is the really cleansed one, and he is pure within as well as without. To dive into the water of the bliss of Brahma-knowledge in the lake of the pure heart is the best of all bathing, and it is only he, whom the wise recognise to be a real pilgrim.

1 *Bṛhad-āraṇyaka*.
2 Ch. 108.

The Upaniṣadic spirit, however, is found in the post-Upaniṣadic period bifurcated into the two main lines of religious thought, *viz.*, Vedānta and Vaiṣṇavism. The Śaṅkarite and the post-Śaṅkarite Vedāntic schools cherished nothing but uncompromising antagonism towards the school of Pūrva-mīmāṃsā, the staunchest advocate of the sacrificial religion of the Vedas. Even Rāmānuja, the great exponent of Vaiṣṇavism, tried to make a compromise between *dharma-jijñāsā* and *brahma-jijñāsā* and held that the former leads to the latter; but Śaṅkara stoutly denied this relation of succession between the two; for, he held that the nature and the ultimate end of the two are diametrically opposite to each other. While the aim of *dharma-jijñāsā* is the attainment of prosperity (*abhyudaya*) in life and the attainment of heaven after death, the aim of *brahma-jijñāsā* is liberation (*mukti*); and while the function of the former is to induce one to perform various sacrificial and ritualistic duties, the function of the latter is only to induce one to know the Brahman, and *to know* the Brahman is *to be* the Brahman. A hankering after the knowledge of the Brahman presupposes no performance of scriptural duties,—it follows rather from a discriminative knowledge of what is permanent and what is transitory (*nityā-nitya-vastu-viveka*), from absolute indifference to the pleasures of life here and hereafter, the capacity for internal and external control and a true desire for being liberated from the fetters of life.

As the Mīmāṁsakas go to the one extreme of saying that religion always involves some kind of activity,—the Vedāntins go to the other extreme of saying that true religion involves no kind of activity whatsoever. The aim of all activities is to produce some sort of effect,—but Brahma-knowledge cannot be the effect of any activity; it is already there, and it is there for all time; it is, however, veiled by our ignorance—by the world-illusion;—the function of the true knowledge of the scriptures is to remove this veil of ignorance from our mind,—and when this veil of the world-illusion is removed Brahma-knowledge will dawn upon us instantaneously and spontaneously. Brahma-knowledge is not something attainable through human effort,—it is rather self-revealed. Brahma-knowledge is not even a mental function,—for, a mental function presupposes the fact that the agent has the power to do or undo it according to his own will,—but we have no such power in the case of Brahma-knowledge. Moreover, as we have noticed before, to know the Brahman is nothing but to be the Brahman, and knowing and being being identical here, no action is implied even in the knowing.

The Vaiṣṇavas, however, represent the spirit of heterodoxy in another way. While the whole emphasis of the Vedāntins is on pure knowledge, the emphasis of the Vaiṣṇavas is on devotion or love. The Vaiṣṇavas always speak very indifferently of heaven and the enjoyment of happiness there,—they discourage even the idea of liberation,—what they want is the blissful realisation of the eternal love of God. It is necessary to remark here that this cult of devotion or love was not and is not limited strictly to the sphere of Vaiṣṇavism,—we have already referred to the Śaivite devotional cult of South India, and even in the Śakta cult of later days (we may mention here the exquisite songs of Rāma-prasāda Sen and others of his time) we find traces of pure devotion and love. But in Northern India and in Eastern India this devotional cult flourished mostly along the line of Vaiṣṇavism and they are commonly taken to be identical.

The innovation made by the Vaiṣṇavas (and all devotional cults in general) is the introduction of the element of divine mercy within the deterministic view of the law of Karma. Germs of the law of Karma can be traced to the ritualistic and sacrificial religious thought of the Vedas, and it is a particularly noticeable fact that practically all the systems of Indian thought accept this theory in some form or other. We have seen that the Saṁhitās and the Brāhmaṇs leave no scope for the interference of the gods in the matter of the fruition of the rites, rituals and sacrifices. But already in the Upaniṣadic period we come across a statement like this,—"This self or soul (*ātmā*) can never be realised through great sayings,—neither by memorising (the scriptures) nor by listening to the scriptures; it is only by him, to whom it reveals itself of its own accord that it can be realised, and to him this soul or self reveals its real form."[1] Herein we find germs of the predominance of the divine will, which reigns supreme over all human efforts, and herein comes the question of divine mercy. Along this line developed the theory of divine mercy of all the devotional cults, and the only religious duty left, therefore, to the followers of these schools, was unconditional self-resignation to the divine will.

Up to the eighth and ninth centuries A.D. the dominating feature of Vaiṣṇavism was this spirit of self-resignation and seeking the haven of the infinite mercy of God. This very spirit indicates that the elaborate system of religious duties, customs, rituals and ceremonies—strict rules for food and dress could find no prominence in the Vaiṣṇava school; whenever they were adopted they were adopted with the purpose of preparing a mental atmosphere favourable to the growth and development of this spirit of devotion and self-surrender. Already in the *Bhāgavata Purāṇa* we find elements of pure love spoken of as the best and highest method through which the direct communion with God becomes possible. There the uncultured rustic cowherd girls of Vṛndāvana are regarded as the best of all religious people for their most sincere and passionate love for Śrīkṛṣṇa, the perfect incarnation of God. Devotion (*bhakti*) in later times was classified under two heads, *viz.*, *vaidhī bhakti*, *i.e.*, devotion that arises through the performance of religious duties, observance of vows and rites, and strict obedience to the rules and regulations laid down in Vaiṣṇava theology; and the other kind of devotion is called *rāgānugā bhakti*, *i.e.* passionate devotion,—or love for God that depends on no extraneous cause,—it is love absolutely for love's sake. The former kind of devotion has always been spoken of as being much inferior to the latter and as such the former is never recognised as devotion proper. This exclusive stress on love has naturally minimised to a considerable extent all the formalities, conventionalism and ceremonialism in religion. Even a man of the lowest origin, such, for example, as a Caṇḍāla, in spite of being a riteless untouchable, has been acclaimed as being much superior to the twice-born

[1] *Kaṭha* (1.2.22).

(Brahmin), by being merely a sincere lover of God; on the other hand, a caste Brahmin, in spite of his loyalty to the rites, customs and duties of Brahminic life *minus* his sincerity of love, has been emphatically declared to be inferior to a Caṇḍāla,—and this really represents the true spirit of Vaiṣṇvism.

Again, the Yoga-school of Indian thought has a religious perspective of its own, and its emphasis is exclusively on the subjective side of religion. Though all sorts of occultism and necromancy prevailed and still now prevail within the school of Haṭha-yoga, and though with a large number of Indian Yogins Haṭha-yoga has become a science of physical feats, serenity prevails within the school of Yoga proper. As a philosophical system Yoga represents a purely idealistic view and it is the mind in all its states and processes that has been held responsible for the whirl of birth and death and consequent sufferings. Religion, according to Yoga, consists in the final arrest of the states and processes of the mind, and the final arrest of the mind means the final arrest of the flux of coming and going and that is the state of final liberation. Yogic Sādhanā, therefore, consists essentially in a process of psychological discipline against a moral background. It is evident from the very nature of Yoga proper that it leaves no scope for idolatry, ritualism and ceremonialism. The dominant trend of Indian thought is idealism; it is the mind with all its principles of defilement that has been held responsible for the world-process. It is for this reason that in practical Sādhanā elements of Yoga have been adopted in almost all the practical systems of Indian religion;—even Vaiṣṇavism with all its love-theories is no exception. In the critical spirit of the old and medieval vernacular poets we shall find this spirit of Yoga acting strongly in unison with the spirit of the other heterodox system.

In spite of their heterogeneous practices, ritualism and ceremonialism the Tāntric schools (both Hindu and Buddhistic) breathe throughout a spirit of revolt against the orthodox schools,—the Hindu Tantras having the same apathy towards the caste-religion or Varṇāśrama-dharma of the Brahminic people as the Buddhist Tantras have against monasticism. We have already seen that the main emphasis of the Tāntrikas is on the practical side of religion, and naturally they discouraged much reading and erudite scholarship, either philosophical or scriptural. The stress of Tantra proper was on Yoga, where discursive knowledge is of little avail. As for the other practices of Tantra, good or bad, their unconventional nature is palpable, and to have these unconventional practices recognised as purely religious practices the Tantras had to decry strongly the conventional practices of both Brahminism and Buddhism. Because of the extremely unconventional nature of the practices, the Tāntrikas had to launch the bitterest attack on the commonly accepted practices and religious views of the orthodox systems. The importance of this critical and revolutionary spirit of the Tantras lies in the fact that the earliest literature of our language (we mean the songs of the Sahajiyā Buddhists) inherited much of its spirit of revolt and criticism directly from the Buddhist Tantras.

It will be noticed that the above critics of orthodox Brahminism were all theists; but the severest attack came from the atheists of whom the Cārvākas, the Jainas and the Buddhists deserve mention here. Already in the Upaniṣads we find mention of schools of naturalism which recognised no ultimate conscious Being as the author of the universe, but thought of the world-process as a product of the course of nature. The materialists are generally spoken of in early texts as the Lokāyata school or the school which admits the truth only of the visible world. In early Pali texts we find mention of many pre-Buddhistic heretical ascetics, of whom mention may be made of Sañjaya, the sceptic, Ajita Keśakambalin, the materialist, Purāṇa-kaśyapa, the indifferentist, Maṣkarin Gośāla, the wandering ascetic, and Kakuda Kātyāyana.[1] The Cārvāka school of thought deserves special mention here. The Cārvākas were not believers in any kind of divinity,—the whole world-process including the psychosis, has been explained by them as the creation of matter. Let a man be happy so long as he lives;—life is short and none can escape the jaws of death; and if once this

1 See B. M. Barua, M.A., D. Lit., *A History of Pre-Buddhistic Indian Philosophy*

body is burnt to ashes there is no returning back;'[1] let one, therefore, eat, drink and be merry. The Cārvākas strongly defied the authority of the scriptures. It has been said that religion is nothing but a device of the cunning priests for earning livelihood as they have no other resources. It is said,—"There is no heaven, no emancipation, no soul,—nothing belonging to the after-world,—never are the duties, prescribed according to the castes and the different stages of life; capable of producing any effect. All fire-sacrifices, the three Vedas, the ascetic practice of holding three sticks (bound together), the practice of rubbing the body with ashes—are inventions of stupid and coward people for the earning of their livelihood."[2] It has been further said,—"If it be true that an animal, when killed in the Jyotiṣṭoma-sacrifice goes to heaven—why then should not the sacrificer kill his own father in the sacrifice? If the funeral rite of offering food, drink and other gifts to the departed may produce satisfaction in them, then the supply of oil to an extinct lamp should also increase its flames. Utterly futile is the contemplation of providing food for those who have departed this life,—for, had there been any truth in this practice, one might have had his satisfaction on his way while gifts were being offered to him in his house. If those who are in heaven can be satisfied by offering of gifts here on earth, then why should not offerings be placed on the lower floor of the house for the satisfaction of those who are above the roof?"[3] It is therefore strongly recommended that one should live joyously as long as one lives,—one should borrow money to procure butter;—if body be once burnt to ashes, it can never return. If after dissociating himself from this particular body a man goes to a different

1 *Sarva-darśana-saṁgraha* (Govt. Oriental ([Hindu] Series), Vol. 1, p. 12.
2 *Ibid.*, p. 13.
3 *Ibid*,, pp. 13-14.
It is interesting to note here some of the verses of the *Viṣṇu-purāṇa* which breathe exactly the same spirit.

nihatasya paśor yajñe svarga-prāptir yadīṣyate |
sva-pitā yajamānena tadā kiṁ na nihanyate ||
tṛptaye jāyate puṁso bhuktam anyena cet tataḥ |
dadyāc chrāddhaṁ śramāyānnaṁ na vaheyuḥ pravāśinaḥ ||

Viṣṇu-purāṇa, 3. 18. 85, quoted in the commentary on the *Sarva-darśana-saṁgraha*, p. 13.

region, why should not he come back many times again through his deep affection for the relatives? So, all these are meaningless talks having absolutely no reality behind. It stands obvious that the Brahmins invented all the funeral rites only to find out a source for their livelihood—they have got absolutely no other justification. Those are hypocritical, cunning and demonic people, who have composed all the Vedas,—and it is really strange that meaningless mutterings like *jarbharī*, *turpharī* etc., are said to be the sayings of learned Pundits. The obscene practice that the wife of the sacrificer should hold the penis of the horse in the horse-sacrifice and all such other practices are prescribed by base hypocrites, and all the injunctions in the Vedas regarding the eating of meat are the sayings of none but the goblins and the demons, who are particularly fond of meat.[1]

The Buddhists and the Jainas, though atheists, were not anti-religious like the Cārvākas. From sacrificial rituals and ceremonies the ground of religion was shifted to a humanitarian plane and the ethical aspect of religion received a great emphasis. Notwithstanding all the differences in metaphysical and theological view-points Buddhism and Jainism had a common front to push in their defiance against the authority of the Vedas, in their absolute denial of any ultimate reality in the form of any Supreme Being, in their emphasis on the cardinal ethical virtues,—particularly on the principle of non-violence. As we have hinted, Jainism viewed religion from a distinctly different perspective from that of the Upaniṣadic or the other Brahminical schools. The ultimate aim is salvation (*mokṣa*),—which can only be attained by the eradication of the Karmas which stick to the soul like dust particles to a body besmeared with oil, and thus bind the soul to this world of sufferings. This inrush of Karma is to be stopped by various kinds of control (*samvara*) and *nirjarā* or the purging off of the Karmas from the soul. The controls are generally the vows of non-injury, truthfulness, abstinence from stealing, sex-control, non-acceptance of the objects of desire, gentle and holy talk, full control over

[1] *Sarva-darśana-saṁgraha* [Govt. Oriental (Hindu) Series], Vol. I, p. 15.

body, speech, and mind, habits of forgiveness, humility, penance, meditation on the real nature of the world and man, and principles of right conduct (*caritra*). *Ahiṃsā* or non-injury is regarded as the highest virtue in Jainism as well as in Buddhism, and in their practical religious conduct the Jains take the greatest precaution to avoid the slightest injury to the smallest of insects.[1] The Buddhists brought about a revolution not only in the religious sphere, but also in the sphere of philosophical thought. The truth, which Śākyasiṁha realised through his great renunciation and profound meditation and by the realisation of which he became the Buddha or the prfectly enlightened one is the truth of *pratītya-samutpāda* or dependent origination which presents an entirely new perspective in the field of philosophy. The fundamental notions of causality, substance, time and space underwent complete change and the general tendency of all logical and metaphysical enquiries was directed not towards any thesis but towards contradicting all kinds of thesis of the established schools. From the religious side, the authority of the Vedas was openly challenged and the efficacy of the rituals and sacrifices was stoutly denied. Moreover the inhuman cruelties inflicted on the beasts in the different kinds of sacrifices was severely condemned. The existence of any ultimate reality, at least in the form of the Supreme Being, was denied or at least strict silence was maintained on all such ontological points; the *summum bonum* of life was declared to be the final liberation from this life of suffering by a strict code of moral

[1] It is to be noticed that orthodox Jainism like other dogmatic schools incorporated various dogmatic beliefs like the self-revealing eternal nature of Jainism as a religion, the godhood of the Tirthaṅkaras and many others of this nature; and a fighting within Jainism itself began between the two main sects, *viz*., the Śvetāmbaras (*i.e.*, wearers of white cloth) and the Digambaras (*i.e.*, the naked). The peculiar beliefs of the Digambaras are that the Tirthaṅkaras live without food, that a monk, possessing property and wearing clothes, cannot attain liberation and that no woman is entitled to liberation. The Jaina monks generally bear clothes of a blanket, an alms-bowl, a stick, a broom to sweep the ground, a piece of cloth to cover his mouth lest any insect may enter it by chance. The Digambaras bear a similar outfit, but they always remain naked and carry brooms of peacock's feather or long hairs of the tail of animals ((*cāmara*). The monks have their head shaven; there is often the custom of plucking the hair out and this plucking of the hair is sometimes regarded as a cardinal religious practice.

discipline. Thus the sacrificial religion of the Vedas was replaced by the Buddhists by the principles of moral virtues and good conduct (*śīlācāra*). Leaving aside the innovations of later Mahāyāna Buddhism or Tāntric Buddhism where Buddhism developed innumerable gods and goddesses and the paraphernalia of worship, partly as a reaction against the negativistic regorism, partly through the influence of Hindu faiths, and mainly through the influence of indigenous religious cults or such other cults of the neighbouring localities, Buddhism denied godhood unreservedly and even the existence of any supreme creator of the universe as no positive evidence of any such being can ever be demonstrated. The spirit of monastic Buddhism on this point is best illustrated in the *Tevijja Sutta* of the *Dīghanikāya* where the belief in the existence of Brahmā (the creator) and the belief in the Brahminical religious systems have been compared to the funny belief of a foolish man in the existence of some beautiful girl somewhere and his wish to enjoy her without knowing absolutely anything about her and her whereabouts.

The Buddhists were strongly opposed to the caste-system and the Varṇāśrama religion of the caste Hindus. A great campaign against the caste-system is found in the *Vajrasūcī* of Aśvaghoṣa where the author tried to prove on the basis of the evidences found in the Vedic literature and the standard Brahminical texts like the *Manu-saṁhitā*, the *Mahābhārata*, etc., that the Brahmins as a class can never be superior to the other castes and that the superiority or the inferiority of man can never be determined by the accidental fact of birth. The orthodoxy and conventionalism of the Śramaṇas and the Brāhmaṇas[1] were constantly criticised by

[1] It should be noted here that wherever we find criticism of the Buddhists against the Brahmins in the Pali texts (and we come across such criticism very frequently) we find mention of the Śramaṇas as one of the ancient orthodox sects along with the Brahmanical sect. These Śramaṇas seem to be an orthodox sect of ascetics who were somewhat akin to the Buddhists in their insistence on the misery and sufferings of Saṁsāra, in the emphasis on compassion and Ahiṁsā and in their disregard of caste system. But it seems they were somewhat dogmatic in view and formality prevailed in their asceticism which made them target of criticism from the monastic Buddhists. In this connection see an article by Winternitz in the journal *Indian Culture* (Vo 1. No. 2) 'Jainas in Indian Literature.'

the Buddhists. Whenever and wherever we find mention of the Śramaṇas and the Brāhmaṇas we find them as representing the mistaken or distorted spirit of religion as contrasted to the true spirit of religion represented by the well-disciplined and perfectly enlightened Buddhists.[1] Without entering into the details, let us give here a few specimen of criticism that were levelled by the Buddhists against these orthodox sects. A good specimen of popular criticism is to be found in the *Vatthupama-sutta* where Buddha preached to the audience that a man can be said to have bathed only when he has become pure in heart.[2] At this a Brahmin from among the audience asked Buddha,—"Does your Holiness go to the Bāhukā river to bathe?" The Lord replied,—"What's the need of going to the Bāhukā river,—what may it do?" The Brahmin said,—"O Gautama, the river Bāhukā is known to many and recognised by many as associated with Mokṣa and virtue and as rendering liberation and destroying sin; many people wash away their sin of past deeds in the river Bāhukā". Then the Lord addressed the following verse—"Indeed there are (sacred) rivers like the Bāhukā, Adhikakkā, Gayā, Sundarikā, Sarasvatī, Prayāga and the Bāhumatī; there the fool, the evil-doers take their bath everyday; but surely they are not purified thereby. What will the Sundarikā do? What can the Prayāga and the Bāhukā do? He who does harm to living beings and who is the doer of all evil deeds, is never purified by (the water of) these rivers."[3] Another instance of the criticism of the same nature can be cited from the dialogue between the nun Puṇṇikā and a Brahmin in the *Therī-gāthā*. Puṇṇikā asks the Brahmin, who was bathing early in the morning in an extremely cold weather,—"I indeed used to plunge into water in cold weather with a view to bring water,—but that was only out of fear of punishment or rebuke from the ladies I served; but of whom

[1] *Cf. pagāḍhā ettha na dissanti eke samaṇa-bahmaṇā |*
taṁ tu desaṁ na jānanti yena gacchanti subbatā || — *Padhāna-sutta.*

[2] *ayaṁ vuccati bhikkhu sināto antareṇa sinānena.*

[3] *bāhukam adhikakkañ ca gayaṁ sundarikam api |*
sarasvatiṁ payāgañ ca atha bāhumatiṁ nadiṁ ||
kiṁ sundarikā karissati, kiṁ payāgā, kiṁ bāhukā nadī ||
veriṁ katakibbisaṁ naraṁ na hi naṁ sodhaye pāpakamminaṁ ||

are you so much afraid, O Brāhmaṇa, that you plunge into water and bear extreme cold with a shivering body?" "The reason is known to you",—replied the Brahmin,—"why then this question? I acquire virtue and destroy the effect of my evil deeds (by bathing). Whoever perfoms evil deeds, whether an old man or young, will escape the fruition of such evil acts by taking bath in holy water." "Who is the fool of fools," asked Puṇṇikā "that has instructed you that the effects of evil-deeds can be washed away by bathing in the water? Had it been the fact, all frogs and tortoises and snakes and porpoises and other aquatic creatures would certainly have gone to heaven. Should all sheep, boar, fish hunters, thieves and murderers and other evil-doers be liberated from all evil deeds by their bathing in water? If this river should wash away all the sins you have accumulated by your former evil deeds, she should wash away all your merits too;—but what should remain then? You do not care to cast away that (*i.e.*, evil deeds) through the fear of which you are plunging every day into water,—the effects of evil deeds will never be washed away by cold water."[1] The nun then adds that if a man is really conscious of the direful effects of the evil deeds and if sin has become something repulsive to him, let him not try to flee from sin or to wash away his sin in water, let him take refuge in the Buddha and adopt his creed and lead a life of discipline and righteousness.

But though Buddhism first began with a freedom of thought and spirit of revolt against orthodoxy, orthodoxy in practical religious life gradually crept into Buddhism itself and the ethical rigorism, strictness of rules and regulations,—austere practices of penance, vows and fastings

[1] *ko nu mate idakkhāsi ajānatassa ajānato* |
udakābhisecanā nāma pāpa-kammā pamuccati ||
saggaṁ nūna gamissanti sabba-maṇḍūka-kacchapā |
nāgā ca susumārā ca ye caññe udakecarā ||
orabbhikā sukarikā macchikā miga-bandhakā |
corā ca vajjhaghāṭā ca ye caññe pāpa-kammino |
udakābhisecanā te pi pāpa-kammā pamuccare ||
sace imā nadiyo te pāpaṁ pubbekataṁ vaheyyuṁ |
puññaṁ pi mā vaheyyuṁ tena tvaṁ parivāhiro assa ||
yassa brāhmaṇa tvaṁ bhīto sadā udakam otari |
tam eva brahme mā kāsi mā te sītaṁ chaviṁ hane ||
Therī-gāthā, (xii, 240-244).

prescribed for the monastic life again made the monks objects of criticism. We have noticed before that a large section of people with more liberal views, freedom of philosophic thought and a generous outlook seceded from the orthodox body. But in course of time when Tāntricism made its way in Buddhism, the Tāntric School again revolted against both the monasticism and scholasticism of Hīnayāna Buddhism and the intellectual pedantry of the Mahāyānists; the Tāntrikas advocated their esoteric practice which were held to be the surest and at the same time the easiest way to liberation. In the Buddhist Tantras we always find that austere practices and penances inflicting disciplinary rigorism on body and mind can never conduce to the attainment of perfection; perfect enlightenment must be attained through an easy process—through the enjoyment of the five objects of desire.[1] So the hard rules of discipline, the practices of fasting, bathing, purifying the body and the mind through strict rules and regulations should all be avoided,[2] and the most pleasant and easiest way of attaining perfection is through initiation in the *tattva* and the practice of yoga in company with the Prajñā (*i.e.*, the female counterpart). The austere penances and vows only make a man sorry, and make his face disfigured; through this pain and sorrow the mind can never be expected to attain perfection.[3] It is, therefore, enjoined, —'Do not cast away the five objects of desire and do not inflict strain on the body through penance; try to attain *bodhi* (*i.e.*, perfect knowledge) in a pleasant way by follow-

[1] *sarva-kāmo-pabhogaiś ca sevyamānair yathecchataḥ* |
anena khalu yogena laghu buddhatvam āpnuyāt ||
duṣkarair niyamais tīvraiḥ sevyamāno na siddhati |
sarva-kāmo-pabhogais tu sevayaṁś cā' śu siddhati ||
Śrī-guhya-samāja, Ch. VII (G.O.S).

[2] *na kaṣṭa-kalpanāṁ kuryāt upavāso na ca kriyām* |
snānaṁ śaucaṁ na caivā'tra grāma-dharmaṁ vivarjayet ||
Advaya-siddhi MS. (C.L. B.No. 13124) pp.35(B)-36A.

This verse is also found in the *Citta-viśuddhi-prakaraṇa*, Verse No. 58.

[3] *Vajra-ḍāka-tantra*, quoted in the Catalogue of Sanskrit Buddhist MSS. J.R.S.B., Vol. I. p. 105. This verse is quoted in the commentary of the Caryā-pada, No. 1, and is said to belong to the *Śrī-samāja*; it is not, however, found in the *Śrī-guhya-samāja-tantra* published in G.O.S.

ing the injunction of the science of esoteric yoga.[1] It has been said in the *Citta-viśuddhi-prakaraṇa* of Āryadeva that bathing in the holy water of the Ganges is of no avail; for, if the water of the Ganges had the capacity of purifying man's body, it would have the capacity of purifying the body even of a dog and the dog also would have been entitled to liberation by bathing in the Ganges. Again, there are fishermen who dive in the water of the Ganges, why should not they be liberated from the fetters of this world? And there are fish in the water of the Ganges; what prevents these poor creatures from attaining Mokṣa? Mokṣa is never possible through going on pilgrimage or bathing, it is to be attained only through the purification of mind, by purging it of all the blemishes of subjectivity and objectivity.[2]

But the fun is that though Tāntricism condemned orthodoxy in the strongest possible terms, it developed within its province the most elaborate form of practices. In formalism, ceremonialism, ritualism, magic, sorcery and in the most complicated system of worship accompanied by the muttering of innumerable Mantras Tāntricism superseded all the other orthodox systems. Vajra-yāna Buddhism, which is the most general name for Buddhist Tāntricism as a whole, developed all possible rites and practices, both conventional and unconventional. Though the secret yogic practice is often spoken of in Vajra-yāna, it was not emphasised as the only method for realising the truth, and hence was the importance attached also to all rules of worship, muttering of the Mantras, describing of the circles and hundred other rituals and ceremonies. Again there arose another group of Yogins within the province of esoteric Buddhism, who revolted against this formal nature of Vajra-yāna and stressed some esoteric yogic practice to be the only method for realising the highest truth or attaining perfection; this school is known as Sahajiyā Buddhism.

We have discussed before at some length the salient

[1] *Pañca-krama*, Ch. I, MS. (B.N. Sans. No. 65, 66) p. 1 (A). This verse is quoted in the commentary of the Caryā-pada (No. 1) as belonging to the *Śrī-samāja* : but it is not found in the text published in G.O.S.

[2] Verses (59-68).

features of this Buddhist Sahajiyā cult. If we analyse and examine the ideas of the Buddhist Sahajiyās we shall find that, as an off-shoot of Tāntric Buddhism, it embodies the heterodoxy of Buddhism in general mixed up with the spirit of Tāntricism. In its aversion towards discursive reason and scholastic erudition and in its stress on the practical side of religion we may find the spirit of Tantra and Yoga working together on it. Again the influence of the Tantra as well as of the Vedānta is palpable in the view that truth can never be found outside—it is to be intuited within. In the highest stress laid by the Sahajiyās on Sahaja-realisation or self-realisation as the *summum bonum* of the religious life we may trace the old Upaniṣadic spirit under the Buddhistic garb. Ideas, derived from different lines of thought, have merged together in a popular way in the songs and Dohās of these later Buddhist poets. In the Jaina Dohās we have almost a similar admixture against a popular Jaina background. The devotional line of thought or the spirit of love is, however, conspicuous by its absence from the Buddhist and Jaina songs and Dohās; but it predominates in the songs and Dohās of the medieval period. The fact will be demonstrated when we shall deal with the salient features of the Vaiṣṇava Sahajiyās and the Bāuls of Bengal in a succeeding chapter, and with those of the innumerable Sahajiyā and Sūfī poets of Upper and Northern India in an appendix. Besides the inherited elements from older thoughts the medieval poets received cognate thoughts and ideas also from Sūfī-istic Islam. As we shall have occasion to turn to the question in detail in future, we need not discuss it now.

(ii) *The Idea of Sahaja*

The criticism made by the Buddhist Sahajiyās, with which the Jaina mystics also joined their voice, defines the Sahajiyā school more negatively than positively. In the positive side, however, the conception of the Sahaja or the ultimate innate nature of all the objects and beings will give us a definite idea about the fundamental tenets of the school.

The word 'Sahaja' literally means that which is born or

which originates with the birth or origination of any entity (*saha jāyate iti sahajaḥ*). It is, therefore, what all the Dharmas possess by virtue of their very existence, and is thus the quintessence of all the Dharmas. As Mahā-sukha is the quintessence of all the Dharmas, this Mahā-sukha-nature is the Sahaja-nature of all the Dharmas. In the *Hevajra-tantra* we find,—"The whole world is of the nature of Sahaja—for Sahaja is the quintessence (*svarūpa*) of all; this quintessence is Nirvāṇa to those who posssess the perfectly pure Citta."[1] But though this Sahaja in the form of Mahā-sukha is realised in and through a physiological process, it should never be conceived as something belonging to the body; though it is within the body, it is not something physical.[2] As the quintessence of all, it is the absolute reality, both immanent and transcendent.

We find in the Upaniṣads that the Brahman as the ultimate nature of our self and of the external world transcends all intellectual comprehension and verbal expression. Similar is the position of the Sahajiyās, who hold that the Sahaja nature is neither definable nor accessible to our mind, nor expressible by speech. As the Brahman is to be realised within, so also this Sahaja-nature is to be intuited within (*svasaṃvedya*). We find in the Upaniṣads that when one realises the self as the Brahman, there is neither the knower (*jñātā*) nor the knowable (*jñeya*) nor the knowledge (*jñāna*); for, in such a transcendental state, "where everything becomes the self, who will see whom and by what means, and who will know whom and by what means?"[3] This Upaniṣadic principle has also been adopted by the Sahajiyās in speaking of the Sahaja nature. It is said in the *Hevajra-tantra*,—"Sahaja can neither be explained by any man nor can be expressed by any speech; it is realised by

1 *tasmāt sahajaṁ jagat sarvaṁ sahajaṁ svarūpam ucyate* |
svarūpam eva nirvāṇaṁ viśuddhā-kāra-cetasā(aḥ?) ||
Hevajra-tantra, MS (A.S.B. No. 11317) p. 36(B).
Cf. also, *svabhāvaṁ sahajam ityuktaṁ sarvā-kāraika-sambaram* |
Ibid., MS. p. 30(A).

2 *dehastho'pi na dehajaḥ* ||
Hevajra-tantra, MS. p. 3(A).

3 *yatra tvasya sarvam ātmaivā'bhūt tat kena kaṁ paśyet, kena kaṁ vijānīyāt* |
Bṛhad-āraṇyako-paniṣat. (4-5-1-5).

the self through the merit of serving at the feet of the Guru."[1] In the *Guhya-siddhi* also it is said that this truth is to be attained through personal intuition,—the tongue can never speak anything of it.[2] That is an all-pervading supreme state where there is neither body nor speech nor any work.[3] It has very nicely been said in a song of Kānha-pāda—"Whatever is related to the mind and to all the Āgamas (scriptures) and religious texts and the beads (for counting the time of taking the name of God)—all are confusing and anomalous. Say, how Sahaja can be explained,—(for) neither body nor speech nor mind can enter into it. In vain does the Guru preach to the disciple, for, how can he explain that which transcends the capacity of all verbal means? Whoever will explain it will misrepresent it; here the preceptor is dumb and the disciple is deaf. Asks Kānha,—how then is that jewel of the Jinas?—it is just as the deaf is made to understand by the dumb (*i.e.*, through the movement of the lips, or by the facial expressions, or by the suggestions by postures and gestures)."[4] Tāḍaka-pāda also says,—"How can what is beyond the path of speech be explained?"[5] Again we find,—"The Sahaja stage can never be explained by the preceptor, neither can it be understood by the disciple,—it is like the flow of nectar;—

[1] *nā'nyena kathyate sahajaṁ na kasminn abhilapyate |*
ātmanā jñāyate puṇyād guru-pādo-pasevayā ||
Hevajra-tantra, MS. p. 22(B).

[2] *sva-saṁvedyaṁ tu tat tattvaṁ vaktuṁ nā'syaḥ pāryate |*
Guhya-siddhi, MS. (C.L.B. No. 13124) p. 14(A).

[3] *yatra na kāryo na vāk-cittaṁ sthānaṁ yat sarvagaṁ param |*
Ibid., MS. p. 15(A).

[4] *jo maṇa-goara ālā jālā |*
āgama pothī iṣṭā-mālā ||
bhaṇa kaiseṁ sahaja bola bā jāya |
kāa-vāk-cia jasu ṇa samāya ||
āle guru uesai sīsa |
vāk-pathātīta kāhiva kīsa ||
je taiṁ bolī te tavi ṭāla |
guru bova se sīsā kāla ||
bhaṇai kāhnu jiṇa-raaṇa bi kaisā |
kāla bobeṁ saṁvohia jaisā ||
Song No. 40.

For the reading of the last line of the verse see the article "*Caryā-padera Pāṭha*" by the present writer in the *Śrī-bhāratī*, Vol. I, No. 7.

[5] *vāk-pathātīta kāhi vakhāṇī ||*
Ibid., Song No. 37.

to whom and by what means can it be explained?"[1] Tillo-pāda says in his Dohās,—Sahaja is a state where all the thought-constructions are dead (*i.e.*, destroyed) and the vital wind (which is the vehicle of the defiled Citta) is also destroyed,—the secret of this truth is to be intuited by the self,—how can it be explained (by others)? The truth (*tatta*=*tattva*) is inaccessible to the ordinary foolish people, and it is also unknown and unknowable to scholars,—but it is never inaccessible to that fortunate and meritorious one who by services has propitiated the Guru.[2] Saraha-pāda also says in his Dohā,—What can be known through meditation of that, which is without knowability? How can that be explained which transcends all speech?[3] In the commentary of the Dohā it is said,—whatever is a production of the mind is false; that is the truth, which is never mentally constructed.[4] Again it is said by Saraha-pāda,—where neither mind nor the vital wind moves, nor is there any function of the sun and the moon, there should the Sahaja-citta rest,—this is the advice of Saraha.[5] Where the mind dies out and the vital wind is also destroyed,—that is the supreme Mahā-sukha, it does not remain steady nor does it go anywhere (or, it never becomes expressible through words).[6] In the Sahaja state the individual mind enters the Sahaja as water enters into water.[7] The nature of the self can never be explained by others;

[1] *ṇau taṁ vāahi guru kahi ṇau taṁ vujjhai sīsa* |
sahajā-vattho amia rasa kāsu kahijjai kīsa ||
Quoted in the *Kriyā-saṁgraha-nāma-pañjikā.*
MS. (B. N. Sans. No. 31) p. 37(B).

[2] *tu marai jahi pavaṇa tahi līṇo hoi ṇirāsa* |
saa (saṁveaṇa tatta-phalu) sa kahijjai kīsa ||
vaḍha aṇā-loa-agocara-tatta paṇḍia-loa agamma |
jo guru-pā(a-pasaṇṇa tāhi ki citta agamma) ||
Dohākoṣa of Tillo-pāda, Verses 7-8, Dr. P. C. Bagchi's Edition.

[3] *jhāṇa-rahia ki kīai jhāne* |
jo avāa tahi kāhi vakhāṇe ||
Dohākoṣa of Saraha-pāda, Dr. P. C. Bagchi's Edition.

[4] *iti tāvan mṛṣā sarvaṁ (yāvad) yāvad vikalpyate* |
tat satyaṁ (tat) tathābhūtaṁ tattvaṁ yan na vikalpyate ||
Quoted in the Com. *Ibid.*

[5] *jahi maṇa pavaṇa na sañcarai ravi sasi ṇāha pavesa* |
tahi vaḍha citta visāma karu sarahem kahia uesa || *Ibid.*

[6] *jahi maṇa marai pavaṇa ho kkhaa jāi* |
ehu se parama-mahāsuha rahia kahimpi na jāi || *Ibid.*

[7] *ṇia maṇa muṇahu re niuṇe joi* |
jima jala jalahi milante soi || *Ibid.*

it can be caused to be realised only through the instructions of the Guru,—none else can make one realise it.[1] The subtle and varied emotions resulting from the realisation of truth is not something capable of being expressed through words,—that stage of bliss is absolutely free from all mental constructions—a supreme world is revealed there.[2] There intellect fails,—mind dies out, all pride and self-conceit vanish away,—mysterious is that Sahaja,—it is a master magician—how can it be bound by meditation?[3] It is free from all the letters and colours and qualities, it can neither be spoken of, nor can it be known.[4] That great Lord of transcendental bliss cannot be spoken of,—just as the pleasure derived from sex-union cannot be explained to an unmarried girl who has never personally experienced it.[5] Unless the body, speech and mind are destroyed, none can experience the bliss of his Sahaja-nature.[6] Kānha-pāda also says in his *Dohākoṣa*,—Only he who revels in Sahaja and who realises his jewel of mind (as the Bodhi-citta) can realise the course of religion,—others cannot understand it even if it is explained to them.

It is, therefore, clear from what is stated above that the nature of Sahaja cannot be defined,—it can only somehow be described. It will be evident that this Sahaja is the Brahman of the Upaniṣads and the Vedānta. It is the *Nirvāṇa-dhātu* of canonical Buddhism, it is the *tathatā* (thatness) of Aśvaghoṣa, it is the negatively described absolute reality of Nāgārjuna, which transcends the four logical categories,—it is the *Abhūta-parikalpa* or the increate absolute with the potency of all objectivity and subjectivity but in itself bereft of all dualism,—or the pure consciousness (*vijñapti-mātratā*) of the Vijnāna-vādins. It is again the Vajra-dhātu

1 *ṇia-sahāva ṇau kahiau aṇṇeṁ* |
dīsai guruuvaeseṁ ṇa aṇṇeṁ || *Ibid.*
2 *are putto tatto vicitta rasa kahaṇa ṇa sakkai tatthu* |
kappa-rahia suha-ṭhāṇu varajagu uajjai tatthu || *Ibid.*
3 *buddhi vināsai maṇa marai jahi (tuṭṭai) ahimāṇa* |
so māāmaa parama-kalu tahī kimvajjhai jhāṇa || *Ibid.*
4 *akkhara-vaṇṇo parama-guṇa rahije* |
bhaṇai ṇa jāṇai emai kahiaje || *Ibid.*
5 *so paramesaru kāsu kahijjai* |
suraa kumārī jima paḍijjai || *Ibid.*
6 *kāa-vāa-maṇu jāva ṇa bhijjai* |
sahaja-sahāve tāva ṇa rajjai || *Ibid.*

or the Vajra-sattva of the Vajra-yānists. It is the Bodhi-citta in the form of the unity of Śūnyatā and Karuṇā, it is the Mahā-sukha or the Supreme Bliss. All these ideas have merged in the idea of Sahaja of the Sahajiyās. In describing Sahaja Tillo-pāda says in his Dohās,—When in the Sahaja stage the Citta and the vacuity enter into an union of bliss all the objects of senses vanish away.[1] Sahaja is without beginning and without end;—this non-dual state of Sahaja is only explained by the venerable Guru.[2] When (in the Sahaja) the Citta vanishes, the Acitta (*i.e.*, negation) also vanishes; the state of non-dual unity (*samarasa*) is free from both existence and non-existence.[3] This transcendental truth is free from all merit and demerit,— for there cannot be any merit or demerit in what is realisable only within.[4] It is bereft of all colour and form,—it is perfect in the form of all.[5] In Sahaja the self is void, the world is void,—all the three worlds are void; in pure Sahaja there is neither merit nor sin.[6] Saraha-pāda also says,—"In Sahaja there is no duality; it is perfect like the sky. The intuition of this ultimate truth destroys all attachment and it shines through the darkness of attachment like a full moon in the night.[7] Sahaja cannot be heard with the ears, neither can it be seen with the eyes; it is not affected by air nor burnt by fire; it is not wet in intense rain, it neither increases nor decreases, it neither exists nor does it die out with the decay of the body; the Sahaja bliss is only an oneness of emotions,—it is oneness in all.[8] Our mind and the vital wind are unsteady like the horse;—

[1] Dohā No. 5 (Dr. Bagchi's edition).

[2] *āi-rahia ehu anta-rahia* |
varaguru-pāa a(ddaa-kahia) || *Ibid.*, Dohā No. 6.

[3] *Ibid.*, Dohā No. 11.

[4] *guṇa-doṣa-rahia ehu paramattha* |
saasaṁveaṇa kevi ṇattha || *Ibid.*, Dohā No. 29.

[5] *vaṇṇa vi vajjai ākii vihuṇṇā* |
savvāāre so sampuṇṇā || *Ibid.*, Dohā No. 32.

[6] *hau suṇṇa jagu suṇṇa tihua(ṇa) suṇṇa* |
(nimmala sahaje ṇa pāpa ṇa puṇṇa) || *Ibid.*, Dohā No. 34.

[7] Dohās of Saraha. p. 11, Verses 16-17.

[8] *saṅka-pāsa toḍahu guru-vaaṇeṁ* |
na suṇai soṇau dīsai ṇaaṇeṁ ||
pavaṇa vahante ṇau so hallai |
jalana jalante ṇau so ujjhai ||
ghaṇa varisante ṇau so mmai |
nau vajjai ṇau khaahi paissai ||

but in the Sahaja-nature both of them remain steady. When the mind thus ceases to function and all other ties are torn aside, all the differences in the nature of things vanish; and at that time there is neither the Brahmin nor the Śūdra.[1] Sahaja cannot be realised in any of its particular aspects—it is an intuition of the whole, the one underlying reality pervading and permeating all diversity. As the truth of the lotus can never be found either in the stalk, or in the leaves, or in the petals or in the smell of the lotus, or in the filament,—it lies rather in the totality of all these parts,—so also Sahaja is the totality which can only be realised in a perfectly non-dual state of the mind.[2] From it originate all, in it all merge again,—but it itself is free from all existence and non-existence,—it never originates at all.[3] For such Sahaja a man must do away with the positive as well as the negative functions of his mind and remain like a pure child absolutely depending on the instructions of the Guru,[4] and when the mind thus remains absolutely inactive in the Sahaja, all the cycles of birth and death are at once stopped.[5] So long as one does not realise the true nature of the self as the ultimate truth one cannot realise the transcendental reality underlying all phenomena.[6] This realisation of the self as the ultimate truth is not possible either through meditation or the muttering of the Mantras.[7] All the external forms are to be realised as pure void,—and the mind also must be beheld as pure void; and through this realisation of the essencelessness of the objects (*dharma-nairātmya*) and also of the subject (*pudgula-nairātmya*) the Sahaja-reality reveals itself in

ṇau vaṭṭai ṇa taṇunte ṇa vaccai |
samarasa sahajānanda jāṇijjai ||
Ibid., p. 12 (Verses 3-6).

1 *javvem maṇa atthamaṇa*, etc. | *Ibid.*

2 *saṇḍa-puaṇi-dala-kamala-gandha-kesara varaṇālem* |
chaḍḍahu veṇima na karahu sosa ṇa laggahu vaḍha ālem ||
Ibid.

3 *Ibid.*

4 *Ibid.*

5 *Ibid.*

6 *jāva ṇa appahim para pariāṇasi* |
tāva ki dehāṇuttara pāvasi || *Ibid.*

7 *saraha bhaṇai vaḍha jāṇau appā* |
ṇau so dheā na dhāraṇa jappā || *Ibid.*

the heart of the Sādhaka.[1] This Supreme Lord (of Sahaja) is neither seen coming nor seen going; nor is he seen remaining within; he is a waveless sea of perfect purity.[2] In Sahaja knowledge there is neither 'without' nor 'within,'—it pervades the fourteen worlds in its non-dual form.[3] "There is some one formless hiding himself within our body,—he who knows him is liberated."[4] As a lunar gem in deep darkness brightens all things by its lustre, so also the Supreme Mahā-sukha or the Sahaja drives away all the miseries of life at once.[5] The truth is neither in the house (*i.e.*, in the body) nor in the forest (*i.e.*, in the external objects),—the truth is in the absolute purity of the Citta which is free from all the Vikalpas.[6]

Kānha-pāda also says that Sahaja is without any wave, it is free from all the defilements,—it is free from both merit and sin—there is absolutely nothing in it.[7] It is unchanging, without thought-constructions, without any transformation or corruption; it neither rises nor sets,—here mind has no function at all, this is what is called Nirvāṇa.[8]

It is to be noticed in this connection that though Buddhism as a religion began its course as an uncompromising atheistic school, believing neither in God nor in the self or the soul-substance, it gradually showed a theistic tendency in course of its evolution. Beginning with the Tathatā-vāda of Aśvaghoṣa and the *Vijñapti-mātratā* or the *Abhūta-parikalpa* of Asaṅga and Vasubandhu, Buddhism

1 *Ibid.*

2 *āvanta ṇa dīssai janta ṇahi acchanta ṇa muṇiai* |
ṇittaraṅga paramesuru ṇikkalaṅka dhāhijjai || *Ibid.*

3 *jima vāhira tima avbhantaru* |
caudaha bhuvaneṁ ṭhiau ṇirantaru || *Ibid.*

4 *asarira (koi) sarirahi lukko* |
jo tahi jāṇai so tahi mukko || *Ibid*

5 *ghorāndhāreṁ candamaṇi jima ujjoa karei* |
parama-mahāsuha ekku-khaṇe duriāsesa harei || *Ibid.*

6 *ṇau ghare ṇau vaṇeṁ vohi ṭhiu ehu pariāṇahu bheu* |
ṇimmala-citta-sahāvatā karahu avikala seu || *Ibid.*

7 *ṇittaraṅga sama sahaja-rūa saala-kalusa-virahie* |
pāpa-puṇṇa-rahie kuccha ṇāhi kāṇhu phuḍa kahie ||
(Dr. P. C. Bagchi's Edition) Verse No. 10.

8 *ṇiccala ṇivviappa ṇivviāra* |
uaa-atthamaṇa-rahia susāra
aiso so ṇivvāṇa bhaṇijjai |
jahiṁ maṇa māṇasa kimpi ṇa kijjai
Verse No. 20.

was coming closer and closer to the Upaniṣadic conception of the Brahman as the Supreme Being. In the conception of the Vajra-sattva and the Lord Śrī-Mahā-sukha of the Vajra-yānists we have seen how the monistic conception of the Supreme Being is clearly established. In the conception of the Sahaja or the *Svābhāvika-kāya* (the body of the ultimate nature) of the Sahajiyās the same tendency of conceiving it just in the image of the monistic Supreme Being is sometimes manifest. Often the Upaniṣadic description of the Brahman as having hands and legs on all sides,—having eyes, heads and faces on all sides,—having ears in all the worlds on all sides—and as pervading the whole universe,—are all applied to this Sahaja.[1] And this Sahaja is none but the self,—and all the worlds are the transformations of this one Sahaja-self,—all the universe is pervaded by the Sahaja-self,—and nothing else is to be found anywhere.[2] All the various phenomena produced by the deeds (*karma*) of the beings are nothing but the modes and modifications of the self-revealed Sahaja; but though they are Sahaja in the ultimate nature, they are produced in their varieties through mentation (*bodhanāt*) in the form of the subject and the object.[3] The Sahaja is itself the sustainer (*bhartā*), itself the performer (*kartā*), itself the king, itself the Lord[4].

1 *sarvataḥ pāṇi-pādādyaṁ sarvato 'kṣi-śiromukham* |
sarvataḥ śrutimat loke sarvam āvṛtya tiṣṭhati ||
eṣa svābhāvikaḥ kāyaḥ śūnyatā-karuṇā-dvayaḥ |
napuṁsaka iti khyāto yuganaddha iti kvacit ||
Śrī-sambara, quoted in the *Subhāṣita-saṁgraha*, Bendall's Edition.
Cf. sarvataḥ pāṇi-pādaṁ tat, etc. *Śvetāśvataro-paniṣat*, 3-16; *Gītā*, 13-13.

2 *mad-bhāva(ṁ) hi jagat sarvaṁ mad-bhāvaṁ bhuvana-trayam* |
mayā vyāptam idaṁ sarvaṁ nā'nyamayaṁ dṛśyate jagat ||
Hevajra-tantra, MS. (RASB. No. 11317.) p. 23(A).

3 *sva-saṁvedyam ayaṁ karma vodhanāt karma jāyate* |
Ibid., MS. p 23(B).

Cf. also the Commentary:—*yat kiñcit dṛśyate sattvānāṁ karma-vipāka-janitaṁ vaicitryaṁ sthāvaraṁ jaṅgamādikaṁ tad eva karma* | *yady etat karmotpadyate sva-saṁvedyāt* | *kathaṁ tarhi mahāmudrā-siddhiḥ* | *tadahumāha* (?), *bodhanād iti bodho grāhya-grāhaka-rupeṇa pratipattiḥ* | *tasmāt karmotpadyate* | *na punaḥ viśvasya sahajaika-rasa-bhāvāt* |
Hevajra-pāñjikā or *Yoga-ratna-mālā*, Ms. (Cambridge, Add. No. 1699) p. 32(B).

Cf. also, *Dākārṇava*:—
sambha kamma jima bhāvaha rui
bhava nivvāṇa ṇa disai koi |
(Dr. N. C. Chaudhuri's edition) p. 144.

4 *svayaṁ bhartā svayaṁ kartā svayaṁ rājā svayaṁ prabhuḥ* |
Hevajra-tantra, MS. p. 23(B).

It is the life of the animate, it is the supreme and immutable,—it is all-pervading and resides in all the bodies,—it is the great life (the vital process)—and the whole universe is imbued with it,—all the existent and the non-existent and everything else proceed from it and it alone. It is the Being of the nature of pure consciousness,—it is the eternal sovereign personality,—it is the Jīva (the individual personality),—it is time,—it is the ego.[1] Tillo-pāda says in a Dohā,—"I am the universe,—I am the Buddha,—I am perfect purity,—I am the non-cognition (*amanasiāra*)—I am the destroyer of the cycle of existence."[2] And this nature of the self is its Sahaja-nature. Saraha-pāda also says,— "One is the Lord explained in all the scriptures and he manifests himself (as the variety of all phenomena) through his own will."[3] In the *Dākārṇava* it is addressed to Sahaja,—"Thou art the cause of all the Dharmas,—but who art thou Sahaja, mysteriously unknown to all?"[4] Again it has been said,—"Only Sahaja-nature is seen (—nothing else is there),—salute to the Lord of all the Suras (gods) and the Asuras! The senses do not know where it is,—worship it through the songs (*gāthā*)."[5]

The reading of the last line given in the commentary of the *Dohākoṣa* (Dohā No. 6) of Kānha-pāda is "*svayaṁ kartā svayaṁ hartā svayaṁ rājā svayaṁ prabhuḥ*," and "*hartā*" is further explained as the destructive form (*svayam eva saṁhāra-rūpaḥ*) of the Lord. [The Ms. of the Commentary on the Dohakoṣa of Kānha-pāda in the possession of the writer, MS. Cambridge Add. No. 1699, p. 43(A)].

[1] *sa eva prāṇināṁ prāṇaḥ sa eva paramā-kṣaraḥ* |
sarva-vyāpi sa evā'sau sarva-dehe vyavasthitaḥ ||
sa evā'sau mahā-prāṇaḥ sa evā'sau jaganmayaḥ |
bhāvā-bhāvau tad-udbhūtau anyāni yāni tāni ca ||
sattvaṁ vijñāna-rūpañ ca puruṣaṁ purāṇam īśvaram |
ātmā jīvañca sarvañca kālaḥ pudgala eva ca ||
Hevajra-tantra, MS. (ASB. No. 11317) p. 27(A).

[2] *hāu jagu hāu buddha (hāu) nirañjana* |
(hāu amanasiāra bhava-bhañjana) |
Tillo-pāda's *Dohākoṣa* (Dr. P. C. Bagchi's Edition), Dohā No. 16

[3] *ekku deva vahu āgama disai* |
appaṇu icche phuḍa paḍihāsai ||
Dohākoṣa (Dr. P. C. Bagchi's Edition).

[4] *kāraṇu sabbha dhammaha tummii* |
ke acchasi sahaja—sarūa ṇa gāi ||
Dākārṇava (Ed. by Dr. N. C. Chaudhuri), p. 138.

[5] *kevala sahaja-sahāu ri disai namahu surāsura tihuaṇa nāhai* |
indiya loa ṇa jānai koi parama mahāsuha pujahu gāhai ||
Ibid., p. 143.

Chapter IV

THE PRACTICES OF THE SAHAJIYĀS AND THE STATE OF SUPREME BLISS (MAHĀ-SUKHA)

We have said that the Tāntric systems, whether Hindu or Buddhist, do not profess to discover and preach any truth anew; their main function is to indicate practical methods for the realisation of truth. The Sahajiyā cult, as an off-shoot of Tāntric Buddhism, lays the highest stress on the practical method for realising the Sahaja-nature of the self and of all the Dharmas. We, however, do not propose to go into all the details; we shall give here a very brief account of the main practices and also of the state of supreme bliss produced through this process of Sādhanā.

(i) *The Guru-vāda*

The most important thing in connection with the practical aspect of the Sahajiyā religion is the selection of a proper preceptor. The whole field of Indian philosophy and religion is characterised by a unanimous emphasis on the Guru-vāda or the doctrine of the preceptor. It will be seen that in a sense all the systems of Indian philosophy and religion are mystic,—for according to all the systems truth always transcends intellectual apprehension or discursive speculation,—it is to be intuited within through the help of the preceptor, who has already realised it. Truth is transmitted from the preceptor to the disciple just as light from one lamp to the other. The only way of knowing the truth is, therefore, to seek the grace of the Guru, who, and who alone, can make a man realise the Supreme Reality. It is believed that the true preceptor in his non-dual state identifies himself with the disciple and performs from within the disciple all that is necessary for the latter's spiritual uplift. The true disciple becomes an instrument in the hands of the true preceptor. It is for this reason that in Indian religions the Guru is held in the highest esteem. Sometimes the Guru is a substitute even for God, or at least God is to be realised through the medium of the person of the Guru, who stands as the living proof for the existence of God. To ordinary people God is a mere time-honoured belief; but the preceptor opens the eyes of the disciple and makes him realise the existence of God. Tāntricism, which lays emphasis on the practical aspect of relgion, naturally, lays equal stress on the function of the Guru. Moreover, many of the Tāntric practices are secret practices involving complex processes of esoteric yoga. Because of this stringent nature of the Tāntric practice the help of the Guru is enjoined to be sought at every step. These intricate esoteric practices, when properly and systematically carried out, may lead a man to the highest spiritual elevation,—on the other hand there is the chance of physical and mental aberration at every step, and if they are not pursued very cautiously and methodically with the guidance and directions of the experienced Guru they may lead, and are very likely to lead, a man into the darkest abyss of hell. Because of their stringent nature these practices have repeatedly been declared in all the Tantras as the secret of all secrets (*guhyād guhyam*), and therefore, there is no other way of being initiated into this method of Yoga save the practical help of the Guru. In almost all the Tantras the Guru is always praised in the superlative terms and is declared to be the highest reality itself.[1] Almost all the Caryā-songs speak highly of the Guru, who is the only help in the path of Sādhanā; the yogins are warned of the pitfalls of the path and are enjoined repeatedly to seek the help of the Guru, wherever there is an iota of doubt in mind and wherever there is the slighest difficulty. We shall see later on that the theory of Guru-vāda, as we find in the Dohās and the Caryā-songs, may be recognised as one of the main characteristics of all the religious sects represented by our old and medieval literature.[2]

(ii) *The importance of the Body in the Sādhanā*

In connection with the practical aspect of the Buddhist

[1] See the first part of the *Subhāṣita-saṁgraha*, edited by Cecil Bendall, where various quotations are to be found from various Buddhist Tāntric texts in praise of the Guru and also defining the nature of a true preceptor.

[2] *Vide Infra*, Ch. V, Ch. VII, Appendix (A).

Sahajiyā cult we should also notice that along with the uncompromising spirit of revolt against all formalities and orthodoxy in religion, great emphasis is laid in the Sahajiyā literature on the human body, which is conceived as a microcosm of the universe. This feature, we have hinted, predominates in all the Tantras in general, wherever the yogic element prevails; but as the Sahajiyās laid their whole stress on the yogic element this theory of the body being the epitome of the whole universe was most emphasised. In the *Hevajra-tantra* we find that the Lord (*Bhagavān*) was asked by a Bodhisattva whether there was any necessity at all of this physcial world and the physical body, everything being in reality nothing but pure void. To this the reply of the Lord was that without the body there was no possibility of the realisation of the great bliss and here lies the importance of the body.[1] But though the truth is within the body and arises out of it, it should never be confused to be something physical.[2] In the *Śrī-kāla-cakra* we find that without the body there cannot be any perfection, neither can the supreme bliss be realised in this life without the body,—it is for this reason that the body with the nervous system is so important for yoga; if perfection (*siddhi*) of the body be attained, all kinds of perfection in the three worlds are very easily obtained.[3] In discouraging going on pilgrimage and bathing in the sacred rivers, Saraha says,—"Here (within this body) is the Ganges and the Jumna, here the 'Gaṅgā-sāgara' (the mouth of the Ganges), here are Prayāga and Banaras,—here the sun and the moon. Here are the sacred places, here the *Pīṭhas* and the *Upa-pīṭhas*—I have not seen a place of pilgrimage and an abode of bliss like my body."[4] The *Tattva* is within

1 *dehā-bhāve kutaḥ saukhyam*, etc.
Hevajra-tantra, MS. p. 36(A).

2 *dehastho' pi na dehajaḥ. Ibid.*

3 *kāyā-bhāve na siddhir na ca parama-sukhaṁ prāpyate janmanī 'ha ||*
tasmāt kāyā-ṛtha-hetoh pratidina-samaye bhāvayet nāḍī-yogam |
kāye siddhe anya-siddhis tribhuvana-nilaye kiṅkaratvaṁ prayāti ||
Śrī-kāla-cakra-tantra, MS. (Cambridge, Add. 236 (4) p. 33(B).

4 *etthu se surasarī jamunā etthu se gaṅgā-sāaru |*
etthu paāga vaṇārasi etthu se canda divāaru ||
khettu pīṭha upapīṭha etthu maiṁ bhamai pariṭṭhao |
deha-sarisaa tittha maiṁ suha aṇṇa ṇa diṭṭhao
Dohākoṣa of Saraha. Nos. 47, 48 (Dr. P. C. Bagchi's Edition).

he house of our body; yet, curious indeed it is, that we generally roam about in the whole world in search of it. It is nicely said by Saraha,—"He is within the house,—but you are enquiring about him outside. You are seeing your husband within, yet are asking the neighbours as to his whereabouts." "Know thyself, O fool," says Saraha,—"the truth is neither to be meditated nor to be held in the body as a Dhāraṇī, neither is it to be muttered as a Mantra."[1] The scholars explain all the scriptures,—but do not know the Buddha residing within the body.[2] "Some one bodiless is hiding himself in the body,—he who knows him there (in the body) is liberated."[3] In the Caryā-songs also the body is highly spoken of as the abode of truth. Thus Kānha-pāda says in a song,—"The yogin Kānha has become a Kāpālī,[4] and has entered into the practices of yoga, and he is sporting in the city of his body in a non-dual form."[5] Again he says,—"Make the five Tathāgatas the five oars and, O Kānha, steer the body on and tear off the snare of illusion."[6] The image of the body being the boat and a pure mind the oar for proceeding on to the way of realising the truth is very popular with the poets of the Caryā-songs.

The body being thus recognised as the abode of all truth the fundamental principles of Mahāyāna as transformed into Vajra-yāna began to be located within the

[1] *gharem̐ acchai vāhire pucchai |*
pai dekkhai paḍivesī pucchai ||
saraha bhaṇai vaḍha jāṇau appā |
ṇau so dhea na dhāraṇa jappā ||

[2] *paṇḍia saala sattha bakkhāṇai |*
dehahim̐ buddha vasanta ṇa jāṇai ||

[3] *asarira (koi sarīahi lukko |*
jo tahi jāṇai so tahi mukko ||

[4] Kāpālī is the general name given to the Tāntric Yogins, but here, in the commentary of the Caryās (and also in the commentary of the *Hevajra-tantra*, MS. Cambridge, Add. No. 1699) the word is derived in the following way:—*kam̐ mahā-sukham̐ pālayati'ti kāpālikaḥ, i.e.*, he who nurses "Ka" which means Mahā-sukha is a Kāpālika.

[5] Song No. 11.

[6] *pañca tathāgata kia keḍuāla |*
bāhaa kāa kānhila māā-jāla ||
Ibid., Song No. 13.

Cf. kāa ṇāvaḍi khāṇṭi maṇa keḍuāla |
sadguru-vaaṇe dhara patavāla ||
cīa thira kari dha(ra)hu re nāi |
āna upāye pāra ṇa jāi ||
Ibid., Song No. 38.

physical system. Thus, corresponding to the six nerve-plexuses (*ṣaṭ-cakra*), or the six lotuses as they are also called, along the spinal cord,[1] as conceived in the Hindu Tantras as well as in the other texts on yoga, the Buddhists conceived of three plexuses or lotuses, with which they identified the three Kāyas. Thus the lowest Cakra in the region of the navel represents the lowest Kāya, *i.e.*, the Nirmāṇa-kāya (body of transformation); the Cakra in the heart is identified with the Dharma-kāya, (*i.e.*, the body of ultimate reality as the cosmic unity); and the Cakra just below the neck is said to be the Sambhoga-kāya (the body of bliss).[2] The Vajra-kāya or the Sahaja-kāya, which is the fourth Kāya with the Tāntric Buddhists, is located in the Uṣṇīṣa-kamala, or the Sahasrāra of the Hindus. It is also called the Mahā-sukha-cakra or the Mahā-sukha-kamala, being the seat of supreme realisation.

We have seen that the Bodhicitta is constituted of two factors, *viz.*, Śūnyatā and Karuṇā, or Prajñā and Upāya. Among the nerves of the body, which are innumerable, thirty-two are more important,[3] of which again three are the most important, two by the two sides of the spinal cord and one in the middle; with these two side-nerves are identified the cardinal principles of Prajñā and Upāya, and the middle nerve, which is the meeting-place of the other two nerves, is spoken of as the path for the Sahaja, or rather Avadhūtī-mārga or simply Avadhūtikā. Avadhūtī is explained as being that, through the effulgent nature of which all sins are destroyed,[4] or that which washes away

1 These are (1) Mūlādhāra-cakra, or the sacri-coccygeal plexus, situated between the penis and the anus and facing down with four petals of red colour; (2) Svādhiṣṭhāna-cakra, or sacral plexus, near the root of the penis with six petals of the colour of vermilion; (3) Maṇipura-cakra, or the lumber plexus in the region of the navel with ten petals of the colour of the cloud; (4) Anāhata-cakra in the heart with twelve petals of the colour of Bandhuka-flower (red); (5) Viśuddha-cakra or the laryngeal and pharyngeal plexus at the junction of the spinal chord and the medulla oblangata with sixteen petals of smoky colour; and (6) Ājñā-cakra between the eye-brows with two petals of white colours. Above all, there is the Sahasrāra-cakra or lotus (*padma*) in the highest cerebral region.

2 In the natural order, however, the Cakra in the heart, being next to the Cakra of Nirmāṇa-kāya, ought to have been the Sambhoga-kāya and the Cakra below the neck ought to have been the Dharma-kāya; this would have been consistent with the general order of the Kāyas.

3 See *Śrī-sampuṭikā*, MS. p. 3(B).

4 Commentary on the *Dohākoṣa* of Kānha-pāda, Dohā No. 4. (MS. B. N. Sans. No. 47) p. 39(B).

the beginningless thought-construction of existence,[1] or that which removes the evils of afflictions very easily.[2] The two nerves on the left and the right, which are identified with Prajñā and Upāya, and which meet together to produce the Bodhicitta, are variously termed in the Buddhist Tantras and the Caryā-songs. The nerve in the right which is the Upāya and which in the Hindu Tantras and the yoga literature is most generally known as the Piṅgalā, is also called *rasanā*, *sūrya*, *ravi*, *prāṇa*, *camana*, *kāli*, *bindu*, *yamunā*, *rakta*, *rajas*, *bhāva*, *puruṣa*, *grāhya*, *vyañjana* (consonants) and also the syllable *vaṃ*. Again the nerve in the left, which is the Prajñā, and which is known generally as the nerve Iḍā, is also called *lalanā*, *candra*, *śaśin*, *apāna*, *dhamana*, *āli*, *nāda*, *gaṅgā*, *śukra*, *tamas*, *abhāva*, (also *nirvāṇa*), *prakṛti*, *grāhaka*, *svara* (vowel) and also '*e*'.[3] Without entering into the details of the significance of these names, it may be said that the two nerves represent the principle of duality and the middle nerve (known as Suṣumnā or Avadhūtikā) represents the principle of absolute unity.

(*iii*) *The Esoteric Practice*

Coming to the question of the esoteric practice of the Sahajiyās, the first thing that we should take notice of is the importance attached to the process of Kāya-sādhana or the yogic practices for making the body strong and fit for higher realisations. This principle and practice of Kāya-sādhana is, we shall see, common to all schools of esoteric yoga and the exclusive emphasis of the Nātha-siddhas was on this Kāya-sādhana.[4] Yoga in general involves psycho-physiological processes; it is therefore that higher kinds of yoga should never be entered upon without a mature or perfect body. For this purpose of making the body mature or perfect the practices of Haṭha-yoga are to be adopted. It is for this reason that the Buddhist Siddhācāryas were, in the practical field, great Haṭha-yogins. In the Caryā-

[1] Comm. on Caryā No. 2.

[2] Comm. on *Dohākoṣa* of Kānha-pāda, Dohā No. 4 (comm. discovered by MM. Śāstri).

[3] For a detailed study of the significance of these names, see *An Introduction to Tāntric Buddhism* by the present writer.

[4] *Vide Infra*.

songs we find frequent reference to the strengthening of the 'Skandhas' or the elements whose aggregate constitutes the body. Until and unless the 'Skandhas' are strengthened, or, in other words, the body is made ripe[1] through practice of Haṭha-yoga, the supreme realisation, known in the Buddhist fold as Mahā-sukha becomes a lulling sleep of the senses or something like a swoon. It will be a blunder to confuse this state of swoon with the state of Mahā-sukha. It has been said in the *Rati-vajra* that if the body and the mind fall into a swoon in the practice of yoga, how can there be perfection in yoga?[2] The yogin has, therefore, been repeatedly advised to acquire a strong body before entering on the yogic process for the attainment of Mahā-sukha.

It has been explained before how the principles of Prajñā and Upāya were identified with the female and the male (or even with the female organ and the male organ which are known also as the lotus and the thunder), and Bodhicitta was identified with the bliss produced through the union of the female and the male. The actual esoteric practice of the Buddhist Sahajiyās is the production of this Bodhicitta in the Nirmāṇa-cakra or the Maṇipura-cakra (in the region of the navel) through processes of Haṭha-yoga and then to give it an upward motion so as to make it pass through the Dharma-cakra and the Sambhoga-cakra and then make it motionless in the Uṣṇīṣa-kamala where it produces Sahaja of the nature of Mahā-sukha. It is held that the Bodhicitta has two aspects; in the ordinary restless aspect (*i.e.*, in the form of gross sexual pleasure which accompanies the discharge) it is called *Saṁvṛta*, and in the motionless aspect of intense bliss it is called the *Vivṛta* or the *Pāramārthika*. This *Saṁvṛta* and *Pāramārthika* aspects of the Bodhicitta represent the *Saṁvṛti-satya*, *i.e.*, the phenomenal or the provisional aspect of reality and the *Pāramārthika*, *i.e.*, the ultimate reality of Mahāyāna philosophy. The yogic Sādhanā of the Sahajiyās is employed first for the production of Bodhicitta through the union of

1 For ripe (*pakva*) and unripe (*apakva*) body, see *Infra*.

2 *mūrcchite skandha-vijñāne kutaḥ siddhir aninditā* ||
Quoted in the commentary of the Caryā-song No. 1

the Prajñā and the Upāya and then for transforming the *Saṁvṛta* Bodhicitta into *Pāramārthika*. The contention of the Sahajiyās is that so long as the intense bliss produced through the union of the Prajñā and the Upāya remains in the region of Maṇipura-cakra or in the region of the navel which is the Nirmāṇa-cakra or the gross physical plane of bondage and suffering, it keeps the yogin in the world of grossness. But as according to standard Mahāyāna philosophy the Bodhicitta, after its production, must march upwards through ten stages known as the *Bodhicitta-bhūmis* and reach the highest state of *Dharma-megha* and attain Buddhahood there, so according to the view of the Sahajiyās this flow of bliss must be made to march upwards through the different Kāyas (corresponding to the *Bhūmis*) and finally reach the region of Vajra-kāya or Sahaja-kāya. In the process of upward march the bliss first produced goes on acquiring a higher nature and when it reaches the Uṣṇīṣa-kamala or the Vajra-kāya or Sahaja-kāya it becomes Mahā-sukha, where all kinds of duality vanish in a unique realisation of supreme bliss.

(iv) *The Middle Path in the Esoteric Sādhanā*

A dominant feature of Mahāyāna is its stress on the middle path avoiding the opposite extremes of views. Thus the philosophical system of Nāgārjuna is known as the 'Mādhyamika' system, or the philosophical school of the middle course, and it is held that Nāgārjuna's school is a school of the middle course in the sense that he steered clear a transcendental path which denies the views of the positivists as well as the negativists. The philosophy of the *Abhūta-parikalpa* of Vasubandhu as expounded in his well-known treatise *Madhyānta-vibhāga* is again a challenge to both the extreme realists (like the Sarvāsti-vādins) and the extreme negativists (like the Mādhyamikas),[1] and the Vijnāna-vādins always professed to be the followers of the middle path. Apart from these philosophical speculations we find in the religious sphere on the whole that the Mahāyānists were opposed to the Idea of Nirvāṇa as much

[1] The Mādhyamika school was always criticised by the Vijñāna-vādins (as also by the Vedāntins) as a pure negativistic school.

as to that of existence in the world of suffering (*bhava* or *saṃsāra*); and according to them the final state is neither the *Bhava*, nor the *Nirvāṇa*,—it is rather a state of non-duality where *Bhava* and *Nirvāṇa* become one and the same. In connection with the idea of *Advaya* or *Yuganaddha* we have seen that the final state is that where all kinds of duality are absorbed in a principle of non-duality. This principle was adopted also by the Sahajiyās in their process of yoga. We have seen that the nerves in the right and the left in the microcosm of the body represent the principles of duality; their separate function which binds one to the world of sufferings must, therefore, be checked by the Yogin and they must unite with the middle nerve and function there conjointly. The middle nerve is, therefore, the middle path which leads to the non-dual state of Sahaja.

The flow of Bodhicitta must be regulated along the middle nerve, and this is the most important and at the same time the most difficult part of the Sādhanā, and it is for this reason that in the Caryā-padas and the *Dohākoṣas* as well as in many of the Buddhist Tāntric texts we find repeated warnings to the novice to take practical suggestions from the preceptor at this stage. If the flow of Bodhicitta moves either left or right, the whole thing is spoiled. In the Caryā-padas, therefore, we find repeated warnings not to go either right or left, but to steer clear through the middle path. We often find injunctions in the Caryās for securing perfect control on the two nerves in the right and the left and to join them together (*i.e.*, to make them function together) in the middle nerve. Thus in a song Lui-pā says, "I have intuited the (non-dual truth) through the suggestion (of the preceptor). I have sat where the couple of the nerves Dhamana (the nerve in the left) and Camana (the nerve in the right) are united together."[1] Guṇḍarī-pāda says,—"Destroy the mother-in-law (vital breath) in the house (*i.e.*, the body) and control the Maṇimūla,—and split up the sides of the sun and the moon."[2] Again

[1] *bhaṇai lui āmhe sāne diṭhā* ǀ (*jhāne diṭhā*—Bagchi)
dhamaṇa camaṇa beṇi pāṇḍi baiṭhā ǁ Song No. 1.

[2] *sāsu gharem ghāli koñcā tāla* ǀ
cānda-suja-beṇi pakhā phāla ǁ
Song No. 4.

Cāṭilla-pāda says,—"The deep river of existence is flowing on in a tremendous flow; there is mud on either side of the river, but the middle is unfathomable. For the sake of 'Dharma'[1] (*i.e.*, for the realisation of the non-essential nature of all the Dharmas) Cāṭilla has built up a bridge, and people, desirous of going to the other shore, can now cross (the river of existence) fearlessly.... After walking up the bridge go neither right nor left,—near is the *Bodhi*, do not go far."[2] From the yoga point of view this river of existence refers to the nervous system mainly with the three principal nerves, which are described in the commentary as *ābhāsa-traya* (*viz.*, Śūnya, Ati-śūnya and Mahā-śūnya), which are the principles of defilement and therefore also the cause of all existence. The two sides, *i.e.*, the two nerves on the left and the right are muddy, *i.e.*, they are the paths which lead to the principles of defilement,[3]—and the middle nerve leads to the depth of the truth and so it is unfathomable. The bridge however, signifies the establishment of the unity between the two aspects of the Bodhicitta, *viz.*, *Saṁvṛti* and *Pāramārthika*,[4] in other words, it is the way to realise as well as demonstrate how the physical Bodhicitta can be transformed into the ultimate Bodhicitta through processes of yoga. Cāṭilla-pāda warns that when one is on the bridge, *i.e.*, when one is engaged in transforming the *Saṁvṛti* Bodhicitta into the *Pāramārthika* through the yogic process, one should go neither left nor right,—the *Bodhi* is to be attained through the middle nerve. Kānha-pāda says in one of his songs,—"The path (*i.e.*, the right path) is obstructed by the *Āli* and the *Kāli*."[5] Again we find,—he (Kānha) enters the lotus-pool of Sahaja by breaking the two posts of '*e*' (representing Prajñā, or the

[1] The original word is *dhāma* which may be derived from the Sanskrit word *dharma*; but Dr. Sukumar Sen suggests that the original word *dhāma* refers to Dhāma-pāda, a disciple of Cāṭilla-pāda.

[2] *bhavanai gahaṇa gambhīra vegeṁ bāhī* |
duānte cikhila mājhe na thāhī ||
dhāmārthe cāṭila sāṅkama gaḍhai |
pāragāmi loa nibhara tarai ||
. . . .
sāṅkamata caḍile dāhiṇa bāma mā hohi |
niyaḍi bohi dūra mā jāhi || Song No. 5.

[3] *vāma-dakṣiṇaṁ cikhilam iti prakṛti-doṣa-paṅkā-nuliptam* | Comm.

[4] *Cf.* Comm. *sa(ṁ)kramam iti saṁvṛtti-paramārthayor aikyam.*

[5] Song No. 7.

left nerve) and '*vaṁ*' (representing Upāya or the right nerve).[1] Again we see that after entering into the yogic practice Kānha has made the *Āli* and the *Kāli* the anklets of his legs and the sun and the moon his earrings.[2] Both these metaphors signify that Kānha has got full control over the *Āli* and the *Kāli* or the moon and the sun (which refer to the two principles of Prajñā and Upāya as well as to the two nerves). Kānha says that he has realised the wave (*i.e.*, the vibration of bliss) in the middle course.[3] In his Dohās also he says that he has broken off the two nerves *lalanā-rasanā* or *ravi-śaśī* in the two sides.[4] Kambalāmbara-pāda says that after pressing the left and the right (nerves) and keeping close to the middle way he has been able to realise supreme bliss.[5] Again Ḍombī-pāda says in a song,—"The boat is steered through the middle of the Ganges and the Jumna; there the exhilerated lady (*i.e.*, Nairātmā, absorbed in the Sahaja-bliss) smoothly carries her children (*i.e.*, the yogin) to the other shore. Steer on,—steer on Oh Ḍombī, (exclaims the poet), time is high up in the way; through the (blessings of the) lotus-feet of the Guru we shall go to the land of the Jinas (*i.e.*, the self-controlled ones). Five oars (taken in the commentary to indicate the five-fold instructions given in the *Pañca-krama*) are moving;—when in the way tie up the rope of the boat with the *pīṭha*, (*i.e.*, arrest the flow of the Bodhicitta, which is compared here to the boat, in the Maṇi-mūla). Throw out water with the pot of void, so that water may not enter through the joint. The moon and the sun are the two wheels, and (the unity of) creation and destruction is the mast (*pulinda*); the two paths to the left and the right are not seen,—steer the boat at your own pleasure."[6] Śānti-pāda also says that he is roaming avoiding the two ways in the left and the right.[7] In another song of

1 Song No. 9.

2 *āli kāli ghaṇṭā neura caraṇe* |
ravi śaśī kuṇḍala kiu ābharaṇe || Song No. 11.

3 *mājha beṇī taraṅgama muniā* || Song No. 13.

4 *lalaṇā-rasaṇā ravi-sasi tuḍia veṇṇa vipāse* | Dohā No. 5.

5 *bāma-dāhiṇa cāpi mili mili māṅgā* |
bāṭata milila mahāsuha sāṅgā || Song No. 8.

6 Song No. 14.

7 Song No. 15.

Vīṇā-pāda he says that he has made a *vīṇā* (*i.e.*, lyre) of which the sun is the gourd (*lāu*) and the moon is the string and Avadhūtī is the stand. On hearing the tune of the *Āli* and the *Kāli*, he says, the mighty elephant has entered Samarasa.[1] Here the sun which is said to be the gourd and the moon which is said to be the string, are but the two nerves in the two sides, and the stand (*daṇḍa*) is the middle nerve. When the two nerves in the left and the right are controlled and fitted to the middle one, an *anāhata* sound[2] is produced and it leads the elephant (*i.e.*, *citta*) to the state of Samarasa. Saraha-pāda says, "In the right and the left are canals and falls,—the straight path is the safe path."[3]

We need not multiply the instances and the analogies given in connection with the yogic process of controlling the two nerves on the two sides and the raising of the Bodhi-citta along the middle nerve. But what is the process for giving the Bodhi-citta an upward motion? The *Apāna* wind, it is held, has always a downward motion the *Prāṇa* an upward motion; the yogin, therefore, should arrest the course of both the *Prāṇa* and the *Apāna* and then make them flow through the middle nerve and with his flow of the vital wind within the middle nerve the Bodhi-citta will also flow upward and reach the Uṣṇīṣa-kamala,—and thereby Mahā-sukha will be produced. The Bodhi-citta should then be made steady by making steady the breath, and this state of Yoga is the ultimate stage for the yogin.

In this production of the Bodhi-citta four stages, associated with the four *Cakras* or lotuses, are distinctly marked, and on the basis of these four stages we find mention of the four Mudrās (*viz.*, *Karma-mudrā*, *Dharma-mudrā*, *Mahā-mudrā* and *Samaya-mudrā*), which are the four stages of yoga. There are again four mental states called the four moments (*viz.*, *Vicitra*, *Vipāka*, *Vimarda* and *Vilakṣaṇa*,[4]

[1] *suja lāu sasi lāgeli tāntī* l
aṇahā dāṇḍī eki kiata avadhūtī ||
* * * *
āli kāli beṇi sāri suṇiā l
gaavara samarasa sāndhi guṇiā || Song No. 17.

[2] See *An Introduction to Tāntric Buddhism* by the present writer.

[3] *bāma dāhiṇa jo khāla bikhalā* l
saraha bhaṇai bāpā ujuvāṭa bhāilā || Song No. 32.

[4] *Vide Catur-mudrā* in the *Advaya-vajra-saṃgraha* (G.O.S.).
Also *Samputikā*, MS., p. 10 (A); *Hevajra-pañjikā*, MS., p. 2 (B).

and four kinds of bliss, *viz.*, *Ānanda*, *Paramānanda*, *Viramānanda* and *Sahajānanda*. *Ānanda* is the bliss when the Bodhicitta is in the Nirmāṇa-cakra, *Paramānanda* in the Dharma-cakra, *Viramānanda* in the Sambhoga-cakra and *Sahajānanda* is more intense; *Viramānanda* means the detachment from the worldly pleasure, and *Sahajānanda* is the final bliss.[1]

(v) *The Yogic Sādhanā of the Sahajiyās and the Female Force*

Another thing that deserves special attention in connection with the yogic practice of the Sahajiyā Buddhists is the conception of the female force. In the Caryā-songs we find frequent references to this female force variously called as the Caṇḍālī, Ḍombī, Śavarī, Yoginī, Nairāmaṇi, Sahaja-sundarī, etc. and we also find frequent mention of the union of the yogin with this personified female deity.

This Yoginī or the Sahaja-damsel should not be confused with the woman of flesh and blood, associated with the actual yogic practices; she is but an internal force of the nature of vacuity (*Śūnyatā*) or essencelessness (*nairātmā*) and great bliss residing in the different plexuses in different stages of yogic practice.

In the Hindu Tantras we find that in the Mūlādhāra-cakra (which is the lowest of the Cakras) remains coiled an electric force known as the Serpent-power (coiled like a serpent) or the Kula-kuṇḍalinī Śakti, and the Sādhanā consists in rousing this Śakti, lying dormant in the Mūlādhāra, and making her unite with the Śiva in the Sahasrāra; and we have seen that the union of the Śakti with the Śiva is what is meant by perfection in Tāntric Yoga. Corresponding to this Kula-kuṇḍalinī Śakti of the Hindu Tantras we find the conception of a fire-force of the Buddhists in the Nirmāṇa-kāya, and she is generally described as the Caṇḍālī. Thus it is said by Kānha-pāda in one of his songs,—"One is that lotus, sixty-four are the petals,—the Ḍombī climbs upon it and dances."[2] In the *Hevajra-tantra* we find, "The Caṇḍālī burns in the navel and she burns the five Tathāgatas

[1] *Śrī-kāla-cakra-tantra*, MS., p. 57(A); *Hevajra-tantra*, MS., p. 27(B).

[2] *eka so padumā cauṣaṭṭhi pākhuḍī* |
tahiṁ caḍi nācaa ḍombī bāpuḍī || Song No. 10.

and the goddesses like Locanā and others, and when all is burnt, the moon pours down the syllable *huṁ*.''[1] This Caṇḍālī is the goddess Nairātmā or Avadhūtikā or Prajñā, and when she is roused through the yogic practice in the navel, all the five Skandhas or the material elements represented by the five Tathāgatas and all the goddesses like Locanā and others associated with these Tathāgatas are burnt away, and when all is burnt the moon, which represents the Bodhi-citta, pours down *huṁ*, which again represents the ultimate knowledge (*vajra-jñāna*).[2] In a song of Guñjarīpāda we find,—"The lotus and the thunder meet together in the middle and through their union Caṇḍālī is ablaze; that blazing fire is in contact with the house of the Ḍombī—I take the moon and pour water. Neither scorching heat nor smoke is found, but it enters the sky through the peak of mount Meru.''[3] When the lotus and the thunder are united through the emotion of Mahā-sukha (which is happily compared to a gush of wind) Caṇḍālī is ablaze in the Nir-

[1] *caṇḍālī jvalitā nābhau dahati pañca-tathāgatān* |
dahati ca locanādīni dagdhe huṁ sravate śaśī ||
Hevajra-tantra., MS., p. 4(B).

[2] In the *Hevajra-pañjikā* we find as many as four interpretation of this verse. In the first interpretation we find that *Caṇḍā* means Prajñā as she is of very fierce (*caṇḍa*) nature in controlling all the great and minor afflictions (*kleśopakleśa*) and *Āli* means Vajra-sattva; therefore *Caṇḍālī* means the union of Prajñā with the Vajra-sattva; and as a result of that union the fire of great emotion (*mahā-rāga*) burns away the five Skandhas and the five elements of earth, etc. (*Cf. locanādīnī'ti pṛthivyā-dīniti*) and the *Śaśī* as the Vajra-sattva adopts the nature of *huṁ*, (it may be remembered in this connection that *huṁ* is the *bīja mantra* of the Vajra-sattva). The second interpretation is almost the same as the first. Another sectarian view (*sampradāya-vyākhyā*) is that *Caṇḍā* is Prajñā, or the left nerve (*i.e.*, flowing from the left nostril) and *Āli* is Upāya or the right nerve; when they are combined together through the instructions of the preceptor, it is called *Caṇḍālī*; *Nābhi* indicates the middle, *i.e.*, the Avadhūtikā (*i.e.*, the middle nerve) through which the fire of great emotion (*mahā-rāgāgni*) all the five Skandhas and the material elements (earth, etc.) are burnt, and when they are burnt the knowledge of the Mahā-sukha is produced. Again, another sectarian explanation is,—*Caṇḍā* is Prajñā, *i.e.*, Śūnyatā-knowledge,—and *Āli* means the mind full of universal compassion; *caṇḍālī* then means a commingling of these Śūnyatā and Karuṇā and when it is thus combined *Śaśī*, *i.e.*, the Vajra-dhara attains an illuminating Samādhi (*prabhāsvaramaya-samādhi*) where the world of the past, present and the future is realised to be one and unchanging. [(*Vide Hevajra-pañjikā*, MS., pp. 9 (B)-10(B).]

[3] *kamala kuliśa mājheṁ bhaia miali* |
samatā joeṁ jalia caṇḍālī ||
ḍāha ḍombī-ghare lāgeli āgi |
sasahara lai siñcahuṁ pāṇī ||
nau khara jālā dhūma na disai |
meru-śikhara lai gaaṇa paisai ||
Song No. 47.

māṇa-cakra in the navel.[1] In contact with this fire of Mahā-sukha the house (*i.e.*, the store of all complexes, desires and root-instincts) is burnt, but the moon (*i.e.*, Bodhi-citta) pours water in the fire. This fire of Mahā-sukha has neither heat nor smoke, but it enters into vacuity (*gaaṇa*) through the spinal column (mount Meru).

In the *Sādhana-mālā* we find that Mahā-mudrā resides in the navel and she is the producer of Mahā-sukha, and for intense scorch she is described as of the nature of fire. She is of the nature of the first vowel, she is taken to be the wisdom by the Buddhas,—she remains pervading the three elements (*tri-dhātu*), and is never known by lay people (*pṛthag-jana*).[2]

In the *Samputikā* this Caṇḍālī is depicted as the female counterpart of the Vajra-sattva; she is absorbed in him, as Prajñā and when roused by the yogic practice she becomes ablaze in the region of the navel. She is known as the goddess Nairātmā as well as the Vasanta-tilaka, she consumes in her thousand heaps of fire—her lustre is like the dazzle of the lightning; at the time of the yogic practice (of making oneself a god) the Śakti moves throughout the whole body with all her power,—she burns the Dharma-cakra in the heart and then through the Sambhoga-cakra proceeds forward and enters the Cakra in the head and then after burning everything and producing bliss returns to the region of the navel again.[3] In the commentary on the *Marma-kalikā-tantra* we find a description of the nature of this Caṇḍālī. It is said to be of the nature of a peculiar affection produced

[1] *Cf.* the Com. *kamala-kuliśam ityādi* | *prajñopāya-samatām satyākṣara-mahā-sukha-rāgā-nilā-vartān nābhau nirmāṇa-cakre caṇḍālī jvalitā mama* |
Ibid., p. 72 (Śāstrī's edition).

[2] *Sādhana-mālā*, Vol. II, p. 448 (G.O.S.).

[3] *tasyaiva sahajā prajñā sthitā tadgata-rūpiṇī* |
karma-māruta-nirddhūtā jvalantī'ha nābhi-maṇḍale ||
nairātmeti vikhyātā vasanta-tilakā smṛtā |
bala-grasat-sahasrāgnī vidyuc-chaṭā-samaprabhā ||
devatā-yoga-kāle roma-kūpāgra-sandhiṣu |
niścaranti diśo daśaḥ sarvān tarjayanti surāsurān ||
hṛdaye dharma-cakram dagdhvā sambhoga-cakrataḥ |
nāsā-randhreṇa niṣkramya dakṣiṇena samantataḥ ||
urṇā-koṣa-gatenāpi randhreṇa daśa-dikṣu vai |
buddhānām bodhisattvānām nāsā-randhreṇa vāmataḥ ||
praviśanti śikhā-cakre samadahya viniṣkramet |
pūrvoktenaiva randhreṇa sikhāyām praviśet punaḥ ||
dagdhānām sarva-buddhānām ānandam janayet tataḥ |
nābhi-maṇḍalam āgatya sthitā bhavati purvavat ||
Śrī-samputikā, MS., pp. 48(B)-49(A).

through the application of all yoga-practices with the instructions of the preceptor,—it is like juice extracted from sugarcanes through pressure,—like great light produced in the wood through friction,—like the pleasure produced in the couples through their intense love in copulation,—like cream produced in milk through churning,—like the most substantial thing (*ghṛta*) produced in cream through the power of heat,—like hard pottery produced from mud through the power of whirling,—like the best potency (wine) produced in grapes, etc., through medicinal processes, like the actual presentation of the desired one through the power of attraction produced in Mantra, etc.[1] Thus it seems from all these descriptions that the goddess Caṇḍālī is nothing but an internal force produced through the yogic process and that the rising of the Caṇḍālī marks the first perception of the Mahā-sukha produced through esoteric yogic practices; when in her upward march she reaches the Uṣṇīṣa-kamala, she becomes of the nature of pure Mahā-sukha. This conception of Śakti of the Buddhist Sahajiyās is an adoption of the general Tāntric conception of the Śakti mixed up with the principle of the destructive fire, or the fire-force situated in the navel as postulated and emphasised by the Nātha-yogins.[2] When through the yogic-process this Śakti is made to move upwards and is gradually dissociated from the principles of grossness and defilement, she gradually reveals to the yogin her pure nature of bliss and in the region of the lotus in the head, *i.e.*, in the highest state completely dissociated from the principle of grossness and defilement, she becomes pure Mahā-sukha.

In the upward march the Caṇḍālī is often described as the Ḍombī and when in the Mahā-sukha-kamala, she is the Sahaja-damsel (*Sahaja-sundarī*) with whom the perfect yogin is always united. In the Caryā-padas we often find that the

[1] *tatra ca śrī-matī caṇḍālī yoga-sakala-śakti-nidhāne guru-vākyādiṣu saṁyoga-śakti-samutpādita-viśiṣṭa-rāgavat* | *ikṣvādiṣu pīḍana-śakti-samupajāta-divya-rasavat* | *kāṣṭhādiṣu śayanīya (?)-śakti-samutpādita-mahālokavat* | *maithuneṣu dampati-prīti-śakti-samutpādita-sukhavat* | *kṣīrādiṣu dhārā-śakti-samutpādita-sāravat* | *navanīteṣu jvāla-śakti-samutpādita-viśiṣṭa-sāravat* | *mṛttikādiṣu āvartana-śakti-samutpādita-taijasavat* | *drākṣādiṣu bhaiṣajya-śakti-samutpādita-bala-viśeṣavat mantrādiṣu ākarṣaṇa-śakti-samutpādita-saphala-vāñchitavat* |

Com. on *Marma-kalikā-tantra*, MS., p. 39 (B).

[2] *Vide Infra* Ch. IX.

yogin is sporting with the goddess Nairātmā in the Sambhoga-kāya near the neck. Thus Savara-pāda says in a song,—"(I chew the) betel-leaf of my heart and chew camphor in great bliss,—and then with the goddess Nairāmaṇi in the neck I pass the night in Mahā-sukha."[1] Here the 'betel-leaf of heart' stands for the luminous Citta, and camphor (*kāpura=karpūra*) for semen.[2] Nairāmaṇi (or *Nirāmaṇi*) is the goddess Nairātmā or Prajñā,—neck implies the Sambhoga-cakra, and night implies the darkness of ignorance and afflictions. In a song of Kānha-pāda we find that the uninitiate speak ill of the Ḍombī (*Nairātmā*) but the wise never separate her from the neck, *i.e.*, from the Sambhoga-kāya.[3] In another song of Śavara-pāda we find that the yogin remains awake with the damsel Nairātmā awakened in the neck (*i.e.*, the Sambhoga-cakra).[4] In a song of Guṇḍarī-pāda we find,—"After pressing the three (*i.e.*, after purifying and controlling the three nerves), I embrace the Yoginī. . . .O Yoginī, (exclaims the yogin) I shall not live even for a moment without thee,—I shall kiss thy lips and drink the lotus-juice."[5] In another song of Kānha-pāda we find,—"Outside the city, O Ḍombī, is thy cottage; thou goest just touching the Brahmins and the shaven-headed (and never reveal thyself to them). O Ḍombī, I shall keep company with thee and it is for this purpose that I have become a naked Kāpālī without aversions. There is one lotus and sixty-four are the petals,—the dear Ḍombī climbs on it and dances there. Honestly do I ask thee, on whose boat dost thou come and go? The Ḍombī sells the loom and also the flat basket (made of bamboo). For thee have I done

1 *hia tāṁvolā mahāsuhe kāpura khāi* l
suna nirāmaṇi kaṇṭhe laiā mahāsuhe rāti pohāi ||
Song No. 28.

2 *Cf. śukraṁ karpūrakaṁ matam* l
Hevajra-tantra, MS., p. 44 (A).

3 *keho keho tohore biruā bolai* l
bidujaṇa loa tore kaṇṭha na melai ||
Caryā-pada, Song No. 18.

4 *kaṇṭhe nairāmaṇi bāli jāgante upāḍī* ||
Ibid, Song No. 50.

5 *tiaḍḍā cāpī joini de aṅkavālī* l
. . . .
joini tāi vinu khaṇahi na jīvami l
to muha cumvī kamala-rasa pīvami ||
Song No. 4.

away with this drama of life. Thou art the Ḍombī and I am the Kāpālī, for thee have I put on a garland of bones. The Ḍombī destroys the lake and eats up the lotus-stalk. I shall kill thee, Ḍombī, and take thy life."[1] Here, the Ḍombī is the Nairātmā and we have already seen that as a Ḍombī (*i.e.*, a woman of the Ḍoma-caste) cannot be touched by a Brahmin because of her low caste, so also the Nairātmā cannot be realised by the orthodox Brahmin, as she transcends all sense-perception.[2] She, therefore, lives outside the city, *i.e.*, outside the world of senses. In the metaphor of selling the loom and the basket of bamboo there seems to be a pun on some of the words; *tanti* in the vernacular means a loom, but it may also be associated with the Sanskrit word *tantrī* or *tantra*, the thread of mental constructions; the word *cāṁgeḍā* means a basket (made of bamboo), but the commentary explains it as *viṣayābhāsam*, *i.e.*, the defiling principle of objectivity. The lake mentioned above is the body and the lotus-stalk is the Bodhi-citta; and the Ḍombī, unless she is perfectly purified, spoils both of them. It is for this reason that the Ḍombī should be purified and made steady in order to attain the Bodhi-citta. This latter Ḍombī, however, seems to be the vital wind, impure and uncontrolled, and in the *Hevajra-tantra* we find that the element of air is represented by the goddess Ḍombī.[3] In a song Vīṇā-pāda, who has made a lyre with the sun, the moon and the Avadhūtī, says that when the lyre produces sound, the Vajradhara (the yogin himself) dances and the goddess (*Nairātmā*) sings and thus the drama of the Buddha is played.[4] Kānha-pāda says in another song,—"Of what nature is, O Ḍombī, thy cleverness?—the aristocrats are outside thee and the Kāpālīs are within (*i.e.*, the arrogant pundits and the orthodox priests can never have any access to the Sahaja-Nairātmā, but only the Kāpālī yogins can realise her). Thou hast spoiled everything, through the law of cause and effect thou hast destroy-

[1] Song No. 10.

[2] *asparśā bhavati yasmāt tasmāt ḍombī prakathyate* |
Hevajra-tantra, MS., p. 2 (B).

[3] *Cf.* Earth is Pukkaśī, water Śavarī, fire Caṇḍālī and air is the Ḍombī.
Hevajra-tantra, MS., p. 26 (A).

[4] *nācanti vājila gānti dei* |
buddha nāṭaka visamā hoi || Song No. 17.

ed the moon. (The significance is that the Nairātmā, when covered with the veils of ignorance, deceives the whole world through illusory knowledge, in that respect she spoils the moon, *i.e.*, the Bodhi-citta). Some speak ill of thee, but the learned never cast thee off from the neck (*i.e.* the Sambhoga-cakra). Thou art the *Kāma-caṇḍālī*,—there is no woman more cunning and unfaithful than the Ḍombī."[1] In another song of Kānha-pāda we find a beautiful analogy of marriage with the Ḍombī. First follows a wedding procession in which existence and extinction are made the musical instruments *paṭaha* and *mādala* and the mind and the vital wind are similarly made two other musical instruments,—the drum is proclaiming a victorious sound and Kānha is on his march for marrying the Ḍombī. By marrying the Ḍombī the gain is the escape from birth, and the transcendental region (*ānatu-dhāma=anuttara-dhāma*) of Mahā-sukha is obtained as the dowry. After marriage day and night pass away in sex-discourse and the night is passed in the bright company of the Yoginī (*i.e.*, the dark night of ignorance vanishes away at the appearance of the effulgent Sahaja-knowledge). The yogin who is in love with the Ḍombī never leaves her even for a moment and always remains mad in the Sahaja-bliss.[2] In a song of Kukkurī-pāda we find it put into the mouth of the Nairātmā,—"I am free from all hopes and desires and the void mind is my husband,—the nature of the realisation of bliss that proceeds from me cannot be expressed."[3] In another song, Śavara-pāda says, "High is the mountain (*i.e.*, the spinal column) and there on it (*i.e.*, in the Mahā-sukha-cakra which is above the spinal column) sits the Śabarī girl; she is decked with the coloured feathers of the peacock and with a garland of jequirity on her neck. O exhilarated Śavara, O mad Śavara, (exclaims the girl on the mountain), do not revel in worldly pleasure; I am thy dear consort of the name of *Sahaja-sundarī* (*i.e.*, beautiful Sahaja-lady). Many are the trees on the mountain

[1] Song No. 18.

[2] Song No. 19.

[3] *hāṁhu nirāsī kha-maṇa-bhatārī* |
mohara vigoā kahaṇa na jāi ||
Song No. 20.

whose branches touch the sky,—the Śavarī girl decked with earrings and the thunder plays alone in this forest. The bed-stead of the three elements (*viz.*, body, speech and mind) are placed and the Śavara spreads the bed in great bliss, and the serpent-like Śavara (*i.e.*, the *citta*) and the goddess Nairātmā (who destroys all the afflictions) pass their night of love on that bed."[1] In another song of Bhusuka-pāda he says,—"I have steered the thunder-boat through the canal of the lotus,—and have left off all the afflictions after reaching the non-dual Bengal. To-day Bhusuka has indeed become a Bengalee, for he has taken Caṇḍālī as his own wife."[2] Here the Vajra (the thunder) stands for the Citta-vajra (*i.e.*, the adamantine mind) and the lotus stands for the Prajñā, and through their union the non-dual truth (Bengal) is obtained.[3] By making Caṇḍālī (produced through the union of the thunder and the lotus) his wife, the yogin has realised the purely non-dual truth.

[1] *ūcā ūcā pāvata tahim basai savarī bālī* ।
moraṅgi pīccha parahiṇa savarī gīvata guñjarī mālī ॥
umata savaro pāgala savaro mā kara gulī guhaḍā tohori ।
ṇia gharinī nāme sahaja sundarī ॥
nānā taruvara maulila re gaaṇata lāgelī ḍālī ।
ekelī savarī e baṇa hiṇḍai karṇa-kuṇḍala-vajradhārī ॥
tia dhāu khāṭa paḍilā savara mahāsukhe seji chāilī ।
savaro bhujaṅga nairāmaṇi dārī pemma rāti pohāilī ॥
Song No. 28.

Cf. also. *varagiri sihara uttuṅga muṇi savare jahi kia vāsa* ।
Dohākoṣa of Kānha-pāda, Dohā No. 25.

[2] *bāja nāva pāḍi pāuā khāle bāhiu* ।
adaa-vaṅgāle kleśa luḍiu ॥
āji bhusu baṅgālī bhailī ।
ṇia gharinī caṇḍālī lelī ॥
Song No. 49.

[3] It is to be noticed that Bengal here represents non-duality. (*Cf.* also, *baṅge jāyā nilesi* etc. Song No. 39). How it came to be so we do not know. MM. Hara prasāda Śāstrī, however, says in his introduction to the *Bauddha-Gān-O-Dohā* (Intro., p. 12) that in the Sahajiyā School there are three ways of Sādhanā—*viz.*, Avadhūtī, Caṇḍālī and Ḍombī, or Vaṅgālī (*i.e.*, Bengalee). In the Avadhūtī there is only duality, Caṇḍālī seems to be a mixture of dualism as well as non-dualism, but in Ḍombī there is only uncompromising non-duality. In Bengal, continues MM. Śāstrī, there was a predominance of monistic thought and therefore the author Bhusuka says that he has become a Bengalee or a pure non-dualist. We, however, do not know on the authority of what text or texts MM. Śāstrī has made these observations. We have never come across any text explaining or even mentioning these three ways of Sahajiyā Sādhanā and it seems a puzzle to us why Avadhūtī should represent dualism. His assertion that Bengal has always stood particularly for non-dual knowledge does not also seem to be historically correct.

(*vi*) *The Final State of Bodhi-citta or the State of Mahā-sukha*

From our previous discussions it will be clear that the question of the production of the Bodhi-citta and its upward march through the different Kāyas to the Uṣṇīṣa-kamala so as to be transformed there into Mahā-sukha is closely associated with the question of raising the Śakti from the lowest pole of phenomenalism to the highest pole of absolute truth. When the Śakti reaches the Vajra-kāya or the Sahaja-kāya she becomes Śūnyatā herself,—and our prefected Citta becomes the lord Vajra-sattva; real Mahā-sukha follows only when this Śūnyatā is united in the Sahaja-kāya with the Vajra-sattva.

There are, however, some signs which are observed by the yogin when the ultimate state is produced. In the *Śrī-guhya-samāja* we find mention of five such signs: the first is of the form of a mirage, the second of the form of smoke, the third in the form of a firefly, the fourth is like a burning lamp and the fifth is like the stainless sky.[1] These signs are rather significant. In the commentary on the *Marma-kalikā-tantra* it has been explained that the sign of mirage signifies the knowledge about the nature of the world, which at that time appears to the yogin to be as illusory as a mirage. When the illusory nature of the Dharmas is thus realised, there remains no appearance (*pratibhāsa*) and, therefore, everything appears to be smoky, a mere illusory happening through the collocation of the causes and conditions like the origination of an elephant in magic; this dependent origination (*pratītya-samutpāda*) is the smoky nature of the world and hence is the second sign.[2] Again, as for the third sign it is said that as the firefly shines in the sky now and then for a single moment, so also in this stage perfect knowledge appears through the void-nature of the Dharmas like momentary

[1] *prathamaṁ marīcikākāraṁ dhūmrākāraṁ dvitīyakam |*
tṛtīyaṁ khadyotākāraṁ caturthaṁ dīpavaj jvalam ||
pañcaman tu sadā-lokaṁ nirabhraṁ gagana-sannibham |
Śrī-guhya-samāja-tantra, Ch.XVIII, p. 164, (G.O.S.)

[2] *māyā-gajādiva(t) māyā-gajaḥ pratītya-samutapanno niḥsvabhāva iti viśvam eva pratītya-samutpāda-rūpaṁ dhūmaṁ paśyatītyarthaḥ |*
Com. on the *Marma-kalikā-tantra*, MS. (BN. Sans. No. 83), p. 45(B).

flashes and hence is the appropriateness of the third sign.[1] In the fourth stage knowledge becomes as bright as a burning lamp and in the fifth or the final stage it becomes like the clear blue mid-day sky of autumn. These signs are referred to also by the *Śrī-kalā-cakra-tantra*;[2] but there as well as in the *Saḍaṅga* it is found that smoke is the first sign and mirage is the second.[3]

But what is the condition of the yogin when the Bodhi-citta is produced and the ultimate realisation is obtained? It is said in the *Vyakta-bhāvānugata-tattva-siddhi*[4] that at that time all the senses are absorbed within, all thought-constructions are destroyed, all the seeds of existence are annihilated; it is full of lustre of bliss,—it is like the vacant sky and yet cool and congenial.[5] It is said elsewhere that at that stage it seems as if the senses are all asleep,—the mind enters within,—and the body completely absorbed in supreme bliss seems to be without any function.[6] In the Caryā-padas we find many songs describing this ultimate stage of perfection or the realisation of the Sahaja-nature in the form of Mahā-sukha. Kānha-pāda in a song compares himself, when absorbed in the Sahaja bliss, to an intoxicated elephant; like the elephant he has trampled down all the posts of '*e*' and '*vaṁ*' or the moon and the sun and torn asunder all the various ties, and like the elephant under strong intoxication has entered the lake of the lotus and become perfectly

[1] *yathā khadyotaḥ khe ākaśe kṣaṇaṁ ksaṇaṁ dyotate tathaiva. . . . . . . .bhāvena śūnyatāyāṁ jñāna(ṁ) yāti. . . . . . . .iti tṛtīyaṁ cihnam* |
Ibid., MS., p. 45(B).

[2] *Cf. śūnye dhūmādi*, etc. MS. (Cambridge, Add. 1364), p. 33(B).
dhūmādīnāṁ nimitta-grahaṇam api, etc., *Ibid.*, p. 110(A).

[3] *Cf. śūnyād dhūmo marīciḥ prakaṭa-vimala-khadyota eva pradīpaḥ* |
Ibid., MS., pp. 109(A)-110(A).
Also *Cf. tatra gurūpadeśena prathamaṁ yogī dhūmaṁ paśyati na marīcikām iti* |
Saḍaṅga quoted in the com. on the *Marma-kalikā-tantra*, MS., p. 45(A).

[4] The text is ascribed in the *Subhāṣita-saṁgraha* (p. 63) to Saraha-pāda, but we do not find mention of the author anywhere in the MS. of the text we have at our disposal.

[5] *viniviṣṭendriya-vargo naṣṭa-vikalpaḥ samāpta-bhava-bījaḥ* |
ānandābhamayo'sau(?) gagana-samo 'py adahaḥ śītalaḥ svāduḥ ||
Vyakta-bhāvānugata-tattva-siddhi, MS. (C.L.B. No. 13124), p. 89(B).

[6] *indriyāṇi svapantī'va mano'ntarviśatī'va ca* |
naṣṭa-ceṣṭa ivā'bhāti kāyaḥ sat-sukha-mūrcchitaḥ ||
Quoted in the *Kriyā-saṁgraha-pañjikā*, MS. (BN. Sans. No. 31), p. 76(B); also in the Com. on the Caryā-pada No. 1 (Śāstrī's Edition).

pacified there.[1] Mahīdhara-pāda says in a song that he has identified himself with the three wooden boards (*i.e.*, the three kinds of bliss as belonging to the body, speech and mind), or, in other words, he has identified the bliss of the body with that of the speech and that again with that of the mind and finally identified all with the self,[2] and there follows a tremendous roar of the spontaneous *anaha* (*anāhata*) sound;—on hearing that sound the arch-enemy, Māra, and all the desires and afflictions of the body vanish away. The exhilarated elephant of Citta is marching on—and in the sky it is always rubbing the sun and the moon (*i.e.*, all principles of duality). Both vice and merit are destroyed, the chain is torn away—the posts trampled, and the sound of the sky is raising—the Citta enters into Nirvāṇa. The Citta neglects all the three worlds, drinks the great liquor (of Mahā-sukha) and revels in intoxication; thus he becomes the lord of the five objects, *i.e.*, becomes the Vajra-sattva himself,—and no enemy is then to be found anywhere. In the scorching heat of the rays (of Mahā-sukha) he has entered the skirt of the sky. Mahīdhara says, "When here I sink within—nothing is seen by me."[3] Bhusukapāda says in a song,[4] "The clouds of compassion are shining always after pressing down the duality of existence and non-existence. The wonderful has risen up in the sky,—behold, Bhusuka, the Sahaja-nature! On seeing and hearing it (*i.e.*, the Sahaja-nature) all the senses are destroyed and the mind within revels in solitude."[5] As all darkness vanishes with the rise of the bright moon in the sky, so also all darkness of ignorance is removed through the rise of the Bodhi-citta and through the realisation of the Sahaja-bliss the ultimate reality underlying the objects is also realised.

[1] *kānhu vilasaa āsava-mātā* |
sahaja nalini-vana paisi nivitā ||
Caryā-pada, Song No. 9.

[2] *Cf. Śrī-guhya-samāja*, Ch. II, p. 11 (G.O.S.).

[3] Caryā-pada, Song No. 16.

[4] *Ibid.*, Song. No. 30.

[5] The text is—
nihure ṇia mana ṇa de ulāsa ||
But the Commentary says,—*nibhṛtena nirvikalpākāreṇa nija-manaḥ bodhi-cittaṁ vijra-guroḥ prasādāt sahajollāsaṁ dadātī'ti* | So in light of the commentary the reading of the text should be,—*nihure ṇia maṇa de ulāsa* || *Cf.* also the Sanskrit rendering of the Tibetan version of the line by Dr. Bagchi—
nija-manasi ullāsaṁ dadāti || *Materials for, etc.*, p. 67.

PART II

THE MEDIAEVAL SAHAJIYĀ SCHOOLS

CHAPTER V

THE VAIṢṆAVA SAHAJIYĀ CULT

(i) *Transition from Buddhist Sahajiyā to Vaiṣṇava Sahajiyā*

THE Vaiṣṇava Sahajiyā movement of Bengal marks the evolution of the Buddhist Sahajiyā cult in a different channel as strongly influenced by the love-religion of Bengal Vaiṣṇavism. The Vaiṣṇava Sahajiyā cult has a considerable literature to its credit. As many as two hundred and fifty manuscripts of small texts containing the various doctrines and practices of the cult are preserved in the Manuscript Library of the Calcutta University and about an equal number of texts (many of them being common with those preserved in the Manuscript Library of the Calcutta University) belong to the Manuscript Library of the Vaṅgīya Sāhitya-pariṣad. These texts, however, do not possess much intrinsic literary value and as such their contribution to Bengali literature would not have been of much importance but for fact that they help us in studying a large number of lyrical songs belonging both to the Sahajiyā Vaiṣṇava and the standard Vaiṣṇava cults, both of which accepted the ideal of Parakīyā love as contrasted with the ideal of Svakīyā love in their doctrines.[1]

These love-lyrics, belonging to the province of Vaiṣṇavism, combine in them a genuine poetic vein of an absorbing human interest with an avowedly religious sentiment and as such they offer a good specimen of how far it may be possible for erotic sentiment, aesthetic sentiment and religious sentiment to combine in popular poetry. In the history of the Vaiṣṇava literature of Bengal the most important factor is the gradual evolution of the ideal of Parakīyā love; but whereas the ideal of Parakīyā love was merely recognised as a theological speculation in standard Vaiṣṇavism, it was accepted even in its practical bearing by the Sahajiyās. In the history of Bengal Vaiṣṇavism there seems

[1] For the ideals of Svakīyā and Parakīyā see *infra*, p. 124.

to have been a process of interaction between the two sects —the practice of the Sahajiyās influencing to a great extent the ideal of the Vaiṣṇava poets, and the ideal of the Vaiṣṇavas in its turn influencing the practices of the Sahajiyās. Though the story of the love-episodes of Caṇḍīdāsa, the greatest love poet of Bengal, with the washer-woman, Rāmī, is still shrouded in mastery and as such cannot be credited historically as supplying proof of Caṇḍīdāsa himself being an exponent of the Sahajiyā practice, yet we should remember that tradition always indicates possibility. Judging from the heaps of tradition centering round the figure of poet Caṇḍīdāsa and also from the number of Sahajiyā poems ascribed to him, it will not be far out of the mark to hold that there might have been some truth in the tradition of Caṇḍīdāsa himself being a Sahajiyā Sādhaka and that his practical culture of the divinisation of human love had supplied him with the deep inspiration that made him the immortal poet of the Rādhā-Kṛṣṇa songs. The indebtedness of Śrī-Caitanya to the love-lyrics of Jayadeva, Vidyāpati and Caṇḍīdāsa is well-known through the *Caitanya-caritāmṛta* (a standard biography of Caitanya) and the songs of some other poets; the inspiration derived from these songs was not negligible in moulding Caitanya's ideal of divine love. Apart from the controversy over the religious view-point of Caṇḍīdāsa and its influence on Caitanya's ideal of love, it may be held that the general history of the Vaiṣṇava Sahajiyā movement with its stress on Parakīyā love was closely related to the general devotional movement of Bengal; it is because of this close relation between the two that the rich field of Bengali lyrics cannot be fully and properly studied without a proper study of the Sahajiyā religion and literature.

The lyrics belonging to the Vaiṣṇava Sahajiyā school are generally ascribed to the well-known poet Caṇḍīdāsa and to some other poets like Vidyāpati, Rūpa, Sanātana, Vṛndāvana-dāsa, Kṛṣṇa-dāsa Kavirāja, Narahari, Narottama, Locana, Caitanya-dāsa and others, and the innumerable Sahajiyā texts are also ascribed to their authorship.

Such assignment, which was evidently made with a view to securing authoritative support from the great Vaiṣṇava poets and thinkers for the unconventional practice of the Sahajiyās, need not be credited historically. In their zeal for propaganda these Sahajiyās have held all the great poets like Jayadeva, Vidyāpati, Caṇḍīdāsa and others, and the great Vaiṣṇava apostles like Rūpa, Sanātana, Svarūpa Dāmodara, Jīva Gosvāmī and others to be the exponents of Sahajiyā practice. Even Śrī-Caitanya himself has been held by some of the Sahajiyās as having practised Sahaja Sādhanā with female companions and attained perfection through it,[1] as lord Buddha was held by the Buddhist Sahajiyās as having practised Sahaja Sādhanā in company of his consort Gopā. It seems, however, that almost all the songs (including the enigmatic songs ascribed to Caṇḍīdāsa well-known as the *Rāgātmika Padas*) and the texts were composed by the exponents of the Sahajiyā cult in the post-Caitanya period, and mostly in or after the seventeenth century A.D.

We have hinted on several occasions that the secret yogic practices, round which grew the paraphernalia of the different Sahajiyā cults, belong neither strictly to the Buddhist fold nor exclusively to the Hindu fold; they are essentially yogic practices, which by their association with different theological systems, either Buddhist or Hindu, have given rise to different religious cults. The most important of the secret practices is the yogic control of the sex-pleasure so as to transform it into transcendental bliss, which is at the same time conducive to the health both of the body and the mind. This yogic practice with its accessories, being associated with the philosophy of Śiva and Śakti,

[1] It is curiously held by a section of the Sahajiyās that Caitanya practised Sahaja Sādhanā in company of Sāṭhi, daughter of Sārvabhauma, and it was because of this fact that the mother of Sāṭhi once said that she would have her daughter a widow. (*Cf. Caitanya-caritāmṛta, Madhya-līlā;* Ch. XV). The Sahajiyās hold that all the great Vaiṣṇava apostles of standard Vaiṣṇavism practised Sahaja Sādhanā with some female companion. Thus it is said in the *Vivarta-vilāsa* of Akiñcana-dāsa,—*śrī rūp karilā sādhanā mirār sahite* | *bhaṭṭa raghu-nāth kailā karṇ-bāi sāthe* || *lakṣmī hīrā sane karilā gomsāi sanātan* | *māhāmantra preme sevā sadā ācaraṇ* || *gosāñi lokanāth caṇḍālinī-kanyā saṅge* | *dohā jan anurāg premer taraṅge* || *goyālinī piṅgalā se braja-devī sama* | *gosāñi kṛṣṇa-dās sadāi ācaraṇa* || *śyāmā nāpitānīr saṅge śrī-jīv gomsāi* | *parama se bhāv kailā yār sīmā nāi* || *raghu-nāth gosvāmī pīriti ullāse* | *mīrā-bāi saṅge teha rādhā kuṇḍa-bāse* || *gaur-priyā saṅge gopāl bhaṭṭa gomsāi* | *karaye sādhan anya kichu nāi* || *rāy rāmānanda yaje deva-kanyā saṅge* | *āropete sthiti teha kriyār taraṅge* ||

Vaṅga-sāhitya-paricaya, Vol. II, p. 1650.

stands at the centre of the net-work of the Hindu Tāntric systems, and when associated with the speculations on Prajñā and Upāya of later Buddhism, has given rise to the Tāntric Buddhist cults including the Buddhist Sahajiyā system; and again, when associated with the speculations on Kṛṣṇa and Rādhā conceived as Rasa and Rati in Bengal Vaiṣṇavism, the same yogic practice and discipline has been responsible for the growth and development of the Vaiṣṇava Sahajiyā movement of Bengal. It will, therefore, be incorrect to say, as has really been said by some scholars, that the Vaiṣṇava Sahajiyā movement of Bengal is a purely post-Caitanya movement having no relation whatsoever with the earlier Buddhist Sahajiyās and that the two cults are distinct fundamentally. A close study of the literture of the Vaiṣṇava Sahajiyās will leave no room for doubting the clear fact that it records nothing but the spirit and practices of the earlier Buddhist and Hindu Tāntric cults, of course in a distinctly transformed form, wrought through the evolution of centuries in different religious and cultural environments. The psycho-physiological yogic processes, frequently referred to in the lyrical songs of the Vaiṣṇava Sahajiyās and also in the innumerable short and long texts, embodying the doctrines of the cult, are fundamentally the same as are found in the Hindu Tantras a well as in the Buddhist Tantras and the Buddhist songs and Dohās. There are sometimes discrepancies only in details and differences more often pertain to terminology and phraseology than to conception.[1]

[1] We may point out here that in the literature of the Vaiṣṇava Sahajiyās we find reference not only to the sexo-yogic practices of the Tāntrics, but also to the important yogic practice of drinking the nectar oozing from the moon situated beneath the lotus of Sahasrāra, which practice was emphasised by the Nātha-yogins (*vide infra*, Ch. IX.) *Cf.*:—

candra uday haile sudhāmṛta kṣare I
pite nā pāiyā cakor pipāsāte mare ||

* * * *

sahasra-dal hay mastak bhitare I
akṣay nāmete tathā āche sarovare ||
udar bhitar āche māna sarovare I
tathā haite phul gela sahasra-dal upare ||
ūrddhva-mukhe adho-mukhe haiyā nāsār I
sarva-kāl mūl bastu āche tār bhitar || *etc.*

Ānanda-bhairava, vide Sahajiyā-sāhitya (edited by M. M. Bose, M.A., pp. 132-133).

It is very interesting to note in this connection that like some of the texts of the Sahajiyā Buddhists some of the Bengali texts of Sahajiyā Vaiṣṇavism, composed some time between the seventeenth and the nineteenth centuries, are introduced in the form of a dialogue between Śiva and Śakti, who are depicted as discussing the secrets of the Vaiṣṇava Sahajiyā Sādhanā,[1] and in the *Ānanda-bhairava* it is hinted that Hara or Śiva himself practised this Sahaja Sādhanā in the company of the different Śaktis in the country of the Kucnīs (women belonging to the Koc tribe).[2]

We have discussed before at length the salient features of the Buddhist Sahajiyā cult and literature. The Vaiṣṇava Sahajiyās, like other medieval schools who were Sahajiyās in a broader sense, and of whom we shall speak in detail in the next chapter, harped on the same string. But we have seen that the angle of vision from which the different schools of Indian religious thought criticised one another was different. Consequently, whereas the criticism of the Buddhist Sahajiyās represents an admixture of the spirit of Buddhism, Vedānta, Tantra and Yoga, the criticism of the Vaiṣṇava Sahajiyās is marked by a dominating spirit of love, which is the watchword of their Sādhanā, although, however, the lurking influence of Yoga and Tantra is not

Again, *haile saday jvālā-jvalan nay*
biṣāmṛta āche tathā ।
biṣ māre gāy amṛte jīyāy
eki adbhut kathā ॥
Amṛta-rasāvalī, *Ibid.*, p. 163.

Cf. also:— *cānder kāche avalā ye āche*
sei ye raseri sār ॥
biṣete amṛte milan ekatre
ke bujhe marama tār ॥

These principles of *biṣa* (poison) and *amṛta* (nectar), which represent the principles of the Sun and the Moon of the yogins (*vide infra*, Ch. IX) were transformed by the Vaiṣṇava Sahajiyās into the principles of *kāma* (carnal desire) and *prema* (pure love).

Cf. *biṣ kheye yevā jārite pāre* । *sei se sādhak rāgete tare* ॥
sādhane sādhak pakvita nay । *biṣ khele seho nāi bācay* ॥
biṣete amṛte ekui hay । *biṣ jārī kare amṛtamay* ॥
Vide Sj. S., Song No. 82.

[1] See *Āgama-grantha* and *Ānanda-bhairava* edited by Mr. M. M. Bose in *Sj. S.*; see also the bibliography of seventy-nine Sahajiyā texts with short notes on them by Mr. M. M. Bose in a pamphlet reprinted from the J. D. L., Vol. XVI.

[2] *ek ek guṇe kaila ekek prakṛti* । *harake bhajaye save bhāv upapati* ॥
śakti jāne rasa-tattva ār jāne śaṅkare । *sahaj bastu āsvādila kucani nagare* ॥
The dalliances of Śiva with the Kucnīs is very well known in the *Śivāyanas* of Bengali literature.

altogether missing. The Buddhist Sahajiyās, we have seen, inherited from the Yogic and Tāntric schools in general the spirit that all truth underlying the universe as a whole is contained in the microcosm of the human body; this belief, we shall presently see, was brought by the Vaiṣṇava Sahajiyās to a deeper significance, which inspired them to declare to the world abroad, "Hearken men, my brothers,—man is the truth above all truths,—there is nothing above that."[1] Again, the same spirit of Guruvāda that characterises the songs, Dohās and other Sanskritic texts of the Buddhist Sahajiyās as also the literature of the medieval saints, characterises also the songs and other texts of the Vaiṣṇava Sahajiyās.[2] Again, as many of the Buddhist Siddhācāryas and medieval saints employed an extremely enigmatic and paradoxical style in their songs in describing the secrets of their Sādhanā, so also it was the custom with the Vaiṣṇava Sahajiyās to couch the secrets of their cult under a similar enigmatic style. Many of the songs ascribed to Caṇḍīdāsa are good specimens of such an enigmatic style. Thus it is clear that in spirit as well as in literary representation the relation between the Buddhist Sahajiyās and the Vaiṣṇava Sahajiyās clearly shows an easy gliding from the one to the other.

Historically it seems that the fall of the Pāla dynasty of Bengal marked also the fall of Buddhism in the province and that there was something like a Hindu revival during the reign of the Senas, who succeeded the Pālas. Vaiṣṇavism, based mainly on the love-dalliances of the cowherd Kṛṣṇa with the cowherd girl Rādhā, began to gain popularity during the reign of the Senas and the first Bengali Vaiṣṇava poet to sing the sweet immortal songs of Rādhā-Kṛṣṇa was Jayadeva, who is said to have been the court-poet of the last Sena King Lakṣmaṇasena in the last half of the twelfth century A.D. Caṇḍīdāsa of the fourteenth century popularised the legends and ideals of

[1] *śuna he mānuṣ bhāi* |
savār upare *mānuṣ satya*
tāhār upare nāi ||

Song ascribed to Caṇḍīdāsa.

[2] *Vide* the songs on Guru collected in the anthology *Sahajiyā Sāhitya* by Mr. Bose.

the love of Rādhā and Kṛṣṇa through his exquisite lyrical poems. Similar lyrics were composed also by poet Vidyāpati of Mithilā, who was contemporaneous with Caṇḍīdās and enjoyed enormous popularity in Bengal; this widespread popularity of the Rādhā-Kṛṣṇa songs began to influence the mind of the people belonging to all sub strata of the society. It was through the influence of this love-ideal of the Rādhā-Kṛṣṇa songs that the ideology of the Buddhist Sahajiyās gradually began to change, and the change of methodology was consequent on the change of ideology.

With the popularity of the Rādhā-Kṛṣṇa songs the ideal of Parakīyā Rati, or the unconventional love between man and woman not bound by the conjugal tie, became emphasised. In almost all the theological discussions of the Vaiṣṇavas of the post-Caitanya period the superiority of this ideal of Parakīyā love to that of Svakīyā was variously demonstrated. In his *Typical Selections from Old Bengali Literature* (Vol. II, pp. 1638-1643) Dr. D. C. Sen has quoted two old documents, belonging to the first half of the eighteenth century, where we find that regular debates were arranged between the Vaiṣṇava exponents of the Parakīyā and the Svakīyā ideals of love, and in the debates the upholders of the Svakīyā view were sadly defeated and had to sign documents admitting the supremacy of the Parakīyā ideal of love. This will help us in guessing how much influence this Parakīyā ideal did exert on the people of the time belonging to the Vaiṣṇava fold. This ideal of Parakīyā love has been the strongest factor in moulding the doctrines of the Sahajiyā Vaiṣṇavism of Bengal.

It is customary to sneer at the Vaiṣṇava Sahajiyā cult as an order of debauchery under the cloak of religion. Abuses and aberrations there are in every religion, and there is no denial of the fact that debauchery found its field of play in the Tāntric schools, both of Hinduism and Buddhism and in the school of the Vaiṣṇava Sahajiyās, but that should not be the only point for consideration in judging the value of these religious orders. As students of literature, religion and culture, let us, like the wise swan, drink only milk out of a mixture of milk and water.

We have pointed out before that the innumerable texts available on the doctrines and practices of the Sahajiyās few can be said to possess much intrinsic merit; but the lyrics of the Sahajiyās, whoever might have been their author, really reached a high pitch of poetry and philosophy, and these songs assigned a sublime value to human love; and with this deification of human love humanity as a whole has also been deified, and heaven above and earth below have met together in the songs of the Vaiṣṇava Sahajiyā poets.

(ii) *The mode of Transformation*

Let us now follow the mode of transformation of the ideology of the Buddhist Sahajiyās into that of the Vaiṣṇava Sahajiyās. The final aim of the Buddhist Sahajiyās, apart from the customary way of describing it as the Vacuity, or the Prajñā, or the Bodhi-citta, was supreme bliss,—and this conception of the final state of the Buddhist Sahajiyās differed from that of the early Buddhists in this that the Mahā-sukha state of Nirvāṇa is a definitely positive state, while the earlier Buddhistic tendency was towards negation; again, the conception of the Buddhist Sahajiyās differs from the general conception of the final state of the different schools of yoga in this that it is not a state of absolute dissolution; though it is a state of arrest and a negative state in so far as it involes the arrest of all states and processes of mind, it is a positive state of supreme bliss. Of course, sometimes this state of supreme bliss has been criticised as a state of mere thought-construction,—and Nirvāṇa has been defined as a pure state of negation bereft of all sorts of thought-constructions;[1] but in general Mahā-sukha itself, bereft of subjectivity and objectivity, has been held to be the final state—the state of vacuity and perfect enlightenment. The final state of Mahā-sukha as the state of Sahaja of the Buddhists is also the final state of

[1] *yāvān kaścit vikalpaḥ prabhavati manasi tyājya-rūpo hi tāvān*
yo' sāvānanda-rūpaḥ parama-sukha-karaḥ so'pi saṁkalpa-mātraḥ |
yo vā vairāgya-bhāvas tadapi tad ubhayaṁ tad bhavasyā'gra-hetu
nirvāṇān nānyad asti kvacid api viṣaye nirvikalpātma-cittāt ||
Apratiṣṭhāna-prakāśa of Nāgārjuna-pāda, quoted in the Com. on the Caryā Nos. 8 and 13 (Śāstrī's edition).

Sahaja with the Vaiṣṇava Sahajiyās; but the Vaiṣṇavas conceived this Sahaja state as the state of supreme love, and this supreme love has been conceived as the primordial substance which underlies the world-process as a whole. But how can this Sahaja be the ultimate reality? It is the ultimate reality inasmuch as it is the non-dual state of the unity of Śiva and Śakti, which are but the two aspects of the absolute reality as conceived in the Hindu Tantras.[1] Again in the Buddhist school it is the non-dual state of unity of Prajñā and Upāya which are also the two aspects of the absolute reality.[2] The principles of Śiva and Śakti or Upāya and Prajñā are represented by man and woman, and it is, therefore, that when through the process of Sādhanā man and woman can realise their pure nature as Śiva and Śakti, or Upāya and Prajñā, the supreme bliss arising out of the union of the two becomes the highest state whereby one can realise the ultimate nature of the absolute reality. Now the conception of Kṛṣṇa and Rādhā of the Vaiṣṇavas was interpreted by the Sahajiyās in a sense akin to the conception of Śiva and Śakti, or Upāya and Prajñā,—and all males and females were thought of as physical manifestation of the principles of Kṛṣṇa and Rādhā. So, the highest state of union of the two, which is the state of supreme love, is the final state of Sahaja. Thus the theological speculations centering round the love-dalliances of Rādhā and Kṛṣṇa in standard Vaiṣṇavism could very easily be assimilated by the Sahajiyās into their cult. Moreover, the standard Vaiṣṇava schools of devotion were all deadly against the final aim of liberation either in any sense of negation, or in the merging of the individual self in the absolute. The supreme state of the Vaiṣṇavas is no state of absolute cessation, or annihilation,—it is a positive state, though of a supra-mental nature, of the eternal flow of divine love—like the smooth and incessant flow of oil. This ideal of the final positive state of love could very well be utilised by the Sahajiyās in a slightly modified way and thus the Sahajiyās could gradually associate their practices with the

[1] *Vide infra*, Ch. XIV.
[2] *Infra*, Ch. XIV, *Supra*, Ch. I.

whole network of Bengal Vaiṣṇava theology. And once the practices of the Sahajiyās could be thus associated with the Vaiṣṇava theology, their whole ideology and methodology began to be influenced palpably by those of standard Vaiṣṇavism.

The main deviation of the Vaiṣṇava Sahajiyās under the sway of Vaiṣṇavism was towards a psychological development, and it will be more correct to speak of it as an innovation through a process of gradual transformation. The Tāntric schools, which emphasised the sexo-yogic practice (and all schools did not certainly emphasise or encourage it), were essentially schools of psycho-physiological yogic practices; but already in the Buddhist Sahajiyā we find a tendency towards the psychological development. There we sometimes find it explained that the most intense sex-emotion, produced under a perfect control of yoga, has the capacity of suspending the ordinary states and processes of the mind and producing a non-dual state of supreme bliss, where, absorbed in the unfathomable depth of emotion, our mind shakes off all its relation to objects and all its character as the subject; and this unique state of bliss is the absolute state of Sahaja-realisation. This psycholoical aspect of the Sādhanā was, however, most empasised in the school of the Vaiṣṇava Sahajiyās, with whom the Sahaja Sādhanā soon developed more into a religion of psychological discipline in the culture of love than a religion of mere psycho-physiological yogic process. In fact, the importance of the Vaiṣṇava Sahajiyās consists in the high pitch which they reached in their enquiry and practical culture of love-psychology and in the new interpretation of our whole being offered in the light of love. It was a religious process of the divinisation of human love and the consequent discovery of the divine in man. As we have said before, the psycho-physiological yogic process was there, but its yogic aspect was dominated by the psychological aspect of the Sahajiyās with which we are mainly interested in our present study.

(iii) *The Psychological Aspect of the Sādhanā of the Vaiṣṇava Sahajiyās*

(A) The Ideal of Love

The psychological aspect of the Sahaja-sādhanā of the Vaiṣṇavas grew mainly with the philosophy of Rādhā and Kṛṣṇa and the eternal love between them in the land of eternity. It is, therefore, necessary, first of all, to elucidate the philosophy of Rādhā-Kṛṣṇa and their eternal love as conceived by the Vaiṣṇavas. According to the philosophical and theological works of Bengal Vaiṣṇavism (popularly known as Gauḍīya Vaiṣṇavism) Rādhā is nothing but the transfiguration of the infinite potency of love contained in the very nature of Kṛṣṇa. The ultimate Being, it is held, may be conceived in three of its states, either as the unqualified Brahman, or as the Paramātman, the indwelling principle of all beings, or as the Bhagavān, the active and qualified God. Kṛṣṇa as Bhagavān possesses three powers, *viz.*, *Svarūpa-śakti*, *i.e.*, the power which He possesses by virtue of His ultimate nature, *Jīva-śakti* or the power through which all the beings are produced (also known as the *Taṭasthā-śakti*, the accidental power), and the *Māyā-śakti*, through which evolves the material world. This *Svarūpa-śakti* of the Lord has again three attributes, *viz.*, the attribute of existence (*sat*), the attribute of pure consciousness (*cit*) and the attribute of bliss (*ānanda*). The potency of the three attributes acts like three powers, in the nature of God, which are known as *Sandhinī* (the power of existence), *Saṁvit* (the power of consciousness) and *Hlādinī* (the power of bliss which is of the nature of infinite love). The transfiguration of this power of bliss or love is Rādhā, and as such the very being of Rādhā is already involved in the very nature of Kṛṣṇa and the two are one and the same in the ultimate principle. Why then the apparent separation of Rādhā from Kṛṣṇa? It is for the self-realisation of Kṛṣṇa. God has within His nature two aspects, the enjoyer and the enjoyed, and without the reality of the enjoyed He cannot even realise His own nature as the enjoyer. Rādhā represents the eternal enjoyed while Kṛṣṇa is the eternal enjoyer, —and the enjoyed and the enjoyer being co-relative, the reality of the one involves the reality of the other; or, in other words Rādhā as the eternal enjoyed is as much real as Kṛṣṇa the eternal enjoyer. This inseparable relation between the two is the eternal love-dalliance of Kṛṣṇa with Rādhā,—and as Rādhā is eternally realising the value of her whole being with reference to her relation to the eternal enjoyer Kṛṣṇa, Kṛṣṇa too is eternally enjoying Rādhā to realise the infinite potency of love and bliss that is in him. This mutual relation of love is the secret of the whole drama enacted in the eternal land of Vṛndāvana. This eternal sport (*līlā*) or love-dalliance of Rādhā and Kṛṣṇa does not presuppose any kind of shortcoming or imperfection in the nature of the ultimate reality, it follows from the very nature of the ultimate reality as such.

This relation of eternal love between Rādhā and Kṛṣṇa has been conceived and expressed in the Vaiṣṇava theology and literature anthropomorphically through analogies of human love. So, to understand the nature of this divine love, human love has been analysed psychologically into all its varieties and niceties to the minutest details, and it has been found on analysis that divine love can be expressed only through the analogy of the most intense and the most romantic and unconventional love that exists between a man and a woman who become bound together by the ideal of love for love's sake. Post-nuptial love is not the highest ideal of love so far as the intensity of emotion is concerned,—for long association and acquaintance devour the strange mystery, which is the salt of love, and social convention and legal compulsion take away much from the passion in it and thus make it commonplace and attenuated. The highest ideal of human love, which is the most intense, is the love that exists most privately between couples, who are absolutely free in their love from any consideration of loss and gain, who defy the society and transgress the law and make love the be-all and end-all of life. This is the ideal of Parakīyā love,[1] which is the best human analogy for divine love. It is because of this theological ideal that in none of the legends of Rādhā-Kṛṣṇa is Rādhā depicted as the

[1] Parakīyā love literally means the love of a man for a woman, who legally belongs to another man.

wife of Kṛṣṇa, she is generally depicted as the wife of another cowherd, or as a maid just attaining the prime of youth.

Śrī-Caitanya, as he has been docetically conceived by his followers, combined in him the enjoyer and the enjoyed,—and it has been said that he was of the ultimate nature of Kṛṣṇa hallowed with the lustre of the supreme emotion of Rādhā (*rādhā-bhāva-dyuti-suvalita*). This speaks of the religious attitude of Caitanya. Though he himself became often conscious of his true self as none but Kṛṣṇa, his dominating religious attitude was *Rādhā-bhāva* or the love attitude of Rādhā towards Kṛṣṇa. This *Rādhā-bhāva*, or the religious attitude of the devotee towards God as the attitude of the most unconventional romantic love of a woman towards her beloved, may be recognised as the fundamental tone of the religion preached by Caitanya, not so much by sermons and teachings as by his tears and frequent love-trances.

The religious attitude of the Vaiṣṇava poets of Bengal, as represented in the innumerable love-lyrics, composed by them, was not, however, exactly the same as that of Caitanya. The attitude of the Vaiṣṇava poets was *Sakhi-bhāva* rather than *Rādhā-bhāva*. Śri-Caitanya placed himself in the position of Rādhā and longed with all the tormenting pangs of heart for union with his beloved Kṛṣṇa; but the Vaiṣṇava poets, headed by Jayadeva, Caṇḍīdāsa and Vidyāpati, placed themselves rather in the position of the Sakhis, or the female companions of Rādhā and Kṛṣṇa, who did never long for their union with Kṛṣna,—but ever longed for the opportunity of witnessing from a distance the eternal love-making of Rādhā and Kṛṣṇa in the supra-natural land of Vṛndāvana (*aprākṛta-vṛndāvana*). This eternal *līlā* is the eternal truth, and, therefore, it is this eternal *līlā*—the playful love-making of Rādhā and Kṛṣṇa, which the Vaiṣṇava poets desired to enjoy. If we analyse the *Gīta-govinda* of Jayadeva we shall find not even a single statement which shows the poet's desire to have union with Kṛṣṇa as Rādhā had,—he only sings praises of the *līlā* of Radhā and Kṛṣṇa and hankers after chance just to have a peep into the divine *līlā*, and this peep into the divine *līlā* is the highest spiritual gain which these poets could think of. The exclamation—"Glorious be the secret dalliances of Rādhā and Kṛṣṇa on the bank of the Jumna"[1] sounds the key-note of the Vaiṣṇava attitude of Jayadeva. The same is the attitude of Caṇḍīdās and Vidyāpati, who were absorbed in the *līlā* of Rādhā-Kṛṣṇa, who indulged themselves in making comments on the *līlā*,—and longed to have the chance to stand by when Rādhā and Kṛṣṇa were united in their love.[2]

It is to be noted that in the religious discourse, which took place between Śrī-Caitanya and Rāy Rāmānanda,[3] the latter stressed *Sakhī-bhāva* as the best means for realising divine love. The theological explanation of this *Sakhī-bhāva* is not far to seek. The general Vaiṣṇava view is that Jīva being the *Taṭasthā Śakti* of Kṛṣṇa is, after all, a Prakṛti and its pride as being the Puruṣa (*puruṣābhimāna*) must be removed before it can be permitted to have its proper place in the eternal region of *Svarūpa-śakti*, and even then only as a Sakhī, rather than as Rādhā, and never as Kṛṣṇa.

To put the poetical utterances of the Vaiṣṇava poets in a clear theological form we should say that, according to them, the absolute reality has from the very beginning divided itself for the sake of self-realisation into two counterparts as the enjoyer and the enjoyed, or as Kṛṣṇa and Rādhā; these Kṛṣṇa and Rādhā are not mere abstract notions,—neither are they purely legendary figures invented through the imagination of the poets,—they are concrete in their divine form and represent the original concrete type of the two aspects of the nature of the absolute as the lover and the beloved having their eternal dalliances in the supra-

1 *rādhā-mādhavayor jayanti yamunā-kūle rahaḥ-kelayaḥ* ||
Gīta-govinda, (1. 1).

2 *Cf.* *āji malayānila mṛdu mṛdu bahata*
niramala cāṁda prakāśa |
bhāva-bhare gadagada cāmara ḍhulāyata
pāśe rahi caṇḍīdāsa ||
Songs of Caṇḍīdās, Pariṣat edition.

Again, *duhuṁ jana ākula duhuṁ karu kora* |
duhuṁ daraśane bidyāpati bhora ||
Pada-kalpa-taru, Song No. 484.

3 *Caitanya-caritāmṛta*, *Madhya-līlā*, Ch. viii.

natural land of Vṛndāvana.[1] The historical personages of Rādhā and Kṛṣṇa as the cowherd boy and the cowherd girl in the geographical area of Vṛndāvana are but the temporal manifestation of the eternal type, a condescension of the supra-natural in the natural form so as to help man to understand the eternal in terms of the temporal.[2] The Vaiṣṇava poets sang of the historical love-episodes of Rādhā and Kṛṣṇa with the belief that corresponding to these love-episodes on earth there are the eternal love-episodes of Rādhā-Kṛṣṇa in the *Aprākṛta* or supra-natural Vṛndāvana and the historical episodes will enable them to form an idea of and to have a peep into the eternal episodes, the realisation of which is the *summum bonum* of the spiritual life.

We have seen that the religious approach of Śrī-Caitanya, as depicted by Kṛṣṇadās Kavirāj in his work, the *Caitanya-caritāmṛta*, was somewhat different from that of the Vaiṣṇava poets. The post-Caitayna Vaiṣṇava poets stuck mainly to the tradition of the pre-Caitanya Vaiṣṇava poets in their poetic treatment of the love-episodes of Rādhā and Kṛṣṇa and the Vaiṣṇava Sahajiyās received their philosophy of Rādhā-Kṛṣṇa from these Vaiṣṇava poets. The Sahajiyās believed in the eternal dalliances of Rādhā-Kṛṣṇa in the highest spiritual land,—but they further held that the eternal concrete spiritual type manifested itself not only in the historical personages of Rādhā and Kṛṣna, but that it reveals itself in actual men and women themselves. Every man has within him the spiritual essence of Kṛṣṇa, which is his Svarūpa

[1] *Cf.* *sekhāne hay ki* || *nitya rās hay* || *nitya mahotsav hay* || etc.
Deha-kaḍacā by Narottam, B.S.P.P. Vol. IV. No. I.

Again, *rādhā-kṛṣṇa rasa-prem ekui se hay* ।
nitya nitya dhvaṁsa nāi nitya birājay ||
Sahaja-upāsanā-tattva by Taruṇī-raman, B. S. P. P., B. S. 1335, No. 4.

Again, *nitya-līlā-kṛṣṇer nāhika pārāpār* ।
aviśrām bahe līlā yena gaṅgā dhār ||
Siddhānta-candrodaya of Mukunda-dās, (Published by Muṇīndra-nandī p. 58; See also pp. 58-64).

nija-śakti śrī-rādhikā lañā nanda-suta ।
bṛndāvane nitya-līlā karaye adbhuta ||
Ibid., p. 91.

se kṛṣṇa rādhikār hayen prāṇa-pati ।
rādhā saha nitya-līlā kare divā rāti || *Ibid.*

[2] Vide, *Rati-vilāsa-paddhati*, MS. (C.U., 572).

(real nature) associated with his lower existence, which is his physical form or Rūpa, and exactly in the same way every woman possesses within her a lower self associated with her physical existence, which is her Rūpa,—but within this Rūpa resides the Svarūpa of the woman, which is her ultimate nature as Rādhā. It is none but Kṛṣṇa and Rādhā who reside within men and women, and it is this Kṛṣṇa and this Rādhā that are making dalliances as men and women.[1] These *rūpa-līlā* and *svarūpā-līlā* of Rādhā-Kṛṣṇa have also been explained as the *prākṛta-līlā* and *aprākṛta-līlā* (*i.e.*, sports in the natural plane and the supra-natural plane).[2] This view of holding men and women to be nothing but physical manifestation of Rādhā and Kṛṣṇa seems to have been inherited by the Vaiṣṇava Sahajiyās from the earlier Tāntric philosophy. In the Hindu Tantras, we have seen, all men and women have been held to be nothing but the incarnations of Śiva and Śakti manifested in the physical form,—and in the Buddhist philosophy they have been spoken of as the embodiment of Upāya and Prajñā respectively, and this philosophy has most probably influenced the Vaiṣṇava Sahijiyās in their belief of men and women being Kṛṣṇa and Rādhā in their Svarūpa. We have pointed out before that many of the Vaiṣṇava Sahajiyā texts are introduced in the form of the earlier Āgamas and Nigamas, and in these texts Kṛṣṇa and Rādhā have always been explained as nothing but the different forms of Śiva and Śakti, and we have also pointed out that Śiva has sometimes been described as practising the Sahaja Sādhanā with Śakti as Kṛṣṇa with Rādhā.

Even in a popular Vaiṣṇava text like the *Brahma-saṁhitā*, which was brought by Śri-Caitanya himself from South India, the Tāntric influence on Vaiṣṇavism is palpable. In the fifth chapter (which only is available now-a-days) of the *Brahma-saṁhitā* we find that the lotus of thousand

[1] *prakaṭa haite jadi kabhu mane hay* ।
rūpāvesa hayiā tave līlā āsvāday ||
sarva para-rasa-tattva kariyā āśray ।
rasamay deha dhari ras āsvāday ||
Dvipako-jjvala, MS. (C. U., No. 564), p. 13(A).
Again,—*manuṣya svarūpe kare kautuka bihār* ||
Campaka-kalikā, B.S.P.P., B.S. 1307, No. 1.

[2] See *Rati-vilāsa-paddhati*, MS. (C. U. No. 572), pp. 3(A)-3(B).

petals in the cerebrum-region is described as Gokula, the abode of Kṛṣṇa. Within the lotus we find description also of the Tāntric *yantra* (the physiological machinery through which truth is to be realised) as also of the *kīlaka* (the wedge, the support). Śiva of the nature of the *liṅga* (the symbol of the male productive energy) is described as the Lord Nārāyaṇa and Śakti of the nature of the *yoni* (the symbol of the female productive energy) is described as Ramā Devī (the consort of Nārāyaṇa).[1] Again it has been said in the *Srī-haya-śīrṣa-pañcarātra*, "Hari (the saviour) as the Paramātman is the Lord, Śrī is called his power (*śakti*); goddess Śrī is the Prakṛti and Keśava is the Puruṣa; the goddess can never be without Viṣṇu and Hari (Viṣṇu) cannot be without the goddess, born in the lotus.[2] It has also been said in the *Viṣṇu-purāṇa*,—"The mother of the world is eternal and she remains inseparable with Viṣṇu; as Viṣṇu is all-permeating so also is she."[3]

It is very interesting to note in this connection that there is a small poetical work, entitled *Sādhaka-rañjana*,[4] by Kamalā-kānta (who flourished in the first half of the nineteenth century) where the yogic Kulu-kuṇḍalinī Śakti has been conceived exactly in the image of Rādhā; she is described in exactly the same way with the same imageries and even in the same diction as Rādhā is described in the Vaiṣṇava literature. The rise of the Śakti to meet Śiva in the Sahasrāra has been sung as the coming out of Rādhā to meet her beloved in private.[5] The

[1] See *Brahma-saṁhitā*, Ch. V, verses (2-10). (Baharampur edition).

[2] *paramātmā harir devas tac chaktiḥ śrīr ihoditā* I
śrīr devī prakṛtiḥ proktā keśavaḥ puruṣaḥ smṛtaḥ ||
na viṣṇunā vinā devī na hariḥ padmajāṁ vinā ||
Quoted in the *Bhagavat-sandarbha* of the *Ṣaṭ-sandarbha* of Jīva Gosvāmi.

[3] *nityaiva sā jagan-mātā viṣṇoḥ śrīr anapāyinī* I
yathā sarvo-gato viṣṇus tathaiveyaṁ dvijottama ||
Cf. also:—*aparaṁ tv akṣaraṁ yā sā prakṛtir jaḍa-rūpikā* I
śrīḥ parā prakṛtiḥ proktā cetanā viṣṇu-saṁśrayā ||
Quoted in the *Bhagavat-sandarbha*.

[4] Edited jointly by Messrs. Basanta Ranjan Ray and Atal Bihari Ghosh.
Sāhitya-pariṣad-granthāvalī, No. 71.

[5] We are quoting here a few specimens:—
gaja-pati-nandita gati avilambe I
kuñcita keśa niveśa nitambe ||
cāru caraṇa gati ābharaṇa-vṛnde I
nakhara-mukura-kara himakara ninde ||

9

philosophical concepts of the pairs Śiva-Śakti and Kṛṣṇa-Rādhā were generally confused; and as a matter of fact Puruṣa-Prakṛti, Śiva-Śakti and Kṛṣṇa-Rādhā mean all the same in popular theology. This fact has helped the development of the theological belief in the Vaiṣṇava Sahajiyā school that men and women are but the Rūpa of the Svarūpa as Kṛṣṇa and Rādhā. But the important point to be remembered in this connection is that while in the Sahajiyā Sādhanā the Kṛṣṇahood of man has been admitted it has never been admitted in the Standard Vaiṣṇava school under any circumstances.

According to the Vaiṣṇava Sahajiyās the region of Sahaja is an ideal transcendental region and it is generally styled as the 'land of eternity' (*nityer deśa*)—this is the Nitya-Vṛndāvana or the eternal Vṛndāvana as contrasted with the other two kinds of Vṛndāvana, *viz.*, Mana-Vṛndāvana and Nava-Vṛndāvana or Vana-Vṛndāvana. By Nava-Vṛndāvana the Sahajiyās refer to the geographical Vṛndāvana, and by Mana-Vṛndāvana the Vṛndāvana of the mental plane of the Sādhaka, and the Nitya-Vṛndāvana transcends both. In this Nitya-Vṛndāvana (also called the

urasi sarasī-ruha bāmā 1
kari-kara śikhara nitambinī rāmā ||
mṛga-pati dūra śikhara-mukha cāya 1
kaṭi-taṭa kṣīṇa sucañcala bāya ||
nābhi gabhīra nīraja-bihāra 1
īṣat bikaca kamala-kuca bhāra ||
bāhu-latā alase sakhī aṅge 1
dolita deha suneha taraṅge ||
sumadhura hāsa prakāśai bālā 1
bālātapa-ruci nayana biśālā ||

* * * *

ratana-vedi para sura-taru-mūla 1
maṇimaya mandira tahi ānukūla ||
sahacarī saṅga praveśai nārī 1
kamalākānta heri balihārī ||

Sādhaka-rañjana, pp. 3-4.

Again,—

kadamva kusuma janu *satata sihare tanu*
yadavadhi nirakhilām tāre 1
jadi pāsarite cāi *āpanā pāsari jāi*
enā dukha kahiva kāhāre ||
sei se jīvana mor *rasikera mana-cor*
ramaṇī raser siromaṇi 1
parihari loka-lāje *rākhiva hṛday mājhe*
nā chāḍiva divasa-rajanī ||
hena anumāni tāre *bāndhi hṛdi kārāgāre*
nayāna pahari diye rākhi,
kāminī kariye curi *hṛdaya pañjare pūri*
animekhe hena rūpa dekhi || etc., *Ibid.*, p. 10.

gupta-candra-pura) resides Sahaja of the nature of pure love which flows between Rādhā and Kṛṣṇa in and through their eternal dalliances. This Sahaja as the Supreme Delight is the ultimate substance underlying the whole world[1] and it can never be realised as such in the gross material world of ours.[2] But how should then men and women of this world attain Sahaja? It is said in reply that there is a passage or transition from this world to the other,—or rather this gross world can itself be transformed into the Nitya-Vṛndāvana by the process of spiritual culture, and the principle of nescience, which is responsible for the grossness of the world can thus be removed. This removal of the fundamental principle of nescience and of the principle of grossness with it through a process of continual psychological discipline, is the primary requisite for Sahaja Sādhanā,—and when this is effected it is revealed to the Sādhaka that the difference between this world and that is more imaginary than real. At that moment there remains no distinction between our physical existence and our spiritual existence.[3] It has been said in a poem ascribed Caṇḍīdās, "Great is the difference between this world and that,—this is the truth known to all ordinary people; but there is a way of transition from the one to the other,—don't speak of it to any one else."[4]

Again,— *cañcala capalā jiniye prabalā abalā mṛdu madhu hāse* I
sumani unmani laiye *aṅginī dhāila brahma-nivāse* ||
unmata-beśā bigalita-keśā maṇimaya ābharaṇa sāje I
timira bināśi bege dhāy rūpasī jhunu jhunu nūpura bāje ||
jāti kula nāśiye upanita āsiye amṛta sarovara tīre I
prema-bhare ramaṇī sihare pulake tanu manda samīre ||

* * * *

keli samāpana kāminīr āgamana harapura ādi saroje I
kula-patha bhediye mūlādhāre āsiye punarapi ramaṇī birāje ||
badana prakāśe śaśadhara bariṣe bilasai purahara aṅge I
kamalākānta heri mukha-maṇḍala bhāsai prema-taraṅge ||
Ibid., p. 34.

1 *rasa bai bastu nāi e tina bhuvane* || Sj. S. Song No. 59.

2 *Cf.* *sahaj kathāṭi ye janā jāne* I
bhayer kathā kahiba kāre I
jagat bāṁcile āmi se mari I
dvigun bhay tāhāri mane ||
ekalā bāṁcile jagat mare ||
jagat ḍubile āmi se tari ||
Amṛta-rasāvalī, Sj. S. P. 161.

Here *jagat* means the changing gross reality.

3 *śrī-rūp svarūp hay svarūp śrī-rūp* ||
Ratna-sāra, MS. (C. U. 1111), p. 18(B).

4 *se deśe e deśe* *anek antar*
jānaye sakal loke I

We have seen that Sahaja as the absolute reality of the nature of pure love involves within it two factors, *i.e.*, the enjoyer and the enjoyed, represented in the Nitya-Vṛndāvana by Kṛṣṇa and Rādhā. These principles of the enjoyer and the enjoyed are known in the Sahajiyā school as the Puruṣa and the Prakṛti, manifested on earth as the male and the female.[1] It has been said in a song (ascribed to Caṇḍīdās)—"There are two currents in the lake of love, which can be realised only by the *Rasikas* (*i.e.*, people versed in Rasa). When the two currents remain united together in one, the *Rasika* realises the truth of union."[2]

se deśe e deśe *miśāmiśi āche*
e kathā koya nā kāke ||
Sj. S. Song No 84.

1 *paramātmār dui nāma dhare dui rūp* l
eimate ek hayyā dharaye svarūp ||
tāhe dui bhed hay puruṣ prakṛti l
sakaler mūl hay sei rasa-murati ||
. . . . .
paramātmā puruṣ prakṛti dui rūp l
sahasra-dale bās kare raser svarūp ||
Ratna-sāra, MS. (C.U. No. 1111), p. 52(B).

Again *Cf.* *rasa āsvādan lāgi hailā dui murtti* l
ei hetu kṛṣṇa hay puruṣ prakṛti ||
prakṛti nā haile kṛṣṇa sevā-janya nay l
ei hetu prakṛti-bhāv karaye āśray ||
Dvīpako-jjvala-grantha, MS. (C.U. No. 564) pp. 1(B)-2(A).

Also,— *ek brahma jakhan dvitiya nāhi ār* l
sei kāle suni isvar karen vicār ||
apurvva raser cheṣṭā apurvva karan l
kemane haive ihā karen bhāvan ||
bhāvite bhāvite ek uday haila l
manete ānanda haiyā bibhvol haila
ardha aṅga haite āmi prakṛti haiva l
aṁśinī rādhikā nām tāhār haiva ||
. . . . . .
āpani raser murtti kariva dhāraṇ l
rasa āsvadiva āmi kariyā jatan ||
Ibd., pp 11(B)-12(A). (*Cf. Bṛhad-āraṇyaka*, 1,4,1-3.)

Again, *ei ye sahaj-bastu sahaj tār gati* l
. . . .
nārī puruṣ rūpe satata bihare ||
Prema-vilāsa of Yugal-Kiśor Dās.
Vide, *Vaṅga-sāhitya-paricay*, Vol. II, p. 1662.

Again, *sei rūpete kare kuñjete bihār* l
sei kṛṣṇa ei rādhā ekui ākār ||
rādhā haite nirākār raser svarūp l
ataev dui rūp hay ek rūp ||
Rādhā-rasa-kārikā, *Vide Vaṅga-sāhitya-paricay*, Vol. III, p. 1671.

2 *prema-sarovare duiṭi dhārā* l
āsvādan kare rasik yārā ||
dui dhārā yakhan ekatre thāke l
takhan rasik yugal dekhe ||
Songs of Caṇḍīdās.

Through man and woman flow these two currents of love,—man and woman are, therefore, the gross manifestations of the same principles of which Kṛṣna and Rādhā are the pure spiritual representations. Man and woman, in other words, are manifestations on earth of the eternal types that are enjoying each other in their eternal Vṛndāvana, and the bliss of intense love that is enjoyed by man and woman through their mutual attachment even in the physical body is but a gross transformation of the eternal purest love that exists only in Vṛndāvana. Man and woman as the representatives of the two flows of love are known in the Sahajiyā literature as Rasa (the ultimate emotion as the enjoyer) and Rati (*i.e.*, the object of Rasa), or as Kāma (the lover that attracts towards him the beloved) and Madana (the exciting cause of love in the lover).[1] In standard Vaiṣṇavism also Kṛṣṇa is known as Kāma or Kandarpa, as he attracts the mind of all creatures towards Him,—while Rādhā is Madana or the object that renders pleasure to the enjoyer. Sahaja is the emotion of the purest love flowing between Rasa and Rati or Kāma and Madana. For the realisation of this Sahaja-nature, therefore, a particular pair of man and woman should first of all realise their true self as Rasa and Rati or Kṛṣṇa and Rādhā,—and it is only when such a realisation is perfect that they become entitled to realise the Sahaja through their intense mutual love. This realisation of the true nature of man as Kṛṣṇa and that of woman as Rādhā is technically known as the principle of *āropa* or the attribution of divinity to man. Through continual psychological discipline man and woman

[1] *Cf.* *paraspar nāyak nāyikā ananga rati* ।
satasiddha bhāve hay brajete basati ॥
Rati-vilāsa-paddhati, MS. (C. U. No. 572), p. 12(A).

Again,— *ratir svarūp śrī-rādhikā sundarī* ।
kāmer citta ākarṣay rūper laharī ॥
Rāgamayi-kaṇā, MS. (C. U. No. 581), p. 8(B).

Again,— *jay jay sarvvādi bastu rasa-rāj kām* ।
jay jay sarvva-śreṣṭha rasa nitya dhām ॥
prākṛta aprākṛta ār mahā aprākṛte ।
bihār karicha tumi nij svecchā mate ॥
svayaṁ kām nitya vastu rasa ratimay ।
prākṛta aprākṛta ādi tumi mahāśray ॥
eka vastu puruṣ prakṛti rūp haiyā ।
vilāsaha bahu-rūp dhari dui kāyā ॥ etc.
Sahaja-upāsanā-tattva of Taruṇī-ramaṇ, B. S. P. P., B. S. 1335, No. 4.

must first of all completely forget their lower animal-selves and attribute Kṛṣṇahood to man and Rādhāhood to woman. Through this process of attribution there will gradually dawn the realisation of the true nature of the two as Kṛṣṇa and Rādhā. When man and woman can thus realise themselves as Kṛṣṇa and Rādhā in their true nature, the love that exists between them transcends the category of gross sensuality,—it becomes love divine, and the realisation of such an emotion of love is realisation of the Sahaja.

(B) The Theory of Āropa

The above, in a nut-shell, is the fundamental basis of the religious creed of the Vaiṣṇava Sahajiyās expressed in their lyrical poems and other prose and poetical works. The principle of Āropa is the most important in the process of Sahaja Sādhanā.[1] We have seen that the Sahajiyās have spoken of two aspects of man, *viz.*, the aspect of physical existence which is the Rūpa and the aspect of spiritual existence (as Kṛṣṇa or Rādhā as the case may be) which is the Svarūpa (*i.e.*, true spiritual self). This Svarūpa must be attributed to and realised in the Rūpa to attain any kind of spiritual gain.[2] But this Āropa of Svarūpa to Rūpa does not mean the negation of the Rūpa; it is rather the act of imbuing every atom of the Rūpa with the Svarūpa. The Sahajiyās are deadly against the principle of denying the value of life on earth and undervaluing our human love. The gross physical form with all its charm and beauty is as real as our spiritual existence, for it is this charm of physical beauty,—the maddening passion, which we call human love, that leads us gradually to a new region where we can find a glimpse of divine love. The spiritual existence

[1] *Cf. chāḍi jap tap sādhaha ārop*
ekatā kariyā mane |
Rāgātmika songs, ascribed to Caṇḍīdās, Mr. Bose's edition. Song No. 1.

[2] *Cf. svarūpe ārop yār rasik nāgar tār*
prāpti have madana-mohan |

* * * *

se deśer rajakinī hay raser adhikārī
rādhikā-svarūp tār prāṇ |
tumi-ta ramaṇer guru seha raser kalpa-taru
tār sane dās abhimān ||

Ibid., Song. No. 5.

of man in divine love does not mean the negation of human love,—it is this human love, beginning in the form of carnal desires and progressing gradually through a process of continual physical and psychological discipline towards an emotion of supreme bliss, boundless and unfathomable in extent and depth, that itself becomes the love divine—the highest spiritual gain. There is no categorical distinction in kind between human love and divine love;—it is human love, transformed by strict physical and psychological discipline, that becomes divine. Divine love is rather an emergence from the carnal desires of man as the full-blown lotus, with all its beauty and grandeur above the surface of water, is an emergence from the mud lying much below. Here there is a difference of outlook among the Sahajiyās and the standard Vaiṣṇavas of Bengal. Kṛṣṇadās Kavirāj has unambiguously declared in the *Caitanya-caritāmṛta* that *kāma* (love in its grosser aspect) and *prema* (divine love) are characteristically distinct in their nature like iron and gold, and while the keynote of *kāma* is the fulfilment of selfish desires, the keynote of *prema* is self-elimination and the fulfilment of the divine desires in and through our whole being. But the Sahajiyās, while agreeing to the latter part of the statement, do not agree to the former part of it. The same flow of emotion, they hold, that becomes *kāma* in association with the selfish desires, transforms itself into *prema* when dissociated from such desires through physical and psychological discipline. *Prema* is but the purified form of *kāma*, and as such the former has its origin in the latter.[1] There cannot be *prema* without *kāma*, and hence, *prema* cannot be attained through the absolute negation of *kāma*; it is to be attained rather through the transformation of *kāma*. The *prema* of the Sahajiyās is not the emotion of the most intense devotion of man towards God,—it is the most intense emotion of love existing between Kṛṣṇa and Rādhā residing as the Svarūpa in the Rūpa of every man

[1] *seita ujjal rahe rase ḍhākā aṅga* | *kām haite janmme prem nahe kāmasaṅga* || *lauhake karaye sonā lauha parasiyā* | *taiche kām haite prem dekha bicāriā* || *paraser gun śriṣṭa (śreṣṭa, sic) tāhe lauha hem* | *kāmer kaṭhin gun parasite prem* || *kāma-bastu candra-kānti paras pāthar* | *prema-bastu sukhamay nirmal bhāskar* || *agnir bhitare lauha thākaye jāvat* | *hemer sadṛsi bastu thākaye tāvat* || *agni-tej sukhāile puna lauha hay* | *ei mate kām prem jāniha niścay* ||
Ratna-sāra, MS. (C.U. No.1111), p. 32 (B).

and woman. It is from this point of view that Caṇḍīdās exclaimed,—"Harken men, my brothers, man is the truth above all truths,—there is nothing above that." In another song of the Sahajiyās we find,—Humanity is the essence of divinity,—and man becomes God in the strength of his love; man is the highest in the world, for it is only he who revels in supreme love.[1] The religion of the Vaiṣṇava Sahajiyās was thus a religion of humanity. The Sahajiyās have not gods or God other than man. Even Rādhā and Kṛṣṇa are never regarded as deities to be worshipped,—they represent principles to be realised in humanity. Humanity itself is thus viewed from a sublime perspective.

What is then the real significance of the Āropa of the Sahajiyās? It is nothing but viewing our whole being in all its physical, biological and psychological aspects from an ontological point of view. And when everything is thus viewed from the ontological perspective, human love acquires an ontological significance. This act of viewing all the gross realities of body and mind from the perspective of the eternal is what is meant by the mixing up of the Rūpa and the Svarūpa.[2] When such an understanding dawns on man there remains to him no difference between the

[1] *mānuṣ dever sār* |
yār prem jagate pracār ||
jagater śreṣṭha mānuṣ yāre bali |
prema-pīriti-rase mānuṣ kare keli ||
Sj. S. Song No. 27.

[2] *rūpete svarūpe dui eku kari*
miśāl kariyā thuve ||
Sj. S. Song No. 32.

Again,

svarūp rūpete ekatra kariyā
miśāl kariyā thuve |
sei se ratite ekānta karile
tave se śrī-matī pāve ||
Ibid., Song. No. 42.

ārope svarūp bhajite pārile
pāive śrī-matī rādhā ||
Ibid., Song No. 66.

Again,

e rati e rati ekatra kariyā
sekhāne se rati thuve |
rati rati duhe ekatra karile
sekhāne dekhite pāve ||
svarūpe ārop ei rasa-kūp
sakal sādhan sāra |
svarūp bujhiyā sādhanā karile
sādhak haite pāra || etc.
Ibid., Song No. 57.

Rūpa and the Svarūpa.[1] The Svarūpa remains in the Rūpa just like the scent of a flower permeating every atom of it. It is said in a song,—"Many speak of Svarūpa,—but it is not the gross reality (of our sense perception).........It is of the nature of the scent of the lotus. Who is the man capable of knowing it?........If one worships this Svarūpa, one will be able to discover the 'real man';—but without the Āropa one is bound to go to hell."[2] As the Svarūpa permeates the Rūpa, it is to be realised through the Rūpa.[3] It is said in the *Ratna-sāra* that one can attain the supra-natural land of Vraja, only by loving and worshipping the human form.[4] Man realises his ultimate nature as the pure emotion of love through his most beloved sweetheart.[5] Man cannot realise his love-nature without being in relation to his sweetheart, it is through the touch of the sweetheart that the lamp is lit within. It is said in a poem of Caṇḍīdās that man by himself can never realise his own grace and loveliness,—it is for this reason that there is a continual burning within; he ponders within, but himself does not know what his heart wants and what makes him so uneasy! The inward longing is for the beloved,—without whom there is the burning sensation in the heart that makes a man dead while living. This death in love is the most covetable death,—and he who knows the real nature of this death accords to it the most hearty reception, and he is the only man who

1 *āropiyā rūp haiyā svarūp kabhu nā bāsio bhinna* ||
Ibid., Song No. 26.

2 *svarūp svarūp aneke kay* I *jīva-lok kabhu svarūp nay* ||
* * * *
padma-gandha hay tāhār gati I *tāhāre cinite kār śakati* ||
* * * *
svarūp bhajile mānuṣ pāve I *ārop chāḍile narake yāve* ||
Ibid., Song No. 68.

3 *parakīā bhāve ati raser ulyās* I *braja bine ihār anyatra nahe bās* || *ihā jāni kara save kāyik bhajan* I *śrī-rūp āśraye kara rasa āsvādan* ||
Ratna-sāra, MS. (C.U. 1111), 18(B).

Again,
aiche kriyā siddhi pāi rūpāśrita dharma I
Vivartta-vilāsa of Akiñcana Dās, *Vaṅga-sāhitya-paricay*, Vol. II, p. 1651.

4 *mānuṣ bigraha bhaji braja prāpti have* I
MS. (C.U. 1111), p. 55(B).

5 *rādhā-kṛṣṇa-prāpti nahe anugata bine* I
Rādhā-rasa-kārikā, *Vaṅga-sāhitya-paricay*, Vol. II, p. 1668.

really lives through his death in love.[1] Through their terrestrial love man and woman proceed towards their divine love,[2]—through the love of body arises in man and woman pure love between their inner selves as Kṛṣṇa and Rādhā.[3] It is for this reason that it has been said in a song that the beloved is the pitcher to fetch water in from the lake of love. Again it has been said that as milk does not thicken without being boiled over the fire, so also the love of man does not become intense enough to be transformed into divine love without the woman of his heart, who serves as the oven to boil and thicken love.[4]

(C) The Stringency of Sahaja-Sādhanā

As love with Āropa leads one to Vṛndāvana, love of the Rūpa without the Āropa of the Svarūpa leads one nowhere but to hell.[5] The Sahaja-sādhaka must not be an ordinary man—the *sāmānya mānuṣ* who lives within the province of desires and instincts,—or the man of passions (*rager mānuṣ*).

āpan mādhurī dekhite nā pāi
sadāi antar jvale I
āpanā āpani karaye bhāvani
ki haila ki haila bale ||
mānuṣ abhāve mana mariciyā
tarāse āchāḍ khāy I
āchāḍ khāiyā kare chaṭ-phaṭ
jīyante mariyā yāy ||
tāhār maraṇ jāne kon jan
keman maraṇ sei I
ye jan jānaye sei se jiyaye
maraṇ bāṭiyā lei ||

Rāgātmika Pada, Mr. Bose's edition, Song No. 14.

[2] *prākṛta mānuṣ deha śarvva mūl hay* I *aprākṛta bastu sei dehete barttay* ||

Nameless MS. (C.U. No. 5961), p. 7.

Again,

sei deha rati jāyā kṛṣṇete barttay I *krame krame rati śola-ānā hay* ||

Ibid., p. 11.

[3] *Cf.* *raser kāraṇe rasikā rasik*
kāyādi ghaṭane ras I
rasik kāraṇ rasikā hoyata
yāhāte prema-bilās ||
sthūlata puruṣe kāma sūkṣma gati
sthūlata prakṛti rati I
duhuka ghaṭane se ras hoyata
eve tāhe nāhi gāti ||

Rāgātmika Pada, Mr. Bose's edition, Song No. 13.

[4] *agni-kuṇḍa bine nahe dugdha-āvarttan* || *prakṛtir saṅge yei agni-kuṇḍa āche* I *ataeva gosvāmīrā tāhā yajiyāche* ||

Vivartta-vilāsa of Akiñcan Dās, *Vaṅga-sāhitya-paricay*, p. 1649.

[5] *Cf.* *se rūp lāvaṇya rasa sañcār* I *mane āropita siddha bicār* ||
sekhāne ekhāne ekui rūp I *marame jānive raser kūp* ||
yadi man caḍe ārop chāḍi I *e ghor narake rahive paḍi* ||

Sj. S. Song No. 41.

He must rise above the level of ordinary animal existence and become the man 'unborn' (*ayoni mānuṣ*) and thence the *sahaja mānuṣ* or the 'man eternal' (*nityer mānuṣ*).[1] In the same way Sahaja cannot be attained through the *sāmānya rati* or the ordinary woman,—it is to be attained through the *biśeṣa rati* or the extraordinary woman who has herself become of the nature of Rādhā. In the culture of love the man of the physical body must be realised by the woman as the 'eternal man,' *i.e.*, the man as Rasa or Kṛṣṇa; and similarly the woman of the physical body must be realised by the man as the 'extraordinary woman,' *i.e.*, the woman as pure Rati or Rādhā. When the *sāmānya* (ordinary) man or woman thus becomes transformed into the *viśeṣa* (extraordinary), he or she becomes fit for undertaking the culture of supreme love.[2] In the *Ujjvala-nīlamaṇi* of Rūpa Gosvāmī we find description of three kinds of Rati, *viz.*, *Samarthā*, *Samañjasā* and *Sādhāraṇī*. *Samarthā Rati* is the woman who unites with the beloved with no selfish motive of self-satisfaction—the only desire in her is to give her beloved the highest satisfaction by complete self-surrender. Among the lady-loves of Kṛṣṇa Rādhā is the only example of *Samarthā Rati*. The *Samañjasā Rati*, however, wishes to have equal share of enjoyment with the lover,—Rukmiṇī and others are examples of this class. The *Sādhāraṇī Rati* or the most ordinary Rati is the woman who is inspired in love-union only with the desire

[1] *Cf.* *mānuṣ mānuṣ* *trividha prakār*
mānuṣ bāchiyā leha ।
sahaj mānuṣ *ayoni mānuṣ*
saṁskārā mānuṣa-deha ॥ etc.
Ibid, Song No. 22.

Cf. also—
rāger mānuṣ *nityer mānuṣ*
ekatra kariyā nive ।
paraśe paraś *ekānta kariyā*
rūpe miśāiyā thuve ॥
eise mānuṣe *āsak kariyā*
rati se bujhiyā nive ।
rūpa rati tāhe *ekānta kariyā*
hṛdete mānuṣ have ॥
Ibid, Song No. 47.

[2] See *Rāgātmika Padas*, edited by Mr. Bose, Song Nos. 2 and 3.
Cf. also—
sāmānyā prakṛti *pārkṛta se rati*
paraś nā kara tār ॥ etc.
Sj. S. Song No. 15.

of self-satisfaction,—and Kubjā represents a Rati of this class. The Sahajiyās accepted this classification of Ratis and according to them the *Samarthā Rati* is the only Rati suited for the culture of love.

The Sahajiyās lay stringent conditions regarding the practice of love. It has frequently been said that for the attainment of true love a man must become dead first of all, —dead in the sense that the animal in him must be eradicated, giving scope for full play to the divine in him; in plainer words, his body and mind must be placed above even the possibility of susceptibility to the lower animal instincts and must be imbued through and through with the radiant glow of his Svarūpa. This strictness has also been frequently emphasised by the condition that a man must do completely away with his nature as a man and transform his nature to that of a woman before he takes the vow of love. Here also the emphasis is really on the total transformation of the ordinary attitude of man towards a woman.

The stringency of Sahaja-sādhanā and the great danger sure to result from the slightest deviation have been repeatedly sung by the Sahajiyā poets in enigmatic statements. The process of Sādhanā has frequently been compared to the process of diving deep in the ocean without getting wet in the least,[1]—or to the process of making the frog dance before the serpent, or to wreathe the peaks of mount Sumeru with a piece of thread, or to bind the elephant with the help of the spider's net.[2]

This stringency in the Sahaja-sādhanā leads to the importance of strict physical and mental discipline without

[1] *Cf.* *kalaṅka sāgare sinān karivi*
elaiyā māthār keś ।
nīre nā bhijivi jal nā chuivi
sama duḥkha sukha kleś ॥
Song ascribed to Caṇḍīdās.

Again,
samudre paśiva nīre nā tītiva
nāhi duḥkha sukha kleś ॥
Song ascribed to Caṇḍīdās.

[2] *sāper mukhete bhekere nācāvi*
tave ta rasik-rāj ॥
ye jan catur sumeru śikhar
sūtāy gāthite pāre ।
mākasāra jāle mātaṅga bāndhile
e ras milāye tāre ॥
Song ascribed to Caṇḍīdās.

which it is simply disastrous to enter upon such a course of Sādhanā. It is for this reason that three stages have been marked in the course of Sādhanā, *viz.*, *Pravarta*, or the stage of the beginner; *Sādhaka*, *i.e.*, an advanced stage,—and *Siddha* or the perfect stage. Closely associated with these three stages of Sādhanā are the five *Āśrayas* (Refuges), *viz.*, *Nāma* (divine name), *Mantra*, *Bhāva* (divine emotion), *Prema* (*love*) and *Rasa* (bliss). *Nāma* and *Mantra* are associated with the stage of *Pravarta*, *Bhāva* with the second stage of *Sādhaka* and *Prema* and *Rasa* are associated with the third stage of *Siddha*.[1] It has been repeatedly enjoined that the Sādhanā in company of a woman can be entered upon only in the Sādhaka stage and real love can be realised only in the perfect stage and never before. In the question of perfection equal stress is laid on the perfection of body as on the perfection of mind; for, the Sahaja can never be realised without a perfect body.[2] Herein comes the question on Kāya-sādhana or the culture of body, which is very often stressed in the Sahajiyā texts on practical Sādhanā.[3] We have seen that this question of Kāya-sādhana plays an important part in the Sādhanā of the Buddhist Sahajiyās,[4]—and the esoteric yogic practice of the Vaiṣṇava Sahajiyās being substantially the same, the question of Kāya-sādhana is equally emphasised in the Vaiṣṇava school.

Again we have seen that in all schools of esoteric yogic practice the body has been held to be the abode of all truth. The same view is equally emphasised in the Vaiṣṇava Sahajiyā school. It is said in a song ascribed to Caṇḍīdās that truth resides in the body.[5] It is said in the *Ratnasāra* that if one can realise the truth of the body (*bhāṇḍa*)

[1] *Vide Āśraya-nirṇaya*, MS. (C.U. 566, 575).

[2] *apakva dehete e kām sādhile*
i-kul u-kul yāy ।
bāman haiyā bāhu pasāriyā
cā̃nd dharivāre cāy ॥
Song ascribed to Narottam, Sj. S.

[3] *Vide Dvīpakojjvala-grantha*, MS. (C.U. No. 564).

[4] *Vide supra*, pp. 92-93.

[5] *bastu āche deha bartlamāne* ॥
Cf. also—
rasa-bastu thāke sei rasik svarīre । *piriti murati hay prem nām dhare* ॥
Dvīpakojjvala-grantha, MS. (C.U. No. 564), p. 10(B).

one will be able to realise the truth of the universe (*brahmāṇḍa*). The realisation of the truth of the body leads to the realisation of the truth of the self, and the truth of the self is the truth of Vṛndāvana. All truth of Kṛṣṇa and Rādhā is to be known from the own body.[1] In the *Caitta*(*tra*, *sic*)-*rūpa-padma-mālā*[2] we find that the *Caitta-rūpa* is the Sahaja-rūpa and this *Caitta-rūpa* or Sahaja-rūpa resides in the different lotuses of the body.

The important point to be noticed in this connection is that as the psychological Sādhanā of love of the Vaiṣṇava-Sahajiyās gradually evolved from the psycho-physiological Yogic Sādhanā of the Tāntrics and the Buddhist Sahajiyās, the culture of love of the Vaiṣṇava Sahajiyās was always based on the psycho-physiological Yogic Sādhanā. It is for this reason that in Sahajiyā texts and songs we find hints on the Yogic Sādhanā associated with the culture of love. Any attempt at the culture of love without being conversant with the secrets of Yogic practices will lead not only to failure, but to extremely direful results. The ideal love of the Vaiṣṇava Sahajiyās can be realised only in a perfectly purified body and mind, whence all the principles of defilement are absolutely eradicated. This state has been said to be the state of *Viśuddha-sattva*. By the purification of body and mind there is first the subsidence of the elements of *Tamas* (inertia) and *Rajas* (energy) and there is the predominance of the element of *Sattva* (intellegence-stuff); but even above the state of *Sattva* is the state of *Śuddha-sattva* (or pure intelligence-stuff); and by further purification *Suddha-sattva* is transformed into *Viśuddha-sattva*. This state of *Viśuddha-sattva* is a transcendental state where there is neither the natural nor the supra-natural,—and pure love is possible only in such a state.[3]

[1] *bhāṇḍake jānile jāni brahmāṇḍer tattva* l *pūrvvete kahila jata bhāṇḍar māhārttya* || *bhāṇḍa bicārile jāni āpan māhārtta* l *āpanā jānile jāni bṛndāvana tattva* || . . . *bhāṇḍa haite jāni jata kṛṣṇara mahimā* l *bhāṇḍa haite jāni rādhā-prema tattva sīmā* ||
MS. (C.U. No. 1111), p. 54(B).

[2] MS. (C.U. No. 592).

[3] *sartta-raja-tamopare surddha-satva nām* l *tātpare bisurddhasartta premer ākṣān* || *prākṛtā-prākṛta tāke kahite nā pāri* l
Rati-vilāsa-paddhati, MS. (C.U. No. 572), p. 24(A).

For the realisation of the ultimate nature as pure love the lover and the beloved must be identical physically, mentally and spiritually; they must be of one body, one mind and one soul. It has been said,—"Do away with the idea of the two and be of one body, if you have the desire for real love; very difficult is this Sādhanā of love, says Dvija-Caṇḍīdās." "All the accessories of love—the separate existences of the lover and the beloved must merge in a unique flow of love,—then and then only this Sādhanā will be fulfilled."[1] About the nature of this love it has enigmatically been said,—"Love-making sits on love-making—and love (*bhāva*) is over that; above that love resides a higher love, and over that remains what may be said to be the highest consummation. In love resides the thrill of joy, and over that thrill the flow,—and there is the flow over the flow,—and that bliss who should know?"[2] "There is the flower over the fruit and the scent is over that,—and on that scent are these letters three (*i.e.*, *pī*—*ri*—*ti*=love; Skt. *prīti*), —great riddle is it to understand!" Again,—"There is the fruit over the flower,—and over that is the wave,—and there is wave above wave,—who does this secret know?"[3] It is extremely difficult to follow these and many such other enigmatic descriptions of love closely and literally,—and we doubt if every one of these statements can be explained rigorously. Such paradoxical statements were made only to emphasise the transcendental nature of the Sahaja love. It is said,—"There is water on earth and above that water rises thewave; love remains above that wave, does anybody know anything about it?"[4] It is about this transcendental love that Caṇḍīdās exclaimed,

[1] Songs ascribed to Caṇḍīdās (Sāhitya-pariṣat edition).

[2] *pīriti upare pīriti baisaye*
tāhār upare bhāv ।
bhāver upare bhāver basati
tāhār upare lābh ||
premer mājhāre pulaker sthān
pulaka upāre dhārā ।
dhārār upare dhārār basati
e sukh bujhaye kārā || *Ibid.*

[3] *Ibid.*

[4] *mṛttikā upare jaler basati*
tāhār upare ḍheu ।
tāhār upare pīriti basati
tāhā ki jānaye keu ||

—"The love of the washerwoman is like tested gold,—there is no tinge of sexuality in it."

Thus the Sādhanā of love of the Vaiṣṇava Sahajiyās is a transcendence from the finite to the infinite,—from the enjoyment of the external object to the realisation of the self which in its ultimate character is but of the nature of pure love. When real love dawns in the heart of the Sādhaka the beloved becomes to him a mere symbol for infinite love,—the whole universe with all its grandeur and mystery contracts in the body of the sweetheart,—not only that, she becomes a symbol for the supreme truth. In such a state of love did Caṇḍīdās, the great lover, exclaim to his sweetheart Rāmī, the wahserwoman:— "Hearest Rāmī, O thou washerwoman,—I knew thy feet to be a cool retreat and so I took shelter there. Thou art to me the revealer of the Vedas, thou art to me as the consort of the Saviour Lord Śiva,—thou art the iris of my eyes;—my worship of love towards thee is my morning, noon-tide and evening services,—thou art the necklace of my neck. The body of the washerwoman is of the nature of the eternal maid Rādhā (*kiśorī-svarūpa*),—there is no scent of sensuality in it,—the love of the wahserwoman is tested gold,—says Baḍu Caṇḍīdās."[1]

(iv) Sahaja-realisation of the Self and the Not-Self

We have said that the final aim of the Vaiṣṇava Sahajiyās through a culture of love is the realisation of the Sahaja nature not only of the self, but also of the external objects, or in other words, of the world as a whole. The realisation of the Sahaja-nature of the not-self, they contend, follows

[1] Caṇḍīdās says, in a similar song—"One confession of my heart—repeatedly am I making to thee,—hearest Rāmī, thou washerwoman,—I have taken shelter under thy feet only because I learnt them to be a cool retreat. The form of the washerwoman is of the nature of the eternal maid, Rādhā,—no scent of sensuality is there;—if I do not see thee my mind is upset,—and it is pacified just at the sight of thee. Thou art, O washerwoman, my consort,—thou art my mother—my father,—all the religious functions performed thrice a day are nothing but worshipping thee,—thou art Gāyatrī, the mother of the Vedas. Thou art the mother of all speech, the wife of Lord Śiva,—the necklace of my neck,—thou art heaven, earth and hell and every thing,—thou art the iris of my eyes. . . .I cannot forget the sweetness of thy beauty,—how am I to make thee my own? Thou art my Tantra, thou art all my Mantras, thou art all the bliss of my prayer. My days fly on in thinking who else in these three worlds may be so much my one,—and through the order of goddess Bāsuli exclaims Caṇḍīdās,—the feet of the washerwoman are the highest truth."

from the realisation of the Sahaja-nature of the self.[1] The Sahaja (of the nature of supreme love) that underlies the self as its ultimate reality, underlies also the not-self,—and both the self and the not-self are mere transformations of the same Sahaja, the plurality of objects with all their differences owes its origin only to the illusory nature of our sense-perceptions.[2] The duality of self and external objects is said to be due to a mere confusion of the senses, and it exists only as long as there is no attainment of self-knowledge. The senses are playing with the objects; but in reality the objects and the self are one and the same in their ultimate nature. When knowledge of the self dawns on man any differentiation like this and that becomes impossible,—and at that time, there is not the least cognition of duality and the whole universe is realised as of the nature of the self.[3] Thus it is contended that the realisation of the Sahaja-nature of the self as pure love automatically leads one also to the realisation of the ultimate nature of the external world.

In the Tantras we find that the world proceeds from the bliss which is the cessation of all duality and which is the nature of the ultimate reality. It has been said in the Upaniṣad,—"Bliss (*ānanda*) is to be known as Brahman, and from bliss proceeds all the objects, and through bliss they live and in bliss do they return and merge."[4] We find an echo of the same truth in the utterances of the Sahajiyās, who say that all the beings are born in Sahaja, they live in Sahaja and again return to Sahaja.[5] The Sahaja is the Rasa, the supreme emotion of love, the quintessence in every body.[6]

1 *āpan jānaye jei jagat jānay* l
jagater jan tār anta nāhi pāy ||
Ratna-sāra, MS. (C.U. No. 1111), p. 19(A).

2 *Cf. tumi śudhu bastu-jñāne dekhitecha bhram* l
natuvā sakali hay ātmār e kram ||
kothā kīṭ kothā iṭ kothāy bā kāṭh l
māyā-baśe tumi śudhu dekh e bibhrāṭ ||
Ibid.

3 *Ibid.*

4 *Taittirīyopaniṣat* (3.6).

5 *sahajete jiv janme sahaje bināśe* l
sahajete khāy piye sahajete bhāse ||
sahajete yāy jiv dekhaha bhāviyā l
sahaj sandhān keha nā pāya khujiyā ||
Ratna-sāra, MS. (C. U. No. 11111), p. 19(A).

6 *rasa bastu thāke sei rasik sarīre* l
pīriti murati hay prem nām dhare ||
Dvīpakojjvala, MS. (C.U. No. 564), p. 10(B).

It is the primordial emotion—it is *Kāma* and from *Kāma* proceeds everything.[1] There is sometimes the tendency of explaining the two aspects of Sahaja (*i.e.*, Rasa and Rati) under the imagery of the seed and the ovum and the cosmos as follwoing from their union, just as it is explained in the texts of the Tāntric and the Buddhist Sahajiyā schools.[2] Both the self and the not-self being thus the product of Sahaja are homogeneous in their ultimate nature and it is, therefore, that the realisation of the nature of the self through the culture of love leads also to the realisation of the ultimate nature of the not-self.

1 *puruṣ prakṛti kāmei utpatti*
kāmete savār janma 1
paśu pakṣī sav kāmete udbhav
kāmete savār karma ||

* * * *

kām upāsanā kām se sādhanā
kām keli sav tantra 1
kāmer mādhurī śrī-rūpa-mañjari
kām hari-nām mantra ||

Song ascribed to Narottam, Sj. S. Song No. 75.

2 *Cf.* *sthāvar jaṅgam ādi jata deha hay* 1
rati-kām sarva-dehe bilās karay ||

* * * *

sei kām raja-bīj rasa-rati sattā 1
sei sarva rasamay sarvamay karttā ||
Sahaja-upāsanā-tattva of Taruṇī-ramaṇ, B.S.P.P. 1335, No. 4.

Chapter VI

A NON-SECTARIAN APPROACH TO THE DOCTRINES OF THE SAHAJIYĀS

(i) *The Purely Psychological Approach Apart From The Theological*

Apart from the theological speculations advanced by the Vaiṣṇava Sahajiyās in connection with their Sādhanā of love, there can be another approach to their Sādhanā from a purely psychological point of view. The Vaiṣṇava Sahajiyās have always mixed up this psychological principle with the theological spculations of Bengal Vaiṣṇavism, and the ideal of Parakīyā love in the human sphere has generally been associated with an ontological significance. But apart from the ontological significance attached to the ideal of Parakīyā love let us see if some religious significance can pertain to such a kind of love even from the purely psychological point of view. From this psychological point of view it may be said that human love, when dissociated completely from selfish carnal desires, not by a process of violent suppression, but by a slow and gradual process of strict physical and psychological discipline, has the capacity, in its boundless extent and deep intensity, of producing a transcendental state of mind, which is of the same kind as the state of mind produced through the highest state of divine love, or communion with God. We have said before that the arrest of the states and processes of the mind plays the most important part in almost all the religious systems of India. Intense human love, or even sex-emotion, has the capacity of producing a supreme state of arrest. In a unique flow of emotion, uninterrupted by subjective or objective notions there dawns an infinite oneness in the mind, which is recognised to be the highest spiritual experience. This is the state of Samarasa after which all the esoteric schools of yoga aspired. The Tāntrics of Hindu as well as of Buddhist schools would often recommend the attainment of such a state of mind through the attainment of intense bliss by a strictly yogic regulation of the sex-act, while the Vaiṣṇava Sahajiyās added the psychological element of love to it. The final aim, however, in all such cases was the attainment of an infinitely blissful state of arrest either purely through a psycho-physiological process of yoga or through the intense emotion of love.

The fundamental principle of the esoteric schools, mentioned above, is that man can never get rid of his sex-propensities even by a life-long struggle of rigorous suppression,—nay, as we have seen, it is in the form of Samarasa or Mahāsukha or Mahābhāva the ultimate nature of our whole being—the ultimate reality from which the world evolves. In the grossest sexual pleasure we have the lowest kind of realisation of the same kind of bliss which follows the realisation of the ultimate reality. It is, therefore, foolish to try to do absolutely away with this fundamental nature of man; the best thing, on the other hand, will be to eliminate the element of grossness from it through physical and psychological discipline.

This theory of the esoteric schools involving the element of sex in religion, may be made subject to severe criticism from the Freudian point of view of modern psycho-analysis,—and there is much cope for such criticism particularly in the field of Vaiṣṇava Sahajiyā cult with all its theory of love, human and divine. But though a Freudian explanation of the whole thing may not be absolutely inadmissible in such religious practices, one fundamental point, which we should never lose sight of even from the empirical point of view, is that though the lotus above the surface of water may have its origin in the mud deep below, mud and the lotus cannot surely be placed in the same scale in our general scheme of valuation.

The main truth of these cults, as we have pointed out, is the possibility of the attainment of an intensely blissful state of arrest, which has been spoken of in these cults as the state of liberation or the state of Brahman-realisation or the state of divine love. This idea that it may be possible to attain liberation through the most intense emotion, or that the state of mind under the most intense emotion of any kind is of the nature of bliss produced by self-realisation, or Brahma-realisation, is not new in the history of Indian religious thought. In the *Bṛhad-āraṇyaka Upaniṣad*, realisation of self has been compared to the transcendental realisation of bliss arising through the deep embrace of a loving woman. Thus it is said,—"As, when deeply embraced by the dear woman, one knows neither anything external nor anything internal, —so also a man deeply embraced by the self (*ātman*) through perfect knowledge knows neither anything external nor anything internal."[1] In the *Bhāgavata-purāṇa* we find that the cowherd girls of Vṛndāvana did attain salvation through their passion towards their beloved Śrīkṛṣṇa, with whom they combined even knowing that it was *jāra* (prosmicuity).[2] It is also cited in this connection that Śiśupāla, king of Cedī, attained liberation through his intense emotion of hatred to Śrīkṛṣṇa.[3] In the *Padma-purāṇa* we find that in ancient times all the great sages of the Daṇḍakāraṇya saw the Lord in the form of Rāma and desired to enjoy Him; all of them afterwards were born in female forms in the land of Gokula and there they enjoyed the Lord with their passions and were

[1] *tadyathā priyayā striyā sampariṣvakto na bāhyaṁ kiñcana veda nā'ntaram evam evā'yaṁ puruṣaḥ prājñena ātmanā sampariṣvakto na bāhyaṁ kiñcana veda nā'ntaram.*
Bṛhadāraṇyako-paniṣat, 4-3-21.

[2] *Bhāgavata-purāṇa*, (10, 29. 11) Vaṅgavāsī edition. This fact described in the *Bhāgavata* has been fully utilised by the Vaiṣṇava Sahajiyās in the following song ascribed to Narahari—

nander nandan karaye bhajan
upapati bhāv layā 1
gopi-anugata braja-jana-rīta
mane āropita hayā ||
ati biparīt braja--jana-rīt
sahaj mānuṣ seha 1
-puruṣ prakṛti haiyā kemane
kāhāre karive leha ||
sākṣāte bhajan kaila gopī-gaṇ
e deśa se deśe dur 1
kothā bṛndāvan kothā braja-jan
kothā prema-rasa-pur || etc. Sj. S. Song, No. 69.

[3] Thus it is said,—"I have already described to you how the king of Cedī (*i.e.*, Śiśupāla) attained salvation even through his hatred of Kṛṣṇa; what wonder then about the (salvation of) girls who were so dear to the Lord? (*i.e.*, what wonder if the cowherd girls have attained salvation through their intense love towards the Lord?) .... By continually applying the emotions of passion (*kāma*), anger, fear, affection unity and friendship to the Lord, people are attaining perfect oneness with the Lord."

uktaṁ purastād etat te caidyaḥ siddhiṁ yathā gataḥ 1
dviṣann api hṛṣikeśaṁ kimetā'dhokṣaja-priyāḥ ||
kāmaṁ krodhaṁ bhayaṁ sneham aikyaṁ sauhṛdam eva ca 1
nityaṁ harau vidadhato yānti tanmayatāṁ hi te ||
Bhāgavata-purāṇa, 10-29-13, 15.

thereby liberated from the ocean of existence. Their liberation was just like the liberation of the demons who approached the Lord with anger, were killed in battle and afterwards attained liberation. Sex-passion and anger are generally the cause of man's downfall in the world, but being united with the Lord with strong emotion the cowherd ladies were all liberated. Those, who worship the Lord through passion, fear or even animosity, will attain Vaikuṇṭha (the land of the Lord),—not to speak of those who worship the Lord through pure devotion.[1]

In their discussion on the nature of aesthetic pleasure some Indian rhetoricians have described it as equal to the bliss of Brahma-realisation. Through the intensity and purity of aesthetic emotion the limitations of mundane life are transcended and in the profound tranquillity of mind the artist enjoys a transcendental bliss equal to the bliss of Brahma-realisation. Viśvanātha Kavirāja says in describing the nature of Rasa that through the intensity of the transcendent emotional appeal of litarature our mind becomes out of touch with the objective world, and due to the separation of mind from the objective world there is the subsidence of the elements of *Rajas* (energy-stuff) and *Tamas* (mass-stuff) and there is the emergence of *Sattva* (intelligence-stuff); as a result of this emergence of the *Sattva* element there is the spontaneous rise in mind of a unique bliss of the nature of pure consciousness untouched by the notion of any other knowable,—and as such it is of the nature of Brahma-realisation.[2] The quintessence of this Rasa is an emotion of supramundane sublimity and nicety, which removes all the limitations of our mind and expands it to a limitless extent. It is only by the meritorious few that such Rasa is realised in its entirety and in its changeless unique character.

This view that it may be possible to attain a state of arrest through the intensity of any kind of emotion or sensation has been emphasised by the Śaiva mystics of Kāśmira also. It has been said by Abhinava Gupta in his

[1] *Padma-purāṇa, Uttara-khaṇḍa*, verses 64-68.
[2] *sattvo-drekād akhaṇḍa-sva-prakāśā-nanda-cinmayaḥ* I
vedyā-ntara-sparśa-śūnyo brahmā-svāda-sahodaraḥ ||

Sāhitya-darpaṇa, Ch. III.

Tantrā-loka that when our mind ceases to form all kinds of false thought-constructions (*vikalpa*), we realise our motionless true self as Śiva; even if a beast attains such a state of mental equilibrium it attains the state of Śiva.[1] The state of homogeneity that is produced in the mind through the absorbing interest of pleasureable sensation of sight, sound and touch leads one to the realisation of the ultimate motionless nature of the self,—and the bliss that is derived from such experience is but a playful manifestation of the blissful nature of the ultimate Being.[2] We find a very clear exposition of this view in the *Spanda-kārikā* and the *Vijñāna-bhairava*. The *Spanda-pradīpikā* (*Spanda-kārikā*) says that for the realisation of the self as the Śiva one has to make his mind absolutely motionless,—the absolutely motionless state of mind is liberation.[3] When the self passes on from its active state of the doer and the knower to its absolutely motionless inactive state, it is no more disturbed by the pernicious memory (*ku-smṛti*) of its past active states; but by passing into the inactive motionless state the self does not lose its nature as the ultimate subject. It is said that two states of the self can be distinguished, *viz.*, the state of pure agency (*kartṛtva*) and the state of being the effect (*kāryatva*). Of the two states the state of being the effect is capable of being destroyed, but the agent is indestructible. This is to say that all outward efforts or activities, which are but the manifestation of the disturbed agent may vanish; but with the vanishing of the active efforts the self as the supreme agent does not die out.[4] The implication is that the outward efforts or activities may die out, but the deep internal emotional states produced thereby do not die out with them. The intense emotional state of our mind which is not limited by any

[1] *Tantrā-loka*, (1.211, 216).

[2] *tata eva samasto'yaṁ ānanda-rasa-vibhramaḥ* |
tathā hi madhure gīte sparśe vā candanādike ||
mādhyastha-vigame yāsau hṛdaye spandamānatā |
ānanda-śaktiḥ saivoktā yataḥ sahṛdayo janaḥ || *Ibid* (3.209-10).

[3] *yadā kṣobhaḥ pralīyeta tadā syāt paramaṁ padam* |
Spanda-kārikā, Ch. I, Verse No. 9, Vizianagram Sanskrit Series.

[4] *avasthāyugalaṁ cātra kārya-kartṛtva-śabditam* |
kāryatā kṣayiṇī tatra kartṛtvaṁ punar akṣayam ||
kāryo-nmukhaḥ prayatno yaḥ kevalaṁ so'tra lupyate |
tasmiṁ lupte vilupto'smī'ty abudhaḥ pratipadyate ||
Ibid., Verses 14, 15,

notion of space, time and dimension approximates the nature of the indestructible true self which is the omniscient pure intelligence.[1] When even the ordinary emotions of our daily life attain a high degree of intensity, our mind attains a state of equilibrium which leads to the realisation of our self as 'the motionless one'. It is said that when a man is very angry or highly pleased, or is in a state of extreme bewilderment, even when he runs fast away (through some emotion of fear or joy), he attains a state which may be said to be the *spanda*, or the ultimate potential nature of the self.[2] When in such a state the sun and the moon go down in the great void, the man in the walking state will feel himself as if fallen into profound, dreamless sleep,—he shall have no other cognition or emotion regarding his body or the world outside,—that is the unveiled state of the self.[3] When the spatio-temporal character of the knower and the knowable is gone the self remains as a pure flow of consciousness, a

[1] *Cf.* *na tu yo'ntarmukho bhāvaḥ sarvajñatva-guṇā-spadam* |
tasya lopaḥ kadācit syād anyasyā'nupalambhanāt ||
Ibid. Verse 16.

[2] *ati-kruddhaḥ prahṛṣṭo vā kiṁ karomī'ti vā mṛśan* |
dhāvan vā yat padaṁ gacchet tatra spandaḥ pratiṣṭhitaḥ ||
Ibid., Ch. II., Verse 6.

It is said that even when a man very eagerly waits for the command of any other person with the firm resolution that whatever will be ordered by the latter must be carried out, he will, through the intensity of his eagerness and the firmness of his resolution, attain a state of equilibrium; through such a condition of mind his inhaling and exhaling breath (the sun and the moon, *i.e.*, *prāṇa* and *apāna*) will enter the middle nerve Suṣumnā, which is the passage for the transcendental region, and all the motion of the sun and the moon (*i.e.* inhalling and exhaling) will stop there.

yām avasthāṁ samālambya yad ayaṁ mama vakṣyati |
tad avaśyaṁ kariṣye'ham iti saṁkalpya tiṣṭhati ||
tāṁ āśrityorddhva-mārgeṇa candra-sūryāvubhāvapi |
sauṣumne'dhvany astamito hitvā brahmāṇḍa-gocaram ||
Ibid., Ch. II, Verses 7, 8.

It is explained in the commentary that whenever, due to whatever reason it may be, one is under the compulsion of carrying out the order of any other man, due to the intensity of concentration of the former just to receive the order of the latter, all the mental states of the former will die out, and because of the dying out of all the mental states his consciousness must attain the ultimate state of perfect tranquillity, and through the practice of such acts of endurance he realises the ultimate truth .

idaṁ tu tātparyam, kenacit kāraṇena avaśya-karaṇīya-vacasā prabhaviṣṇunā kārayitavya-vastu-vivakṣayā ākṣiptasya puṁsaḥ tad-vacana-śuśrūṣāmātra-niviḍā-vadhānatvāt samasta-vṛtti-pratyastamaye sati, saṁvit turīyāṁ daśām avaśyamevāviśati, tat-pratyavamarśā-bhyāsāt paratattvo-palabdhiḥ

Ibid., Comm. by Rāmakaṇṭha, pp, 77-78

[3] *tadā tasmin mahāvyomni pralīna-śaśi-bhāskare* |
sauṣupta-padavan mūḍhaḥ prabuddhaḥ syād anāvṛtaḥ ||
Ch. II, Verse No. 9.

stream of colourless emotion. This flow of pure emotion, which is not determined by any quality whatsover, is the pure nature of the self.

In the *Vijñāna-bhairava* we find corroboration of what is stated in the *Spanda-pradīpikā*. There it is said that to attain the state of Bhairava, or rather to realise the ultimate nature of the self, one has to realise the ultimate nature of the self and of objects as pure consciousness bereft of all waves of mentation. But how to attain such a state of Bhairava? The *Vijñāna-bhairava* enjoins that such a state may be attained through a state of arrest produced by any intense emotion or even sensation. Just as after the ringing of a bell the main sound dies out leaving behind a continuous unqualified lingering vibration, so also after the mind is deeply disturbed by a strong emotion (like the sex-emotion), there follows a flow of unqualified lingering emotion, and that oneness of emotion becomes to the Sādhaka as of the same nature as the unqualified bliss resulting from the realisation of the self.[1] Through kissing and embracing of woman there follows an over-flood of joy which proceeds from within and amounts to the bliss of self-realisation. If we are very glad at any time on any account,—or if we meet any of our nearest and dearest ones after a long separation, there is an excess of emotion, through the meditation on which it is possible to merge oneself in the 'thatness.'[2] If we take meal to our heart's content after we are very hungry and if we take some palatable drink after we are very thirsty, there follows a contented joy of relish through which also we may attain Māhāsukha (great bliss). Through the qualityless intense joy that may follow from attending to music or to any such other object the yogin may merge himself in it and realise 'thatness' thereby. The mind should be kept fast wherever there is the satisfaction of mind,—for, thereby will the ultimate nature of the self as supreme bliss be reveal-

1 *śakti-saṅgama-saṁkṣubdha-śaktyā-veśā-vasānikam* |
yat-sukhaṁ brahma-tattvasya tat-sukhaṁ svākyam ucyate ||
Vijñāna-bhairava, Sl. 69. See also the commentary on the verse by Kṣemarāja.

2 *ānande mahati prāpte dṛṣṭe vā bāndhave cirāt* |
ānandam udgataṁ dhyātvā tallayas tan-manā bhavet ||
Ibid., Verse 71.

ed to us.[1] Through the sudden arrest or careful control of any of the senses the particular sense enters into the non-dual vacuity and the soul shines there in its ultimate nature.[2] Whenever the mind is disturbed either through knowledge or through ignorance, mind attains the ultimate state as an after-effect of this disturbance. If a man stands by the side of a great hole like a well, etc., and then looks upwards, his mind will be bereft of all thought-constructions and the states of mind will be suspended. In our deep emotions of anger, fear, sorrow,—or in the emotion produced in a lonely cave, or in the emotion resulting from flying away from the battle field, or in the emotion of strong curiosity or of hunger there is a state which may be said to be identical with the state of the Brahman.[3]

(ii) *Criticism from The Yoga Point of View*

From the above it will be clear that the view that it may be possible to attain some religious experience through an intense emotion or even through some strong sensation is not very uncommon in the field of Indian religious thought. But as this view is closely associated with the question of a state of arrest, which is so much emphasised in the Pātañjala system of yoga, it will not be unfair to make some comment on it from the yoga point of view.

The exponents of yoga have admitted the fact that it may be possible to attain a state of arrest even through

[1] *yatra yatra manas-tuṣṭir manas tatraiva dhārayet* |
tatra tatra parā-nanda-svarūpaṁ saṁpravartate ||
Ibid, Verse 74.

[2] *yasya kasye 'ndriyasyā'pi vyāghātāc ca nirodhataḥ* |
praviṣṭasyā'dvaye śūnye tatrai 'vā'tmā prakāśate || *Ibid.*, Verse 89.

The author goes so far as to say that if any one first pinches a particular limb with a pointed needle and then concentrates his mind on the place of painful sensation he will attain a stainless state of Bhairava. (*Ibid.*, Verse 93.) When our mind is deeply absorbed in any object of sex-passion, anger, greed, infatuation, pride and jealousy, through the deep absorption in the emotion the distinctive features of the objects vanish away and what remains is the ultimate reality. (*Ibid.*, Verse 101).

[3] *Ibid.*, Verse 118.

The reading of the verse in the edition we are using is as follows:—
kṣutādyante bhaye śoke gahvare vā raṇāddrute |
kutūhale kṣudhādyante brahma-sattvāmayī daśā ||

But the reading of the verse as quoted in the commentary on the *Spanda-sūtras* by Utpalācāryya is as follows:—
krodhādyante bhaye śoke gahvare vāraṇe raṇe |
kutūhale kṣudhādyante brahma-sattā-samīpagā ||
Vide., p. 51.

some strong sensation or emotion; but that kind of arrest of mind is very transitory and as such falls far short of the final state of Samādhi. Samādhi of yoga proper does not mean a temporary arrest of mind,—it means a permanent state of arrest which removes all our afflictions and which eradicates all mental complexes and root-instincts that serve as the seed of the future recurrence of life and suffering.

In the yoga scheme of psychology there have been recognised five planes of mind, which are technically known as the five *citta-bhūmis*. These are, (1) *kṣipta*, (2) *mūḍha*, (3) *vikṣipta*, (4) *ekāgra* and (5) *niruddha*. The *kṣipta* state is the ordinary unsteady state of mind which is always changing from one object to another. The second state is the state in which mind, under the sway of some strong sensation or emotion, lies infatuated, as it were. In this state there is the excess of the *tamas* (*i.e.*, the gross material stuff) and under the sway of the *tamas* mind falls asleep, or, swooning, as it were. The third state is the state of *vikṣipta*, which is distinguished from the *kṣipta* state by the possibility therein of temporary arrest of the mental states. It is the momentary steadiness that the mind may have amidst its unsteady changes. The other two states are *ekāgra* (one-pointed) and *niruddha* (perfectly arrested). Of these two *ekāgra* state has been explained by Vācaspati in his commentary as *eka-tāna*, which literally means 'one-tuned,' *i.e.*, the state where all the mental states attain an oneness in deep concentration on some particular object of meditation. This *ekāgra* state leads to the next state which is the state of final arrest (*niruddha*).

Now of the five planes (*bhūmi*) of the mind only the last two are recognised as the planes of yoga proper. Temporary arrest may be possible in the *mūḍha* and *vikṣipta* planes also,—but they cannot be recognised as states of yoga as there is the possibility of their relapse to ordinary active states at any moment. The important thing in yoga proper is not therefore somehow to attain a state of arrest, but to well-prepare the planes of mind for Samādhi. If the plane be well-prepared even active states cannot disturb the mind.

If we examine the states of Samādhi described particularly by the Kaśmīra-school of Śaivism, we shall be tempted to say that many of these states can be classed as the *mūḍha* state of mind and only a few of them fall within the state of *ekāgra*. There is no denial of the fact that when we are deeply absorbed in any intense emotion, we transcend our ordinary physical, biological and psychological existence,—and even it may be admitted that such states of transcendental emotion approximate in nature deep religious experience, but the question remains, how far it will be correct to accept all such states to be identical with our supreme religious experience. In states of great hunger, anger, jealousy, fear, curiosity, sex-passions, etc., there may be a temporary sleep of the ordinary mental states and processes,—but they being outside the plane of yoga may at any time relapse into activity, and for this reason such states should never be confused with the final state of Samādhi.

To judge the state of Samarasa of the Tāntriks or of Mahā-sukha of the Buddhist Sahajiyās, or the state of supreme love of the Vaiṣṇava Sahajiyās, we should first of all examine the *citta-bhūmi* in which such a realisation is possible. If the realisation be in any of the first three planes of the *citta*, *i.e.*, if it be a mere state of sleep of the senses, or just like a state of swoon of a temporary nature then it cannot be recognised as a state of yoga proper. Everything, therefore, depends on the plane of *citta*. The Tāntriks and the Sahajiyās were conscious of this truth and they laid sufficient stress on it. All the stringent conditions laid by the Tāntriks and the Sahajiyās for the esoteric practice may be viewed from the yoga point of view as conditions for a proper plane of *citta* where the absorption of the psychical processes may amount to a state of Samādhi. Whenever the esoteric practice is resorted to in a lower plane the result produced must be dangerous; it is for this reason that the Sahajiyās repeatedly declared that a real Sahajiyā Sādhaka is rarely found even among crores (*koṭike goṭik hay*).

CHAPTER VII

THE BĀULS OF BENGAL

(i) *General Nature of the Bāul Sect*

FAR from the empty noise and busy bustle of urban life, flourished in the villages of Bengal an order of singers, still extant,—an institution of immense literary and religious interest; for, the songs of these bards are as much noted for their naiveté and sponteneity of expression as for the spiritual intensity of their content. The 'unpremeditated art' of their 'first fine careless raptures' lifts us to a level of experience where the æsthetic and the religious work together for a unique spiritual transport. Indeed we can say about these songs what Keats says about the songs of the Nightingales of heaven,—

> ... ... divine melodious truth
> Philosophic numbers smooth.

When a number of these Bāul songs were collected by revered Kṣitimohan Sen, a close associate of the poet Rabindranath Tagore in Santineketan, and were made public[1] they presented a pleasant surprise to the enlightened public both for the lofty and subtle sentiments they embodied and the spontaneity and nicety of expression. We are quoting below some lines from these songs.

> 'O thou cruel and hasty enthusiast, wouldst thou make a fry of the buds of your mind by applying heat of fire? Wouldst thou make flower bloom and scatter fragrance all round without giving it the time? Lo, here is my supreme preceptor—my Lord, He makes the bud unfold itself through ages—He has no haste in this!'[2]

There must not be unusual haste in spiritual life for having all the buds of mind unfolded all at once. Mild heat

[1] The songs were first published in an anthology of old and modern Bengali songs, entitled *Baṅgavāṇī*, edited by Lalitmohan Chatterjee and Charu Chandra Banerjee.

[2] *niṭhur garaji, tui ki mānas-mukul bhājbi āgune etc.* The song was composed by Madan. *Vide*, Kṣitimohan Sen, *Bāṁlār Bāul*, *Calcutta*, 1954, p. 63.

from the sun and the moon—from the unknown stars above —helps the bud in expressing itself in exquisite colour and scent; but it takes some scheduled time; if in our hectic effort to shorten the time to the minimum we apply heat of fire to it, it will be fried—it will never bloom. The artist behind the whole cosmic process teaches us the same lesson; the cosmic process is a process in millions and billions of ages—it is a process for unfolding whatever colour and scent lie dorment in it—for unfolding the true meaning of the universe; but the Supreme One makes the flower of the Universe bloom slowly and gradually in time. When the original creator shows no impatience—why should we?

Biśā Bhuṁimālī[1] says in a song, 'The lotus of my heart is going on blooming and blooming for ages; in it are bound together both Thou and I—what help for it now!'[2] The implication is that the life-process of man binds both God and man in a bond of creative comradeship, for as the poet Tagore puts it, 'the creation in me is Yours as well as mine'; so both has a common interest in the unfolding of this lotus, and both become bound together in the common interest.

Iśān Yugi, the preceptor of Madan, sings in one of his songs,—'Hail be to me to me—a flute which receives the blow from Thy own mouth. No grief for me—no grumble from me if I become spent up after this blowing by Thee even for once.'[3] The flute has its wounds in life which make holes; but all the wounds are compensated when the Supreme One blows His own breath through the holes of life's wounds.

In a song (probably by Kṛṣṇakānta Pāṭhak[4]) we find the lotus waiting in the morning for the beloved—the sun. All the other flowers have bloomed, but the lotus has been waiting and waiting, for it says, 'I would not open my eyes if I cannot see him (my beloved, the sun) just at my first glance; so I entreat ye all (all the other flowers), ye whisper into my ears through all your scent,—he has come—he has come in the sky in the east.' All the hidden wealth and

[1] He hails from East Bengal. *Vide*, Kṣitimohan Sen, *Bāṁlār Bāul*, Calcutta, 1954, p. 63.

[2] *hṛday kamal calteche phuṭe*, etc.

[3] *dhanya āmi—bāṁśite tor āpan mukher phuṁk* etc.

[4] *Vide*, Kṣitimohan Sen, *Loc. cit.* The song is, *āmi melum nā nayan etc.*

grandeur of the spiritual aspirant have meaning with reference only to the Supreme Beloved; so the progreess of whole life should be directed to the glancing of the Beloved and the Beloved only.

In speaking of the deep spiritual experience one Bāul[1] sings,—"My eyes close up in the dimness of my sweet realisation. The lotus has drawn back all its petals in the shore of vast dimness."[2] The profound mystic experience is the vast dimness in which merges the individual self with all the mental states and processes.

These songs, the Bāul themselves have said, have to be approached not with the arogance of philosophic erudition, nor with the customary way of scholarly scansion, but with a softness of feeling and a meekness of spirit. The traditional philosophers and academicians have been snubbed by the Bāuls in the characteristic piquant way. It has been said in a song, 'Who is this man, a dealer and expert in gold, that has entered the flower-garden? He rubs his touchstone against the (petals of the) lotus, Oh the fun, Oh the fun!'[3] Applying an academic way of scanning to songs bearing religious experience is just like applying the touchstone to the petals of the lotus with a view to evaluating the lotus.

But academicians as we are, if we are anything at all, we cannot avoid the academic way of approach. Pandit Kṣitimohan Sen was no doubt a pioneer in collecting the Bāul songs and in popularising them among the élite of our country; but only a small number of the songs from among the songs he has collected were published. The literature was therefore very scanty. The next notable attempt was made by Maulavi Muhmmad Mansur Uddin, M.A., who published[4] about hundred Bāul songs under the caption *Hārāmaṇi* (the lost jewel). The number of songs increased considerably in the enlarged edition of the book published by the University of Calcutta. Dr. Upendranath Bhattacharyya, M.A., D.Phil, who had conducted extensive

[1] Padma-locan of Midnapore. *Vide*, Kṣitimohan Sen, *Loc. cit.*

[2] *āmār ḍublo nayan raser timire* etc.

[3] *phuler bane ke ḍhukeche re sonār jahari*
nikṣe ghaṣaye kamal ā mari ā mari || Kṣitimohan Sen, *Bāmlār Bāul*, p. 50.

[4] With a foreward by Rabindranath Tagore.

field work in this direction has been able to collect a large number of Bāul songs and he has published more than five hundred songs in his commendable work *Bāṁlār Bāul O Bāul Gān* (the Bāuls and Bāul songs of Bengal) published in 1957. The next note-worthy publication is from the University of Calcutta which, contains about four hundred songs of Lalan Fakir, the most reputed of the Bāul composers.[1] Two hundred and ninety-seven songs of Lalan Fakir have also been published by M. Mansur Uddin, M.A., in the Bengali journal *Sāhitya Patrikā* from Dacca (1958). We may incidentally refer also to the publication of two hundred forty songs of Pāglā Kānāi by Dr. P. M. Islam of the Rajshai University.[2] Pāglā Kānāi was not known particularly as a Bāul poet, but if we compare the songs composed by Pāglā Kānāi with those composed by the well known Bāul singer Lalan Fakir we shall find no characteristic difference except that the songs of Lalan Fakir include a few songs on an esoteric sexo-yogic practice.

Judging from the songs hitherto available to us, it is extremely difficult to ascertain who the Bāul poets exactly were. We, for the past few decades, have been influenced in this matter by the ideas propagated by the poet Tagore in his poems and writings, and also by the writings and speeches of his close associate, Pandit Kṣitimohan Sen; for them Bāul represents more a spirit of unconventional approach to divinity through unassumed love and piety than any precise religious cult. As a matter of fact, these unlettered village-singers, known as the Bāuls, belong to the lower ranks of both the Muslim and the Hindu communities of Bengal and they are composed partly of householders and mainly of mendicants. The Bāuls belonging to the Hindu community are generally Vaiṣṇavite in their faith and those belonging to the Muslim community are generally Sūfī-istic and in both the schools the emphasis is on the mystic conception of divine love. The word *bāul*[3]

[1] *Vide*, *Lālan-gītikā* edited jointly by Dr. Matilal Das, M.A., Ph.D., and Sri Pijus Kanti Mahapatra, M.A., Calcutta University, 1959.

[2] *Vide*, Dr. M. Islam, *Kavi Pāglā Kānāi*, Dacca, 1959.

[3] We find the use of the world *bāul* in the *Caitanya-bhāgavata* of Vṛndāvana-dās as also in the *Caitanya-caritāmṛta* of Kṛṣṇa-dās Kavirāj. *Cf.* the well-known enigmatic message that was sent by Advaitācarya to Caitanya (*Caitanya-caritāmṛta*, *Antya-līlā*, Ch. xix).

with its Hindi variant *bāur* may be variously derived; it may be derived from the Sanskrit word *vātula* (affected by wind-disease, *i.e.*, mad, crazy), or from *vyākula* (impatiently eager);[1] both these derivations are consistent with the modern sense of the word, which denotes inspired people with an ecstatic eagerness for a spiritual life where one can realise one's union with the eternal Beloved—the 'Man of the heart'. The name Bāu las also its cognate form Āul can very well be associated also with the Arabic word *awliya* (plural of *wali*, a word originally meaning "near," which is used for 'friend,' or 'devotee'), that refers to a class of perfect men.[2] With the Bengali word *bāul* we may also compare the Sūfī word *Diwānā* which means mad, *i.e.*, free from all social responsibilites.

Religious people with different modes of Sādhanā are included within the Bāul sect; in spite of the differences in modes of Sādhanā, their general religious feature is characterised by a common spirit of extreme unconventionalism. Pandit Kṣitimohan Sen and the poet Tagore have emphasised that aspect of the Bāul songs where the mystery of the infinite being defined in terms of the finite has been very naively and nicely expressed and the pangs of the human heart for union with the 'Man of the heart' (*maner mānuṣ*) has dominated. But in his recent researches on the subject Dr. Upendranath Bhattacharya has practically challenged the validity of the older view and has tried to establish that the distinctive feature of the religion of the Bāuls is represented by the doctrines and practices of a secret cult involving sexo-yogic relations. There is truth in the assertion of Dr. Bhattacharya inasmuch as, in a general way, the Sādhakas of the Vaiṣṇava Sahajiyā order, and orders akin to it, with their secret practices involving the 'four moons'[3] (*cāri candra*), were also known as the Bāul. But it

Cf. also:— *bāuliyā biśvāşere nā dive āsite* ||
prabhu kahe bāulliyā aiche kene kara 1 *etc.*
Caitanya-caritāmṛta, *Ādi-līlā*, Ch. XII.

An earlier referece of the word is found in the *Śrī-kṛṣṇa-vijaya* of Mālādhar Basu (second half of the sixteenth century). See *fn.* of p. 529 of the C. U. edition.

[1] These indifferent mendicants are also sometimes known by the name *Āul* which may be derived from the Skt. word *ākula*.

[2] *Vide Studies in Islamic Mysticism*, by R. S. Nicholson.

[3] The 'four moons' imply semen, ovum, stool and urine.

seems that out of their doctrines and practices their search for the 'unknown bird' (*acin pākhī*) that mysteriously comes in and goes out of this cage of the human body emerged as the most striking feature. This life-long search for the 'unknown bird' got itself mingled with the Vaiṣṇavite and Sūfī-istic devotional approach to the divinity. This striking feature of the songs of the Bāuls attracted well known poets and composer of songs of the second half of the nineteenth century to compose poems in the pattern of the Bāul songs, though, however, these poets and composers were not in any way attracted to the secret sexo-yogic practices of the Bāuls. Even the well known Bengali lyric poet Biharilal Chakravarti of the second half of the nineteenth century was irresistably tempted to compose hundred songs in the pattern of the Bāul songs and he himself called these songs Bāul songs. Similarly Harinath Majumdar of the late nineteenth century composed many Bāul songs in a *nom de plume*. So it will not be correct to say that the spirit of the Bāul songs of which we speak to-day is but an attribution to the Bāul songs of our own ideas, or the ideas of Pandit Kṣitimohan Sen and of the poet Tagore; it emerged as a distinctive feature of the Bāul songs by the middle of the nineteenth century, if not earlier.

As for the doctrines and practices of the orders who resorted to a Sādhanā of the 'four moons', or sexo-yogic practices akin to it, we have made a study of it already in the previous chapters. We shall not, therefore, in the present context, deal with Bāul songs referring to such secret practices; we, on the other hand, shall restrict our study to the Bāul songs that celebrate the 'Man of the heart' and speak of the mystic love these Bāuls cherish for this 'Man of the heart'.

The Bāuls are somewhat strange people, peculiar in their manners and customs, habits and practices. They refuse to be guided by any cannon or convention, social, or religious. Freedom of spirit is their watch-word and they take to an unsophisticated way of life in which the more natural inclinations of the mind are not restrained by social institutions. They proceed in a direction opposite to that followed by the general run of people. They avoid all religion in which the natural piety of the soul is overshadowed by the useless paraphernalia of ritualism and ceremony on the one hand and pedantry and hypocrisy on the other. It is for this reason that the Bāuls would call their path *ulṭā* (*i.e.*, the reverse) path and would call the process of their spiritual advance as the process of proceeding against the current.[1] It is said in a beautiful song,—

"Reverse are the modes and manners of the man who is a real appreciator of the true emotional life and who is a lover of true love; none is sure about the how and the when of his behaviour.

"Such a man is affected neither by the weal nor by the woe of the world, and constantly realises the delight of love; it appears that his eyes are floating on the water of delight; sometimes he laughs alone in his own mood, sometimes he cries alone.

"He lights the lamp of love and sits on and on with his mind immersed in the fathomless depth of the sea of emotion; he has in his hand the key for happiness, but he never seeks it.

"Awkwardly wild are all his manners and customs,—and the other extremely wonderful fact is that the glory of the full-moon closes round him for all time; and further, this moon ceases not to shine day and night—there is no setting of the moon of his heart.

"He is as much satisfied with mud as with sandal-paste; no hankering has he after name and fame, equal are to him all that are far and near; he builds his house in the sky, even if the fourteen worlds are burnt to ashes."[2]

1 *naphcher ulṭā nāo bāio, re manurā* । etc.
Vicitrā, B. S. 1335, Caitra.

anurāgī rasik yārā bācche tārā ujān bāṁke ।
yakhan nadīr "humā" ḍāke jāgāy tarīr phāṁke phāṁke ।
Hārāmaṇi, collected and edited by Mr. M. Mansur Uddin, M.A. Song No. 46.

ujān jale pāḍi dharā re guru āmār ghoṭla nā ।
bhaver naukā khāni uu-ḍuu guru pāḍī pelam nā ।
Ibid, Song No. 47.

2 *bhāver bhāvuk premer premik hay re ye jan* ।
o tār biparīt rīti paddhati; ke jāne kakhan se thāke kyāman ।
(*bhāver mānus*)

tār nāi ānanda nirānanda, labhi nitya premānanda,
ānanda-salile yyāna tār bhāsche du'nayan;
o se kabhu āpan mane hāse, āvār kakhan bā kare rodan ।
(*bhāver mānus*)

It may be observed in this connection that this *ulṭā* path, with all its theological as well as yogic implications, was the path spoken of and adopted by all the medieval saints of India, and a detailed study of it will be found in a succeeding chapter where we shall deal with the cult of the Nātha-yogins. It may be further noted that the Sūfīs, whose influence on the Bāuls was immense, were also Sādhakas in the 'reverse path' exactly in the same sense as explained above. Thus, as R. A. Nicholson puts it,—"Unification (tawhid) is defined as 'the absoluteness of the Divine nature realised in the passing-away of the human nature,' so that 'the man's last state reverts to his first state and he becomes even as he was before he existed'."[1]

(ii) *The Bāuls and the Sahajiyās*

The Bāul poets are Sahajiyās in a general sense of the term. We have said before that a general consideration of the tenets of the Sahajïyās will lead to the conclusion that the different Sahajiyā sects would style them as Sahajiyās for two reasons. In the first place, they are Sahajiyās inasmuch as the ultimate reality, in whatever form it may be, was always conceived by them as the Sahaja, *i.e.*, that which is inborn or the quintessence which all the animate and the inanimate possess by virtue of their very existence; the realisation of this Sahaja was regarded by the Sahajiyās as the highest attainment of spiritual yearning. Secondly, the Sahajiyās are Sahajiyās inasmuch as they condemned in

se juālāiye premer bāti, bose thāke divā rāti,
bhāv-sāgare ākul pāthāre ḍuvāiyā man;
o tār hasta-gata sukher cāvi, tavu kare nā sukh anveṣaṇ I
(bhāver mānuṣ)
cāl calan sakal beāḍā, ār eyāk kāṇḍa sṛṣṭi-chāḍā,
pūrṇimār cāṁd hṛday byāḍā tār āche sarva-kṣaṇ;
se śaśir niśi diśi samān uday, se cāṁder nāire asta gaman I
(tār hṛday-cāṁder)
tār candane hay yyāman prīti, pāṁk dileo hay temni tṛpti,
cāynā se sukhyāti, tār tulya par āpan;
se āsmāne bānāy ghar bāḍī, dagdha holeo e codda-bhuvan ||

Bāul-saṅgīt, collected in the anthology *Vividha-dharma-saṅgīt*, edited by Mr. Prasannakumār Sen (published in V.S. 1314). Song No. 461.

[1] *The Idea of Personality in Sufism, p.* 13.

Cf. also—"Hence the upward movement of the Absolute from the sphere of manifestation back to the unmanifested Essence takes place in and through the unitive experience of the soul;" *vide*, Nicholson, *Studies in Islamic Mysticism*, p. 84.

the strongest language they could command all kinds of insincerity and artificiality in life and religion and at the same time recommended the most natural path for the attainment of truth. We shall see later on[1] that in this general sense the host of the Santa poets (including the Śikh poets and the Indian Sūfī poets) of upper, central and northern India were all Sahajiyās. In the Bāuls of Bengal, therefore, we find the continuity of the Sahajiyā movement, the first systematised form of which is found in the school of the Buddhist Sahajiyās. When we shall analyse the tenets of the Bāuls, as embodied in their songs that are available to us, we shall find that the doctrines of the earlier Sahajiyās form the real background of their religion,—although Sūfī-ism of Islam have introduced a new spirit in it. A study of the Bāul songs will, therefore, naturally lead us, first to a study of their Sahajiyā background and then to the line and colour that have been given to it by Sūfī-ism.

In speaking of the earlier Sahajiyā background of the Bāuls we mean mainly the schools of Buddhist Sahajiyā and of Vaiṣṇava Sahajiyā. Though there are no positive data to enable us to ascertain the exact time when the Vaiṣṇava Sahajiyā movement first began and when it reached its fullest development, yet it seems that the Vaiṣṇava Sahajiyās were earlier than the Bāuls.[2] There are however some instances of striking similarity between the creeds of the earlier Sahajiyās and these the Bāuls which definitely points a genealogical connection between them. The songs and Dohās of the earlier Sahajiyās are characterised by a spirit of heterodoxy and criticism, which is likewise a feature of the songs of the Bāuls. Secondly, the earlier Sahajiyās lay strong emphasis on Guru-vāda, and so do the Bāuls as it will appear from their 'Murshid' songs. Thirdly, we have seen that according to the earlier Sahajiyās the human body is the microcosm, or rather the epitome of the universe and that truth resides within and is to be realised within;—this is exactly the belief shared by the Bāuls. Finally, the earlier Sahajiyās conceived of the ultimate reality as the Sahaja and

1 *Vide* Appendix A.
2 The word Baul is used in the present discourse always in its restricted denotation.

this conception of the Sahaja is also found in the songs of the Bāuls; and like the earlier Sahajiyās the Bāuls also a advocate the most natural path for the realisation of this Sahaja-nature.

But the earlier Sahajiyā cult underwent a notable transformation in the hands of the Bāuls; for, the Bāuls, by deviation and innovation, effected a great change both in the ideology and practice of the Sahajiyās. The difference in ideology is palpable in the conception of Sahaja. The Buddhist Sahajiyās conceived Sahaja as Mahā-sukha which is the unity of the duality represented by man and woman as Upāya and Prajñā. The method for the realisation of this Sahaja consisted, therefore, essentially in a sexo-yogic practice. To this, however, the Vaiṣṇavas supplied the element of love. But here, in the Vaiṣṇava school also, Sahaja was conceived as supreme love which can be realised by the union of Kṛṣṇa and Rādhā who reside in the corporeal form of man and woman. The process of Sādhanā is also, therefore, a process of the Divinisation of the human love. But we have seen that this love is not the love of the nature of the most intense yearning of human soul towards God, it is the yearning of man for woman, or of woman for man. In all their theories of love and speculations on the lover and the beloved, the Vaiṣṇava Sahajiyās never speak of any love beyond the purest and the most perfect form of human love and of any lover and beloved other than man and woman, who are themselves incarnations of the eternal Lover and the Beloved. But the Bāuls conceived Sahaja as the innermost eternal Beloved who is the 'Man of the heart' (*maner mānuṣ*). The Bāuls also speak of love and union, but this love means the love between the human personality and the Divine Beloved within and in this love man realises his union with the Divine, or in other words he merges his personal existence in the Beloved that resides within this temple of the body. Great has been the influence of Sūfīism on the Bāuls in the evolution of this new conception of Sahaja and in the difference in their religious approach. But a little penetration into the nature of Sahaja, variously described in the songs and Dohās of the Buddhist Sahajiyās, will show that the germ of such evolution was already there in the ideas of the Buddhist Sahajiyās. We have already made it clear that in spite of the conventional way of describing the Sahaja under a Buddhistic garb, the Sahaja of the Buddhist Sahajiyās often implies a supreme Being residing within. It has been said in a Dohā of Saraha-pāda that some One Formless is residing within this form of ours,—he who knows Him becomes liberated.[1] Again it is said,—"He is within your house (of body), and you are looking for him outside! You are beholding your husband (within), and asking for his whereabouts to your neighbours!"[2] These and such other verses will supply us with a clue to the tendency of the Buddhist Sahajiyās of conceiving the Sahaja as a Being, who became gradually transformed into a Personal God with whom it may be possible to have personal relations. This tendency of the earlier Sahajiyās paved the way for the evolution of the conception of the 'Man of the heart' under the strong say of Sūfī-ism.

It may be observed that the literature of the Santa poets of upper, central and northern India also represent, as will be demonstrated later,[3] the spirit of Sūfī-ism against the background of the earlier Sahajiyās. In this respect the Bāul songs of Bengal have the closest affinity with the songs of the medieval saints of the other parts of India. As Sūfī-ism is so important a factor in the religious tenets of the medieval saints of India, we propose to deal with the nature and extent of the influence of Sūfī-ism on the Bāuls in some detail. Our present study will also help us in the future study of the cognate literature of the medieval saints of other parts of India.[4]

(iii) *The Bāuls and the Sūfīs*

(A) A Brief History of Sūfī-ism in India and particularly in Bengal

In all probability Sūfī-ism began to make its way in India in the eleventh century A.D. and apostles like Shah Sultan Rumi (who came to Bengal in 1053 A.D.),

[1] *Vide* p. 90
[2] *Vide* p. 90
[3] *Vide* Appendix A.
[4] *Vide* Appendix A.

Sayad Nathar Shah (who carried Sūfī-ism to the Deccan for the first time and died there in 1039 A.D.), Makhdum Sayad 'Ali 'Uluvvi 'al Huzurri (who setteld in Lahore) are the preachers of this first period.[1] But Sūfī-ism as a religious school began to influence the mind of the Indian people on a large scale from the end of the twelfth century and the two orders of Sūfī-ism that gained sufficient ground on the soil of India by this time are the Chishti and the Suhrawardi orders. The renowned apostle Khwajah Mu'-inu-d-din Chisti, who settled in Delhi in 1193 was the founder of the Chishti Order in India. The Suhrawardi Order was also almost synchronously founded by Shyak Baha'u-d-din Dhakriya Multani (born in Multan in 1169 and died in 1266). These two Sūfī-istic orders soon succeeded in attracting a considerable number of Indian people to accept their tenets. Another Sūfī-istic Order, *viz.*, the Quadiri Order was introduced and popularised in India during the fifteenth century A.D. by Sayad Muhammad Ghauth Gilani, who came to India in 1482. Another Sūfī-istic Order was introduced in India by the end of the fifteenth century by Khwajah Muhammad Bakvi Billah, it is the Naqshbandi Order. Badi'u-d-din Shah-i-Madar founded another important Sūfī-istic Order in the fourteenth century A.D., which is known as the Madari Order.

The Pantheistic or rather the Panentheistic mysticism of the Upaniṣads, the devotional mysticism mainly in the Vaiṣṇavite line and the Sahajiyā movements offered Sūfī-ism a ready field and this will account for the speedy growth and spread of Sūfī-istic faith in India. Moreover, from the twelfth century A.D. the history of India represents a history of contact, conflict and compromise—political, cultural and religious. In this period of contact Sūfī-ism, as transformed in India, could very well serve as a medium of compromise and it is this additional possibility that may be held responsible for the wide-spread popularity of the Sūfī-istic thoughts.

Sūfī-ism entered Bengal rather as an overflow from Northern India. There are as many as seven Sūfī-istic orders in Bengal, of which the Suhrawardi Order, introduced

[1] *Vide* Dr. M. Anamul Haq, M.A., Ph.D., *Vaṅge Sūfī-prabhāva*, Ch. III.

by Makhdum Shaykh Jalalu'-d-din Tabriyi (death 1125 A.D.), seems to be the earliest. The Chishti Order was introduced probably by the North Indian saint Shaykh Faridu'-d-din Shakraganj (death 1269 A.D.). Shah Safiu'-d-din Shahi (1290? 1295) of Pāṇḍuā (in Hughli) was in all probability the first apostle of the Qadadari Order. The Madari Order was perhaps introduced in Bengal by Shah Madar himself as an itinerant mendicant. Another popular Sūfī-istic Order of Bengal is the Adhami Order, more pūpularly known as the Khidwari branch. The Naqshbandi Order was perhaps introduced first by Shaykh Hamid Danishmand in the seventeenth century. The other Order of Sūfī-ism in Bengal is the Qadiri Order, which was introduced probably by Abdul Kadir Gilani in the sixteenth century.[1] We need not enter here into the detailed history of how the Sūfī-movement spread with all its branches and sub-branches in Bengal; it will be sufficient for us to know that different orders of Sūfī-ism did penetrate into Bengal, and did very easily and promptly recruit large number of converts. The Sūfī-istic ideas that were thus introduced were soon assimilated with the prevalent Sahajiyā ideas and the results of this amalgam has been the Bāuls of Bengal.

(B) Influence of Sūfī-ism on the General Nature of Bāul Sect

(a) *The Influence of Sama*

In gauging the nature and extent of the influence of Sūfī-ism on the Bāuls we may observe in the first place that the out-pouring of the heart through songs was an important religious mode with the Bāuls; in this we may find on the one hand the influence of Bengal Vaiṣṇavism, which attached much importance to music as a medium of holy communion, and on the other hand the influence of the Sūfī-istic custom of 'Sama' (*i.e.*, song and dance).[2] The effect of

[1] *Ibid.*, Ch. III.

[2] Dr. Anamul Huq postulates the influence of Sufī-istic Sama even in the Vaiṣṇava religious function of *Kīrtana* (*i.e.*, singing in congregation); but the custom of such singing and dancing is found among the Southern Vaiṣṇavite saints, the Ālvars, from sometime the sixth or seventh century A.D.; the postulation of Sufī influence on this point, therefore, does not seem warrantable. Prediction to such religious practice of *Kīrtana* is also found in the *Bhāgavata-purāṇa*, *e.g.*,—*kṛṣṇavarṇaṁ twiṣā-kṛṣṇaṁ sāṅgo-pāṅgā-stra-pārṣadam/ yajñaiḥ saṁkīr-tana-prāyair yajanti hi sumedhasaḥ* || (11.5.32, Vaṅgavāsi edition).

music, the Sūfīs hold, helps one much in passing into the *fana*, *i.e.*, in passing away of consciousness in mystic union with God.

(*b*) *Importance of the Murshid*

Secondly, we may consider the importance that is laid by the Sūfīs on Guru-vāda. We have seen how Guru-vāda is ingrained in the religious thoughts of India in general, and how in the spiritual life God has sometimes been replaced by the Guru. The Sūfīs laid the same stress on the Murshid or the Shaykh, *i.e.*, the preceptor or spiritual guide. The view of Sūfī-ism on this point will be best illustrated if we quote here the view contained in the *Awarifu-l-Ma' arif*. It is said,—"When he (*i.e.*, the Murid or the disciple) is possessed of manners, he taketh in love a place in the Shaikh's heart; and is agreeable to God's sight. Because, with mercy, favour and care, God ever looketh at the hearts of His own friends (the darvishes).

"Thus, by dwelling in the Shaikh's heart, the constant blessings of God's mercy and of his endless bounty, comprehend his existence: and the Shaik's acceptance becometh his mark of the acceptance of God, Muhammad, and of all Shaikhs."[1]

In the 'Murshidā-songs' of the Bāuls we find a mixture of the Indian spirit with the spirit of Sūfī-ism. The excellence of the 'Murshidā-songs' of the Bāuls consists in there pathos, in their expression of the groaning and the beating heart of the restless aspirers; additional charm has been imparted to the songs by the unconditional self-resignation of the Murid or the disciple, who has accepted the Murshid as a sure mast in the boundless heaving sea of existence,—like a lamp in the abyss of darkness. "To and fro is tossing my boat with a jingling sound in the rough wind," proceeds the cry from a heart,—"O my Murshid, yet let me live in my hope in thee. Clouds have thickened in the west and the roarings are now on,—torn is the rope of my helm,—and the boat is moving in the whirl; yet, O my Murshid, let me live in my hope in thee! The waves sweep from helm to prow,—and all my

[1] *Awarifu-l-Ma'arif*, translated by H. Wilberforce Clarke, p. 18.

merchandise, more precious than gem and diamond, is being swept away by the current; yet, O my Murshid, let me live in my hope in thee."[1] Songs of this type may be found abundantly in the Bāul literature of Bengal.

(c) *Heterodoxy of the Bāuls*

The next point to be noted is the heterodox spirit of the Bāuls. In this, as we have said, the background of Sahajiyā thought cannot be overlooked; but the influence of Sūfī-ism is also not less noteworthy. As essentially a cult of love-mysticism Sūfī-ism, in spite of the rites and customs that gradually developed around it, breathes a spirit of heterodoxy in general. It is rightly said,—"Transacting as it were directly with the Divine Being, the Sūfīs throw off the shackles of the positive religion; pious rebels, they neither fast nor make pilgrimages to the temple of Mecca,[2] nay, they forget their prayers; for with God there is no other language than the silent language of the heart. From excess of religion they have no religion at all. Thus is confirmed the trite saying that "extremes meet." "The perfection of a man's state," says Jami, "and the utmost degree to which

[1] *ūnur jhūnūr bāje nāo āmār*
nihāilyā bātāse re murṣid,
railām tor āśe ।
paścime sājila myāgh re dyāoyāy dila re ḍāk ।
āmar chiḍila hāler pānas naukāy khāila pāk ||
murṣid, railām tor āśe ||
āgā bāiyā oṭhe ḍheu re pāchā bāyyā re yāy ।
āmār hirālāl māṇikkar bārā sote lāiyā yāy ||
murṣid, railām tor aśe ||
See *Bhārati*, B.S., 1331, Bhādra.

Cf. also—*tomār caraṇ pāva boile re,*
guru, baḍa āśā chila ।
* * * *
cātak raila myāgher āśe, myāgh paḍila anya dyāśe,
cātak bāṁcave kise ||
āmār āśā-nadīr kule baiyā re,
guru, kāndte janam gela ।
baḍa āśā chila || (Own collection).

[2] *Cf.* the Bāul song:—
(mor) yāite to cāy nā re man makkā madinā ।
(ei ye) bandhu āmār āche, āmi raire tāri kāche
(āmi) pāgal haitām dūre raitām
tāre cintām re yadi nā ।
(āmar) nāi mandir nāi masjed,
nāi pūjā ki bakred,
tile tile mor makkā kāśī
pale pale sudinā ||
Vide '*Bāṅlār Prāṇa-vastu*' by Kṣitimohan Sen. *Pravāsī*, B.S. 1337, Caitra.

saints may attain is to be without an attribute, and without a mark." The most fervent zeal sinks into the coldest indifference about religion.[1]

The mystics in all countries are as much opposed to the paraphernalia of practices, rites and customs as to scriptures and speculative literature. The mystics do not believe in the powers of our discursive reason, which, it is held, is limited by its very nature. It is, therefore, that all attempts to comprehend the ultimate truth through intellectual pursuits are bound by nature to be sadly baffled.[2] But though truth cannot be known, it can be intuited or realised within,—it can be realised in the Sahaja (natural) path through the secret communion of love. In love we become one with the reality and it is in this union of love that the mystery of the whole universe is revealed to us. The mystery of the universe can never be understood unless it is revealed in love.[3] It is for this reason that the mystics discard all ceremony and ritualism on the one hand and scholasticism and discursive erudition on the other and proceeds straight in the path of love. It is said in a song,—"O my lord, I hear thy call, but I cannot come,—for, the sham Guru and Murshid block my way. If that, which ought to cool the body when immersed, begins to burn all around, then, tell me, Master, where on earth I shall find a foothold!—my spiritual endeavour for 'unity' dies away in differences of plurality. Many are the locks in thy gate, *viz.*, the scriptures, the Qur'an and rosaries;—showiness mars the endeavour and is the greatest impediment,—Madan cries in remorse."[4] It is said in another song, "Grass by no means grows on the beaten

[1] *The Dabistan, or School of Manners*, translated by David Shea and Anthony Troyer; preliminary discourse, pp. clxiv-clxv.

[2] *Cf. duniyār bhojer bāji, mollā kāji,*
bhāvle pāgal paṇḍit jñānī | etc.
Bāul-saṅgīt, collected in *Vividha-dharma-saṅgīt*, p. 123

[3] *ki ha'te ki hay dekhi sāmi daradīr mane* |
āmi ār miche bhāvi kyāne |
* * * * *
brahma-jñānī pa'ḍe tantra, bheve ma'lo e paryanta,
pele nā tār ādi anta, maner bhrānti gela nā;
yata yogī ṛṣi yoga-tapasvī, ār yata tīrtha-vāsī,
ka're brata ekādasī, śānti pela nā mane || *Ibid*, p. 247.

[4] *tomār path ḍhāikāche mandire masjede* |
(tomār) ḍāk śune sāmi calte nā pāi
rukhā dāmḍāy gurute murśede || *etc.*
Baṅlār Prāṇa-vastu by Kṣitimohan Sen, *Pravāsī*, B.S. 1337, Caitra.

foot-tract void; so, how would they find the living 'Sahaja' (*i.e.*, the Man of the heart) they that leave not custom-beaten way? The heart-flow comes out when custom is shed away. Cast away thy fears, to Biśā Balā sayeth,—the path shines out clear, when ties are all loosened."[1] Religion, it is held, cannot be confined to ritualistic observances,—it is a functioning of the whole being extending over the entire gamut of human experiences. If we try to confine religion to any code of rituals and practices we shall be strangely fettered by the very means of liberation. If a necklace of wish-yielding gem loses its wish-yielding capacity, the necklace itself will be nothing but a chain.[2] We have said that as a Sahajiyā sect the Bāuls would always advocate the Sahaja (*i.e.*, the most natural) path for the spiritual life. It is said, "If thou wouldst visualise that Man, thou must be natural in Sādhanā and must go to the land of Sahaja."[3]

(*d*) *Body as the Microcosm of the Universe*

We have seen that the Sahajiyās recognised the human body as the microcosm of the universe and that, according to them, Sahaja as the ultimate reality resides within this human form as our true self or the ultimate nature. This is exactly the view that has been contended by the Sūfī mystics. The Bāuls also cherished the same doctrine. The human body has always been described as the temple of the Dear One.[4] In vain, they say, are people mad after going on pilgimage,—in vain are they searchng the Beloved in temples and mosques and in other places. Thus it is said,

[1] *gatā-gater bāṁjhā pathe* l *ājāya nā ghās kona mate* ||
rīte pathei calen yārā l *jyānta sahaja pā(ye)n ki tārā ?*
niyam rīt chāḍāyyā gele l *maram raser daraś mele* ||
kay 'balā' bhay chāḍre 'biśā' l *khasle bāṁdhan milve diśā* ||
Ibid, p. 855.

[2] *āmār centa-maṇi hār,*
yadi hārāy centa tār
tave eman bāndhan bāndhte pāre
(ye) chāḍāy sādhya kār ? *Ibid*, p. 855.

[3] *yadi bheṭvi se mānuṣe*
tave, sādhane sahaj havi,
tor yāite have sahaj deśe l
Ibid, p. 850.

[4] *Cf.* "The mosque that is built in the hearts of the saints
Is the place of worship for all, for God dwells there."
Masnavi of Jalalu'ddin, quoted in *The Idea of Personality* by Nicholson, p. 57.

"The Man of the house is dwelling in the house,—in vain have you become mad by searching Him outside. It is for your own fault that you are roaming about for ever. You have been to Gayā, Benares (*Kāśī*), and Vṛndāvana,—and have travelled through many rivers and forests and other places of pilgrimage; but say,—have you seen in all these anything of Him of Whom you have heard? Through false illusion you have lost all your power of understanding,—with jewel tied in your own skirt, you have been swimming in search of it. With care you might have easily got the gem,—but you are losing everything carelessly,—the jewel shines so near to your eyes, but alas! you are keeping your eyes shut—and you do not see."[1] Again it is said, "Search, O brother, for the Lord, who is the kind sympathiser of the poor (*dīna-daradī sāṁī*), in the company of enlightenment as thy preceptor. The heart deceiving, blurs the eye and a single hair hides the mountain truth! The Lord in His lone seat looks. What humour enjoys my Lord at the folly and laughs! Carefully proceed in your spiritual effort; may be, you will find wealth very near; says Lālan, search your own house, truth is not very far!"[2]

(*e*) *The Man of the Heart*

In the songs of the Bāuls we hear much of the 'Man of the Heart' Whose abode is the human body and Whose seat is the human heart. Poetically this 'Man of the Heart' has variously been depicted as the Supreme Beloved, the poet himself being the passionate lover. The songs embody

[1] *Phakir-cānder Bāul Saṅgīt* (collected in the *Vividha-dharma-saṅgīt*), p. 220. See also—

pañca bhūte ka're jhagḍā, dile chāre khāre sonār ākhḍā,
mānav deher māṇik mākḍā, tā'ke cinlām nā I
Ibid, p. 249.

[2] *kothā āche re dīn-daradī sāṁi,*
cetan gurur saṅge laye khavar kara bhāi I
cakṣu āndhār deler dhokāy, keśer āḍe pāhāḍ lukāy,
ki raṅga sāṁi dekhche sadāi, base nigam ṭhāṁi I
* * * *
sumje bhave sādhan kara, nikaṭe dhana pete pāra,
lālan kay nij mokām ḍhora, bahu dūre nāi I
Hārāmaṇi, edited by M. Mansur Uddin, Song No. 3.

Cf. also—
āmār e ghar-khānāy ke birāj kare I
tāre janam bhare ekvār dekhlem nāre II etc.
Ibid, Song No. 5.

throughout the pangs of separation for the 'Man of the Heart' and a maddening desire to be united with Him. This Bāul doctrine of divine love naturally brings in the question of its similarity or dissimilarity with the Vaiṣṇava conception of love with which we are familiar in Bengal. In a general way it may be said that the intensity of divine love, which we find in the songs of the Bāuls was influenced, no doubt, to a considerable extent by the general *prema* (love) movement of Bengal. But when we analyse the conception of love, as enunciated in the school of Bengal Vaiṣṇavism, it appears that this theory of love is based on a principle of duality, theological, if not metaphysical. Theologically the Vaiṣṇavas have conceived some kind of duality between God and the individual (*jīva*) and this principle of duality brings in the question of devotion, which gradually culminates in the conception of passionate love. Metaphysically, however, the relation between God and the individual has often been spoken of as incomprehensible (*acintya*); it is a relation of non-dualism, and yet of dualism and this principle of dualism in non-dualism is something that transcends intellectual comprehension. In their theology, however, the conception of dualism prevails, and all poetical and metaphorical descriptions of love seem to be based on this theological speculation. But the Bāul conception of love is ultimately based on a non-dualistic belief, the dualism is either illusory or metaphorical.

The difference between the Bāul conception of love and the Vaiṣṇava Sahajiyā conception of love is however palpable. The love of the Vaiṣṇava Sahajiyās exists between individual beings as Rādhā and Kṛṣṇa, but not between the individual and the Absolute; it is the love between Rādhā and Kṛṣṇa that ultimately leads to the realisation of the Absolute. The love of the Bāuls is, on the contrary, the love directly between the Sahaja as the ultimate reality on the one hand and the individual on the other. To conform to the emotional approach of the Bāuls the Sahaja has gradually transformed itself into a Personal God, or the Supreme Being with whom it may be possible to have personal relations. The mode of transformation of the conception of Sahaja into a Personal God has already been indicated at the very outset. This Sahaja as the Personal God is the 'Man of the Heart.' From this point of view the love-union of the Bāuls with the 'Man of the Heart' really means the realisation of the Sahaja or the ultimate nature of Self. The love, of which we hear so much in the songs of the Bāuls, is the love between our human personality and the Divine Personality residing in the human as the true self. The Beloved as the Divine Personality residing in us is our Sahaja-nature, and the lover is the human personality, falsely viewed as separate from this Divine Personality. Love here really implies self-love, the gradual passing away of the human into the Divine.

The creed of the Bāuls is thus fundamentally based on the question of self-realisation. From the days of Upaniṣadic mysticism this question of self-realisation has been the pivot round which the religious thoughts of India have mainly revolved. The minor religious sects like the different branches of the Sahajiyās are saturated through and through with this Upaniṣadic spirit of self-realisation. In this spirit, however, Sūfī-ism is intimately related to Upaniṣadic mysticism, although the element of love which is conspicuous in Sūfī-ism is not stressed in the Upaniṣads. It is because of this striking similarity in spirit that scholars have often postulated influence of Indian thought on the evolution of Sūfī-ism itself. Without entering into the controversy involved in such postulations it may be said, that the religious contents of Sūfī-ism were in no way foreign to the mass-mind of India; it is for this reason that Sūfī-ism was very easily acceptable to the masses. But whenever we should discuss the influence of Sūfī-ism on the evolution of the minor religious sects like the Bāuls of Bengal and the Santa poets of Upper and Northern India we should never lose sight of the Indian background prepared by Upaniṣadic mysticism and the devotional movements mainly in the Vaiṣṇavite line. The fact seems to be that the popular composite religious consciousness which was formed by an unconscious admixture of Upaniṣadic mysticism and the devotional fervour of the Vaiṣṇavas was further modified by the kindred thoughts of Sūfī-ism where the spirit of the

Upaniṣads and that of later Vaiṣṇavism are found combined together.

Let us now turn our attention to the Sūfī-istic conception of the divinity and the ideal of love as conceived by the Sūfīs. The whole ideology of the Sūfī mystics is also shaped and coloured on a Pantheistic or rather a Panentheistic canvas. The creation proceeds from God, the Absolute, as His self-manifested attribute, mode or modification. The sum-total of the manifested attributes of God is the universe. Hallaj, the well-known Sūfī poet, who was done to death because of his novel belief of *Anal'haqq* (*i.e.*, I am the truth), says that "the essence of God's essence is love. Before the creation God loved Himself in absolute unity and through love revealed Himself to Himself alone. Then, desiring to behold that love-in-aloneness, that love without otherness and duality, as an external object, He brought forth from non-existene an image of Himself, endowed with all His attributes and names. This Divine image is Adam, in and by whom God is made manifest—divinity objectified in humanity."[1] We find a very beautiful echo of this Sūfī-istic principle in the *Jñāna-sāgar* of Ālirājā[2]. There it is said that the Absolute was alone in the beginning; but it could not realise the infinite potency of love that was in it without a dual; in love therefore it created a dual out of its ownself,—and the dual was Muhammad. This first pair represent the original lover and the beloved. Because of this fact that God in His absolute aloneness could not realise His love and a second was required as the beloved, love cannot be realised in the world without there being a pair.[3] The whole universe thus proceeds from the Love of God. Love is the

[1] Nicholson, *Studies in Islamic Mysticism*, p. 80.

[2] Sāhitya-Pariṣat Series, No. 59. It is an Islamic Yogic text in Bengali which has mixed up Sūfī-istic ideas with the ideology of the Vaiṣṇava Sahajiyās and the Nāthists.

[3] *prathame āchila prabhu ek nirañjan* ।
prema-rase ḍuvi kaila yugal sṛjan ‖
prem-rase bhuli prabhu jāhāke sṛjila ।
mohāmmad buli nām gaurave rākhila ‖
* * * * *

pratham bhāvuk prabhu bhāvinī janmila ।
mohāmmad kari nām trijagate haila ‖
bhāvak bulie prabhu ār se bhāvinī ।
ei se yugal nām dharila āpani ‖
* * * *

underlying principle of the cosmic process as a whole. The fact has very nicely been put in the *Jñāna-sāgar*, mentioned above. It is said there that the universe has its origin in love, and the chaos is systematised into the cosmos through the bond of love. There is love between fire and air, between earth and water; without this love neither heaven, nor earth, nor the nether world would have originated at all. There is love between heaven and the skies, between heaven and earth, between hell and the nether world in which it lies, and thus are the three worlds supported in love. There is love between the sun, the moon, the planets and the stars and in love are they all fixed into the sky above. There is love between the sea and its water, between the moon and the night and the sun and the day;—the tree is fixed to the earth by its root, the black-bee is attached to the lotus, fish is bound to the water, man is bound to the woman—and all in love. The body is in love with the mind and the mind with the vital wind. In love does the mother conceive the child, in love does the earth hold fast the root of the tree, in love does the tree hold fast the branches and the flowers and fruits,—in love does the fruit accumulate juice in its kernel,—thus is the whole creative process supported in love.[1]

This Love of God as the *raison d'être* of the whole universal process brings in the question of self-revelation for self-realisation. The whole universe thus serves as a mirror where the love and beauty of the Absolute are reflected.[2] This manifestation of the love and beauty of the Absolute has reached perfection in the personality of man and it is for this reason that "Man is the microcosm in which all attributes (of the Absolute) are united, and in him alone does the Absolute become conscious of itself in all its diverse aspects. To put it in another way, the Absolute, having completely realised itself in human nature, returns into itself

bhāvak bhābinī nām buliye yugal ।
yug haite siddhi karma hay je sakal ॥
yugal nā haile keha nā pāre calite ।
yug bine prem ras nā pare bhugite ॥
ek ek prem nā hay kadācan ।
yugal haile yogya pirīti bhajan ॥
Jñāna-sāgar, pp. 24-25.

Cf. Bṛhadāraṇyako-paniṣat, see infra, ch. xiv.

1 *Jñāna-sāgar*, p. 26, pp. 33-35. *Cf.* the poem *Philosophy of Love* by Shelley.

2 *Dabistan*, Vol. III, p. 227.

through the medium of human nature; or more intimately God and man become one in the Perfect Man—the enraptured prophet or saint—whose religious function as a mediator between man and God corresponds to his metaphysical function as a unifying principle by means of which the opposed terms of reality and appearance are harmonised."[1] It has been said in the *Ibnu'l-Arabi* that "When God willed in respect of His beautiful names (attributes), which are beyond enumeration, that their essence (*a'yan*) or if you wish, you may say "His essence '(*aynuhu*)'—should be seen, He caused them to be seen in a microcosmic being (*kawn jami'*) which, inasmuch as it is endowed with existence, contains the whole object of vision, and through which the inmost consciousness (*sivī*) of God becomes manifested to Him."[2] Man thus represents in him a synthesis of the create and the increate,—of the finite and the infinite.

As the best manifestation of the life-principle man serves as the connecting link between the noumenon and the phenomenal creation. Man thus synthesises within his nature two aspects of existence, which are called in Sūfī-ism the *nasut*, which is his human personality and the *lahut*, which is his Divine personality. The pangs of separation from which humanity suffers follow from the false notion of dualism between this human personality and the Divine in man.

This conception of the Divine and the human combined in man may well be affiliated with the Upaniṣadic conception of the *Paramātman* and the *Jīvātman*. They are like two birds living in friendly terms on the same tree,—one of them (i.e., *Jīvātman*) tastes the sweet fruit of world-experience, but the other never touches it, but gazes on and on.[3] This Divine in us is dearer to us than our son, than wealth—than everything else.[4] Immortal becomes the beloved of the man who adores this inner self as the dearest one.[5] That Divine personality is the ear of our ears, eye of our eyes,

[1] Nicholson, *loc. cit.*
[2] Quoted by Nicholson, *loc. cit.*
[3] *Muṇḍakopaniṣat* (3.1.1); *Śvetā°* (4.6). *Cf.* the poem *Two Birds* by Tagore in *Sonār Tari*.
[4] *Bṛhadāraṇyaka* (1.4.8).
[5] *Ibid* (1.4.8).

word of our words, mind of our minds and life of our lives.[1] He resides in the heart of man and is to be known in the heart of man.[2]

But while the Upaniṣads speak of the love between the Divine personality and the human personality more or less metaphorically, the whole emphasis of the Sūfīs and the Bāuls is on love.

Through ecstasy of the purest love the mystic passes in the *fana*, which is the passing-away of the human in the Divine. The fire of love burns into ashes the bundle of complexes from which emerges the false notion of the 'I-ness', and through pangs of heart the ice of 'I-ness' melts into flow of tears and the 'I' in man and the 'He' in man become one and the same. This is the truth which was perceived by Hallaj in his mystic trance, and which inspired him to exclaim to the world abroad *Ana'l haqq*—'I and the truth are one'! In such a moment did he declare:—

> I am He whom I love, and He whom I love is I.
> We are two spirits dwelling in one body,
> If thou seest me, thou seest Him;
> And if thou seest Him, thou seest us both.

So long as there is even an iota of dualism, the door of the divine temple remains banged against us and our Eternal Beloved dwelling within refuses to respond to our call. It is only after the melting away of the human personality that the door is opened and the screen before our eyes is removed leaving the lover and the beloved unified in bond of infinite love.[3]

The Divine Personality, Who is the eternal Beloved of

[1] *Kena°* (1.2).
[2] *Śvetā°* (4.17).
[3] This truth has been very poetically and nicely illustrated by the Sūfī poet Jalalu'ddin Rumi through the following story in his *Masnavi*:—
"A man knocked at the door of his friend. The latter asked: 'Who art thou, my dear?'—'It is I',—'In this case, be off; I cannot at present receive thee; there is no place at my board for one who is still *raw*; such a man cannot be sufficiently dressed (that is matured) and cured of hypocrisy, but by the fire of sepration and refusal.' The unfortunate man departed. He employed a whole year in travelling, consuming himself in the flames of desire and affliction, caused by the absence of his friend. Matured and perfected by his long trial he again approached the door of his friend and knocked modestly, fearful that an uncivil word might again fall from his own lips.—'Who is there?' was asked from the interior of the house—'Dear friend, it is thyself who art at the door'.—'Because it is myself, enter to-day; this house can contain no other than I'." *Vide*, *Dabistan*, Vol. III, p. 292, F.N. 1.

the human personality and with whom man becomes one in his ecstasy of love, is the indwelling principle not only of the self, but also of the not-self. It is for this reason that the sights and sounds of the external world always bear love-message of the Beloved to the responsive heart of the mystic lover. In love are we all separated from the Beloved with whom we were once one,—and in love again shall we proceed in the regressive way and realise our true original self being one with the Beloved.

In the conception of the 'Man of the heart' of the Bāuls we find a happy mixture of the conception of the *Paramātman* of the Upaniṣads, the Sahaja of the Sahajiyās and the Sūfīistic conception of the Beloved. The mystic attitude of the Bāuls is best expressed in the wonder how that Infinite has objectified itself in the finite,—how through the whole being of the finite that Infinite is expressing itself in infinite ways and thereby realising itself in infinite varieties. It is not through any intellectual speculation,—but through the ecstasy of love that the truth has revealed itself to the lover, that there is 'some one unknown' living within his corporeal form. Thus the Bāul says,—"Methinks, by this time I have become mad; otherwise, why should I feel so troubled inside every now and then? When I remain quiet with the undisturbed mind, I see that Some One speaks loudly from within,—"I am here, here I am'! In the dimness of the sky of my heart, methinks, I see Some One come to my side; He moves, He speaks, He plays,—He smiles,—He indulges in hundred other sports! . . . . If I try to leave Him off and live alone, I cannot; it seems, He has settled His dwelling in the core of my heart."[1] It is like an 'unknown bird' that comes within the cage of this corporeal form,—and it is the greatest wonder with the Bāul, how the 'unknown bird' is playing its eternal play of coming and going,—the play of

[1] Bāul song, collected in *Vividha-dharma-saṅgīt*, pp. 228-29. *Cf.* also:—

mānuṣ hāoyāy cale hāoyāy phire,
mānuṣ hāoyār sane ray
deher mājhe āche re sonār mānuṣ ḍākle kathā kay ।
tomār maner madhye ār ek man āche go—
tumi man miśāo sei maner sāthe ।
deher mājhe āche re mānuṣ ḍākle kathā kay ॥
—*Hārāmaṇi*, p. 2.

self-manifestation and of returning once more to itself.[1] Though the bird lives in the cage of the human body, it floats in the boundless sky high above.[2] The life-long search of the Bāul is for this 'unknown bird', which is felt to be very near, singing within and enchanting us by its beauty and sweetness of song,—but which we are not being able to find out. It is always playing the game of hide and seek, as it were. In the pang of his heart the Bāul says,—"Where has the 'Bird of Beauty' hidden itself by deceiving me? I roam about in search,—but cannot find it out,—it has flown far away.

". . . . .Very affectionate is that bird, and it comes of itself and invites me to talk, if even I forget it; but if I attempt to catch hold of it, it escapes my grasp,—and alas! it has made me mad!

"O my brethren, if any of you have seen that 'Bird of Beauty', catch it once for me; if I once can get hold of it, I shall keep it tamed with care for ever in the cage of my heart."[3] It is after this 'some one unknown' that the Bāul has run mad.[4] The vision of the unknown, the call of the Infinite, the secret touch of the Beloved have made the Bāul peculiarly indifferent to the social life on earth,—and have made him come outside the limitations of earthly considerations. It is the beauty of the Formless residing within all

1 *khāṁcār bhitar acin pākhī*
kemne āse yāy I —*Hārāmaṇi*, p. 4.

2 *maner manurāy pākhī gahīnete caḍere*
nadīr jal śukhāye gelere
pākhī śūnye uḍān chāḍere
māṭir deha layre I —*Ibid*, pp. 4-5.

Cf. "The bird of (the soul of) my heart is a holy bird;
the ninth heaven, its dwelling;
Of the cage of the body, vexed of the world, stated.
From the head of this dust-heap (the world), the bird of the soul how flieth?
At the door of that threshold, its nest, the (mighty)
falcon (wordly) attachments maketh.
When the bird of the heart fleeth, its abode is the lofty
Sidrah tree;
The resting-place of our falcon (soul), know (to be) the
pinnacle of the ninth heaven (God's throne), etc.
—*Divān-i-Hāfiz*, translated by Clarke, Part II, p. 772.

3 *āmāy diye phāṁki, rūper pākhī, kothāy lukā'lo* I
āmi ghure byāḍāi dyākhā nā pāi, uḍiye ye pālālo I *etc.*
Song of Kāṅgāl Harinath, collected in *Vividha-dharma-Sangit*, pp. 179-80.

4 *āmāre pāgal ka're ye jan pālāy,*
kothā gele pāva tāy I *etc.*
—Song of Kāṅgāl Harināth, *Ibid*, p. 215.

forms that has entrapped the heart of the Bāul—and he weeps and weeps. This incessant weeping in secret gives him a peep into the beauty that pervades the whole universe by its matchless glow and grandeur. In such a state when he looks at the sky, the divine beauty appears before him floating with the clouds; the splendour of that beauty moves from star to star and the heart is illumined by its flash.[1] Through the whole cosmic process the one Lord-Beloved is playing the play of self-expression and self-realisation, endless is His sport—incomprehensible is its mystery.[2]

But though the Beloved is pervading the whole universe, the best way of finding Him out is to search within and to realise Him through the realisation of the self. Like the full moon He is in the sky of our heart,—but heaps of clouds have gathered over the moon; spiritual endeavour consists in driving the clouds away with the instructions of the true preceptor and to let the moon shine unobstructed in its own lustre.[3] In the mystery of the self lies the mystery of the Lord and to know the former is to know the latter.[4] It has been said by Kāṅgāl Harināth,—"O the mad, thy 'Bird of Beauty' is sitting in its nest in the bower of thy heart, find it out there; offer it fruits of devotion and water of love, and it will be tamed for ever."[5] Phakir-cānd says in a song,—"O my mind, let me tell thee,—the 'Man of the heart' is in the heart and search for Him there; why art thou roaming from

1 Song of Kāṅgāl Harināth, *Ibid*, p. 216.

2 *sāiṁjīr līlā bujhvi kṣyāpā keman kare* l
līlāte nāire sīmā kon samay kon rūp dhare l
Song of Lālan Phakir, *Hārāmaṇi*, Song No. 28.

3 *āche pūrṇimār cānd meghe ḍhākā* l
cānder nīce bindu sakhā,
megher āḍe cānd rayeche
megh keṭe cānd uday karā;
seḍā keval kathār kathā l
madan bale andhakāre banda haye rali ekā,
yāhār āche murśid sakhā sei se pāve cānder dekhā l
Ibid, Song No. 84.

4 *āpanār janma latā, jāna ge tār mukti kothā,*
lālan kay have śeṣe sāṅi paricay l *Ibid*, Song N9. 12.
See also Songs Nos. 16, 17.

Cf. also—*yār nām ālek mānuṣ āleke ray* l
śuddha prema-rasik bine ke tāre pāy l
ras rati anusāre, nigūḍha bhed jānte pāre,
ratite mati jhare, mūl khaṇḍa hay l
līlāy nirañjan āmār, ādh līle kallena pracār,
jānle āpanār janmer bicār, sav jānā hay l etc.
Ibid, Song No. 36.

5 *Bāul-song*, collected in the *Vividha-dharma-saṅgīt*, p. 180.

country to country?—never have I seen a greater fool than thee."[1] "In man resides the Lord, why hast thou not known Him with thy common sense? . . . . In eternal union does that Beloved dally in the heart,—He dallies in the heart with all the gates shut—and from the side of man, he (man) shuts up all the doors of the chamber of his heart with the strength of love and therein gazes at the beauty of the Beloved."[2] It is the screen of illusion,—the shade over the eyes that prevents us from beholding the beauty of the 'Man of the heart'; it is this illusion that lengthens the distance between man and the 'Unknown One.' Man often feels that it is not he, but that 'Unknown One' that is moving and working through him,—but yet alas,—because of the shade over the eyes,—he cannot catch at the 'Unknown One."[3] 'In man,' says Lālan, 'resides that Jewel of Man,'—but ah me, that Jewel I could not recognise!'[4] Lālan says in another beautiful song that 'changeless beauty' resides within the house of this man,—it is to be realised there. It is through the medium of the human form that the divine beauty is to be realised. The truth is metaphorically explained in the following lines:—"At the gate of that 'Divine Beauty' there is the revered Śrī-rūpa (*i.e.*, the human form and personality), and the lock and the key for 'Divine Beauty' are in his hand; one, who will be a devotee of the Śrī-rūpa, will obtain the lock and the key; Phakira

1 *yākhan āmār maner mānuṣ kothāy pāi* ।
yār tare mana-khede prāṇ kānde sarvadāi । *re* ।
* * * *
phikir-cānd kay manare tomāre,
o tor maner mānuṣ hṛde āche, khuṁje ne tāre;
kyān ghure byāḍās deś bideśe, yāman hāvā ār to
dekhi nāi re ।

Song of Praphulla Bandyopādhyāya, disciple of Phikir-cānd, *Ibid*, pp. 214-15.

It may be noted that the disciples of Phikir-cānd used to compose songs of their own in the name of the Guru.

2 *mānuṣe gosāṁi birāj kare,*
kyān cinline sāmānya jñāne re ।
* * * *
nitya yoge sāṁi bihare, bihare hṛd baddha ka're;
o hṛd baddha ka're rāger jore, hāre re re rūp nehāre—
Song by an unknown author, *Ibid*, p. 247.

3 *Vide* Song of Lālan, *Hārāmaṇi*, Song No. 35.

4 *ei mānuṣe āchae re man*
yāre bale mānuṣ-ratan,
lālan bale peye se dhan pārlām nā cinte ।
Ibid, Song No. 6.

Lālan says that such people will be able to get hold of that one who escapes all grasp."[1]

The love celebrated in the Bāul songs is mutual, inasmuch as it induces on the one hand the Infinite Absolute to find self-expression in the finite and relative nature of the manifested world, including human personality which is the highest expression of the Absolute,—and, on the other hand, inspires man to find his true nature by gradually dissolving his separate existence and passing away into his original being in God. We have seen that man is the marginal being, or a finite-infinite being; when associated with principles of illusory defilement, he passes on to his purely finite nature of animal existence, when he suffers bondage on all sides; but when he purifies himself in love, the principles of defilement in him being all burn away, he passes again on to his true divine nature and becomes liberated by transcending all limitations of finitude. In such a state, when the apparent difference between humanity and divinity is totally removed through love, man becomes one with the Reality itself. It is in such a state that the Bāul exclaims that the self is everything—everything proceeds from the self.[2]

1 *rūper ghare aṭal rūp bihāre*
ceye dekh nā tāre ।
* * * *
o se rūper darajāy, śrī-rūp mahāśay,
rūper tālā-cāvi tār hāte sadāy;
ye jan śrī-rūp gata have, tālā-cāvi pāve,
phakir lālan bale adharā dharve tārā ||
Ibid, Song No. 7.

2 *bicār kariyā dekhi sakalei āmi* ।
* * * *
āmi haite āllā rasul, āmi haite kūl,
āmi haite āsmān jamin, āmā haitei sav (bhula?) ।
marva marva deśer lok mor kathā yadi lay,
āpani cinile dekha khodā cinā yāy ।
Vicitrā, B. S. 1335, Caitra.

In the same strain did the Sūfī poet exclaim—
None lives but his life is from mine, and every willing soul is obedient to my will;
And there is no speaker but tells his tale with my words, nor any seen but sees with the sight of mine eye;
And no silent listener but hears with my hearing, nor any one that grasps but with my strength and might;
And in the whole creation there is none save me that speaks or sees or hears.
Nicholson, *The Idea of Personality in Sufi-ism*, p. 21.
Cf. also *Dabistan*, Vol. I, Preliminary Discourses, p. clxvi.

But we should notice that though love is the main religious mode of the Bāuls, the element of yoga is in no way less important in their Sādhanā. The element of love is generally associated with elements of yoga in the Bāul sect as it is in Sūfī-ism. The *modus operandi* of the Bāuls who take to the Sādhanā of the 'four moons' is essentially yogic. But elements of yoga are resorted to also by the devout Bāuls as a process of purification and concentration.

(iv) *Poet Tagore and the Bāul Songs*

The Bāul songs, with the ingrained spirit of freedom, the mystic conception of divinity and love and also with the charm of their tune, leading the mind to supreme renunciation and indifference, had strong influence in the evolution of the poetico-religious mind of poet Tagore. Tagore says in *The Religion of Man* that in his youth he could not harmonise his inner spiritual demands with his relationship with the monotheistic church with which he was closely associated. After a long struggle with the feeling that he was 'using a mask to hide the living face of truth,' he severed his connection with the church. "About this time," says the poet, "one day I chanced to hear a song from a beggar belonging to the Bāul sect of Bengal. ...What struck me in this simple song was a religious expression that was neither grossly concrete, full of crude details, nor metaphysical in its rarefied transcendentalism. At the same time it was alive with an emotional sincerity. It spokes of an intense yearning of the heart for the divine which is in Man and not in the temple, or scriptures, in images and symbols. The worshipper addresses his songs to Man the ideal..."[1] Again he says,—"Since then I have often tried to meet these people, and sought to understand them through their songs, which are their only form of worship. One is often surprised to find in many of these verses a striking originality of sentiment and diction; for, at their best, they are spontaneously individual in their expressions."[2]

In another place the poet says,—"Those, who have gone through my writings, know that I have expressed my love

[1] *The Religion of Man*, Ch. VII, *The Man of My Heart*, p. 110.
[2] *The Religion of Man*, p. 111.

towards the Bāul songs in many of my writings. When I was in Śilāidaha I would frequently meet these Bāuls and I had occasion to have discourses with them. I have fitted the tune of the Bāuls to many of my songs, and in many other songs the tune of the Bāuls has consciously or unconsciously been mixed up with other musical modes and modifications. It will be easily understood from the above that the tune as well as the message of the Bāuls had at one time absorbed my mind as if they were its very element."[1]

The conception of the 'Man of the heart', as confessed by Tagore himself, deeply stirred his poetic mind even in his youth. Tagore, with the Upaniṣadic background of his mind prepared in his early days by his father as well as by the whole environment of his life, naturally tried to assimilate the message of the Bāuls with the Upaniṣadic doctrines.

We have indicated in the introduction that through all his songs and poems Tagore sings of an Infinite Being, Who is seeking His self-expression through the whole creative process for self-realisation,—and the best expression of the Divine personality is through the human personality, and throughout the life-process of man there is going on this continual process of love-making between the human and the Divine. This human personality and the Divine personality, both of which remain combined in the nature of man, are the 'I' and the 'You', the 'Lover' and the 'Beloved' so much spoken of by poet Tagore in his songs and poems. In singing of this 'I' and the 'You' in man, between man and the 'Man of the heart', Tagore has been the greatest of the Bāuls of Bengal.

[1] Foreword to *Hārāmaṇi* by Tagore.

PART III

THE NĀTH CULT

CHAPTER VIII

LEGEND AND HISTORY

ANOTHER obscure religious cult, that has influenced the growth of Bengali literature as also the literature in many other modern Indian languages to a considerable extent from an early period, is Nāthism. As an All-India religious movement Nāthism enjoyed and is still enjoying immense popularity. The religious and literary history of Nāthism in Bengal is, therefore, intimately connected with that of many other provinces of India as also of the Himalayan regions like Nepal and Tibet. There are many yogic texts in Sanskrit either directly ascribed to the Nāth-gurus (mainly to Gorakh-nāth), or somehow associated with the cult. The Nāth literature in the vernaculars consists mainly of longer narrative poems of the nature of ballads and also stray songs. A general survey of the nature and extent of Nāth literature with particular reference to Bengali will be found in the Appendix (B); a detailed list of Sanskrit and Hindi texts ascribed to Gorakh-nāth may be found in the Hindi book *Nātha-sampradāya* by Prof. Hazariprasad Dwivedi.[1]

(i) *Origin of the Nāth Cult*

The problem of the origin and development of the Nāth cult in India, including the Nāth movement of Bengal, is as yet shrouded in the mist of legends and myths. From the heaps of traditional accounts it is possible for us only to form an idea of the extent of popularity which the cult enjoyed and is still enjoying in the soil of India; but no definite history of its origin and development can be constructed with the data that we have at our disposal. We have, however, made it clear on several occasions that the historical study is not our primary concern,—we are rather interested in the religious contents relating to our literature; but as the mythical and semi-historic accounts will help us to a great extent to under-

[1] Published by Hindustani Academy, Allahabad, 1950.

stand the religious nature of the cullt, we propose to make here a brief study of them.

The Nāth cult is essentially a yogic cult; but among the innumerable yogic sects of India the cult is characterised as the Nāth cult due mainly to the fact that its stalwarts generally bear the title of 'Nāth', and the word Nāth has been dealt with in some of the standard Sanskrit texts as a philosophic concept for a state of surpeme existence. Various theories are current among scholars as to the nature and origin of this cult. Some take it to be essentially a crypto-Buddhist or an esoteric Buddhist cult, which later seceded from the Buddhist fold and transformed itself into a Śaivite cult. Others, on the other hand, are of opinion that the Nāth cult is essentially a Śaitvite cult, which, in course of its evolution, was assimilated within esoteric Buddhism and it is for this reason that we find in it a hotchpotch of esoteric Buddhism and yogic Śaivism. But before indulging in such speculations we should first of all be sure of what the Nāth cult stands for. The Nāth cult seems to represent a particular phase of the Siddha cult of India. This Siddha cult is a very old religious cult with its main emphasis on a psycho-chemical process of yoga, known as the Kāya-sādhana or the culture of body with a view to making it perfect and immutable and thereby attaining an immortal spiritual life.

To escape death, as we shall see, was the central point round which grew the details of the Siddha cult, and the Siddhas in general hold "that death may either be put off *ad libitum* by a special course of restrengthening and revitalising the body so as to put it permanently *en rapport* with the world of sense, or be ended definitively by dematerialising and spiritualising the body, according to prescription, so that it disappears in time in a celestial form from the world of sense, and finds its permanent abode in the transcendental glory of God."[1] This Siddha school seems to be closely associated with the Indian school of Rasāyana and it is sometimes held that the Siddha school was originally based on the

[1] *Vide*, *The Doctrinal Culture and Tradition of the Siddhas* by Dr. V. V. Raman Śāstrī M.A., Ph.D., F.R.A.S., M.R.A.S., in the *Cultural Heritage of India*, Srī Ramakrishna Centenary Memorial, Vol. II, pp. 303-319.

theories and practices of the Rasāyana school.[1] This Rasāyana school has been accepted as a school of Indian philosophy in the *Sarva-darśana-saṁgraha* of Sāyaṇa-Mādhava. The school is styled there as the *Raseśvara-darśana* and the doctrines of the school are explained with reference to well-known texts on Rasāyana. The school is, however, recognised here as a Śaivite school. Rasāyana or alchemy is an ancient science of the pre-Christian origin having immense popularity in different parts of the world. In India, however, instead of being purely a chemical science, it developed theological speculations and already in fairly old medical texts we find references to the view that *siddhi* or perfection can be attained by making the body immutable with the help of *Rasa* (*i.e.*, some chemical substance). There is a popular tradition that the Siddhas were "a band of death-defying theriacal and therapeutic alchemists indebted in all respects to Bhoga, a pre-Christian Tāoist immigrant from China, who, in his methods of keying up the body of impure matter through 'reverberation' and 'projection' to the pitch of practically cancelling demise, merely sought to promulgate the lesser athanasic precepts of Lao-tse, since the vital objective of the Tāo-Teh-King is the transfiguration of the immortalised ethereal body into a permanent garment of celestial virtue, in order to fit it to associate to eternity with the Tāo."[2]

Patañjali, the great exponent of yoga, who flourished most probably some time between the second and the sixth century A.D.,[3] says in the *Kaivalya-pāda* of his yoga-aphorism that *siddhi* can be attained even by the application of herb or medicine (*auṣadhi*).[4] In the commentary on this aphorism Vyāsa and Vācaspati say that this *siddhi* by *auṣadhi* refers to the schools of yogins who attained perfection with the help of Rasāyana.[5] We shall presently see that the *Rasa* of the Rasāyana school was replaced, in the cult of the

[1] For the details of the fundamental points of similarity between the Nāth school and the school of Rasāyana, see *infra*, Ch. IX, Sec. V.

[2] Dr. Raman Śāstrī, *Loc, cit.*

[3] See *History of Indian Philosophy* by Dr. S. N. Dasgupta, Vol. I.

[4] *janmauṣadhi-mantra-tapaḥ-samādhijāḥ siddhayaḥ* I

[5] *auṣadhibhiḥ asura-bhavaneṣu rasāyanety evam ādi etc.* I *Comm. of Vyāsa. auṣdhi-siddhim āha—"asura-bhavaneṣu" iti* I *manuṣyo hi kutaścin nimittād asura-bhavanam upasamprāptah kamanīyābhir asura-kanyābhir upanītam rasāyanam upayujyājarā-maraṇatvam anyāńca siddhir āsādayati ihaiva vā rasāyanopayogena* I *yathā māṇḍavyo muniḥ, rasopayogād bindhyavāsī iti* I Vācaspati.

Nāth Siddhas, by the nectar oozing from the moon situated in the Sahasrāra and the whole chemical process was changed into a psycho-chemical process of Haṭha-yoga. From the above it seems plausible to hold that the *siddha mārga* evolved gradually from the ancient school of Rasāyana. The theory of the Sun and the Moon as expounded by the Nāth Siddhas[1] and the principle of being immortal by drinking the nectar oozing from the Moon are found explained in the second Brāhmaṇa of the *Bṛhad-jābālopaniṣat*.[2] Of course the *Bṛhad-jābālopaniṣat* is not one of those Upaniṣads that are recognised by scholars to be authentic and fairly early in origin, and therefore the occurrence of the principles of the Nāth cult in this text may not help us much in ascertaining the exact time when these doctrines were prevalent; but the fact will at least hint at an antiquity of the tradition. What we can be sure of on this point is that the science of Rasāyana was accepted much prior to the advent of Patañjali by a section of yogins for the attainment of the immutability of the body and for the attainment of many other supernatural powers and that escape from death through the perfection of body was regarded by these yogins as the highest achievement in religious life. As this is essentially the position held also by the Nāth Siddhas, the history of the Nāth yogins may be traced back to a period prior to Patañjali.

From the above discussions it will be clear that any hypothesis about the possibility of the Nāth cult being originally an esoteric Buddhist cult and seceding from Buddhism in course of time to assume a Śaivite air is based purely on a misconception of the fundamental nature of the cult. Such a misconception arises also from the reliance on some popular traditions current in Eastern India. In Eastern India, particularly in the Himalayan regions (in Nepal and Tibet), many of the traditions of the Nāth Siddhas got mixed up with those of the Buddhist Siddhācāryas. The reason for such a mixture and confusion is not very far to seek. If we analyse and examine the different schools of esoterism, which go by the name of Tāntric Buddhism, or Śāktaism, or Śaivism, we shall find that in their composite practical nature they

[1] *Vide infra.*

[2] *Vide infra.*

contain mainly two elements: one is the paraphernalia of rites and rituals of a heterogeneous nature, which are neither Hindu nor Buddhistic in origin, but represent a common stock of heritage to all the popular religious systems of India; the other element is the element of yoga in its various forms, which also is a common heritage. We have hinted before[1] that at different periods in the history of Indian religion these paraphernalia of practices together with the various yogic elements got themselves associated with the different schools of Hindu and Buddhist philosophy, giving rise to the different esoteric schools. This fact has been responsible for so much mixture and confusion among the views and practices of these esoteric schools.

If we are to recognise any fundamental philosophy in the Hindu Tāntric systems, we should say that it is the philosophy of Śiva and Śakti with all ontological and cosmological speculations on them; and we have seen before that all the yogic practices of the Tāntric Buddhists have also grown with the fundamental ideology of Prajñā and Upāya, which is essentially the same as that of Śiva and Śakti. The traditional belief of Hinduism is that Śiva is the original instructor of all yoga,—the Tāntric Buddhists also believe that Lord Buddha, or rather lord Vajra-sattva (or Hevjra, or Heruka), who is conceived just as Śiva, is the original instructor of all secret yoga. The traditional belief of the Nāths is that Ādi-nāth is the first in the list of the chronology of the Nāths,—and all secrets of yoga proceed from him. This Ādi-nāth is none but Śiva of the Hindus,[2] and Buddha, in the form of the Vajra-sattva, of the Buddhists; and as a matter of fact we frequently come across the epithets of 'Ādi-nātha' and 'Bhūta-nātha' applied to the Vajra-sattva or Hevajra in the Buddhist Tantras as they are frequently applied to Śiva in the Hindu Tantras. We have also pointed out that some of the important Buddhist Tantras are introduced as a dialogue between the lord and the compassionate lady just as many of the Hindu Tantras are, and according to the literary traditions of the Nāths also, we find that Matsyendra-nāth

[1] *Supra*, introduction.

[2] *Cf. sakaler pradhān siddhā bandiva bholā-nāth.* l
Gopi-candrer Sannyās, by Sukur Mahammad (C.U.), p. 397.

(the first among the human Gurus) received the secret of yoga in the form of a fish when it was being disclosed to the Goddess in a castle on the Kṣīrodasea. The theory of the Sun and the Moon of the Buddhists has correspondence in the Nāth cult. It is because of the general similarities of this nature that Tāntric Buddhism seems allied to the other yogic sects. The final state of yoga is called the Sahaja state or Sahaja-samādhi or Śūnya-samādhi by the Buddhist Sahajiyās and this idea is to be met with also in the literature ascribed to the Nāths. In the two versions of the *Akula-vīra-tantra*[1] (authorship attributed to Matsyendra-nāth) we find a detailed description of the state of Sahaja; there it is defined as a state of perfect equilibrium, which transcends all our perceptual knowledge with positive and negative attributes. In that state of perfect quietude the yogin becomes one with the whole universe and realises a non-dual existence. In such a state "He himself is the goddess, himself the God, himself the disciple, himself the preceptor; he is at once the meditation, the meditator and the divinity (meditated upon)."[2] It is very easy to see that this Sahaja is the same as the Sahaja described in the Buddhist Tantras and the Buddhist Dohās and songs. In the vernacular literature on the Nāth cult we frequently meet with this conception of Sahaja or Sahaja-Śūnya, particularly in the old Hindi poems ascribed to Gorakh-nāth and in similar poems ascribed to Nāth-Siddhas like Carpaṭi, Jālandhar, Caurańgī and others.[3] In the *Haṭhayoga-pradīpikā* (which is a standard

[1] See *Kaula-jñāna-nirṇaya*, edited by Dr. P. C. Bagchi, Calcutta Sanskrit Series, No. III.

[2] *svayaṁ devī svayaṁ devaḥ svayaṁ śiṣyaḥ svayaṁ guruḥ* |
svayaṁ dhyānaṁ svayaṁ dhyātā svayaṁ sarvatra devatā ||
(*Akula*, A, p. 26).
sa brahmā sa hariścaiva sa rudraś caive'śvaras tathā ||
sa śivaḥ śāśvato devaḥ sa ca somārka-śańkaraḥ |
sa viśākhyo mayurākṣo arhanto budham eva ca ||
svayaṁ devī svayaṁ devaḥ svayaṁ śiṣyaḥ svayaṁ guruḥ |
svayaṁ dhyānaṁ svayaṁ dhyātā svayaṁ sarveśvaro guruḥ ||
(*Akula*, B, pp. 116-118).
Vide Dr. Bagchi's introduction, pp. 55-56.

[3] See *Gorakh-bānī* edited by P. D. Barthwāl, Prayāg, 1943. See also the text of the *Gorakh-bodh* as quoted by Dr. Mohan Singh in his work on Gorakhnath and also similar literature of the medieval yogic saints illustrated at the end of the same text. Also Dr. Dharmavīra Bhāratī, *Siddha-sāhitya* (in Hindi), Allahabad, 1955, Ch. V; Dr. Barthwal, *Yoga-pravāha*, Banaras, 1947, pp. 69-75.

text on Haṭha-yoga) we find that the Buddhist theory of the four kinds of Śūnya, *viz.*, Śūnya, Ati-śūnya, Mahā-śūnya and Sahaja-śūnya (or Sarva-śūnya)[1] is associated with the four stages of sound produced through yogic practices.[2] Again, the Nāth literature (including the Sanskrit and vernacular texts) is sometimes characterised by a spirit of heterodoxy and criticism similar to that of the Tāntric Buddhists.[3] It is found further that in the texts ascribed to the Nāths holy places of pilgrimage located within the human organism are described under several categories, viz., *Pīṭha*, *Upapīṭha*, *Kṣetra*, *Upakṣetra*, *Sandoha*, etc., and this is the custom also with the Buddhist and the Hindu Tantras.[4] As for the technical yoga terminology, it can be said that they have been common to all the esoteric yogic schools.

The most important thing common to all schools of esoterism is the culture of the body or Kāya-sādhana through the processes of Haṭha-yoga. We have seen before that though Kāya-sādhana was not the final aim of the Buddhist and the Vaiṣṇava Sahajiyās, the process of Kāya-sādhana was regarded in both the sects as an indispensable accessory for the realisation of the Sahaja-nature as supreme bliss or supreme love.

The fact of such a similarity and mixture has been responsible for the frequent association of the Nāth cult with the cult of the Tāntric Buddhists in myths and legends. But judging from the literary records and the legends and traditions still prevalent among the yogins of the Nāth order it appears that the Nāth cult has grown with a general air of Śaivism. It is noticeable that not only is there the tradition of Mahādeva or Śiva being the original instructor of the cult, but that Gorakh-nāth, the most renowned and most important yogin of the sect, has frequently been identified with Śiva or deified as such. The deity of the cult, where traditional or iconographic record of the deity is available, is found to be Śiva; the places of pilgrimage of the yogins of

1 *Vide supra*, pp. 51-53.
2 *Vide*, *Haṭha-yoga-pradīpikā*, Iyangar's edition (4. 70-75).
3 *Vide Gorakh-bānī*, ed. by Dr. Barthwal.
4 *Vide*, *Kaula-jñāna-nirṇaya*, introduction, p. 57.

this order[1] are generally of Śaivite importance and the temples there often contain an image of Śiva or the phallic symbol of the lord. Again in dress and other accessories the Nāth yogins are depicted just like images of Śiva, who himself is the greatest of yogins. The Siddhas of the Nāth cult are sometimes described in vernacular literature as fond of intoxicants like *Siddhi* and *Gāñjā* just as Śiva is.[2] '*Vam, Vam*' is the peculiar mystic sound of the Nāth yogins as it is of Śiva himself. It is also noticeable that in the *Vallāla-carita* the priests of the Yogī caste of Bengal have been spoken of as *rudraja brāhmaṇa* (*i.e.*, Brahmins deriving their origin from Rudra or Śiva),—and as a matter of fact the Yogīs of Bengal even in the present day speak of themselves as belonging to the *Śiva-gotra* (*i.e.*, the Śiva-lineage).[3]

But in spite of all these, the general similarity in tone and practice has been responsible for the confused identification of the later Buddhist apostles with the Nāth yogins, and it may be probably for this reason that Matsyendra-nāth, who is taken to be the first of the human exponents of the Nāth cult, has been deified in Nepal as Avalokiteśvara, and even at the present day the Buddhists of that land hold annual procession in honour of the deified Matsyendra-nāth. It is also perhaps for this reason that Matsyendra-nāth is identified in Tibetan traditions with Lui-pā (or Luyi-pā), who is generally taken to be the first among the Buddhist Siddhācāryas.[4] In the Sanskrit commentary on the Caryā-song No. 21 we find a quotation of a few lines (composed in the language similar to that of the Caryā-songs), which is ascribed to Mīna-nāth (commonly accepted as identical

[1] For detailed descriptions of such places see Briggs, Chs. V and VI.

[2] As a typical instance we may cite the following description of Hāḍiphā or Jālandharīpā in the version of the *Gopi-candrer Sannyās* by Sukur Mahammad:—

takhane āniyā dila siddher jhulī ||
sooā kuclā siddhā haste kari nila |
sooā man dhutrār phal tāthe miśāila ||
sooā man kuclā siddhā ekatra kariyā |
mukhe tule dila nāth śiva nām liyā ||
(C. U. edition, Part II, pp. 431-432).

[3] *Vide* introduction to *Mayanāmatīr Gān* by Dr. N. K. Bhaṭṭaśālī, p. iv.

[4] *Vide* introduction to the *Bauddha-Gān-O-Dohā* by MM. H. P. Śāstrī.

with Matsyendra-nāth)[1] and MM. H. P. Śāstrī, on the evidence of it went so far as to say that the Nāth yogins (who, according to MM. Śāstrī, flourished some time before the Buddhist Siddhācāryas) also composed Bengali songs exactly in the manner of the songs of the Buddhist Siddhācāryas. The hazardous leap involved in the inference of MM. Śāstrī seems to be too long to justify his inference. Of course, many Sanskrit texts and Hindi texts are ascribed to Gorakh-nāth, who has even been recognised as the first prose-writer in Hindi (or Panjabi),[2] but we cannot be sure that the heap of literature (either in Sanskrit or vernacular) ascribed to Gorakh are not later texts, embodying some of the doctrines of the cult.

The general similarity among the esoteric yogic sects of the later Buddhists and the Śaivites seems to be responsible also for the tradition that many of the Siddhas of the Nāth cult, including the most renowned Gorakh-nāth, hailed from the Buddhist fold as seceders. According to the evidence of Tāranāth the name of Gorakh-nāth, when he belonged to the Buddhist fold, was Anaṅga-vajra. MM. Śāstrī says that the Buddhist name of Gorakh-nāth was Ramaṇa-vajra.[3] It is said that the Nepalese Buddhists are much displeased with Gorakh-nāth and hate him as a seceder.[4] In the index of the *Pag Sam Jon Zang* Mr. S. C. Das says,—"Gaurakṣa—a cowherd, who being initiated into Tāntric Buddhism became the well known sage Gaurakṣa, whose religious school survives in the yogee sect, who go under the designaton of Nāth."[5] Though we are not quite sure of the history either of the Nāths or of the Buddhist Siddhācāryas, yet a consideration of the general circumstances lead us to believe that all these traditions have more confusion for their

kahanti guru paramārthera bāṭa |
karmma kuraṅga samādhika pāṭa ||
kamala bikasila kahiha ṇa jamarā |
kamala madhu pivivi dhoke na bhamarā ||
Ibid p., 38.

[2] Vide Applendix (B). In Bengali, however, though we have vernacular literature on Gorakh-nāth there is no vernacular text ascribed to Gorakh-nāth; here there is no tradition whatsover of Gorakh-nāth being an author of Bengali literature at any time.

[3] *Vide* introduction to the *Bauddha-Gān-O-Dohā* by MM. Śāstrī, p. 16.

[4] *Ibid.*

[5] *Pag Sam Jon Zang*, Index, p. ix.

genesis than historical facts. We may note here also the queer suggestion about the identification of Gorakh with Ārya Asaṅga, or even with Nāgārjuna, the well known Buddhist scholar.[1] Whatever might have been the history of the origin and development of the Nāth cult and the cult of the Buddhist Siddhācāryas, the fact is that Mīna-nāth, Matsyendra-nāth,[2] Gorakṣa-nāth, Jālandharī and Cauraṅgīnāth, who are the most prominent among the Nāths, were all included in the list of the Buddhist Siddhācāryas and were sometimes credited with some works on esoteric Buddhism, which were translated into Tibetan.

Dr. B. M. Barua sugests that—in the Nāthism of Bengal as in that of other places, one may trace the recrudescence and continuity of the doctrines and practices of the Ājīvikas, who were a factor, as noted before in the religious history of Bengal. The points of similarity between the Ājīvikas and the Nāths may, according to Dr. Barua, briefly be noted thus:

(1) Both sects recognised three supreme Personalities in their religious tradition, the Ājīvikas: Nanda-vatsa, Kṛśa Sāmkṛtyāyana and Maṣkarin Gośāla; the Nāths: Mīna-nāth, Matsyendra-nāth and Gorakṣa-nāth.

(2) Both sects admitted singing and dancing as two important modes of religious expression.

(3) Both sects believed that in order to reach the human state a soul must pass through eighty-four hundred thousand stages.

(4) Both aspired after *Ananta-mānasa* or Sahasrāra as the highest condition of soul reachable through Haṭha-yoga, in which Prāṇāyāma or control of the vital wind is the essential feature.

(5) Both were Caturaṅgīs (*Cauraṅgīs*) in the sense that their religious life was to stand the fourfold test of ascetics, *viz.*, *parama-tapassitā* (great privation), *parama-lukhatā* (great austerity), *parama-jegucchitā* (great loathness to wrong-doing), and *parama-pavivittatā* (great aloofness from the world).

[1] *Vide* Introductory note by Mr. Daljit Singh to the *Gorakh-nath and Mediaeval Hindu Mysticism* of Dr. Mohan Singh (p. xiii).

[2] In the Tibetan as well as in the Indian traditions Mīna-nāth and Matsyendra nāth are sometimes held to be different, while according to the Bengali tradition the two are generally held identical.

In criticism of the views of Dr. Barua we may say that though there may be some important points of similarity in some of the views, practices and traditions of the Ājīvikas and the Nāth Siddhas, there seems to be no similarity in their theological speculations. The Ājīvikas were indeed wandering saints, who would often have recourse to some of the important Haṭha-yogic practices; but these Haṭha-yogic practices were no monopoly of any particular religious sect; they were and still are important factors in the practical aspect of many of the Indian religious systems. It is a particular theological system growing round these important Haṭha-yogic practices that have given a distinctiveness to Nāthism as a religious sect. The tenets of the Ājīvikas are not yet clearly known; but as far as they are known, they do not seem to represent any close resemblance with the speculations of the Nāth Siddhas.

The similarity in the tradition of three supreme personalities, of which Dr. Barua speaks, is indeed noticeable and the tradition of the Tri-nāth (three Nāths) is still current in many parts of East-Bengal and North-Bengal and there are still extant religious functions which are generally accompanied by popular songs in honour of the Tri-nāth. In these functions, however, the Tri-nāth have frankly become the trinity.[1] About the second point, though we find that Gorakṣa-nāth transformed himself through his yogic power into a dancing girl and rescued his preceptor from the country of Kadalī by dancing and singing,—that seems to have been a mere trick to enter into the country of women, and as such need not be recognised to be any important religious mode of the Nāths. Of course the episode of the captivity of Mīna-nāth in the land of Kadalī and his rescue by Gorakṣa may allegorically be interpreted as the bondage of the human soul[2] through worldly pleasure and its redemp-

[1] The present writer may speak of one function in honour of the Tri-nāth in some parts of East-Bengal. The function is known as *Tennāther Melā* (the congregation of the three Nāths) and is generally held with the purpose of preventing some family calamity and of gaining prosperity for the family or for an individual. In the function, however, the three Nāths are confusedly identified with the trinity, *viz.*, Brahmā, Viṣṇu and Śiva and three pipes of *Gāñjā* are offered to them, which are then smoked. In the songs, however, the Tri-nāth is regarded, as one deity.

[2] There being the Upaniṣadic analogy between the fish (*mīna*) and the human soul.

tion through practices of yoga, and in that case the dancing and singing of Gorakṣa in the form of the dancing girl may be held important as a religious method; but from a study of the fundamental tenets or the yogic practices of the Nāths it does not seem to be the fact that dancing and singing were any important method of religious expression with the Nāth yogins. Many Kānphaṭ yogins are, however, found begging from door to door singing songs,—but this singing seems to be simply the profession of a beggar—and nothing more. About the third point we may note that the number eighty-four, as we shall presently see, was held to be a mystic number not only by the Nāths, but by various other schools and we find enough of it in popular literature, both Sanskrit and vernacular. The fourth and fifth points are noteworthy inasmuch as the Ājīvikas like the Nāths were wandering yogins who emphasised processes of Haṭha-yoga and were also great ascetics.

(ii) *Traditions of the eighty-four Siddhas and the nine Nāths*

All yogins, who have attained perfection in the practice of yoga, were honoured with the general epithet of Siddha, or Siddhā (as in the vernacular). The Buddhist Sahajiyā yogins of much renown are commonly known as the Siddhācāryas and the apostles among the Nāth yogins are also called Siddhas; it is for this reason that there has been a popular confusion of the Buddhist Siddhācāryas and the Nāth yogins in the chronology of the Siddhas. Through such a confused amalgamation has arisen the tradition of the eighty-four Siddhas. In the lists available we shall find that some of the Buddhist Siddhācāryas and Nāth yogins have been included indiscriminately. This tradition of the eighty-four Siddhas is very important inasmuch as the tradition is found frequently mentioned in the vernacular literature of different periods. In the *Varṇa-ratṇā-kara*[1] we find a list of the eighty-four Siddhas, where

[1] MS. preserved in the A.S.B. No. 4834; the author Kavi-śekharācārya Jyotirīśvara was a court-poet of King Hari-siṁha Deva of Mithilā, who reigned from 1300-1321 A.D. *Vide* introduction to the *Baudha-Gān-O-Dohā* by MM. Śāstrī, p. 35.

the names of seventy-six Siddhas really occur.[1] In the first chapter of the *Haṭha-yoga-pradīpikā* we find a list of yogins, who are called the Mahā-siddhas.[2] We find here many of the important names common with those found in the list given in the *Varṇa-ratnā-kara*. This tradition of the eighty-four Siddhas is very popular in Tibetan Buddhism also. Albert Gruenwedel has given the full list of these eighty-four Siddhas from data available from the Tibetan sources.[3] This list of the Siddhas has also been discovered in Java

[1] The list gives the names as follows:—(1) Mīna-nāth, (2) Gorakṣa-nāth, (3) Caurańgī-nāth, (4) Cāmarī-nāth, (5) Tanti-pā, (6) Hāli-pā, (7) Kedārī-pā, (8) Dhońga-pā, (9) Dāri-pā, (10) Viru-pā, (11) Kapālī, (12) Kamārī, (13) Kāṇha, (14) Kanakhala, (15) Mekhala, (16) Unmana, (17) Kāṇḍali, (18) Dhovī, (19) Jālandhara, (20) Tońgī, (21) Mavaha, (22) Nāgārjuna, (23) Daulī, (24) Bhisāla, (25) Acitī, (26) Campaka, (27) Ḍheṇṭasa, (28) Bhumbharī, (29) Bākali, (30) Tujī, (31) Carpaṭī, (32) Bhāde, (33) Cāndana, (34) Kāmarī, (35) Karavat (36) Dharma-pāpatańga, (37) Bhadra. (38) Pātali-bhadra. (39) Palihiha, (40) Bhānu, (41) Mīna, (42) Nirdaya, (43) Savara, (44) Sānti, (45) Bhartṛhari, (46) Bhīṣaṇa, (47) Bhaṭī, (48) Gagana-pā, (49) Gamāra, (50) Meṇurā, (51) Kumārī, (52) Jīvana, (53) Aghosādhava, (54) Girivara, (55) Siyārī, (56) Nāgavāli, (57) Bibhavat, (58) Sārańga, (59) Vivikidhaja, (60) Magara-dhaja, (61) Acita, (62) Bicita, (63) Necaka, (64) Cāṭala, (65) Nācana, (66) Bhīlo, (67) Pāhila, (68) Pāsala, (69) Kamalakańgāri, (70) Cipila, (71) Govinda, (72) Bhīma, (73) Bhairava, (74) Bhadra, (75) Bhamarī, (76) Bhuru-kuṭī.

[2] The list includes the names of the following Siddhas:—Ādi-nātha, Matsyendra, Śābara, Ānanda-bhairava, Caurańgī, Mīna, Gorakṣa, Virupākṣa, Bileśay, Manthāna, Bhairava, Siddhi, Buddha (Siddha-bodha, see *Bhāratavarṣīya Upāsaka-sampradāya*, Vol. II, pp. 136-137), Kanthaḍi, Koranṭaka, Surānanda, Siddha-pāda, Carpaṭi, Kāneri, Nityanātha, Nirāñjana, Kapālī, Bindu-nātha, Kāka-caṇḍīśvara, Ahvaya (Maya?), Allāma, Prabhu-deva, Ghoḍā,colī, Ṭiṇṭiṇi, Bhānukī, Nāradeva, Khaṇḍakapālika and others. See *Haṭha-yoga-pradīpikā*, Ch. 1., verses (5-9) (Iyangar's edition).

[3] The list available through the Tibetan sources is as follows:—(1) Lūhi-pā (Matsyendra or Matsyāntrād), (2) Līlā-pā, (3) Virū-pā, (4) Dombi Heruka, (5) Śābara (or Śabari), (6) Saraha (or Rāhula-bhadra), (7) Kańkāli, (8) Mīna (or Vajrapāda), (9) Gorakṣa, (10) Caurańgī, (11) Vīṇā, (12) Śānti (or Ratnākara Śānti), (13) Tanti, (14) Carmari (or Carmāra), (15) Khaḍga, (16) Nāgārjuna, (17) Kṛṣṇa-cārī (orKānha-pāda, Kanapa, Karana), (18) Kāṇera (Kāṇarī, or Āryadeva), (19) Sthagana (or Thagana), (20) Nāḍa-pā (or Yaśobhadra), (21) Śāli-pā (or Sṛgāla-pāda), (22) Tilo-pā (or Tailika-pāda), (23) Chatra, (24) Bhadra (or Bhāde), (25) Dvikhanḍī (or Dokhanḍī), (26) Ajogi (or Yogi-pāda), (27) Kaḍa-pāda (orKāla), (28) Dhovī (or Dhombhi), (29) Kańkaṇa, (30) Kambala (or Kamari), (31) Teṅki (or Damgi), (32) Bhade (or Bhandhe, Bhāṇḍārī), (33) Tandhī (or Tandhe), (34) Kukkuri, (35) Cubji (or Kusūli), (36) Dharma, (37) Mahī, (38) Acintya (Acinta, Acinti), (39) Babhahi (or Bhalaha), (40) Nalina, (41) Bhusuku (or Śānti-deva), (42) Indra-bhūti, (43) Megha-pāda (or Meko), (44) Kutrhā), (or Kuṭhāli), (45) Karmāra, (46) Jālandhari, (47) Rāhula, (48) Gharbari (or Gharma-pāda), (49) Dhakri (or Tokri), (50) Medinī, (51) Pańkaja, (52) Ghaṇṭā (or Vajra-ghaṇṭa), (53) Yogī, (54) Celuka (or Caluka) (55) Vāguri (? Guṇḍarī), (56) Luñcaka (or Lucika), (57) Nirguṇa, (58) Jayānanda, (59) Carṣaṭī (or Pacari, Pācala), (60) Campaka, (61) Viṣaṇa (or Bhikhana), (62) Bhali (or Teli, Tailī), (63) Kumari (or Kumbhakāra), (64) Cārpaṭi (or Javari), (65) Maṇi-bhadrā, (66) Mekhalā, (67) Mańkhalā

and has been published by Van Manen from Holland.[1] The tradition is very popular also in the South.[2]

We are not, however, prepared to give any historical credit to the list of these eighty-four Siddhas or even to the tradition of the eighly-four Siddhas. If we just examine the lists of these eighty-four Siddhas it will appear that they are anomalous lists containing names of many Buddhist Siddhācāryas who flourished during some time near about the tenth to the twelfth century A.D., and within the list of these Buddhist Siddhācāryas the name of the most reputed Nāths have been incorporated for reasons discussed before. This tradition of the eighty-four Siddhas is occasionally referred to in the Nāth literature of Bengal as well as in the Santa literature and Sūfī literature of Western and Northern India.[3] It has been rightly held by some scholars that this number eighty-four is rather a mystic than a historical number, and for ourselves we have sufficient reason to be convinced of the purely mystic nature of this number. The significant mention of this number eighty-four is found in the belief of the Ājīvikas, who held that soul must pass through eighty-four hundred thousand stages before attaining the human state.[4] In the *Maitrāyaṇī Upaniṣat* we find mention of eighty-four thousand states of birth.[5] In some of the Tantras and Purāṇas also we find reference to the eighty-four lacs of *yonis* or birth in different states.[6] The

(or Kaṅakha), (68) Kala-kala, (69) Kanthaḍi (or Pantali), (70) Dhahuli (or Dauḍī), (71) Udhali (or Uḍḍiya), (72) Kapāla, (73) Kilı, (74) Puṣkara (or Sāgara), (75) Sarva-bhakṣa (or Sābhikṣa), (76) Nāga-bodhi, (77) Dārika, (78) Puttal (or Putuli) (79) Panaha (or Upanāhī), (80) Kokilā (or Kokilī), (81) Anaṅga, (82) Lakṣmiṅkarā, (83) Sāmudra (or Samuda), (84) Bhali-pā (or Byāḍi or Byāli). *Vide, introduction* to the *Śūnya-purāṇa* by Dr. Shahidullah, pp. 3-4; *Kalyāṇa* (an article *Caurāsī Siddha Tathā Nātha-sampradāya* by Bhagavatīprasād Siṁhaji) *Yogāṅka* number.

[1] *Vide* B. S. P. P.—The Presidential Address of MM. H. P. Śāstrī, B.S. 1329.

[2] *Vide* Dr. Raman Śāstrī, *loc. cit.*

[3] Sometimes the number of the Siddhas is said not to be merely eighty-four, but eighty-four million, and that shows that the mystic number became mythical, at least so far as the vernacular poets were concerned.

Cf. The Vijak of Kabir by Ahmad Shah, Śākhī, No. 257, p. 209.

[4] *Dīgha-nikāya*, Vol. I., p. 54.

[5] Third *prapāṭhaka*.

[6] *Tantra-tattva*—by S. C. Bhaṭṭācārya, Vol. I, pp. 21-22.

There is also the popular belief of eighty-four *Kuṇḍas* (bowel-shaped vessel) in the city of Yama in which the convicted are doomed.

Cf. emata dharmar barata avahela jehi jan |
caurāśi kuṇḍeta jam ta pele tatakhan ||
Śūnya-purāṇa, Tīkā-pāvana, p. 52.

number of the Buddhist *dhammakhandas* (i.e., *dharma-skandha* or branches of doctrines, division of the *dharma* or scripture) is eighty-four, or rather eighty-four thousand. It has been said in the Pāli text *Gaṁdha-vaṁsa* that those scholars, who will write commentaries, notes etc. on the Pāli texts containing the eighty-four thousand *dhamma-khandas*, or will cause others to write such works, will gather immense merit equal to the merit derived from building eighty-four thousand shrines, constructing eighty-four thousand images of Buddhas, establishing eighty-four thousand monasteries. It has further been said that he, who makes a good collection of the sayings of Buddha, or causes others to do it, and who scribes, or causes to be scribed the sayings of Buddha in the form of a manuscript, and who gives or causes others to give materials for preparinc such a manuscript and to preserve it, will amass immense virtue equal to that, which is gathered by building eighty-four thousand shrines and erecting eighty-four thousand monasteries.[1] Statements of similar nature are also found in later Buddhistic texts.[2] In the Pāli text *Anāgata-vaṁsa* we find that when Maitreya, the future Buddha, will renounce the world, moved by universal compassion, eighty-four thousand friends, kinsmen and princesses will follow him, and eighty-four thousand Brahmins, versed in the Vedas, will also accompany him. The mystic nature of the number eighty-four will also appear from the fact that the commonly accepted number of the yogic postures (*āsana*) is said to be eighty-four in the Yogic and Tāntric texts; and it has sometimes been held that the number of the yogic postures are eighty-four million because of the fact that the number of the different stages in the evolution of a creature is eighty-four million,[3]—and of these eighty-four million only eighty-four are prominent, and so they are described in detail. As a matter of fact, we do not find even these eighty-four *Āsanas* described anywhere, only a few of them being described in the Yogic and Tāntric literature. We may also note that

[1] *Gaṁdha-vaṁsa*, (last Chapter).

[2] *Guṇa-kāraṇḍa-vyūha*, p. 41, pp. 76-77. In this connection see also *Amitāyur-dhyāna-sūtra*, *The Sacred Books of the East*, Vol. XLIX.

[3] *Gorakṣa-paddhati* (verse 8); *Gorakṣa-saṁhitā* (verse 7); *Gheraṇḍa-saṁhitā* (2. 1-2) etc.; *Sundara-dāsa* (*Sundara-granthāvali*, Vol. I, p. 41).

sometimes the number of the beads in the rosary of a Kānphaṭ yogin is also eighty-four. In the *Skanda-purāṇa* we have detailed description of the eighty-four *Śiva-liṅgas* (*i.e.* phallic symbols of lord Śiva) in eighty-four conscecutive chapters.[1] All these taken together will convince one of the mystic nature of the number eighty-four, and this will justify the doubt about the historical nature of the tradition of the eighty-four Siddhas.

Side by side with the tradition of the eighty-four Siddhas we find the tradition of the nine Nāths.[2] In the ceremonies on the occasion of the initiation into the order of Kānphaṭ yogins there is the custom of worshipping the nine Nātns and the eighty-four Siddhas.[3] But even in this tradition of the nine Nāths, there is no agreement among the lists, and all sorts of mythical accounts are found concerning them. In the *Soḍaśa-nityatantra* quoted in the *Gorakṣa-siddhānta-saṁgraha* we find mention of the nine Nāths who are said to have preached the Tantras in the different ages. In the *Tantra-mahārṇava* (quoted in the same text) eight Nāths are said to be residing in the eight directions and one in the centre. These Nāths are Gorakṣa-nāth in the east (residing in the forest of Jagannātha?), Jālandhara in the northern region (Uttara-patha, in a forest near Jvālā-mukhī ?), Nāgārjuna (in a forest near Godāvarī in the south?), Dattātreya in the west (to the west of the river Sarasvatī?), Devadatta in the South-West, Jaḍa Bharata in the North-West, Ādināth in the land of Kurukṣetra in the Midland and Matsyendra-nāth in the South-East in a land near the sea-coast.[4] We notice further that the Kāpālika-school was introduced by the Nāths and there are twelve personalities, to whom was revealed the truth of this school. They are,

[1] *Skanda-purāṇa, Avantya-khaṇḍa, Caturaśīti-liṅga-māhātmya.*

[2] 'The sixty-four yoginis, the fifty-two heroes, the six ascetics, the eighty-four Siddhas, the nine Naths, paid homage (to Nanak)'—*Janam-sakhi* of Bābā Nanak—Trumpp, prefatory remarks, p. vii.

Cf. also:—'By having heard (his name) the Siddhas, Pirs, God and Naths (have been made),'—*Japa*, 9, Trumpp.

'Remembering that name the nine Naths of spotless emancipation, Sanak and the others were saved.

To which being attached the eighty-four Siddhas and Buddhas (and) Ambarika crossed the water of existence;'—*Panegyric of Amardas*, Trumpp, p. 700.

[3] Briggs, p. 33, p. 136.

[4] *Vide Gorakṣa-siddhānta-saṁgraha*, pp. (44-45). Note that the ninth Nāth in the *Iśāna-koṇa* is not described.

Ādi-nāth, Anādi, Kāla, Vaikālika, Karāla, Vikarāla, Mahākāla, Kāla-bhairava-nāth, Vaṭuka, Bhūta-nāth, Vīra-nāth and Śrī-kaṇṭha. Again, twelve are the apostles, who are said to be the founders of the cult (*mārga-pravartaka*),—they are Nāgārjuna, Jaḍa-bharata, Hariścandra, Satya-nāth, Bhīma-nāth, Gorakṣa, Carpaṭa, Avadya, Vairāgya, Kanthādhārī, Jālandhara and Malayārjuna.[1] In another list we find the following names of the nine Nāths; Gorakṣa-nāth, Matsyendra-nāth, Carpaṭa-nāth, Maṅgala-nāth, Ghugo-nāth, Gopī-nāth, Prāṇa-nāth, Sūrat-nāth and Camba-nāth.[2] These Nāths are believed to be immortal demigods and preachers of the sect for all ages, and it is also believed that they are still living in the Himalayan region; sometimes they are regarded as the guardian spirits of the Himalayan peaks.[3]

[1] *Śābara-tantra*, quoted in the *Gorakṣa-siddhānta-saṁgraha.*

[2] *The Legends of the Punjab*, by R. Temple, pp. 18-19, Vol. I, referred to by Briggs, p. 136. In another list again many of the nine Naths are identified with the Hindu gods. Thus (1) Oṁkāra Ādi-nātha (Lord of Lords) is identified with Śiva, (2) Shelnātha (Lord of the Arrow Shaft) with Kṛṣṇa or Rāmacandra; (3) Santosa-nātha (Lord of Gratification) with Viṣṇu, (4) Acalacambhunātha (Lord of Wondrous Immortality ?) with Hanumāna or Lakṣmaṇa; (5) Gajabalī Gajakaṇṭha-nātha (Lord of the Elephant's strength and Neck) with Gaṇeśa Gaja-karṇa; (6) Prajā-nāth, or Udai-nātha (Lord of the People ?) with Pārvatī; (7) Māyā-rupī Macchendra-nātha, Guru of Gorakha-nātha, (8) Gathepinde Ricayakari (?), or Naranṭhar, Śambhujaiti Guru Gorakha-nātha; (9) Jñāna-svarūpa or Purakh-Siddh Gauranjwenātha, or Purān Bhagat. Briggs, pp. 136-37. Almost a similar list of the nine Naths has been given by Kitts. It runs as follows:—Oṁkāri-nāth, Viṣṇu Saṁtok-nāth, Viṣṇu; Gajboli, Gajāna (Gajānana ?), Hanumān; Acaleśvar, Gaṇpati; Udayanāth, Sūrya; Pārvati Prem, Mahādeo; Santhanāth, Brahmā;Gyāniji Siddhacewarng Jagannāth; Māvārūpī Matsya. *Ibid*, p. 137.

[3] In the *Yogi-sampradāyā-viṣkṛti*, referred to before, we find an account of the incarnation of the nine Nārāyaṇas as the nine Nāths. Here, however, popular imagination seems to have run riot. It is said that towards the end of the Dvāparayuga the earth was heavy with sin, and the attention of Mahādeva, the Lord Sovereign, was drawn to the fact. Moved to pity the Lord at once sent sage Nārada to Badarikāśrama, where the nine Nārṇyaṇas (who were the sons of Ṛṣabha-rājā) of the name of Kavi-nārāyaṇa, Kara-bhājana (who were the sons of Ṛṣabha-rāja) of the name of Kavi-nārāyaṇa, Kara-bhājana Nā°, Antarikṣa Nā°, Prabuddha Nā°, Avirhotri Nā°, Pippalāyana Nā°, Camasa Nā°, Hari Nā° and Drumila Nā° were holding discussions on self-knowledge. Nārada intimated to the Nārāyaṇas the will of the lord, who would have the Nārāyaṇas come down to the world to preach the secrets of yoga to people so that they may be liberated. The Nārāyaṇas went to Vaikuṇṭha to take counsel from Viṣṇu as to how to carry out the will of lord Śiva. Viṣṇu, accompanied by the Nārāyaṇas, went to Kailāsa to receive instructions from the Lord, and with His instructions the nine Nārāyaṇas incarnated themselves in the form of the nine Nāths, *viz.*, Matsyendra, Gorakṣa, Gahini, Jvālendra, Kāriṇa-pā, Carpaṭa, Revana, Bhartṛ and Gopī-candra. It was settled that Matsyendra would be initiated by the Lord Himself, Gorakṣa, Carpaṭi and Revana by Matsyendra, Gahini by Gorakṣa: Jvālendra would be initiated by the Lord,—Kariṇa-pā, Bhartṛ and Gopī-candra by Jvālendra. (*Vide* Ch. 1.).

In this connection, we may take note of the different accounts given of the Nāthgurus. The Mārāṭhi tradition may be illistrated thus[1]:

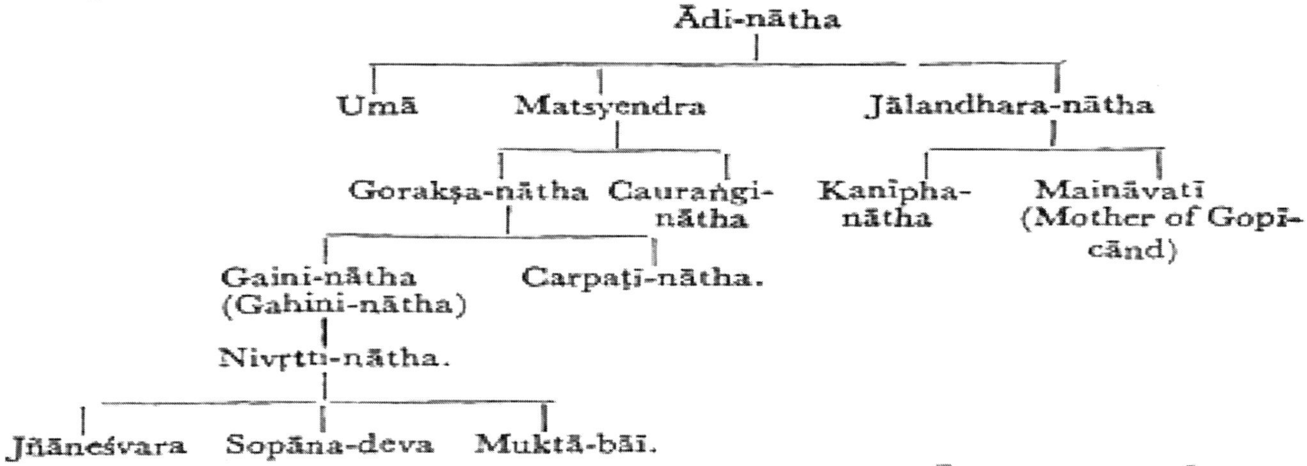

According to the chronology of Bahiṇā Bāī Ādi-nātha (Śiva) taught the secrets of Yoga to Pārvatī and Matsyendra managed to hear them; Matsyendra taught them to Gorakh-nāth, he to Gahinī, Gahinī to Nivṛtti-nāth, he to Jñāneś-vara, he to Saccidānanda and further to Viśvambhara, he to Rāghava (Caitanya), he to Keśava-caitanya, and Keśava to Bāvāji Caitanya, he to Tokobā (Tukārāma) and Tokobā to Bahiṇā Bāī (1700 A.D.).[2] Another chronology runs thus:

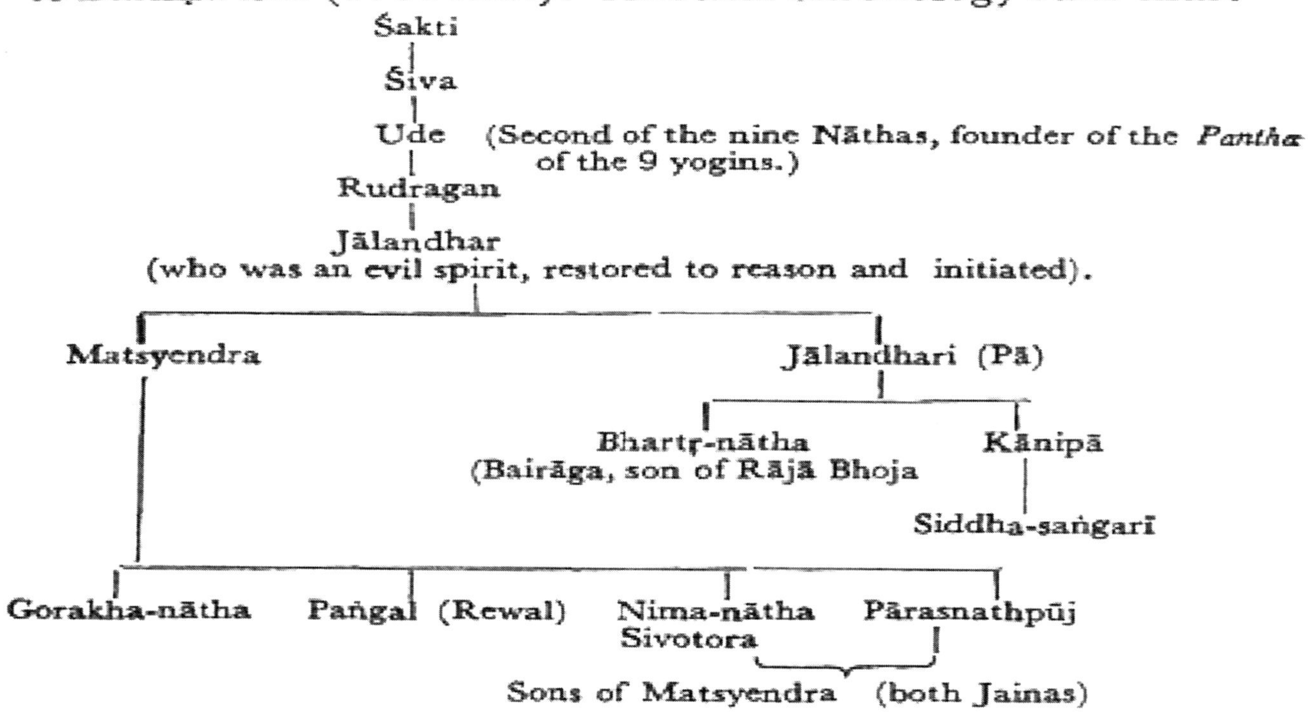

[1] *Vide*, *Śrī-jñāneśvara-caritra* by Mr. Pāṅgārakara pp. 60-78.
[2] Briggs, *loc. cit.*

Various lists of the nine Nāths are found also in the literature of the Santa poets. It will be easy to see from the above that as no strictly historical importance can be attached to the lists of the eighty-four Siddhas so also no historical importance can be attached to these chronologies of the Nāth-gurus.

According to the accounts found in Bengali, Mīna-nāth or Matsyendra-nāth (the two being held identical according to the Bengali tradition) and Jālandharī-pā (more commonly known as the Hāḍi-siddhā) were the direct disciples of Ādi-nāth or Śiva; Gorakh-nāth was the disciple of Mīna-nāth and queen Mayanāmatī (mother of Gopī-cānd) was the disciple of Gorakh-nāth; Kānhu-pā or Kānu-pā was the disciple of Jālandharī-pā or Hāḍi-siddha,[1] who also initiated King Gopī-cānd to the yogic order. Kānu-pā had his disciple Bāil Bhādāi. Many of the Nāth Siddhas are referred to also in the *Dharma-maṅgala* literature. Sahadeva Cakravartī, as we shall see, made a regular mixture of the legends of the Nāth literature and the Dharma literature. In many other texts of the Dharma literature we find the prominent Nāth Siddhas and also other sages descending on earth, along with the various gods, on the occasion of some ritualistic and sacrificial ceremonies held in honour of the Dharma-ṭhākura. In the *Dharma-pūja-vidhāna* we find the custom of worshipping many of these Nāth Siddhas along with some gods, goddesses and demi-gods of the Dharmites.[2] The most prominent names, which we come acoross in the legends of the Nāth literature of Bengal, are (1) Mīna-nāth, (2) Gorakh-nāth, (3) Jālandharī-pā, (4) Kānu-pā, (5) Maināmatī and (6) Gopī-cānd. Various are the legendary and mythical accounts that have grown round the names of these personalities in Nepal, Tibet, Bengal and in various other provinces of India. We need not enter into the details of these legends or

[1] *tave yadi pṛthivīte yāila har-gaurī* ǀ
mīna-nāth hāḍiphāe karanta cākari ‖
mīna-nāther cākari kare jati gorakhāi ǀ
hāḍiphār sevā kare kānāphā jogāi ‖
Gorakṣa-vijaya, p. 10.

[2] *Dharma-pūjā-vidhāna*, p. 133.

the controversies of the historical and geographical questions pertaining to them; a brief survey of the various accounts will, however, be found in the Appendix (C).

CHAPTER IX

THE RELIGION OF THE NĀTH SIDDHAS

THE religious views of the Nāth Siddhas are as much obscured by the insufficiency and anomaly of accounts as is the history of the whole cult. The distinctive features of their yogic practices as also the theories behind them are not found explained systematically in any of the Sanskrit or non-Sanskrit texts, associated with the cult somehow or other. The Sanskrit texts are mainly texts on Haṭha-yoga in general and the vernacular texts are generally poetical texts on legends and myths. The method of treatment of the present writer has, therefore, been to analyse and examine all the available data and to give a systematic exposition of them so as to give a general idea about the nature of the cult.

(i) *General Air of Supernaturalism*

The general religious nature of Nāthism is characterised by a wide-spread belief in occult power attained through the practice of yoga. All the legends are permeated through and through with a spirit of supernaturalism more in the form of the display of magical feats and sorcery by the Siddhas than in the form of occasional interference from the gods and goddesses, or any other supernatural being. Occultism is an inseparable ingredient of popular religious consciousness,—nay, it is often the salt of popular religious belief. In the history of Indian religion occultism is associated with religious beliefs and practices from the time of the *Atharva-veda*, and henceforth it is associated with all esoteric religious systems in the Hindu, Buddhist and other religious schools. In Pāli literature we find occasional reference to the belief in the *Iddhis* (i.e., *ṛddhi*) or occult powers attainable through religious practices. We find frequent reference to the ten supernatural powers (*daśa-bala*) and also to the six supernatural faculties (*abhijñā*) which are attainable by a Buddhist adept. Patañjali, the great propounder of yoga, who dealt primarily with the psychological aspect of yoga, also devoted a full chapter of the *Yoga-sūtra* to the different kinds of supernatural powers (*vibhutis*) attainable through concentration of mind on different objects or on different centres of the body. The eight supernatural faculties, viz., *Aṇimā* (the power of becoming as small as an atom), *Mahimā* (the power of becoming big), *Laghimā* (the power of assuming excessive lightness at will), *Garimā* (the power of becoming as heavy as one likes), *Prāpti* (the power of obtaining everything at will), *Prakāmya* (the power of obtaining all objects of pleasure at will), *Iśitva* (the power of obtaining supremacy over everything) and *Vaśitva* (the power of subduing, fascinating or bewitching) are well known in the school of yoga.[1] It is held that through the practices of Haṭha-yoga "the gross body begins to acquire something of the nature of the subtle body and to possess something of its relations with the life-energy; that becomes a greater force more powerfully felt and yet capable of a lighter and freer and more resolvable physical actions, powers which culminate in the Haṭhayogic *śiddhis* or extraordinary powers of *garimā, mahimā, aṇimā* and *laghimā*."[2] These powers are generally known as the eight powers of lord Śiva himself, who is the lord of yoga.

The Nāth Siddhas (including Mayanāmatī, who too was versed in the mystic knowlege of yoga) displayed throughout these eight supernatural powers. Thus we find in the *Gorakṣa-vijaya* that when Śiva granted the boon to a princess that she should get Gorakh as her husband, the great Yogin Gorakh, assumed the form of a child of six months before the princess and expressed the desire of sucking her breasts. The princess got offended and insisted on having Gorakh as her husband; Gorakh could not agree to her proposal, but gave her his old patched and ragged garment and asked her to wash it in water and to drink that water. This would, he assured, give her a son. She obeyed and the words of Gorakh came to be true. After that Gorakh was sitting under a *Bakula* tree and at that time Kānu-pā was passing through the sky above. Gorakh could know of it

[1] To these eight another is often added, which is *Kāmāvasāyitva* (i.e., the power of suppressing desire, self-denial or mortification).

[2] *The Synthesis of Yoga* by Aurobindo Ghose, *Ārya*, 1918, pp. 404-405.

by the shadow of the Siddha falling below; he got offended and sent his pair of wooden sandals to go up and bind the arrogant Siddha down and the order of Gorakh was instantaneously carried out. Again, when Gorakh resolved to enter into the country of Kadalī in the guise of a Brahmin in order to rescue his Guru, he sent Laṅga and Mahā-laṅga (two attendants on Gorakh) to Viśva-karmā asking the latter to supply him at once with a golden sacred thread, a pair of golden ear-rings, golden frontal marks, golden umbrella, stick, etc., and everything was readily and most obediently supplied by Viśva-karmā. When Gorakh again demanded for the necessaries for assuming the form of a dancing girl, Viśva-karmā supplied him with all golden articles at once. The Nāths seldom walked on earth, they moved in the air and would traverse hundreds of miles within the twinkle of an eye. To remove the illusion of Guru Mīna-nāth and to recover him to his sense, Gorakh-nāth displayed various yogic powers before the Guru. He first split into two Binduk-nāth (who was born to Mīna-nāth in Kadalī), then washed his (Binduk-nāth's) body in the manner of a washerman and dried it up in the sun,—and then revived him once more just by the fillip of his fingers. Mayanāmatī and her preceptor Hāḍi-siddhā displayed magical powers at every step in all the versions of the story of Gopī-cānd. They could know everything by their *dhiyāna* (*i.e.*, *dhyāna*, meditation) or *mahā-jñāna* (great mystic knowledge) and could do anything and everything they liked with the help of a mere *Huṁkāra* (*i.e.*, the sound of the mystic syllable *huṁ*) or such other Tāntric mystic syllables.[1] At the time of Mayanāmatī's initiation by Gorakh in her childhood, Gorakh made a full grown banian tree from its seed within the time of twelve *Daṇḍas*.[2] Again, twelve crores of Yogins with thirteen crores of disciples, who assembled on the occasion of Mayanā's initiation, and whose assemblage occupied the space that could be traversed in six months, could be served with the rice that was cooked

[1] In the Rangpur version of the story we always find that Hāḍipā or Mayanāmatī did everything by the muttering of *tuḍu tuḍu*; *tuḍu tuḍu* here, however, represents the muttering of the mystic syllables.

[2] One *Daṇḍa* is approximate to 24 minutes.

from a single grain of paddy,—and yet after all had eaten to their heart's content, the food for one Siddha was still left in the earthen pot.[1]

In the description of Hāḍi-siddhā we find that he makes ear-rings of the sun and the moon, and lord Indra himself fans him; he cooks his food in the moon and eats his food on the back of the tortoise,—and goddess Lakṣmī herself prepares food for him. The five daughters of Indra remove the leaves on which he takes his food and Suvacanī[2] supplies him with betel-nut, the Nāga-girls of Netherland prepare his tobacco-pipe and Meghanāl, son of Yama, comes forward to serve him with a fan. He walks with his golden sandals and if he gets hold of Yama he beats him severely.[3] Before Gopī-cānd agreed to accept Hāḍi-siddhā as his Guru, he (Gopī-cānd) wanted to be convinced of the yogic powers of the latter. In one of the versions of the song we find that at the challenge of the king, the Siddha at once got ready, rolled thrice on the ground and got his body pasted with eighty maunds of dust,—made the rope round his loins with eighty maunds of jute, put on a cap made of eighty four maunds of iron, held in hand an iron stick weighing eighty three maunds, and put on a pair of iron sandals weighing eighty two maunds. The Hāḍi got ready and came out of his cell and drank water with twenty two maunds of pea. He stretched his hands which reached the sky above; he stretched his legs which reached the netherland below; the hairs of his body stood like palm trees and the cap on his head reached the mountain Kailāsa. When the Hāḍi Siddhā began to move, mother earth began to quake with cracking sound; when the Hāḍi stood up his head struck against heaven above; when he began to move with a broom, a broken spade, a basket to carry rubbish, and an earthen water jar on head, he crossed fortytwo *Krośas*[4] in one single step, and wherever he placed his feet, the foot-prints made large tanks. When he arrived at the port of Kaliṅkā, he first made a *Huṁkāra* for broom, and innu-

[1] *Gopī-candrer Pāṁcālī* (C.U.), p. 344.
[2] An indigenous demi-goddess of Bengal.
[3] *Gopī-candrer Gān, Bujhān Khaṇḍa,* (C.U.), p. 61.
[4] A *Krośa* is a little more than two miles.

merable brooms poured down from above and began to cleanse the market automatically; then he made another *Humkāra* for baskets and innumerable baskets began to remove rubbish automatically; when he made *Humkāra* for the spade, innumerable spades began to scrape the ground automatically; similarly innumerable earthen jars began to pour down water. Hāḍipā then went to the house of Mayanā and asked from her something to eat. Mayanā asked him to take his bath and then to take meal. Hāḍipā went to the river to bathe, released in the river a piece of torn cloth with twelve knots and thereby the water was dried up; the merchants in their stranded boats began to weep; fish, shark, dolphin, crocodile—all began to cry in the dry bed of the river; Hāḍipā took pity on them, pressed the piece of cloth with twelve knots and the river became once more overflooded with water. He then entered the coconut-garden of the king and sat on his yogic posture and all coconuts dropped down before him; he spilt them up with his nail, drank water and ate up the nut and the coconuts returned to the trees and remained hanging just as before. By that time Mayanā finished her cooking and invited Hāḍipā to take meal; the meal prepared was taken by the Hāḍi all at once,—but that could not appease his hunger. He then took seven bags of dried paddy, three bags of salted onion and swallowed the whole thing with twenty-two jars of water.[1] Similar other magical feats were displayed by the Hāḍi as proof of his yogic power. He cut a man into two and revived him at will within the twinkle of an eye; he transferred the head of queen Adunā to the trunk of queen Padunā and *vice versa* and again set everything right. When he was buried under the stable, he tore off all his bondage of rope and chain by means of a single *Humkāra*; the chain of hand became transformed into a rosary of beads; the heavy stone on his chest became the outer garment of yoga (*yoga-paṭṭa*); the rope with which he was bound became the rope of his loins; and the grave was transformed into an under-ground cave

[1] *Vide Gopī-candrer Gān, Bujhān Khaṇḍa* (C.U.), pp. 80-85. *Cf.* also *Gopī-candrer Sannyās*, pp. 440-441.

where Hāḍi remained absorbed in his yoga-meditation.[1] These are some of the types of magical powers displayed by the Siddhas, mainly by Gorakh, Hāḍipā and Mayanā-matī. We need not multiply instances. Similar legends of magical powers displayed by the Nāth Siddhas are found abundantly also in the Nāth literature of other vernaculars. This curious blending of supernaturalism and occultism with the most realistic description of the story and the keen human interest involved in the pathos of the great renunciation of a young king like Gopī-candra, has infused Nāth literature with a peculiar literary charm.

In the literary field, at least so far as Bengali literature is concerned, this emphasis on occultism in the Nāth literature sharply makes it distinct from the literature belonging to similar esoteric schools, we mean the literature of the Buddhist Sahajiyās, the Vaiṣṇava Sahajiyās, the Bāuls and such other schools of Bengal. We have seen before how a spirit of revolt against occultism and outward show of austere practices characterises the literature of the different Sahajiyā sects including the literature of the Sūfī poets. Very frequently and severely did Kabir criticise the sect of the Gorakh-yogins in his poems; so have also his followers including Nānak, the Sikh prophet.

Judging from the religious point of view such occultism represents only the popularly adumbrated superficial feature of Nāthism. It is not also a fact that such display of supernatural power characterises all literature belonging to the Nāth cult. In some of the Hindi texts on Gorakh and Matsyendra and in some texts of Hindi literature ascribed to Gorakh-nāth we find the same spirit of heterodoxy as is found in the Sahajiyā literature, and there the Nāths have joined with the Sahajiyās in their spirit of criticism. The perusal of an early Hindi text like the *Gorakh-bodh* or *Gorakh-bānī* will tempt one to believe that there is no difference between Nāthism and the various other Sahajiyā cults in their religious attitude. The other fragments of literature ascribed to Gorakh and to Carpaṭa (who also has been included in the list of the Siddhas and is well-known in Hindi and Punjabi

[1] *Gopī-candrer Sannyās*, p. 418.

Nāth literature as a great Siddha of the Nāth Sect) will lead once to the same conclusion.[1] In the Sanskrit texts on yoga, which are ascribed to the authorship of Gorakh-nāth, or are traditionally associated with the name of Gorakh and are believed to represent the religious views and practices of the Nāth-yogins, we often find criticism levelled against other orthodox religious systems from the stand-point of yoga. We may for instance refer to the *Gorakṣa-siddhānta-saṁgraha*,[2] where we find many orthodox schools severely criticised from the point of view of yoga and there the supremacy of the yoga-school has been established with help of the texts belonging to various yogic schools.[3] In the sixth chapter of the *Siddha-siddhānta-paddhati* we find description of the real yogin, and in the fifth chapter of the *Gorakṣa-saṁhitā* we find an elaborate description of the final state of yoga. From these descriptions it will appear that the state of non-duality, bereft of all disturbance of mentation, is the final state of yoga. On this point these yogins, as he have said, appear homogeneous in spirit with the Buddhist Sahajiyā yogins. In the small texts, entitled *Amanaska-vivaraṇa* and *Yoga-bīja*[4] belonging to the yogic cult of the Siddhas, we find the same spirit of criticism.[5] A very faint echo of this spirit of yoga literature in general is sometimes found also in Bengali Nāth literature, where the path of yoga is eulogised to king Gopī-cānd either by his mother Mayanāmatī or by his Guru Hāḍi-siddhā.[6]

It will be doing the worst sort of injustice to Nāthism as a popular religious sect to hold that in its origin and nature it had noting in it worth considering but the practices

1 For such literature ascribed to Gorakh and Carpaṭa, see Dr. Mohan Singh's work on Gorakh-nath, and see *Gorakh-bānī* edited by Dr. Barthwal. Aslo see *Yoga-pravāha* (in Hindi) by Dr. Barthwal.

2 The text is a compendium of news and views on the yogic cult of Gorakṣa collected from the Sanskrit texts that are traditionally associated with the cult as embodying the doctrines of the cult.

3 *Vide*, pp. 1-9; 12 *et seq*; 23-24; 49, 54, etc.

Gopī-nāth Kavirāja's edition.

Cf. also *Kaula-jñāna-nirṇaya* ascribed to Matsyendra, particularly *Akula-vīra-tantra* included in it.

4 The two texts are published in the Vasumatī series of Bengal in a collection of many small yogic texts published under the general caption of *Śāstra-śataka*.

5 *Cf.* *Amanaska-vivaraṇa*, verse No. 1.

6 *Cf.* *Gopī-candrer Gān* (C.U., Part I), p. 70; *Gopī-candrer Sannyās* (C.U., Part II), p. 433, etc.

of Haṭha-yoga with the only end of attaining some occult powers. It is the wild, though sweet, imagination of the uninitiated village poets that is responsible for the growth of so much occultism in the Nāth cult at the cost of the truth in the cult which is certainly worth considering. Behind the legends and traditions found in popular poetry we occasionally find glimpses of light, with the help of which we shall try in the following pages to catch at the inner truth of the cult.

(*ii*) *The final End of the Nāth Siddhas*

What was the final aim of the Nāth Siddhas and what was the means (*Sādhanā*) through which this end was to be attained? If we are to give the answer in a nutshell, we should say that the final aim of the Nāth Siddhas was the attainment of Śivahood in and through the attainment of immortality,[1] and the means of attaining it was primarily Haṭha-yoga. The question of escaping death may be taken to be the most salient feature of Haṭha-yoga in general as contrasted to the other forms of yoga, *viz.*, Mantra-yoga, Laya-yoga and Rāja-yoga. The latter three schools are idealistic in their philosophical outlook and, therefore, lay the greatest emphasis on the final arrest of the mind and the attainment of liberation thereby (liberation from the whirl of coming and going); the emphasis of Haṭha-yoga seems to be primarily on the physical or physiological practices which remove disease, decay and death. In the description of the benefits attainable through the practices of yoga we frequently meet with statements that through such and such yogic practices the yogin gets rid of all diseases, his old body becomes rejuvenated, his body becomes changeless like a mountain; he becomes a victor over *Kāla* (*i.e.*, time) and a deceiver of *Kāla*; he becomes a victor over Death (*mṛtyuñjaya*). Patañjali, the great propounder of yoga, gives Haṭha-yoga but a subsidiary place—it is resorted to only for gaining a control over the physical and the physiological systems, and this control necessarily affects psychological states and conditions, and a perfect control over the psycho-

[1] *Cf. jīv thaiṁ sīv hoibā prāṇī*—from a created being one must become the Śiva Himself. *Sikhyā Darasan* collected in *Gorakh-bānī* (ed. by Dr. Barthwal).

logical states leads to final liberation. In this final state of liberation the Puruṣa or the 'seer' remains in his pure essential nature. This final aim of yoga as the final arrest of mind has often been admitted also by Haṭha-yoga, and in some of the standard texts Haṭha-yoga has been made subservient to Rāja-yoga (*i.e.*, the yoga *par excellence*, which is the yoga of meditation);[1] but considering the general tone of Haṭha-yoga it seems that the very approach of Haṭha-yoga was somewhat different from the approach of the other schools of yoga. There is indeed the question of liberation in Haṭha-yoga,—but here the conception of liberation itself is different from that of the other schools of thought. Liberation here means immortality first in a perfect body (*siddha-deha*) and then in a divine body (*divya-deha*), and this is the *Siddhi* or the perfection after which the Siddhas aspired.

The final aim of the Nāth Siddhas is *Jīvan-mukti* or liberation while living, and this state of liberation is what is meant by immortality. While the other schools of thought regard the final dissolution of the body or its final dissociation from the spirit indispensable for liberation, the Siddhas seek liberation in a transformed or transmaterialised body, which is the perfect body. What is this perfect body or the divine body? It is an indestructible spiritual body, absolutely free from the principles of defilement or the principles of *aśuddha-māyā*; but it is associated with principles of *viśuddha-māyā* which prevents it from becoming absolutely static and acts as the absolutely purified dynamic principle for its further evolution through subtler stages to lead it to the final state of *parā-mukti*. The yogins in their perfect body are prompted by the principles of *viśuddha-māyā* to benevolent activities rendering spiritual guidance to innumerable religious aspirants—and this state is the fittest state for becoming a Guru or spiritual preceptor. It is for this reason that the Siddhas are the true preceptors in the world. Further, due to the absolute dissociation of the *aśuddha-māyā* these benevolent activities of the Siddhas cannot any more bind them down to the world of suffering.

[1] *kevalaṁ rāja-yogāya haṭha-vidyopadiśyate* ||
Haṭha-yoga-pradīpikā, (1-2).

This active state of the Siddha, which helps the religious aspirants on the one hand and evolves its final state of *parā-mukti* on the other, may very well be compared to the Bodhisattvahood of the Buddhists, where there is the principle of activity in the form of universal compassion, which uplifts the suffering beings on the one hand, and, on the other hand, makes the Bodhisattva march forward through the ten stages of *Bodhisattva-bhūmi* towards the final goal of Buddhahood.

In the *Yoga-vīja*, a small yogic text, we find that the body is of two kinds, *viz.*, unripe (*apakva*) and ripe (*pakva*). The unripe body is the body not disciplined by yoga, and the ripe body is the body disciplined by yoga. Through the fire of yoga the body becomes supra-material and above all sorrows and sufferings, while the unripe material body of ordinary people becomes the cause of all sorrow and sufferings. Such a yoga body (*yoga-deha*) is rare even to the gods; it is a body bereft of all limitations and bondage and at the same time possessing great powers; it is limitless like the sky but purer even than the sky.[1] The great yogin with his perfect body moves in the world according to his own will,—and as this perfect body is produced through the burning away of his physical body through the fire of yoga there is no further death for him. Where an ordinary man lives (in his physical form) the yogin is dead,—and where there is the death for all (in the physical form) there is no death for the yogin. He has no duty of his own,—but at the same time is not defiled by any activity,—he is liberated while living—and is always living in his true body, which

[1] *apakvāḥ paripakvāś ca dvi-vidhā dehinaḥ smṛtāḥ* 1
apakvā yoga-hīnāstu pakvā yogena dehinaḥ ||
pakvā yogāgninā dehī ajaḍaḥ śoka-varjitaḥ 1
jaḍas tat pārthivo jñeyaḥ apakvo duḥkhado bhavet ||
śarīreṇa jitāḥ sarve śarīraṁ yogibhir jitam 1
tat kathaṁ kurute teṣāṁ sarva-duḥkhādikaṁ phalam ||
mahā-bhūtāni tattvāni saṁhṛtāni krameṇa ca 1
sapta-dhātumayo deho dagdho yogā-gninā śanaiḥ ||
devair api na labhyate yoga-deho mahābalaḥ ||
cheda-bandhair vimukto' sau nānā-śakti-dharaḥ puraḥ 1
yathā-kāśas tatāh dehaḥ ākāśād api nirmalaḥ ||
Verses 33, 34, 46, 48, 49 and 50.
Vasumatī edition (in the collection of *Śāstra-śataka*).

is bereft of all defilement.[1] A deathless ripe body of this type is the first requisite for a Siddha; for such a ripe body helps the Siddhas in attaining the final state of *Parā-mukti*.[2]

As pre-eminently a Śaivite school the aim of the Nāth cult was the attainment of Śivahood or the state of Maheśvara. Immortality is recognised to be the quintessence of the ultimate nature of the Lord; to attain the state of *Parā-mukti* in and through the state of *Jīvan-mukti* is, therefore, virtually the same as to attain the state of Maheśvara. It is for this reason that in common belief we find great Nāth Siddhas like Matsyendra and Gorakh often identified with Śiva or Maheśvara. It will not be correct to think therefore that the Nāth cult is essentially an atheistic school of alchemy. The real significance of the attainment of immortality is the attainment of the state of the Great Lord.

The legendary accounts, given in the Nāth literature of the life and activities of the Nāth Siddhas, including king Gopī-cānd's mother Mayanāmatī and king Gopī-cānd himself, will corroborate our statement on the final aim of the Nāth yogins and their general religious attitude. The myths, legends, traditions and stories have all behind them the quest of immortality,—an escape from the clutching jaws of decay and the cruel snatch of death. It is easily detectable in the stories of the Nāth literature that what differentiates the Siddhas from ordinary men is their power of control over death and decay. Yama, the king of death, had no hold over the Nāth Siddhas,[3] and whenever he, in the course of the execution of his ordinary daily duties, forgot this important fact and transgressed the limit of his power and foolishly

[1] *saṁsaret ca punas tāni svecchayā vijitendriyaḥ* ।
maraṇaṁ tasya kiṁ devī pṛcchasīndu-nibhā-nane ॥
nāsau maraṇam āpnoti punar yoga-balena tat ।
puraiva mṛta evāsau mṛtasya maraṇaṁ kutaḥ ॥
maraṇaṁ yatra sarveṣāṁ tatrāsau sakhi jīvati ।
yatra jīvanti mūḍhās te tatrāsau mriyate sadā ॥
kartavyaṁ naiva tasyāsti kṛtenāsau na lipyate ।
jīvan-muktaḥ sadā svasthaḥ sarva-doṣa-vivarjitaḥ ॥
Ibid., verses (53-56).

[2] *Cf.* *marau ve jogī marau, marau, maraṇ hai mīṭhā* ।
tis maraṇī marau, jis maraṇī gorakh mari dīṭhā ॥
Gorakh-bānī, Sabadī, 26.

[3] *Cf.* *jahāṁ anaṁta sidhāṁ mili ārati gāī* ।
tahāṁ jam kī bav na nauḍī āī ॥ *Gorakh-bānī, pada* 61.

extended his hands over any of the Siddhas, the poor Lord of Death was taught a very good lesson by the Siddhas. In the *Gorakṣa-vijaya* or the *Mīna-cetana* we find, when Gorakh heard from Kānu-pā of the captivity of his Guru Mīna-nāth in the land of Kadalī among the wicked women, he took up his mystic bag (*siddha-jhuli*), put on his loose garment and the pair of wooden sandals, held his staff in hand and at once entered the city of Yama. Yama was seated on his throne in the open assembly and at the sight of Gorakh he rose from his seat in reverence and humbly enquired about the cause of his (Gorakh's) sudden visit to the city of the dead. Gorakh took Yama severely to task for summoning his Guru Mīna-nāth and thus poking his (Yama's) nose in the affairs of the immortal Siddhas. Gorakh further remarked that if Yama would have the audacity of meddling with the affairs of the Siddhas he (Gorakh) would drag him (Yama) to Brahmā himself and let him (Yama) learn from Brahmā the exact limitations of his lordship. Gorakh rebuked Yama strongly in a high spirit, threatened him with an immediate order of dismissal and the ruin of his capital; and as a matter of fact when Gorakh stood up angrily with his hanging bag and loose garment of patched cloth and began to utter the *Huṁkāra*, Yama began to tremble with his whole kingdom. Yama got afraid, felt helpless and immediately lay before Gorakh all the files of official records; Gorakh examined them one by one, picked up the file containing the decree on his Guru,—effaced the name of his Guru from the list of the dead, upset the decree of Yama and then left the city leaving behind a strict warning.[1]

The story of the fall of Mīna-nāth among the women of Kadalī signifies that worldly enjoyment in the form of the satisfaction of carnal desires leads a man to disease and decay; and death in that case becomes the inevitable catastrophe of the drama of life. The self-oblivion of Mīna-nāth symbolises man's oblivion of his true immortal nature;—and the charms of Kadalī represents the snares of life. What was repeatedly emphasised by Gorakh in his enigmatic songs

[1] *Gorakṣa-vijaya*, pp. 45-48.

in the guise of the dancing girl to recall his self-forgotten Guru to true judgement, is that the life of pleasure in company of beautiful women leads to the inevitable end of death, while the only way of escaping death and being immortal even in this very life is to have recourse to the path of yoga.[1] This is the cardinal truth which Mīna-nāth, inspite of all his former Sādhanā, lost sight of through the curse of goddess Durgā, the same curse symbolising the eternal curse of Nescience on humanity: and this is the cardinal truth which was variously explained through various imageries by the worthy disciple Gorakh to his Guru. In his songs as the dancing girl Gorakh repeatedly pointed out that the Guru was going to die a most ordinary death in the company of women; he (Gorakh) therefore urged him to have recourse to the yogic processes of making the body perfect, which has been spoken as Kāya-sādhana[2] or the cultivation of the body through the processes of yoga. This Kāya-sādhana is the most important thing in the Nāth literature and Kāya-siddhi or the perfection of body may be taken to be the summum bonum after which the yogins were aspiring.

It may also be pointed out that the original question of Durgā (who may be taken to be the Prakṛti or the embodiment of the principle of phenomenalism) to Śiva (who is the changeless truth in its ultimate form), with which the *Gorakṣa-vijaya*, or the *Mīna-cetena* begins, is,—"Why is it, my lord, that thou art immortal, and mortal am I? Advise

[1] *Cf. tomhā sama puruṣa je nāhi kona dese* l *gali gele mohāras yāu mātra ses* || *kadalīr rājā tumhi mīna adhikārī* l *uṭhite nā pāra mātra āpanā samvari* ||.... *sādha sādha āpanā kāyā mādaleta bole* l *sarva dhan hārāilā kāminīr kole* ||.... *guru haiyā nā bujha āpanār bol* l *kāyā sukhāila tohmār kāminīr kol* || *abhay bhāṇḍār guru nirbhaye nila hari* l *sudhā ghar gṛha tumi rahicha pāsarī* ||.... *kāyā sādha kāyā sādha guru mocandar* l [*tumi guru mocandar jagata īśvar* ||] etc. *Ibid.*, pp. 21 *et seq. Cf.* also pp. 106 *et seq.*

[2] *Cf. nācanti je gorakhnāth ghāgharer role* l
[*kāyā sādha kāyā sādha mādale hena bole* ||]
navīn kukile jena ādha ādha bole l
kāyā sādha kāyā sādha mandirāe bole || *Gorakṣa-vijaya*, pp. 94-95.
sādha sādha āpanā kāyā mādaleta bole l
sarva dhan hārailā kāminīr kole ||

* * *

kayā sādha kāyā sādha guru mocandar l
[*tumi guru mocandar jagata īśvar* || *Ibid*, p. 98.
kāyā sādha kāyā sādha āhmi putra bali l *Ibid*, 130.

me the truth, O lord, so that I also may be immortal for ages."[1] It was in answer to this question of Durgā or Pārvatī that the secret of Haṭha-yoga was expounded by Śiva to his beloved consort, which the first Siddha Mīna-nāth managed to hear in the form of a fish, and which was afterwards preached and popularised by the latter all over the world.

This quest of immortality and the secret of its attainment through yoga is the pivot round which the whole cycle of the stories of Māṇik-candra and his son Gopī-candra revolved. There we find, when Mayanāmatī came to know that due to the spells employed by the subjects of the king through the practice of some malevolent Tāntric rites king Māṇik-candra was about to fall a prey to Death, she hastened to the kingdom and asked the king to learn *Mahājñāna* (*i.e.*, the secrets of yoga) from her, which, she repeatedly assured, would enable him to defy the decree of Death; but the king declined and as a result he met with the ordinary mortal end. It has been said that the disregard of *Mahājñāna* was the plea for Yama for extending his hands on to the king.[2] However, after the death of the king Yama sent one of his officers with summons to bring the life (*jiu*=*jīva*) of the king; Mayanā in her meditation saw the messenger of Yama near the king and offered him a pony in exchange of the life of the king. The next day two officers came, and Mayanā bribed them with the life of a maid-servant; on the fourth day came four, who were bribed with the life of Mayanā's brother; on the fifth day again came five officers, and Mayanā offered them an amount of five hundred rupees in cash for buying sweet-meats and eating to their heart's content. But this time Godā-yama, the messenger, would not be satisfied without the life of the king. At this Mayanā

1 *tumhī kene tara gosāñi āmhi kene mari* I
hena tattva kaha dev joge joge tari || *Gorakṣa-vijay*, p. 12.
Cf. avadhū sakti soi jo sabahīm soṣai I
sīv soi jo sab ko poṣai || *Gorakh-bānī*,
Gorakh-Gaṇeś Guṣṭi, 44.

2 *Cf. tīrir ghārer jñān dekhi rājā jñān kaile helā* I
ai dine bhāḍuyā yam pāti gyāla khyālā ||
Gopī-candrer Gān (C.U., Part I), p. 12.

flew into rage and began to tremble,—she at once muttered within the *Mahā-mantra*, transformed herself through her yogic power into Caṇḍī and again into Kālī with her large sword (*khāḍā*=Skt. *khaḍga*) and attacked the whole host of the Yamas, caught hold of some of them and belaboured them severely and the Yamas flew away somehow with their lives. Godā-yama (who seems to have been the leader of the party) was in a fix; helpless as he was, he, with his elder brother Āvāla-yama, went to Śiva. With the advice of Śiva the Yamas extracted from the king his life in the absence of Mayanā who was sent for water and they flew away in the form of golden black-bees. Mayanā could know of this from the river and at once pursued Godā-yama and entered the palace of Death. Through her spell all the inhabitants of the palace at once got attacked with severe headache, and some flew away in fear. By her *Huṁkāra* Mayanā caught hold of Godā-yama, bound him down and began to beat him severely with an iron rod. Godā, however, begged most humbly Mayanā's mercy and agreed to give her back the life of her husband, which, Godā said, was kept in the market place. Mayanā followed Godā, who somehow managed to slip from her hands and escaped. Godā went straight to the queen of Yama and sought her protection; she took pity on Godā and hid him in a corner covering him with straw; but Mayanā could know everything in her meditation and chased him there in the form of a serpent. Godā transformed himself into a mouse, Mayanā chased it in the form of lacs of cats; Godā became a pigeon, —Mayanā pursued it in the form of innumerable hawks. In this way Godā-yama tried to escape by transforming himself into innumerable beings in land, water and air,— but he did not succeed. Mayanā at last caught hold of Godā who was compelled to let loose the life of Māṇikcandra. Lord Śiva and Gorakh, Mayanā's Guru, however, interfered in the matter and the prestige of Death was somehow saved by coming to respectable terms with Mayanā. The whole story, in its full-fledged form, is nothing but a popular myth; but the spirit that is hidden behind and serves as the nucleus of the whole detail is that a perfect yogin conquers death completely,—and so much is his control over death that he may deal with Death at any time in any way he pleases.[1]

We may further note that Mayanā became *Satī* with her husband, but fire could not burn Mayanā. At the instance of his queens, Gopī-cānd put Mayanā to cruel and direful tests. She was thrown into fire, but even her garment was not stained with smoke; she was drowned in water bound within a bag, but mother Gaṅgā herself came forward to welcome her in her (Gaṅgā's) lap; she walked on a bridge made of hair; she walked on the edge of a razor; she was shut up for full seven days and nights within a boiler containing boiling oil, which was being heated from below constantly; she crossed all the rivers in the boat made of the husk of a corn, but nothing could bring about her death, neither was any part of her body damaged in any way.[2] Mayanā herself declared to her son Gopī-cānd,—"By the practice of the mystic knowledge one becomes immortal, (and the course of life will retard towards immortality from its natural flow towards death and decay) just like the current of the tide-wave running backward. Through the boon granted by Gorakh-nāth I am deathless; I can remain in the void for full fourteen ages,—in water for full thirteen ages, in the fire for twelve years. When the creation will sink below and finally dissovle, and the earth will be not and there will remain only all-pervading water, the sun and the moon will set for ever and the whole universe will be destroyed,—I shall float on for ever,—I shall have no death."[3]

Jālandhari-pā or Hāḍi-siddhā also gave ample proof of his

[1] The story of Mayanāmatī's initiation by Gorakh-nāth in her childhood shows that Gorakh was moved at the idea that even a chaste and beautiful girl like Mayanā should meet with the same fate as other ordinary mortals, and he then initiated her into the cult of yoga to make her immortal. After her initiation Gorakh declared,—'Death himself has now given a written bond (not to extend his hands over Mayanā).' He further declared that Mayanā would never be burnt in fire, drowned in water, pierced through by any weapon; if she should die in the day-time he (Gorakh) would not let the sun go, but would bind him down,—if she should die at home, he would not let Yama go, but bind him down,—if she should die of a cut from a flat sword (*khāḍā*=a large sacrificial knife), he would bind goddess Caṇḍī (who generally bears such a weapon) down,—Mayanā would survive even the sun and the moon. *Gopī candrer Pāṁcālī*, (C.U. Part II), p. 345.

[2] See *Gopī-candrer Pāṁcālī* (C.U. Part II), pp. 366-369; *Govinda-candra-gīta* (Mr. Śīl's edition), pp. 71-73; *Gopī-candrer Gān, Bujhān Khaṇḍa*, (C.U., Part I), pp. 87-130, etc.

[3] *Govinda-candra Gīt* (Mr. Śīl's edition), pp. 70-71.

control over Death. In describing the extraordinary yogic power of Hāḍipā Mayanā says to Gopī-cānd that whenever Hāḍipā chances to catch hold of Yama or any of his officers he beats them severely for full eight hours, and there is no escape for Yama from the hands of the Hāḍi.[1] When Gopī-cānd accepted Hāḍipā as his Guru, renounced the world and left the palace with his Guru, the king was unable to keep pace with the Guru in the path through the dense forest, created by the *Huṁkāra* of the Hāḍi and he was lagging behind. The police officers of Yama, so to speak, availed themselves of this opportunity and attacked Gopī-cānd and extracted his life from him[2] and went to the city of Death. After sometimes Hāḍipā looked back and found the king dead. The yogin flew into fierce rage, ordered all the tigers of the forest to guard the corpse of the king and himself went straight to the city of the dead, inflicted severe punishment on all, beginning with the king to the lowest of the officers. The king of Death begged his (Hāḍipā's) pardon and promptly ordered his officers to return the life of king Gopī-cānd.[3] These popular legends are significant. Of course the imagination of the poets has often exaggerated the yogic powers of the Siddhas and put the yogic truths in extremely popular legendary form,—but the truth behind is the truth of immortality attainable through Haṭha-yoga.

A very important fact to notice in this connection is that the keynote of the story of Gopī-cānd's great renunciation also is the quest of immortality. It was his own mother Mayanāmatī, who compelled the king by hook or by crook to leave his loving wives, his boundless wealth and immense power and to take the vow of a Nāth yogin in his budding youth at the age of eighteen. Mayanā lamented that she had none else to call her a mother excepting Gopī-cānd,—yet

[1] *dauḍiyā byāḍāite jadi jamer lagya pāy* l *cilācāṅgi diyā jamaka tin pahar kilāy* ||
māriyā dhariyā jamaka karuṇā sikhāy l *hyāna sādhya nāi jamer palāiyā eḍāy* ||
Gopī-candrer Gān (C.U., Part I), p. 61.

[2] It may be remembered in this connection that in the ordinary course the king had only eighteen years' longevity.

[3] See *Gopī-candrer Gān*, (C.U. Part I), pp. 202-207. In another place Hāḍi-siddhā with the help of a *Huṁkāra* called upon the sovereign Yama with all his followers and officers to make a good road for him and Gopī-cānd; Yama readily obeyed the order and went out with all the necessary implements to construct a long road fo: them. *Ibid.*, pp. 213-217.

she did insist on (his Gopī-cānd's) becoming the disciple of Hāḍipā and taking the vow of a yogin; the unwillingness of the king and his conspiracy with the queens was of no avail. What was there in Mayanā that dominated over her ordinary motherly affection? It was the hope of immortality for her only son, who otherwise, in the course of his ordinary life of worldly enjoyment, would have died a premature death at the age of eighteen. She was not by nature a heartless witch,—it was for a higher gain that she acted heartlessly for the time being to compel her son to be a yogin.[1]

The ideal of immortality in the *Siddha-deha* as propounded by the yogins of the Siddha-school exerted considerable influence also on the Orissa school of Vaiṣṇavism of the sixteenth century. Though the general conception of the final state as described by the exponents of this school was mainly in the line of the *Bhagavad-gītā*, the ideal of immortality in the *Siddha-deha* was there.[2] We find there instructions on yoga for making the body immutable.[3] The yogic system involving the control over the sun and the moon[4] was advised to be adopted for the perfection of the body.[5]

Here we should note that though there was a general similarity in the methods adopted by the Nāth yogins, the Buddhist Sahajiyās, the Vaiṣṇava Sahajiyās and the followers of the Nirguṇa-school of Hindi poetry mainly in the practices of Kāya-sādhana, yet there were fundamental differences in their aims and attitude. Thus, while the former schools held the realisation of the ultimate nature of the self as well as of the not-self, either in the form of perfect enlightenment, which is great bliss (as in the case of the Buddhists) or in the form of perfect love (as in the case of the Vaiṣṇavas) or as the 'Incomprehensible Beloved' (as in the Nirguṇa school of Northern and Western India), to be the final aim

[1] *Gopī-candrer Pāṁcālī*, (C.U. Part II), pp. 326-331.

[2] *Vide*, *Brahma-śaṅkali* of Acyutānanda Dāsa, Prācī-grantha-mālā series, No. 6, p. 2, 3.

[3] *yantra binyāsi tantra kaha* I
yemante rahiva e deha || *Ibid.*, p. 4.

[4] *Vide Infra.*

[5] *Brahma-śaṅkali*, p. 15.
cf. also *candra sūryaṅku kale goṣṭhi*
biṣama brahma agni uṭhi ||
pralaya tāku na bādhai I
teveṭi siddha aṅga hai || *Ibid*, p. 17.

of all Sādhanā, the Nāth yogins employed all the yogic practices for the attainment of immortality and Maheśvara-hood thereby. Of course, this final immortal state of the yogin has also been spoken of as the state of liberation or the state of the Sahaja, yet a difference in the general outlook as well as in the religious approach is on the whole perceptible. It is thus difference in outlook and approach and also the differences in practices, of which we shall speak later on, that necessitate the postulation of a line of demarcation between the different Sahajiyā schools on the one hand and the school of the Nāth yogins on the other.

(*iii*) *The Means*

(A) Ulṭā-sādhanā or the Regressive Process

Coming to the question of the practical Sādhanā we find that the Nāth Siddhas called their Sādhanā Kāya-sādhana (culture of the body) with a view to attaining Kāya-siddhi (perfection of the body). The process has frequently been styled in the vernaculars as the Ulṭā-sādhanā, or the regressive process[1] and the epithet is doubly significant. The yoga practices of the Nāth Siddhas is *Ulṭā* or regressive, firstly in the sense that it involves yogic processes which give a regressive or upward motion to the whole biological as well as psychological systems which in their ordinary nature possess a downward tendency; and secondly, in the sense that such yogic practices lead the Siddha to his original ultimate nature as the immortal *Being* in his perfect or divine body, back from the ordinary

[1] *āe guru ūlaṭiyā yog dhara*
nija mantra karaha svoran I
ūlaṭiyā ānā
khāl jor bharite kāraṇ ||
bhāla kaha yae putra jati gorakhāi I
kāyā tomhār sthir kara-
tripini dea je sthānā (thānā ?)
Gorakṣa-vijaya, p. 115.
ūlaṭi sādhite jog gāe bal nāi ||
Ibid, p. 116.

jadi se sādhivā kāyā ulaṭi dhar jog ||
ulaṭiyā dhar guru sumerur kalā I
pākiche māthār keśa hai jāiva kālā ||
Ibid, p. 145. etc.

Cf. *gigani caḍhi pīvai pāṇi* I
ulaṭi sakalī āp ghari āṇī ||
Gorakh-bodh, Verse No. 38.

avadhū bolyā tat bicārī, pṛthvī maiṁ bakbālī I *Gorakh-bānī*, p. 97.
dasavaiṁ dvār niraṁjan unaman bāsā, sabadaiṁ ulaṭi samāṁuāṁ I
Ibid, p. 98.

creative process of *becoming*. We have had several occasions to dwell on the two aspects of the reality underlying the universal process as a whole; *viz.*, Śiva as the noumenal aspect, or pure consciousness and perfect rest and the Śakti as the phenomenal aspect of world-activity—the aspect of change and evolution. As most of the schools of yoga take the body to be the epitome of the universe, and the life-process, including its physical, biological and psychological aspects, to be a microcosm of the world-process, the life-process in the physical body is also believed to possess these two aspects, *viz.*, the Śiva aspect of perfect rest in the divine or the perfect body, and the Śakti aspect of activity in the physical body of continual change. Śakti in her ordinary course of phenomenal manifestation leads to change, death and decay—to the whirl of coming and going. The aim of the yogin is to stop this ordinary downward course of Śakti, downward in the sense of a phenomenal manifestation, and to give her, through physical and psychological, or rather physico-psychical efforts, an upward motion so that by a regressive process she may once more proceed backward to be united with Śiva and be absorbed in the nature of Śiva who is the Motionless Immortal Being. According to Tāntric and Haṭha-yogic belief, we have already seen, the region of the body below the naval is the region of Śakti, while the region above the navel is the region of Śiva; the former is called the domain of *Pravṛtti* or activity and change, while the latter is the domain of *Nivṛtti* or rest. It is generally believed that Śakti, or the principle of change, resides coiled as a serpent in the nature of the world-force in the lowest nervous plexus situated just on the lowest extremity of the spinal chord, while Śiva, the principle of rest, is situated in the Sahasrāra[1] or the lotus of thousand petals in the head. The Sahasrāra and the Mūlādhāra (the highest and the lowest plexuses) are the two poles within which evolves the whole creative process. Yoga consists in the raising of the Śakti from the lowest region of change and activity to the highest

[1] In many of the Tantras and texts on yoga Ājñā-cakra or the plexus or lotus just below the Sahasrāra is described as the abode of Śiva, Sahasrāra being the plexus where there is the realisation of the perfect union of Śiva and Śakti.

region of rest so as to be united with and absorbed in Śiva. This union of Śiva and Śakti symbolises in the wider sense the stoppage of the ordinary process of becoming and the retrogression of the whole world-process for the attainment of the changeless state of the Immortal Being. How is this retrogression to be effected? By a perfect control over the physical, biological and psychological process and by setting a regressive motion in them through slow and gradual processes of yoga;—this is what is meant by the Ulṭā-sādhana. Because of this *Ulṭā* nature of the Sādhana, the language of the songs in which the secret of the Sādhana is couched is also generally of a *Ulṭā* nature, or extremely paradoxical and enigmatic.[1] The process has also been explained under the imagery of proceeding against the current (*ujāna-sādhana*).[2]

All spiritual or religious endeavours are processes of Ulṭā-sādhana in a general sense inasmuch as they give a higher or upward tendency to our lower being. It has been said in a popular Buddhist verse that when an intense thirst is felt within for something higher, the mind becomes no more perturbed by desires, and at that state one is said to be in an upward current.[3] We have referred before to the word *parāvṛtti* found in Mahāyānic texts. In the *Mahāyāna-sūtrālaṅkāra* we hear of the *parāvṛtti* of the five senses, of the mind, of the sex-act, etc.[4] It seems to us that the real significance of the word *parāvṛtti* is just the same as the Ulṭā-sādhana. It is the process of introversion, a reversal of the world of *pravṛtti* to the state of *nivṛtti*. We have seen also that the Pañca-śākhā school of Orissa Vaiṣṇavism was influenced to a considerable extent by the ideal of Kāya-sādhana of the Siddha school; these Vaiṣṇavas also have often spoken of

[1] *Cf. guru mīna-nāth re ulṭā ulṭā dhārā* ।
pukura mure dhāna śukāiyā ugāra-tale bāḍā ॥ *etc.*
Quoted in the introduction of the *Gorakṣa-vijaya* by Munsi Abdul Karim. *Cf.* also a similar song in the *Dharma-maṅgala* of Sahadev Cakravartī, B.S.P.P., B.S., 1304. See the Appendix E.

[2] *Cf. saṭ-cakra bheda guru khelāuk ujān* । *Gorakṣa-vijaya*, p. 147.

[3] *chanda-jātā avasāye manasā ca phuṭā siyā* ।
kāmesu appaṭibaddha-cittā uddhaṁsoto ti vuccati ॥ *Therī-gāthā*, (1. 12).

[4] IX, Verses (41-46).

the *Ulṭā* process or the *Ujāna* process in their yogic Sādhana.[1] We have further seen that the Sūfīs and the Bāuls of Bengal were Sādhakas of this Ulṭā-sādhana.[2] A very nice exposition of this Ulṭā-sādhana is found in the *Jñānasāgara* of Āli-rājā. There it is said that the process of divine love is a reverse process,—and he who does not know the secret of this reverse process cannot have eternal life. Here the forward becomes the backward and the backward becomes the forward and the world is related to the reality in this inverted law.[3] The way towards perfection has been kept hidden by the Lord and only the unreal path (*asāra panthā*) is kept open before all creatures; it is for this reason that man, after his birth in this world, naturally has recourse to the unreal path and remains absorbed in transitory enjoyment. The reason why the path towards perfection is thus concealed by the Lord from the eyes of ordinary creatures is that the possibility of easy access would have made it cheap; the Lord has enhanced the value and the glory of the path by keeping it secret and extremely difficult of access.[4] All these seem to be an echo of the well-known Upaniṣadic saying that by giving the senses an outward

1 *e pañca-bhūta madhye byāpi* I
khelanti parama svarūpī ||
binā ujāni na balāi I
ke acchi siddha aṅga bahi ||
ulaṭa ujāni calile I
pūrita mānasa-sarovare ||
Brahma-śāṅkali of Achyutānanda Dāsa, (Prācī-grantha-mālā series), p. 26.
Again, *ulaṭi ūrddhvaku kṣepai* || *Ibid.*, p. 7,
hetura mūle dhara ṭāṇi I
bahantā nadīka ujāṇi ||
* * *
ujāna laya-yoga khaṭa I etc. *Ibid.*, p. 11.
yeve tu dhāivu ujāni I
kṣepiva gagana ku pāni ||
teve parame hoi mela I etc. *Ibid.*, p. 17.
Again, *yogīṁkara yoga ujānare siddha hoi* I *Śūnya-saṁhitā*, Ch. XXI. (Prācī-grantha-mālā series), p. 112.

2 *Vide Supra*, pp. 185-86.

3 *pirītī ulṭā rit nā bujhe cature* I
ye nā cine ulṭā se nā jiye saṁsāre ||
samukh bimukh hae bimukh samukh I
pālṭā niyame sav jagat saṁyog II *Jñāna-sāgara*, pp. 36-37.

4 *bimukhe āgam pantha rākhiche gopate* I
calile bimukh panthe siddhi sarva mate ||
samukher sav patha bimuk kariyā I
palaṭi bimuk panthe jāiva caliyā || *Ibid.*, p. 38.

tendency and turning them away from the inward truth the self-created one (Brahmā) gave proof of his jealousy, as it were; it is because of this fact that man generally sees what is external, and not that which is within; but wise people there are, who, in quest of life eternal, have inverted their visual power and realised the self in and through a reverse process.[1]

The process of arrest or control of various sorts, which is the most important function of yoga, is personified in the Bengali texts as 'Khemāi' (from Skt. *Kṣema*—safety, security, tranquillity),[2] who has been spoken of as the best guard to be placed in the different centres of the body so that the wealth within may not be stolen away by Kāla (death, decay, change).[3] Khemāi has sometimes been depicted as a very smart policeman, who arrests all the evil tendencies, pierces the undisciplined and unsteady elephant of mind with the hook (*aṅkuśa*);[4] it is for this reason that Gorakh-nāth in the form of the dancing girl instructed the captive Guru Mīna-nāth (who was at that time made the king of the country of Kadalī) to give his royal sceptre to Khemāi and to serve him most obediently, and Gorakh

1 *parāñci khāni vyatṛṇat svayambhus*
tasmāt parān paśyati nāntarātman 1
kaścid dhīraḥ pratyag-ātmānam aikṣad
āvṛtta-cakṣur amṛtattvam icchan || *Kaṭha*, (2.4.1.).

2 The word may also be derived from the word *Kṣamā* which has its dialectal variant as *Khemā*. This *Khemā* has its secondary meaning as stoppage (as in *khemā deoyā*) and hence the word has acquired the sense of 'restraint'.
Cf. *dvitīe ajapā jāna cāri beda sār* 1
saddāe japae jīv kṣemā nāi tār ||
Gorakṣa-vijaya, p. 192.

3 *bhananta gorakh-nāth rūḍā rākhau, nagarī cor malāyā* ||
Gorakh-bānī, *Pada*, 10.

Again, *cetani paharai kotvāl boliye, tām cor na jhaṁkai dvār* ||
Ibid, *Pada*, 27.

4 *khemāir hāte guru nā dilā je dhanu* 1
kāma-rase dhanu dilā bhedilek tanu || *Ibid.*, p. 124.
khemāire aṅkuśa diyā manāi pāgal || *Ibid.*, p. 141.
māgh māsete guru hima kharaśān 1
kṣemāir cākarī kari rākhaha parāṇ || *Ibid.*, p. 143.
khemāire aṅkuś māra hastiyār muṇḍe || *Ibid.*, p. 150.
ehi cari dhaut jan sarir alay 1
kām krodha lobha moha ehi cāri hae ||
ei cāri janere dhariā daḍ kari 1
sakale miliyā kara khemāir cākari || *Ibid.*, p. 151.

assured him that he (Khemāi) would be the best man to rule the country (of this body).[1]

The purification of and the control over the muscles, sinews, nerves, ducts and the nerve-centres through the processes of *Āsana* (posture), *Dhauti* (washing), *Bandha* (different kinds of arrest), *Mudrā*, *Prāṇāyāma* and other process of Haṭha-yoga are generally prescribed to be directed towards the final aim of the transformation and transubstantiation of the body. Closely associated with the question of transubstantiation of the body is the question of attaining full control over the mind. An echo of the general Indian trend of idealism is also found here and there in the stories of the Nāth literature.[2] We have seen that the control of the mind is the yoga *par excellence*, and it is held that the vital wind is the vehicle of this mind, and the control of the vital wind through the processes of *Prāṇāyāma* leads to the control of the mind. With the arrest of the vital wind the mind becomes arrested, and it is for this reason that the arrest of the *vāyu* (*i.e.*, the vital wind) has been held very important in the Nāth literature as in the literature of other religious schools containing discourses on yoga.

Kāya-sādhana of the Nāth Siddhas implies, on the whole, a slow and gradual process of continual purification, rejuvenation and transubstantiation of the body through various yogic processes. It has been said that through the fire of yoga (*i.e.*, the purifying processes of yoga) the ordinary body of change and decay is burnt away and from the process of purification and rejuvenation results a new immutable divine body as a transformation of the old. Without entering into the details of this Kāya-sādhana, let us discuss

1 *Cf.* *pāṭe rājā daḍa kari khemāir sane mili* |
kāmer galāte dey lohār jiñjali ||
sakala chāḍiyā guru khemāire kara rājā |
bhakṣiyā garala candra kāyā kara tajā || *Ibid.*, p. 152.
Also Ibid., p. 159.

2 *biṣam śikal bānde manake nā deya ṭhāi* |
manake bāndhile bāchā taler lāgāl pāi ||
ei saṁsār mājhe man ḍākāt baḍa |
bipad pāthāre man dāgā dive baḍa ||
man rājā prajā man māyā phanda |
man bāndha tan cinta śuna gopi-candra || etc.
Gopī-candrer Sannyās (C.U., Part II) p. 435.

here at some length a particular form of yoga that was most emphasised in Kāya-sādhana.

(B) *Kāya-sādhana*

(*a*) The Theory of the Sun and the Moon

To understand fully the secrets of Kāya-sādhana we should first of all understand the theory of the sun and the moon as postulated in yoga.

The sun and the moon are very frequently to be met with in the Tāntric and yogic texts and it is held that yoga consists in the unification of the sun and the moon. The sun and the moon refer generally to the two important nerves in the right and the left and their union generally refers to the union of the two currents of the vital wind, *Prāṇa* and *Apāna* or inhalation and exhalation.[1] But the sun and the moon have got a deeper meaning still. In the *Siddhasiddhānta-paddhati* (ascribed to Gorakh) we find that the physical body emerges from the collocation of five factors, *viz.*, *Karma* (activity), *Kāma* (desire), *Candra* (the moon), *Sūrya* (the sun) and *Agni* (fire).[2] Of these the first two are rather the conditions of the visible body (*piṇḍa*), while the other three are the primary elements of which the body is made. Of these three again the sun and fire are generally held to be the same. Then the primary elements out of which the visible body is made are reduced to two, *viz.*, the sun and the moon. The moon represents the elements of *Rasa* or *Soma*, (*i.e.*, the quintessence in the form of the juice) and the sun is the element of fire, and, therefore, the body is called the product of *Agni* and *Soma*.[3] *Rasa* as *Soma* is the food (*upabhogya*) while fire as the consumer is the eater (*bhoktā*),[4] and through the well-proportioned combination

[1] The word Haṭha-yoga really signifies the union of the *ha*, *i.e.*, the sun and the *ṭha*, *i.e.*, the moon.

Vide, *Haṭha-yoga-pradīpikā*.

[2] *karma kāmaś candraḥ sūryo' gnir iti pratyakṣa-karaṇa-pañcakam* (1.62).

[3] *agai-somā-tmako deho vindur yad ubhayā-tmakaḥ* ||

Quoted in the commentary by Dravyeśa Jhā on the above aphorism.

Cf. *agni-ṣomā-tmakaṁ viśvaṁ ity agnir ācakṣate* |

Bṛhaj-jābālo-paniṣat, (9.1).

[4] *Cf.* *gām āviśya bhūtāni dhārayāmy aham ojasā* |
puṣṇāmi cauṣadhīḥ sarvāḥ somo bhūtvā rasātmakaḥ ||
ahaṁ vaiśvānaro bhūtvā prāṇināṁ deham āśritaḥ |
prāṇā-pāna-samāyuktaḥ pacāmy annaṁ caturvidham ||

Gītā, (15.13-14).

of the consumer and the consumed the whole creation is sustained. The sun and the moon as *Agni* and *Soma* respectively are manifested in the physical world as the seed of the father and the ovum of the mother, through the combination of which proceeds the visible body,[1] and thus *Agni* and *Soma* are the two primordial elements of which the whole creation is made. The moon, in addition to the one digit (*kalā*), which is the digit of nectar, and which it possesses by virtue of its own nature, possesses sixteen other *kalās* which are explained here as the sixteen modes in which the moon functions.[2] The sun, again, in addition to its own digit of self-luminosity, possesses twelve other digits, which are the modes in which the element of the sun functions.[3] This theory of the sun and the moon with its cosmological significance is found explained in the second *Brāhmaṇa* of the *Bṛhaj-jābālo-paniṣat*.

In the yogic texts in general the moon and the sun represent the two elements underlying physical existence,—*viz.*, the element of creation and preservation and the element of change and destruction.[4] The moon as the principle of non-change and immortality resides in the region of Śiva and the sun as the principle of change and destruction resides in the region of Śakti. The moon and the sun are thus associated with Śiva and Śakti. The moon is the depository of

[1] *kiñca sūryā—gni-rūpaṁ pituḥ śukraṁ soma-rūpaṁ ca mātṛ-rajaḥ, ubhayoḥ saṁyoge piṇḍotpattir, etc.* *Vide*, Comm. referred to above.

[2] *ullolā, kallolinī, uccalantī, unmādinī, taraṁginī, śoṣiṇī, lampaṭā, pravṛttiḥ, laharī, lolā, lelihānā, prasarantī, pravāhā, saumyā, prasannatā, plavantī l evaṁ candrasya ṣoḍaśa-kalā saptadaśī kalā nivṛttiḥ sā'mṛta-kalā l*

Siddha-siddhānta-paddhati (1.63).

Cf. *Tantrā-loka* (3.138).

[3] *tāpinī, grāsikā, ugrā, ākuñcanī, śoṣiṇī, pravodhanī, smarā, ākarṣaṇī, tuṣṭi-varddhinī, ūrmi-rekhā, kiraṇavatī, prabhāvatī'ti dvādaśa-kalā sūryasya, trayodaśī sva-prakāśatā nija-kalā l*

Siddha-siddhānta-paddhati (1.66).

[4] In some places, however, the sun is not identified with the destructive fire,—it is described as situated in the middle as the middle principle.

ūrddhve tu saṁsthitā sṛṣṭiḥ paramānanda-dāyinī ||
pīyūṣa-vṛṣṭiṁ varṣantī baindavī paramā kalā ||
adhaḥ saṁhārakṛj jñeyo mahān agniḥ kṛtāntakaḥ l
ghoro jvālāvalī-yukto durdharṣo jyotiṣāṁ nidhiḥ ||
tayor madhye paraṁ teja ubhayānanda-sundaram l
avatāraḥ sa vijñeya ubhābhyāṁ vyāpakaḥ śivaḥ ||
paraspara-samāviṣṭau candre' gniṣṭītibhe śaśī l
candraṁ sṛṣṭiṁ vijānīyād agniḥ saṁhāra ucyate ||
avatāro raviḥ prokto madhyasthaḥ parameśvaraḥ l

Quoted in the comm. on the *Tantrā-loka* (3.67) by Jayaratha.

Amṛta or ambrosia which gives immortality, while the sun is the fire of destruction (*kālāgni*).[1] The moon is situated just below the Sahasrāra or the lotus of thousand petals in the cerebrum region,—it is facing downwards; and the sun is situated in the region of the navel or in the lowest plexus (*Mūlādhāra*) facing upwards. It is held that *bindu* which is the quintessence of the body is of two kinds, *viz.*, the yellowish white *bindu* (*pāṇḍura-bindu*) and the red *bindu* (*lohita-bindu*),—the former is of the nature of semen (*śukra*), while the latter is of the nature of ovum (*mahā-rajas*); the *bindu* (*i.e.* the white *bindu* or semen) is contained in the moon in the upper region, while the ovum is contained in the sun in the navel; this *bindu* is Śiva and that is the moon,—and the *rajas* is Śakti, which is the sun.[2] Thus it seems that the conception of the moon and the sun has been associated with that of Śiva and Śakti, and metaphysically the moon and the sun represent the nature of Śiva and Śakti, respectively. The sun, we have seen, is called *Kālāgni* or the fire of destruction, and it is also called Rudra (*i.e.* the Dire One) as opposed to Śiva (the All-good One). In the *Kaula-jñāna-nirṇaya* this *Kālāgni* as Rudra is associated with Śakti and is said to be seated in the lower region (*Mūlādhāra*) within the mouth of the *Vāḍavā*. It is held that there are seven lower regions called *pātāla* and seven upper regions called heaven. Creation lasts as long as the *Kālāgni* remains in the lower region, but when it burns upwards, dissolution

1 *bujhāile nā bujha guru yādrer* (*andher*) *lakṣaṇ* I
yamreta eḍiyā kara garal bhakṣaṇ || *Gorakṣa-vijaya*, p. 134.
nābhi-deśe vasaty eko bhāskaro dahanā-tmakah I
amṛtā-tmā sthito nityaṁ tālu-mūle ca candramāh ||
varṣaty adho-mukhaś candro grasaty ūrddhva-mukho ravih I
jñātavyā karaṇī tatra jathā piyūṣam āpyate ||
Gorakṣa-paddhati, 2nd *Śataka*, *verses* (32-33). (Bombay Edition).

Generally the sun is described in the naval: but the *Gorakṣa-saṁhitā* (Ch. IV, verse 152) and the*Kaula-jñāna-nirṇaya* (Ch. II. verse 3)it is described in the lowest lotus or the Mūlādhāra.

2 *sa punar dvividho binduḥ pāṇḍuro lohitas tathā* I
pāṇḍurah śukram ityāhur lohitākhyo mahārajaḥ ||
sindūra-drava-saṁkāśaṁ nābhi-sthāne sthitaṁ rajaḥ I
śaśi-sthāne sthito bindus tayor aikyaṁ sudurlabhaṁ ||
bindu śivo rajaḥ śaktiś candro bindu rajo raviḥ I
anayoḥ saṅgamād eva prāpyate paramaṁ padam ||
Gorakṣa-paddhati, p. 35 (verses 71-73).

Also, *Gorakṣa-saṁhitā* (Prasanna Kaviratna's edition), pp. 29-30 (verse, 80-82). *Cf.* also, *Gorakṣa-sāra-saṁgraha*, p. 41.

starts.[1] In the Buddhist Tantras and the Buddhist Sahajiyā songs these principles of the sun and the moon have been conceived as the fire-force in the Nirmāṇa-kāya (*i.e.* the plexus of 'the body of transformation') and as the Bodhi-citta in the Uṣṇīṣa-kamala respectively. The fire-force in the Nirmāṇa-kāya (situated, according to the Buddhists, in the navel region) is described as the goddess Caṇḍālī. This point has been discussed before in detail.[2]

The Sādhanā of the Haṭha-yogins consists, on the whole, in the act of combining the sun with the moon after getting complete mastery over them. In describing the yogic power of Hāḍi-siddhā Mayanāmatī frequently refers to the fact that Hāḍi-siddhā has made the sun and the moon his ear-rings.[3] Though the statement is found in our literature only to describe the mythical power of Hāḍi-siddhā, with whom everything impossible became possible, there is a deeper yogic significance behind. These principles of the sun and the moon have been referred to in the *Gorakṣa-vijaya* under various imageries.[4]

This act of combining the sun with the moon or the perfect control over them then implies many things in practical yoga. It implies, firstly, the retrogressive process of turning the cosmic manifestation back to its original form of rest, and this is effected by the yogins by rousing Śakti and uniting her with Śiva in the Sahasrāra. The combination of the sun and the moon implies secondly the yogic practice in which the male and the female unite and the combined substance of the seed and the ovum is sucked within by the yogin or the yoginī, as the case may be,

[1] *Kaula-jñāna-nirṇaya, Ch.* II.

[2] *Vide supra*, pp. 99-106

[3] *edeśiyāhāḍi nāy baṅga-deśe ghar* ।
cāndra-suruj rākheche dui kāner kuṇḍal ॥
Gopī-candrer Gān (C.U. Part I), p. 61.
yam rājā hay yār nijer cākar ।
candra sūrya dui jan kuṇḍal kāner ॥
Gopī-candrer Sannyās (C.U. Part II), pp. 440-441.

[4] *e.g. śanivāre bahe bāyu śūnye mahātithi* ।
pūrvve ule bhāskar paścime jvale bāti ॥
nivite nā dio bāti jvāla ghana ghana ।
ājukā chāpāi rākha amūlya ratan ॥
ravivār bahe bāū laiyā ādya mūl ।
āgun pāniye gura ek samatul ॥
āgun pāniye jadi hae milāmili ।
nivi jāiva āguni raiyā jāiva chāli ॥ *Gorakṣa-vijaya*, p. 140.

through some secret yogic processes.[1] Again the practice of purifying and controlling the nerves like Iḍā and Piṅgalā by controlling *Prāṇa* and *Apāna* through processes of *Prāṇāyāma* is what is meant by combining the sun and the moon. The three important nerves Iḍā, Piṅgalā and Suṣumnā in the left, right and the middle are frequently described in the yogic texts as of the nature of the moon, the sun, and fire (*Soma* or *Candra*, *Sūrya* and *Agni*), respectively. In the Nāth cult, however, the commingling of the sun and the moon has the deeper significance of transforming the material body of change to an immutable body of perfection. How can that be effected? It can be effected by a perfect control over the destructive force of the sun and then rejuvenating the whole body with the nectar oozing from the moon. We have seen that the sun represents the principle of destruction and the moon that of creation. The yogin tries to avoid both the extremes and have recourse to a principle of eternal conservation, which can be effected only by the perfect commingling of the principle of destruction and creation. This is what is meant by the real commingling of the sun and the moon.[2]

It is held in practical yoga that the quintessence of the visible body is distilled in the form of *Soma* or nectar (*amṛta*) and is reposited in the moon in the Sahasrāra. There is a curved duct from the moon below the Sahasrāra up to the hollow in the palatal region; it is well-known in yoga physiology as the *Śaṅkhinī*. This is the *baṅka nāla* (*i.e.* the curved duct) frequently mentioned in the vernaculars through which the *mahā-rasa* (*i.e. Soma-rasa*) passes. This curved

[1] *Cf. Vajrolī-mudrā.*

[2] *beṅkā nāle sādha guru nā kariyā helā* || *Gorakṣa-vijaya*, p. 147.

Kabir in his songs frequently speaks of this *baṅka-nāla*. The Orissa Vaiṣṇavas also speak of it in connection with their Sādhanā.

Cf. *nirodha karala triveṇī* I
baṅka-nālara sikha pare I
kamāra nāla yeuṁ ṭhāre ||
ūrddhva-mukhare kari ṭhaṇā I
mahā-śūnyare mo bhajanā || *Brahma-śāṅkali*, p. 3.

Again *ujāni dhara bāyu ṭāṇi* I
kṣipa ākāśa mārge pānī ||
baṅku nālare ṭhula kara I
nāsikā agre dṛṣṭi dhara || etc.
Ibid., pp. 20-21.

avadhu saṁkhanī nāli siv saṁcaryā, sukhmani paiṭhā jīv I
wātā garbhi basaṁtaḍāṁ, baṁka nāli ras pīv || *Mācīṁdra-Gorakh-bodh*, collected in *Gorakh-bānī*, 60.

duct *Śaṅkhinī* is described in the *Gorakṣa-vijaya* as the serpent with mouths at both ends.[1] The mouth of this *Śaṅkhinī*, through which the *Soma* or the *Amṛta* pours down from the moon is called the *Daśama-dvāra* or the tenth door of the body as distinguished from the other nine ordinary doors.[2] This tenth door is the most important in yoga and is frequently referred to in old and medieval Bengali literature and it is frequently mentioned also in the Hindi texts on yoga.[3] Through this tenth door nectar trickles down from the moon, ordinary people knows nothing of its secret.[4] In the ordinary course the nectar, trickling down from the moon through this tenth door, falls in the fire of the sun and is eaten up or dried up by the sun. The quintessence of the body in the form of *Soma* or *Amṛta* being thus dried

1 *budh bāre bahe bāyu bujha āpe āp* l
phirāi khelāo guru dui mukhā sāp ||
cāpile garjjiyā uṭhe biraha nāginī l
sāpinī nā haye guru surasā saṅkhinī ||
Goraksa-vijaya, p. 141
jyaiṣṭha māseta guru bhānu kharaśān l
surasā sāpinī tole kailās samān || *I bid.*, p. 143.
saruyā saṁkhinī saṅge ekā bhedi kāl l
paricay kari hāsā bandi kara kāl || *Ibid.*, p. 144.

2 *ekaṁ mukha-randhraṁ rāja-dantā-ntare, etad eva śaṅkhinī daśamadvāram ity ucyate* l
Amaraugha-śāsana (Kashmir Series of Texts and Studies), p. 11.
See also:—*ṣaṣṭhaṁ tālu-cākraṁ tatrā'mṛta-dhārāpravāhaḥ ghaṇṭikā-mūla-randhra-rāja-dantāṁ śaṁkhinī-bibaraṁ daśama-dvāram*, etc.
Siddha-siddhānta-paddhati (2,6).
Cf. *daśami duārata cihṇa dekhaiā* l
āila garāhaka apaṇe bahiā || *Caryā-pada* No. 3.
This tenth door has been explained in the comentary as the *vairocana-dvāra*, or the most supreme gate (*vairocana* being generally held supreme in the pantheou of many of the Buddhistic esoteric schools).
Cf. also—*iḍā piṅgalā susamanā sandhī* l
mana pavana tāta kaila bandī ||
daśamī duyāre dilo kapāṭa l
eve caḍiloṁ mo se yoga bāṭa ||
Śrī-kṛṣṇa-kīrtana (Sāhitya Pariṣat edition), p. 359.
dasaveṁ dvāre dei kapāṭ l *Gorakh khojī auraī bāṭ* ||
Gorakh-bānī, Śabadī, 135.
bhediyā daśamī dvār khāl jor bhara ||
Gorakṣa-vijaya, p. 139.
iṅgalā piṅgalā dui nadīr ye mājhe l
daśamīte tāli diyā rahivā sahaje || *Ibid.*, p. 144.
daśamīr dvār bhedi ḍhoke ḍhoke tola l
ujāuk mahā-ras bharauk khāla jora ll *Ibid.*, p. 145.

3 *Cf.* *dasam duārā agam apārā param puruṣa kī ghāṭī* l
Beni, *Ādigrantha*, p. 974, quoted by Dr. Mohan Singh.

4 *gagan sikhar āchai aṁbar pāṁṇīṁ* l
maratāṁ mūḍhāṁ lokāṁ maram na jāṇīṁ ||
Gorakh-bāni, Pada 5.

up, the body falls a victim to the fire of destruction (*Kālāgni*),[1] —this is how in the natural course of things death becomes the inevitable catastrophe of life. This ordinary course of the flow of nectar must be checked and regulated and this is the only way of deceiving Kāla (Time) and becoming immortal. The tenth door must be shut up or well guarded, —and this has figuratively been hinted in the vernaculars by the phrase 'locking up the tenth door' or 'placing sentinels' there. If this door remains open the *Mahā-rasa*, which is the best wealth of man, will be stolen away by the Sun or Death.[2] On the other hand, if this *Mahā-rasa* can be saved from the sun and if the yogin can himself drink this nectar, the yogin will undoubtedly become immortal.

How to save this *Amṛta* from the sun? Various are the yogic processes described in Haṭha-yogic and Tāntric texts.

1 *nābhi-mūle vaset sūryas tālu-mūle ca candramāḥ* I
amṛtaṁ grasate sūryas tato mṛtyu-vaśo naraḥ ||
Gorakṣa-saṁhitā (I, 85),

Cf. *candrāt sāraḥ sravati vapuṣas tena mṛtyur narāṇāṁ* I
tad badhnīyāt sukaraṇam ato nānyathā kārya-siddhiḥ ||
Gorakṣa-paddhati, verse 15.

vimala salila sosa jāi jai kālāgni paiṭhai II
Dohā-koṣa of Kānha-pada, Dohā No. 14.

Also—*tṛṣā nāgile jal āse śūnya haite* I
tṛṣā lāgile jal tor khāy hutāśane ||
Gopī-candrer Gān (C.U. Part I), p. 72.

Again—*kadācit nija candra nā karivā vyay* I
bāra batsarer āyu eka dine kṣay II *Garakṣa-vijaya*, p. 188.

2 *ḍuvila tomhār naukā kāchi gela chiḍi* I
tomhār sakal bharā karileka curi ||

* * *

gurur bacan tomār kichu nāi bhāy I
yatheka sampad tomār tuli dilā nāe ||

* * *

pradiva nivile bāpu ki kariva taile I
ki kāj bāndhile yāil jal nā thākile II
sikhaḍ kāṭile tave paḍe gāch I
bini jale kathāte jie māch ||
laḍivāre sakti nāhi gurur sakati I
dvār-khān mukta kari karilā basati ||
mukta dvār pāi cor haila satāntar I
sarva dhan hari nila śūnya haila ghar ||
Gorakṣa-vijaya, pp. 107-108.

Again—*nagare manusya nāhi ghare ghare cāl* I
āndhale dokān diyā kharid kare kāl || *Ibid.*, p. 138.

[There is a pun on the last line. The literal meaning is,—the blind is kept in charge of the shop and the deaf buys everything; the blind is the igorant and the uninitiated, while the deaf is Death (*Kāla*) who pays no heed to the request of any body.]

Again—*dvitīya prahara rātri kāla nidrā ghor* I
ojaner tail māpi lai jāe cor II *Ibid.*, p. 139.

Of all the processes the process known as *Khecarī-mudrā* has been held to be the most important. It is the process of turning the tongue backwards into the hollow above so as to reach the mouth of the *Rāja-danta* or of the *Śaṅkhinī* (which is the tenth door) and of fixing the sight between the eye-brows. The tongue thus extended backwards shuts up the tenth door and the nectar, thus saved, is drunk by the yogin himself. This *Khecarī-mudrā* has been praised eloquently in all the yogic texts as the best and the surest way of becoming immortal. It is held that this yogic process has the capacity of controlling all kinds of secretion, and if a yogin practises *Khecarī* his *bindu* (seed) will remain undisturbed even if he is closely embraced by a woman. This process of drinking the nectar by the practice of the *Mudrās* and the *Bandhas* is the way to eternal life.[1] In some of the texts this secretion of nectar from the moon is associated with the rousing of Kuṇḍalinī Śakti and it is held that the rousing of Śakti in the Sahasrāra is instrumental to the trickling down of the nectar,—and sometimes Śakti herself is depicted as the drinker of the nectar. This liquid, trickling from the moon, is also called the wine of the immortals (*amara-vāruṇī*), and as the gods have become immortal by drinking *Amṛta* or the ambrosial wine, so the yogins become immortal by drinking this wine trickling from the moon.[2] Drinking of wine and eating of meat, which are indispensable to a Tāntric Sādhaka, are explained by the

[1] *Cf.* *rasanāṁ ūrddhvagāṁ kṛtvā kṣaṇā-rdham api tiṣṭhati* |
viṣair vimucyate yogī vyādhi-mṛtyu-jarā-dibhiḥ ||
ūrddhva-jihvaḥ sthiro bhūtvā soma-pānaṁ karoti yaḥ |
māsā-rddhena na sandeho mṛtyuṁ jayati yoga-vit ||
nityaṁ soma-kalā-pūrṇaṁ śarīre yasya yoginaḥ |
takṣakenāpi daṣṭasya viṣaṁ tasya na sarpati ||
indhanāni yathā vahnis tala-vartiṁ ca dīpakaḥ |
tathā soma-kālā-pūrṇaṁ dehi dehaṁ na muñcati || *etc.*

Gorakṣa-paddhati, pp. 37, 38 (Bombay edition).

These verses are repeated in many other similar texts.

Cf. again—*ghaṇṭā-koṭi-kapola-koṭara-kuṭī-jihvā-gra-madhyā-śrayā-cchaṅkhiny āgata-rāja-danta-vivaraṁ prānto-rddhva-vaktreṇa yat* | *samprāptaṁ hanu-randhra-mūla-vidhinā yac candra-toyaṁ mukhe tatsarvaṁ ravi-kāla-rūpa-sadane rakṣet parā sāraṇā* || *etc.*

Amaraugha-śāsana, p. 1 *et seq.*

[2] See *Gorakh-bānī*, *Pada* 28.

Nāth yogins as the drinking of the nectar from the moon and turning the tongue backwards in the hollow above.[1]

We have seen that the moon has sixteen digits. The secretion of the *Soma-rasa* in the *Kālāgni* (the solar fire of destruction) is sometimes figuratively called the eating up of the digits of the moon by the *Rāhu*,[2] the passage from the moon to the *Kālāgni* being conceived as the *Rāhu*. The idea of the disappearance of the digits of the moon one by one and the reappearance of the digits in order has given rise to the theory of the *Tithis* (i.e. the lunar day, or the thirtieth part of a whole lunation), including the *Pūrṇimā* (full-moon) and the *Amāvasyā* (*i.e.*, the night of the newmoon),—the processes of disappearance and reappearance of the digits being represented as the black and the white fortnight.[3]

The conservation and the yogic regulation of the *Mahā-rasa* are at the centre of the yogic Sādhanā of the Nāth Siddhas. The Nāth Siddhas (as well as the Buddhist Siddhācāryas) admitted six parts of yoga, viz., *Āsana*, *Prāṇāyāma*, *Pratyāhāra*, *Dhāraṇā*, *Dhyāna* and *Samādhi*,[4] excluding the two parts, viz., *Yama*, *i.e.*, restraint and *Niyama* or discipline of the Pātañjala system. It will be observed that in the Pātañjala system *Yama*, *Niyama* and *Āsana*

1 *mukh-khāni chāl guru jihvā-khāni phāl* I
amar pāṭane jena yete kare hāl ||
ucca nic bhūmi-khāni tāte kṛṣi hay I
jadi haye gṛha-vāsī se bhūmi caṣay || *Gorakṣa-vijaya*, p. 138.

Cf. *gomāṁsaṁ bhakṣayen nityaṁ pived amara-vāruṇīm* I
kulīnaṁ tam ahaṁ manye itare kula-ghātakāḥ ||
go-śabdeno'ditā jihvā tat-praveśo hi tāluni I
go-māṁsa-bhakṣaṇaṁ tat tu mahā-pātaka-nāśanam ||
jihvā-praveśa-sambhūta-vahnino 'tpāditaḥ khalu I
candrāt sravati yaḥ sāraḥ sā syād amara-vāruṇī ||
Gorakṣa-paddhati, pp. 3839 (Bombay edition).

2 Rāhu is the mythical demon that devours the moon, which fact is held responsible for the eclipse.

3 *Cf.* The Commentary on the line—*cañcala cīe paiṭho kāla* ||
Caryā-pada No. 1.

prakṛtyā-bhāṣa-doṣa-vaśāt cañcalyatayā prakṛta-sattvena (*ā*, *sic*) *cyuti-rūpo hi-rāhuḥ* I *sa eva kālaḥ* I *kṛṣṇa-pratipaddaśāyām praviṣṭaḥ* I *yasmāt nandā-bhadrā jayā-riktā-pūrṇā-tithi-krameṇa samvṛtti-bodhi-citta-mṛgāṅkaṁ śoṣaṁ nayatīti* I
Comm. on the Song No. 1 (Śāstri's edition).

Cf. also:—*kālāgniś cyutā-vasthā kṛṣṇa-pratipat-praveśa-kāla-pravṛtta iti* I
Comm. on the Dohā No. 14 of Kānha-pāda.

4 *āsanaṁ prāṇa-saṁrodhaḥ pratyāhārāś ca dhāraṇā* I
dhyānaṁ samādhir etāni yogāṅgāni vadanti ṣaṭ ||

Cf. *Maitrāyaṇīya Upaniṣat* (Cowell's edition. Ch. VI. p. 129), where the six *Aṅgas* are described as *Pratyāhāra*, *Dhyāna*, *Prāṇāyāma*, *Dhāraṇā*, *Tarka* and *Samādhi*.

are physical and moral discipline for the control of the mind, *Prāṇāyāma* a vital process for the arrest of the mind, and *Pratyāhāra*, *Dhāraṇā*, *Dhyāna*, etc. are purely psychological processes for the final concentration and arrest of the mind; all these processes are associated in the Nāth cult with the process of retaining the *Mahā-rasa* and the yogic regulation of its secretion for the transubstantiation of the body and thus attaining a life eternal.[1]

(*b*) The Sun and the Moon as Woman and Man

There is, however, another aspect of the theory of the sun and the moon. We have seen that the sun is the *Rajas* and the moon is the *Bindu*,[2] the sun is associated with Śakti and the moon with Śiva—and the moon must be saved from the destructive sun. In the grosser aspect, man must save himself from the clutches of woman, who has been always depicted in the Nāth literature as the tigress. Charmed and allured by her, man loses vital energy. She has generally been spoken of as the enchantress of the day and the tigress of the night. The Nāth Siddhas were strict celibates, and it appears from the Nāth literature in all the vernaculars that women are regarded as the greatest danger in the path of yoga and they are given no status higher than that of ferocious tigresses always bent on sucking the blood of the prey. The fall of Mīna-nāth in the company of the women of Kadalī or the queen of Ceylon and his rescue by Gorakh-nāth seem to be a popular poetical version of the general attitude of the Nāths towards women in general. In his enigmatic counsels to the Guru Gorakh-nāth said,—"The breath of women dries up the body and youth vanishes day by day. Foolish are the people who understand nothing and make pets of tigresses in every house; in the day the tigress becomes the world-enchantress and at night she dries up the whole body. The milk is stolen and the tigress boils it, and the cat

1 *candrā-mṛtamayīṁ dhārāṁ pratyāharati bhāskaraḥ* I
yat pratyāharaṇam tasyāḥ pratyāhāraḥ sa ucyate ||
Gorakṣa-paddhati, p. 74.

2 *Vide supra.*
Cf. also—*yathā yoniś ca liṅgaṁ ca saṁyogāt sravato'mṛtam* I
tathā'mṛtāgni-saṁyogād dravatas te na saṁśayaḥ ||
Tantrā-loka (4, 131).

(death?) is sitting by; the essence of milk is thrown down on the ground and only the vacant vessel remains in the sky."[1] Similar verses ascribed to Gorakh-nāth are also found in Hindi.[2] If we follow the words of reproof that Gorakh-nāth levelled against his fallen Guru, we shall be convinced of the uncompromisingly adverse attitude of the Nāths against women, who are generally termed as thieves, dacoits, pirates, thirsty tigresses and hypocrite cats. In one place Gorakh says,—"You have handed over your store to the gang of dacoits, you have employed the mouse as guard for the pepper plant and the cat for thickly boiled milk; you have kept logs of wood to the custody of the carpenter, the cow to the tiger, wealth to plunderers, the frog to the serpent, bulbous root to the boar and arum to the porcupine; you have kept the mouse as the guard of the granary, kept plantains before the crow, offered fish to the rustic rogue, dry fuel to fire. You have lost whatever merchandise you had at your disposal, exhausted your store and created sensation in the vicinity; you are living with your neighbours who are thieves and frauds."[3] Enigmatic statements of this nature casting serious reflection on the nature of women abound in the *Gorakṣa-vijaya*, or the *Mīna-cetana* and also

1 *Gorakṣa-vijaya*, pp. 186-187.
Cf. also—*hera dekha bāghinī āise* l
neter āṁcale carma-maṇḍita kariyā
ghar ghar bāghinī poṣe ||
Song of Gorakha-nāth in the *Dharma-maṅgala* of Sahadev, B.S.P.P. 1304.

2 *Cf.* *guru jī aisā kām na kijai, jāṁte amī mahāṁ-ras chījai* ||

* * *

goḍe bhae ugamage peṭ bhaiā dhiladhilā kes vagale ke paṁkhā l
amī mahā-ras bāghini sokhā tāte ghor mathan bhai aṁkhā ||
divas kau bāghini suri nari mohai rātī sāir sokhai l
murakh lokā aṁdhalā pasūā niti prati bāghani pokhai ||
dāmi kāḍhi bāghani lai āiā māu kahai merā puti bihāiā l
golī lakḍī kau ghuṇi lāiā tin ḍāl mūl saṇi khāiā ||
bāghni jiṁda bi bāghani biṁda bi bāghani hamārī kāṁiā l
ini bāghani trailokī khāī badati gorakhu rāiā ||
Quoted by Dr. Mohan Singh in his *Gorakhnāth* etc, part II, p. 3.
Cf. *etaiṁ kacchu kathīlā guru sarbaiṁ cai bholai* l
sarba ras khoīlā guru bāghaṁnī cai kholai ||
nācata gorakh-nāth ghūṁgharī cai ghālaiṁ l
sarbai kamāī khoī guru bāghanīṁ cai racaiṁ || *Gorakh-bānī*, *Pada*, 2.
Also *Ibid*, *Pada* 43, 48.

3 *Gorakṣa-vijaya*, pp. 121-23.
Gopī-candrer Pāṁcālī, (pp. 340-41).

in the songs of Gopī-cānd. Similar words, phrases and imageries were freely used also by Mayanāmatī, who was bent on saving her only son from the clutches of his youthful wives.[1] We need not multiply illustrations. It will be clear from the above that in a grosser sense *Māha-rasa* means the seed, and the Sādhanā consists in saving the same from any kind of discharge, and it has been emphatically declared in all texts of yoga that he, who has been able to give an upward flow to the fluid, is a god, and not a man.

This attitude towards women, as found in the Nāth cult, seems to have influenced the tone of the poets of the Nirguṇa School (as the school is styled and defined by Dr. Barthwal) of Hindi poetry headed by Kabir. Kabir and his followers, just like the Nāths, spoke of women in no better terms than as ferocious tigresses always seeking opportunity to prey upon men and to suck their vitality.[2]

(C) Points of Similarity and Difference in the Practical Aspect of Yoga between the Nāth Cult and other Esoteric Schools

It is important to note in this connection that in the practical aspect of yoga the system of Kabir, as also that of a

[1] In one place Mayanā says to Gopī-cānd:—All men serve women gratis; the *Mahā-rasa* within the body is worth thousands of chests filled with gem; and when that wealth is lost man becomes subdued by a woman. A lioness is she and casts her eyes like the tigress: she leaves aside the bones and the flesh and sucks up the *Mahā-rasa*. Woman deals in the wealth of man, and the allured man goes on serving her gratis. With his plough and bulls man cultivates the field of others,—there is the loss of the bulls and of the seed in the bargain. Though steel is used in the plough it decays in earth. If the bat eats up the soft stem of the plantain-tree the fruits cannot grow,—if the newly grown bamboo is pierced through by insects, how can it stand any weight? *Gopīcandrer Sannyās* (C.U. part II), p. 438. *Cf.* aslo *Gopi-candrer Gān*, pp. 71, *et seq.*

[2] *Vide Kāmī Nāra Kau Aṅga-Kabīra-Granthā-valī* (Śyāma-sundar Dās's edition), pp. 39-41; *Atha Nārī Nimdā Ko Aṅga—Sundara-Granthā-vali*, Vol. II, pp. 347 *et seq.*

Cf. alslo—*din kā mohinī rāt kā bāghinī*
palak palak lahu coṣe 1
duniyā sav bāurā ho ke
ghar ghar bāghinī poṣe 11 Ascribed to Tulasīdās.

Cf. also the fowloiing poem of Palṭu-dās:—*bhāg re bhāg phakir kā bālakā kanak kāminī dui bāgh lāge* 1 *mār legī paḍā eīciyāyagā bhaeā bekuf tu nahī bhāge* || *sṛṅgo ṛsi nārae kā mārakā khāy gayi bace na koyi jau lākh tyāge* 1 *palṭudās kahe ek upāy hai baiṭha saṅta-sangamā nitya jāge* 1

Vide Bhāratvarsīya Upāsaka-sampradāya by A. K. Datta, Vol. I, pp. 255-256.

host of other medieval Hindi poets, was essentially the same as that of the Nāth yogins described above. Of course, there is a remarkable difference in the religious attitude, but in spite of all differences in views and the religious approach, the yogic process seems to have been substantially the same. In his religious approach Kabir, with other poets of his school, is known to us more as representing a devotional school of mysticism, characterised by a spirit of heterodoxy, than as a school professing faith in yogic practice; but the fact remains that the poems of Kabir and the works of many other poets of this school speak of a system of yogic practice behind their devotional fervour.[1] In his work *Nirguṇa school of Hindi poetry* Dr. P. D. Barthwal has given an exposition of the yogic practices referred to in the works of this school of poets, and a perusal of the book will convince one of the inherent similarity in yogic practice of this school with that of its predecessors, *viz.*, the Nāth Siddhas. The theory of the sun and the moon and the question of the secretion of nectar referred to above play the most important part in these medieval schools. It is perhaps because of this similarity in yogic Sādhanā and the similarity of the general tone of extreme repulsion against women as a class, that the Kabir-panth has traditionally been affiliated with the Gorakhpanth and Kabir has been believed to have had met Gorakhnāth and have had religious discourses with him.

An important point to note is the difference in the religious approach as well as in method among the Nāth Siddhas on the one hand and the Buddhist Sahajiyās on the other. We have said before that though both the sects were cognate Haṭha-yogic sects there is a sharp difference in the professed final aim as well as in practices of yoga. The final aim of the Nāths, we have seen, is the attainment of immortality; while the final goal of the Buddhist Sahajiyās is the attainment of Mahā-sukha. The Nāth Siddhas believed in the reality of birth and death and tried to avoid the whirl by transubstantiating the material body of change to subtle etherial body and that again finally to a perfect divine body; but the Buddhist Sahajiyās inherited from the

[1] See *Infra*, the Appendix (A).

earlier schools of Buddhism the spirit of extreme idealism and tried to avoid the whirl of birth and death by realising the void-nature of the self and of all the Dharmas, and they further contended that the void-nature of the self and the not-self can be realised only through the realisation Mahā-sukha. The emphasis of the Nāths is on the yogic process of transubstantiating this corporal body of death and decay,—and the emphasis of the Buddhist Sahajiyās is on the sexo-yogic practice, which transforms the ordinary sex-pleasure to a higher and deeper emotion of bliss. Of course, the Kāya-sādhana of the Nāthists is also there in the practices of the Buddhists,[1] and we also find occasional references in the Dohās and the Caryā songs to the flow of nectar and the process of drinking it by the yogin with the purpose of making the *Skandha* (the elements, the aggregate of which constitutes the physical body) firm and stable and becoming *ajara* and *amara* (diseaseless and deathless); we find occasional references to the drinking of the nectar or the honey of the lotus in the head by the black-bee of the mind, and also to the pouring down of water from the moon of Bodhicitta, full in its sixteen digits, into the fire below. Though in some cases these expressions and imageries may be explained figuratively, yet it appears that the practice of the Buddhists for the realisation of the Mahā-sukha was intimately connected with the Kāya-sādhana of the Nāths.[2] The conception of the *Vāruṇī* or the ambrosial liquor is also found in the Caryā-padas,[3] and this *Vārūṇī* may more satisfactorily be explained in the sense of the amborsial liquor of the Nāth yogins than figuratively as the flow of Mahā-sukha or grossly as the flow of the Bodhicitta as semen virile. What we want to emphasise is that while one school had recourse to the Sādhanā from a particular

[1] *Supra*, p. 108.

[2] For a detailed study of the similarity between the Sādhanā of the Nāth Siddhas and that of the Buddhist Siddhācāryas the reader may consult the book *Siddha-sāhitya* by Dr. Dharmavir Bharati, Allahabad, 1955 (in Hindi).

[3] *eka se śuṇḍini dui ghare sāndhaa* |
ciana bākalaa bāruṇi bāndhaa ||
sahaje thira kari bāruṇi sāndhe |
jeṁ ajarāmara hoi diḍha kāndhe || Caryā Song, No. 3.

Cf. *ekā strī bhujyate dvābhyām āgatā candra-maṇḍalāt* |
tṛtīyo yaḥ punas tābhyāṁ sa bhaved ajarāmaraḥ ||
Gorakṣa-paddhati, p. 74 (Verse 31) (Bombay Edition).

outlook the other approached the yogic practices from a different point of view and while the emphasis of the one is on some particular aspect of the Sādhanā, the emphasis of the other was on another.

It is because of these differences that while the Nāth Siddhas were vehemently opposed to the association of women in any way with their Sādhanā and described them as the greatest impediment in their march towards immortality, the Buddhist Sahajiyās eulogised women in all possible glowing terms as the incarnation of Prajñā, or Śūnyatā herself, and her company was regarded as indispensable for the attainment of perfection in spiritual life. Of course we have seen before[1] that the Prajñā or the Yoginī or the Mudrā spoken of by the Buddhist Sahajiyās is not always the corporeal women; she is the Nairātmā or Śūnyatā or the Sahaja-damsel. But it will be equally a great mistake to try to interpret the Mudrā always in this idealised sense and thus to explain away the necessity of the compnay of women in the Sahaja-sādhanā.

We have noted before that the Mahā-sukha of the Buddhist Sahajiyās was not a purely physiological sensation,—there was a psychological element involved in it.[2] This psychological aspect in the Sādhanā (associated with the sex-emotion and sex-pleasure) is conspicuous by its absence in the Nāth school. The Vaiṣṇava Sahajiyā cult, we have seen, was based primarily on the divinisation of the sex-emotion by both physiological and psychological discipline. The Mahā-sukha as the Sahaja-nature of the self and the not-self was transformed into the emotion of supreme love in the Vaiṣṇava school. Neither Mahā-sukha nor supreme love of the purest and the most intense nature is attainable without the help of the chosen woman and it is for this reason that the Buddhists always spoke of her as the incarnation of Prajñā and the Vaiṣṇavas of Mahābhāva (*i.e.*, the supreme emotion of love as personified by Rādhā), —and this attitude of the Sahajiyās, both Buddhist and Vaiṣṇava, will present a sharp contrast to that of the Nāth Siddhas in general. The important point, however, to be

[1] *Supra*, pp. 99 *et seq.*
[2] *Supra*, Ch. V.

noted in this connection is that in spite of this general attitude of aversion towards women, the Nāth Siddhas also practised some well-known processes of yoga like Vajraulī, Amaraulī, Sahajaulī,[1] etc. in the company of women. But these practices are yogic practices, pure and simple, in which women are neither philosophised upon, nor idealised.

(iv) *The Vedic Soma-sacrifice and the Drinking of Nectar in the Yogic Schools*

The most important part of the Sādhanā of the Nāth Siddhas, *viz.*, the drinking of the nectar called *Soma*, oozing from the moon, can very well be associated with the Vedic rite of *Soma*-sacrifice, in which the *Soma*-juice was drunk and also offered to the gods and it was believed that the *Soma*-juice rejuvenates and envigorates the body and gives the drinker, whether god or man, eternal life in heaven or earth. This *Soma*-juice was prepared from a particular climbing plant (well known as the *Soma*-plant, Sacrostema Viminalis or Asclepias Acida), which was said to grow luxuriantly on the mountains of India and Persia, and it is very frequently referred to in connection with sacrifice in the Vedic literature as well as in the Avesta. The relation between the *Soma*-plant and the moon was held very mysterious. The plant itself was often called 'the moon-plant' and it was believed that the plant received its exhilarating and envigorating juice directly from the moon. As a matter of fact the moon is generally believed to be mysteriously related to all the medicinal herbs and it is held that the juice of the herbs, that possesses capacity of curing diseases and conferring longevity, comes from the moon. In the *Viṣṇu-purāṇa* (1.22) Brahmā is said to have appointed *Soma* or the moon to be the monarch of planets, of plants, of sacrifices, and penances, and one of the names of the moon is *Oṣadhi-pati* or *Oṣadhīśa*, i.e., 'the lord of herbs.'[2] So intimate is the relation between the plant *Soma* and the moon that in Vedic as well as post-Vedic literature the moon

[1] For these processes of yoga see *Haṭha-yoga-pradīpikā* (3/83-100). They are to be found in other standard works on Haṭha-yoga also.

[2] Dictionary of Monier Williams, p. 1137.

herself is called *Soma*. The *Soma*-plant was believed to possess sixteen leaves corresponding to the sixteen digits of the moon,[1] the leaves disappear one by one with the digits of the moon in the black fortnight and again reappear with the reappearance of the digits of the moon in the white fortnight. The mythical legend goes in the Purāṇas that "at the churning of the ocean after all sorts of medicinal plants and healing herbs are thrown in, three of the precious things said to be produced are *Soma* 'the moon,' *Amṛta* 'nectar,' and *Surā* 'spirituous liquor,' and in the other legends this nectar is said to be preserved in the body of the moon.[2] It will be easy from the above to detect the striking similarity of the conception of the moon and *Amṛta* or *Soma* of the yogins with those of the Vedic and post-Vedic traditions, —and it will also be easy to see how the Vedic religious function of sacrifice was transformed into a yogic practice, in both the cases there being the question of drinking *Soma* to gain eternal life.

(*v*) *The Rasāyana School and the Nāth Cult*

We have said before in connection with the history of the Nāth cult that in ideology as well as in methodology the yoga-system of the Nāth Siddhas is strikingly similar to that of the Rasāyana school. The Sādhanā of the Nāth Siddhas is essentially a Sādhanā of *transubstantiation and transfiguration*. We have already referred to the popular traditions prevalent among the people of the Nāth sect even to-day that the Siddhas like Matsyendra-nāth, Gorakh-nāth and others are still living in their subtle super-material body in the hilly regions of the Himalayas. These popular beliefs of a mythological nature have their root in the theological speculations of the sect. It has been said in the *Yoga-vīja* that the perfect body of the yogin is subtler than the subtlest, yet grosser than the grossest; the yogin can transform his body according to his will—and his form is above all disease and death. He plays in the three worlds

[1] We may note here that in the yogic texts *Amṛta* is often thought of trickling down from the lotus of sixteen petals (*ṣoḍaśa-patra-padma-galitam*, *Gorakṣa-paddhati*, p. 76, verse 57), which corresponds to the moon with the sixteen digits.

[2] Monier Williams, p. 1137.

sportively wherever he likes, and can assume any and every form through his incomprehensible power.[1] The same belief is to be found also in the Rasāyana school.[2] The Rasāyana school is fundamentally based on the ideal of *Jīvan-mukti* and the method advocated is that of transubstantiation with the help of *Rasa* or chemical element (generally mercury) and thus making the body immutable.[3] This Rasāyana, though primarily a school of chemical science, was associated with theological speculations, and renowned personalities like Nāgārjuna (the alchemist), Vyāḍi, Vyajapyāyana and others are recognised to have been the stalwarts of the school. It is believed that many are the gods, demons, sages and men, who have attained the immutable divine body with the help of *Rasa* and have thus become *Jīvan-mukta*.[4] The theological aim of the school can be postulated from the first chapter of the *Rasārṇava* where Bhairava (lord Śiva) explains the principles of Rasāyana to the goddess, and these principles, he says, are the best and the surest way to attaining perfection. The question of the goddess is, how to attain *Jīvan-mukti*. The Lord replies that the secret of *Jīvan-mukti* is rarely known even to the gods. The conception of post-mortem liberation is totally worthless; for in that case all creatures are entitled

1 *sūkṣmāt sūkṣmataro dehaḥ sthūlāt sthūlo jaḍāj jaḍaḥ* I
icchā-rūpo hi yogīndraḥ svatantras tv ajarā-maraḥ ||
krīḍati triṣu lokeṣu līlayā yatra kutracit I
acintya-śaktimān yogī nānā-rūpāṇi dhārayan || (Verses 51-52).

2 *evaṁ rasa-saṁsiddho duḥkha-jarā-maraṇa-varjito guṇavān* I
khe-gamanena ca nityaṁ saṁcarate sakala-bhuvaneṣu ||
dātā bhuvana-tritaye sraṣṭā so'pīha padma-yonir iva I
bhartā viṣṇur iva syāt saṁhartā rudravad bhavati ||
Rasa-hṛdaya-tantra (Āyurvedīya-grantha-māla, Vol. I, 19. 63-64).

Again.—*svadehe khe-caratvaṁ ca śivatvaṁ yena labhyate* I
tādṛśe tu rasa-jñāne nityā-bhyāsaṁ kuru priye ||
Rasārṇava, edited by Prof. P. C. Roy (Bibliotheca Indica).

3 *apare māheśvarāḥ parameśvara-tādātmy-vādino'pi piṇḍa-sthairye sārvā-bhimatā jīvan-muktiḥ setsyatī'ty āsthāya piṇḍa-sthairyo-pāyaṁ pāradādi-pada-vedanīyaṁ rasam eva saṁgirante* I
Sarva-darśana-saṁgraha (Govt. Oriental Hindu Series, Vol. I), p. 202.

4 *devāḥ kecin maheśā-dyā daityāḥ kāvya-puraḥsarāḥ* I
munayo vālakhilyā-dyā nṛpaḥ someśvarādayaḥ ||
govinda-bhagavat-pādācāryo govinda-nāyakaḥ I
carvaṭiḥ kapilo vyāliḥ kāpāliḥ kandalāyanaḥ ||
ete'nye bahavaḥ siddhā jīvan-muktāś caranti hi I
tanuṁ rasamayīṁ prāpya tadātmaka-kathā-caṇāḥ ||
Quoted in the *Sarva-darśana-saṁgraha*, p. 204.

to it by virtue of their mortal nature.[1] Again post-mortem liberation, spoken of in the six systems of philosophy, is a mere inferential speculation inasmuch as no positive proof of such liberation is available at all. On the other hand the state of *Jīvan-mukti* by making the body immutable is as positive as anything.[2] To be something knowable, liberation must have a 'knower'; the demise of the knower excludes the possibility of the knowable, and hence the conception of post-mortem liberation is as fictitious as anything.[3] For *mukti* worth the name, the *Piṇḍa* (the body, must be preserved and perfected and liberation is thus attainable only through the perfection and preservation of the body by the application of *Rasa* (which, according to the school of Rasāyana, is mercury), also by the control of the vital wind.[4] The *Rasa* or *Pārada* is believed to be vested with the mysterious capacity of transforming a base metal into gold and thus by constant rejuvenation and envigoration through a process of transubstantiation the *Rasa* can make every creature immortal. It has been said that *Rasa* is called *Pārada* because it leads one to the other

1 *ajarā-mara-dehasya śiva-tādātmya-vedanam* ।
jīvan-muktir mahā-devi devānām api durlabhā ||
piṇḍa-pāte ca yo mokṣaḥ sa ca mokṣo nirarthakaḥ ।
piṇḍe tu patite devi garddabho'pi vimucyate || (Verses 4-5).

2 *saḍ-darśane'pi muktis tu darśitā piṇḍa-pātane* ।
karā-malakavat sā'pi pratyakṣā no'palabhyate ||
tasmāt taṁ rakṣayet piṇḍaṁ rasaiś caiva rasāyanaiḥ ।
Quoted in the *Sarva-darśana-saṁgraha*, p. 203.

Cf. Also—*iti dhana-śarīra-bhogān matvā' nityāṁ sadaiva yatanīyam* ।
muktis tasya jñānāt taccābhyāsāt sa ca sthire dehe ||
Rasa-hṛdaya-tantra (I. 10) (Āyurvedīya Grantha-mālā No. 1.

Again,—*asminneva śarīre yeṣāṁ paramātmano na saṁvedaḥ* ।
deha-tyāgād ūrddhvaṁ teṣāṁ tad brahma dūrataram ||
brahmādayo yajante yasmin divyāṁ tanuṁ samāśritya ।
jīvan-mūktāś cānye kalpānta-sthāyino munayaḥ ||
tasmāj jīvan-muktiṁ samīhamānena yoginā prathamam ।
divyā tanur vidheyā hara-gaurī-sṛṣṭi-saṁyogāt || *Ibid* (1.21-23).

3 *rasāṅkameya-mārgo'kto jīva-mokṣo'nyathā tu na* ।
pramāṇāntara-vādeṣu yukti-bhedā-valambiṣu ||
jñātṛ-jñeyam idam viddhi sarva-tantreṣu sammatam ।
nājīvan jñāsyasi jñeyaṁ yad atostyeva jīvanam ||
Raseśvara-siddhānta, quoted in the *Sarva-darśana-saṁgraha*, p. 207.

4 *Vide, Ibid.* (Verses 18-22).

shore of the world.[1] It is the quintessence of lord Śiva.[2] The *Rasa* is again said to be the seed of Hara (*i.e.*, Śiva) and *Abhra* (mica) is the ovum of Gaurī; the substance that is produced through the combination of the two elements makes creatures immortal.[3] This state of immortality attainable through the application of *Rasa* has frequently been spoken of also in the standard works on Indian medical sciences as the state of *Jivan-mukti*, which has been eulogised as the only state of real perfection. We have hinted that the *Rasa* of Rasāyana, variously described as the most powerful element and called the *Bindu* of lord Śiva himself,[4] has been replaced in the Nāth cult by the *Somarasa* oozing from the moon in the Sahasrāra. We may also note that in the *Rasārṇava* the two primordial elements, of which the physical body is produced, have been described as the vital wind (*vāyu*) and the *Rasa* and according to this school the only way of making the body ever-lasting is the control over the vital wind and the scientific application of the *Rasa*; this is the case also with the yoga-system of the Nāth Siddhas, where the control of the vital wind and the proper regulation of the secretion of the *Soma* are regarded as of paramount importance.

It should be noted in this connection that the alchemists generally use the two words *Siddha-deha* and *Divya-deha* as synonymous, evidently because both are free from corruption, mortality and the defects belonging to the ordinary human frame; but a distinction should be made between the aim of

1 *saṁsārasya paraṁ pāraṁ dattesau pāradaḥ smṛtaḥ* ।
Quoted in the *Sarva-darśana-saṁgraha*, p. 202.

2 *pārādo gadito yasmāt parārthaṁ sādhakottamaiḥ* ।
supto'yaṁ mat-samo devi mama pratyaṅga-sambhavaḥ ॥
mama deha-raso yasmād rasas tenāyam ucyate । *Ibid*, p. 202.

3 *ye cātyakta-śarīrā hara-gaurī-sṛṣṭijāṁ tanuṁ prāptāḥ* ।
muktās te rasa-siddhā mantra-gaṇaḥ kiṁkaro yeṣāṁ ॥
Ibid., p. 203.

abhrakas tava bījaṁ tu mama bījaṁ tu pāradaḥ ।
anayor melanaṁ devi mṛtyu-dāridrya-nāśanam ॥
Ibid., p. 204.

4 In many of the texts on Rasāyana *Rasa* has been held identical with Śiva and as such it is said to be vested with the same potency as Śiva himself, *Cf.*

darśanāt tasya bhakṣaṇāt sparśanāt smaraṇād api ।
pūjanād rasa-dānāc ca dṛśyate saḍ vidhaṁ phalam ॥
kedārādīni liṅgāni pṛthivyāṁ yāni kānicit ।
tāni dṛṣṭvā tu yat puṇyaṁ tat-puṇyaṁ rasa-darśanāt ॥
Rasārṇava.

Cf. also similar other verses quoted in the *Sarva-darśana-saṁgraha*, p. 208.

the Nāth Siddhas and the Rasa Siddhas on the one hand and that of the Siddhas of the *Śuddha-marga* (pure path) on the other. The Nāth Siddhas and the Rasa Siddhas are known to be closely allied with each other regarding the ultimate object of their aspiration which consists in making the body a proof against death and decay and always responsive to the stimulus of the world of senses and capable of wielding immense power. But both of them are to be sharply distinguished from the adepts of the pure path. In the view of the latter, for instance, the incorruptible body is of two kinds, *viz.*, the one of the *Jīvan-mukta* and the other of the *Parā-mukta*. The former is the pure body of *Śuddha-māyā* known as *Praṇava-tanu* or *Mantra-tanu*, a body into which the corruptible body of *Māyā* in its triple aspect is finally transmuted. It is deathless and free from disintegration, but disappears in the end in higher *Mukti* in the Body of Pure Light, or Divine Body, called *Divya-deha* or *Jñāna-deha* of *Mahā-māyā*, which being absolutely spiritual (*cinmaya*) is beyond the farthest reaches of matter. In Tāntric phraseology the two bodies are known respectively as *Baindava* and *Śākta*. That the Nāths also in certain places discriminate between *Siddha-deha* and *Divya-deha* as the exponents of the other mystic cults do, is evident from their reference to the two distinct stages of *Amara* add *Avināśī* as Relative and Absolute Immortality. This contrast between the two conceptions of Kāya-siddhi is brought in an interesting manner in the disputation between Gorakṣa-nāth and Allam-prabhu as recorded in the *Bhaviṣyat-purāṇa-prabhu-liṅga-līlā*.[1]

[1] Ch. X (Verses 50-79): *Vide* Introduction to the *Liṅga-dhāraṇa-candrikā* by M. R. Sakhare, pp. 341-343. The present writer is indebted to MM. Gopinath Kabiraj for this information.

PART IV

THE DHARMA CULT OF BENGAL

Chapter X

GENERAL NATURE OF THE CULT

Another popular religious cult, known as the Dharma cult, developed in Bengal out of the admixture of some relics of decaying Buddhism, popular Hindu ideas and practices, a large number of indigenous beliefs and ceremonies, and ingredients derived also from Islam. This cult is responsible for the rise and growth in Bengal of a type of literature which deserves attention because of its quantitative as well as qualitative importance. The cult is called the Dharma cult for the reason that the main deity, around whom the paraphernalia of worship, ceremonies and practices gathered, and whose boundless grace and unquestionable supremacy have been demonstrated by a large number of poets in their semi-epical poems, is the Lord Dharma, or, as popularly known, the Dharma-ṭhākura. Credit must be given in this case also to the late MM. H. P. Śāstrī, who played the pioneer's part in bringing to the notice of the public the existence of such a religious cult and the literature on it.

Dharma cult is a local cult of Western Bengal and is prevalent even in the present days in some districts. The fact that the Dharma cult originated and spread only in some parts of Western Bengal is proved beyond doubt by the local references found in the ritualistic works and the Dharma-maṅgalas; and the sacred places and rivers mentioned in these works have already been localised in different parts of West Bengal, known as Rāḍha.[1] The stone-images of Dharma-ṭhākura are still found in West Bengal and are still worshipped in the temples of Dharma. Again, all the poets of the Dharma-maṅgala literature, whose works have been discovered up till now, belong to the districts of West Bengal. Moreover, in connection with the salutations found in the opening chapter of some of the Dharma-maṅgalas to

[1] *Vide Discovery of Living Buddhism in Bengal* by MM. H. P. Śāstrī; and also the introductory articles by Dr. M. Shahidullah, Mr. Basantakumar Chatterjee and Mr. Charuchandra Banerjee in the *Śūnya-purāṇa*, edited by Mr. Charuchandra Banerjee.

the different gods and goddesses worshipped in the temples of the different localities all over Bengal, we find that Dharma-ṭhākura, in all his names and forms, belongs only to the villages of West Bengal.[1] It is also clear from the references that are found in the texts that this cult of Dharma was current among the low-class people like the Hāḍis, Ḍomas, Bāgdis, Fishermen, Carpenters and the like. Archeological investigations have revealed that ideas and practices similar to those of the Dharma cult are to be found also in some parts of Orissa, particularly in Mayurbhanja and its vicinities.[2] From a comparative study of the thoughts, beliefs and practices of the crypto-Buddhistic cults of Orissa (as Mr. N. N. Bose calls them) and the various forms of the Dharma cult found in the South-Western part of Bengal, it will appear that they are essentially the same in so far as all of them represent only a mixture of later Buddhistic ideas and practices with the popular Hindu beliefs and practices including a mass of the beliefs and practices of the Non-Aryan aborigines.

In our present study we are not very much interested in the ceremonial aspect of the cult; we are concerned with it only in so far as it concerns our literature, or in so far as it supplied inspiration to a good number of poets to compose fairly bulky poetical works to eulogise the sovereign power of Lord Dharma. A detailed account of the extent and the nature of the literature that was inspired by this cult, with a discussion on the controversy over the time of composition and the authorship of the works, will be found in the Appendix (D).

The Dharma cult is the result of a popular commingling of a host of heterogeneous beliefs and practices; it will therefore be incorrect to style it purely Buddhistic or Hindu or indigenous either in origin or in nature,—it is as much a hotch-potch in its origin as it is in its developed form and nature. Critical analysis of the constituent elements reveals

[1] *Vide* MS. entitled *Dharmer Bandanā* (C. U. 2470), pp. 1(B)-2(B). Also see *Sarva-deva Bandanā* in the *Śrī-dharma-maṅgala* of Māṇik Gāṅguli, edited by MM. H. P. Śāstrī and Dr. D. C. Sen, pp. 6-7. *Cf.* also the *Anādi-maṅgala* or *Śrī-dharma-purāṇa* of Rām-dās Ādak, edited by Mr. B. K. Chatterjee, M.A., from the Sāhitya-pariṣat, pp. 5-6.

[2] *Vide Modern Buddhism And Its Followers In Orissa* by Mr. N. N. Bose.

that, as a popular religious cult, Dharma cult owes many of its elements to that form of later Buddhism, which is known as Mantra-yāna and laterly, and most commonly, as Vajra-yāna. The liturgical texts, *viz.*, the *Śūnya-purāṇa* and particularly the compendium entitled the *Dharma-pūjā-vidhāna*,[1] will at once remind one of the liturgical texts of Mantra-yāna or Vajra-yāna. Of course, in these vernacular works we find but a very faint trace of the earlier practices, we mean those of Tāntric Buddhism, they being replaced by innumerable local and indigenous practices. In the process of assimilating the local indigenous practices the liturgical works of the Dharma cult show the same tendency as is found in the liturgical works of Tāntric Buddhism. With the *Śūnya-purāṇa* and the *Dharma-pūjā-vidhāna* of the Dharma cult (excluding the portions on consmogonical speculations) we may compare more particularly one well-known compendium of the religious practices of Vajra-yāna Buddhism, *viz.*, the *Kriyā-saṁgraha.*[2] This text begins with the details of the construction of the Vihāra (which is not here the monastery of the monks or the nuns, but frankly the temple of gods and goddesses), worship of various gods and goddesses, and hundred other ceremonies and practices including placing of the jar (*kalasa*), ablution, fire-sacrifice, etc. These are found also in the *Śūnya-purāṇa.*[3] The *Kriyā-saṁgraha*, however, assumes a pseudo-Buddhistic form by professing occasionally that the final aim of all these rituals and ceremonies is the realisation of Bodhicitta with a view to attaining liberation not merely of the self but of the whole universe. But along with this avowedly Buddhistic purpose even the performance

[1] Edited by Mr. Nani Gopal Banerjee, Sāhitya-pariṣad-granthāvali, No. 56.

[2] We have not been able to discover this text; we have at our disposal in rotograph a commentary on the text by Kuladatta, entitled *Kriyā-saṁgraha-pañjikā* (manuscript preserved in the Bibliotheque Nationale, Paris, Sanscrit31). A copy of the manuscript of this commentary is also preserved in the Asiatic Society of Bengal (MS. Nos. 3854, 4728). In the *Dharma-koṣa-saṁgraha* of Vajrācārya Amṛtānanda of the Mahābodhi-Vihāra in Lalita-pattana (MS. preserved in A.S.B., No. 8055) we find, in connection with the enumeration of the types of Buddhistic literature found in Nepal, mention of this *Kriyā-saṁgraha* and also a brief note on the nature of its contents. The nature and the contents of the text, however, can fully be known through the perusal of the commentary of Kuladatta.

[3] *Cf.* the details of constructing the temple of Dharma or Nirañjana, found in the *Śūnya-purāṇa*. See the chapters of *Atha Dvāra Mocana*, *Atha Ghar Dekhā*, *Atha Dānapatir Ghar Dekhā*, etc.

of fire-sacrifice and the sacrifice of animals to the goddesses are also prescribed in this text in complete oblivion of the fact that Lord Buddha began his religious career as a living protest against the sacrificial religion of the Vedas and the cruelty to animals involved therein. The chapters on fire-sacrifice (*Homa* or *Yajña*) found in the liturgical texts of the Dharma cult may be a faint echo of this prototype. In the *Kriyā-saṁgraha* we find that the offering to the goddess Hāriti consists of fish, blood of animals, meat along with all other articles; in the *Śūnya-purāṇa* also we find that the goddess associated with Dharma is very fond of animal-sacrifice.[1]

But admitting the fact of this relation between the liturgical works of the Dharma cult with some liturgical works of Tāntric Buddhism, how far will it be correct to say that the nature of the Dharma cult is essentially Buddhistic? In our opinion, though it may be true to call the Dharma cult Buddhistic from a popular point of view, it is not true from the critical point of view; for, the heterogeneous practices which go by the name of Tāntric Buddhism have nothing in them Buddhistic but an outward colouring effected through the introduction of some stray Buddhistic terms and ideas used generally in a transformed and deteriorated form, and also through the introduction of a pantheon gradually evolved from the docetic conception of Buddhahood. Some Nepalese Buddhistic practices are, indeed, found in the practices of the Dharma cult;[2] but it is plain to see that these are local practices which are neither Hindu nor Buddhistic either in nature or in origin. The theory propounded by MM. H. P. Śāstrī that the stone-images of Dharma-ṭhākura (*Dharmaśilā*), which are found abundantly in Western Bengal, and the shape of which approximates the shape of a tortoise, are nothing but the miniature forms of the Nepalese Bud-

[1] See the chapter on *Atha Devīr Manui* in the *Śūnya-purāṇa*. It is a noticeable fact in this connection that goddess Hāriti occupies an important position in some of the Buddhist Tāntric texts and in Nepal images of gooddess Hāriti are frequently found side by side with the supreme Lord in the Buddhist temples. In the Dharma cult also Lord Dharma is often found associated with goddess Śītalā, who is supposed by scholars to be the transformed form of the Buddhist goddess Hāriti (both being goddesses associated with irruption).

[2] As for instance, we may note the use of lime in the worship of Dharma, and also in the worship of goddess Śītalā (generally associated with Dharma) who is taken to be goddess Hāriti of Tāntric Buddhism.

dhist representation of the *Stūpa* with the five Bodhisattvas inscribed on them,[1] is not, however, clear and convincing. It is not also a fact that all the stone-images of Dharma are of the shape of a tortoise. In the liturgical texts, however, we find occasional reference to the tortoise on whose back the "wooden sandals" of Dharma are to be placed. This tortoise is so well-known a mythological figure in the Hindu Purāṇic literature that Buddhistic interpretation of it seems unwarranted. As a matter of fact this importance of the tortoise in a religion may betray its indigenous nature and origin. As for the idea of Dharma, who is the Lord Supreme, it will be more correct to say that he represents the conception of the Lord Supreme found in the religious beliefs of India than to say that he represents the idea of Buddha. The idea of the Lord Supreme, as conceived in all forms of Tāntric Buddhism, is, as we have already hinted, almost the same as conceived in many systems of Hindu theology. The followers of the Dharma cult have proceeded a step farther than the Tāntric Buddhists and Dharma here represents the formless Brahman of the Upaniṣads, the Lord Śiva of the Śaivites and the Tāntrics, Viṣṇu of the general Vaiṣṇavites, Kṛṣṇa of the Kṛṣṇite Vaiṣṇavas and Rāma of the Rāmite Vaiṣṇavas, and again sometimes the Sun-god of the Sun-worshippers. The followers of the Dharma cult seem to have altogether forgotten that this Supreme deity may have something to do with the Buddha of the Buddhists; and excepting two remarks that the original place of Dharma is the land of Ceylon and the Deity Dharma is much revered in the land of Ceylon,[2] there is no direct evidence in the liturgical works or in the Maṅgala literature of the knowledge of the Dharmites that their religion and their deity have anything to do with Buddhism and the Buddha. Even the above

[1] See an article by MM. H. P. Śāstrī in the *Nārāyaṇa*, 1322 B.S., *Māgha*.

[2] *Vide*, *Śūnya-purāṇa*, pp. 100, 219.

The triangular land (*tekanā medinī*) of Dharma referred to in the *Śūnya-purāṇa* seems to be Ceylon; but we should notice in this connection that in the *Dharma-maṅgala* of Dvija-rām-candra we find *Siṁhala* to be a village situated somewhere in West Bengal. *Cf.*

bālighāṭ surānadī dekhe bāma-bhite |
rākhila siṁhal grām dekhite dekhite ||
MS. C. U. No. 2464, p. 6(A).

But nowhere in the *Dharma-maṅgalas* do we find any tradition of this *Siṁhala*'s being the original place (*ādya sthāna*) of Dharma.

remarks seem to be a mere tradition transmitted to the Dharmites and their import may not be clear to the Dharmites themselves.

So when we say that the Dharma cult is a crypto-Buddhist cult, we should remember that it can be said to be Buddhistic only in so far as it bears faint relation to that form of later Buddhism more than ninety per cent of which belong to religious systems other than Buddhism. We have seen in an earlier chapter that various forms of Tāntric Buddhism were prevalent in Bengal up to the twelfth century A.D. The revival of Hinduism with the rise of the Senas of Bengal and the Muslim invasion of Bengal dealt a death blow to all schools of professed Buddhism in Bengal. It is a well-known fact that many of the Vihāras, which were important centres of Buddhism, were mistaken by the Mahomedan invaders to be the forts of the enemy and were destroyed. But, as it has rightly been pointed out by MM. H. P. Śāstrī, no religious movement of long-standing cultural influence can be eradicated all at once from a land by any other religious movement or political and religious causes. Buddhism, even in its Tāntric form, was pushed aside and was gradually assimilated into the cognate religious systems among the Hindus and the Muslims, and the Dharma cult is the outcome of such a popular assimilation. It is to be noted that the yogic element, which forms the most important factor of Sahajiyā Buddhism, had no influence on the Dharma cult and save some yogic imageries and phrases found occasionally used in the liturgical works,[1] no reference to yoga of any sort is to be found in the Dharma cult.

Before passing on to the next topic we think it necessary

[1] *Cf. mana haila naukā pavana keraāla |*
sunāra naukā rūpāra keraāla ||
Śūnya-purāṇa, p. 105.

"The mind becomes the boat and the vital wind the oar; golden is the boat and of silver is the oar."

mana kara naukā pavana keraāla |
āpuni to nirañjana hoilā kāṇḍāra || *Ibid.*, p. 209.

"Make your mind the boat and the vital wind the oar; Nirañjana himself has become the helmsman." *Cf.* also—"Make your mind the boat and the vital wind the oar,—and make your mind concentrated, and then only can you expect to go to the other shore. When the *Dāna-pati* (*i.e.*, the man who met all the expenses for Dharma-worship) heard the oracle, his mind became the boat and his vital wind was stopped. Of silver was the boat and of gold was the oar,—and Dharma-rāja himself became the helmsman." *Ibid.*, p. 41.

to say here a few words about the probability of some Muslim influence on the Dharma cult. After the Mahomedan invasion of Bengal in the thirteenth century, the Muslims began gradually to settle in the land and to exert political, religious and cultural influence on the people. It seems that the followers of the Dharma cult with their monotheistic belief in the formless God could easily have friendly terms with the Muslims who had the same monotheistic belief in the formless God and who were particularly antagonistic to the politheistic belief of popular Hinduism. There seems to be palpable influence of the Muslims in the description of Dharma of later days.[1] The Muslims of Bengal were in their turn variously influenced by these minor cults of Bengal, and as a matter of fact we find that in the popular Muslim literature of Bengal the Muslims used all the terminology of the Dharma cult and the Nātha cult in their description of God.

It seems that the followers of Dharma suffered much for their religious beliefs and practices from the Caste Hindus and when the Mahomedans entered Bengal as a conquering power the Dharmites took shelter under them, and when the caste Hindus were being persecuted in the hands of the Mahomedans for their beliefs and practices 'the ancient grudge' which the Dharmites had against the Hindus was laurelled. We find in the *Yama-purāṇa* of the *Śūnya-purāṇa* that the messenger of Yama assumed the form of a human being and entered the city where Rāmāi lived in the form of a Hindu ghost. Rāmāi came forward and inscribed some mark on the forehead of the ghost (so as to initiate him to the Dharma cult), but the latter chained Rāmāi hand and foot and took him to Dharma-rāja Yama, who ordered Rāmāi to be cut into two with the help of a saw. But Rāmāi began to meditate on the *Karatār* (the Lord) and the saw could not pierce him; he was then successively cast into fire with hands and legs tied up and into the ocean with a slab of stone on his chest; but in each case Rāmāi was saved by the

[1] *Cf.* *hāte lile tira kāmaṭha pāya diyā muiā* |
gauḍe balāna giyā dharma mahā-rāja ||
Dharma-pūjā-vidhāna, p. 215.

As has been suggested by Dr. Shahidullah Dharma is described here just in the image of a Muslim emperor of Bengal.

Karatār. The historical fact behind the legend is the persecution of the Dharmites by the Caste Hindus.[1] We find that some of the poets of the *Dharma-maṅgalas* as first refused to comply with the request of Dharma to compose any poem in his honour for the fear of social persecution and it was after repeated assurance that the Lord could persuade them to compose poems.[2] The story of the wrath of Lord Nirañjana (*Nirañjaner Ruśmā*) found in the *Śūnya-purāṇa* as well as in the *Dharma-pūjā-vidhāna* points out the simple fact that the Muslim conquest of Bengal and the persecution of the Hindus by the Muslims were regarded by Dharmites to be the gracious device of the Lord himself to save the Dharmites from the hands of the persecuting Hindus.[3] In the *Dharma-pūjā-vidhāna* the story of the wrath of Nirañjana was followed by many pseudo-Urdu verses, which are ascribed to Rāmāi Paṇḍit. Here Rāmāi eulogises the religion of the Muslims and condemns that of the Hindus and prefers the practices of the former. As a matter of fact there are some customs in the Dharma cult which are essentially Muslim. As for instance, we find in the liturgical texts the custom of sacrificing goats or duck or pigeon before Dharma by cutting their throat in a particular manner (*javāi*—Arabic *Yavah*), which is peculiarly a Muslim custom. Again, the animals or the birds are to be sacrificed with their face westward. In other places we find much importance given to the western direction in connection with the worship of Dharma or the accessory ceremonies. The description of the gates invariably begins with the description of the western gate. Much importance is also attached to the moon, who is depicted as

[1] See introduction to the *Śūnya-purāṇa* by Dr. Shahidullah, p. 35.

[2] *Vide Dhm.* of Māṇik-gāṅguli, p. 9..

[3] There we find that when the Brahminic people of Maldah began to tax the *Saddharmīs* (*i.e.*, the Dharmites who professed to be the *Saddharmīs*), topersecute them and to kill them, Lord Nirañjana got much angry in Vaikuṇṭha and revealed himself as the *Khodā* (God) of the Muslims in the village of Jājpura; he was seated on a horse with a black hat on and with a bow and arrow in hands, and all the gods and goddesses of the Hindu pantheon gladly put on the dress of Muslim soldiers to accompany the lord. The lord, however, with his army broke all the temples of the Hindus, plundered the Hindus, ravaged them and persecuted them, and the Dharmites were saved. Jājpura, a village in the district of Hugli, is described in the Dharma-maṅgala literature as very important place of the Dharmites, and there is also the tradition in later *Dharma-maṅgalas* that Dharma revealed himself as a Muslim (*javana-avatāra*) in the place. *jājapurer dehārā bandiva ekaman* | *jei khāne avatār haila javan* || MS. entitled *Dharmer Bandanā* (C.U. No. 2470), p. 1(B).

the *Koṭāla* (gate-keeper) of the western direction. This importance given to the western direction and the moon undoubtedly bears testimony to the Muslim influence.[1] It is also to be noted in this connection that one of the most important incidents of the *Dharma-maṅgalas* is the incident of making the sun rise in the west by Dharma in response to the prayers of Lāusen. The incident is described in detail in all the *Dharma-maṅgalas*. Instead of taking this incident simply as an instance of the display of supernatural power by the devotee of Dharma, will it be far wide of the mark to infer that the whole incident was construed only to explain from the stand-point of the Dharmites why the west was regarded so important by them? Again, we find that some importance is also attached to Friday which is an auspicious day with the Muslims. All these practices, however, seem to have been introduced into the Dharma cult in later times in course of its evolution.

[1] See a discussion by Dr. B. M. Barua, M.A., D.Lit., in the *Śanivārer Ciṭhi* B.S. 1345, *Pauṣa*.

Chapter XI

SPECULATIONS ON THE CONCEPTION OF DHARMA

(i) *Hindu Conceptions of Dharma*

As the Dharma cult represents a composite form of religion developing from a popular adoption of diverse religious practices, rites and ceremonies, so also is the idea of Dharma, which has been the receptacle of various conceptions of the sovereign deity found in various religious thoughts. Here, as we have hinted before, we have the unconscious mixture of the conception of the Upaniṣadic Brahman with the Puruṣa of the Sāṃkhya, Śiva of the Tantra, Viṣṇu, Kṛṣṇa and Rāma of the Vaiṣṇavas, Yama, the lord of justice and death, and also with Dharma, the popularly conceived godhead in general. These ideas of the Supreme Being have again coalesced with the idea of the supreme deity variously conceived in later Buddhism.

The idea of Dharma as the godhead has a fairly old history in the Hindu texts. The word *dharma* ordinarily means that which is to be held fast or kept, or that which holds fast or keeps, or law, statute, religion, piety, right, justice, equity, virtue, merit, nature or character of entities, an essential of characteristic quality, mark, peculiarity of an entity, or the entity itself. In its Vedic form (*dharman*) it meant the maintainer, the supporter, the arranger. When popularly personified, Dharma means the lord of all laws and ordinances, the lord of justice, the central figure of all religion, and in this last aspect Dharma is popularly conceived as God, the Lord Supreme, who is maintaining the whole world by administering order, discipline and justice. Even in the present day the custom among the common run of people is to swear by the name of Dharma, to appeal to Dharma for redress from distress, to invoke the blessings of Dharma in time of calamities,—and in all these cases Dharma is none but the supreme deity or God Himself. From as early a time as the time of the Vedas, the word

Dharma is found used in its variously personified forms. In the *Śatapatha-brāhmaṇa* (13.4.3) we find in connection with the enumeration of the kings and the subjects of all quarters and localities that Dharma Indra was the king of the gods. Here Dharma is identified with Indra, the lord supreme of the later Vedic literature.[1] In the Purāṇic literature we find mention of another Dharma, who is Righteousness, Justice, Law or Virtue personified; he was born from the right chest of Brahmā and had three offsprings, Śama, Kāma and Harṣa. Dharma or Dharma-rāja is well-known in the Purāṇic and epic literature of Sanskrit as the epithet of Yama who is the God of justice and the king of death. Even in popular Buddhistic literature Yama is widely known as the Dharma-rāja.[2] Dharma is, again, one of the attendants of the Sun-god; he is Justice or Virtue, identified with Viṣṇu; he is Prajāpati, and is said to be the son-in-law of Dakṣa. We find mention of many other personalities in the Purāṇic literature of the name of Dharma who were notable for various virtues and activities.

Of all these, however, Yama, the king of death and justice, is the most widely known by the name of Dharma or Dharma-rāja. In the *Mahābhārata* Yudhiṣṭhira is traditionally described as the son of Yama, and he himself was known as *Dharma-putra* (*i.e.*, the son of Dharma) and the epithet Dharma-rāja is also found frequently used for him. It is a very popular story of the *Mahābhārata* that Dharma in the guise of a Yakṣa put a few questions to Yudhiṣṭhira and the answers given by the latter was to the entire satisfaction of Dharma and Yudhiṣṭhira obtained boons from him. When Yudhiṣṭhira was bewildered at the superhuman form and glow of the disguised Yakṣa, the latter declared,—"I am Dharma, your father of supreme power—and am come here only to see you. My body is constituted of fame, truth, self-control, purity, simplicity (*ārjava*), modesty, steadiness (*acāpalya*), bounty, penance and physical and mental discipline (*brahmacarya*); non-violence, equity, peace,

[1] *Vide* B. K. Chatterjee's introduction to the *Śrī-dharma-purāṇa* of Mayūra-bhaṭṭa.

[2] *Vide Kāraṇḍa-vyūha*—printed in Calcutta in 1873 by Satyavrata Sāmaśrami in a series of Jaina works.

moral virtue, purity and non-exhilaration are my senses."[1] This Dharma once more came to test the righteousness of Yudhiṣṭhira in the guise of a dog when the latter was about to enter heaven (*Mahā-prasthānika-parva*, Ch. 3). In the *Skanda-purāṇa*, Yama, the son of Sūrya, is depicted as a great sage (*ṛṣi*) of the name of Dharma or Dharma-rāja. He was practising austere penances to propitiate *Mahādeva* (*i.e.*, Śiva). The gods (including Indra) got frightened at the penances of Dharma and sent down a celestial damsel, Varddhiṇī by name, to disturb the penance of Dharma. In course of a dialogue with her Dharma said,—"I am Yama to all beings who are evil-doers,—and I am *Dharma* to all self-controlled people."[2] Lord Śiva was propitiated by the penances of Dharma and as desired by the latter the forest *Dharmā-raṇya* became a sacred place for pilgrimage through the boon of Śiva. Dharma himself preferred to be transformed into a bull and became the mount of Śiva.[3]

In the Bengali Manuscript Library of the Calcutta University we have a manuscript entitled *Dharma-itihāsa* (*i.e.*, the history of Dharma, MS., C. U. No. 6152) which is ascribed to the poet Guṇa-rāja-khān.[4] The Dharma of the text is none but the Lord Supreme, and it has been demonstrated with reference to the stories of the Rāmāyaṇa and the Mahābhārata how the genuine devotees in different times and places were, under various critical circumstances, protected through the infinite grace of the Lord.

Traditions in the Dharma cult often show a great tendency to identify Dharma, or Dharma-rāja with the Dharma-rāja Yama. As a matter of fact Yama himself, seated on his *Vāhana* (mount) or buffalo, is often identified with the Dharma-rāja of the Dharmites in many places of West-Bengal and the festivities in connection with the *gājana* of Dharma are known as the festivities of Dharma-rāja Yama.

[1] *Mahābhārata*, *Vana-parva*, Ch. 312.

[2] *yamo' haṁ sarva-bhūtānāṁ duṣṭānāṁ karma-kāriṇām |*
dharma-rūpo hi sarveṣāṁ manujānāṁ jitātmanām ||
sa dharmo' haṁ varārohe dadāmi tava durlabham |
tat-sarvaṁ prārthaya tvam me śīghraṁ cāpasarasāṁ vare ||
Dharmā-raṇya-khaṇḍa (417-18) included within the *Brahma-khaṇḍa*.

[3] *Skanda-purāṇa, Brahma-khaṇḍa, Setu-māhātmya*, Ch. III.

[4] We do not think that this Guṇa-rāja-khān is the same as Mālādhara Vasu, the well-known translator of the *Bhāgavata* in the pre-Caitanya period.

Often it has been found that in worshipping Dharma-rāja the priests utter the Mantra,—'Salute to Dharma-rāja, who is Yama and who is of various forms' (*namaste bahurūpāya yamāya dharma-rājāya*).[1] In the ritualistic texts also we find corroboration of the fact. In the chapters on the river *Vaitaraṇī* of the *Śūnya-purāṇa* we find that Dharma himself is acting as the helmsman and carrying all the devotees of Dharma to heaven, which is situated on the other side of the direful river *Vaitaraṇī*. Rāmāi Paṇḍita himself is here helping all lay people on board. The name of the river *Vaitaraṇī* is so closely associated with the name of Yama in Hindu mythology that it takes no time to recognise that this Dharma-rāja is none but Dharma-rāja Yama.[2] In a chapter of the *Dharma-pūjā-vidhāna* we find the deity of the Dharmites unconsciously identified with Yama seated on his *Vāhana* of buffalo and accompanied by his well-known clerk, Citra-gupta, and his attendants, Kāla and Vikāla with iron chains in their hands; he is found administering law to all people of the world.[3]

In the liturgical texts of the Dharma cult the tradition of Dharma's identity with Yama seems to be less popular than the tradition of his identity with Śiva and Viṣṇu; in the *Dharma-maṅgalas* again the tradition of the Śaivite nature of Dharma seems to be in a dwindling condition and the Vaiṣṇavite nature, either in the form of Viṣṇu in general or Kṛṣṇa or Rāma in particular, predominates. But before we deal in detail with this question it will be helpful to us

[1] *Vide* an article *Rāḍha-bhramaṇa* by Pañcānan Banerjee, B.S.P.P., 1314 B.S. It is interesting to compare with the above Mantra the ordinary Mantra of *Yama-tarpaṇa:—yamāya dharma-rājāya mṛtyave cāntakāya ca* etc.

[2] Of course, in some other chapters (*viz.*, the chapters on *Yama-purāṇa*, *Yama-dūta-samvāda*, *Yama-rāja-samvāda*) we find that the Purāṇic Dharma-rāja Yama and Dharma-rāja are differentiated. It is demonstrated with legends that Dharma-rāja Yama has no sovereignty over people who are devotees of Dharma-rāja Nirañjana or the *Karatār* and that, being sadly harassed on several occasions, Dharma-rāja Yama with the help of Rāmāi Paṇḍit made an exhaustive list of the priests and devotees of Dharma-ṭhākura of the five ages (including the void-age) so that he might instruct his officers not to meddle with them. About this disagreement of traditions we have nothing more to say than that here in the Dharma cult, which offers the best specimen of the religious psychology of untrained masses, nothing but anomaly and confusion can be expected.

[3] pp. 249 *et seq.* In one line of this chapter, however, Dharma and Yama are spoken of as two (*Yama dharma duijan bogyā āchen-deva-sabhāy*); but in fact they are treated as one throughout the whole chapter.

to investigate into and examine the Buddhistic substratum of lord Dharma.

(ii) *Buddhistic Substratum of Dharma*

In the Sanskrit dictionary *Amarakoṣa* Dharma-rāja has been mentioned as a synonym for Buddha;[1] in the Jātaka stories also the epithet Dharma-rāja refers to Buddha. It may be noted that the Dharmites still observe the days of *Buddha-pūrṇimā* (*i.e.*, *Baiśākhī purṇimā*, the birthday of Buddha) and *Aṣāḍhī pūrṇimā* (the day on which *Dharma-cakra* was first preached by Buddha) as highly auspicious festive days. But it will not be fair to surmise from such identifications that Dharma or the Dharma-rāja, or rather the Dharma-ṭhākura of the Dharma cult directly represents Buddha. In discussing the Buddhistic substratum of the idea of Dharma we should remember that the Buddhism we are referring to here is not the Buddhism with which we are acquainted in any of the standard Buddhistic schools; it is that phase of later Buddhism which is so-called mainly historically as maintaining in a transformed and modified form the continuity of the older thought. We may illustrate the exact nature of the relation of the Dharma cult with standard Buddhism with reference to an episode of the popular Pāli text *Milinda-pañha*. The question of king Milinda is whether the man who is reborn is the same as the man who is dead or is an absolutely new man. It is indeed very difficult to answer the question directly in consistence with the theory of momentariness of the Buddhists. The answer of the Elder Nāgasena is, therefore, indirect; he says that the man who is newly born is neither the same as the former, nor is he absolutely a new man; but in spite of the absence of personal identity the latter is to be associated with the former only because of the fact that the former is mysteriously responsible for the existence of the latter. The argument of Bhadanta Nāgasena may very aptly be repeated here in connection with the exact relation between the Dharma cult and Buddhism, or the conception of the Dharma-ṭhākura and the conception of the ultimate

[1] *sarvajñaḥ sugato buddho dharma-tathāgataḥ* I

reality propounded in Mahayāna Buddhism. It may be repeated here that it will be wrong to suppose that any particular Buddhistic conception of the reality has, through processes of long transformation, coalesced with the Hindu conceptions of the supreme deity and has thus given rise to the composite conception of the Dharma-ṭhākura. Dharma-ṭhākura represents as much infiltration of ideas from popular Hinduism as from popular Buddhism, and this explains his extremely heterogeneous nature. In investigating into the Buddhistic substratum of the conception of Dharma, there fore, we shall only indicate the different lines in which Buddhistic ideas might have infiltrated in the mind of ordinary masses to give rise to the conception of a deity of such heterogeneous nature.

We have seen before that the philosophic ideas of Mahāyāna Buddhism, with the spirit of catholicity and adaptation, had an innate tendency towards approximating the Upaniṣadic spirit. Whatever may be the position of Nāgārjuna and his followers, who have been the centre of great controversy, the conception of the ultimate reality of the Vijñānavādins as pure consciousness or the absolute uncreate cannot but be held to be positive in nature. The Tathatāvāda of Aśvaghoṣa admits the Tathatā-nature (*i.e.*, the nature of the Dharmas as thatness) to be something substantial, permanent and unchanging and as such it is something positive, though formless and unqualified. The conception of the *Vijñapti-mātratā* or the *Abhūta-parikalpa*, which is of the nature of consciousness, bereft of the duality of the knower and the knowable, seems to be just the previous step of the conception of the Brahman which in its absolute and unqualified nature transcends all knowledge, knower and knowability. It has always been vehemently argued by the Vijñānavādins that Śūnyatā was never spoken of by the Lord as pure 'nothing'; while it is the negation of all duality, it implies at the same time the reality of pure-consciousness or the absolute uncreate, which is unchanging, unthinkable, all-good, eternal, all-bliss, the ultimate element of the nature of liberation.

Again in the docetic conception of the Tri-kāya in the Mahāyāna system the Dharma-kāya or the body of the cosmic unity, or the organised totality of things, though not as a purely philosophical concept, but as an object of religious consciousness, approximates the idea of the Brahman. The word Dharma-kāya is often explained as the body of law; and it may also be remembered that Buddha is said to have told his disciples that his teachings should be recognised as his own immortal body. But the word *dharma* is generally used in the Mahāyāna texts in the sense of 'entity'; and the Dharma-kāya means the 'thatness' (*tathatā-rūpa*) of all the entities, it is in other words the *dharma-dhātu* or the primordial element underlying all that exists. It has been also termed as the Svabhāva-kāya, *i.e.*, the body of the ultimate nature. It is described as devoid of all characters, but possessing eternal and innumerable qualities. It is neither the mind, nor matter, nor something different from the both.[1]

This docetic conception of Buddhahood as implied in the theory of Tri-kāya gradually transformed itself in the monotheistic conception of a Being and latterly in the clear conception of a personal God. The Dharma-kāya Buddha became the Lord Supreme, the Sambhoga-kāya Buddha became the Dhyāni-Buddhas (*viz.*, Vairocana, Akṣobhya and others) and the Nirmāṇa-kāya Buddha gave the idea of the human Buddhas (*Mānuṣī* Buddha).

All these various philosophical concepts about the ultimate reality in the different schools of Buddhism, including the docetic conception of Buddha as conceived in the theory of the Tri-kāya, lost their special significance in a popular

[1] The nature of the Dharma-kāya is described in the *Avataṁsaka-sūtra* in the following manner,—"The Dharma-kāya though manifesting itself in the triple world, is free from impurities and desires. It unfolds itself here, there, and everywhere responding the call of Karma. It is not an individual reality, it is not a false existence, but is universal and pure. It comes from nowhere, it goes to nowhere; it does not assert itself, nor is it subject to annihilation. It is for ever serene and eternal. It is the One, devoid of all determinations. This body of Dharma has no boundary, no quarters, but is embodied in all bodies. Its freedom or spontaneity is incomprehensible, its spiritual presence in things corporeal is incomprehensible. All forms of corporeality are involved therein, it is able to create all things. Assuming any concrete material body as required by the nature and condition of Karma, it illuminates all creations. Though it is the treasure of intelligence, it is void of particularity. There is no place in the universe where this body does not prevail. The universe becomes, but this body for ever remains. It is free from all opposites and contrarieties, yet it it is working in all things to lead them to Nirvāṇa." Quoted in Suzuki's *Outlines of Mahāyāna Buddhism*, pp. 223-224.

idea of a Supreme Being in later schools of Tāntric Buddhism, and the most common name by which He was known among the Tāntric Buddhists was the Lord Vajra-sattva.[1] Though it became customary with the Buddhist Tāntrikas to describe this Vajra-sattva with all sorts of negative attributes (of course, in addition to the positive ones), it is very easy to see that the conception of the Vajra-sattva behind all these positive and negative attributes is definitely positive and is that of a personal God. All Buddhistic ideas, *viz.*, the idea of Śūnyatā, the idea of pure consciousness, the idea of the Bodhicitta, the idea of Mahā-sukha began in later days to acquire cosmological and ontological significance in the form of an all-pervading Being. The origin of the Dharma-ṭhākura with all his positive and negative, Buddhistic and Hindu attributes may historically be associated with the conception of this Lord Supreme of the later Buddhistic schools.

In connection with the evolution of the conception of Dharma the question of its relation with the Dharma of the three 'jewels' of Buddhism (*viz.*, Buddha, Dharma and Saṅgha) naturally attracts our notice. MM. H. P. Śāstrī and others have propounded the theory that in later times Buddha, the first of the three jewels, was naturally eliminated by the lay Buddhists with the growing influence of revived Hinduism, and the third jewel Saṅgha became the *Śaṅkha* (conch-shell), which is very important in connection with Hindu worship; and the second jewel, *viz.*, Dharma became identified with the Buddhist *Stūpa*, which was worshipped as something like the symbol of Dharma,—and the *Stūpa* became the Dharma-ṭhākura of the Dharma cult in the form of a tortoise. In propounding such a theory, however, we should proceed a bit cautiously. As for the transformation of Saṅgha into *Śaṅkha* we may say that the frequent mention of *Śaṅkha* with various other necessaries of worship in the *Śūnya-purāṇa* cannot convince one of its Buddhistic origin; for *Śaṅkha* is no less important as one of the necessaries of worship in the proper Hindu liturgy than in the cult of Dharma. The story of Viṣṇu's killing Śaṅkhāsura and giving the *Śaṅkha* to Padmālaya's son, as narrated in the Oḍiyā text *Siddhānta-*

[1] *Vide-Supra*, pp. 28-29.

ḍambara, seems to us to have nothing in it to warrant the origin of this *Śaṅkha* in the Saṅgha of the Buddhists.[1] Of course in the *Dharma-pūjā-vidhāna* we find a few confused lines on *Śaṅkha;* what we can at most infer from this is that *Śaṅkha* was held important in the worship of Dharma.[2] We sometimes find also salutation to *Śaṅkha* in connection with the opening chapter of salutation in the Dharma-maṅgalas.[3] This importance of *Śaṅkha* has nothing in it which may help us to construe some kind of relation between *Śaṅkha* and the Buddhist *Saṅgha* on any convincing ground.

We have already pointed out that Śūnyatā and Karuṇā, transformed as Prajñā and Upāya, were held very important in Tāntric Buddhism, and a tendency was manifest to interpret this Prajñā and Upāya as static and dynamic, or negative and positive, as female and male, and so on. Gradually the three jewels Buddha, Dharma and Saṅgha came to be interpreted in terms of Prajñā, Upāya and the world produced by them; Upāya as the male principle was identified with Buddha, and necessarily Dharma became Prajñā or the female principle and Saṅgha came to be interpreted as phenomenal world which is produced through the union of Prajñā and Upāya.[4] Some scholars maintain that these transformed

[1] "We scarcely think it would be very wide of the mark to infer from this that the word Sankha here means nothing but a Buddhistic Sangha. In this interpretation of Sankha as Sangha, we are supported by the Sunya-Purāṇa, in which Sankha is very frequently used for Sangha. The common people in their ignorance of the teachings of Buddhism and its terminology, either misspelt Sangha as Sankha or mistook Sankha for Sangha which really means a congregation of Buddhistic monks." *Modern Buddhism And Its Followers, etc.*, by N. N. Bose, p. 19.

[2] It should however be remembered in this connection that in the Dharma-maṅgalas we frequently come across the details of Dharma-worship; but there we do not find any special attention paid to this *Śaṅkha*.

[3] *Cf* *śola śaṅkha bandi a asaṅkhya lakṣa muni |*
e cāri paṇḍit banda e cārī āmani ||
MS. entitled *Dharmer Bandanā*, C. U. No. 2470, p. 1(A).

It may be noted here that in the *gājana* of Śiva, which is prevalent in some district of East Bengal, and which is nothing but a Śaivite version of the *Dharmer gājana* of West Bengal (see *infra*, p. 279 F. N. No. 3) we find a few fragmentary verses on the origin and importance of *Śaṅkha*, and we may further notice that Gaurī or Pārvatī (*i.e.*, the consort of Śiva) is particularly fond of putting on the bracelet made of *Śaṅkha*. We are quoting here some fragmentary verses:—*sapta samudre janmen śaṅkha śona tār kathā | gaurīke dhariyā nila akṣay baṭ-talā || śāś (?) khān kariyā śaṅkha tuliyā thuila ḍāle | paban bātāse śaṅkha śiva rām bale || hena bā śaṅkha śuddha nayare kon nare bale || śrī-phāl kuṇḍal devī gāy haila gharma | biśva-karmā kāṭiyā dilā daś bhāi śaṅkha || daś bhāi śaṅkha devī pare daś haste | kon śaṅkhe bādya ghaṇṭā kon śaṅkhe jal | śiver ālay āmār yamer nāhi dāy | koṭi koṭi praṇām kari mahādever pāy ||* (Own collection).

[4] For a detailed discussion on the point see the chapter on Cosmogony, *infra*.

forms of the three jewels are still now preserved in the Jagannātha temple of Puri. There the two male figures, with a female figure in the middle, widely known in their Hinduised nomenclature as Jagannātha and Balarāma with the image of Subhadrā in the middle, are in all probability the representations of the three jewels of Buddha, Dharma and Saṅgha transformed as Upāya, Prajñā and their son, *i.e.*, the phenomenal world. In the esoteric Buddhist literature the epithet Jagannātha (*i.e.*, the lord of the world) is widely used before Buddha or rather the Lord Supreme, and it is also a well-known adjective used before the Lord Supreme of the Hindus,—and thus through the medium of the epithet Jagannātha, the first of the three jewels could very easily be Hinduised and the Hinduisation of the other two was but a matter of course. This theory of the transformation of Buddha, the first jewel of the Buddhists, into Jagannātha (and later on frankly conceived as Kṛṣṇa) has its corroboration in the tradition of the literature of the Dharma cult. Jayadeva, the famous Vaiṣṇava lyric poet, described Buddha as the ninth incarnation of Viṣṇu; and in the literature of the Dharma cult we find in connection with the description of the incarnations of God that in the ninth incarnation God was born as Jagannātha, who is none but lord Buddha, and he settled his residence on the sea-coast, where he has relieved the whole world by distributing to all (irrespective of caste and creed) his *Prasāda* (*i.e.*, the food offered to God and supposed to be accepted by him.)[1] In another place we find that in this incarnation of Jagannātha the lord revealed himself to the Hindus and Muslims, who were all united together in his (*i.e.*, Jagannātha's) place, and in the country of Gauḍa (*i.e.*, in Bengal) he has revealed himself as the Dharma-rāja.[2]

But though Buddha was the first of the jewels and had his prominence also in the temple of Jagannātha, he could not enjoy universal sovereignty for several reasons. In the

[1] *Dharma-pūjā-vidhāna*, pp. 206-207; also p. 208. See also *Govinda-vijaya* of Śyāma-dās, Vaṅgavāsī-edition, p. 3.

It may be pointed out here that in the ten incarnation of Viṣṇu, inscribed on the gateway of the temple of Jagannātha in Puri, Buddha, the ninth incarnation, has been replaced by Jagannātha.

[2] *Dharma-pūjā-vidhāna*, pp. 214-15.

first place, from the metaphysical standpoint Dharma represents Prajñā or Śūnyatā, which being the ultimate source of all origination and being often interpreted as the noumenal aspect of the reality, was infused with more cosmological and ontological value than Buddha, who represents Upāya or Karuṇā, metaphysically explained as the aspect of phenomenalism. This metaphysical valuation might have been there in the mind of common people in the form of a time-honoured tradition, and this may be why Dharma could supersede the claim of Buddha in being recognised as the supreme divinity among the Dharmites. In the second place, in later times lay people had no idea about what these three jewels might be; they could recognise only Dharma, who was, in common faith and tradition, known to them as the Supreme Lord, the Sovereign Deity over the universe,—some Invisible power administering law and justice; consequently Dharma became gradually recognised as the Lord Supreme. Moreover, with the growing influence of Hinduism it was not possible for ordinary people of lower social order to accept any one but Dharma out of the three jewels as their Lord.

The Dharma-ṭhākura of the Dharma cult is not generally associated with any Śakti or female counterpart. In the *Dharma-pūjā-vidhāna*, however, we find a goddess, Kāminyā by name, whose worship follows the worship of Dharma along with the worship of many other gods and goddesses, and she is the goddess for removing blindness and leprosy. This Kāminyā is sometimes described as something like a Śakti of Dharma,[1] and as a matter of fact some of her descriptions resemble the description of the goddess variously described in the Buddhist and the Hindu Tantras. But the

[1] *oṁkāra-bhūta-vedāya kāminā-sahitāya ca |*
mama sarvārtha-siddhy-arthaṁ dharma-rāja namo'stute ||
Dharma-pūjā-vidhāna, p. 86.
oṁ nā'stikāyāṁ tathā devaṁ kāminā-sahitaṁ prabho |
āyur-ārogyaṁ aiśvaryaṁ sampattiṁ dehi me sadā ||
Ibid, p. 87.
ullūka-vāhanaṁ dharmaṁ kāmikhyā(?)-sahitaṁ śivam |
dhauta-kunde (ndu)-dhavalaṁ sarva-sampat-phala-pradam ||
Ibid, p. 77.

This last verse is found in the *Śrī-dharma-maṅgala* of Māṇik Gāṅguli as:—
uluka (sic. kaṁ)-vāhanaṁ dharmaṁ kāminyā sahitaṁ (sic. -te) śivam |
dhauta-kundendu-dhavala-kāyaṁ dhyāyed dharmaṁ namāmy aham ||
p. 4.

more important fact is that Dharma-ṭhākura, as the Sovereign Deity, has frequently been identified with Śiva and as such is always associated with his Śakti as *Bhagavatī*, *Ādi-devī*, *Ādi-śakti*, or as Bāśulī, Caṇḍī, Durgā, Pārvatī, etc. In the liturgical texts Dharma-ṭhākura is frequently styled as *Maheś-vara* (the great lord) or *Mahādeva* (the great deity), *Devadeva* (the God of gods)—epithets which are commonly used before the well-known deity Śiva. In some temples of Dharma Dharma-ṭhākura has been transformed completely into Śiva.[1] In the well-known religious ceremony of West Bengal known as the *Gājana* of Dharma, which is the most celebrated function of the Dharmites current even to the present day, Dharma has been frankly made Śiva and the *Gājana* of Dharma really means the *Gājana* of Śiva. In the book *Ādyer Gambhīrā* by Mr. Haridās Pālit[2] we find an elaborate account of the *Gājana* of Dharma. Even a cursory glance on the verses that are sung with dancing and beating of double drums will show how confusedly Śiva and Dharma have been mixed together in these ceremonies and the verses themselves are really fragments found in the liturgical works of the Dharma cult and the Śivāyanas of Bengal. It is very interesting to note that this ceremony of *Gājana* is also found in some districts of East Bengal in the form of *Nīla-pūjā*, (*i.e.*, the worship of the deity Nīla), and this elaborate religious ceremony, which takes place in the last week of the Bengali year and takes about a week's time to be completed, is never suspected by the people in these districts to be anything but a Hindu religious function primarily concerned

1 It is interesting to note here an incident described by MM. H. P. Śāstrī in an article in the Bengali monthly *Nārāyaṇa* (B.S. 1322, *Māgha*) in connection with the transformation of Dharma to Śiva. In a temple of Dharma MM. Śāstrī found a priest dividing into two equal portions the offerings to be presented to Dharma. He asked out of curiosity why such a division was made. The reply of the priest was—"He is Dharma and Śiva at the same time and hence is the division." On further enquiry MM. Śāstrī came to learn that the Mantra with which the offerings were presented to the deity was,—"Salute be to Śiva, who is Dharma-rāja" (*śivāya dharma-rājāya namaḥ*). After several years of his first visit MM. Śāstrī went there once more and found that by this time a *Gaurī-paṭṭa* (a symbolic representation of the female organ of the Śakti generally found placed beneath the symbolic representation of the male organ of Śiva) was placed by the Brahmins beneath the stone-image of Dharma so as to Hinduise him completely.

2 Published under the auspices of the Māladaha National Educational Institute, B.S. 1319.

with the Hindu deity Lord Śiva.[1] The fragmentary verses that are generally recited in connection with the various ceremonies of this function have striking affinity with the verses found in the liturgical works of the Dharma cult and also in the *Gājana* of Dharma of West Bengal not only in matter and spirit, but sometimes in language also with slight deviations.[2]

The conceptions of Śiva and Śakti or the primordial male and the female have their bearing on the literature of the

[1] A very brief account of this *Gājana* of East Bengal will be found in the *Vaṅga-Sāhitya-paricaya*, Part I, of Dr. D. C. Sen (published by the University of Calcutta), pp. 159-161.

[2] We have collected from some villages in the district of Backergunge the fragmentary verses akin to those found in the liturgical works of the Dharma cult. They are recited in connection with the *Nīla-pūjā* ceremony. It will be interesting to note that the cosmogonical ideas found in these verses are the same as found in the literature of the Dharma cult. We shall discuss this point later on in our discussion on cosmogony. Lord Śiva is occasionally styled here as Dharma or Dharma-rāja. In the *Dharma-pūjā-vidhāna* (pp. 242-45) we find a discussion on the origin and growth of the foetus; exactly a similar verse is found among the verses that are recited on the occasion of the *Nīla-pūjā*. We find in the liturgical works of the Dharma cult salutation and prayers to the four quarters with a presiding deity in each; the same custom is also found in the *Gājana* of Śiva, and the peculiar fact to be noticed is this that here as well as in Dharma cult the ceremony begins from the west, which is not surely a Hindu practice. This practice however, seems significant and its significance has been explained before (*Supra*, p. 306). We are quoting here a specimen of the verses recited in *Dikbandanā*:—

paścim paścim ādi paricay dvārī
maṇimay muktār hār ।
śuddha kaṇṭhe kāñcan dvār ।
kāñcan dvāre bākya nāme takya (?) *rudra sthāpita* ।
tān rājā śrī-jagannāth bāhinī
tār dharma puruṣe dharma dharma hār ।
tānāre sevile mukti kata pāi
nā yāya yama-purī śiva-purī ṭhāi ॥
āgam bed gāyatrī bāṇī
kāñcan duāre den puṣpāñjali ।
he sādhuli, dik paścim, kārtik ganeś mahādev saṅginī,
dik paścim sapta-tāl kāṭhi
tine saṅge bālā khāṭi ॥

Similar verses are recited in accompaniment with dances and beating of drums in the other three quarters, the presiding deity in the north being Śrī-sabhā-liṅga, in the east Śrī-muṇḍa-cakra and in the south Śrī-vaidya-nātha. Again, we have in the liturgical works of the Dharma cult descriptions of the construction of the temple of Dharma (commonly known as *dharmera deula*); with them we may compare the following verses on *gṛha-nirmāṇa*, *i.e.*, constructing the house (for the Lord) on occasion of Śiva's *Gājana*:—

sapta samudre sthān sthiti tīrtha barānasi ।
yāita bahiyā kare stav ṣāiṭa ṣāiṭa ṛṣi ॥
ṛṣi gaṇe kare stav bhāciyā nirañjan ।
ghṛta śāil jukhiyā kare deul sṛjan ।
arjun kāṭen pāthar dānave māre hurā ।
kānde kariyā bahe dik sonār pāiṭkarā ॥
rajata kāñcan kāñcan sāire ।
rajata kāñcan kāñcan pāire ॥
śveta cāmare chāiyā cāri cāl ।

Dharma cult particularly in connection with the portions on cosmogony and cosmology,—and as we have to deal in detail with these ideas in a separate chapter, we do not propose to deal with them here.

The point to be emphasised here is that in the Buddhist Tantras a tendency was manifest always to conceive the Supreme Lord in the image of Śiva and the female counterpart of the Lord in the image of Śakti, and these Lord and Lady of the Buddhists were in still later times identified completely with the Śiva and Śakti of the Hindus. In the section on cosmogony of the *Śūnya-purāṇa* we find that goddess Ādyā, who is also called Gaurī (Durgā and Pārvatī), was unable to control her youth and sent *Kāma* (Cupid) to the Lord who was absorbed in deep meditation on the river Ballukā; *Kāma* disturbed the meditation of the *Karatār*. The whole scene here has been confusedly borrowed from the tradition of the disturbance of Śiva's meditation by Cupid for his (Śiva's) marriage with Pārvatī, Dharma-ṭhākura being conceived here exactly in the image of lord Śiva. This identification is not, however, complete in the literature of the Dharma cult; there Lord Śiva has not yet been able to cast off or hide away completely his Buddhistic attributes,—

cāri cāl cāri pāir coyārī chanda I
ei ghar khānā dekhāy yena batriśer banda ||
medinī haila potā ākāś haila cāl I
sāgar dekhāy yena parvat samān ||
gayā talāiyā ghar tīrtha bārānasī I
ghare basiyā harinām duyāre tulasī ||
maiśā (?) *samāgam kāñcan doyār* I
kāñcan doyār nay kedār doyār ||
kedār doyār nay muktir doyār I
muktir doyār nay siṁher doyār ||
pañca pāthar laiyā śiv basila āpani I
mandire āsilen ṭhākurāṇī ||

Again in the *Śūnya-purāṇa*, the *Dharma-pūjā-vidhāna* and the *Śrī-dharma maṅgāla* of Mayūra-bhaṭṭa (B. K. Chatterjee's edition) we have funny legendary accounts of the origin of the metal copper, of the *Beta*-stick (*beta*=Skt. *vetra*), of the double drum (*ḍhāk*), etc., which are of great importance in connection with Dharma-worship. Similar legendary accounts (of course with more Hindu tinge) are found also in the fragmentary verses which we have collected in connection with Śiva's *Gājana* in East Bengal. Space will not allow us to quote them here and to compare them side by side with the accounts that are found in the Dharma-maṅgala literature. We have in our collection accounts of the origin of corn, of *Beta*, *Dhāka*, *Śaṅkha*, iron, thread, copper, the earthen pots and earthen vessel for incense (*dhūpati*), of incense, etc.

In the chapter on the cultivation of lands (*Atha Cāṣa*) which seems to be a fragment inserted in the Dharma literature from the Bengali Śaivite literature, the Lord Supreme of the Dharmites has become lord Śiva, as conceived in the Bengali Śivāyanas.

there is still something of later Buddhism round the figure of Lord Śiva.

This conception of the Supreme Lord and the consort, as expounded in later Buddhism, developed itself into the idea of the Ādi-Buddha and Ādi-Prajña in Nepalese Buddhism. This Ādi-Buddha or the primordial Enlightened One is the Self-created One (*Svayambhū*) of the *Svayambhū-purāṇa*.[1] He is described there as the Lord Supreme, who is worshipped by all the gods, Yakṣas and Rakṣas in the mountain of Gaurī-śṛṅga in the country of Nepal. He is described as of the nature of the ultimate substance (*dharma-dhātu*). He is often conceived as lord Vairocana with the other four Tathāgatas placed in the four quarters round him. Again, the Lord is often said to be Śākya-muni, who is called both Jagannātha as well as Dharma-rāja.[2] This Lord Supreme is called both Svayambhū (*i.e.*, the Self-originated One) and Śambhu (literally, the Lord of Welfare), which is the most common epithet applied to Lord Śiva; the name Śiva also implies that the deity is welfare itself. The Ādi-Buddha, who is the Svayambhū and who is called the Dharma-rāja is sometimes described as of the nature of the three jewels (*tri-ratna*).[3] It appears from the above that the three jewels were sometimes conceived in later times as the three attributes of the Ādi-Buddha. In the same text, again, Mañju-śrī is conceived as the Lord and he also is called the Dharma-rāja.[4] The Ādi-Buddha and the Ādi-prajñā have frankly been explained in the *Svayambhū-purāṇa* as of the Nature of Upāya and Prajñā or Karuṇā and Śūnyatā, and have again been described as Śiva and Śakti.[5] In the *Dharma-koṣa-saṁgraha*[6] we find

[1] *Bṛhat Sayambhū-purāṇa*, edited by H. P. Śāstrī, (Bibliotheca Indica).

[2] *Ibid*, p. 21.

[3] *namo buddhāya dharmāya saṅghāya ca svayambhuve |*
tri-ratna-mūrtaye tasmai ādi-buddha-svayambhuve ||
śrī-svayambhū me śaraṇaṁ ratna-traya-svarūpiṇam |
sarva-pratidiśā me'dya svayambhuve kṛtāñjali ||

Ibid., p. 119.

[4] *cf. nāmnā ca dharma-rājo' yaṁ patnibhyaḥ saha saṁyutam ||*

Ibid, p. 149. F. N.; also p. 157.

[5] *Ibid.*, pp. 179-180. See also the Chapter on Cosmogony, *infra*.

[6] This work, which is preserved in manuscript in the Asiatic Society of Bengal (No. 8055), was written by Vajrācārya Amatānanda of the Mahābodhi-vihāra Lalita-paṭṭana, who was the first Residency Pundit in Nepal at the request of Brian Hodgson in N. S. 946 (*i.e.*, 1826 A.C.). Mr. Hodgson has made a good use of this work in his papers on the language and literature of

this idea of the Ādi-Buddha and Ādi-prājñā variously explained. It is said there that the Lord is called Ādi-Buddha, because he is the first knowable, and can only be inwardly intuited as he has no form to be perceived. He is called Nirañjana, because there is no stain (*añjana*=collyrium) in him, he being of the nature and form of the void like the sky. He is formless, supportless (*nirādhāra*); he is the Upāya, he is the Mahāvairocana.[1] This Ādi-Buddha is the Dharma-rāja. He is Dharma-rāja because he is the lord of all the entities (*dharmāṇāṁ rājā*), or because he shines in the world in his justice (*dharmād rājate saṁsāre rājate*), or because all the entities, or all justice shine from him (*dharma rājate yastmāt*).[2] He is also called Dharmeśa, because he is the lord of all the divine virtues like the ten *kuśalas* (*i.e.*, ten Buddhistic acts of righteousness) and is also the lord of all people who possess these virtues.[3] In another place he is explained to be Dharma-rāja, because he is associated with the knowledge of the perfectly pure ultimate element of all the Dharmas.[4] Again it is said, Dharma means the *Dharma-dhātu* (*i.e.*, the ultimate element behind the Dharmas) and the ultimate support of this *Dharma-dhātu*; and he who shines with the *Dharma-dhātu*, is called the Dharma-rāja.[5] He is the *Dharma-dhātu* in the form of Mahā-sukha or great Bliss. He is also called the lord of all beings—the Prajāpati.[6] It will be clear from the above that Ādi-Buddha, the Lord Supreme of Nepalese Buddhism, who was of the nature of Upāya, as contrasted with Prajñā, was widely known also as Dharma-rāja, and that will make it very clear how the Lord

Nepalese Buddhism (*vide*, A Descriptive Catalogue of Sanskrit MSS in the Government Collection, under the care of the A.S.B.—prepared by H. P. Śāstrī, pp. 192-193). The text is evidently not very old; but we attach importance to it only because of the fact that being composed by an orthodox Pundit of Nepal, it is likely to contain genuine information, at least so far as Nepalese Buddhism is concerned.

[1] He is called Mahā-vairocana, because, he is great (*mahān*) and at the same time illuminates or rather enlightens everything *viśeṣeṇa rocayati sarvaṁ mahāṁścāsau*—MS. p. 1(B).

[2] *Dharma-koṣa,-saṁgraha*, MS p. 3(*A*).

[3] *dharmeśaḥ* I *dharmāṇāṁ daśa-kuśalādīnāṁ īśaḥ dhāraṇā-tmakānāṁ saṁsārikānāṁ ca* I *Ibid*. MS. p. 8(B).

[4] *su-viśuddha-dharma-dhātu-jñāna-yogena dharma-rāṭ* I *Ibid*. MS. p. 8(B).

[5] *dharmo dharma-dhātuḥ, (tasya) sādhiṣṭhānaṁ yatra, tena vā-rājata iti dharma-rāṭ* I *Ibid* MS. p. 63(A).

[6] *Ibid*. MS. p. 63(B).

Supreme of the later Buddhists can also be associated with the Dharma-ṭhākura of Western Bengal and some parts of Orissa.

The above will confirm our previous statement that Dharma-ṭhākura does not represent the conception of any particular deity,—he rather represents the general idea of Godhead or of the sovereign deity over the universe, and as such he has been associated consciously with all the conceptions of Godhead or of the sovereign deity popularly current in Bengal and Orissa from the tenth century A.D. It is interesting to note that there is a Hindi text, entitled *Dharma-parīkṣā*[1] which relates the character of Jina Deva as the principal God of the Jainas and Jina Deva is styled in the text as Dharma.

After all these speculations on the origin and nature of Dharma, the supreme deity of the Dharma literature, let us now see how he is actually depicted in the literature of the Dharma cult, and these illustrations will, we hope, guarantee the relevancy and correctitude of our speculations.

[1] *Dharma-parīkṣā*, MS. No. 122, *vide Annual Report On The Search For Hindi MSS for the year* 1900—prepared by Śyāmasundar Dās (published by the Government of U.P., India).

CHAPTER XII

DHARMA AS DESCRIBED IN THE DHARMA LITERATURE

IN the Dharma-maṅgala literature, which flourished comparatively late, the nature of Dharma is found more simplified than in the liturgical works. In the Dharma-maṅgalas we have almost nothing Buddhistic in the conception of Dharma, he being completely Hinduised; the composite nature of Dharma is better illustrated in the descriptions of the Lord found in the liturgical works. In these descriptions of Dharma we should notice the importance that has been attached to the idea of Śūnyatā in various forms as the quintessence of Dharma or as an attribute of Dharma. Vacuity is the support of Dharma—it itself is the essential nature of Dharma. This Śūnya or Śūnyatā has been variously spoken of in the liturgical works of the Dharma cult but rarely in the Dharma-maṅgalas. It will be a great mistake to think that the Dharmites inherited this idea from the Buddhists as a philosophical idea; it was rather transmitted to them through a long process of change in the popular religious psychology,—and we are inclined to believe that whenever the Dharmites spoke of the Śūnya or the Śūnyatā, they simply inherited the idea as a social heritage without being conscious of what the term did actually imply. So much emphasised was the idea of Śūnyatā as the nature of the ultimate reality in Buddhistic philosophy, religion and literature for centuries in India and outside, and so widespread and deep-rooted was its influence on the mass through the enthusiasm of the Mahāyānists, that the association of the idea of voidness with that of the ultimate reality became a tradition. We have already pointed out that in Tāntric Buddhism, roughly and widely known as Vajra-yāna, practically almost all the heterogeneous elements are non-Buddhistic when considered in relation to the ethico-religious spirit of Buddhism; but attempt has always been made to give all these practices a Buddhistic garb mainly through the frequent use of the word Śūnyatā and more frequently its synonym Vajra, which was believed to be something like the magician's wand having the capacity of transforming everything non-Buddhistic into Buddhistic. In the Dharma cult of Bengal and similar religious beliefs and practices of Orissa, and also in the Vaiṣṇavism of Orissa the lingering effect of the tradition is best exhibited. This Śūnya was made much use of also in the yogic literature of the Muslims of Bengal.[1] It is indeed very interesting to notice that the staunch apostles of Vaiṣṇavism of Orissa in the sixteenth century, *viz.*, Acyutānanda Dāsa, Balarāma Dāsa, Jagannātha Dāsa, Ananta Dāsa, Yaśovanta Dāsa and Caitanya Dāsa, who were all contemporaries and who propagated Vaiṣṇavism as professed followers of Caitanya, described Lord Kṛṣṇa as the *Śūnya-puruṣa*[2] and made him none but the incarnation of Śūnyatā,[3] the ultimate void.

1 *E.g. saṁsāre phakīr sūnya jape śūnya nām* l *śūnya hante phakirer siddhi sarva kām* || *nām sūnya kām sūnya sūnye yār sthiti* l *se sūnyer saṅge kare phakir pirīti* || *sūnyeta parama haṁsa sūnye brahma-jñān* l *yathāte parama-haṁas tathā yogo-dhyān* || *je jāne haṁser tattva sei sār yogī* l *sei sav suddha yogī hae sūnya bhogī* || *siddhā ek sūnyo ek ei se yugal* l *je save ei tattva pāle se tanu nirmal* ||

Jñāna-sāgara by Ali Rājā *alias* Kānu Fakir, edited by Munshi Abdul Karim, Sāhitya-pariṣat Series, No. 59, p. 22.

Again,—*śūnya sūkṣma tanu hae rūp śūnyākār* l *rūper sāgare siddhi jathā baṇijār* || *śūnya sindhu hante byakta ruper sāgar.........mīrttikār ghaṭha-rūpe jagate pracār* l *mṛttikār bhāṇḍamule śūnya tanu sār* || *Ibid.*, p. 42.

2 *śūnya-puruṣa śūnya pare bandha* ||
śūnya-puruṣa udāsare rahe l
śūnya-puruṣa savu māyā bhyāye ||
śūnya-puruṣa dayālu aṭai l
śūnya-puruṣa sarva-ghaṭe rahi ||
śūnya-puruṣa kare naṭa ghuṭa l
śūnya-puruṣa jāne chanda-kuṭa ||
śūnya-puruṣa śūnare mārai l
marī śūnya puṇya gati karai ||
śūnya-mantre śūnya-puruṣa dharā l
daṇḍu thāi rājā hoiṇa tvarā ||

* * *

śūnya-puruṣare eteka teja l
śūnya hoi bhogya karai rājya ||
śūnya-puruṣa alage rahacchi l
śūnya pare rahi līlā kārucchi ||

Śūnya-saṁhitā (Edward Press, Cuttack), Ch. VII, pp. 52-53.

Again.—
tathī upare anakṣara l
tā pare śūnya nirākāra ||
śūnya upare mahāśūnya l
śuna rādhika dei mana ||
rūpa arūpa tahī nāhī l
se mahāśūnya ye bolai || etc.

Prema-bhakti-brahma-gītā, Yaśovanta-dāsa, (Prācī-grantha-mālā No. 17), p. 19.

3 See *Virāṭ-gītā* of Balarāma-dāsa, quoted in *Modern Buddhism* etc. by Mr. N. Basu, p. 40. Also, *Brahmāṇḍa-bhūgola-gītā* of Balarāma-dāsa, quoted in *Modern*

Another term, which is also frequently used as an epithet of Dharma and often rather as a synonym for Dharma, is Nirañjana, whch means "the stainless one." The use of the word Nirañjana is not, however, very uncommon in Hindu philosophical and theological texts; but its use seems to be more common in the Buddhist than in the Hindu fold; and it is very frequently and aptly used as an epithet of the reality, which in its ultimate void-nature is stainless like the sky above. In the liturgical works of the Dharma cult queer derivations of the word Nirañjana are offered which are purely arbitrary in nature.[1] This epithet or rather the synonym Nirañjana for the ultimate reality or the formless Supreme Being became very popular in all the vernacular literature, and in fact it has been very widely used by the Dharmites, the Nāthists, the Bāuls, the Sūfī poets, the Nirguṇī-poets of Hindi literature and also by the Sikh poets.

(*i*) *Dharma—confusedly described as the Lord Supreme in the liturgical works*

Let us now examine the descriptions of Dharma that are found in the *Dharma-pūjā-vidhāna* in connection with the meditation on and prayers and salutation to Dharma. The most important, however, is the meditation of Dharma, which runs as follows:—"Let that Lord of the form of vacuity, who has neither end, nor middle, nor beginning, neither hands and legs, nor body and voice, neither form, nor any primordial shape, nor fear and death, nor even birth,—who is accessible only to the greatest of the yogins in deep meditation, who belongs to all the sects (or who permeates all the petals of the lotuses within the body), who is bereft of all mental construction, who is one, stainless, and giver of the boon of immortality, protect me."[2]

Buddhism etc. See also many other similar extracts quoted by Mr. Basu in his work from the standard works of the other poets.—*Modern Buddhism,* etc. Ch. III.

[1] Thus, for instance, we find in the *Śūnya-purāṇa,*—

nīrete nirmala kāa nāma nirañjana |

i.e., he is called Nirañjana because his body is washed clean by primordial water.—p. 14.

[2] *oṁ yasyā'ntaṁ nā'di-madhyaṁ na ca kara-caraṇaṁ nā'sti kāyo ninādaṁ*
nā'kāraṁ nā'di-rūpaṁ na ca bhaya-maraṇaṁ nā'sti janmaiva yasya |
yogīndra-dhyāna-gamyaṁ sakala-dala-gataṁ sarva-saṅkalpa-hīnaṁ
tatraiko'pi nirañjano' mara-varadaḥ, pātu māṁ śūnya-mūrtiḥ ||
Dharma-pūjā-vidhāna, p. 70.

Again,—"I am invoking the Lord, who is the giver of all the fruits of desire, who has nothing like a shape, nor any seat to perform yoga, who is the absence of all and at the same time the abode of all, and who is adorned with all the postures and gestures (*sarva-mudrā-suśobhitam*). Come down, O the voidlord and take your seat here."[1] Lord Dharma is said to have incarnated into the world only to relieve all the beings of the three worlds from their bondage.[2] And this tone is just the same as is found in the Buddhist Tantras in connection with the invocation of the Lord Supreme. Dharma is again spoken of here as immersing his form in the sea of consciousness which is of the nature of supreme bliss.[3] Seated on his mount Ullūka he is the lord of the nature of the unity of Brahmā (the creator), Viṣṇu (the preserver) and Śiva (the destroyer). He is the great, the Brahman of the beginningless luminous form. He is adored in all the fourteen worlds and is of the form of perfect void. He is knowledge and consciousness, pure and changeless, innocent and formless and is to be known as the syllable "Oṁ"; he transcends all qualities, is the underlying reality not yet manifest in existence (*avyakta*); he is the transcendent reality, he is the Brahman.[4] He is perfectly pure, all-good, quiet, without beginning and end;—he is the life of the world and is of the form of lustre and bliss; he is not determinable by the four quarters, time and space (*a-dig-deśa-kāla-vyavacchedanīyam*). He has incarnated himself on the bank of the river Ballukā (which is in the district of Burdwan) seated on his favourite mount Ullūka and he is to be known only through the injunctions of the fifth Veda (*i.e.* the canonical or rather the liturgical works of the Dharmites).[5] Lord

[1] *Ibid*, p. 70.

[2] *trailokya-uddhāra-hetustvam avatīrṇo'si bhūtale* || *Ibid*, p. 72.

[3] *paramā-nanda-bodhā-bdhi-nimagna-nija-mūrtaye* | *Ibid*, p. 72.

[4] *Ibid*, p. 75.

[5] *Ibid*, p. 76. Similar descriptions of Dharma abound in the *Dharma-pūjā-vidhāna*; thus it is said,—"He is the Nirañjana, who is neither space (*sthāna*), nor fame, who has neither the lotus-like feet, nor any form, nor any primary colour; who is neither the seer nor sight, neither the hearer nor hearing, neither white, nor yellow, nor red, nor golden, neither like the sun, nor the moon, nor fire,—he neither rises, nor sets; he is stainless, of the form of the syllable "Oṁ", the supreme abode, unqualified, supportless, unchanging and all-void (*sarva-śūnyam-yam*). He is neither the full-grown tree, nor the root, nor the seed, nor the shoot, nor the branch, nor leaves, nor the trunk, nor the foliage; neither the flower, nor the scent, nor the fruit, nor the shade. (*Ibid*, p. 77) He is

Dharma has been saluted as the presiding deity over the gods (*devā-dhideva*), as the lord of the gods (*deveśa*), as the unity of all the gods (*sarva-deva*), as the primordial deity (*ādi-deva*), as the lord of the world (*jagannātha*), as the bestower of perfection (*siddhi-dātā*), the lord of all yoga (*yogeśvara*), as the incomprehensible deity (*acintya-devatā*) and as the saviour of all, giver of happiness and liberation and the supreme deity of vacuity (*śūnya-deveśa*). He is eternal, of pure quintessence (*śuddha-sattva*), of the form of compassion (*karuṇāmaya-mūrti*), and having the supreme virtue of contentedness (*santoṣa-śīla*).

If we examine the descriptions given above as specimen we shall find that some of the descriptions are almost the same as are to be found in the Buddhist Tantras in connection with the meditation of, and the salutation to, the supreme deity, and many of the attributes are taken frankly from the attributes of the divinities of the Hindu pantheon. It is, however, noticeable that in the descriptions of Dharma the negative tendency outweighs the positive.[1] This dominance of the negative tendency even in the most popular religion cannot but be recognised as the dwindling influence of Buddhism with its emphasis on the negative aspect of

neither the up nor the down,—neither Śiva nor Śakti, neither male nor female, nor the astral body (*liṅga-mūrti*), he possesses neither hands, nor legs, neither form nor shade; he is neither the five elements, nor the seven seas, nor the quarters, neither mountains nor peaks, neither Brahmā, nor Indra, nor Viṣṇu nor Rudra. He is neither the universe (*brahmāṇḍa-khaṇḍa*), nor the seed of time (*kāla-bījam*), neither the preceptor, nor the disciple, nor the planets, stars and heaps of clouds; neither the Vedas, nor the scriptures, nor the prayer offered thrice a day, nor the hymns; neither Mantra, nor the muttering, nor meditation, nor fire-sacrifice, nor gifts to or worship of gods. He is profoundly quiet, void in the form of Nirvāṇa, and is the ultimate substance of the universe. He is in the netherlands, in the invisible region (*antarikṣa*), in the four quarters, in the sky, in all the mountains and seas, in the root-syllable (*bīja-mantra*) and other Mantras, in the plants, in the land of the gods and the demons, in flowers and leaves and in the blade of grass, in iron, wood and ash, in earth, water and air,—in the static and the dynamic, he is all-pervading and one. (*Ibid*, pp. 78-79).

1 In addition to what is illustrated above compare also:—

nā'sti rūpaṁ nā'sti dehaṁ na'sti kāyo ninādam I
nā'sti janma nā'sti mūrttis tasmai śrī-dharmāya namaḥ ||
nirañjanaṁ nirākāraṁ sūnya-rūpaṁ jagad-gurum I
nirālambe sthitaṁ nityaṁ cintayāmi nirañjanam ||
nirañjanaṁ nirākāraṁ nirvikalpaṁ mahātmānam I
nirlepa-puruṣaṁ devaṁ sarva-lokaika-nāthakam ||
oṁkāra-bindu-sahitaṁ nirākāra-nirañjanam I
ādy-anta-rahitaṁ śūnya-rūpaṁ devaṁ nirañjanam ||

Ibid, pp. 90-91.

the reality. In connection with the salutation to Dharma salutations are offered to all kinds of void, *viz.*, great-void (*mahā-śūnya*), supreme void (*parama-śūnya*) etc.[1]

In the *Śūnya-purāṇa* we find similar descriptions of Dharma. By combining all the positive and negative attributes applied to him nothing can be said of him but that he is the Supreme Lord. He is saluted in his form of vacuity (*śūnya-rūpam*), as formless, saviour from calamities, the supreme of all the gods.[2] He is the *Karatāra* (the supreme lord), he comes from the void and has his support in the void.[3] He himself is the unity of the triad Brahmā, Viṣṇu and Mahādeva (*i.e.*, Śiva).[4] He is the supreme lord transcending both voidness and non-voidness.[5] In the beginning the Lord was moving alone in great-void (*mahā-śūnya*), having only void as his support, and the whole cosmos came out of the great void only through the will of the Lord. In the *Deva-sthāna* of the *Śūnya-purāṇa* we find that Brahmā is performing austere penances for the Lord by making his body the instrument for the yogic Sādhanā, and Viṣṇu is also invoking the Lord; Śiva is performing penances with his head down and legs up and singing the praise of the Lord with his horn and drum; Indra (*Purandara*) is performing penance for Dharma by inflicting severe torture on his body and all the yogins and sages are holding austere penances to propitiate him. For the bath of the Lord, Hanūmān digs a pond with his *vajra*-nails (*vajja-nakha*) and constructs four *ghats* in the four quarters—one of gold, one of silver, one of copper and the other of pearl, and fills up the pond with the water of the river Bhogavatī (*i.e.*, the Ganges of the Netherland). The Lord then gets into a golden palanquin and goes to bathe accompanied by all the gods including Brahmā, Viṣṇu, Śiva, Indra and by all the sages like Vaśiṣṭha, Nārada and others.[6]

It is needless to repeat here that in these descriptions

1 *Śūnya-purāṇa*, p. 93.
2 *Śūnya-purāṇa*, p. 152.
3 *Ibid*, p. 218.
4 *Ibid*, p. 218.
5 *gaganā-gagana (sic,-nā) -pāraṁ paraṁ parameśvaraṁ etc.* *Ibid*, p. 228.
6 See *Atha Mukti-snāna*, *Śūnya-purāṇa*, pp. 179-181. Also, *Atha Dharma-pūjā*, *Ibid*, p. 175 *et seq.*

Dharma has often been identified with Śiva, Viṣṇu (or Nārāyaṇa) and Kṛṣṇa.[1] The abode of Dharma wavers from Kailāsa to Vaikuṇṭha, showing thereby the tendency of identifying Dharma sometimes with Śiva and sometimes with Viṣṇu. Though Śūnya has been made much use of in describing Dharma and though his formless and non-essential nature has been variously emphasised, yet Dharma is conceived always as a personal God with a form.[2]

(ii) *Dharma as the Sun-god*

Dharma has sometimes been described as the sun, and there is a two-fold reason behind it. In the first place Dharma is luminous by nature and so is the sun and hence the identity. Secondly, Dahrma is Śūnya and Śūnya is of the shape of a zero and, therefore, Dharma is of the shape of a zero;[3] and as the sun is also of the shape of a zero, Dharma is identified with the sun. Moreover, Dharma moves in the void, and void is the sky, and the sun moves in the sky and hence the sun is Dharma.[4] The Sun-god,

[1] *Vide Dharma-pujā-vidhāna*, p. 79.

[2] We may note here the reply of Rāmāi Paṇḍita made to some questions put to him. He says,—"My home is in Ballukā and I worship the Formless One; I meditate on the void and adore the form of the Lord." *Śūnya-purāṇa*, p. 165. It is indeed funny to see that one who worships the formless and meditates on the void should adore any particular form or figure of the Lord! In another place, however, Ulluka, the mount of Dharma, puts the following questions to Dharma, —"Who is the Lord (*Karatār*) in this world and who is work or action (*karma*)? Who is the being pervading the fourteen worlds? Who has made *Khalla* (? a canal, a cut, a creek, a trench, a deephole) and *Bihalla* (?) and who has made the *Salla* (Śāla tree?) in the mountain? Who is transformed into hands and legs? Who does infuse the blooming flowers with scent and who does create and destroy the sun and the moon? Who does make water flow in the rivers, from whose body does the heavenly river Ganges flow and who has made her (*i.e.*, the Ganges) flow in a zigzag course? Who has placed the mountains on their firm basis and who does reside in the void? Who does come from the Śūnya and goes to the Śūnya, and who does make the Śūnya his support and then meditate on the Śūnya? Who does bear fruits in the form of the tree? Who does rain the form of the cloud? Who does accept worship in every house and who is called the mother of the world?" To every one of these questions the reply of Dharma is that it is he himself who is responsible for this universal process and for all that are in it. *Ibid*, pp. 211-12.

[3] *Cf. śūnya-bhuvanaṁ* l *śnūyaṁ bartulā-kāraṁ bhavatī'ti śūnya-bhuvanaṁ* l *bindvā-kāraṁ* l

Dharma-koṣa-saṁgraha, MS. p. 2(A).

[4] *śūnya-mārge sthitaṁ nityaṁ śūnya-deva-divākaram* l
tam ahaṁ bhajāmi śrī-dharmāya namaḥ ||

Dharma-pūjā-vidhāna, p. 89.

Cf. also :
nirālambe rathe mārge śūnya-mūrttiṁ divākaraṁ etc. *Ibid*, p. 51.
maṇḍalaṁ vartulā-kāraṁ śūnya-dehaṁ mahābalam l
eka-cakra-dharaṁ devaṁ taṁ sūryaṁ praṇamāyaham || *Ibid*, p. 52.

who is of the form of zero, or in other words circular in shape, is described as the cause of creation, preservation and destruction and as such is of the nature of the three *guṇas* (i.e. *sattva*, *rajas* and *tamas*) and also of the nature of the triad, Brahmā, Viṣṇu and Śiva, who represent the three *guṇas* respectively.[1] In the *Dharma-pūjā-vidhāna* we find the Dharmites presenting offerrings to the Sun-god, who is subsequently identified with Dharma. He is described as the lord (*gosāñi*), who takes ablution and offers his Brahminic prayers in the bathing-ghat of the river Campā.[2] Yet at the same time he rises on the shore of the seven seas in a chariot, which is decorated with vermilion, diamond, coral and pearl. Seven horses of pure white colour carry the golden chariot of the Lord which has been decked with sixteen flowers. Sixteen attendants are holding the chain of the chariot, the galaxy of the twelve Ādityas are sitting within, and Indra, the king of the gods, is holding the umbrella over the Lord who is shining on his golden pedestal with a garland of golden lotus round his neck. The lord is then entreated to turn his attention to the beings of the world, for whom wealth and welfare are solicited.[3] The descriptions of the Sun-god, seated in his golden chariot of seven white horses, and the way in which he is approached by his devotees for bestowing health and wealth on all beneath at once remind one of the Vedic hymns of similar contents.[4] The similarity is indeed striking, and that may suggest some link between them through popular traditions. In the *Bāra-māsi* of the *Śūnya-purāṇa* we find the worshipper of Dharma presenting offerings to the twelve *Ādityas* (suns,) who are spoken of as twelve brothers. Again we find, Lord Dharma rises from his sleep early in the morning and Ullūka offers to him his prayer; eight horses of white colour carry the golden chariot of the Lord and the Lord rises

[1] *Ibid*, p. 51.
Again, *udaya-kāle brahma-svarūpaṁ madhyāhne maheśam* I
asta-kāle svayaṁ viṣṇus tri-mūrttiś ca divākaram II *Ibid*, p. 52.

[2] *Ibid*, p. 123. *Cf. Śūnya-purāṇa*, p. 149.
Campā or Cāṁpāi is river in the district of Bankura, and it is described as a very important and sacred river of the Dharmites.

[3] *Vide*, *Dharma-pūjā-vidhāna*, pp. 123-25.

[4] *Vide*, *Ṛg-veda*, (1.22.8), (1.24.4), (1.35.2,4-5) etc.

as the luminous sun.[1] In the east is situated the golden temple of the Lord. The devotees invoke the Lord to rise up from his sleep and to relieve the whole world from darkness. Then the Lord awakes and asks for his chariot and horses, which are prepared for him instantly. The Lord then climbs on his chariot and the crown on his head touches the sky, and Indra begins to shiver in fear in heaven and the serpent Vāsuki in the Netherland. When the Lord of the world thus rises on his chariot with a sacred thread of nine folds round his neck[2] and shining with his radiant lustre like a wonder to all beneath, some think of him to be very near, and some to be far off. Thd Lord removes the sorrow of the poor beneath by distributing immense wealth.[3]

(iii) *Dharma of the Dharma-maṅgalas*

(A) Dharma as Viṣṇu in general

In the ritualistic works Dharma is often called *Svarūpa-nārāyaṇa* and there is also the custom of presenting *Tulasī* leaves to his feet; he has lotus-like hands like Viṣṇu, Vaikuṇṭha is his abode. The transformation of Dharma into some form of Viṣṇu was almost complete in the Dharma-maṅgala literature. The Dharma-maṅgala literature, which is now available to us, is of very late origin and flourished under the sway of Vaiṣṇavism both of the Rāma cult and the Kṛṣṇa cult; it is for this reason that Dharma of the Dharma-maṅgalas is mostly identified with Viṣṇu in general and Kṛṣṇa and Rāma in particular. It is only sporadically here and there in the cosmogonical discussions and in some other places that we hear in the Dharma-maṅgalas of the *Śūnya-mūrtti* of Dharma or of his "formless form" with all his negative and positive attributes.[4] The older tradition of the identification of Dharma with Śiva

[1] P. 150.

[2] It is to be noted that lord Sūrya (*Sūrya-ṭhākura*) of the folk-songs of Bengal also wears the sacred thread of nine folds round his neck.

[3] See *Atha Dharma-sājana*, *Śūnya-purāṇa*, pp. 159 *et seq*.

[4] See, *Dhm*. of Ghana-rāma (Vaṅgavāsī edition). See also *Ibid*, pp. 31, 148, 205, 962.

Also *Dhm*. of Māṇik Gāṅguli, pp. 112, 156.

Dharmāyaṇa of Nara-siṁha Vasu. Vol. 1, MS. (C. U. No. 3224), p. 7(A).

seems to have dwindled away by this time. Though Dharma is sometimes spoken of as the lord of Caṇḍī, and is worshipped with *Vilva-patra*[1] which is particularly dear to Lord Śiva, and though his abode is located in Kailāsa, yet it seems that with the rise of the various Śākta and Vaiṣṇava cults Śaivism was rapidly losing ground. This was why the tradition of Dharma as Śiva was gradually passing into oblivion in the Dharma-maṅgala literature; and not only that, we sometimes find Śiva introduced in the Dharma-maṅgalas only to obey Lord Dharma and help him in his struggles against the goddesses. The general descriptions of Dharma that are found in the various Dharma-maṅgalas are the popular descriptions sometimes of the unqualified Brahman of the Upaniṣads and sometimes of the Puruṣa of the Sāṁkhya and sometimes of a mixture of them in the most confused manner with the legendary accounts of the various incarnations of Viṣṇu and his activities in various ages as are found in the Purāṇic literature.[2] Again sometimes we find Dharma in the assembly of the gods, including Indra, Brahmā, Viṣṇu, Śiva, Varuṇa and others, seeking advice from them as to the right measure to be taken to keep up his prestige, which was very frequently at stake in the hands of the devotees of Śakti. In the attempt to introduce his worship on earth by establishing his almighty power Dharma-ṭhākura had no plain sailing; his devotee Lāusen was at every step challenged by the devotees of Śakti either in the form of beasts or in the form of men, and whenever his devotee was thus challenged out Lord felt a sudden jerk in his royal seat either in Kailāsa or in Vaikuṇṭha and he would enquire from Ullūka, and more generally from Hanūmān, as to what might have been the cause of that trouble; they would in reply describe the miserable plight in which his devotees might have been. In almost all cases our Dharma-ṭhākura was very helpless and we find him always seeking advice and practical help from his companion and instructor Ullūka and mainly from his

[1] *Dhm.* of Ghana-rāma, p. 68; also *Ibid.*, p. 102, 111.

[2] See the descriptions of Dharma in the *Dhm.* of Rāma-nārāyaṇa (MS. C.U. No. 2450), pp. 4(B)-5(A), and pp. 16(A) *et seq. Dhm.* of Ghana-rāma, p. 2, 102; *Dhm.* of Māṇik Gāṅguli, p. 1, pp 4-5. etc.

chief agent or executor, Hanūmān. But in cases of more serious and emergent nature Dharma-ṭhākura would call for an assembly attended by all the prominent gods (goddesses being conspicuous by their absence) and would seek advice from them all.

In the Maṅgala literature we generally find Dharma in the form of Viṣṇu of dark blue colour with four hands with the conch-shell, disc (*cakra*), mace (*gadā*) and lotus; he has ear-rings, his *Kaustubha* jewel is suspended on his chest, he has his yellow garment and lotus-eyes and he is with his mount Garuḍa. Whenever we find the Lord appearing before the devotee, the devotee would never believe him to be Dharma unless and until he would appear before him in his form of Viṣṇu with four hands. A typical case is the trouble that was created by a dog in the way when Dharma was proceeding to Hākanda to rise in the west at the request of his devotee Lāusen. The dog obstinately obstructed the path of the Lord and would not allow him to pass on without disclosing his identity. The Lord told him that he was Dharma himself; but the dog intentionally refused to believe him to be Dharma unless and until he was in his form with four hands and in blue colour; at last the Lord had to comply with the request of the devout dog and assumed the form of Viṣṇu,[1] and when the Lord asked the dog to pray for any boon it liked, the dog asked the boon of being a *Tulasī*-leaf so that he might have the rare fortune of sticking to the lotus feet of the Lord constantly.[2] In the *Dharma-pūjā-vidhāna* and some of the Dharma-maṅgalas the ten incarnations of Viṣṇu have been described as the ten incarnations of Dharma. The Dharma-ṭhākura of Mayanā-pur is known as *Yātrā-siddhi* and the people of the locality believe *Yātrā-siddhi* to be identical with Viṣṇu.[3] In the work entitled *Yātrā-siddhi-rāyer Paddhati* there is a Sanskrit hymn addressed to Dharma; the poet of the work (which seems to be very recent in origin) has gone even so far as to make Lord Dharma indulge in love-dalliances

[1] See the chapter on *Paścima-udaya*, found in almost all the Dharma-maṅgalas.

[2] *Dhm.* of Ghana-rāma, pp. 260-261.

[3] *Vide*, B.S.P.P., B.S., 1813, No. 2.

with the cowherd girls in the water of the river Ballukā.[1] In the Dharma-maṅgalas devotees have, in connection with the praise of the Lord, always referred to many of the Purāṇic incidents where the Lord had shown kindness to his devotees and given them proper shelter. It is mentioned that Dharma protected Prahlāda from the hands of Hiraṇyakaśipu, gave shelter to Dhruva and placed him in the fixed heavenly region, saved Sudhanvā and Ajāmila, protected the Pāṇḍavas in all their calamities, saved the honour and chastity of Draupadī when she was being molested by the evil sons of Dhṛtarāṣṭra; he was all through the charioteer of Arjuna, killed the demon Rāvaṇa and saved Sītā, deceived Brahmā, the creator, and taught him a very good lesson in the land of Vṛndāvana as a cowherd boy and had all sorts of love-dalliances with the cowherd girls of Vṛndāvana. These and many such other descriptions of Dharma-ṭhākura abound in almost all the Dharma-maṅgalas, where we find nothing but a list of some of the more important incidents associated with the different incarnations of Viṣṇu jotted down pell-mell.

(B) Dharma as Rāma

The identification of Dharma-ṭhākura with Rāma in the Dharma-maṅgalas has been brought about mainly through the mediacy of Hanūmān. In the liturgical works Hanūmān is only one of the four *Koṭālas* (gate-keepers) of Dharma, but in the Dharma-maṅgalas he is sometimes the mount of Dharma, sometimes the counsellor and the conscience-keeper of the Lord. In the Ṛg-Veda Ulūka (the owl) has been described as the mount of Dharma-rāja Yama, and probably the tradition has come down to the Dharmites;[2]

[1] *prabhinnā-ñjana-ballūkā-jala-keli-kalotsukam*
yodhayantaṁ vihārantaṁ cakraṁ kvacid gopān etc. ||
Vide, B.S.P.P., B.S. 1313, No. 2, p. 94.

[2] Much speculations are made by scholars as to the exact nature and significance of this Mount Ullūka or Uluka associated with Dharma, and it is also a matter of controversy whether Uluka here is actually the bird owl, or is any other personality. As a matter of fact in the *Śūnya-purāṇa* and also in the *Dharma-pūjā-vidhāna* Uluka is more a personality than a mere bird. He is often called a sage or the great sage (*Muni or Mahā-muni*). From the very beginning Dharma-ṭhākura did nothing without the advice of Uluka and in fact the latter seems to be much wiser than the lord himself. But in the Dharma-maṅgalas Uluka is generally depicted as the bird owl and in the legend of Hariścandra of the Dharma-

but in later times Ulūka seems to have practically been outsted by Hanūmān. Hanūmān, the ape-god, has a special place in the history of our literature. However strong in their supernatural power and in their tenacity of purpose in quarrels and intrigues, the gods and goddesses of our literature seem to have been all through very weak physically, and whenever any gigantic work had to be performed, Hanūmān was invariably approached by all the gods and goddesses. We find him also a good assistant to Viśvakarmā, the great mechanic of the universe. Hanūmān, therefore, served not only Rāma-candra of the Bengali Rāmāyaṇas—he has served Caṇḍī in the Caṇḍī-maṅgalas, Manasā, the serpent goddess, in the Manasā-maṅgalas, and every one took advantage of his gigantic physical strength and his obedient nature. Dharma-ṭhākura, therefore, was wise enough to have Hanūmān constantly at has dispoal to have all the difficult tasks done by him. But by being thus constantly accompanied and obeyed by Hanūmān, Dharma-ṭhākura could no longer retain his Dharma-nature and gradually became transformed into Rāma-candra himself.

maṅgalas he plays an important part. The owl, which was the Mount of Dharma, was once sitting on the branch of a tree, when he was pierced through by an arrow aimed at by Luhicandra, son of Hariścandra; the bird cursed the family of Hariścandra and said that Hariścandra would leave no posterity; it is generally with this curse of the bird Uluka that the Hariścandra legend begins. Saving a few places where Uluka is admitted to be the sage Uluka and the counsellor of Dharma, Uluka is depicted in the Dharma-maṅgalas as a mere bird, the place of sage Uluka being practically usurped by Hanūmān. The name Uluka, however, is well-known in Purānic literature as the name of different notable personalities. In the Purāṇas Uluka is a name of Indra himself; another Uluka was the son of sage Viśvāmitra,—another the son of Śakuni. In the *Mahābhārata* we find mention of a king of the name of Uluka; another Uluka was an ambassador in the *Mahābhārata*. Again the Vaiśeṣika system of Indian Philosophy is also known as the philosophy of Uluka; in the Vaiśeṣika system *Dharma* has variously been explained (of course, in a sense entirely different from that of the Dharma of the Dharma cult). Mr. B. K. Chatterjee in his introduction to the *Dharma-maṅgala* of Mayūra-bhaṭṭa is disposed to think that the Dharma cult of Bengal may be a continuation of the religious cult propounded by Uluka in a very early period, and hence is the importance of Uluka in the Dharma-maṅgalas. But such a surmise does not seem to us plausible at all for various reasons. There is nothing in the Dharma cult which can even very remotely be associated with anything of the Vaiśeṣika system; moreover, it is doubtful whether the Vaiśeṣika system of thought represents any religious sect. If the religious doctrines of Uluka were something different, that being entirely unknown to us, the question of the possibility of its relation with the Dharma cult cannot be decided. It should also be remembered in this connection that far from representing any philosophical school, the Dharma cult of Bengal, as we have repeatedly pointed out, cannot be said to represent even any particular religious school.

We find in the Dharma-maṅgalas that whenever Dharma-ṭhākura asks Hanūmān to do some arduous and hazardous work, Hanūmān refers to all his (Hanūmān's) heroic deeds of the Rāmāyaṇic period and says that if it were possible for him to do all those great things for the lord at that time, there is no reason why it should not be possible for him to do the same once more for the lord. The lord also occasionally refers to the valour and obedience of Hanūmān that he had shown formerly on various occasions.[1]

As a matter of fact we find Hanūmān often performing the same kind of wonderful feats for the lord in the Dharma-maṅgalas as he did in the Rāmāyaṇas.[2] We have sufficient reasons to believe that at least some of the poets of the Dharma-maṅgalas, such as Ghana-rāma, Sītārāma-dāsa, Rāma-nārāyaṇa and others were devoted to Rāma if they were devoted to any particular deity at all. Ghana-rāma, in many of his colophons, states that his mind is a bee which constantly sticks to the lotus feet of Rāma-candra. Sītārāma-dāsa and others also begin their books or the chapters therein with salutation to Rāma, who is said to be Dharma.

(iv) *The Description of Dharma As All-White*

One very significant point is that the complexion of Dharma-ṭhākura is white, and not only that, everything associated with him is white.[3] In the *Dharma-pūjā-vidhāna* he has been saluted in his form of pure white colour resembling the colour of a fresh Kunda flower and the refreshed moon (*dhauta-kundendu-dhavala*). He wears white garment and bears a white umbrella.[4] His throne or seat is also described white.[5] In his white form he is associated with pure intelligence-stuff.[6] He wears a white garland and also a

[1] As a typical instance compare the dialogue between Dharma and Hanūmān when the former was requesting the latter to protect Lāusen in his (*i.e.*, Lāusen's) childhood from the hands of the thieves.

[2] As an instance we may point out that when Lāusen was crossing the river Ajay to attack Ichāi-ghoṣ he was captured and broughta victim to the Netherland (*Pātāla*) by the river herself; to this Dharma became perturbed and sent Hanūmān to do the needful. Hanūmān went to the place of action and put all the water of the river Ajay into cavities of his ears; the river begged pardon, released Lāusen and then and then only was her water released. *Dhm.* of Rāma-nārāyaṇa, *Dhekura-pālā*, MS. (C. U. No. 2454) pp. 5(A)-5(B).

[3] In the *Viṣṇu-dharmottara* Dharma has been described as of four faces, four hands, adorned with ornaments and of white complexions.

[4] P. 76. [5] *Ibid.*, p. 81. [6] *Ibid.*, p. 84.

white sacred thread.[1] He has a white disc in his hand, white hair on his head and white horses with his white throne.[2] Clad all in white and seated on the white seat that stainless one moves in the chariot of swans, which are also of pure white colour.[3] In the *Śūnya-purāṇa* we see that there are white flags on the gate of Dharma,[4] and he is pleased to sit on the white seat being clad in white garment.[5] In Ghana-rāma we find that the lord was worshipped in all ages with white flowers.[6] Even when in his way to Hākanda to rise in the west in the form of a Brahmacārin with a golden colour and red garments, with the bowl and *kuśa*-grass in hand and with rosary and frontal marks, Dharma-ṭhākura could not dispense with his old white umbrella.[7] In the fragmentary verses that are recited in the ceremony known as the *Gājana* of Dharma (and in the *Gājana* of Śiva in East Bengal) we find the same description of Dharma as all white.[8]

The white-complexioned god of the Hindu Pantheon is lord Śiva. In popular meditation he has been compared to the silver mountain (*rajata-giri-nibha*). In the Tantras he is the *Śveta-bindu* (or the white matter) as opposed to Śakti who is the *rakta-bindu* (or the red matter); he resides in the snow white mountain of Kailāsa. The other popular Hindu deity of white colour is the goddess Sarasvatī, the goddess of learning. She is herself white, is clad in white garment, sits on a white lotus,[9] and has the white swan as

1 *Ibid*, p. 87. 2 *Ibid.*, p. 90.

3 *Ibid.*, *Cf.* also *Anādi-maṅgala* of Rāma-dās Ādak. 4 P. 66.

5 *Śūnya-purāṇa*, p. 67, p. 69, p. 149. *Cf.* also, *Ibid.*, p. 218. 6 P. 176.

7 P. 260. *Cf.* also. *Anādi-maṅgala* of Rāma-dās Ādak, p. 34. Māṇik Gāṅgu says that Dharma has white seat, white paste of sandal besmeared on his body; he has white cloth, white *cāmara* and a pair of white sandals on his feet (*Dhm.* of M. Gāṅguli, p. 1). In other places we find that Dharma has white glow around his body, white cloth, and ornaments; he is besmeared with white sandal-paste; he puts on white shoes and sits on a white throne; he has white frontal mark, white and brilliant matted hair, and a garland of white moons; he has white seat with a white canopy, and with white flags, and his temple is lighted with white glow (*Ibid.*, p. 5, p. 33, p. 212, etc.). White is his residence, white his house and white is the pedestal of the lord with everything else white around. *Ibid.*, p. 48; see also p. 55.

8 *Vid. Ādyer Gambhīrā* by Haridās Pālit, p. 25. See also p. 83. Similar verses are also found among the fragmentary verses we have in our collection in connection with the *Nīla-pūjā* of East Bengal of which we have already spoken.

9 *Cf.* the meditation of Sarvsvatī:—

yā kunde-ndu-tuṣāra-hāra-dhavalā yā śveta-padmā-sanā
yā vīṇā-bara-daṇḍa-maṇḍita-karā yā śubhra-vastrā-vṛtā | *etc.*

her mount. It is customary to worship her with all kinds of white articles; she loves white sandal-paste, white paddy, white flowers, fried paddy of white colour, white curd, etc.[1] In the province of Buddhism also we meet with various form of Sarasvatī, but her pure white colour is generally maintained.

The white colour of Śiva and Sarasvatī seems to have some metaphysical significance. White colour represents perfect purity and knowledge.[2] Metaphysically Śiva is pure consciousness, perfect enlightenment, he is pure intelligence-stuff (*viśuddha-sattva*),—and the white colour of the lord bears a subtle harmony with the metaphysical nature of the lord. Sarasvatī also represents learning and wisdom—she stands for perfect enlightenment. In some of the Purāṇas she has been conceived as representing the *Sattva-guṇa* of the primordial goddess, who is called Ādyā-śakti or Mahālakṣmī, the other two *guṇas viz.*, *Rajas* (energy) and *Tamas* (inertia) being represented by Lakṣmī and Mahākālī respectively.[3] In the Sāṁkhya philosophy pure intlligence-stuff (*Sattva*) has been spoken of as of pure white colour, *Rajas* or energy of red colour, *Tamas* or inertia of black colour. It is for this reason that the colour of Sarasvatī is pure white and everything associated with her and her worship is also white.

Cf. also:

taruṇa-śakalam indor vibhratī śubhra-kāntiḥ
kuca-bhara-namitāṅgī sanniṣaṇṇā-sitā-bje 1

Also:—

viśada-kusuma-tuṣṭā puṇḍarīko-paviṣṭā
dhavala-vasana-veśā mālati-baddha-keśā 1
śaśadhara-kara-varṇā śubhra-tāḍaṅka-karṇā, *etc.*

[1] It is noticeable in this connection that in the autumnal worship of goddess Lakṣmī, which is widely known as the worship of *Kojāgara-Lakṣmī* all the articles of worship are prescribed to be white; even the food and sweet-meats to be offered to her should preferably be white. In this, however, there seems to have been something like a popular confusion. In our religious history Lakṣmī and Sarasvatī have sometimes been confused one for the other, and this will explain the worship of Sarasvatī on the white *Pañcamī* (*i.e.*, the fifth day of new moon) of the month of *Māgha*, which was most probably originally the date for the worship of Lakṣmī as the very name *Śrī-pañcamī* will indicate (see *Sarasvatī* by Mr. Amulya Caraṇ Vidyābhūṣaṇa, Vol. 1). May we infer that as we have the worship of Sarasvatī in the *Śrī-pañcamī* of the month of *Māgha* in the place of the worship of Laskṣmī, so we have the worship of Lakṣmī on the full-moon night of autumn in the place of the worship of Sarasvatī and hence perhaps is the importance of all white articles in the *Kojāgara-Lakṣmī's* worship?

[2] In literature, however, white colour also represents fame and smile (*Cf.* *yaśasi dhavalatā varṇyate hāsakīrtyoḥ*—*Sāhitya-darpaṇa*).

[3] *Vide*, *Sarasvatī* by A. Vidyābhūṣaṇa, Vol. I, p. 119-20.

Coming to Buddhism we find that when Buddha began to be docetically conceived, he was conceived as the embodiment of perfect purity and perfect enlightement. He was pure-consciousness (*vijñapti-mātratā* or *vijñāna-dhātu*) as the ultimate reality,—he is perfect knowledge or wisdom. He has often been described as effulgent by nature (*prakṛti-prabhāsvara*) and as radiating light of knowledge (*prajñā-loka*). Round the physical form of historical Buddha as Siddhārtha or Śakya-siṁha there has always been a glow of perfect purity and enlightenment. Before giving birth to Buddha, Māyā, his mother, dreamt that a white elephant entered her womb and this predicted the birth of Buddha who would attain perfect enlightenment. This notion of perfect purity and enlightenment as the ultimate nature of Buddha or rather of the supreme deity (*Bhagavān*) was to a great extent traditionally carried down even to the latter periods of Tāntricism. It is, therefore, not very unlikely that in the popular description of Dharma-ṭhākura as all white and having everything white associated with him we have an unconscious mixture of the notions of Śiva and Buddha.

CHAPTER XIII

THE THEORY OF THE *PAṆḌITAS*, *KOṬĀLAS*, *ĀMINĪS*, ETC.

LORD Dharma has five *Paṇḍitas* in the five ages, Setāi in the golden age (*Satya-yuga*), Nīlāi in the silver age (*Tretā-yuga*), Kaṁsāi in the copper age (*Dvāpara-yuga*), Rāmāi in the iron age ((*Kali-yuga*) and Goṁsāi in the void-age or the age to come (*Śūnya-yuga* or *Anāgata-yuga*). Setāi is white in colour, Nīlāi is blue, Kaṁsāi yellow, Rāmāi red and Goṁsāi green. The five *Paṇḍitas* are really the five priests of Dharma in the five ages including the age to come.[1] But at the time of the worship of Dharma all the five ages meet together with all the five *Paṇḍitas*, whom we find placed in the five quarters, and these five quarters are again represented by the five gates of the temple of Dharma facing the five quarters. This theory of the gates in the different directions with respective presiding deities over them is also found in the *Gājana* songs of Śiva still now current in West Bengal as well as in East Bengal. In the versions of West Bengal the presiding deities over the southern, western, northern and eastern gates are Jagannātha, Ekādaśa Bhīma, the Sun (*Bhānu-bhāskara-rāya*) and Kāmākhyā of Kāma-rūpa respectively.[2] In the versions of East Bengal the deities in the west, south, east and north are Jagannātha, Vaidyanātha, Śrī-muṇḍa-cakra-vāhinī and Śrī-sabhā-liṅga-vāhinī respectively.[3] Sometimes Jagannātha, Kṣīra-nadī-sāgara, Sūrya-divākara (the sun) and the Himalayas are also saluted in the four directions.[4]

The five priests in the five quarters have again five *Koṭālas*, or guards or rather gate-keepers with them, *viz*., Candra (the moon) in the west, Hanūmān in the south, Sūrya (the sun) in the east, Garuḍa in the north and

[1] The tradition of Paṇḍita Goṁsāi is not found in all the descriptions.
[2] *Vide*, *Ādyer Gambhīrā* by H. Palit.
[3] See *infra*, Appendix D.
[4] See *Vaṅga-sāhitya-paricaya*, Part I, pp. 159-60.

Ulūka in the void. The *Koṭālas*, as they are depicted in the *Śūnya-purāṇa*, seem to be so many attendants on the priests and gate-keepers in the five directions of the Dharma temple; they open doors to the visitors and again shut them up. The association of the sun and the moon with the east and the west is well-known, and the association of Hanūmān with the south is also well-known through the stories of the Rāmāyaṇa (Ceylon, which was the field of activity of Hanūmān being situated to the south of India). So the appointment of these three *Koṭālas* in the three quarters is easily explicable. Guruḍa and Ulūka are well-known as the mounts of Viṣṇu and Dharma-ṭhākura respectively. As Hanūmān, associated with the south, happens to be something like the mount of Rāma-candra, it is perhaps by the law of association that the two other well-known mounts are placed in the other two quarters. In the *Dharma-pūjā-vidhāna*, however, the *Koṭālas* or the guards are differentiated from the gate-keepers (*Dvārī* or *Dvāra-pāla*), who are again attended by four *Pātras* (attendants). The four gate-keepers in the four quarters (the fifth gate of void being omitted here) are, Jharjharī-sundara (or Jharjharikā) or Mahākāla in the west, Jambhava or Tīkṣṇa-damṣṭrā in the south, Mahākāya in the east, and Nandīdeva in the north; and the *Pātras* are Paḍihāra, Hanūmān, Ḍāmaraśāñi and Kāmadeva respectively. We have somewhat detailed description of these *Dvāra-pālas* in the *Dharma-pūjā-vidhāna*.

The *Paṇḍitas* of the five ages are associated with different number of followers, different *Āminīs* or *Ghaṭa-dāsīs* who are female attendants on the Lord. The whole thing can be illustrated with the help of the following Chart (the discrepancies of the descriptions being neglected).

This theory of the five *Paṇḍitas, Koṭālas, Āminīs*, etc., is nothing but a popular adoption of the later Buddhist theory of the *Pañca-tathāgatas*, also known as the five Dhyānī Buddhas.[1] With the growth of the docetic conceptions in Mahāyāna Buddhism the five *skandhas* or elements began to have ontological significance and gradually gave rise

[1] See an article by P. K. Mukherjee in the Bengali monthly *Pravāsī*, (1329 B.S., No. I).

Paṇḍita or priest	Age	Direction	Colour of the paṇḍitas	Followers (gati)	Āminī or Ghaṭadāsī	Koṭāla	Dvārapāla and Pātra	Name of the gates	Water for the bath of Dharma and the cups offered to him	Raw material of the houses seats, bathing ghats, thrones, dams, etc.	Colour of the articles offered to Dharma
Setāi or Śvetāi	Golden (Satya)	West	White	400	Basuyā or Bijayā	Candra (The Moon)	Jharjharī-sundara or Mahākāla (pātra-Paḍihāra)	Paścima-duyāra, or Ahaka	Water of five sacred places; cup of water	Gold	White
Nilāi	Silver (Tretā)	South	Blue	800	Caritrā	Hanūmān	Jambhava or Tikṣṇa-daṁṣṭrā (pātra-Hanūmān)	Laṅkāra duyāra, or Natvaka	Coconut-water; cup of milk	Silver	Blue
Kaṁsāi	Copper (Dvāpara)	East	Yellow	1200	Gaṅgā	Sūrya (The Sun)	Mahākāya (pātra Dāmara-śāñi)	Udaya-duyāra, or Saṁkhāri	Water of tribeṇī: cup of honey	Copper	Copper-colour
Rāmāi	Iron (Kali)	North	Red	1600	Durgā	Garuḍa	Nandīdeva (pātra Kāma-deva)	Gājana-duyāra, or Bhiṣaṇa	Milk of the Kapilā cow, cup of love	Red metal, or bell-metal, stone, pearl, brass	Red
Gosāñi	Void (Śunya) or Future (Anāgata)	Void (Śūnya)	Green	Innumerable	Abhayā	Ulūka	..	Pañcama-duyāra	Empty cup	Diamond	..

to the conception of five deities. In the *Pañca-tathāgata-mudrā-vivaraṇa* of the *Advaya-vajra-saṁgraha* we find that the five *Tathāgatas* are but the modes and modifications of the Dharma-kāya of the Vajrasattva. These five *Tathāgatas*, though originally conceived as the five deities over the five *skandhas*, are later on regarded as the five presiding deities over the five gross elements (*viz.*, earth, water, fire, air and ether) and the five senses (*viz.*, senses of vision, taste, hearing, smell and touch). In later Buddhistic esoteric literature these deities are described with their Bodhisattvas, human Buddhas (*Mānuṣī Buddha*), Śakti (female counterpart), mounts (*vāhana*), postures (*mudrā*), crest, family (*kula*), *bīja-mantra* etc. They are again associated with the five gross elements (*pañca-bhūta*), five kinds of sense perception and the five sense organs. They are again located in the five places within the human body. We are giving a chart overleaf of the whole thing, wherein the controversies over the details are ignored.[1]

If we put side by side and compare the two charts, one illustrating the theory of the five *Tathāgatas*, or the five *Dhyānī* Buddhas and the other illustrating the theory of the five *Paṇḍitas* of the Dharma cult, no room will be left for doubting the fact that the latter is but a transformed version of the former. With the five *Tathāgatas* and the five *Paṇḍitas* we may compare also the popular Islamic tradition of the five *Pīrs* (or saints). It may also be cursorily noticed that the Kabīr Panthis have the belief that the *Sat Puruṣa* (i.e. the Supreme Being) has four different messengers in the four ages, *viz.*, *Sat Sukrit* in the *Satya-yuga*, *Munin-darji* in the *Tretā*, *Karuṇāmaya Ṛṣi* in the *Dvāpara* and *Kabir Saheb* in the *Kali*.

Already in the *Hevajra-tantra* we find that there are four corners and four gates or doors of the Maṇḍala or Cakra (mystic diagram) of goddess Prajñā and four are the

[1] For a detailed study of the subject see an article *Vajra and Vajrasattva* by the present writer in the *Indian Culture*, Vol. VIII, No. 1. See also *Śrī-guhya-samāja* (G. O. S.), *Advaya-vajra-saṁgraha* (G. O. S., Chs. on *Pañca-tathāgata-mudrā-vivaraṇa*, and *Pañcā-kāra*), *Sādhana-mālā* (G. O. S., Vol. II, pp. 445-46), *Hevajra-tantra*, *Paṭala* IX, *Sampuṭikā*, Ch. I, *Pañca-krama*, Ch. I. *The Gods of Northern Buddhism* by A. Getty. *Buddhist Iconography* by Dr. B. Bhaṭṭācārya, pp. 1-8, and *An Introduction to Buddhist Esoterism* by Dr. B. Bhaṭṭācārya, Ch. XIII.

Dhyānī Buddha	Skandha	Direction	Colour	Śakti	Bodhisattva	Human Buddha	Kula (Family)	Mount (Vāhana)	Posture (Mudrā)	Bīja	Element (bhūta), sense-perception, and sense-organ	Location in the human body
Vairocana	Rūpa	Centre	White	Vajradhātveśvarī or Tārā	Samantabhadra or Cakrapāṇi	Krakucchanda	Moha	Dragon	Dharma-cakra	"a", or "oṁ"	Vyoma (ether) Sound (śabda) ear	Head
Akṣobhya	Vijñāna	East	Blue	Locanā	Vajrapāṇi	Kanakamuni	Dveṣa	Elephant	Bhusparśa	"y" or "huṁ"	Mārut (air) Touch (sparśa) Skin	Heart
Ratnasambhava	Vedanā	South	Yellow	Māmakī	Ratnapāṇi	Kāśyapa	Cintāmaṇi	Lion	Varada	"r" or "Svā"	Tejas (fire) Vision (rūpa) Eye	Navel
Amitābha	Saṁjñā	West	Red	Pāṇḍarā	Padmapāṇi, or Avalokiteśvara	Gautama	Rāga	Peacock	Samādhi	"b" or "āh"	Water (ap) Taste (rasa) Tongue	Mouth
Amoghasiddhi	Saṁskāra	North	Green	Āryatārā, or Tārā	Viśvapāṇi	Maitreya	Samaya	Garuḍa	Abhaya Viśvavajra	"l" or, "hā"	Earth (kṣiti) Smell (gandha) Nose	Legs

Śaktis in charge of the four gates; they are Gaurī in the east, Caurī in the south, Vetālī in the west and Ghasmarī in the north; there are other two gooddesses, *viz.*, Bhūcarī and Khecarī in the downward (*adhas*) and upward (*ūrddhva*) directions.[1] These goddesses in the different directions are again said to be the presiding Śaktis over the five sense-perceptions. Again the presiding Śaktis over the five *Skandhas* are said to be Vajrā, Gaurī, Caurī, Vajra-yoginī and Nairātmya-yoginī respectively.[2] These goddesses are placed in the different quarters.[3] Without entering into the anomalous details it will be sufficient for us to note that the conception of the four gates or doors were already there in Tāntric Buddhism. In the exoteric form of northern Buddhism we find the theory of the five Buddhas represented in the Buddhist *Stūpas* or *Caityas* of latter time, where one of the five Buddhas was given prominence to be the Lord Supreme and was placed in the centre and the other four were placed on the four gates or doors on the four sides. Such a scheme is to be found also in the sculptural representation of the later Buddhist *Stūpas* or *Caityas*. Esoterically, however, these *Tathāgatas* and also their Śaktis are placed in the central, eastern, southern, western and northern direc-

1 *cakraṁ pūrvaṁ yathā kathitaṁ hārā-rddhahāra-śobhitam* |
catuṣ-koṇaṁ catur-dvāraṁ vajra-sūtrair alaṁkṛtam ||

* * * *

niḥsṛtā indra-dig-gaurī pūrva-dvāre tu saṁsthitā |
mantha-manthāna-yogena caurikā niḥsṛtā punaḥ ||
niḥsṛtya dakṣiṇe dvāre caurī saddvāla (?)—vālike |
bola-kakkola-yogena vetālī niḥsṛtā punaḥ ||
niḥsṛtya paścime dvāre niṣaṇṇā māra-bhañjanī |
mahā-dvandva-samāpattau niḥsṛtā ghasmarī punaḥ ||
niḥsṛtya uttara-dvāre niṣaṇṇā ghora-rūpiṇī | *etc.*

Hevajra-tantra, M.S pp. 55(B)-56(B).

Cf. also *indre gaurī yame caurī vetālī vāruṇe diśi* |
kaubere ghasmarī caiva adho bhūcharī smṛtā ||
ūrddhve khecarī proktā utpatti-krama-pakṣataḥ | *etc.*

Ibid, MS. P. 25(B).

See also *Sādhana-mālā*, (G. O. S.) Vol. II, p. 445.

2 *rūpe gaurī samākhyātā śabde caurī prakīrtitā* |
vetālī gandha-bhāge ca rase ghasmarī kīrtitā ||
sparśe ca bhūcarī khyātā khecarī dharma-dhātutaḥ |

Hevajra-tantra, MS. P. 25(B).

rūpa-skandhe bhavet vajrā gaurī vedanāyāṁ smṛtā |
saṁjñāyāṁ caurī yoginī saṁskāre vara-yoginī ||
vijñāna-skandha-rūpeṇa sthitā nairātmyā-yoginī | *etc.*

Ibid, MS. P. 15(A).

See also *Sādhana-mālā*, Vol. II, p. 545.

3 *Sādhana-mālā*, Vol. II, p. 444.

tions of the mystic diagram (Maṇḍala) of secret practices. In latter times all these esoteric and exoteric traditions transformed themselves into the scheme of the five gates (including the void-gate) of the temple of Dharma, where the five *Tathāgatas* or the five Buddhas have become the five worshippers of lord Dharma in the five ages in the form of the five *Paṇḍitas.*

The tradition that there are different deities presiding over the different quarters is, however, as old as the Vedas. Thus in the *Atharva-veda* we find that, of the Eastern quarter Agni is the overlord, black serpent is the defender, the Ādityas are the arrows, and homage is paid to the overlord, the defender and the arrows. Similarly, of the Southern quarter Indra is the overlord, cross-lined (serpent) defender, the Fathers the arrows; of the Western quarter Varuṇa is the overlord, the adder defender, food the arrows; of the Northern quarter Soma is the overlord, the constrictor defender and the thunder-bolt arrows, of the fixed quarter (*dhruvā dik*) Viṣṇu is the overlord, the serpent with black-spotted neck defender, the plants the arrows; of the upward quarter Bṛhaspati is the overlord, white serpent defender and rain the arrows.[1]

It will be very interesting also to note, in connection with this Buddhist theory of the *Pañca-tathāgatas* and their Śaktis and the corresponding theory of the five *Paṇḍitas* with the five *Āminīs* as found in the Dharma cult, that this theory has its correspondence also with the Hindu Tantras. We have seen that the five *Tathāgatas*, though originally said to be five deities over the five *Skandhas*, are associated with the five gross elements. These five elements have been represented in the Hindu Tantras by the five (out of the six) lotuses or plexuses, *viz.*, Mūlādhāra representing earth, Svādhiṣṭhāna representing water, Maṇipura representing fire, Anāhata air and Viśuddha ether. There are five presiding gods and five goddesses associated with these lotuses. The gods are, Brahmā, Viṣṇu, Rudra, Īśāna, and Mahādeva respectively; and the goddesses associated with the lotuses are Ḍākinī, Rākiṇī, Lākinī, Kākinī and Śākinī respectively. The *bīja-*

[1] (3.27.-1-6).

mantras of the lotuses are *laṁ, baṁ, raṁ, yaṁ,* and *haṁ*; the *bīja-mantras* of the five *Dhyānī* Buddhas are also almost exactly the same (*i.e., l, b, r, y,* and *oṁ*). The first three gods associated with these lotuses are respectively of red, blue and vermilion colour, and the last two are white. The goddesses are of red, deep blue, dark-green, smoky and white colour.

In the colour scheme, however, there is perfect correspondence between the Buddhist and the Dharmite tradition; they have a faint resemblance with the colour scheme of the Tantras also. The five elements in the five plexuses, *viz.*, earth, water, fire, air and sound are described in some of the texts as of yellow, white, red, smoky and blue colour respectively. Again we find in the Purāṇic literature that there was the tradition of God's having four different colours in the four different ages. God was of white colour in the *Satya-yuga*, red colour in the *Tretā-yuga*, yellow in the *Dvāpara-yuga* and black in the *Kali-yuga*.[1] Rūpa-gosvāmī speaks of the colour scheme as white, red, dark-green and black.[2] It may also be noted that in the *Anāgata-vaṁsa* (a Pāli text describing the tradition of the advent of Maitreya, the future Buddha), there is the description of four gates in the capital city Ketumatī and in the four gates there will be four Kalpa-trees of the blue, yellow, red and white colour.[3] In the *Chāndogyo-paniṣat* we find that of the four Vedas, the first, i.e., the *Ṛg-veda* is spoken of as of the colour of the white portion of the eye, and the second, i.e., the *Sāma-veda* is spoken of as of the colour of the deep blue portion of the eye.[4] Again, of the five material elemnts *Tejas* is described as red, water as white an earth as black.[5] Again, the nerves of the body have been described as secreting four kinds of liquids, which are of white, blue, yellow and red colour.[6]

1 *āsan varṇās trayo hyasya gṛhṇato' nuyugaṁ tanuḥ* |
śuklo raktas tathā pīta idānīṁ kṛṣṇatāṁ gataḥ ||
Bhāgavata-purāṇa, (10. 8. 13).

2 *kathyate varṇa-nāmabhyāṁ śuklaḥ satya-yuge hariḥ* |
rakta-śyāma-kramāt kṛṣṇas tretāyāṁ dvāpare kalau ||
Laghu-bhāgavatā-mṛta of Rūpa-gosvāmi.

3 *Vide verses* (10-20).

4 *Chāndogya*, (1. 7. 4).

5 *Ibid.* (6/4)

6 *Ibid.* (8.6.1).

About the colour of the different articles associated with the worship of Dharma in the five gates, it will be seen that the articles associated with the western gate, which in its turn is associated with Setāi *Paṇḍita*, are all white in colour; similar is the colour scheme of the articles associated with the other gates. Again, as for the metal of the articles it may be noticed that the articles associated with western gate, which is again connected with the *Satya-yuga* or the golden age, are all made up of gold; those of the southern gate, associated with the silver age, are all of silver; those of the eastern gate, associated with the copper age, are all of copper, those of the northern gate, associated with the iron age, are spoken of as made up of some lead metal, or, bell-metal, stone and brass; and those of the fifth gate, associated with the void age or the age to come, are all of diamond. The tradition of Gosāñī *Paṇḍita* of the age to come (*Anāgata-yuga*) may possibly have something to do with the tradition of advent of the future Buddha Maitreya in the *Anāgata* age, as it is described in the Pāli text *Anāgata-vaṁsa*.

CHAPTER XIV

COSMOGONICAL AND COSMOLOGICAL THEORIES IN OLD AND MEDIEVAL VERNACULAR LITERATURES

(1) *A brief Exposition of the Theories*

IN the old and medieval vernaculars of India we find various theories about cosmogony and cosmology. In spite of the differences in details, there is a general similarity in the description. When we shall analyse the ideas found in these theories we shall find that here also, as in other cases, there is a great jumbling of ideas received from various sources of Indian philosophy, theology and mythology. Of all the descriptions found in the vernaculars, the descriptions contained in the literature of the Dharma cult of Bengal seem to be the most detailed and important, and we shall presently see that all the other descriptions found in other types of literature present a striking similarity with the descriptions found in the literature of the Dharma cult. Though the accounts given in the vernaculars are often extremely confused in nature, we must first of all attempt a very brief exposition of these cognate theories and our next and more important task will be to analyse them and to affiliate the constituent elements to the older thoughts and beliefs.[1]

In the *Śūnya-purāṇa* we find that in the beginning there was nothing,—neither any linear mark, nor any form, nor any colour, nor any trace of anything; there was neither the sun nor the moon, nor the day nor the night. There was neither water, nor earth, nor the sky, nor the mountains. The universe was not,—neither was anything mobile or immobile, nor were the temples, nor the gods in them,—there were only all-pervading darkness and haze (*dhundhukāra*)—and in the infinite vacuum the Lord alone was moving in

[1] In this connection see introduction to the *Śūnya-purāṇa* (edited by Mr. C. Banerjee) by Dr. Shahidullah and Mr. B. Chatterjee.

the great void having nothing but void as his support. And in his absolute loneliness the Lord was thinking of creating something, and out of the great vacuum there came out the vital air of the Lord, from which came inhalation and exhalation; from these again proceeded great compassion and from that all the principles of illusion. Then there came out a bubble of water on which the Lord made his seat, but the bubble could not withstand the pressure of the Lord and burst into pieces leaving the Lord once more in the vacuum. Then the Lord sat fixed in the vacuum and in and through his compassion another personality of the name of Nirañjana came out of him. The latter, however, had no hands and legs,—neither had he any father and mother, nor was he born of the seed and the ovum, nor had he any other companion in the great void. This Nirañjana or Dharma then sat on the seat of compassion and passed full fourteen ages in the meditation on the Great (*bambha-jāna*). After fourteen ages of meditation Nirañjana yawned and from his high breath came out the bird Ullūka. The bird began to flee away from the Lord who was calling it from behind; but Ullūka got tired in the infinite void and came back to the Lord. The Lord then took compassion on Ullūka and made his seat on the back of the bird and once more passed fourteen years in meditation. In the meantime Ullūka became much fatigued with hunger and thirst and asked for some drink from the Lord. The Lord gave a little quantity of fluid from his mouth to the bird to drink. Ullūka drank the fluid, but some portion of it fell outside in the void and water came out of it, and both the Lord and his mount were floating on water. But in the heaving water both of them were being tossed roughly and a feather dropped from the body of the bird and the feather became a swan. The Lord then proposed to have some rest on the back of the swan, and the latter agreed, and the Lord once more passed several ages on the back of the swan. But the swan also got tired and flew away in the void leaving the Lord in water. The Lord then touched water with his lotus-like hand, whereby a tortoise came to being, and the Lord passed several ages in meditation on its back. The tortoise also got tired and flew away leaving the Lord and Ullūka on water. Ullūka then advised the Lord to create the world in water. With the instructions of Ullūka the Lord cast off on water his golden sacred-thread, which instantaneously became the serpent Vāsuki of thousand fangs. Then the Lord accumulated a little quantity of dusty substance from his nail and placed it in the form of the world on the head of the serpent Vāsuki. The Lord then went out with the Ullūka to visit the world and the world was increasing with the speed of the Lord. By roaming about in the world the Lord became tired and began to perspire and from the sweat of his body was produced the Ādyā-Śakti (the primordial energy). The Lord built a house for her and placed her there and after creating the river Ballukā engaged himself in meditation once more for fourteen ages. In the meantime Ādyā-Śakti grew young and from her youthful desires proceeded forth Kāma (Cupid) who was sent by Ādyā to the Lord. Kāma went to the Lord, aimed his arrow at him and the Lord was disturbed. The Lord came to know everything from Ullūka and put Kāma in an earthen pot and Kāma became transformed into poison. Ādyā, after some time, became unable to bear the burden of her youth and attempted to commit suicide by swallowing the contents of the earthen pot; but to her astonishment she became pregnant thereby. Three gods were then born to Ādyā, *viz.*, Brahmā, Viṣṇu and Śiva. Just afer their birth all the three went out for penance and meditation, and the Lord also went to test them in the form of a corpse flowing on water. Brahmā could not recognise the Lord in disguise, Viṣṇu also could not recognise him; it was only Śiva, who could recognise the Lord. The Lord became pleased with Śiva, and granted him three eyes (for all the three brothers were born blind). Subsequently at the request of Śiva the other two brothers, *viz.*, Brahmā and Viṣṇu also received eye-sight with the sprinkling of the fluid from the mouth of the Lord. All the three brothers then went back to Ādyā, where they were entrusted by the Lord with the task of creation. Ādyā-Śakti was asked to be the wife of Śiva and to help him in the work of creation. Thus after entrusting the whole task of creation, preservation and destruction to the triad the Lord once more went to the void and remained for ever seated on his mount Ullūka.[1]

The fragmentary accounts of cosmogony found in the *Dharma-pūjā-vidhāna* also tally with those found in the *Śūnya-purāṇa*; the only difference is that Dharma Nirañjana came out of the formless absolute Lord in the form of a luminous body in the void and was asked to create the universe with his three qualities (*guṇas*), *viz*., *sattva*, *rajas* and *tamas*, personified as the triad Brahmā, Viṣṇu and Śiva.[2]

In the Dharma-maṅgalas detailed accounts of cosmogony are found which, though slightly different in details, are substantially the same as found in the *Śūnya-purāṇa*. Thus almost a similar account of cosmology is found in the Dharma-maṅgala of Sahadev Cakravartī.[3] The account given in the Dharma-maṅgala of Sītā-rām Dās also tallies with the account of the *Śūnya-purāṇa* almost verbatim; the only important deviation is that after the world was created Dharma himself assumed the form of a charming damsel and was then himself in union with her. Through their union three gods of the nature of the three *guṇas* were born to them.[4]

In the *Anādi-maṅgala* of Rāmdās Ādak[5] we find that Mahāmāyā was produced from the left side of Dharma. Mahāmāyā or Ādyā-śakti attained her youth. Dharma proposed to Ullūka that as Ādyā was produced from the left part of his body, she should be the wife of the Lord. The proposal appeared obnoxiously repulsive to Ādyā, who tried to flee away in all the directions; but at last she had to give way and the marriage took place in the void through the mediation of Ullūka. Then follows the birth of the triad and the story of Dharma's disguise to test them. Here also it was Śiva, who could recognise the Lord, and the propitiated Lord entrusted Śiva with the charge of creation. But Śiva, with the preponderance of *tamas* in him, created the Yakṣas, Rakṣas, ghosts, genii, demons and

[1] *Śūnya-purāṇa*, *Sṛṣṭi-pattana*, pp. 1-42. In this connection see the introduction to the *Śūnya-purāṇa* by Dr. Shahidullah and Mr. B. K. Chatterjee.

[2] *Dharma-pūjā-vidhāna*, pp. 201-202.

[3] *Vide* B.S.P.P., B.S. 1304.

[4] *Dhm*. of Sitārām Dās, *Sthāpanā-pālā*, MS. (C. U. No. 2469), p. 3(A).

[5] Edited by Mr. B. K. Chatterjee, Sāhitya-pariṣat series, No. 82.

many such other horrible beings. The Lord then put a check to Śiva and asked Brahmā to take the charge of creation. The Lord himself assumed the form of a bear and brought for him (Brahmā) the earth, which lay hidden in the netherland. Then follows the theory of the self-originated Brahmā and the *Manus*, the *Ditis* and the *Aditis*, etc., as it is found in the Purāṇic literature.[1] In Ghana-rāma we find that in the primordial void and darkness the formless supreme Lord first revealed himself in a form which contained the potency of all creation. The Lord desired to create and from his desire for creation was born *Prakṛti* in the form of the most beautiful and charming woman,—and the mind of the Lord was disturbed at the sight of her beauty, and through the distruhance in his mind *Prakṛti* was infused with the three *guṇas* from which again were born the three gods, Brahmā, Viṣṇu and Śiva. Then follows the story of their penance and their test by Dharma in the guise of a corpse. Here also, as in the case of Rāmdās's account, Śiva, who was first entrusted with the charge of creation, created all sorts of horrible beings and then the charge was transferred from him to Brahmā. From Prajāpati Brahmā was first produced *Ahaṅkāra* (egohood), from *Ahaṅkāra* proceeded the five elements and then the four sons of Brahmā (*viz.*, Sanaka, Sananda, Sanat-kumāra and Sanātana) and so on as in the popular Purāṇic accounts.[2] According to the account given by Māṇik Gāṅgulī the triad with the essence of the *guṇas* was produced from the union of the Lord and Śakti and for the triad Śakti again divided herself into three goddesses, *viz.*, Brahmāṇī, Vaiṣṇavī and Śaivī. Then follows the test of the triad. Here we find that all the three gods could recognise the Lord and did welcome him warmly and humbly and the Lord, pleased with the triad, entrusted them with the charge of creation, preservation and destruction. The three Śaktis, *viz.*, Brahmāṇī, Vaiṣṇavī and Śaivī were then united with Brahmā, Viṣṇu and Śiva and the triad with their Śaktis created the manifold universe.[3] The account given by Narasiṁha Vasu in

[1] *Vide Anādi-maṅgala* of Rāmadās Ādak, pp. 7-10.
[2] *See Dhm.* of Ghana-rāma, *Sthāpanā-pālā*, pp. 5-7.
[3] *Dhm.* of Māṇik Gāṅgulī, pp. 9-11.

his *Dharmāyaṇa* comes closer to the Sāṁkhya view of cosmology. From the desire of the Lord for creation in the primordial void *Prakṛti* was born in the form of a beautiful woman, and from the union of *Prakṛti* and the Lord was born a son of the name of *Mahartta* (*i.e., mahat*) and from *Mahartta* came three *Ahaṁkāras* of the nature of three *guṇas*, and from them were born the triad.[1] Then follows the story of the test of the triad and Śiva was entrusted with the charge of creation. But in actual creation we find the Purāṇic story that the Lord with his mysterious *Māyā* (i.e. principle of creative illustion) slept on the snake *Ananta* and from the lotus of his navel proceeded Brahmā, who was always thinking of creation.[2] Brahmā had four sons proceeding from his desire (*mānasa-putra*), *viz.*, Sanaka, Sanātana, Sananda and Sanat-kumāra. And then came the theory of the *Manus*, *Diti*, *Aditi* and others just as in the Purāṇas.

In the *Gājana* songs of West Bengal and East Bengal we find the same conception of cosmogony. In the verses collected by Mr. Haridās Pālit in his book *Ādyer Gambhīrā* we find that in the beginning there was nothing and the Lord (*Gosāñi*) was in the form of the void in the boundless void.[3] Then there was water and the Lord was floating (?) in his void-form.[4] He then ordered a crab to sink down and to bring earth from the bottom,—and the crab brought earth for the Lord. According to one version[5] the Lord made the world with a portion of earth brought by the crab and the world was then placed on the back of a tortoise. According to another version the earth, brought by the crab was of the nature of gold and from it there was an egg and that egg burst into two (one half becoming the earth and the other half the sky?) and the triad, Brahmā, Viṣṇu and Śiva then created the world.[6]

In the fragmentary verses, which the present writer

[1] *mahartta haite haila ahaṅkār tin* l
sartta raja tāmasa trigun bhirnna bhin ||
sartta rūpe birsna rūpa karilā āśray l
rajaguṇa sthiti-kartā brahmār tanay ||
siv tama-gune haila jāhā haite nās l
tāmasa gunete janmila ākās ||

Dharmāyaṇa of Narasiṁha Vasu, Vol. I., MS. (C.U. 3224), p. 7(B).

[2] *Ibid*, MS. pp. 9(A)-9(B). [3] P. 19.

[4] *Ibid*, p. 24. [5] *Ibid*, p. 19. [6] *Ibid*, pp. 24-25.

collected from the district of Bakergunge in East Bengal, and which are sung on the occasion of the *Nīla-pūjā* at the end of the month of *Caitra* similar cosmogonical ideas are found. In one verse we find,—"In the beginning there was neither any cause, nor reason, nor the sky; neither was there water nor earth; neither the within, nor the without, and the Lord was all alone. The Lord then perspired and from his sweat was created the universe.[1] In another song we find that Dharma-rāja, after travelling long on his mount, perspired and from his sweat a phantom was produced and the phantom became magically transformed into a girl; she stood before the Lord and the Lord got enamoured with her; she, however, began to flee in the western direction to escape his hands and rebuked the shameless father who was mad after his own daughter; but the Lord paid no heed to her words and pursued her madly.[2]

In connection with the travelling of Śiva as a mendicant in the market-place (*bajār-sannyāsa*), which is also included in the ceremonies on occasion of the *Nīla-pūjā*, we find the following verse:—"Void was the market place, the earth was not,—*Sannyāsins* (those that have renounced the world), *Tapasvins* (those who practise penances) and *Ṛṣis* (sages) there were none; neither was the day, nor the night. How was the Lord at that time? All the existent was void, the non-existent was also void and the Lord of void was of the body of void; the earth with the seven islands was immersed in water in the void. What was the state of the Lord at that time? He was of the form of an egg. There was no earth, and the boar brought it with the help of his teeth. Lord Śiva then created the earth with the dusty substance of

1 *hetu buddhi nā chila gagan-maṇḍal* |
nāhi jal nāhi sthal bāhire sthāpan ||
bhitar bāhir nāhi keval ekeśvar ||
........carma gharme bhijila |
chiṭāiyā nakṣatra
ei-rūpa sṛṣṭi haila biśvambhar ||

2 *āila re dharma-rāj ulāse (uluke?) caḍiyā* |
ulāse rāse śṛṅga ghāmila |
chāyāya āchila kanyā māyāte jammila ||
piche āchila kanyā sumukhe dāṇḍāla |
tāhā dekhiyā dharma-citta dharaṇ nā yāy |
paścim dike kanyā dhāṇyāiyā yāy ||
etek śuniyā devī balila uttar |
bāp haiyā jhire karte cāy bar || etc.

his body." There is also mention of Nila and Anila in the verses in a rather unmeaning and confused manner.[1]

In the Caṇḍī-maṅgalas of Bengal we find almost a similar conception of cosmogony and cosmology. In the *Caṇḍī-maṅgala* of Māṇik Datta, who flourished in or before the fifteenth century, we find a confused echo of the cosmogonical theory found in the *Śūnya-purāṇa*.[2] In the *Caṇḍī-maṅgala* of Mukundarām Cakravartī (of the sixteenth century) we find that the primordial Lord (Ādi-deva) was thinking of creation in the void, and when he was thus pondering on, Prakṛti came out of his body, and Prakṛti, who was the manifestation of the power (Śakti) of the Ādi-deva, was called the Ādi-devī. The Lord infused his energy in Prakṛti and thereby a son of the name of *Mahān* (i.e. *Mahat*) was born to them; the son of *Mahat* was *Ahaṁkāra* and from *Ahaṁkāra* were born the five (elements), *viz.*, earth, water, fire, air and ether. Again one Lord became three (the Triad) according to the *guṇas*. Of the Triad Brahmā had four sons born of his desire (*mānasa-putra*), but all the four went away for penance leaving behind the phenomenal world. Brahmā, however, got angry and from his anger was born Rudra, who was given six female companions (*viz.* Dhṛti, Vṛddhi, Īśī, Vaśī, Śivā and Aṇimā) and was ordered to create the creatures. Śiva began to create horrible creatures and was at once stopped by Brahmā. For the purpose of creation Brahmā

[1] *bājāre śūnya sthal sannyāsī tapasī ṛṣī* |
nā chila divā niśi ||
śona re bhāi śiver mādār (?) |
takhane āchilā gosāṁi keman avatār ||
hay śūnya nay śūnya śūnya śūnya kāy |
sapta-dvīp pṛthī śūnya chila jalamay ||
śona re bhāi śiver mādār |
takhane āchila gosāṁi dimba-avatār ||
hari giri parvat nā chila māṭi |
barāha āniyā tāy dante kāṭi ||
e śiv pāsara āpanā |
āṅger mayalā diyā kare pṛthivī sthāpanā ||
nile āchilā gosāṁi anile sut |
nile āchilā gosāṁi keman adbhut ||
nile āchilā gosāṁi kabhu nahe jāni |
ek ek kalikā (?) *diyā sevila medinī* ||
māṭi cākā dhariyā phelilām jale |
sthir nā haite ṭal-mal kare ||
deo deo basumātā more deo bar |
bachare bachare haio bālār agrasar ||

[2] See B.S.P.P., 1317; also *Vaṅga-sāhitya-paricaya*, Part I, pp. 300-301.

then divided his body into two parts, one as the female and the other as the male (the latter being named as Svayambhuva Manu). This latter was then requested by Brahmā to create progeny, but Svayambhuva Manu wanted land where the created beings might have their abode. At this Brahmā became perturbed and from his nostril came out the boar who went to the netherland and brought back on his long teeth the earth that lay hidden there; and then creation began as it is described in the Purāṇas.[1] The account given in the *Caṇḍī-maṅgala* of Mādhavācārya, though substantially the same as described above, shows a greater amount of confusion of ideas. Here the Devī was created from the breath of the Lord and Brahmā was born in the navel. Of the triad Brahmā, Viṣṇu and Śiva, the Devī was given to the last for creation. In the *Annadā-maṅgala* of Bhārata-candra also we find a similar account. The *Biṣahari Padmā-purāṇa* of Jīvan Maitra also contains a cosmogonical account of the same nature.[2]

The cosmogonical ideas of the literature of the Nāth cult of Bengal also resemble to a great extent the ideas described above. According to the accounts given in the *Anādi-purāṇa* or *Anādi-caritra*, the *Hāḍa-mālā-grantha*, the *Yogi-tantra-kalā* etc.,[3] Alek-nātha (the incomprehensible one) or Nirañjana Gosāṁi created Anādi Dharma-nātha and from the liquid of the mouth of the former there was water on which Anādi-nātha made his seat. Then Alek-nātha created goddess Kāketukā from the energy of his own body, and she was put to death under the pressure of the feet of Anādi. Ādi-devī, or goddess Kāketukā was then revived through the grace of the Lord and he instructed Anādi to create the beings in union with Ādi. Then the creation began. The serpent Vāsuki was created and was placed in the netherland and on the fang of it was placed the earth of a triangular shape. Then from the fist of Dharma were born the triad, who were deaf an d

[1] *Kavi-kaṅkaṇa Caṇḍī* by Mukundarām.

[2] *Vide Bāṅgalā Puthir Bivaraṇ*, by Har Gopāl Dās Kuṇḍu, B.S.P.P., B.S. 1313, Vol. 3, p. 162.

[3] *Vide Nātha-dharme Sṛṣṭi-tattva* by Rāj-mohan Nāth, B.S.P.P., B.S. 1331, No. 2.

dumb. Then follows a somewhat different version of the test of the triad.

Gorakṣa-vijaya contains a cosmogonical account, which, in spite of slight differences, presents on the whole the same view as described above. In the beginning there was only the *Karatār* and nothing else. The *Karatār* himself was not self-conscious,—it was the potentiality in him that made him self-conscious in the process of manifestation. His manifested form followed his self-consciousness and the principle of change and transformation followed from his manifestation in a form.[1] And then there was the desire of the Lord to create the world and for the purpose he produced Dharma Nirañjana. Dharma was first in a slumbering state, and when he became awakened he found some shadowy entity by his side, who was none but Ādyā (*i.e.*, Ādyā Śakti). The Lord attempted to capture her, but she tried to escape. She was then captured by force and through the union of the Lord and the Ādyā the sun, the moon, the earth and the stars were produced. From the *Huṁkāra* of the Lord was born Brahmā and from his mouth was Viṣṇu. Through the mutual attraction and affection of Ādi and Anādi (Ādi represents Śakti who has a beginning and Anādi represents the beginningless principle) there was sweat and soul, the ego, the four Vedas and fourteen scriptures; water and earth and all the other beings were produced from this sweat.[2] From the different parts of the body of Anādya emanated Śiva and Gaurī (who is the mother of the universe) and all the other Siddhas. The Lord then proposed that some one of them (*i.e.*, either Śiva, or any of the Siddhas) should accept Gaurī as his wife. At this proposal all bent their head out of shame. The Lord then ordered Śiva to accept Gaurī, who (as Anādya told) was but one with Śiva in her ultimate nature. In accordance with the decree of the Lord, Hara and Gaurī came down on earth and they were accompanied by the Siddhas. In his discussion with Ādyā, Anādya says that he, as the ultimate reality, has an unchanging permanent nature of his

[1] *Gorakṣa-vijaya*, edited by Munsi Abdul Karim. Sāhitya-pariṣat Series No. 4, p. 1. Also see Appendix of the text, pp. 4-5.

[2] *Gorakṣa-vijaya*, Appendix (ka), alternative readings from MS. No. 5, p. 1.

own, which is unspeakable, and in that unchanging ultimate nature he remains pervading the whole cosmos in his formless form. As there is the tree from the seed and the seed in the tree, so is the creation form Anādya and Anādya in creation. As cream is produced by the churning of milk, as fire is produced through the rubbing of two logs of wood, so also is the creation. As there is the cycle of the night of the new moon and of the full moon, so there is the process of creation and dissolution. A similar view of cosmogony is found in the *Gopī-candrer Sannyās* by Sukur Mahammad.[1]

In some of the Vaiṣṇava Sahajiyā texts also we find a similar theory of cosmology, more confusedly mixed up with Vaiṣṇava theology and mythology.[2]

It is interesting to note in this connection that in course of the religious discussion that took place between a Portuguese Christian Missionary on the one hand and an orthodox Brahmin on the other in the *Brāhmaṇ-Romānkyāthalik-saṁvād*,[3] of Don Antonio we find ideas of cosmogony and cosmology strikingly similar even in details to the ideas found in the descriptions of the texts belonging to the Dharma cult, Caṇḍī cult and the Nāth cult. This fact clearly indicates that the ideas of cosmogony and cosmology described above are neither provincial nor sectarian in nature; on the other hand they represent the general ideas infiltrated in the mind of the masses.

The cosmogonical ideas and description found in the literature of some other vernaculars of India also bear striking resemblance to those found in Bengali. The cosmogonical descriptions found in the Vaiṣṇava literature of Orissa of the sixteenth century are almost the same as found in the Dharma-maṅgala literature of Bengal. As the point has been discussed and demonstrated in the work *Modern Buddhism and its Followers in Orissa* by N. N. Bose, we need not repeat it here.

The description of the primordial nihil and of the absolute Lord existing all alone in the void is also found in the poems

[1] C. U. Vol. II, pp. 441-444.

[2] *Vide Āgama Grantha* (edited by Mr. M. M. Bose, C. U.). *Cf.* also the Vaiṣṇava text *Goloka-saṁhitā*, *vide* B.S.P.P., B. S., 1309.

[3] Edited by Dr. S. N. Sen, M.A., Ph.D., D.Lit., and published by the University of Calcutta.

of the Santa poets of Hindi literature. Thus Kabīr says,—

When there was no air, and no water,
then who created the universe?
Then was no bud, no flower,
then no womb and no generation.
Then was no learning, no Veda,
then no word, no taste.
Then was no body, no dweller,
no regions below, no earth, no sky, no heaven.
Then was no Guru, no chela, no fathomable and unfathomable,
no worship of Sagun and Nirgun, no two paths.[1]

The creation is due to the activities of Nirañjana, and in the beginning he alone was, and there was nothing else.[2]

In the *Ād-maṅgal* of Kabīr and in his *Ramaiṇīs* we find that in the beginning was the Almighty One (*Samaratha*)—and there was no second to the Lord. There first came consciousness within himself and then proceeded the desire for creation, and six Brahmās were created. The six failed in their task of creation and a seventh was produced by the Lord—and his name was Nirañjana. Nirañjana wanted a *bīja-kheta* (a field to sow in) for procreation and the Lord created a woman for him and the woman had to be the wife of Nirañjana against her will. This woman is none but *Māyā*. Through the union of Nirañjana and *Māyā* three sons of the nature of the three *guṇas* were born, they were Brahmā, Viṣṇu and Maheśvara.[3]

Dādū also says that Nirañjana is never associated with anything else;—water and earth, the static and the dynamic—the earth and the sky, the sun and the moon, water and air, day and night, heat and cold, hunger and thirst—nothing can touch him—nothing can be associated with him.[4]

Sundar-dās also says that in the beginning Nirañjana made out of his own self the five principles (*pañca-tattva*)

[1] *Vide The Bijak of Kabir*, Ahmad Shah, p. 55(7).

[2] *Kabīr-granthāvalī*, edited by Śyāmsundar Dās, p. 162, Padāvalī, 219. *Cf.* also, *Ramaiṇī*, No. 6, *Bījak Kabīr-dās*, Riwām edition.

[3] *See Ād-maṅgal*, *Bījak Kabīr-dās*, Riwām edition; also *The Bijak of Kabir*, by Rev. Ahmad Shah, pp. 41-43. *Cf.* also: *Ramaiṇī* No. 1, Riwām edition; also *Ramaiṇīs*, No. 2, 3.

[4] *Vide Anthology of Dādū*, edited by Mr. K. Sen, p. 590.

of the material elements and also the three *guṇas*. From *rajas* was Brahmā, from *sattva* was Viṣṇu and from *tamas* was Śaṅkara, and the three gods had Satya-loka. Vaikuṇṭha and Kailāsa as their respective abode. Three goddesses, *viz*., Brahmāṇī, Ṭhākurāṇī and Bhavānī were then associated with them. From the triad, in association with their Śaktis, proceeded the universe with all its diversities.[1] As it appears from the glimpses that are found in his works, Tulsī-dās also had a cognate cosmogonical view. The cosmos is produced from the *Māyā* of the Lord and the *Māyā* is conceived as the Ādi-śakti.[2]

(ii) Analysis of the ideas of Cosmogony and Cosmology found in the Vernacular Literature

Let us now proceed with the task of analysing and examining the accounts found in the vernaculars and let us also see how far the ideas can be traced back to older theories, legends and myths. There is a marked tendency among some scholars to hold that the cosmogonical and the cosmological views discussed above are Buddhistic in origin. If we proceed on in a critical way we shall see that there is no distinctive nature of the views found in the vernaculars. As we have said, here there is but a popular and confused mixture of the cosmogonical and cosmological ideas found in the Vedic literature, in the Upaniṣads, the Sāṁkhya system, in the Purāṇic literature, in the Hindu Tantras and in the later phase of Mahāyāna Buddhism mainly expressed through the various Buddhist Tantras. Yet, if any character is to be given to them, it will be more correct to say that they are essentially Hindu; and even the Buddhistic elements are introduced in their Hinduised form.

[1] See the chapter on *Guṇa Utpatti Nisāṁnī—Sundar-granthāvalī*, edited by Purohita Harinārāyaṇa Śarmā, pp. 205-207.
Also *Cf*. the chapter on *Rāmāṣṭaka*, *Ibid*, pp. 159-161.

[2] *ādi-śakti jehi jag upajāyā* | *sou avatarihi mori yaha māyā* ||
Rāma-carita-mānasa, *Bāla-kāṇḍa*.
mana māyā-sambhava parivārā | *jīv carā-car bibidha prakārā* ||
Ibid, *Laṅkā-kāṇḍa*.
sunu rāvaṇ brahmāṇḍa-nikāyā || *pāi jāsu bal biracati māyā* ||
jā ke bal biraṁci hari īsā | *pālata sṛjata harata dasa-sīsā* ||
Sundara-kāṇḍa. Nāgari-pracāriṇī edition.

(A) The Primordial Nihil

Among the various accounts given in the vernaculars the first point to note is that in the beginning there was nothing, and the ultimate Being was floating as the Formless One in the infinite vacuum. The whole universe was then created by him from nothing. Or we shall find that there was the primordial darkness and water and the Lord was there in his formless existence. This idea is, however, to be met with first in the *Ṛg-veda*. There we find,—

"At that time there was neither the aught, nor the naught, neither the earth nor heaven above. What was there to cover all? Wherein was the abode of all? Was there water deep and fathomless?

"No death was then, nor immortality, no distinction between day and night. The One alone breathed without any air,—nothing existed other than that One.

"In the beginning there was darkness shrouded in darkness, indistinct was all—and water was everywhere. The All-pervading One was covered with all the non-existent, and through the *Tapas* or the divine effort arose the 'One'."[1]

The same idea is variously described in the Upaniṣadic literature. In the *Śvetāśvataropaniṣat* we find, "When there was neither darkness, nor day, nor night,—neither the existent nor the non-existent—there was only the All-good One (Śiva); He was changeless, He was the Adorable, He was the creator,—and from Him proceeded eternal enlightenment."[2] In the *Taittiriyopaniṣat* it is said that the non-existent (*Asat*) was in the beginning and from the *Asat* arose the *Sat* and the *Sat* produced its own self by itself.[3] The *Aitareyopaniṣat* says that in the beginning was the self (*Ātmā*) alone and nothing else; it observed itself (*tad aikṣata*) and the beings were produced thereby. Again we find that in the beginning was the *Asat* alone, and from the *Asat* arose the *Sat* and the *Sat* was one and without a second

[1] (10. 129. 1-3). *Cf.*, also,—*devānāṁ yuge prathame'sataḥ sad ajāyata* I (10.72.3).

[2] *yadā tamas tan na divā na rātrir na san na cāsac chiva eva kevalaḥ* I
tadakṣaraṁ tat savitur vareṇyaṁ prajñā ca tasmāt prasṛtā purāṇī I (4.18).

[3] (2.7).

in the beginning. The *Sat* desired that it would be many and energy (*tejas*) arose from it; from *tejas* was water (*āp*) and from *āp* was produced gross matter (*anna*).[1] The *Bṛhad-āraṇyaka* says that the Brahman was alone in the beginning and from Him arose all gods and the universe in all its varieties.[2] Again it is sometimes said that water alone was in the beginning,—from water arose *Satya*, from *Satya* arose the Brahman, from the Brahman Prajāpati (the lord or the creator of the beings) and from the Prajāpati were the gods.[3] Again we find that water was in the beginning and therein was born Prajāpati in the lotus-leaf. He desired to create the universe and the universe gradually proceeded from his desire.[4] The conception of the primordial water is as old as the Vedas[5] and is very popular so far as the Purāṇic literature of India is concerned. A very popular conception found in the Purāṇic literature (and the conception is very old indeed) is that the Supreme Lord was floating in the primordial water and hence is the name *Nārāyaṇa* for him.[6] In later Vaiṣṇava literature we frequently find the Lord sleeping on the surface of the sea. This primordial water has often been philosophised as the water of original cause-potency (*kāraṇa-vāri*). With the account given by Māṇik Datta in his *Caṇḍī-maṅgala* that the Lord was floating on the surface of the primordial water with a lotus-leaf as his support, we may compare the following account given in the *Śukla-yajur-veda*,—"In the beginning was water and only water; and Prajāpati transformed him into air and accepted a Puṣkara-leaf as his support; but he was tossing and tossing etc."[7] As for the account given in many of the Maṅgala-kāvyas that the Lord brought to the surface of water the earth, submerged in water, in

1 *Chāndogya*—(6.2).

2 (4.10-11). *Cf.* also *Nārāyaṇopaniṣat*, (1.1).

3 *Bṛhad-āraṇyaka*, (5.5.1).

4 *Taittirīya Brāhmaṇa*, (1.1.3), *Taittirīya Saṁhitā*, (7.1.5), *Bṛhad-jābālopaniṣat*, (1.1.).

5 *yad devā adaḥ salile susaṁraddhā atiṣṭhata* 1
Ṛg-veda, (10.72.6). *Cf.* also *Ibid*, (10.82.1, 5-6), (10.121.7), (10.190. 1-3); also *infra*, p. 377.

6 *Cf. āpo nārā iti proktā āpo vai nara-sūnavaḥ* 1
tā yad asyāyanaṁ pūrvaṁ tena nārāyaṇaḥ smṛtaḥ || *Manu-saṁhitā*, (1.10).
The same verse occurs in many Purāṇic texts.

7 (5.5.6.4), (5.5.7.5).

the form of a boar, we may refer to the similar description found in the *Śukla-yajur-veda*.[1]

(B) The Conception of Nirañjana—a replica of Prajāpati Brahmā

In the next place we find that the Supreme Being in his state of the Absolute is not the creator of the universe. He produced Dharma or Nirañjana, from whom proceeded the universe, and all the vernacular poets are unanimous on the point. This idea also has its origin in the Vedic and the Upaniṣadic literature. The absolute reality in its unqualified qualitiless form is not the creator of the universe, for the Absolute is neither the Ens, nor the non-Ens,—neither existent, nor non-existent. The creator of the universe is, however, Prajāpati, or Brahmā or the Viśva-karmā as he has variously been conceived in the Vedic and Upaniṣadic literature. This Prajāpati or Brahmā, though often described as the most supreme of all the gods, the god of the gods, is never the same as the Absolute Brahman. In the Vedic literature we find that the vast universal process could not be explained with reference to the well-known gods; there was, therefore, naturally the tendency to conceive of a greater god, who represents no particular aspect or force of nature, but an unified conception representing something like the totality of the forces acting behind the universal process. He is the *Hiraṇya-garbha*—the first radiant manifestation of the Supreme Unmanifest,—as the personification of the creative impulse and the creative force of the Unmanifest. It is said in the *Ṛg-veda* (10.121) that the *Hiraṇya-garbha* arose in the beginning; he as the lord of all the existent; he was the lord of the earth and the sky and he vested all creatures with life and breath; the gods do not dare disobey him, he is the god of the gods. In the Brāhmaṇas, Āraṇyakas and the Upaniṣads we find ample references to this Prajāpati Brahmā, also spoken of as the *Hiraṇya-garbha*, who was the first created,—the first being,—the first born of all the gods. In the Brāhmaṇas and the Upaniṣads we always find Prajāpati Brahmā performing

[1] (7.7. 1.5).

penance for the purpose of creation. Sometimes it is said that Brahmā was born in the primordial water. The eptihet *Hiraṇya-garbha*, applied to Brahmā, points to the fact that he was born of a golden egg supposed to have been formed out of the seed deposited in the water when they were produced as the first creation of the Supreme Lord. In the *Śatapatha-brāhmaṇa* (XI. I, 6. 1-11) we find that Prajāpati was born of a golden egg, which was produced by primordial water through penance. Thus it is said,—"In the beginning there existed here nothing but water, a sea of water. These water desired to propagate their kind. They tortured themselves, they mortified themselves. And when they had mortified themselves a golden egg originated in them. The year did not yet exist at that time; but as long as the duration of a year, this golden egg swam about. After a year a man arose out of it; that was Prajāpati."[1] In the *Chāndogya-upaniṣat* it is said that in the beginning was the *Asat*; from the *Asat* there was the *Sat* and from the *Sat* originated an egg. After one year the egg split up into two and from the golden protion was created the region above and from the silver portion the earth below.[2] We find somewhat detailed description of this *Hiraṇya-garbha* Brahmā also in the *Manu-saṁhitā*. There it is said that once this universe was shrouded in darkness and everything was imperceptible, indistinct—beyond all understanding and all kinds of intellectual comprehension—as if in deep sleep. Then the Self-existent Unmanifest Lord, with an impulse towards creation, manifested Himself in His radiant form, and that Incomprehensible All-pervading One created Himself in a form. With a view to create various kinds of beings from His own body He first created water and deposited His seed in it. The seed in the water transformed itself into a resplendent egg, from which was born Brahmā, the grand-father of all the worlds (*sarva-loka-pitāmaha*). The first person, created by the unmanifest cause-potency, which is eternal and is of the nature of both

1 *A History of Indian Literature*, by Winternitz, p. 223.
2 *Chāndogya*—(3.19).

Ens and non-Ens, is called Brahmā.[1] Brahmā lived in that egg for full one year and after that broke it into two parts through the force of meditation; with the upper part of the egg he made heaven and with the lower part he made the earth, and in between the two regions was created the sky and the eight quarters, etc. Then follows the creation from Brahmā, which of course, was in the line of the Sāṁkhya cosmology.[2] In the vernaculars we find occasional references to this egg; and from what is discussed above about the nature and function of Prajāpati Brahmā, it will be very clear to see that the conception of Nirañjana, as we find variously described in the vernacular literatures, is nothing but a very popular representation of the older conception of Prajāpati Brahmā.

We think, it will not be far wide of the mark to recall in this connection the Vedāntic conception of the two aspects of the ultimate reality or the Brahman, the unqualified inactive absolute aspect, which can only be negatively described; the other aspect is the qualified active aspect which has been described as the *Īśvara*. The Absolute is in no way related to this illusory world; it is the *Īśvara*, as associated with *Māyā* (nescience), that is responsible for the creation of this illusory world.

(C) The Primordial Goddess

The next point to notice is that lord Nirañjana, who personified the creative impulse of the Absolute, desired to create the universe and from the desire emanated the primordial goddess, who is called Ādyā or Ādyā-śakti or Prakṛti or simply the Devī. This also is a very well-known theory absorbing in it many traditions derived from various sources. Already in the *Bṛhad-āraṇyakopaniṣat* we find that in the beginning was the *Ātman* and it became self-conscious and from its self-consciousness proceeded 'Egohood'—(*ahaṁ-nāmā'bhavat*). It never enjoyed, and as it was not possible to enjoy all alone it longed for a companion; it then divided

[1] *yat tat kāraṇam avyaktam nityaṁ sad-asad-ātmakam* I
tad-visṛṣṭaḥ sa puruṣo loke brahm'eti kīrtyate I
Manu-saṁhitā, (1.11).

[2] *Vide Manu-saṁhitā*, Chapter I.

its own self into two as the male and the female, or as the husband and the wife, and from their union proceeded the creation.[1] In another place of the same text we find that the *Ātman* was alone in the beginning. Desirous of issues the *Ātman* wished to have a wife.[2] These two aspects of the Brahman as the male and the female have been variously conceived in the Upaniṣads. Here (in the *Bṛhad-āraṇyaka*), for instance, the mind is said to be the self (*ātmā*), speech the wife (*vāg jāyā*) and life (*prāṇa*) is the issue. In the *Praśnopaniṣat* we find that Prajāpati, desirous of progeny, had recourse to penance and produced the couple (*mithuna*) and the couple consisted of *Rayi* (matter) and *Prāṇa* (the vital force),—the Sun is the *Prāṇa* and the moon is the *Rayi*.[3] In the *Bahvṛcopaniṣat* (which, however, is undoubtedly a text of much later time) it is said that in the beginning was the Goddess (Devī); she created the egg of the world,—and from her were born the gods like Brahmā, Viṣṇu and Śiva.

Though, however, the theory of the female counterpart of the original Lord in connection with cosmogony may be traced back even to the days of the Upaniṣads, this idea, as found in the Purāṇic literature as also in the vernacular literature, seems to have been influenced more by popular Sāṁkhya ideas. Notwithstanding the controversies of the philosophers as to the exact nature of Puruṣa and Prakṛti and the exact relation between them, the general view is that the whole creation proceeds from Prakṛti (or the primordial cosmic substance) in contact with Puruṣa, who is the unchanging principle of pure consciousness. Though some schools of Sāṁkhya hold that creation proceeds from the spontaneous disturbance in the equilibrium of the three qualities in Prakṛti, the more general view is that the creative impulse is supplied to Prakṛti by Puruṣa through his contact just as active power is supplied to inactive iron by magnet through its contact (*sānnidhya*). Through the association or the contact of Puruṣa with Prakṛti the character of the one is infused in the other and the creative process

[1] *Bṛhad-āraṇyaka* (1.4.1-3).
[2] *Ibid* (1.4.17).
[3] *Praśnopaniṣat*, (1.4-5).

follows as a result of the process of infusion. From this philosophical idea of the association of Puruṣa and Prakṛti and the infusion of the character of the one into the other in the process of creation has followed the popular tendency to conceive of Puruṣa as the male and of Prakṛti as the female and of their contact as their union, through which proceeds the visible world. It may be remarked that philosophers also have sometimes taken the analogy of the male and the female in explaining the nature of and the relation between Puruṣa and Prakṛti.

The cosmic process, however, proceeds from Prakṛti. Prakṛti is constituted by nature of three qualities (*guṇa*), *viz.*, *sattva* or the intelligence-stuff, *rajas* or energy and *tamas* or inertia. So long as there is the equilibrium of the three *guṇas* in Prakṛti there is no cosmic process;—the cosmic process follows from the distrubance in the nature of Prakṛti. From the disturbance in Prakṛti first follows the principle of *Mahat* or *Buddhi*, which is "the last limit up to which the subjective and the objective can be assimilated as one indistinguishable point which is neither the one nor the other, but which is the sources of them."[1] From *Mahat* follows the principle of 'egohood' (*ahaṅkāra*), which in its turn generates the eleven senses on the one hand and the five *Tanmātrās* (*i.e.*, the five potentials of the five gross elements) on the other. From these five *Tanmātrās* again follow the five gross elements of earth, water, fire, air and ether. These principles of Puruṣa, Prakṛti, *Mahat*, *Ahaṅkāra*, the eleven senses, the five *Tanmātrās* and the five gross elements taken togeter constitute the twenty-five *Tattvas* or principles of Sāṁkhya metaphysics.

The *Gītā*, the most popular religio-philosophical literature of India, echoes the Sāṁkhya view of cosmology in a rather popular and synthetic way. There we find the idea of the Absolute (which is known as the *Puruṣottama*), which approximates the unqualified Brahman of the Vedānta;[2] but in the active and qualified aspect (*i.e.*, as the *Bhagavān*) He causes Prakṛti to bear the whole universe.[3] Puruṣa and

[1] *The study of Patañjali*, by Dr. S. N. Das Gupta, p. 51.
[2] *Vide Gītā*, (15. 16-18).
[3] *mayā'dhyakṣeṇa prakṛtiḥ sūyate sacarācaram* l
hetunā'nena kaunteya jagad viparivartate l *Gītā* (9.10).

Prakṛti are frequently called in the *Gītā* as the *Kṣetrajña* (literally, the knower of the field) and the *Kṣetra* (the field), and everything, whatsoever, is created through the union of the *Kṣetrajña* and the *Kṣetra*.[1] Puruṣa and Prakṛti are conceived here just as the original male and the female or the father and the mother.[2] This idea of Puruṣa and Prakṛti as the primordial male and the female (or the father and the mother) is to be found in almost all religious systems and literature of India. The same idea of the god and the godeess is to be met with in the Vaiṣṇava literature, in the Śaiva literature and in the Tantras.

In the Purāṇic literature we find but a hotch-potch of the Upaniṣadic and Sāṁkhya ideas with further modification and innovation. Here we generally find a glimpse of the Upaniṣadic idea of the Absolute and then the first manifestation of the Unmanifest in the form of an active personal god with or without the legend of the egg associated with his origin. Then follows Prakṛti from the creative impulse of the Lord as his Śakti (power), and through this introduction of Prakṛti the Sāṁkhya theory becomes interwoven with the ancient legends. The Sāṁkhya theory generally ends with the origination of the gross matter; for the propagation of the human race these Purāṇas generally follow the accounts given in the *Manu-saṁhitā*. On some of the accounts the Tāntric line of thought (which we shall presently discuss) had palpable influence.[3]

The Sāṁkhya idea of Puruṣa and Prakṛti was inherited by the vernaculars through the medium of the Purāṇas in a more anomalous form. The primordial goddess, originating from the sweat, or the smile of lord Dharma (or Nirāñjana,

[1] *yāvat sañjāyate kiñcit sattvaṁ sthāvara-jaṅgamam* |
kṣetra-kṣetrajña-saṁyogāt tad viddhi bharatarṣabha ||
Ibid, (13.27).

[2] *Cf. mama yonir mahad brahma tasmin garbbhaṁ dadhāmyaham* |
sambhavaḥ sarva-bhūtānāṁ tato bhavati bhārata ||
sarva-yoniṣu kaunteya mūrtayaḥ sambhavanti yāḥ |
tāsāṁ brahma mahad-yonir ahaṁ bīja-pradaḥ pitā ||

[3] For specimens of discussions on cosmogony and cosmology in the Purāṇic and such other popular literatures see *Bhāgavata-purāṇa* (3.5. 23-38); *Garuḍa-purāṇa* (*Pūrva-khaṇḍa*, Ch. IV); *Padma-purāṇa* (*Sṛṣṭi khaṇḍa*, Ch. II); *Padma-purāṇa* (*Kriyā-yoga-sāra*, Ch. II); *Brahma-vaivarta-purāṇa* (*Brahma-khaṇḍa*, Ch. III); *Śiva-purāṇa* (*Jñāna-saṁhitā*, Chs. V and VI); *Sanat-kumāra-saṁhitā*, Ch. III, *Vāyavīya-saṁhitā*, Ch. VIII; *Khila-harivaṁśa* (Ch. I, verses 21 *et seq.*); *Devī-purāṇa*, (Ch. AXIX), etc.

or the Ādi-deva) has frequently been styled as Prakṛti,[1] and the idea of Prakṛti brought with it the ideas of the *guṇas*, which were transformed and personified as the triad. We have seen that through the union of lord Nirañjana and the Prakṛti (who is depicted as a very beautiful woman) were produced three sons, Brahmā, Viṣṇu and Śiva of the nature of the three *guṇas*, *viz.*, *sattva*, *rajas* and *tamas*; and these three sons were then entrusted with the charge of the creation of the world. This, however, represents the general and popular Sāṁkhya view of the contact of Puruṣa with Prakṛti and the creation of the world through the activities of the three qualities of Prakṛti. We have seen that according to the version given in the *Dharmāyaṇa* of Narasiṁha Vasu the son born to Prakṛti by Nirañjana was *Mahat*, and from *Mahat* originated *Ahaṁkāra* and the three *guṇas*. In the version, found in the *Caṇḍī-maṅgala* of Mukunda-rāma also we find that through the infusion of the energy of the Lord in Prakṛti a son of the name of *Mahat* was born to them, the son of *Mahat* was *Ahaṁkāra*, who again had five sons who represent the five gross elements.

It is to be noted that the primordial goddess had emanated from the Lord. The Lord and the goddess have then been conceived in the vernaculars as the Ādi-deva and the Ādi-devī. Sometimes they have been conceived as the Ādi and the Anādi; the Lord is the beginningless eternal One; while the Goddess, emanating from the body of the Lord, is the produced one. The creation, however, proceeds from the Ādi-devī, and the Ādi-deva returns to his meditation after the goddess has been created. In this theory of the Ādi-deva and the Ādi-devī the vernaculars seem to have been more influenced by the Śaiva and Śākta ideas (as they are found in the Śaiva and Śākta texts and in the Tantras in general) than by the Sāṁkhya theory of Puruṣa and Prakṛti. We have already pointed out that though in a popular way Puruṣa and Prakṛti of the Sāṁkhya system have somehow been related together in the process of cosmic evolution, metaphysically they are two distinct and self-

[1] It should be noted in this connection that the word Prakṛti in classical Sanskrit literature as well as in the Purāṇic literature became frankly synoymous with the word Śakti or Ādi-devi, the primordial gooddess.

sufficient realities and it is because of the distinct nature of Puruṣa and Prakṛti that various controversies have arisen as to the exact nature of the relation. In the Tantras and other Śaiva and Śākta literatures the primordial god and the primordial goddess, or Śiva and Śakti, as they are commonly called, are not two distinct ultimate realities; they represent two aspects of the absolute reality and sometimes Śakti is conceived as contained in Śiva as his kinetic energy. The absolute truth is a union of Śiva and Śakti. Śiva represents pure consciousness which is inactive—the static aspect of the ultimate reality;—while Śakti represents the world-force—the dynamic aspect of the ultimate reality; Śiva is *Nivṛtti* (state of rest) and Śakti is *Pravṛtti* (the state of activity) and in the ultimate state they remain in a union of oneness. This is the principle of non-duality (*advaya*) which is explained in the Tāntric texts under the imagery of *maithuna* (conjugal intercourse) or *Kāma-kalā* (as it is called in the texts *Kāma-kalā-vilāsa*, *Devī-upaniṣat* and such other texts).[1] In the *Kāma-kalā-vilāsa* we find that Śiva or Maheśa is pure illumination (*prakāśa-mātra-tanu*) or the abstract self-shining thought with all the principles of activity contracted within it (*antar-līna-vimarśaḥ*); Śakti is the principle of activity or the inherent activity of thought (*vimarṣa or kriyā-śakti*) and she contains in her the seed of the future world (*bhāvi-carācara-bījam*). Śiva, however, realises himself through Śakti, and, therefore, it is said that Śakti is the clear looking-glass in which the form and beauty of Śiva is reflected. The philosophical implication is that pure abstract thought cannot realise its own nature unless it comes back to itself through its own activity, and when thus it returns to itself through *vimarśa*, it becomes 'egohood' or *ahaṁkāra*, which is called "the mass produced through the union of Śiva and Śakti" (*śiva-śakti-mithunapiṇḍa*).[2] In the gross sense this Śiva is the white-matter (*sita-bindu*) or seed or semen, while Śakti is the red-matter (*śoṇa-bindu*), and I-ness or egohood is the son born to them. This conception of Śiva and Śakti has also

[1] *Vide supra*, p. 30.
[2] *Kāma-kalā-vilāsa* (Kasmir Series Texts and Studies, No. XII), Verse No. 5.

been interpreted as matter and energy, which are the two essential component parts of all entity. In everything that exists there must be two things,—that which exists and the power or energy by virtue of which it exists or acts; this matter that exists is the Śiva and the energy of existence is Śakti[1] and there is an inseparable relation between them, the one cannot be without the other. Śiva without Śakti is absolutely helpless in doing anything whatsoever,—he himself cannot even vibrate without the help of Śakti.[2] It is Śakti who creates the universe and preserves it and again destroys it at her own will.[3] It is to be noted that sometimes Śiva has been conceived as the absolute, Śakti with the seed of all manifestation and creation is contained in the very nature of Śiva. Though in many places we find that the one absolute truth divides itself into two aspects as Śiva and Śakti and manifests itself in the world-process and realises itself through it, yet inother places we find that Śiva manifests his power in the form of Śakti only for the purpose of self-realisation,—for, the universal abstract thought-principle cannot realise its ownself without the conscious activities in the form of the world-process.[4] But whether Śakti be contained in the nature of Śiva, or, Śiva and Śakti be the two aspects of the absolute reality, Śakti is directly responsible for the creation of the visible world—either as the energy (*i.e.*, the world-force), or as the principle of illusion (*māyā*) as she is known in the popular Vedāntic line of thought. It is because of

1 *yasya yasya padārthasya yā yā śaktir uditā* |
sā tu sarveśvarī devī sa tu sarvo maheśvaraḥ ||
—*Vāmakeśvara-tantra*, (7/31).

2 *śivaḥ śaktyā yukto yadi bhavati śaktaḥ prabhavitum*
na ced evaṁ devo na khalu kuśalaḥ spanditum api ||
—*Ānanda-laharī* or *Saundarya-laharī*, I, ascribed to Śaṅkarācārya.

Cf. also

sā devī paramā devī śivābhinnā śivaṅkarī |
śivābhinnā tayā hīnaḥ śivo'pi hi nirarthakaḥ ||
Sūta-saṁhitā.

paro hi śakti-rahitaḥ śaktaḥ kārtuṁ na kincaṅa |
śaktas tu parameśānī śaktyā yukto yadā bhavet ||
Vāmakeśvara-tantra. (4-6).

3 *śaktiḥ karoti brahmāṇḍaṁ sā vai pālayate'khilam* |
icchayā saṁharatyeṣā jagad etac carā-caram ||
Devī-bhāgavata.

4 On the nature of and the relation between Śiva and Śakti see *Tantra-tattva* (in Bengali) by Śiva-candra Vidyārṇava Bhaṭṭācārya, Part I, the chapter on the philosophy of Śakti (*Śakti-tattva*), pp. 225 *et seq.*

this that we find in the vernaculars that before the actual cosmological process begins the original goddess comes out of the body of the Lord and herself creates the whole universe. The emanation of the Śakti in the form of a woman from the body of the Lord is to be frequently met with in the Purāṇic and Tāntric texts, and there is no doubt that this idea was received by all the vernacular poets through the Purāṇas and the Tantras. But the oldest basis of the tradition is to be found in the *Ṛg-veda* where it is said that the Father became desirous of meeting his own youthful Daughter and had sex-intercourse with her.[1] Sāyaṇa explains the Father as Prajāpati and the Daughter as Uṣā (Dawn). There is an echo of this fact of the Father meeting the Daughter also in the *Aitareya Brāhmaṇa*,[2] *Tāṇḍya-mahā-brāhmaṇa*[3] and the *Śatapatha-brāhmaṇa*.[4]

The three *guṇas* of Prakṛti as conceived in the Sāṁkhya system were ascribed to Śakti in the Tāntric and Purāṇic texts, and we frequently find that the triad, *viz.*, Brahmā, Viṣṇu and Śiva, who are put in the charge of creation, preservation and destruction, are the three sons of the original Śakti; and they are of the nature of the three *guṇas*, *viz.*, *sattva*, *rajas* and *tamas*. In the *Mahā-bhāgavata* we find that in the beginning the universe was without the sun and the moon; there was neither the day nor the night, nor fire nor the directions,—the whole universe was without touch, sight and sound, etc., and it was bereft of all the luminaries. At that time there was only Prakṛti as the supreme reality. When there was the desire for creation in her, she, though formless, assumed the form of a goddess and at once created a personality with the three *guṇas* she had within her; but the person (*Puruṣa*) was without consciousness. She then infused her own creative impulse in that Puruṣa and the Puruṣa thus endowed with power created three personalities of the name of Brahmā, Viṣṇu and Śiva, who were of the nature of the three *guṇas*.[5] The

1 (10.61.5-7). 2 (3.33). 3 (8.2.10). 4 (1.6.2.1.)

5 *brahmādyāḥ puruṣās trayo nija-guṇais tat-svecchayā kalpitāḥ* I
Mahā-bhāgavata, quoted in the *Tantra-tattva*, Part I, p. 235.

Also—*tataḥ sā svecchayā svīyai rajaḥ-sattva-tamo-guṇaiḥ* I
sasarja puruṣaṁ sadyaś caitanya-parivarjitam ||
taṁ jātaṁ puruṣaṁ vīkṣya sattvā-di-tri-guṇātmakam I
sisṛkṣāṁ ātmanas tasmin samākrāmayad icchayā ||

idea of the Śaktis, emanating from the original Śakti and being united with the triad for the purpose of creation, is also found in these Tantras.[1] In the Śaiva and the Śākta Tantras we find that the original Śakti has three qualities in her, *viz.*, *Icchā* (*i.e.*, the volitional nature), *Jñāna* (*i.e.*, the cognitive nature), and *Kriyā* (*i.e.*, active nature). In the *Gorakṣa-saṁhitā* these *Icchā*, *Jñāna* and *Kriyā* are spoken of as the three goddesses, *viz.*, *Gaurī*, *Brāhmī* and *Vaiṣṇavī*, who are contained in the nature of *Praṇava*.[2] Again it is said in this connection that with the three component parts of *Praṇava* (*i.e.*, *a*, *u*, and *m*) are associated the three *guṇas* and the triad.[3] The triad and the three Śaktis being thus associated with the *Praṇava* could very easily get associated with one another,—and it is for this reason that in the vernacular texts we find the three Śaktis, *viz.*, *Gaurī* (or *Rudrāṇī*), *Brāhmī* (or *Brahmāṇī*) and *Vaiṣṇavī* (who represent respectively the three aspect of the original Śakti, *viz.*, *Icchā*, *Jñāna* and *Kriyā*) are generally associated with the triad Śiva, Brahmā and Viṣṇu as their female counterparts. There is also reference to the penance of the triad to propitiate the original Śakti,[4] and also to the fact that by this austere penances Śambhu could obtain the goddess as his wife;[5] and we think that these traditions with much poetic innovations, additions and alterations have found place in the cosmogonical traditions of the vernaculars. The story of the god's or goddess's assuming the form of a corpse to test the triad does not, however, seem to be very old—but as we have seen, the tradition of the penance of the triad seems to have some older basis behind it,—and it seems that the tradition of the penance of the triad with

tataḥ sa śaktimān sraṣṭā puruṣa-trayaṁ guṇa-trayaiḥ ।
trayo-babhūvuḥ puruṣā brahmā-viṣṇu-śivāhvayāḥ ॥
Mahā-bhāgavata Ch. I, verses 51-53. (Quoted in the *Tantra-tattva*).

1 *Cf. Ibid*, Ch. I, verses 55-56; Ch. II, verse 23.

2 *icchā-jñāna-kriyā śaktir gaurī brāhmī'ti vaiṣṇavī* ।
tridhā-śaktiḥ sthitā yata tat-paraṁ jyotir omiti ॥ *Gorakṣa-saṁhitā*, (5.3).

3 *Ibid*, (5.4).

4 *yāṁ ārādhya viriñcir asya jagataḥ sraṣṭā hariḥ pālakaḥ* ।
saṁhartā giriśaḥ svayaṁ samabhavad dhyeyā ca yā yogibhiḥ ॥
Mahā-bhāgavata, (1.1).

5 *yā svecchayā'sya jagataḥ pravidhāya sṛṣṭiṁ*
samprāpya janma ca tathā patiṁ āpa śambhuṁ ।
ugrais tapobhir api yāṁ samavāpya patnīṁ
śambhuḥ padaṁ hṛdi dadhe paripātu sā vaḥ ॥ *Ibid*, (1.2).

the mixture of popular poetic imagination has obtained its full-fledged form in the story of the test of the triad. In the *Bṛhad-dharma-purāṇa*,[1] however, we find a detailed account of the story of the test of the triad; but the text has rightly been suspected by scholars to be of much later origin and as such the story might have been borrowed in its full-fledged form from the accounts given in the vernaculars.

(iii) *Buddhist Element in the accounts of the Cosmogony and Cosmology of the Vernaculars*

It will appear from what is discussed above that the accounts of cosmogony and cosmology given in the vernaculars are based fundamentally on the Hindu ideas, philosophical, theological, mythological and traditional. Yet we should notice that the later Buddhistic ideas of cosmogony and cosmology have also got mixed up with the Hindu ideas and legends in the accounts given in the vernaculars. But we beg to remind that the popular Buddhistic cosmogonical ideas, found mainly in the Buddhist Tantras and in the Nepalese Buddhistic traditions, are nothing but popular adoption of various Hindu ideas under a Buddhistic garb. In the whole field of Mahāyānic thought we find an inherent tendency of compromise with the Hindu thoughts and ideas,—the ideas of cosmogony and cosmology also seem to have evolved gradually on the Hindu line.

We have seen that in Vijñāna-vāda Buddhism Śūnyatā was conceived as something like the ultimate substance or the primordial element, from which evolves the visible world. This idea of Śūnyatā, we have said before, was inherited by the later vernacular poets, not as any philosophical concept, but merely as a popular idea floating in the air. It is therefore that we see in the descriptions of the vernaculars that the primordial divinity, who is responsible for the creation of the universe, was himself void by nature. He was moving in the void and the Lord of the void created the universe out of the great void. Again we have seen[2] that the conception of Dharma as described in the verna-

[1] Edited by H. P. Śāstri, Bibliotheca Indica, New Series, No. 668.
[2] *Vide supra*, Ch. XI.

culars reminds one at some places of the Mahāyānic conception of the Dharma-kāya of Buddha which is the 'thatness' underlying all phenomena. Dharma-kāya is the cosmic oneness from which proceeds the diversity of the cosmic process. In the descriptions of the vernaculars we find that the cosmic process emanates from Dharma. In this idea also some influence of the Mahāyānic conception of Dharma-kāya with all its cosmological implications may plausibly be postulated.

From the mythological point of view we find it described in the *Kāraṇḍa-vyūha* that being desirous of creating the universe the original lord (Ādi-buddha) first created the Bodhisattva Avalokiteśvara; from the eyes of Avalokiteśvara originated the sun and the moon, Maheśvara from his forehead Brahmā and others from the two shoulders, Nārāyaṇa from his heart, Sarasvatī from the teeth, air from the mouth, the earth from the feet, Varuṇa from his udder; from among all these gods Avalokiteśvara selected Maheśvara, whom he predicted to be the creator in the age of Kali under the name of the Ādi-deva.[1] It is needless to say that mythological accounts of this type have nothing Buddhistic in them in the fundamental nature.

The Buddhistic influence on the cosmogony and cosmology of the vernaculars is, however, considerably palpable in the conception of the Ādi-deva and the Ādi-devī, with whom the later Buddhistic conceptions of the Ādi-buddha and the Ādi-deva or the Ādi-prajñā or simply Prajñā has got mixed up. We have seen before that this Ādi-buddha and the Ādi-prajñā are nothing but the transformation of the Mahāyānic idea of Śūnyatā and Karuṇā in the image of Prakṛti and Puruṣa or Śakti and Śiva.[2] To understand the cosmological significance of the conception of the Ādi-deva and the Ādi-devī, we should, therefore, discuss the cosmological significance of Śūnyatā and Karuṇā as it is explained in the Buddhist Tāntric texts.

We have seen that in later Mahāyāna texts, we mean the Buddhist Tantras, Bodhicitta was conceived of as the

[1] *Kāraṇḍa-vyūha* (printed in 1873 in Calcutta by Satyavrata Sāmaśramī in a series of Jaina works), pp. 14-15.
[2] *Supra*, pp. 29 *et seq*.

highest reality of the nature of the ultimate substance from which everything originates. This absolute ultimate substance have two elements in it, *viz.*, Śūnyatā and Karuṇā, or Prajñā and Upāya. Cosmologically Prajñā is pure consciousness and perfect enlightenment, and is the principle of pure passivity; Upāya is the world-force,—it is the dynamic principle, through the activities of which the phenomenal world comes into existence. The metaphysical implication is that Śūnyatā as perfect enlightenment or pure consciousnes is purely inactive; it is the principle of universal compassion that disturbs her and causes waves of mentation in that pure consciousness and these waves of mentation are fundamentally responsible for the existence of the phenomenal world. This principle of Upāya as the dynamic force behind the evolution of the world-process is a means, it is held, for leading all sentient beings to the ultimate goal of perfect purification and liberation; and the idea here seems to be akin to the popular Sāṁkhya view that the activities of Prakṛti are finally aimed at the liberation of Puruṣa. It is clear to see, that this cosmological and ontological significance of Prajñā and Upāya are exactly the same as that of Śiva and Śakti, and, as we have already noticed, the only difference is that pure consciousness, which is absolutely passive by nature and represents the negative aspect of the reality, is conceived as the Lord in the Hindu schools, and it is conceived as the goddess in Buddhism; and whereas the active or the positive element is the goddess according to the Hindu view, it is the Lord according to the Buddhist view. But notwithstanding this difference in notion, Prajñā and Upāya have throughout been drawn in the image of Śiva and Śakti. As in the Hindu Tantras Śiva and Śakti are conceived of sometimes as constituting the two aspects of one absolute reality,—but sometimes again Śiva is in many places depicted as the absolute reality, Śakti being included in his nature;—so also is the case with Prajñā and Upāya,—sometimes they are explained as two aspects of the one reality, and sometimes, Prajñā being the absolute reality, Upāya is said to be included in her nature. In either case the relation between the two is inseparable as is in the case of Śiva and Śakti.

These conceptions of Prajñā and Upāya have important ontological and cosmological bearing on the four schools of Nepalese Buddhism.[1] The Svābhāvika school holds that there is no immaterial ultimate truth in the form of the soul substance; matter is the primordial substance, from which the world proceeds. This matter as the ultimate substance has two modes which are called *Pravṛtti* and *Nivṛtti*, action and rest, dynamic and static, concrete and abstract. Matter is eternal as a crude mass (however infinitely attenuated in in *Nivṛtti*) and so are the powers of matter. The proper state of existence of these powers is the state of *Nivṛtti* or rest as the abstraction from all phenomena. When these powers pass from the state of rest into their causal and transitory state of activity the phenomenal world comes into existence, and it again ceases to exist when the powers repass from *Pravṛtti* to *Nivṛtti*. This *Nivṛtti* is the Prajñā[2] and *Pravṛtti* is the Upāya. We have seen that Prajñā and Upāya are deified as the Ādi-prajñā and the Ādi-buddha, and the visible world is said to be created through their union. Buddha as the principle of active power first proceeds from *Nivṛtti* or Ādi-prajñā and then associates with her and from their union proceeds the actual visible world. The principle is symbolised as Prajñā being first the mother and then the wife of the Buddha. The well-known triad—Buddha, Dharma and Saṅgha—has often been explained, as we have seen, as Upāya (Buddha), Prajñā (Dharma) and the world (Saṅgha) produced through the union. In some of the Nepalese schools of Buddhism Prajñā as Dharma is given the highest prominence in the scheme of the triad and Buddha emanates from Prajñā. In some of the Hindu Tantras also we find that the goddess has been given more prominence than the Lord, the former being conceived as the first principle. In some places, it has been pointed out, the primordial Lord is seen floating in water. What is this water? It is, according to some of the Tantras, Śakti, who is pervading the whole universe in the form of water. This belief influenced the Nepalese Buddhists also, who have

[1] The four schools are:—(*i*) Svābhāvika, (*ii*) Aiśvarika, (*iii*) Kārmika and (*iv*) Yātnika.

[2] *Vide Illustrations of the Literature, etc.*, by Hodgson, p. 149.

often conceived of Ādi-prajñā in the form of primordial water.[1] This Ādi-buddha and Ādi-prajñā or Ādi-devī are the original father and mother of the world.[2] In the *Svayambhu-purāṇa* Prajñā is described as the Śakti of Śiva, as the mother of the three worlds, the void of the voids—the mother of the Buddhas,—the mother of all the gods.[3] Again, all female creatures are said to be the incarnations of Prajñā while all males are the incarnations of Buddha (*Upāya*). Again the Lord symbolises the generative power while the lady symbolises the productive power. The Lord is the seed (*bindu*) and the lady is the ovum (*rajas*),—and from their union proceeds the Bodhicitta, from which everything is born. The Ādi-prajñā or the Ādi-śakti is also spoken of as of the triangular form (*tri-koṇākāra*, which is the symbol of the productive power) as she is described in the Hindu Tantras also.

From the above it will be clear that, in the conception of the Ādi-deva and the Ādi-devī of the vernaculars (or of the Ādi and the Anādi as we find in the Nāth literature), we find a popular mixture of Puruṣa and Prakṛti of the Sāṁkhya system, of Śiva and Śakti as we find in Tāntricism in general, and the Ādi-buddha and the Ādi-prajña of the different schools of later Buddhism. It may cursorily be noticed that in the Taoism of China we find a similar conception of cosmogony, where it is held that the universe proceeds from the primordial parents Tao and Tai or rather from the original male and the female, *yang* and *yin*.

(*iv*) *Similarity of the Descriptions of the Vernaculars with those of other Literatures*

The cosmogonical and cosmological descriptions found in other parts of the world offer points of similarity with the

[1] *Cf. parjñā jalamayā-kārā* | *prajñā strī-liṅgatvāt drava-rūpā tato jalā-kārā* ||
Dharmakoṣa-saṁgraha, MS. p. 5(B).

[2] *Devendra-paripṛcchā-tantra*, quoted in the *Subhāṣita-saṁgraha*, p. 76 (MS). It is interesting to note how Prajñā and Upāya have sometimes been saluted as the mother and the father of the world just in the manner and even in the language in which poet Kālidāsa has saluted Pārvatī and Maheśvara in the first verse of the first canto of the *Raghu-vaṁśa*.

vāgarthāviva sampṛktau jyotsnā-candramasāviva |
jagatām pitarāvādyau prajño-pāyāv-upāsmahe ||
Dharma-koṣa-saṁgraha, MS. p. 10(B).

[3] *Svayambhu-purāṇa*, edited by H. P. Śāstrī (Bibliotheca Indica), pp. 179-180.

descriptions given above. The *Voluspa*, which supplies us with cosmogonic account of the Scandinavian branch of the Teutons, begins as follows:—

"There was, in times of old, where Ymir dwelt,
nor land nor sea, nor gelid waves;
earth existed not, nor heaven above;
there was a chaotic chasm,
and verdure nowhere."[1]

Some Babylonian descriptions also begin in a similar manner; thus:—

"When above unnamed was the heaven,
(And) earth below by a name was uncalled,
Apsu (the deep) in the beginning (ristu) being their together,
(And) the flood (Mammu) of Tiamat the mother of them all,
Their waters were embosomed together (in one place),
But no reed had been harvested, no marsh-plant seen;
At that time the gods had not appeared, any one (of them)
By no name were they called, no destiny (was fixed)."[2]

The belief that water was the primordial element is found in many countries. Thus according to the Babylonians "the primal element of the universe was water, symbolised and ruled by Tiamat, the personification of 'Chaos', until she was slain by the god Marduk." This conception of the cosmic ocean is found in some Greek and Egyptian accounts also. The tradition of the well-known cosmic-egg is also found in other countries; thus 'at Eliphantine (of Egypt) it was believed that Khnum had made the cosmic-egg from the mud of the Nile.'[3]

[1] Hasting's *Encyclopaedia of Religion and Ethics*. (The article on Cosmogony and Cosmology).

[2] *Ibid*, p, 129. *Cf.* also:—

"No holy house, no house of the gods in a holy place has yet been built,
No reed had grown, no tree been planted,
No bricks been made, no brick-mould formed,
No house been built, no city founded,
No city built, no man (adam) made to stand upright,
The deep was uncreated, Eridu unbuilt,
The seat of its holy house, the house of the gods, uncreated.
All the earth was sea,
While within the sea was a current." etc. *Ibid.*, p. 129.

[3] Hasting's *Encyclopaedia of Religion and Ethics*, p. 126.

APPENDICES

Appendix (A)

THE RELIGIOUS TENETS OF THE NON-BENGALI MEDIEVAL SAINTS IN RELATION TO THE TENETS OF THE EARLIER BENGALI SAHAJIĀS

We have pointed out on several occasions that most of the medieval saints who gave vent to their religious emotion through the medium of the different vernaculars were Sahajiyās in a general sense. We have also hinted that in the religious tenets as well as in the literary representation of the medieval saints the form and spirit of Sūfī-istic literature acted strongly against the Sahajiyā background. We have seen how in the case of the Bāuls the spirit of Sūfī-ism acted on the spirit of the Sahajiyās and other devotional schools. In point of time some of the Saint-poets of upper, central and northern India flourished earlier than the Bāuls of Bengal, and many of them were contemporary with, if not earlier than the Vaiṣṇava Sahajiyās of Bengal. When, therefore, we speak of the Sahajiyā background of these non-Bengali medieval poets, we mean the Buddhist Sahajiyā movement in particular. A study of the poems of these medieval poets, particularly of the poems of Kabīr, decidedly the most prominent figure of the middle age, will reveal that there is a clear line of continuity from the Buddhist Sahajiyā poets to the medieval poets.[1] But the difference between the earlier school and the medieval schools lies in the element of love and devotion, which is conspicuous by its absence in the Buddhist Sahajiyā school. This element of love and devotion was supplied profusely to the medieval schools by the different devotional movements as well as by Sūfī-ism. Though devotion may be recognised to be one of the characteristics of later Mahāyānic Buddhism, it is not so in the case of the Buddhist Sahajiyā cult, which was pre-eminently an esoteric yogic school. But in spite of this difference the general similarity

[1] For a detailed study of the subject see Dr. Dharmavir Bharati, M.A., D.Phil., *Siddha-sāhitya* (in Hindi), Ch. V, Allahabad, 1955.

in spirit, in literary form and sometimes even in language, is indeed striking. Let us now demonstrate our contention point by point. As, however, we are not attempting here any comprehensive study of the religion and literature of these medieval Saint-poets, but dealing with them in relation to the Bengali literature, only those points will be touched that directly concern our early and medieval literature.

(i) *The Spirit of Revolt and Criticism*

We have seen how heterodoxy—a spirit of revolt and criticism—characterises the religion and literature of the Buddhist Sahajiyās. We have seen that the same spirit of heterodoxy characterises the religion and literature also of the Sūfīs. This spirit may be recognised as a salient feature of the medieval Saint-poets as a whole. In connection with the analysis of the different lines of heterodoxy in the religious history of India we pointed out that elements of love and devotion have often inspired heterodoxy in the religious schools and that these elements of love and devotion influenced the revolutionary spirit of the medieval saints to a great extent. To begin with, we may consider the religious views of Kabīr as expressed in his poems, songs and couplets. At least one-third of the literature of Kabīr (which is fairly large) is devoted to criticism against the orthodox Hindus and Muslims. As a religious apostle Kabīr was neither a Hindu nor a Muslim and criticised both the communities unreservedly. He says,—"The Hindus have died by worshipping the gods and the Turks have died by going on pilgrimage; the yogins have died by matting hair,—none of them have got at the truth."[1] Against caste system Kabīr says,—"If thou thinkest, penalties for deeds,—born a Śūdra, you die a Śūdra,—it is only in the world of illusion that you assume the sacred thread. If birth from Brahmin mother makes you Brahmin, why did you not come by another way? If birth from a Turk mother makes you Turk, why were you not circumcised in the womb? If you milk black and yellow cows together, will you be able

[1] *Kabīr-granthāvalī*. Ed. by Śyām-sundar-dās, Nāgarī-pracāriṇī Granthamālā, No. 33, p. 195.

to distinguish their milk?"[1] Against metaphysical erudition and the recital of the sacred scriptures the criticism of Kabīr was equally strong. He says that people read the four Vedas, but none makes any enquiry about the Lord; the truth has been discovered by Kabīr, and the Pundits are searching the field in vain.[2] The world is dying of reading books,—yet none have become the real Pundit,—if a single letter of the Dear One be learnt, a man becomes a really learned one.[3] Again it is said,—"O brother, thou art misled believing in the six Darshanas; wrapped in the garb of Pakhanda. They came and destroyed the soul and life; the four Vedas are wise and clever, but dumb. The Jainis know not the mystery of Dharma; they pluck leaves and come to God's temple. . . . . . The divine knowledge is outside this way: though it seems near, yet it is far off. To him who knows it is near, for all beings it pervades."[4]

Kabīr says that roaming about on pilgrimage and bathing in the sacred rivers are absolutely futile so long as the mind is not purified through the sincere love of the Lord. The world is tired of going on pilgrimage and bathing in sacred rivers; people settle near the city of Benares and drink transparent water,—but no salvation is there without the name of Hari (the Saviour).[5] Some go to Muttra, some to Dvārakā, some to Puri to see Jagannātha,—but without the association of the saints, and sincere devotion to the Saviour nothing avails at all.[6] Nothing avails in putting on

1 *The Bijak of Kabir* by Ahmad Shah, *Ramaiṇis*, No. 62.

2 *Kabīr-granthāvalī*, p. 36.

3 *Ibid*, p. 39.

4 *The Bijak of Kabir, Ramaiṇīs*, No. 30. *Cf.* also:—

"The Smriti made known three qualities; and the paths of sin and merit were laid down. From reading the Smriti and the Vedas disputings arose: conceit is practised in the garb of Pakhanda. One reads the Vedas and takes honour to himself; for him knot of doubt is not yet unloosed. He reads the Vedas and then he destroys lives: and offers their severed heads to images. Says Kabir, through Pakhanda they troubled many lives. The inward light is not revealed; no one in this life has seen himself." (*Ramaiṇī* No. 31). "Some go on pilgrimage, some shave their heads; others make discourse on Pakhandas, illusion and mantras. Reading the sciences and the Vedas they are swollen with pride, at the end they fill their mouth with ashes." (*Śabdas*, No. 21.)

5 *tīrth kari kari jag muvā ḍuṁghai pāṁṇī nhāi* ।
rāṁmahi rāṁm japaṁtaḍāṁ kāl ghasiṭyāṁ jāi ॥
kāsī kāṁṭhaiṁ ghar karaiṁ pivaiṁ nirmal nīr ।
mukati nahiṁ harināṁv bin yauṁ kahai dās kabīr ॥ *Kabīr-granthāvalī*, p. 37.

6 *Ibid*. *Sādha Kau Aṁg*, p. 49, *Cf.* also:—

"What profit is there by bathing if the mind is full of filth? A fish lives ever in water, yet it never loses its smell. The world perished in visiting the tirthas, in the robe of a yogin or a mendicant or a saint,—that is nothing but self-delusion; nothing can be gained by such hypocrisy. "There is a roof of falsehood, it spreads over earth and sky. In all ten regions its noose is set: it has beset the soul. Devotion, sacrifice and rosary, piety, pilgrimage, fastings and alms,—nine Bhaktis, Vedas, the Book, all these are cloaks of falsehood."[1] What is the good of counting beads if the mind is not controlled?[2] What is the good of shaving the head if the superstitions and the desire are not removed from the mind?[3] What is the good of becoming Vaiṣṇava if true discriminative knowledge is not acquired,—the paintings and the frontal marks are only to deceive people. Everyone is engaged in practices of physical yoga, none is after the union of the mind (with God).[4]

It will be seen from the above and host of such other criticisms made by Kabīr that the tone of Kabīr is harmoniously tuned with that of the earlier Sahajiyās. The resemblance is not only in spirit, but often also in language and imagery. Like Saraha-pāda[5] Kabīr also says,—"What are the naked,—what are the mendicants with skins, if they do not know the true nature of the self? If one becomes a yogin by roaming about naked, why should not the deer of the forest be liberated? If perfection can be attained by shaving head, why should not the sheep enter heaven? . . . . Says Kabīr, hear O brother,—none have attained salvation without the name of Rāma.[6] The Pundits know the Āgamas,

fasting and in bathing in cold water. Through each knowledge of the True Name death has drowned all the ages. Two go to the tirath,—the mind is restless and the heart covetous. Not one sin was blotted out, but ten maunds burden more was loaded. Millions of tirath visited, millions of temples built; but so long as a Sant goes unserved, all works are fruitless." (*The Bijak of Kabir*, pp. 21-22.)

1 *The Bijak of kabir, Śabdas* No. 113, pp. 148-149.

2 *kar pakaraiṁ aṁguri ginaiṁ man dhāvāī cahuṁ vor* |
jāhi phirāṁyāṁ hari milai so bhayā kāṭh kī ṭhaur ||
mālā paharai man-muṣī tāthaiṁ kachū na hoi |
man mālā kauṁ pheratāṁ jug ujiyārā soi ||
Kabīr-granthāvalī, Bheṣa Kau Aṁg, p. 45.

3 *kesoṁ kahā bigaḍiyā je mūṁḍai sau bār* |
man kauṁ kāhe muṁḍie jamaiṁ biṣai bikār || *Ibid*, p. 46.

4 *Kabīr-granthāvalī*, p. 46.

5 *Vide supra*, Ch. III.

6 *kā nāṁgeṁ kā bāṁdhe cāṁm* |
jau nahiṁ cinhasi ātam-rāṁm ||
nāgeṁ phireṁ jog je hoī |
ban kā mṛga mukati gayā koī ||

all sciences and grammars,—Tantra, Mantra and Medicine they know,—yet they die at the end. The yogins, the ascetics, the observers of penances and the Sannyāsins wander about in many a sacred place; those, who are with their hair plucked out, with shaven heads, the silent ones and those with plaited hair—all these die at the end. They have pondered much and given serious consideration to the problems of the world,—but in no way will they be spared. Says Kabīr, take refuge in the Lord and birth and death will be stopped.[1] "If by worshipping stones one can find God, I shall worship a mountain. If by immersion in the water salvation be obtained, the frogs bathe continually. As the frogs, so are these men, again and again they fall into the womb."[2]

The revolutionary lead that was thus given by Kabīr in the early middle period of the vernacular literature was vigorously carried out by a host of poets that followed, and the current still flows on. Dādū of the sixteenth century may be said to have been the worthiest successor of Kabīr. He says,—"The Pundits have bound the world by the net-work of illusion and Karma (various activities); a good preceptor is rarely found, who can show the real path. They speak of the sinful path, believe in illusion and Karma,—none points to the perfectly pure One (Nirañjana) who is very near to us."[3] Worship by love is the real worship,—that is the best kind of prayer; such love involves no activities whatsoever, neither should there be any fixed time and place for it; throughout the whole life—in all moments we may worship the Lord through our incessant flow of love. Dādū says,—"For decency's sake people (the Muslims) fast, invite others for prayer and offer prayer; the business of

mumḍ mūmḍāyaim jau sidhi hoī |
svarga hī bheḍ na pahumtī koī ||

* * *

kahai kabīr sunahu re bhāī |
rāmm nāmm bin kin siddhi pāī ||

Kabīr-granthāvali, Padāvalī No. 132.

1 *Kabīr-granthāvalī Padāvalī* No. 248.

2 *Kabir and the Kabir Panth*, by Rev. G. H. Westcott, M.A. For many such other criticisms of Kabir see pp. 56-70 of the same book.

See also the *Nirguṇa School of Hindi Poetry*, by Dr. P. D. Barthwal, M.A., D.Litt., Ch. II.

3 The Anthology of Dādū, collected and edited by Kṣitimohan Sen, Viśva-bhārati-granthālay, Calcutta, p. 216.

Dādū is with the Lord (Sahib), in what path should he walk? Why this grief, O Dādū,—stand before the Lord every day and every moment, and let your invocation (*azan*) be there where the Lord is in His true nature."[1] The Muslims cut the throat of others and compel them to profess their religion; five times daily do they offer their prayer, but there is no sincere faith in their heart for truth. They do never kill their ego,—but go to kill others; but Dādū says,—how can one attain Khudā (God) without annihilating the self? He, who destroys the body and mind and unites with the Lord, and controls himself through the divine realisation, is the real Awliyā Pir (*i.e.*, preceptor of the Muslim Awliyā sect).[2] Like Kabīr Dādū also repudiated communalism and sectarianism in the strongest possible words. He says,—"The Hindus say,—'mine is the real path.' The Turks say—'mine.' Say, where the path for the Alekha (Skt. *alakṣya*=invisible) may at all be,—He has been realised without a path. Says Dādū, both are mistaken,—both are rustic in their view,—know only that to be the truth which transcends both. In innumerable sects the Great One has been divided into parts; O Dādū, they have left the perfect Lord and are bound by the complexes of illusion.[3] The earth and the sky—to what sect do they belong? Water, air, day and night, the sun and the moon, and others—to what sect do they belong?[4] Without belonging to any particular sect they are serving the Lord incessantly. Pomp and peasantry, erudition and scholasticism can give man no peace,—vain is the pride of literacy, vain is the glory of scriptural knowedge. "I have composed a few verses,—and a few Sākhīs,[5] and there arises the conviction in me that I am wise in the world. May be, listening to the discourses on knowledge some *Śabdas* and *Sākhīs* are mastered;—and simultaneously arises the conviction that there is no match for me. What is the good of composing verses and reciting *Sākhīs* if the truth of the Lord,—

[1] Kṣitimohan Sen, *Dādū* p. 273.

[2] *Ibid.*, p. 274.

[3] *Ibid.*, pp. 275-276.

[4] *ye sab hai kiske paṁth meṁ dhartī aru asmān* 1
pānī pavan din rātkā caṁd sūr rahimān ||
Ibid., p. 276. See also pp. 387-388.

[5] Sākhis are verses which bear testimony to some truth (from Skt. *Sākṣī*).

the ultimate reality—is not realised?"[1] "Hear, O Pundits, sons of Brahmā (*i.e.*, the Brahmins),—Empty is your pot,—and you are not taking cognizance of it; you are talking all about Āgama and Nigama, but in your house there is going on the dance of ghosts (or the five *bhūtas* or material elements). Merely by reading you will never reach the ultimate state,—by reading you will never cross to the other shore; by reading creatures do not reach the goal;—O Dādū, call Him aloud through the pangs of your heart. Vain is the knowledge without the name (of the Lord), by explaining the Vedas and the Purāṇas they only become relieved of the burden on their head. Thoroughly have I pondered over all that are in the Vedas and the Kuran,—the land, where Nirāñjana is available, is not far off from me. Tired are the Pundits by reading on and on,—but none has crossed ashore; I do not know why the whole world is running on with faith in ink and paper. How many Vedas and Kurans have perished only staining heaps of paper,—O Dādū, a real saint is he, who has read a single letter of love."[2] "They serve pebbles and stone and the quintessence of the self is lost to them. When the invisible Lord is residing within, why should we roam about in other places? They wash stone with water which they drink,—the soul worships stone! The soul thus becomes stone,—and many have sunk down thus. They are gathering pebbles in the skirt and are believing them to be bits of diamond; when at the end Hari, the jeweller, will test them, the whole life will be lost."[3] All rites and ceremonies, talking and preaching appear repulsive without Rāma,—vain are all knowledge, yoga and meditation. Wise men there are many,—many are the Pundits, heroes and the bounteous; innumerable are the ways of outward show;—rare is a man who is absorbed in the Lord. All make innumerable outward shows and carry on propaganda and self-advertisement:—but Hari is available only through self-abnegation—none proceeds towards that path.[4] Great

[1] Kṣitimohan Sen, *Dādū* p. 278.
[2] *Ibid.*, p. 281. Also see p. 514.
[3] *Ibid.*, p. 283.
[4] *Ibid*, p. 308.

is the difference between a real saint and a hypocrite who makes parade of outward show,—their difference is just as much as the difference between the earth and the sky. The saint is absorbed in Rāma, the hopes of the hypocrite, fond of show, lie all in the outward world. Innumerable are such hypocrites in the world, rare are the saints; diamond is available in far off lands, but pebbles everywhere.[1] Through illusion have you got your head shaven,—but this is no yoga (union with God) at all; but with the ultimate Lord you have no acquaintance;—the hypocrite never succeed. Without love, goodwill and affection in vain is all toilet; if the soul be not attached to the Lord, why should he recognise you? . . . O, Dādū, the yogin, the Jaṁgama (a Śaivite ascetic), the Sevaḍā (a Jaina saint), the Buddhist monk and the Muslim mendicant, and the six systems of philosophy—all are outward show of hypocrites without Rāma, the Supreme Lord.[2] Whether you make outward dress, get your body pierced with a saw, or remain with your face upwards, or go on pilgrimage,—the Lord will not be found without truth.[3] Illusion has thickened within,—yet outwardly they are assuming the air of one who has renounced all,—they put on a cover of thatched cloth and move in a gay mood. They are controlling the body, but the mind moves on all quarters,—they talk of the dear one,—but make nothing but self-advertisement.[4]

Sundar-dās, the great disciple of Dādū, echoed the voice of his preceptor throughout the volumes of his poems. Like Kabīr, Dādū and a host of other poets Sundar also criticised severely the orthodox rituals and religious practices of both the Hindus and the Mahomadans.[5] Sundar says that he has seen the six systems of Hindu Philosophy, he has seen the Sūfīs and the Śekh,—but none of the sects could satisfy his

[1] Kṣitimohan Sen, *Dādū* p. 310.

[2] *Ibid.*, pp. 311-312.

[3] *sacu bin sāmi nā milai bhāvai bhekh banāi* I
bhāvai karavata urdhamukhī bhāvai tīrath jāi ||
Ibid., p. 313.

See also the questions and answers (No. 5, *Ibid.*, p. 587), which are also found in Kabīr with slight alterations.

[4] *Ibid.*, p. 337.

[5] See *Atha Sahajānanda* in the *Sundar-granthāvalī*, edited by Purohita Harinārāyaṇa Śarmā and published by the Rājasthān Society (Serial No. 1), Verses (2-5).

spiritual demand and it is therefore that he has had recourse to the most natural path.[1] In the *Sarvāṅga-yoga-pradīpikā* Sundar criticises the various religious sects of India severely and exhaustively.[2] Similar criticism has been made by Sundar-dās in the chapter on *Bhrama-vidhvaṁsa Aṣṭaka* where his criticism has been levelled against both the orthodox Hindus and the Muslims.[3] The lifeless orthodoxy and the formalism even of the contemporary Santa-sects, yogic sects and Sūfī sects were also criticised by him.[4]

Nānak, the founder of Śikhism, also echoed the same spirit as is found in Kabīr, Dādū and others. He also criticised the orthodox sects of both the Hindu and the Muslim communities. He says,—

"(Make) kindness the mosque, sincerity the prayer carpet, rectitude (equity) the lawful (food) according to the Kuran.

Modesty circumcision, good conduct fasting, (thus) thou becomest a Musalman."[5]

On going to pilgrimage and bathing in the sacred rivers Nānak says,—"I bathe at a Tīrtha, if I please him; without pleasing him, what shall I do with bathing?"[6] Against scholasticism, Brahminism and philosophical erudition Nānak holds the same view as his predecessors.[7] In a

1 See *Atha Pañca Prabhāva*, *Sundar-granthāvalī* p. 189.

2 *Ibid.*, Vol. I, pp. 88-94.

3 *Ibid.*, Vol. I, pp. 235-238. See also *Savaiyā, Cāmṇak ko Aṁg, Ibid.*, Vol. II, pp. 455-463; *Sāsī Cāmṇak ko Aṁg, Ibid.*, Vol. II, p. 385.

4 *Ibid.*, Vol. II, p. 385.

5 The *Ādi-grantha*, translated from the original Guru-mukhi to English by Dr. Ernest Trumpp. (Printed by order of the Secretary of State for India in Council), p. 194, vii.

6 *Ādi-grantha, Japu* 6; also *Cf. Japu* 21. *Cf.* also:—

tīrath koṭi kīe isnān dīe bahu dān mahā brata dhāre |
des phirio karo bhes tapo dhan kes dhare na mile hari piāre ||
āsan koṭ kare asaṭāṁg dhare bahu niyās kare mukh kāre |
dīn daiāl akāl bhaje bin aṁta ko aṁta ke dhām sidhāre ||

Anthology of Nānak's poems. Published by Bhāiparatāp Siṁha Prītam Siṁha, Amritsar, p. 132.

Cf. also:—*Ibid.* p. 116, 120, 127, pp. 241-42, etc.

7 *Ādi-grantha*, p. 934. *Cf.* "Reading and reading the Pandit explains the Veda, (but) the infatuation of the Maya lulls him to sleep. (*Ibid.*, p. 117).) The Pandit, reading and reading cries aloud, but in him is the infatuation of the Maya and love (to her). (*Ibid*, p. 118.) In going through the six Shastras, in knowing them by heart, in worship, in (applying) the Tilak, in bathing at a Tirtha, in the practice of purity, in the eightyfour ascetic postures tranquillity is not obtained, O dear!" (*Ibid.*, p. 136.) "He (*i.e.*, the Pandit) explains the Smriti, Shastras and the Veda; but being led astray by error he does not know the truth (the Deity)." (*Ibid.*, p. 158, *cf.* also p. 326, ix.) It will appear from the

fine poem Nānak says that it is ridiculous to perform *Ārati*[1] before the Lord in a temple,—for the whole universe is performing *Ārati* before Him. The sun and the moon are the lamps on the plate of the sky, the constellation of stars is the pearl; the wind is carrying incense, the forests in flower are supplying lustre, the spontaneous sound is serving as the drum—and thus is being performed the *Ārati* of the Lord.[2]

The same spirit, as illustrated above, will be found in the devotional lyrics of almost all the poets and poetesses of medieval vernacular literatures of India, including Tulsī-dās, Mīrā-bāī, Rajjabjī, Caraṇ-dās, Sahaj-bāi, Dayā-bāī and other poets and poetesses. If these poets and poetesses stood for anything it was saving religion from degenerating into mere codes of scriptures and time-honoured customs and practices,—the watch-word of all was sincerity of love. The contemporary Sūfī mystic poets (who composed poems in some dialect of Hindi) also had the same spirit as the other devotional lyricists. Thus Rajjab says,—"Amidst the darkness pervading all the quarters the light that will radiate lustre shines within our heart. By dry indifference towards the world and the austere penances inflicting torture on the body, can you expect to destroy the enemy that lies within you, or do you derive any light therefrom?" "Fill the mosque of your life with prayer (*Namaz*) and salute; it is the mind that frequently creates disturbance there; from that calm mosque of life drive away this Kafer mind." "There are as many sects as there are men, and thus the creator created varieties; but salutes of all human hearts are uniting together to form a great stream of salutes to the sea of the Lord Saviour." "The Ganges has her origin at

verses and songs of Nānak that his strongest note was against the Smṛti-śāstra of the orthodox Hindus, and scholastic Brahmanism was made the object of scathing criticism. (See *Ibid.*, pp. 333-334, iv. v. xxii, xxiii.)

[1] Waving light or incense before an idol.

[2] *gagan mai thālu ravi-cand dīpak bane*
tārikā maṇḍalā janak motī ǀ
dhūpumal ānalo pavaṇu cavaro kare
sagal banarāi phūlaṁta joti ǁ
kaisī āratī hoi ǀ
bhav khaṇḍanā terī āratī ǀ
anahatā sabada vājaṁta bherī ǁ

Anthology of Nānak, (Amritsar publication), pp. 190-191.

the feet of the Lord; if the feet of the Lord be within the heart of all lovers, the Ganges of love will flow in the heart of all the devotees; where the courses of all these Ganges meet together it makes a great Tīrtha, and liberation is assured if one bathes in this sacred place." "This universe is the Vedas,—creation in its fullness is the real Kuran. The Pundits and the Kazis are mistaking a heap of dry paper to be the real world, and they are sadly disappointed. Paper is in the heart of the sincere devotee,—and all truth shines on it in letters of sincerity; in the universe where all the hearts have united together shine all the Vedas and the Kuran. Break away the barrier of all artificiality and read the truth of the universe formed by the unity of hearts. Readers are seen in this world of lifeless letters inscribed on the lifeless sheets of paper,—but there are the living Vedas in the life of man, and if you are to read anything, O Rajjab, read those living Vedas of life."[1] Bulleshah, the Sūfī mystic, says,—"O Bulla, people say,—"Thou shouldest sit within the mosque; what is the gain of sitting within the mosque if there is no sincere prayer (*Namaz*) within the heart?" "O Bulla, places of pilgrimage are filled with plunderers,—in the temple reside the deceivers,—and within the mosque are rogues;—but the beloved Lord is outside all." "Khudā (God) is to be found neither in the mosque, nor in the Kābā, nor in the scriptures, nor in the routine-work of prayer (*Namaz*); if something could be understood in a natural way,—the Pundits would create great disturbance." "O Bulla, there is no salvation by pilgrimage to Mecca—if egohood is not cast away from the heart;—diving hundreds of times in the Ganges cannot give you salvation; salvation will be attained only when the ego is completely resigned."[2]

(ii) *Guru-vāda*

Another striking point of similarity in the spirit of the Sahajiyā Buddhists, the Sūfī-ists and the various other Sahajiyās of the medieval period is the stress laid on the Guru or the preceptor. We have seen that as an offshoot of the

[1] See *Bhāratīya Madhya-yuge Sādhanār Dhārā* by Kṣitimohan Sen, pp. 82-83,
[2] *Ibid.* pp. 114-115.

Tāntric system Buddhist Sahajiyā school attached the greatest importance on the really qualified preceptor. The same spirit is to be found in almost all the minor religious systems of the medieval period. The highest stress of the innumerable Santa poets is on the Guru, that of the Sūfī poets is also on the Guru or the Mursid,—that of the Śikhs is still more particularly on the Guru, that of the Nāth yogins is similarly on the Guru, that of the Vaiṣṇava Sahajiyās, and the Āuls, Bāuls, Kartā-Bhajās, Darbesis and other religious sects of Bengal is also on the Guru. The fact is so undisputed and so well known that it seems unnecessary to illustrate it from the sayings of the medieval poets. In the works of Kabīr, Dādū, Nānak, Sundar-dās and others separate chapters will be found entirely devoted to the explanation of the importance of the Guru. It has been held there that truth is a flash of light, which is infused from the preceptor into the disciple just as one candle is lighted from another burning candle. As a matter of fact, this Guru-vāda may be regarded as the special characteristic, not of any particular sect or line of Indian religion, it is rather the special feature of Indian religion as a whole.

(iii) *All Truth within*

We have seen how in the Buddhist Sahajiyā school the physical organism was regarded as the epitome of the universe and how the physical body as such was regarded as the abode of all truth. We have further seen that it is a salient feature also of Sūfī-ism. We have seen how in the Buddhist Tantras all the metaphysical principles with all their corollaries were discovered within the body and how all the sacred mountains, rivers and places of pilgrimage have been located within the physical organism. It has been observed that in the case of the Buddhist Sahajiyās this spirit of regarding the body as the abode of all truth is not a pure and simple case of inheritance from Tāntricism; in many places the influence of Upaniṣadic mysticism is also palpable. In this aspect also the spirit of the medieval Hindi and Bengali literature is strikingly similar to that of the Buddhist Sahajiyā school. We have further noticed before that in this spirit of the medieval schools the influences of Sūfī-ism was immense against the earlier Sahajiyā background.

In Kabīr, though the Vaiṣṇavite spirit on the Dvaitādvaita line together with the Sūfī-istic spirit may sometimes seem dominant, the Tāntric spirit is not also wanting. By Tāntric spirit, in this connection, we mean the principle of making the physical system, including the physiological and biological processes, an instrument for the realisation of truth. A study of the poems of Kabīr will reveal that Kabīr had a yogic system of his own involving the theory of the lotus or plexus, the nervous system and the control of the vital wind.[1] We find here the two important nerves in the left and the right, most commonly known as the Iḍā and Piṅgalā, as the moon and the sun, or the Gaṅgā and the Jamunā.[2] The meeting place of the three nerves Iḍā, Piṅgalā and Suṣumnā is, as usual, described here as the *tri-veṇī* (i.e., the meeting of the three courses).[3] The middle nerve Suṣumnā has always been spoken of (like the Buddhist Sahajiyās) as the path to Sahaja or vacuity (*sahaja śūnya*),[4] and the yoga has always been described as Sahaja yoga and the final state as Sahaja-samādhi or Sahaja-śūnya. The drinking of the nectar pouring from the moon situated on the top of the mount Meru (i.e., the spinal chord) has been held very important by Kabīr.[5] All the medieval Hindi poets akin to Kabīr had a similar system of yoga. Dr. P. D. Barthwal, M.A., D.Litt., in his work, *The Nirguṇa*

1 See the songs of Kabīr in the *Kabīr-granthāvalī*, p. 88. (*ṣaṭ dal kaval nivāsiyā etc.*), p. 96 (*ṣāṭ cakra kī kanak koṭhaḍī etc.*). *Cf.* also—
ulaṭe pavan cakra ṣaṭ bedhā, mera-daṁḍa sarapūrā I
gagan garaji mān suṁni samāṁnāṁ, bāje anahad tūrā || *Ibid.* p. 90.
ulaṭe pavan cakra ṣaṭ bedhā, suṁni surati lai lāgī I
amar na marai marai nahiṁ jīvai, tāhi khoji bairāgī || *Ibid*, p. 91.

2 *Cf.* *caṁd sūr doi khaṁbhavā, baṁka nāli kī ḍorī* I *Ibid*, p. 94.
caṁd sūr doi bhāṭhi kīnhī, suṣamani cigavā lāgī re I *Ibid*, p. 110.
sasihar sūr milāvā, tab anahad ben bajāvā I *Ibid*, p. 146.
See also p. 157, 190, 198, 223, 308 etc.
For Gaṅgā and Yamunā see *Ibid.*, p. 94, p. 306 etc.

3 *Cf. tri-beṇī manāha nhavāie surati milai jau hāthi re* I *Ibid*, p. 88.
ṣaṭ cakra kī gāgarī, tribeṇiṁ saṁgam bāṭ I p. 94.

4 *suṣaman nārī sahaji samāṁniṁ pīvai pivanhārā* I *Ibid*, p. 110.
sahaji suṣamanāṁ kāchai || *Ibid*, p. 110.

5 *Vide supra* ch. ix, iii, (*b*), (*a*).

School of Hindi Poetry, has given an exposition of the yogic system of Kabīr and other poets of his school.[1]

It will be clear from the above that the yogic and the Tāntric influence on Kabīr was no less important than the Vaiṣṇavite and the Sūfī-istic influence. Like the Buddhist poet Saraha-pāda Kabīr also says—Within the form resides the formless, his whereabouts are known to none. Musk is there in the navel cavity, yet the dear is roaming about in the forest (in search of it); exactly in the same way, Rāma is residing within every body, but the world does not perceive. The Lord is residing within the body, through illusion none knows Him,—just as the musk-deer smells the grass of the forest and roams about.[2] Again he says,—"In the lake of the body there is a lotus without parallel, and on it resides the Supreme Being of supreme lustre—of Him there is neither any sign or form."[3] We have seen that the Buddhist Sahajiyās have declared that all the sacred rivers, sacred mountains, places of pilgrimage are within this body, and they localised them within the body.[4] Kabīr also says,—"Within the heart are the Ganges and the Jumna and there is the ghat (bathing step) of *Sahaja śūnya* and Kabīr has created his temple there."[5] Again Kabīr says that the mind is Muttra, heart Dvārakā and the body is the temple of ten gates and lustre shines within.[6]

In Dādū, however, the Sūfī-istic spirit seems to be more prominent. He says,—"O Dādū, in every body resides the jewel of Rāma, but none perceives the Lord; when the Guru gives a light in the hand, people can realise Him there.... The good preceptor has shown, that within the heart is the mosque, here the temple, here is service and salute; why should I then roam about outside? Within is the disciple, within the preceptor, within is advice; in vain

1 See Ch. III of the same work. See also the verses of Carapaṭi, Beṇī, Nāmadev and Guru Nānak quoted at the end of the work *Gorakhnāth and Mediaeval Hindu Mysticism* of Dr. Mohan Singh, M.A., Ph.D., D.Litt.

2 *Kabīr-granthāvalī, Kastūriyā Mṛga Kau Aṁg*, p. 81.
Cf. also the *Kastūrī Mṛga Kau Aṁg* of Dādū—see Sen's edition, pp. 298-299.

3 *Ibid*, p. 237.

4 *Supra*, ch. iv, ii.

5 *gaṁg jamun ur aṁtarai sahaj sumni lyau ghāṭ* |
tahāṁ kabīrai maṭh racyā muni jāna jīvaiṁ bāṭ ||
Kabīr-granthāvalī, p. 18.

6 *man mathurā dil dvārikā, kāyā kāśī jāṁṇi* |
dasavāṁ dvārā dehurā tāmaiṁ joti pichāṁṇi || *Ibid*, p. 44.

people roam about outside with matted hair on their heads."[1] Again,—"In the temple of my body I shall perform my prayer,—none else have access there; there shall I count the beads made of the pearl of mind,—and then will be my Lord pleased. My bath is in the stream of my heart, I wash my mind there; I bow down my head before the Lord and offer me to Him."[2] Again,—"Some run to Dvārakā, some to Benares and some to Muttra; but the Lord is residing in the body. Near is that venerable one,—God is within the body. O Dādū, all are leaving Him aside and are offering their worship outside."[3] Again Dādū says,—"Within the body is the sky, within it is the earth; within the body are the four Vedas, within the body lies their mystery; within the body there is repeated birth; within the body is the beginning and the end,—within the body is God. Within the body are the seven seas, within the body the unknown Lord; within the body is the water of the rivers,—within the body is the truth profound, within the body plays the vital force, within it is Nirvāṇa; within is the service,—within pours the incessant flow (of nectar); in the body are arts,—in it the One Being; in it the glow of love and in it the company of the Lord; in it blooms the lotus, and resides the bee; in it the manifestation, in it resides the seer."[4]

Cf. also— *kāyā madhe koṭi tirath kāyā madhe kāsī* 1
kāyā madhe kavalāpati, kāyā madhai baikuṁṭha bāsī 1
ulaṭi pavan ṣaṭcakra nivāsī, tīrath-rāj gaṁg taṭa bāsī ||
gagan maṁḍal rabi-sasi doi tārā, ulaṭī kūṁcī lāgī kivārā 1
kahai kabīr bhai ujiyārā, paṁca māri ek rahyau ninārā ||
Ibid, Padāvalī, No. 171, p. 145.

Cf. also— *jis kārani taṭi tīrathi jāṁhiṁ, ratan padārath ghaṭ hiṁ māṁhiṁ* 1
Ibid, Padāvalī No. 42, p. 102.

1 *Dādū*, ed. by K. Sen, p. 211.

2 *Ibid*, p. 273.

3 *Ibid*, p. 284; also p. 294.

4 *Ibid*, pp. 601-602. Sundar-dās says in a song,—"In this body (*ghaṭa*) are Viṣṇu, Maheśa, Brahmā and other god and the sage Nārada, in it are Indra and Kubera,—in it is the mount Sumeru; within the body is the sun and the moon, and the seven seas, nine lacs of stars, and the flow of the Ganges and the Godābarī; in it the enjoyer of worldly bliss and also the Gorakh yogin; in it the assembly of the Siddhas, in it resides the soul in her loneliness. Within the body are Muttra and Benares,—in it the householder and the ascetic of the forest, in it the bathing in the Tīrthas; within the body are all dancing and singing and the playing on of the flute: in it the red powder (*phāg*) of the spring, in it the husband and the wife; within it are heaven and the netherlands, in it the decay of time; in it the beings are living for ages and in it they drink nectar to be immortal. When the mystery of the body is known, death and

Nānak also says,—

"For whose sake they go to the bank of a Tirtha.
(That) exquisite jewel is even in the heart.
The Pandit, having read and read, discusses an argument,
(But) does not know the thing that is within."[1]

Again he says,—"The nine regions of the earth are contained in this (human) body; every moment I pay reverence (to it)."[2]

Again,—

"Why do you wander about searching? search should be made in this mind.
Who dwells with thee, O Lord, why should he wander from forest to forest?"[3]

(*iv*) *The conception of Sahaja*

The conception of Sahaja of the medieval poets also shows striking similarity with that of the earlier Sahajiyās. As in the case of the Bāuls of Bengal, the conception of the ultimate reality of these medieval Hindi poets represents a synthesis between the conception of the reality held by the earlier Sahajiyā school and that of the Supreme Beloved held in Sūfī-ism and the then prevalent other devotional schools of India. The ultimate reality being thus conceived as the Supreme Beloved, Sahaja has often been identified with Rāma, where Rāma stands for the Divine Personality as the indwelling principle, with whom it is possible to have relations of love. The Santa-poets flourished mostly before the Bāuls of Bengal; historically, therefore, it seems that the synthesis between the Sahajiyā movement and the Sūfī-movement was brought about first by the poets of Northern and Upper India. The same contingency that was responsible for bringing about such a synthesis in Northern and Upper India was responsible for effecting a similar synthesis also in Bengal.

decay (*kāla*) will not befall anybody, and Sundar says that this mystery can never be fathomed without the help of the right preceptor. *ghaṭ bhitari biṣṇu maheśā* etc., *Sundar-granthāvalī*, p. 886.

[1] *Ādi-grantha*, translated by Trumpp, pp. 213-214, iv.

[2] *Ibid*, p. 298.

[3] *Ibid*, p. 369.

Speaking about Sahaja Kabīr says,—"All speak of the Sahaja,—but none knows what Sahaja actually is. That is really Sahaja, through which a man leaves off all his objects of desire,—that is called Sahaja, which keeps the five (senses) well-controlled,—that is really Sahaja, in which the son, the wife, all wealth and desire remain merged together, and in which Kabīr becomes the maid of Rāma; that is really Sahaja, through which the Lord is realised in a natural way.[1] Like their predecessors the medieval poets also emphasised the unspeakable nature of Sahaja, which is the Lord (*Sāṁi*) or Rāma with them. Though Kabīr, Dādū, Nānak and other Hindi poets of the Nirguṇa-school often speak of the Lord or of Rāma and Kṛṣṇa and frequently conceive themselves as the maid of the Lord (and as a matter of fact there is a considerable number of such poems in Kabīr, Dādū and even in the Śikh poet Nānak who preached the religion of the *Alekh*), it will be a mistake to think that these poets believed in any particular incarnation of God; it has been repeatedly declared by these poets that the Lord or Rāma or Kṛṣṇa is no historical being,—neither is he the incarnation of God; He is the Divine Being, the ultimate formless reality—the non-dual all pervading reality, conceived more as immanent than as transcendent,—and that is the Sahaja of these poets. The ultimate state of bliss is frequently described by Kabīr as the *Sahaja-samādhi* just like the Buddhist Sahajiyās.[2] This state of Sahaja is to be attained through the final arrest of the functions of the mind,[3]—and this Sahaja is the state of vacuity and hence it is often called the *sūni sahaja*.[4] This Sahaja is a non-dual state of supreme bliss (*sukha* or *mahā-sukha*).[5]

1 *Kabīr-granthāvalī*, pp. 41-42.
2 *Ibid*, p. 89, p. 137, p. 217 etc.
3 *Ibid*, p. 159.
4 *Cf*. *kahai kabīr soi jogesvar, sahaj suṁni lyau lāgai* ||
Ibid, *Padāvalī* No. 69, p. 109.
sahaj suṁni maiṁ jini ras cāṣyā, etc. *Ibid*, p. 111.
ṭāryau ṭarai na āvai jāi,
sahaj suṁni mai rahyau samāi || *Ibid*, p. 199. Also p. 269.
sunna sahaj mahi bunata hamārī I *Ibid*, p. 272.
5 *Cf*. *hai koī saṁt sahaj sukh upajai* etc. *Ibid*, p. 138.
kāṭi sakati sib sahaj pragāsyo ekai ek samānā I
kahi kabīr guru bheṭi mahāsukh bhramata rahe man mānām ||
Ibid, p. 316.

The same description of Sahaja is to be found in the poems of Dādū. It is to be observed that the element of yoga-practices is comparatively less in Dādū than in Kabīr,—the sole emphasis of Dādū seems to be on the intensity of devotion and love through which mind attains the perfect state of unity and non-duality and this state is what he calls the state of Sahaja. Dādū speaks of the Lord (*Sāmi* or Rāma) more frequently than Kabīr; but the Lord is none but the formless non-dual ultimate Beloved and that ultimate Beloved is the Sahaja.[1] It is through self-abnegation or the merging of the self in the absolute or, in the language of the Sūfīs, passing away in the Divine Personality in *Fana* that Sahaja can be realised.[2] It is to be realised not through any austere practice, but through a state of passing away or deep immersion through the intensity of supreme love and devotion.[3] About Sahaja Dādū says in a poem,—"When the mind reached the Sahaja state all waves of duality vanished away,—hot and cold became the same,—everything became one."[4] "Bereft of the 'two' is Sahaja,—there joy and sorow become one; that Sahaja neither dies nor lives,—it is the state of complete Nirvāṇa... Hold your mind in the Sahaja vacuity amidst all duality, and by attaining the final state of arrest drink nectar,—and there is no fear of *kāla* (time or death)."[5] "O Dādū, let us proceed to that land of Sahaja where none dies or lives,—there is no fear of the whirl of coming and going,—one realisation for all time. Let us proceed, O Dādū, to the land where neither the sun nor the moon can go,—where there is no access for day and night,—everything remains

tana mahi hoti koṭi upādhi I *ulaṭi bhai sukh sahaji samādhi* ||

* * * * *

kahu kabīr sukh sahaj samāo āpi no ḍaro na avar ḍarāo I etc.

Ibid, p. 318.

[1] *Cf. sūkhima sahaj na sūjhai nirākār niradhār* ||

* * * * *

* * *bhītari rām dikhāi* || etc.

Dādu, edited by K. Sen, p. 313. See also the verse on p. 347.

[2] *Ibid*, p. 259.

[3] *Cf.* *surati sadā sanmukh rahai jahāṁ tahāṁ lava līn* I
sahaj rūp sumiraṇ karai nikarama dādu dīn II

Ibid, p. 424. See also the verse on p. 422.

Also, *prem bhagati jav upajai nihacal sahaj samādh* I

[4] *Ibid*, p. 347.

[5] *Ibid*, verses on pp. 382-383.

merged in Sahaja."[1] When the mind becomes absorbed in Sahaja, one can see without eyes, feel without the body and mutter the name of Brahman without the tongue, one can hear without the ears, walk without the legs and may have consciousness without the mind,—this is really the nature of Sahaja.[2] According to Dādū also this Sahaja is vacuity (*śūnya*) and is pervading the whole universe as the ultimate reality behind all phenomena. "In every place, in every body (*ghaṭa*) and in everything else Sahaja vacuity lies pervading,—there dwells the Stainless One, no quality has any access there."[3] "One and indivisible is the lake, immeasurable is water,—swans are bathing in that lake; void is the lake of Sahaja where the swans (the mind of the saints and the yogins) are sporting."[4] "A tender plant is the self, where blooms the flower of Sahaja; in a Sahaja (natural and easy) process true preceptor gives advice about it, but rare are persons who can understand."[5] All diversity is but the sporting of Sahaja itself. "That vital power (*prāṇa*), that body (*pyāṇḍa*)—that flesh and blood, —those ears and that nose—all are playing wonderful play in Sahaja."[6]

Sundar-dās in his poems on *Sahajānanda* says that after the preceptor had explained to him the nature of Sahaja, he has given up all religious ceremonialism and yogic practices and has been trying to approach Sahaja (the ultimate truth) in a Sahaja (natural and easy) way. This Sahaja is the Brahman, the unified cosmic principle.[7] As a matter of fact it will be seen that almost all the mystic

1 *calu dādū taham jāiye jaham marai na jivaī koi* l
avāgavana bhay ko nahim sadā ek ras hoi ||
calu dādū taham jāiye jaham camd sūr nahim jāi l
rāti divas kī gami nahim nahim sahajaim rahyā samāi || *Ibid*, p. 384.

2 *nain bin dekhibā amg bin pekhibā*
rasan bin bolībā brahma setī l
sravan bin sunībā caraṇ bin cālibā
citta bin cityabā sahaj etī || *Ibid*, p. 416.

3 *Ibid*, p. 459.

4 *Ibid*, p. 461.

5 *Ibid*, p. 484

6 *Ibid*, p. 596.

7 Sundar says,—"That perfectly pure Sahaja is in everything, and with that Sahaja all religious people gather together. Śaṅkara began his Sādhana in this Sahaja (and in the Sahaja way),—Sukdeva, Sanaka and others also followed this Sahaja way. Devotees like Sojā, Pipā, Senā and Dhanā all have drunk of this Sahaja-bliss in the natural way,—Raidās was also a Sādhaka of Sahaja and Guru Dādū also realised infinite bliss in this Sahaja path. *Sundar-granthāvalī*, pp. 303-06.

poets of the medieval period were advocates of Sahaja. Even the Śikh poet Nānak spoke of the Sahaja in the same sense as did Kabīr, Dādū and others. With him also Sahaja is not only the ultimate reality, it is at the same time the Lord—the ultimate Beloved.[1]

(*e*) *Similarity in the Literary Form and Language*

It may be observed in this connection that not only in ideology, but also in the poetic representation, there is a general similarity between the poetry of the Santa and the Sūfī poets and that of the Buddhist Sahajiyās. Often similar imageries, similar phrases and even similar lines are to be found. Thus, for example, Śānti-pāda in a Caryā song says, —*alakkha lakkha na jāi*, *i.e.*, "the imperceptible cannot be perceived"; the same line is to be found in Kabīr several times.[2] We have seen that the highest state of realisation has often been spoken of by Kabīr as vacuity or the sky (*śūnya* or *gagana*) and the ultimate reality—the Sahaja— is also spoken of as void. In a poem Kabīr says,—"There is the sky or the void in the beginning,—void at the end and void also in the middle,[3]—and this indestructible void never comes and goes,[4] neither does any entity come and go in it. When the mind is placed in this vacuity, death bows down its head before a man.[5] These lines instantaneously remind one of the Caryā songs studied before. We have seen that Bhusuka-pāda compared the defiled mind to a deer, beset on all sides with hunters;[6] Kabīr also compares this mind to the deer beset with hunters, *kāla* (time, decay or death) being generally compared to the hunter.[7] Saraha-pāda says in a Dohā, "The Pundits are in the habit of explaining all the Śāstras, but do not know the Buddha,

[1] *jākai antar basai prabhu āpi* I
nānak te jan sahajī samātī ||
Anthology of Nānak, (Amritsar edition), p. 367.

[2] *Kabīr-granthāvalī*, p. 35, p. 229, p. 230, p. 328.

[3] *Ibid*, p. 103.

[4] *Ibid*, p. 103.

[5] *gagan maṁḍal āsan kiyā, kāl gayā sir kūṭi* || *Ibid*, p. 76,

[6] *Supra* Ch. ii.

[7] *aheḍi daum lāiyā, mṛga pukāre roi*
jā ban maiṁ krilā karī, dājhata hai ban soi || *Ibid*, p, 12.
māraum tau mano mṛga kaum, nahiṁ tau mithyā jāṁna || *Ibid*, 30.
kāl aheḍi bhāgā I *Ibid*, p. 89.
kāl aheḍī saṁjha sakārā, sāvaj sasā sakal saṁsārā || *Ibid*, p. 231.

who is residing within the body." The same couplet with a slight change in language is found in Kabīr.[1] In a poem of Bhusuka-pāda we find that Sahaja has been compared to a big tree,[2] Kabīr also compares Sahaja to a big tree in a nice poem.[3] In a Caryā song Kānhu-pāda compared his purified mind, exhilarated with supreme bliss, to an elephant in rut, who is depicted revelling in the lotus-pond of Sahaja. Kabīr also compares Sahaja to a tender plant in blossom, and the mind to an elephant attracted to it.[4] There are poems in Kabīr, which in their entirety can very well be compared with some of the Caryā poems of the Siddhācāryas. Thus the song No. 62, given in the Appendix of the *Kabīr-granthāvalī* (edited by Mr. Śyāma-sundar Dās) can very well be compared with some of the Caryā-padas describing the ecstatic realisation of the Sahaja bliss.[5] The next verse of Kabīr (Appendix, Song No. 63) on the illusory nature of the phenomenal world—and the unreality of all duality also offers striking similarity in idea and representation to some of the Caryā-padas dealing with the same idea. There are some other analogies, such as the analogy of the mute in connection with the realisation of the Sahaja, the analogy of mind's being merged in Sahaja just as salt in the water of the sea, etc.; but they are inherited by all

[1] *Cf.* *paṇḍia saala sattha vakkhāṇai* I
dehahiṁ vuddha vasanta ṇa jāṇai || Dohā of Saraha, p. 68.
paḍhi paḍhi paṁḍita beda bāṣānaiṁ,
bhīṁtari hūti basata na jānaiṁ ||
Kabīr-granthāvalī, Padāvalī, No. 42, p. 102.

[2] Caryā No. 43.

[3] *Cf.* *taravar ek anaṁta mūrati, suratā lehu pichāṁnīṁ* I
sākhā peḍ phūl phal nāṁhīṁ, tākī amṛta bāṁṇī I
puhap bās bhavarā ek rātā, bārā le ur dhariyā I
solaha maṁjhaiṁ pavan jhakorai, ākāse phal phaliyā ||
sahaj samādhi biraṣ yahu sīṁcyā, dharatī jal har soṣyā I
kahai kabīr tās maiṁ celā, jini yahu taravar peṣyā ||
Kabīr-granthāvalī, Padāvalī, No. 166.

[4] *sahaja beli jab phūlaṇ lāgī, ḍāl, kūpal melhī* ||
man kaṁjar jāi bāḍī bilaṁvyā, satgur bāhi belī I
Ibid, Padāvalī, No. 163, p. 142.

[5] The poem of Kabīr runs thus:—
suṣaman nārī sahaj samānī pīvai pīvan hārā ||
avadhū merā man matavārā I
unmad caḍhā ras cākhyā tribhavan bhayā ujiyārā ||
dui pur jori rasāī bhāṭhi piu mahāras bhārī I
kām krodh dui kiye jale tā chūṭi gai saṁsārī ||
pragaṭ pragās jñān guru gammita sati guru te sudhi pāī I
dās kabīr tāsu mad-mātā ucaki na kabahu jāī ||
Kabīr-granthāvalī, p. 282.

these sects from earlier common sources. Saraha-pāda says in another Dohā that those who do not enjoy (with the perfectly purified mind) the perfectly purified objects of enjoyment (viewing them and realising them all as Sahaja in nature) and only hover in the voidness, will have to return to objects (of enjoyment) like a crow, which leaves the mast and hovers over the sea and then turns to the mast once again.[1] The imagery is found in Dādū where he says that the mind must be made firmly fixed in Sahaja which is the mast in the ocean of existence. 'The crow,' he says, 'sat on the mast and took its journey in the ocean; it hovered round and round and got tired and then sat still on the mast of the ship.[2] In another Dohā Saraha says,—"Don't repress the desires for objects,—for see the cases of fish, insects, the elephant, black-bees and the deer" (*i.e.*, they themselves bring about their death by the instinctive attachment towards taste, sight, touch, smell and sound respectively).[3] Almost similar Dohās are found in Tulsīdās, Ravidās, Dādū and others.[4]

Another important point of similarity between the Buddhist Sahajiyā literature and the literature of the medieval vernaculars is the enigmatic style used in describing the secret doctrines of the cults. With this we shall deal in the Appendix (E).

[1] *Dohākoṣa* of Saraha, No. 70 (Dr. Bagchi's edition).

[2] *Dādū*, edited by K. Sen, p. 319.

[3] *visaāsatti ma bandha karu are baḍha saraheṁ vutta* |
mīna paaṅgama kari bhamara pekhaha hariṇaha jutta ||
Dohākoṣa of Saraha, Verse No. 71.

[4] *Cf.* *ali pataṅga mṛga min gaj iyāṁko ekai āṁc* |
tulsī yāko kyā gat, yāko piche pāṁc ||
Dohāvalī, edited by U. N. Mukherjee.

The deer, the fish, the black-bee, the moth, the elephant are (all) destroyed by one (and the same) fault.

In whom are the five incurable faults, how much hope has he?—Ravidās, *Ādi-grantha* (translated by Trumpp), p. 666.

Cf. also:—*bhavaṁrā lubadhī vāskā mohyā nād kuraṁg* |
yauṁ dādū kā man rām sauṁ jyoṁ dīpak jyoti pataṁg ||
Dādū, p. 505.

APPENDIX (B)

GENERAL INFORMATION ABOUT THE LITERATURE OF THE NĀTH CULT IN BENGALI

THE Nāth literature of Bengal consists mainly of longer narrative poems and straty songs. Thanks to the scholarly enthusiasm and literary taste of Dr. Grierson, who, when a civilian in the district of Rangpur in North-Bengal, collected for the first time some versions of the songs concerning Māṇik-candra and his son Gopī-candra or Govinda-candra. In course of the narration of the eventful stories of the royal family the poets described the supernatural power attainted by some of the Nāths, who are generally spoken of as the *Siddhas* or yogins who have attained perfection. The first publication of these narrative poems in the *Journal of the Asiatic Society of Bengal* in 1878 under the caption of *Māṇik-candra Rājār Gān* (song of king Māṇik-candra) readily attracted the notice of the Bengalee scholars to such narrative poems, generally sung by the illiterate villagers in the interiors of Bengal and different versions of the song were soon discovered in different parts of North-Bengal as well as of East-Bengal.[1]

Besides the different verisions of the ballads concerning king Māṇik-candra, his wife Mayanāmatī, and his son

[1] Mr. Śivnāth Śīl discovered a manuscript of one version of the song ascribed to the authorship of Durllabh Mallik and it was published in 1902 under the caption of *Govinda-candra Gīt* and in the sub-heading the text was described by the editor as embodying the doctrine of the Tāntric Buddhists. Mr. Viśveśvar Bhaṭṭācārya soon collected a rather complete version of the song of Māṇik-candra and Gopī-candra from the district of Rangpur. Some manuscripts of some versions of the poem composed by Bhavānī-dās were discovered in the districts of Tippera and Chittagong and a version of the poem composed by the Mahomadan poet Sukur Mamud was discovered in North Bengal. Dr. N. K. Bhaṭṭaśālī also edited a version of the song, which was published under the caption of *Maynāmatīr Gān* under the auspices of the Sāhitya-pariṣat of Dacca.

The *Māṇik-candra Rājār Gān*, collected and published by Dr. Grierson and the versions of the song collected by Mr. Bhaṭṭācārya are substantially the same and the *Gopī-candrer Gīt* edited by Mr. Śil is rather a concise version of the same song with omissions and additions here and there. All the songs on Māṇik-candra, Mayanāmatī and Gopī-candra have been published by the University of Calcutta under the joint editorship of Messrs. Viśveśvar Bhaṭṭā-cārya, D. C. Sen and Basanta Ranjan Rāy in two volumes.

Gopī-candra or Govinda-candra, the other important discovery is the different versions of the songs on Gorakṣa-nāth (popularly known as Gorakh-nāth), mainly based on the story of the down-fall of the great yogin Matsyendra-nāth or Mīna-nāth as a result of the curse of goddess Durgā, and the rescue of the preceptor by his worthy disciple Gorakh-nāth through his yogic stength.[1]

The literature of the Nāth cult of Bengal, like most other types of literature of Bengal, consists practically of songs. All the big and small versions of the poems on Gopī-candra and Gorakh-nāth were, and still are sung mainly by the Yogi-sects and also by the Sūfī-istic Muslims in North-Bengal and East-Bengal. The Yogi-castes of Bengal[2] somehow associate themselves with the Nāth sect that spread almost

[1] A version of the song ascribed to Śyāmdās Sen was edited by Dr. N. K. Bhaṭṭaśāli (published under the auspices of the Dacca Sāhitya-pariṣat) under the caption of *Mīna-cetana*. Many versions of the song, which, in spite of the difference in details, are substantially the same, have been discovered in different parts of the Chittagong Division of East-Bengal. In the manuscripts four names are found for the author of the song, *viz*., Kavīndra-dās, Sekh Fayzulla, Bhīm-Dās and Śyām-dās Sen. A verson of the song has been edited by Munsi Abdul Karim Sāhitya-viśārada. He has prepared the text by comparing the available manuscripts (the alternative readings, omissions and additions being noted in the foot-notes and the appendix). The text has been published by the Vaṅgīya Sāhitya-pariṣat under the heading of *Gorakṣa-vijaya*. The text has been re-edited by Panchanan Mandal under the caption *Gorkha-vijay*, published by Visva-Bharati.

In the *Dharma-maṅgala* of Sahadev Cakravartī the story of the fall of Mīna-nāth and his rescue by Gorakh-nāth has been incorporated within the general story of the Dharma-maṅgalas. There we find that the consort of Śiva once became desirous of knowing the truth behind the world and entreated the lord to explain all secrets to her. Śiva agreed and went with her to the bank of the sacred river Vallakā, where he instructed her in all the secrets of the physical and spiritual life. Mīna-nāth heard these instructions from the womb of a fish; then follow Mīna-nāth's uncharitable remarks on Gaurī (the consort of Śiva),—her curse on him—his fall in the land of Kadali-pāṭan and transformation into a sheep through the charm of the women of that country—his rescue by Gorakh—the meeting of the five Nāths, *viz*., Kālupā, Hāḍipā, Mīna-nāth, Gorakṣa-nāth and Cauraṅgī-nāth—their obeisance to Hara-Gaurī and the installation of Mīna-nāth as a king in Mahānanda (*vide* B.S.P.P., B.S. 1304 p. 286). The secret of the Nāth cult has best been explained (of course enigmatically) in the text *Gorakṣa-vijay*. There are, however some other unpublished yogic texts dealing with the general tenets of yoga akin to that of the Nāth cult, and of these mention may be made of the *Anādi-purāṇa*, or the *Anādi-caritra*, *Hāḍa-mālā-grantha*, *Yogi-tantra-kalā* and *Veda-māla-grantha*. (*Vide*, B. S. P. P., B.S. 1331, No. 2 and B.S.P.P., B.S. 1341, No. 4).

[2] The Yogis of Bengal are about four and a half lac in number and they reside mostly in East-Bengal and North-Bengal. As a caste they bear the title *Nāth* with their name, and are mostly weavers, and sometimes dealers in betel-leaves and lime and sometimes cultivators. The Yogis geneally bury the dead though now-a-days they are adopting the purely Hindu process of cremating the dead with the Hindu ceremonials. For a detailed study of Nāth yogins of Bengal see *Nāthasampradāyer Itihās, Darśan O Sādhan-praṇālī* by Dr Kalyani Mullick, M.A., PhD. (in Bengali, Calcutta 1950).

throughout the whole length and breadth of India sometime during the tenth to twelfth century A.D. ; and in fact, though the Yogis of Bengal are now being gradually assimilated within the composite fold of Hinduism, they retain some old social customs as the characteristic features of their caste. The Yogis (or rather the *Jugis*) generally sing these songs in accompaniment with a musical instrument known as the *Gopī-yantra*, which is a simple instrument made with the bottle-gourd, a bamboo stick and a string attached to them.[1] These songs, particularly the songs of Mīna-nāth and Gorakh-nāth, are very popular also among the Muslims of East-Bengal and some of the versions of the story of Mīna-nāth and Gorakh-nāth have been collected from them.[2] The currency and popularity of such versified stories among the Muslims of Bengal has historical reasons behind it. The Muslims of Bengal are mainly converts from the people of Bengal (both Hindu and non-Hindu), and formerly constituted an integral part of the Bengalees both racially and culturally. The stories of Gorakh-nāth and Gopī-cānd, at least the skeleton of such stories, had been, in all probability, current in Bengal (and not only in Bengal, but in many other parts of India) before the time of the conquest of Bengal by the Muslims in the thirteenth century. Such stories were, therefore, common heritage of the Muslims and the non-Muslims of Bengal. The gradual revival of Hinduism in Bengal, however, introduced Saskritic and Purāṇic stories among the public, and the mind of the Caste Hindus readily responded to this Sanskritic and Purāṇic influence. As a result the popular vernacular stories were naturally pushed in the corner, and were preserved only by the Muslims and the low-class Hindus, who did not come directly under the pale of the Sanskritic and Purāṇic

[1] This is, however, a very popular musical instrument of Bengal. At the suggestion of Sister Nivedita Dr. D. C. Sen was convinced of the fact that this *Gopī-yantra* owes its name to king Gopī-candra of the ballads; but we are not quite sure of the fact. Even at the present time the Bāuls and other Vaiṣṇava beggars of Bengal sing songs from door to door in accompaniment with this instrument.

[2] In the United Provinces the yogi singers are generally called Bhartharīs or Bhartṛharis. They sing the song of Gopī-cānd and Maigan-nāth and the teachings of Bhartṛhari. No Hindu domestic festival is complete unless these Bhartharīs come and sing their songs. They use ochre coloured clothes of the Sannyasins. But they are by religion Mahomedans. They seem to be the descendants of their yogi forefathers and have inherited their yogi songs as well.

influence of revived Hinduism. Moreover, the Caitanya-movement of Bengal over-flooded the soil of the province with innumerable Rādhā-Kṛṣṇa songs and soon it became proverbial in Bengal that there is no song without Kānu (*i.e.*, Kṛṣṇa). So strong was this Vaiṣṇava movement in Bengal and so immense was the lyrical appeal of the Rādhā-kṛṣṇa songs that its influence was felt even by the low-class illiterate section of the Hindus. It is for all these reasons that the indigenous vernacular songs of Bengal, such as the songs of the Nāth literature, practically became obsolete among the Hindus and they are preserved as an ancient heritage largely by the Bengali Muslims and sometimes by the people of the lower substrata of the Hindu community. It may also be noted in this connection that the Nāth cult and the Nāth literature of Bengal with its salient features have inspired the Muslims more than the Hindus in composing a large number of yoga-literature in Bengali. To such a type belong the *Jñāna-sāgara* of Āli Rājā, *Jñāna-pradīpa* and *Jñāna-cautiśā* of Syed Sultan, *Nur-Kandila* of Mohammad Safi, *Vāra-māsyā, Yoga-Kalandar* and *Satya-jñāna-pradīpa* of Mursid.[1] These texts represent a popular mixture of the different kinds of yoga, the yoga of the Sahajiyās and of the Nāths and the Sūfī-istic yogic system. In the course of its evolution Indian Sūfī-ism was variously influenced by the different yoga systems of India,[2] and it was for this reason that Sūfī-istic Islam of India could easily compromise, or rather harmonise itself with the minor religious sects of India which have largely influenced the growth of modern Indian literatures. The Muslim yogic literature of Bengal is but the result of such a compromise.

Besides the stories of Gorakh-nāth and Gopī-cānd, stray songs of the Nāth-gurus, emphasising the vanity of life and the pernicious effect of worldly enjoyment and stressing side by side the importance of yoga as the only path for escaping death and deacy and for attaining liberation, are found among the Yogis and the Muslims of North-Bengal and East-Bengal. Munshi Abdul Karim quotes a poem as a specimen in his introduction to the *Gorakṣa-vijaya*.

[1] *Vide* introduction to *Gorakṣa-vijaya* by Munshi Abdul Karim.
[2] See *Vaṅge Suūphi-prabhāva* by Dr. Enamul Haq.

The present writer had occasions to listen to such songs in the interior of the district of Bakergunge, and such songs are invariably couched in an unintelligible enigmatic style, which generally characterises yogic songs in all the vernaculars of India. The enigmatic song in the Dharma-maṅgala of Sahadev Cakravartī[1] is a typical song of this class. The Nāths became gods or demi-gods in later times in Bengal as well as in other parts of India, and such is specially the case with Gorakh-nāth. There are many popular beliefs in the divinity of Gorakh-nāth. A typical tale of this nature is associated with a custom of East-Bengal, which is known as the "paying off the debt of Gorakh." Gorakh is here depicted as the cattle-god and Māṇik-pīr is his disciple. The ceremony consists in offering milk-made sweetmeats to Gorakh and Māṇik. A song is sung in this connection, in which we find that Māṇik-pīr, the Fakir (or the mendicant), comes to the house of Kālu-ghoṣ with his usual cry of *Vam, Vam* (which is the general custom with the yogi-mendicants); at the sound of *Vam, Vam* Kālu-ghoṣ's mother understands that the Fakir has come to beg for something,—and in consultation with the daughter of Beku Bānu she offers the Fakir five pice (in the name of the five Fakirs, or rather the five Pīrs of the Muslims). Māṇik refuses to accept cash-payment and asks for milk curd; but out of her foolishness Kālu's mother deceives the Fakir and disappoints him. As a result thereof all the cows, calves and even the milk-maid of Kālu-ghoṣ die within a very short time. Kālu's mother realises her folly, solicits the mercy of the Fakir,—and the Fakir takes pity on her, strikes his stick against the ground with the usual sound of *Vam, Vam* and everything becomes all right instantaneously.[2] In some places of North-Bengal Gorakṣa-nāth is taken to be the god of the cow and songs are sung of him in an annual festival.[3] In this transformation of Gorakṣa-nāth to a cow-god the word *gorakṣa* was popularly confused to mean what the word *go-rakṣaka* (*i.e.* the protector of the cows)

1 *Vide*, B.S.P.P., B.S. 1304.

2 *Bāṁlār Śakti*, Vol. iii, No. 3.
Cf. also:—*Rājsāhīr Sonā-pīrer Gān* by Mr. S. N. Das. *Vaṅga-lakṣmī*, Baiśākh, 1347.

3 See *Gorakṣadār Gīta*—*Pravāsī*, B.S. 1329.

means and hence was probably the deification of Gorakṣa-nāth to a god associated with the cow, as Mīna-nāth was with fish. The confused etymological meaning of the word *gorakṣa* seems to be responsible also for the tradition that Gorakṣa-nāth was the son of Śiva by a cow.[1] There are the Punjabi and Nepalese traditions of Gorakh-nāth's being born in cow-dung or upon the dunghill.[2] According to some Tibetan tradition Gorakṣa-nāth was a cowherd.

In the Vaiṣṇava love-lyrics of Bengal we find occasional references to the yogins of the Gorakh order. In a well-known poem of Govinda-dās we find that Kṛṣṇa once disguised himself as a Kānphaṭ yogin to propitiate Rādhā who had got angry with him. He went as a yogin to Rādhā's house exclaiming the name of *Gorakh* and blowing the horn (as is the general custom with such yogins).[3] We also find occasional references to Rādhā's expressing the desire to assume the form of a yoginī with shaven head and rings in the ears (just like the *yoginīs* of Kānphaṭ order) and to wander from place to place in quest of her lover Kṛṣṇa.[4]

It will not be out of place to say a few words about the time and authorship of the long narrative poems that constitute the main portion of Bengali Nāth literature. As for the time of composition of these poems what we can at most say is that the skeleton of the stories may be as old as the eleventh or the twelfth century; but surely the versions of the songs, which are available to us either in manuscript, or in the oral reproduction of the singers, are not very old. There is sometimes a tendency, however, to take account of the linguistic evidence in this connection; but in the

1 *Vide* Briggs' *Goraknāth And The Kānphaṭa Yogis*, p. 183.

2 *Ibid*, pp. 182-183.

3 *gorakh jāgāi* *siṅgā-dhvani karatahi*
jaṭilā bhikha āni dei | *etc.*
Srī-srī-pada-kalpa-taru, edited by S. Roy, Song No. 398.

4 *e.g. muḍāva māthār keś* *dhariva yoginī-beś*
yadi soi piyā nāhi āila |
* * *
geruyā basana *angete pariva*
śaṅkhera kuṇḍala pari |
yoginīr beśe *yāva sei deśe etc.*
Vaiṣṇava-padāvalī, Vasumatī edition, p. 234.
Also:—*keha bale cala ghare dvāre agni diyā* |
kāne pari kuṇḍal caliva yogī hañā ||
Caitanya-bhāgavata, *Madhya*—Ch. xxvii.

examination of the linguistic evidence provincialism is more often than not confused with archaism. It is difficult to determine at this late period of the history of our literature who the original composers of the songs of Gorakh-nāth and Gopī-cānd were; but it seems that these songs were handed down from singer to singer from sometime near about the twelfth century A.D. In course of such transmission the skeleton of the story was supplied with new flesh and blood by different singers and poets in different times and localities. Munshi Abdul Karim in his introduction to the *Gorakṣa-vijaya* argues from the frequency and the prominence of the name of Sekh Fayjulla in the colophons, and also from the evidence of some Sūfī-istic Islamic influence in the version of the *Gorakṣa-vijaya*, that Sekh Fayjulla is the original poet of the *Gorakṣa-vijaya*. But it seems that all the poets, including Sekh Fayjulla himself, received some versions of the poem from earlier sources and to the version they received they made sufficient additions and alterations.

The Nāth literature of Bengal, far from being an isolated phenomenon, is closely connected with the history of the Nāth literature of most of the Indo-Aryan vernaculars, *viz*., Panjabi, Maraṭhi, Midland Hindi and Eastern Hindi and also Oḍiyā. Besides the vernacular texts on Gorakh-nāth and those ascribed to the authorship of Gorakh-nāth there are as many as thirty Sanskrit texts on yoga, ascribed to the authorship of Gorakh.[1] Besides these Sanskrit texts Gorakh-nāth is claimed to have been an early writer of Hindi poetry and he is further claimed to have been the first known Hindi (or Panjabi) prose-writer.[2] Dr. Mohan Singh gives the list

1 Of these mention may be made of the following:—(1) *Amaraugha-śāsana*, (2) *Amara-nātha-saṁvāda*, (3) *Gorakṣa-siddhānta-saṁgraha*, (4) *Caturaśīty-āsana*, (5) *Jñānāmṛta*, (6) *Yoga-cintāmaṇi*, (7) *Yoga-mahimā*, (8) *Yoga-mārtaṇḍa*, (9) *Yoga-siddhānta-paddhati*, (10) *Viveka-mārtaṇḍa*, (11) *Siddha-siddhānta-paddhati*, (12) *Gorakṣa-saṁhitā*, (13) *Gorakṣa-śataka*, *Jñāna-śataka*, (14) *Gorakṣa-kalpa*, (15) *Gorakṣa-gītā*, (16) *Nātha-līlāmṛta*, (17) *Gorakṣopaniṣad*, (18) *Kāya-bodha*, (19) *Yoga-vīja*, (20) *Amanaska-vivaraṇa*, (21) *Siddha-siddhānta-saṁgraha*, etc. *Vide Nātha-sampradāya* (in Hindi by Hazariprasad Dwivedi; also *Goraksha-nāth and Mediaeval Hindu Mysticism*, by Dr. Mohan Singh, and *Gorakhnāth and The Kānphaṭa Yogis*, by G. W. Briggs, Ch. XII.

2 *Vide Nātha-sampradāya* (in Hindi) by Hazariprasad Dwivedi and also *Siddha-sāhitya* (in Hindi) by Dr. Dharmavir Bharati. Also *Gorakhanāth and Mediaeval Hindu Mysticism*, by Dr. Mohan Singh, and *History of Panjabi Literature* by Dr. Mohan Singh.

of as many as twenty-five Hindi works about Gorakh-nāth and his cult mentioned in the State Library, Jodhpur.[1] He also gives illustrations from other poetical works embodying the sayings of Gorakh, and of these the *Gorakh-bodh*, which is taken to be a Hindi work of the fourteenth century, deserves special mention. The most authentic version of the Hindi texts ascribed to the authorship of Gorakh-nāth is to be found in the *Gorakh-bānī* edited with Hindi annotations by Dr. P. D. Barthwal and published by the Hindi Sahitya Sammelan from Prayag in 1955. In his collection Dr. Barthwal has included some twenty-six texts and also some more songs. He has compared the manuscripts available and tried to give a correct reading as far as possible.[2] There are poetical works with the Gopī-cānd legend in old Panjabi, of which mention may be made of the *Udās-Gopī-cānd*.[3] The Gopī-cānd legend is very popular also in the Maraṭhi literature, particularly in folk-lore. The Maraṭhi legends on the Nāths (including Gopī-cānd) can be gathered from the concluding portions of the *Jñāneśvarī*[4] of Śrī-jñāneśvara and also from the widely mythical accounts given in the *Yogi-sampradāyāviṣkṛti*.[5] There is a Hindi version of the

[1] The list is as follows:—*Gan Bodh, Gorakh-Ganesh Gosthi, Mahadev-Gorakh-samvad, Gorakh-Datt Gosthi, Kanthad-bodh, Asht-Mudra, Panchmatri Jog, Abhai Matra, Daya-bodh, Narve-bodh, Ankalishalok, Kafar-vodh, Gorakhnath Ki Satra-Kala, Atam-bodh, Pran Sankhi, Gyan Chautisi, Sankhya Darshan, Rahras, Nathji Ki Tithali, Battris Lecchan, Granth Homavari, Chhand Gorakhnath Ji ka, Kisan Astuti-Kari, Siddh Ikbis Gorakh, Sist Praman Granth*. Besides these the following texts are also said to belong to the sect; *e.g.*, *Tattva-sāra, Brahma-jñāna, Svarūpa-Jñāna*, etc., attributed to Gorakh-nāth. *Asaṅga-vākya* of Bāla-nāth, *Mahāyoga-vākya* of Māṇḍuki-pāva, *Mukti-sarala-vākya* of Vakra-nāth, *Amṛta-prayoga* of Hālika-pāva, etc.

[2] Texts included in the *Gorakh-bānī* edited by Dr. Barthwal are:—

(i) *Sābadī*, (ii) *Pada*, (iii) *Siṣyā Darsan*, (iv) *Prān Saṁkalī*, (v) *Naravaibodh*, (vi) *Ātmabodh*, (vii) *Abhaimātrā Joga*, (viii) *Paṁdraha Tithi*, (ix) *Sapta vār*, (x) *Machiṁdra Gorakhbodh*, (xi) *Romāvalī*, (xii) *Gyān-tilak*, (xiii) *Paṁca-mātrā*.

There are three appendices, the first appendix include the following:—

(i) *Goraṣ Gaṇeś Guṣṭi*, (ii) *Gñānadīpa bodh* (*Goraṣ Datta Guṣṭi*,) (iii) *Mahādev Goraṣ Guṣṭi*, (iv) *Siṣṭa Purāṇ*, (v) *Dayābodh*, (vi) *Kuch Pada*.

The second appendix contains:—

(i) *Sapta Vār Navagraha*, (ii) *Brata*, (iii) *Paṁca Agni*, (iv) *Aṣṭa-Mudrā*, (v) *Caubīs Siddhi*, (vi) *Batīs Lachan*, (vii) *Aṣṭa Cakra*, (viii) *Raha Rāsi*.

The third appendix contains a few songs.

[3] The M.S. of the text is preserved in the Library of the University of the Punjab. (No. 374). Dr. Singh in his work on Gorakh-nāth quotes some portions of the text.

[4] A Maraṭhi commentary on the *Gītā* by Jñāneśvara.

[5] A Hindi work said to be a translation by Candra-nāth yogī, and published by Śiva-nāth Śāstrī, Ahmedabad.

Gopī-cānd song by *Lakṣaṇa-dāsa.*[1] Even at the present day dramas are composed in Marathi and Hindi with the legend of Gopī-cānd, and it is also a popular story of modern Hindi cinema. Dr. D. C. Sen quotes in his *Typical Selections From Old Bengali Literature* a version of the Gopī-cānd song (in a mixed Oḍiyā-Bengali dialect) from the yogis of Mayurbhanj.[2] Stray songs on Gopī-cānd and Gorakh-nāth are popular even at the present day among the yogis of the Punjab, Bombay and Maratha. Songs of Gopī-cānd, similar to those that are found in Bengal, are current as popular folk-lore also in Magahi and in the Bhoj-puri dialect.[3]

The historical reason for this wide-spread popularity of the Nāth literature throughout India is that the Nāth movement was, and still is, an all-Indian movement. The followers of this sect, who are now best known as the Kānphaṭ yogins (because of the peculiar custom of having the ears pierced through before being initiated into the order and also of wearing ear-rings) are found widely scattered all over India. They are occasionally met with separately as wandering mendicants in towns and villages and also in groups in their headquarters. Such Yogins are found abundantly in the Northern Deccan, in the Central Provinces, in Gujrat and Maraṭha, in U.P., Bihar and Bengal, and also in some Himalayan regions, particularly in Nepal. Even at the present day the Kānphaṭ yogins have their quarters and scared places of pilgrimage all over India, the headquarters of Tilla in the Punjab and that of Gorakhpur and Dinodar being the most important.[4] A detailed study of the important Nāth yogins contemporaneous with the most important yogin Gorakh-nāth is to be found in the

1 B.S.P.P., B.S., 1928, No. 2.

2 Mr. G. C. Halder, M.A., has given a short sketch of the Panjabi, Hindustani, Gujrati, Maraṭhi and Bengali versions of the story of Gopī-cānd under the caption of *The Legend of Rājā Gopī-cānd* in a paper read in the sixth Oriental Conference. (*Vide Proceedings of the Sixth Oriental Conference*).

3 *Vide* J.A.S. B., Vol. liv., Part I, 1886.
Also, J.A.S.B., Vol. lii, 1883, *Folk-lore from Eastern Gorakhpur* by Fraser.

4 For the numerical strength of the Kanphaṭ yagins in the different provinces of India and for their sects, sub-sects, vows, customs, quarters and sacred places of pilgrimage see the work of Mr. Briggs. As Mr. Briggs has dealt with these things in detail, the present writer does not propose to enter into the details of the question here.

commendable Hindi book *Nāth-sampradāya* by Dr. Hazari-prasad Dwivedi; he has also given in his book an account of the different sects of yogins of the later times branching out from the Nāth cult.

Whoever might have been the original exponent of the cult, Gorakh-nāth, of all the Nāths, enjoys the most wide-spread celebrity and popularity, and it will be very clear from the heaps of traditions and legends that have gathered round the figure of this great Yogin that, wherever might have been the birth-place of Gorakh-nāth, the field of his activities spread from the Frontier Provinces in the west to Bengal in the east including the Himalayan regions. It is for this reason that literary accounts of Gorakh-nāth's life and activities are found in almost all parts of India. Another point to note is that, though the Kānphaṭ Yogins have their quarters and headquarters, where they generally reside in groups, the custom of going on long pilgrimage to the sacred places scattered all over the country is very popular among them, and it is natural that with their long wanderings they have spread the legends and traditions of their sect to all parts of the country, and this may be recognised as a plausible exaplanation for the inter-mingling of the stories and traditions. In spite of the legendary and mythical nature of the story of king Gopī-cānd, we have reasons to believe that he was a historical person and that his native land was Bengal;[1] but it is because of the reasons stated above that this story of Gopī-cānd plays a very important part in the folk-literature of the different vernaculars. There is a large number of wandering yogins belonging to the Kānphaṭ sect, who beg from door to door, from one part of India to the other part, singing songs on Gorakh-nāth and Gopī-cānd. In Bengal we occasionally find such a class of Hindu Yogins and Muslim Fakirs still singing songs of the Nāths.

We have given before an exposition of the religious background of the Nāth literature of Bengal and some other problems, which are associated with the origin and develop-ment of the cult. Now we shall give a short sketch of the

[1] *Vide Infra*, Appendix (c).

stories with which the Nāth literature of Bengal flourished. The story of Gorakh-nāth runs as follows:—

At the time of the creation of the universe Śiva came out of the mouth of the primordial Lord in the form of a Yogin with matted hair and ear-rings; Mīna-nāth was born as a Siddha and from the bone (*hāḍa*) of the Lord was born Hāḍiphā (*i.e.*, Jālandharīpā); from the ear (*karṇa*) of the Lord was born Kānphā, and Gorakh-nāth with his long hanging bag of mystic importance (*siddha-jhuli*) and his outer garment of patched cloth (*kānthā*) came from the matted hair of the Lord. A beautiful girl of the name of Gaurī was the mother of the world. The Lord then asked some one of the Yogins (including Śiva, who here represents none but Ādi-nāth, traditionally said to be the original Nāth of the Nāth cult) to accept Gaurī as his wife, to which all bent their heads in disapproval. At the suggestion of the Lord then Śiva or Hara accepted Gaurī and came down on earth with her, and all the Siddhas followed them. Mīna-nāth and Hāḍiphā became attendants of (*i.e.*, disciples of) Hara-Gaurī, Gorakh became the attendant of Mīna-nāth and Kānphā of Hāḍiphā, and all of them began to practise austere yoga. Then Gaurī wanted to know from her Lord the supreme truth (*tattva*). For this purpose both the Lord and his consort repaired to the Kṣīroda sea where there was a small beautiful castle raised on the surface of water (*ṭaṅgi*). There the Lord began to explain to his consort all the secret truths, but the goddess fell asleep. Mīna-nāth, however, in the form of a fish (*mīna*) lay beneath the castle and heard all truth from the mouth of the Lord. The Lord came to know of it and cursed Mīna-nāth saying that there would be a time when he would forget all *Tattva*.

Thereafter once in Kailāsa the goddess proposed to Śiva that the Siddhas should marry and lead a domestic life; but the Lord replied that the Siddhas were perfect yogins and above all wordly emotions. The goddess then proposed to put the Siddhas to a test in the form of a beautiful damsel. All the Siddhas, excepting Gorakh, fell victims to the amorous charm of the goddess and every one except Gorakh felt within a desire to enjoy her,—and the desire of the

Siddhas was all approved of by her.[1] Mīna-nāth, as he desired, was destined for the land of Kadalī, where he would keep company to the amorous girls of the land; Hāḍiphā was destined for the country of Mayanāmatī, where he would serve as a sweeper and enjoy the company of Mayanāmatī, the queen;—and Kānphā was destined for the city of Ḍāhukā. Consequently Mīna-nāth, the great yogin, went to the country of Kadalī, where he got enamoured with six hundred women and was passing his days with them in erotic dalliances.[2] Gorakh-nāth, however, came to know of the sad and shameful plight of his Guru and entered the city of Kadalī as a dancing girl. In course of his dancing and singing Gorakh rebuked the preceptor in enigmatic words (so that the women of the country could make no sense out of them) and also explained to him the importance and the processes of yoga. The preceptor gradually came to his senses, recollected his own history and came out of the land with his worthy disciple Gorakh and once more engaged himself in austere practices of yoga.

The other story, *viz.*, the story of Gopī-cānd (or Gopī-candra, Govi-candra, or Govinda-candra), which in its complete version includes also the story of his father Māṇik-candra, runs as follows (the differences in the different versions being here ignored):—

Māṇik-candra was a renowned and pious king of Bengal.

[1] Here we find that the goddess adopted all the vilest means to seduce Gorakh but was sadly defeated in all her attempts. Similar legends are also found in the Dharma-maṅgalas, where the goddess tries to captivate the mind of the hero Lāusen by her charm of body in the for of a beautiful woman; but Lāusen, like Gorakh, could put the goddess to shame by the strength of his character.

[2] In the Dharma-maṅgalas also we find mention of such a country inhabited mainly by women full of carnal desire and it was only through the grace of Lord Dharma that the hero Lāusen could get the upper hand over all the allurements. The country is called in the Nāth literature the *Kadalīr Deśa*. Various attempts have been made to identify this land of Kadalī, the general tendency being to identify it with Kāma-rūpa, which is noted as one of the original centres of Tāntricism, and the *yoni-pīṭha* of the Goddess. But we should also consider another fact in this connection. In the Sanskrit dramas we find occasional reference to the *Kadalī-gṛha* (*i.e.*, a house in the plantain garden) of the kings for love-making with women other than the married ones. The tradition is also continued in the Bengali Maṅgala-kāvyas, where ordinary women, assembled on the occasion of any marriage ceremony get enamoured with the beauty of the bridegroom and wishes to have him allured in the *Kalā-van* (plantain garden). May the name *Kadalī* for the country where Mīna-nāth got allured by vile women have something to do with the above fact?

He had many wives, including Mayanāmatī, the daughter of Tilak-candra. To avoid family quarrels Mayanā was decreed to live separately in the city of Pherusa away from the royal family. In the reign of the pious king the happiness and prosperity of the people knew no bounds; but unfortunately a tyrant with a long beard hailed from East-Bengal and occupied the post of Minister for Revenue. His oppression soon led the subjects to join together in worshipping Dharma with mystic religious rites with a view to putting the king to death. The attempt of the people became fruitful and the future longevity of the king was reduced from eighteen years to six months. Citra Govinda (*i.e.*, Citra-gupta, the record-keeper of the king of death and also something like a personal assistant) opened his record-book and issued summons to the king and Godā-yama was sent to bring the life (*prāṇa*) of the king. Mayanā came to know of the mishap and hastened to the king. She requested the king to get himself initiated into the great mystic wisdom (*mahā-jñāna*) of yoga, so that he might be able to challenge the decree of Death; but the king felt it beneath his dignity to be initiated by his wife and refused the proposal indignantly; as a result death befell the king and he was brought to the city of the dead. But Mayanā at once seized the city of the dead through her mystic power and inflicted all sorts of torment on the officers. The king in charge of the dead was in a fix; but Gorakh-nāth, who was the Guru of Mayanā, brought about some compromise and accordingly Mayanā was endowed with the boon of a son to be born to her. Mayanā came to learn that the life-span of the child was destined to be only eighteen years; she grumbled and it was arranged that the son would be immortal, if he would accept Hāḍi-siddhā as his Guru and attend upon him. The corpse of the king was then cremated in a truly royal manner; Mayanā became Satī by placing herself on the funeral pyre by the side of her husband; but she came back unburnt and in due time gave birth to a son, who was the king Gopī-cānd in question. The prince grew in age and married Adunā, the daughter of king Hariścandra, at the age of twelve (according to some versions at the age of nine), and received his other daughter Padunā as present.[1] The prince ascended the throne and began to enjoy his life to his heart's content in company of the young wives. Mayanā felt that if Gopi-cānd was thus allowed to plunge into wordly enjoyment he would soon die at the age of eighteen. She proposed the king's renunciation of all wealth and beauty, and the acceptance of Hāḍipā as his Guru after taking the vow of a yogin. The king first refused the proposal stoutly and indignantly, and he even went so far as to suspect the character of his mother in connection with Hāḍipā. The mother was shocked and Gorakh, her Guru, cursed Gopī-cānd for uttering such calumny against his mother and decreed afflictions during the period of his *Sannyāsa*. The queen-mother, however, made fresh attempts to convince her son of the vanity of the world and the excellence of the immortal life, which can be attained only through renunciation and yoga. The son was convinced; but when he entered the harem he was once more tutored by the queens and instigated against the mother. The king at the instance of the wives asked his mother to demonstrate her yogic power by standing the ordeals to which she would be put, and the mother agreed. She was put into fire and drowned into water, she was given poison to swallow and made to walk on the edge of a knife and was put under various other direful ordeals of the type; but she came out successful in all cases. According to some of the versions the king, at the instance of the queens, dug a hole under the floor of the stable where Hāḍipā was buried alive; the Siddha resorted to his yogic power and remained absorbed in yogic meditation for a long time and was later on rescued by his disciple Kānupā.[2] Mayanā also asked the Hāḍi-siddhā to demonstrate his supernatural power of yoga before her son and the Siddha performed unbelievable miracles and thereby commanded respect and obeisance from the king. The king ultimately accepted Hāḍipā as his preceptor,

[1] According to the version of Bhavānī-dās Gopī-cānd had four queens, Adunā, Padunā, Ratan-mālā and Kāñcā-sonā (Kāñcan-mālā?). See *Gopī-candrer Gān*, Part II, C.U., p. 332). According to Sukur Mahmmad the four queens were Adunā, Padunā, Candanā and Phandanā.

[2] Such is the tradition also in the Marāṭhi versions of the story. See *Yogi-sampradāyā-viṣkṛti*.

renounced the world at the age of eighteen,[1] got his head shaved and ears split, bore the beggar's *Jhuli* and the patched outer garment (*kānthā*) and took to the vow of the yogin. The Guru, however, put the disciple under various trials and tribulations through his magical power, and the worst of all was that the new yogin was sold to a prostitute of the name of Hīrā, who compelled him (the king) to serve her as the humblest menial as a punishmnt for his refusal to yield to her amorous desires. However, the king bore all these trials with infinite patience and implicit obedience towards the Guru. Mayanā eventually came to know of the sad plight of her son, rebuked Hāḍipā for this maltreatment of her son and demanded the release of her son at once. After long twelve years Hāḍipā came back to the king, cursed the prostitute and all her female attendants to be transformed instantaneously into bats, and conferred the secret wisdom on the king. The king then returned home. He could not first be recognised by the queens; but when recognised, he was welcomed by all and the king began to lead a happy life once more.

[1] In the *Udās Gopī-cānd*, a Panjabi version of the story of Gopi-cānd, we find that Gopī-cānd was made a king at the age of twelve and took *Sannyāsa* at the age of sixteen (*solo barisi kā jogi huā*), and that Gorakh-nāth, and not Hāḍipā, was his Guru. See some portions of the text of *Udās Gopī-cānd* quoted from a MS. at the end of the work of Dr. Mohan Singh.

Appendix (C)

AN ACCOUNT OF THE PROMINENT FIGURES IN THE NĀTH LITERATURE OF BENGAL

In the Nāth literature of Bengal the most important figures are (1) Mīna-nāth, (2) Gorakh-nāth, (3) Jālandharīpā, (4) Kānupā, (5) Gopī-candra and (6) Mayanāmatī. Various accounts, mostly legendary in nature, are found about these important personalities; let us give a brief sketch of them in the following pages.

(i) *Mīna-nāth*[1]

In all the traditions about the Nāths, Mīna-nāth or Matsyendra-nāth figures as the first of the human Gurus. In many of the standard texts on yoga Matysendra-nāth has been saluted as the Ādi-guru. In the yogic texts the names of Matsyendra, Gorakṣa, Jālandhara, Caurańghī and others are commonly found as the stalwarts of Haṭha-yoga, and some yogic practices are specially associated with the names of some of these yogins.[2] References to Mīna-nāth and Gorakṣa-nāth and some other Nāths are also found in some of the Tāntric texts.[3] Mīna-nāth and Matsyendra-nāth (with all the other variants of the name)[4] seem to have been identical, and they came to be two perhaps in course of time. In the Nāth literature the word *Nātha* (which originally means 'the lord') has sometimes been used with an ontological significance and

[1] For a study of these personalities and may others personalities associated with the Nāth cult the reader may consult the following books also:—Dr. Kalyani Mallick, M.A., Ph.D., *Nāthasampradāyer Itihās, Darśan O Sādhana-praṇālī* (in Bengali), Calcutta, 1950; Prof. Hazari Prasad Dwivedi, *Nātha-sampradāya* (in Hindi), Allahabad, 1950; Dr. Dharmavir Bharati, *Siddha-sāhitya* (in Hindi), Allahabad, 1955.

[2] *Cf. Matsyendrā-sana, Gorakṣā-sana, Jālandhara-bandha,* etc.

[3] Sylvan Levi, *Le Nepal*, Vol. I, referred to by Dr. Bagchi.

[4] The popular name is Mīna-nāth in Bengali, Matsyendra in Sanskrit and Machamdar in Hindi and Panjabi (*Cf.* Mocandar in Bengali). The variants of the name found in the *Kaula-jñāna-nirṇaya* (which is ascribed to Matsyendra-nāth) are Macchaghna-pāda, Macchendra-pāda, Matsyendra-pāda, Mīna-pāda, Mīna-nātha, Macchendra-pāda Matsyendra, Macchindra-nātha-pāda. (See Introduction by Dr. Bagchi).

there is sometimes a tendency to interpret the names of the Nāths, particularly of Matsyendra and Gorakṣa, as some transcendental states of mind or soul attainable through the practice of yoga. Abhinava-gupta in his *Tantrāloka* speaks of Macchanda-vibhu and explains it as one who tears the fetters of bondage.[1] Prof. Tucci cites one instance from Durjaya-candra's commentary on *Catuṣpīṭha-tantra*, where *prajñā* is spoken of as *makara-mīna*.[2] In the Hindi text *Gorakh-sār* (which is a loose Hindi translation of the *Gorakṣa-śataka*)[3] Machaṁdara has been explained as one who has controlled his mind, who has known the truth of the six Cakras (nerve-plexus), and who shines in the unflickering lustre of his soul.[4] Traditionally, however, Mīna-nāth has variously been associated with fish, and that perhaps because of his name (as Gorakh-nāth is with the cow, Kukkurī-pāda with the dog, and so on). We have seen that Mīna-nāth received instructions on yoga from Ādi-nāth in the form of a fish.[5] In another legend Matsyendra is said to have come out as a boy from the mouth of a fish.[6] Mīna-nāth is known also by another name, *viz.*, Macchaghna[7] which

[1] *rāgāruṇaṁ granthi-bilāva-kīrṇaṁ*
yo jālamātāna-vitāna-vṛtti I
kalombhitaṁ bāhyapathe cakāra
stān me sa macchanda-vibhuḥ prasannaḥ || (1.7)

In commenting on the verse Yayaratha says—*sa sakala-kula-śāstrāvatārakatayā prasiddhaḥ*.

macchāḥ pāśāḥ samākhyātāś capalāś citta-vṛttayaḥ I
cheditās tu yadā tena macchandas tena kīrtitaḥ ||

ityādy uktyā pāśa-khaṇḍana-svabhāve macchandaḥ, etc., p. 25.
(Kashmir Series of Texts and Studies, No. XXIII, Vol. I).

Also see Introduction to *Kaula-jñāna-nirṇaya* by Dr. P. C. Bagchi, p. 6.

[2] *Kaula-jñāna-nirṇaya*. Introduction by Dr. Bagchi, p. 7.

[3] MS. preserved in the Library of the Mahārāja of Benares and accessible to the writer through the courtesy of the royal family.

[4] MS. No. 300, p. 1(a).
Cf. also:—

lākh caurāsī raba paravarai I
soi karīm je etī karai ||
gorakh soi gyāṁn gami gahai I
mahādev soī man kī lahai ||
sidha soī jo sādhai iti I
nāth soī jo tri-bhuvana jitī ||

Kabīr-granthāvalī, Padāvalī, No. 327.

[5] The sheat-fish according to the Bengali tradition
Cf. *matsya-rūp dhari tathā mīna mocandar* I
jaṅgir lāmāte rahe bogāl sundar ||

Gorakṣa-vijaya, p. 13.

[6] *Vide Yogi-sampradāyāviṣkṛti*, Ch. II.

[7] *Cf. Macchanda* of Abhinava-gupta. It seems to be a confusion with some colloquial variant of the name Matsyendra.

means 'a killer of the fish' and as a matter of fact he has been spoken of as a Kaivarta or a fisherman by caste.[1] According to the *Kaula-jñāna-nirṇaya* Matsyendra, though originally a Brahmin by caste, came to be known as *Matsyaghna* as he acted like a fisherman in Candra-dvīpa first by killing a big fish and discovering the text containing the sacred knowledge from the belly of the fish and by once more rescuing it (the text) by killing the fish that had once more eaten it up. This tradition is also responsible for the location of Mīna-nāth in Candra-dvīpa, which is generally taken by scholars to be some coastal region of East-Bengal.[2] In the pictorial representations of the Siddhācāryas, available in Tibet and Nepal, Mīna-nāth is always associated with the fish,[3] and somewhere he is found eating the intestines of a fish.[4]

According to all the traditions Gorakh-nāth is the disciple of Matsyendra-nāth. In Bengali Nāth literature we find occasional reference to another disciple of Matsyendra of the name of Gābhur-siddhā.[5] We have discussed before the Bengali legend of the downfall of the great yogin Mīna-nāth being seduced by the women of the country of Kadalī. The story has its variant in the story of Matsyendra-nāth being captivated by the two queens of Ceylon (*Sangal*). The yogin was leading a domestic life in the company of the queens and was ultimately discovered by his disciple Gorakh, who entered the palace as a fly.[6] Matsyendra then left Ceylon, but took with him the two sons, *viz*., Pāros-nāth

1 *Kaula-jñāna-nirṇaya*, *Paṭala* xvi (22-37). See also introduction, pp. 8-9.

2 MM. H.P. Śāstrī identifies this Candra-dvīpa with the Candra-dvīpa of the district of Bakergunj. Dr. Bagchi is disposed to identify it with the Sundwip in the district of Noakhali. (See B.S.P.P., B.S. 1329, No. 1; also Introduction to *Kaula-jñāna-nirṇaya* by Dr. Bagchi, pp. 29-32).

3 See B.S.P.P., B.S., 1329, No. 2; also *Kalyāṇa, Yogāṅka*.

4 The Tibetan synonyms for Matsyendra nāth (or Lui-pā with whom he is generally identified) can be restituted in Sanskrit as *matsyodara* or *matsyāntrāda* ("the eater of the intestines of a fish," Levi, *Le Nepal*, 1, p. 355, referred to by Dr. Bagchi). Lui-pā is also described in the *Pag sam jon zans* as a Buddhist sage sprung from the fisherman caste, who was a disciple of Śavarī-pā. In the same work Machendra is said to be the incarnation of Mahādeva as a fisherman in the womb a fish at Kāmarūpa (*Vide* Dr. Bagchi, pp. 22-23).

5 *Cf.* *ek sisya yāche mor jati gorakhāi* I
āra sisya āche mor gābhur siddhāi II *Gorakṣa-vijaya*, p. 130.
Again, *mithu kāle nā dekhilām gābhur sidhār mukh* II *Ibid*, p. 116.

6 In the Bengali legend he entered the city of Kadalī as a dancing girl.

and Nīm-nāth, who were born to them, and the two sons became the founders of the Jain religion.[1] According to the Nepalese and Tibetan traditions, as we have noted before, Matsyendra-nāth is identified with Lui-pā, who is regarded as the Ādi-guru among the Buddhist Siddhācāryas. As S. Levi describes in his *Le Nepal*, Matsyendra is identified with Avalokiteśvara Padma-pāṇi. There is the legend that Gorakṣa once came to Nepal in search of his Guru Matsyendra; but as the mountain was difficult of access he had recourse to the stratagem of binding the nine *nāgas* under a *turtle* and sat on them. Consequently, the sky becoming cloudless, there was drought in the valley for long twelve years. Then Bandhu-datta, the Guru of Narendra-deva, the then King of Nepal, went to mount Kapotala with the king to bring Avalokiteśvara or Matsyendra. They propitiated Matsyendra with worship. Avalokiteśvara was then cleverly brought to Nepal, imprisoned in the form of a black bee and installed in pomp in a place called Bugama. There then followed rain in abundance and thus the country was saved. The Brahminical version, however, narrates the story somewhat differently. Once Gorakṣa-nāth went to Nepal, but he got offended with the people of the country as he was not warmly received. He imprisoned the clouds and put them under his seat for twelve years; consequently there was drought and famine. Fortunately Matsyendra chanced to come to Nepal at the time and, while the Guru was passing by, Gorakṣa stood up to show him respect and thus the clouds were let loose and there was rain in abundance, which saved the whole country. Matsyendra thus in the form of Avalokiteśvara Padma-pāṇi commands universal respect in Nepal still to the present time and is still worshipped in the land with much reverence.[2] There is the celebrated annual procession of *Ratha yātrā* (a procession with Matsyendra as Avalokiteśvara on a decorated chariot) in honour of this

1 *Vide* Dr. Bagchi's Introduction to *Kaula-jñāna-nirṇaya*, p. 15; Briggs, p. 233. For details and variants of the story see Briggs, pp. 72-73,

2 According to the Nepalese tradition Mīna-nāth is the younger brother of Matsyendra and is worshipped almost with equal pomp.

popular god.[1] Matsyendra has, however, been deified in later times in many other places and the images of Matsyendra and his favourite disciple Gorakṣa are found in some shrines of the Nāthists,—and the foot-print of these two demi-gods are also worshipped in some places by the Kānphaṭ yogins. The peculiar custom of having the ears split is also sometimes traditionally believed to have been introduced by Matsyendra-nāth and many are the legends that are associated with such a tradition. There is another tradition which makes Matsyendra-nāth the founder of Kāmarūpa-mahāpīṭha of the so-called Arddha-tryambaka-maṭha, which represents the fourth or Kaula order of Tāntric worship. Again there is a legend recorded in the *Gorakṣa-kimaya-sāra*, which makes Matsyendra-nāth identical with Mahā Viṣṇu Sāṅga, whom some scholars are inclined to identify (though on insufficient ground) with the old Viṣṇu-svāmī.

Attempts have been made to fix up the approximate time of Matsyendra. The time of his advent has been held in the Nepalese tradition synchronous with the reign of Narendra-deva, who flourished in the seventh century A.D., but as the alleged synchronism cannot be historically relied upon because of the extremely mythical nature of the whole tradition, the time of Matsyendra cannot be fixed up with reference to it. Dr. P. C. Bagchi, however, has attempted to fix the date sometime in the tenth century with reference to the date of the manuscript of the *Kaula-jñāna-nirṇaya*. The mention of Matsyendra (as Macchanda) by Abhinava-gupta, who lived towards the beginning of the eleventh century approximately confirms this date. Again the tradition of the identity of Matsyendra with Lui-pā (who flourished in the tenth century)[2] will also put Matsyendra to the same century. The time of Gopī-cānd will also ascribe some such time to Matsyendra.[3] Many of the traditions taken together will strengthen the belief that

[1] For detailed description of this procession and other religious functions in Nepal in honour of Matsyendra see Briggs, pp. 144-145, pp. 231, *et seq*.
[2] *Supra*, pp. 227-228.
[3] *Infra*, pp. 457-459.

Matsyendra, the first Nāth Guru flourished at the latest in the tenth century A.D., perhaps earlier.

(*ii*) *Gorakh-nāth*

Though Mīna-nāth or Matsyendra-nāth was the first of the Nāth Gurus, the most celebrated Nāth Guru was Gorakṣa-nāth. All Indian traditions of later days make him the incarnation of Śiva, who is the divine source of all yoga. It is believed, and there seems to be a considerable amount of truth in the belief, that it was Gorakh, who popularised, if not introduced, the principles and practice of yoga throughout the length and breadth of India. As in the case of Mīna-nāth, the name Gorakṣa-nāth has frequently been explained docetically. Thus in the hymn of Gorakṣa-nāth by Śrīkṛṣṇa in the *Rāja-guhya* it has been said,—"By the letter 'ga' is implied the qualified nature, 'ra' indicates the form and beauty, by 'kṣa' is implied his nature as imperishable Brahman,—salute be to that Śrī-gorakṣa."[1] He is the supreme Brahman of the Brahmans, the gem on the crown of Rudra and others,—and the three worlds are made by him. He is the totality of all the qualities,—he is at the same time the absence of all the qualities,—he resides in qualities in his unqualified nature,—he is both formless and with form. He is worshipped by the gods (in heaven), by men on earth, and by the Nāgas in the netherland. He is all alone, eternal and free from the fetters of existence, he is the supreme Brahman and the imperishable divine lustre. The sky is his temple decked with various gems, and the all-good lord is there with boons of safety and security. He is saluted by Brahmā, Viṣṇu and other gods,—by the sages and other ordinary people and also by all the Siddhas, who are of the essence of knowledge."[2] Such docetic descriptions of Gorakṣa-nāth are also found in the *Śrī-gorakṣa-sahasra-nāma-stotra* (hymns of the thousand names of Śrī-gorakṣa) of the *Kalpa-druma-tantra* and also in the *Brahmāṇḍa-purāṇa*.[3] Bengali literary traditions make him the purest

[1] *ga-kāro guṇa-saṁyukto ra-kāro rūpa-lakṣaṇaḥ* |
kṣa-kāreṇākṣayaṁ brahma śrī-gorakṣa namo'stu te ||
Quoted in the *Gorakṣa-siddhānta-saṁgraha*, p. 42.

[2] *Gorakṣa-siddhānta-saṁgraha*, p. 42.

[3] *Ibid.*, p. 43.

and strongest of all the yogins. The erotic charm even of goddess Durgā herself was repeatedly put to shame by the purity and strength of his character. Most of the renowned medieval saints, who composed songs in vernaculars, paid homage to this great Yogin along with Matsyendra, Carpaṭa, Bhartṛ, Gopī-cānd and others. Kabīr refers to Gorakh several times in his poems and there goes the tradition in the Hindi work *Gorakh-nāth-kī-goṣṭhi* that Kabīr met Gorakh and held religious discourse with him. A similar tradition is found in the *Janam Sākhi* of Bābā-Nānak, where it is said that Nānak met Gorakh-nāth and Matsyendra-nāth and held religious discourse with them. It is further said that when, in course of his long wanderings as a Yogin, Nānak went to Ceylon he was mistaken for Gorakh-nāth.[1] Dādū refers to Gorakh and the doctrine of the innumerable Siddhas. Gahinī-nāth of the twelfth or thirteenth century acknowledges Gorakh to be the great teacher of Pīpā; Guzrati poets also mention Gorakh with reverence. Kṛṣṇadās, a Guzrati poet, sings of Mucchandra and Gorakṣa as two Jaina saints.[2] Rajjabjī, a Rājputanā saint of the nineteenth century, mentions Gorakh with reverence. If we take account of the literature of Nāthism in all parts of India, we shall find that everywhere traditions hold Gorakh to have been the supreme of all the Gurus.

So widely popular has been the great saint Gorakh-nāth among many of the Yogi-sects of India, for a long time comprising a decade of centuries, that countless traditions have grown round the figure of the great yogin, and Mr. Briggs has taken the trouble of collecting many of these traditions in his work on *Gorakh-nāth and The Kānphaṭ Yogis of India*.[3] From these heaps of wild legends, which are often contradictory to one another, and which have grown more with a belief in the divinity of Gorakh than in his human personality, it is now impossible to construct any historical account of the life and teachings of the saint. Traditions generally agree to hold him to be the disciple of Matsyendra. Matsyendra, we have seen, was most probably a saint of

1 See *Janam Sākhi*, Trumpp's translation.
2 Dr. Mohan Singh, *op, cit.*, p. 8.
3 See also the work of Dr. Mohan Singh.

the tenth century A.D.; Gorakṣa then must also be placed sometimes in the tenth century, or at least in the first half of the eleventh century. Traditionally Gorakh is regarded by the orthodox Kānphaṭ yogins to be unborn and deathless; he is the immortal saint, believed to be living still now in some hilly region of the Himalayas. Gorakh has sometimes been held to be the Guru even of the triad, *viz.*, Brahmā, Viṣṇu and Śiva, and there is the story of Viṣṇu's creating the world in the primordial water from a handful of ashes from the eternal fire (*dhuni*) of Gorakh in the netherworld (*Pātāla*). There are also stories of Gorakh's fighting with many goddesses in different Śākta centres and the goddesses in every case had to bend their heads before the mighty Yogin.[1] Various are the legends even about his birth in the human form. We have seen that in the Bengali work *Gorakṣa-vijaya* he is said to have come of the matted hair of Mahādeva.[2] There is also the story of his being born on a dung-hill from a quantity of ashes, which was given by Mahādeva to a barren lady to swallow in order to have a child, and which was thrown away in disregard on a dung-hill. Yet another legend would make him born of a cow by Mahādeva. Apart from these legendary accounts traditions would show that he was born in some low caste family.

There are controversial legends about the birth place of Gorakh. The mythical account says that he lived in the Punjab at Peshwar (?) in the Satya (*kṛta*) yuga, at Gorakhpur in the Tretā yuga, at Hurmy beyond Dwārakā in the Dvāpara yuga and at Gorakhmari (Gorakhmandi) in Kathiwar in the Kali yuga. It is also said that Gorakh appeared in the Kali yuga in the form of the Śeṣa Nāga. According to the Nepalese tradition Gorakh lived at Gorakh in Western Nepal in a cave. The cave and the town are said to have obtained their name from Gorakhnāth, and even the national name *Gurkha* is sometimes explained with reference to Gorakh. Others would again make Gorakh-nāth the original inhabitant of Gorakhpur in

[1] For many such stories see *Yogi-sampradāyā-viṣkṛti*.

[2] *Cf. jaṭā bhedi nikalila jati gorakh-nātha* |
siddha jhuli siddha kāthā tāhār galāte ||

U.P., and the name of the city is also explained with reference to the name of the saint. As a matter of fact Gorakhpur is one of the most important centres of the Kānphaṭ Yogis even to the present day. Some Nepalese tradition would again hold that Gorakh came to Kāṭhmuṇḍu from the Punjab. He is again claimed as a saint of Oudh. The monks of Gorakhpur hold that he came to the United Provinces from the Punjab, and that his chief seat was at Tilla, in Jhelum. Traditions in Kacch (Sindh) would have him in the Punjab. Yogis at Nasik hold that Gorakh went from Nepal to the Punjab and thence to other parts of India. Dr. Mohan Singh holds that Gorakh was an original inhabitant of some place round the area of Peshwar. But from the preponderance of traditions and from the importance which all the Kānphaṭ Yogis attach to Tilla in Jhelum of the Punjab, it will appear that Gorakh was an original inhabitant of the Punjab, at least a considerable portion of his life-time was spent in the province. But at the same time it seems that Gorakh travelled throughout the whole of India and legends associate his life and activities with Afganistan, Beluchistan, the Punjab, North-Western Provinces, Sind, Guzrat and Maraṭha in the west, north and south, and with Ceylon in the extreme south, with U.P. in the middle, and with Nepal, Assam and Bengal in the east.

In the Nāth literature of Bengal Gorakh-nāth figures prominently as the disciple of Mīna-nāth and the preceptor of queen Mayanāmatī, mother of king Gopī-cānd. But in the literature of the other vernaculars "Gorakh is said to have been the teacher of Puran, son of Salbahan of Sialkot; of Bharthrihari, step brother of Vikramaditya of Ujjain; of Raja Gopi Chand of Ujjain, Rangpur, Dharanagri, or Kanchanpur; of queen Lunan Chamari and queen Sundran of Assam (or Orissa?); of Ranjha of Jhang; of Gugga Pir of Rajputna; of Baba Ratan of Peshwar; of Dharmanath, who migrated to Western India; of king Ajaipal and Venapal; of Kapila muni and Balnath; of the holy Prophet Muhammad; of Madar; of Luharipa; of Ismail, a Siddha; of Ratan Sain, the hero of Padumavati by Jayasi."[1] The tradition of

[1] Dr. Mohan Singh, *op. cit.*, p. 7.

Gorakh's holding religious discourse with Kabīr and Nānak, the most important poets of the Santas and the Śikhs respectively, have already been mentioned. All these traditions convince one only of the extent of popularity which Gorakh has been enjoying in the religious history of a vast country like India.

(iii) *Jālandharī-pā*

So far as the Gopī-cānd legend is concerned, Jālandharī-pā figures as the most important as he was the Guru of Gopī-cānd himself. Jālandharī and Matsyendra were direct disciples of Ādi-nāth and as Matsyendra was destined by goddess Durgā to be snared by the women of Kadalī, Jālandharī-pā was destined, as desired by him, to lead the life of a sweeper (which was the work of a Hāḍi) and enjoy the company of queen Mayanāmatī. In the Nāth literature of Bengal Jālandharī-pā is better known as Hāḍi-pā.[1] It may be noticed in this connection that while Mīna or Matsyendra and Gorakṣa generally bore the title of *Nāth* with their name, Jālandharī (or Hāḍi-pā) as also his disciple Kānu-pā bore the title of 'pā'[2] (and seldom Nāth) with their names. It is perhaps because of this fact that Jālandharī-pā has been traditionally held to be the introducer of the 'Pā' sect among the Kānphaṭ Yogins. He has also been held responsible for the practice of splitting the ears. It is said that when king Bhartṛ was initiated by Jālandharī into the Yogi-cult, the former asked for some distinctive mark,—and the splitting of ears and wearing long ear-rings were the distinctive marks which he was allowed to have.[3] The Augharī sect of yogins also trace their origin to Jālandharī.

According to the Tibetan tradition Jālandharī is identical

[1] In the *Gorakṣa-vijaya* we find that this Siddha originated from the bone (*hāḍa*) of Mahādeva and hence the name Hāḍi-pā. But the more plausible reason for the name seems to be his desire to take up the meanest profession of a Hāḍi (a very low class people with the general occupation of the sweeper), if, however, that would allow him a chance to enjoy a woman like goddess Durgā.

[2] This *pā* is, however, nothing but the colloquial form of the Sanskrit word *pāda* commonly used as a mark of reverence with the names of the *Siddhācāryas*. The use of *pāda* as a mark of reverence is found in many other religious sects also. The form *phā* as in Hāḍi-phā, Kānu-phā, etc., seems to be nothing but the East Bengal dialectal aspirated form of *pā*.

[3] Briggs, p. 9.

with the Buddhist Siddha Bāla-pāda, who was born in Sind in a rich Śūdra family. He courted Buddhism and was practising yoga in the province of Udayana. Thence he went to Jālandhar of the Punjab and was henceforth known as Jālandharī.[1] He travelled from Jālandhar to Nepal and thence to Avanti, where he made many disciples including Kṛṣṇā-cārya. He then came to Bengal in the guise of a Hāḍi, performed miracles, and was recognised by queen Mayanāmatī, who made her son king Gopī-cānd his disciple. Gopī-cānd, however, took the Siddha to be a cheat and the Siddha was buried alive and was rescued later on by his disciple Kṛṣṇācārya after twelve years.[2] This legend of Jālandharī being buried alive by king Gopī-cānd (at the instance of his queens and minister) and his rescue by Kṛṣṇācārya is found in all the traditions,—Bengali, Hindi, Maraṭhi and Tibetan. In the *Gorakṣa-vijaya* we find that Kānu-pā was informed of the sad plight of the Guru by Gorakṣa-nāth. In the thirty-sixth song of the Caryāpadas we find Kānhu-pāda (or Kṛṣṇācārya-pāda) mentioning Jālandharī-pā as his Guru. We are loathe to believe that this Jālandharī-pā and Kānhu-pā of the Buddhist fold are identical with the Nāth Siddhas of the same name. Jālandharī is said to have been the Guru also of king Bhartṛhari of Ujjain, whose renunciation of the royal wealth and enjoyment for taking the vow of a yogin is associated with the same popular pathos as that of king Gopī-cānd. In Western India songs on Bhartṛ are as truly popular as those on Gopī-cānd. Other traditions, however, make Bhartṛ the disciple of Gorakh.

(iv) *Kānu-pā*

Kānu-pā[3] was the worthy disciple of Hāḍi-pā. Like

[1] We find mention of some Jālandhar-gaḍ in the Dharma-maṅgala literature (*cf.* Māṇik-gāṅgulī, p. 70; Dvija Rām-candra, MS. C. U. No. 2464, p. 2) which seems to be some native state in Bengal.

[2] *Vide*, a note on the Antiquity of Chittagong compiled from the Tibetan works *Pag Sam Jon Zang* of Sumpa Khanpo and *Khabad Dun Dan* of Lama Tāranāth by S. C. Das, (J.A.S.B., 1898).

[3] Kānu-pā is variously named as Kānuphā, Kānpha, Kāhnāi, Kānāi, Kāluphā, Kālaphā, etc., all of which are dialectal variants of the Sanskrit name Kṛṣṇapāda.

Mīna-nāth and Jālandharī Kānu-pā was destined for the city of Ḍāhukā[1] in the south, where he would have the opportunity of enjoying a woman like Durgā in her amorous guise. Though there is thus the indication of the fall also of Kānu-pā, we do not get any account of his fall in any of the stories either relating to Gorakh-nāth or Gopī-cānd. On the other hand we find that Kānu-pā once met Gorakh in his way, informed him of the fall of his Guru Mīna-nāth in the country of Kadalī and was in his turn informed by Gorakh of the sad plight of his own Guru Hāḍi-pā, who was buried under the floor of the stable by king Gopī-cānd. Kānu-pā at once hastened to the city of Gopī-cānd (in Meherkul or the city of Pāṭikā)[2] and rescued his Guru by devising various means. All the poets are, however, silent as to what happened to Kānu-pā after the rescue of the Guru. In the *Gopī-candrer Sannyās* by Sukur Mahammad there is, however, further indication of Kānu-pā's trials in the city of Ḍāhukā with the curse from his own Guru Jālandharī, with whom he (Kānu-pā) played false in order to save Gopī-cānd from the wrath of Jālandharī. It was further decreed by the Guru at the supplications of Mayanāmatī that Kānu-pā would be rescued from his trials in the city of Ḍāhukā by his disciple Bāil Bhādāi. But nothing whatsoever is heard of Kānu-pā in the literature. These stories of the rescue of Jālandharī by his disciple Kānu-pā are also found in the legends of Western and Northern India,—but there Kānu-pā seems to be more commonly known as Kānarī-nāth.

The question as to whether the Kānu-pā of the Nāth literature is identical with the Kānhu-pāda, or Kṛṣṇācārya-pāda of the Caryā-songs has rightly attracted the notice of scholars.[3] We have already noticed the important fact that Kānu-pā of the Caryā-songs has, at least in one place, spoken of Jālandharī-pā as his Guru. But in spite of this

1 The city is also called Dāhurā, Vahaḍi, Ḍārāv, etc.

2 For these cities and the controversies over their identification in different parts of East Bengal and North Bengal see the introduction to the *Gopī-candrer Gān* (C.U.) by Mr Viśveśvar Bhaṭṭācārya.

3 See *Hājār Bacharer Purāṇ Bāṅgalāy Siddhā Kānupār Gīt O Doṁhā* by Dr. M. Shahidullah, Dacca Sāhitya Pariṣat Granthāvali, No. 10.

coincidence, the identity of the two is still now a matter of speculation. Again, even in the esoteric Buddhist field we find that many Tāntric works including the important commentary on the *Hevajra-tantra* (known as the *Hevajra-pañjikā* or *Yoga-ratnamālā*) are ascribed to Kṛṣṇācārya, and we have nothing to be sure that the authors of all these works are the same; on the other hand there is reason to believe that there were more than one person of the same name belonging to the Buddhist fold. Rai S. C. Das, Bahadur in his edition of the *Pag Sam Jon Zang* has given short accounts of at least three Kṛṣṇācaryas; of these one of the Kṛṣṇācāryas had his disciple in Bhāde, who has been included in the lists of the eighty-four Siddhas. This Bhāde has undoubtedly given rise to Bāil Bhādāi of the Bengali Nāth literature.

(v) *Gopī-candra or Govinda-candra*

Almost all the legends about Gopī-candra or Gopī-cānd describe him as a powerful king of Bengal. But literary records of Bengal do not agree on the point of localising the kingdom of Gopī-cānd. On the whole two conflicting claims are found; according to some versions of the songs the locality of the whole story of Gopī-cānd is North Bengal in or near about the district of Rangpur, while in many other versions the locality is said to be in the district of Tippera. As a matter of fact the topographical references found in some of the versions lead us to North Bengal and there are traditions in those parts of North Bengal of Gopī-cānd's being a king of the vicinity; but the topographical references in some other versions will again lead one to think that the locality must be somewhere in the district of Tippera in East Bengal.[1] The fact may be that the empire of Gopī-cānd extended over parts of East Bengal as well as of North Bengal and hence are the traditions in both the places. The legend of Gopī-cānd has already been described. We shall deal here very briefly with some of the questions pertaining to the probable time of his reign. He was perhaps a Gandha-

[1] For the discussion on the Topography see Mr. V. Bhaṭṭācārya's introduction to C.U. edition. See also B.S.P.P., 1328, No. 2.

baṇik (literally a seller of perfumes) by caste, and the tradition of his family relation with Cānd Beṇe, the important merchant that figures in our early and medieval literature, will also corroborate this tradition. According to the version of Bhavānī-dās Gopī-cānd left no posterity; while local traditions both in Rangpur and Tippera show that he left a son Bhava-candra or Udayacandra by name. According to the Hindi and Marathi tradition Gopī-cānd had a sister of the name of Campāvatī, who, after Gopī-cānd had taken his vow of Sannyāsa, tried to dissuade him,—but was at last herself convinced of the superiority of the yogic life.[1] European scholars like Buchanan Hamilton, Glazier and Grierson held that the family of Gopī-candra was somehow related to the family of the Pāla kings of Bengal. Some hold that Māṇik-candra, who was the father of Gopī-candra, was the brother of Dharma-pāla, and after the death of Māṇik-candra there followed war between Dharma-pāla and Mayanāmatī, mother of Gopī-cānd, and Gopī-cānd inherited the throne after Dharma-pāla had been defeated and killed; some again hold that Dharma-pāla was the brother-in-law of Mayanāmatī. Grierson, however, held that Māṇik-candra was not the brother, but some rival of, or native prince under the sway of king Dharma-pāla. This theory of the relation of Gopī-cānd or his father with Dharma-pāla has been discarded by scholars, as no credible evidence on the point is available. Of the few important historical documents available on Gopī-cānd we may consider first of all the rock-inscription of Tirumalai placed by Rajendra-cola of the Deccan. According to this inscription Rajendra-cola defeated Dharma-pāla of Daṇḍabhukti, Raṇasūra of Southern Rāḍha, Govinda-candra of Vaṅga and Mahīpāla of Northern Rāḍha. We have seen that Gopī-candra is also wellknown as Govinda-candra, and Vaṅga would originally mean East Bengal, and there is also the tradition, as we have seen, of Gopī-cānd being a king of East-Bengal; associating these facts together it may be presumed that king Govinda-candra, referred to in the

[1] *Cf. Yogi-sampradāyā-viṣkṛti*, Ch. 42. *Cf.* also the Hindi version of the Gopī-cānd song, B.S.P.P., 1328, No. 2, p. 52.

Tirumalai inscription, is the Gopī-cānd of the Nāth literature. Rajendra-cola flourished in the first quarter of the eleventh century; if the identity of the Govinda-candra of the inscription and that of Nāth literature be accepted then Gopī-cānd or Govindra-candra may be taken to have flourished in the first half of the eleventh century; and this fixing of time approximately tallies, we have seen, with the time of Matsyendra-nāth, who might have flourished in the tenth century.

The discovery of three copper-plates in the districts of Faridpur and Dacca in East Bengal, containing the genealogy of some Candra-dynasty of East Bengal, has thrown a flood of light on the question of the identification of Gopī-cānd. The genealogy of the Candra-dynasty, found in these inscriptions, runs as follows:—

Pūrṇa-candra
|
Suvarṇa-candra
|
Trailokya-candra
|
Śrī-candra

According to Durlabh Mallik the father and grand-father of Māṇik-candra were Suvarṇa-candra and Dhāḍi-candra respectively. Dr. N. K. Bhaṭṭaśālī has tried to explain Dhāḍi-candra as referring to Pūrṇa-candra. According to the Maraṭhi and Hindi tradition Tilak-candra or Trailokya-candra was the father of Gopī-candra. Again Mayanāmatī herself has sometimes been spoken of as the daughter of Tilak-candra. On the whole the names of Suvarṇa-candra and Trailokya-candra are found common in the inscriptions and in the Nāth literature and this has led scholars to suppose that Gopī-candra came out of the Candra dynasty of East Bengal. Experts have given their opinion that these copper inscriptions belong to the tenth or eleventh century A.C., and therefore Gopī-cānd might have flourished some time near about this time. Another fact to be considered in this connection is that Deva-gaṇa, grand-father of Bhadreśvara, who again was father of Sureśvara, well-known author of the *Śabda-pradīpa*, was the court physician of king Govinda-candra; Sureśvara flourished probably in the latter half of the eleventh century,—his great grand-father Deva-gaṇa then flourished perhaps sometime in the second half of the tenth century or in the first half of the eleventh century. But the difficulty is that there is nothing to be sure that the Govinda-candra referred to by Sureśvara in the introduction of his work is identical with the Govinda-candra or Gopī-cānd in question.

(vi) *Mayanāmatī*

Before we conclude the chapter we should say a few words about Mayanāmatī, who is important not only as the mother of king Gopī-cānd, but also as a woman well versed in yoga and having miraculous power thereby. In some of the versions she is said to be the daughter of some king, Tilak-cānd by name, and her name in her childhood was Śiśumatī (and Suvadanī according to another version). According to the Tibetan tradition she was the sister of Bhartṛ, the king of Malvar, mentioned above. A modern author Candra-nāth yogin speaks of her as the *Dharma-bahin* of king Bhartṛ of Ujjain.[1] In the Hindi version of the story of Gopī-cānd she is said to be the daughter of Candra-sena of Dhārā-nagar. From her very childhood she showed signs of possessing wonderful yogic powers and this attracted the notice of the great yogin Gorakh-nāth, who initiated her into the Nāth cult. Gopī-cānd, we have seen, once cast serious aspersions against the mother and the legend of the curse of goddess Durgā towards Hāḍi-pā to be enthralled in the city of Mehera-kula in the company of queen Mayanāmatī, lends some support to such a suspicion; but the suspicion of the son was stoutly denied by the mother and the poets have also very cleverly handled the situation. Mayanāmatī is depicted in the Nāth literature as a Tāntric Ḍākinī, which means the woman of mystic wisdom. As the Ḍākinī is deified in the Tantras as the goddess of mystic wisdom, or some sort of a demi-goddess having mystic wisdom as well as supernatural powers, so

[1] *Yogi-sampradāyā-viṣkṛti*, Ch. 39.

Mayanāmatī has also been deified in later times as some one midway between a witch and a goddess and she has also sometimes been identified with Caṇḍī or Kālī, and she is still now worshipped in some parts of North Bengal with animal sacrifice by priests belonging to the Rāja-vaṁśa caste. Mr. V. Bhaṭṭācārya has presented us with one of the interesting songs that are recited on the occasion of the worship of Mayanā-buḍī.

APPENDIX (D)

GENERAL INFORMATIONS ABOUT THE DHARMA LITERATURE OF BENGAL

In giving an idea of the literature belonging to the Dharma cult we should first of all mention the two liturgical works available on the cult, the *Śūnya-purāṇa*[1] ascribed to Rāmāi Paṇḍit, who is traditionally supposed to be the founder of the cult in the age of Kali, and the other, the *Dharma-pūjā-vidhāna* which is also ascribed to Rāmāi Paṇḍit, as well as to Raghu-nandana. These liturgical texts represent popular literature of a composite nature in a very loosely versified diction, which embody topics on cosmogony, liturgy, legends about Dharma-worship, building of temples, rituals, ceremonies and indigenous practices, all centering round the godhead of Dharma. There is a great deal of controversy over the authenticity of these texts and the time of their composition and their authorship. As our present study is not primarily historical, we do not propose to enter into the details of these controversies; for our purpose it is necessary to state briefly the conclusions, which we have arrived at by a minute study of the data available on the points at issue.

As for the *Śūnya-purāṇa*, which is ascribed to Rāmāi Paṇḍit, there are sufficient reasons to belive that the text in its published form does not represent the contents of a single book composed at any particular point of time by any particular author. On the other hand the text seems to be a collection of versified accounts of the Dharma cult

[1] Edited by Mr. N. N. Vasu for the first time and published from the Sāhitya Pariṣat and then by Mr. Charu Chandra Banerjee from the Vasumatī Office. The name *Śūnya-purāṇa* was used for the book for the first time by the editor Mr. N. N. Vasu and the naming seems to be arbitrary, for no such name of the book is found in any manuscript (the original manuscript of Mr. Vasu is not, however, available to the public). In one place of the text the book is called *Āgama-purāṇa*, and it is also traditionally called the *Hākanda-purāṇa*. MM. H. P. Śāstrī named it as *Rāmāi Paṇḍiter Paddhati*. However, as the book became widely known by the name of *Śūnya-purāṇa* the name was retained in the second edition by Mr. Banerjee.

which grew during the thirteenth and the seventeenth, centuries among the adherents of this cult. It will be observed that the same topics under the same heading have been introduced thrice or even four times within the text with slightly different readings. There is no order in the arrangement,—cosmogonical, liturgical, ceremonial and legendary accounts have been introduced here and there pell-mell. Linguistic differences are also noticeable in different chapters. All these go to prove that the text is more of the nature of a compilation than the authentic version from a single hand. With the pseudo-archaic forms introduced late in the composition of the verses the language of the *Śūnya-purāṇa* in general presents no archaic character which might justify its claim to have been composed sometime during the fourteenth or the fifteenth century. From the heaps of traditional accounts that have gathered round the figure of Rāmāi Paṇḍit we are loathe to explain away the personality of Rāmāi as purely fictitious. We may not, and we should not, accept all the mythical and semi-mythical accounts given in the *Śrī-dharma-purāṇa* ascribed to Mayūra-bhaṭṭa,[1] or in the *Yātrā-siddha-rāyer Paddhati*;[2] but nevertheless Rāmāi seems to have been a historical personage.

Rāmāi was held in all Dharma-maṅgala literature to have been the founder of the Dharma cult. The fact may historically be explained in the following manner. A mass of crude local religious ideas and practices of purely indigenous origin got mixed up with some crypto-Buddhist ideas and practices and with these again were incorporated many Hindu ideas and practices in course of time. This curiously composite whole, which could neither be recognised as any form of Buddhism, nor any form of Hinduism, was perhaps modified and loosely codified into a popular religious system by Rāmāi Paṇḍit and henceforth Rāmāi Paṇḍit has been enjoying the credit of being the founder of the cult. Attempts have been made by scholars to determine the time of Rāmāi Paṇḍit, but it appears to us

[1] Edited by Mr. Basanta Kumar Chatterjee and published by the Sāhitya Pariṣat.

[2] Portions of the work containing the accout of Rāmāi Paṇḍit are quoted in the introduction to the *Śūnya-purāṇa* (Pariṣat edition) by Mr. N. N. Vasu.

that no such convincing data are available as may warrant the fixing up of the date historically. One way of forming some idea about the time of Rāmāi is to trace the history of later Buddhism in Bengal, from which evolved this mixed religion among the ordinary people, and from a consideration of the course of evolution of later Buddhism it appears that Rāmāi Paṇḍit might have appeared in or about the twelfth century A.D. As we have said, detailed accounts of Rāmāi Paṇḍit and his heirs are given in the *Śrī-dharma-maṅgala* of Mayūra-bhaṭṭa, edited by Mr. B. K. Chatterjee as well as in the *Paddhati* of Yātrāsiddha Rāya;[1] but for various reasons we are not prepared to believe in the historicity of these accounts. The accounts given there are all of an extremely legendary nature.[2] It may cursorily be mentioned here that in the ritualistic texts as well as in the Dharma-maṅgalas we find occasional references to Mārkaṇḍeya Muni in connection with the worship of Dharma, and sometimes he is depicted as the instructor of Rāmāi in the matter of Dharma-worship. This seems to be nothing but an attempt somehow to connect the Dharma cult with the Purāṇic Hindu legends. Attempts have also been made by scholars to connect the legends of the Dharma cult with those of the Nāth literature and to determine the time of Rāmāi Paṇḍit with the help of the personages of the Nāth literature.[3] In the *Śūnya-purāṇa*

1 *Vide* B.S.P.P., B.S. 1313, No. 2.

2 Thus, for instance, it has been said that at the end of the Dvāpara age Viśvanātha, a Brahmin of the city of Dvārikā, with his wife Kamalā, worshipped Viṣṇu desirous of a child; long time passed without any issue and then the couple went out on pilgrimage and observed austere penances in sacred places with the purpose of having a son born to them—but all was in vain; being thus sadly disappointed they were one day about to commit suicide, but were saved by sage Mārkaṇḍeya who taught them the right method of worshipping Viṣṇu who is here plainly identified with Dharma-rāja. They followed his advice, propitiated Viṣṇu or Dharma and had a son born to them,—and as the son was born in the Rāma Tīrtha, the son was called Rāmāi. It has been said in this connection that the child was born in the white Pañcamī of the month of Vaiśākha on Sunday and the Star was *Bharaṇī* (*vaiśākhī sita-pañcamī nakṣatra bharaṇī I ravivār śubha yoge prasave brāhmaṇī* ‖ p. 13). The same account is found in the *Paddhati* of Yātrāsiddha-rāya (See introduction to the *Śūnya-purāṇa*, edited by Mr. N. N. Vasu). But it has been pointed out by Dr. Shahidullah that there cannot be any Sunday in the month of Vaiśākha with white Pañcamī and the star *Bharaṇī* (see introductory article of Dr. Shahidullah in the *Śūnya-purāṇa*, edited by Mr. C. C. Banerjee, p. 35) and this speaks of the imaginary nature of the whole account.

3 See an article on Rāmāi Paṇḍit by Dr. Binay Kumar Sen, M.A., Ph.D., in the *Calcutta Review*, August, 1924.

we find that king Haricandra erected a temple of Dharma and with his chief queen Madanā worshipped Dharma with pomp and pageantry avowedly with the purpose of having a son born to them. This Haricandra has been identified with king Hariścandra of Sābhār in the district of Dacca. Two daughters of Hariścandra, *viz.*, Adunā and Padunā were given in marriage to the renowned king Gopī-candra or Govinda-candra, who flourished in the eleventh century.[1] The Tibetan historian Lama Tāranāth has also mentioned the name of Haricandra, who was a king in Bengal in the eleventh century. But the story of Haricandra (or rather Hariścandra), found in the Dharma-maṅgala literature, seems to be purely mythical, and like the story of the sage Mārkaṇḍeya and the fragments of many other Purāṇic stories, this well-known story of Haricandra or Hariścandra has been interwoven with the main story of the Dharma-maṅgala literature. This story of Hariścandra was current in India as a very popular story from the time of the Vedas. This story is found in the *Aitareya Brāhmaṇa, Kauṣītakī Brāhmaṇa* and in many other places of the Vedic literature.[2] The same story is told in the *Mahābhārata* in a slightly different form as the story of Karṇa's offering the flesh of his son to Lord Viṣṇu, disguised as a Brahmin-guest. In the Vedic literature the story of Hariścandra begins with the question of having a son by propitiating God Varuṇa; it is therefore, very likely that the same story was told in connection with Rañjāvatī's having a son born to her by propitiating Lord Dharma. We may point out here that, not only king Hariścandra, but even Lord Nārāyaṇa has in some versions of the Dharma-maṅgalas been held to have been the first worshipper of Dharma.[3] Moreover, it has rightly been pointed out that no stone-image of

[1] *Vide supra.*

[2] *Vide, A History of Indian Literature* by Winternitz pp. 211-216: also introduction to the *Śrī-dharma-purāṇa* of Mayūrabhaṭṭa by B. K. Chatterjee, pp. 44-45.

[3] In the Dharma-maṅgalas we often find a chronology of the twelve worshippers of Dharma. According to the chronology given by Māṇik Gāṅgulī the first worshipper was Lord Nārāyaṇa on the shore of the Kṣīroda sea; the second was the King of the gods (Indra?), the third was king Mahīsura, the fourth was Kuvadatta of Cāpāya; the fifth Haricandra, who sacrificed his son to Lord Dharma; the sixth was Kāśī of the Rāja-vaṁśa, the seventh was Rañjāvatī, who laid herself on spikes in order to have a son; the eighth was Lāusen; the ninth was Jayasiṁha, who worshipped Dharma on the bank of

Dharma-ṭhākura or any trace of Dharma-worship is found in any locality of Dacca, or East Bengal as a whole,—whereas stone-images of Dharma-ṭhākura and various traces of Dharma-worship are found abundantly in West Bengal; under the circumstances it is unwarranted to place king Haricandra, the first worshipper of Dharma, in the village Sābhār of the Dacca district.[1]

of the Lake Tāra; the tenth worship was in Kaṅura and the twelfth worshid was in connection with the death of Ichāi-ghoṣ (*Śrī-dharma-maṅgala*, p. 225). According to Ghana-rām the first worshipper of Dharma was Mahārāja Bhoja; the second was Dhūpadatta, who erected a temple of Dharma in Māṇik-dvīpa; the third was Mathura-ghoṣ and the fourth the Brahmin Mahīmukha; the fifth was Kālu-ghoṣ who was born from the sweat of Dharma; the sixth was king Hariścandra, the seventh was the son of Sadā Ḍoma; the eighth was Āsāī Caṇḍāla; the ninth the Brahmin Mahīpāla; the tenth was Śivadatta of the Bārui caste (*i.e.*, people dealing in betel leaves); the eleventh was Harihara Bāiti and the twelfth was Lāusen (*Śrī-dharma-maṅgala* of Ghana-rām, p. 272). According to Rūp-rām again, the first worship was offered by the Brahmin Harihara, to whom Dharma appeared in the form of a Brahmacārin, the second was made by the son of a cowherd (*goāl koṅār*) who built a golden house for Dharma in Sonārapura; the third was made by Isāi Caṇḍāla, who offered Dharma a tank of wine and a dam of cakes (*mader pukhur dila piṭhār jāṅgāl*); the fourth worship was made by the son of a merchant, the fifth by Puradatta and the sixth by king Hariścandra with his wife Madanā (and the author confesses in this connection that the story of Hariścandra is famous in the Purāṇa, named *Kāśī-khaṇḍa*); the seventh was by Sadā Ḍoma who offered wine and meat to Dharma; the eighth was by Ananta Vāsuki, ninth by Kharjjura-nandana (?),—and the tenth by the Bāiti of Gauḍa; the eleventh worship was by Rañjāvatī and the twelfth and the last by Lāusen. [See MS. C. U. 3279, pp. 85 (A)—85 (B)]. The list according to the *Anādi-maṅgala* of Rāmdās Ādak is as follows:—Dvija Harihara, Urvaśī Muni, Sadā-śiva in the form of Sadā Ḍoma, on the bank of the river Bullukā (by whom?), Māndhātā, Yudhiṣṭhira, Hariścandra, worship in Gauḍa (by whom?) etc., the twelfth being Lāusen (see p. 245). Such a chronology of the twelve worshippers of Dharma in the Kaliyuga are found in many of the Dharma-maṅgalas by other poets with some alterations. It is needless to repeat here that no historical importance should be attached to these chronologies which are purely legendary and myhical in nature. It is also to be noted that the number of worshippers of Dharma-ṭhākura in the Kaliyuga is twelve only because of the fact that twelve is the mystic number of the Dharma cult, and the worship of Dharma is called *Bārmati*. The ceremonies of the worship take place in twelve consecutive days beginning from the third Tithi of the light half of the month of Vaiśākha. In the Dharma-pūjā twelve flowers, twelve items of all ritualistic articles are required; the male devotees required are twelve and the number of the female devotees is also twelve; even the chapters in the Dharma-maṅgalas are twelve. Mr. B. K. Chatterjee likes to connect this custom of the Dharma cult with the Vedic custom of Twelve days' sacrifice (*vide* Introduction to *Śrī-dharma-maṅgala* of Mayūra-bhaṭṭa, p. 245). In the *Dharma-pūjā-vidhāna* we find that in every age there are seven devotees (*bhakta*) of Dharma. In the Satya age the devotees are,—Brahmā, Ulūka, Nārada, Vasumati, Durgā, Indra and Gaṅgā; in the Treta age Vali, Māndhātā, Sāgara, Kārttika, Kālughoṣa, Venupura, and Bhaṭṭa-dharādhara; in the Dvāpara age Rāvaṇa, Indra-kumāra, Śaṅkha, Śrī-rāma, Gāndhārī, Bhagīratha, Bhāskara and Pakṣirāja (*i.e.*, Garuḍa); in the Kali age Kapilā, Nārāyaṇa, Maṇirāja, Bhaṭṭa, Muṇḍira Ghoṣa, Pūrva-datta, Bhīṣmaka, Kauntaka, Bighneśvara, Āsāya Caṇḍāla, Varuṇa, Magara, Manoratha Paṇḍita, Pakṣasāreṅga, Sādhupura Datta and Dhanakuvera (p. 8). The number in the Kaliyuga evidently exceeds seven and becomes fifteen.

[1] Introduction to the *Śrī-dharma-maṅgala* of Mayūra-bhaṭṭa by Mr. B. K. Chatterjee, p. 45.

Rāmāi Paṇḍit was in later times transformed into a purely mythical figure by being associated with the other four exponents of the cult, *viz.*, Śetai, Nīlāi, Kaṁsāi and Goṁsāi.[1] In the Dharma-maṅgalas of the later period Rāmāi Paṇḍit is found to be the instructor of Queen Rañjāvatī, mother of Lāusen, the hero of the Dharma-maṅgalas. This Rañjāvatī is said to have been the sister-in-law of the emperor of Gauḍa. In no one of the Dharma-maṅgalas do we find mention of the name of this emperor of Gauḍa; but it is said that he was the son of Dharma-pāla.[2] Dharma-pāla is a famous king of the Pāla dynaty of Bengal, who ascended the throne in 815 A.D. He had two sons of whom Tribhuvana-pāla, the elder of the two, died prematurely during the lifetime of his father; consequently Deva-pāla, the younger son, became the emperor of Gauḍa after Dharma-pāla. If we are to accept the account given by Ghana-rām, Rañjāvatī was the sister-in-law of king Deva-pāla, who flourished in the ninth century A.D., and Rāmāi Paṇḍit being the instructor of Rañjāvatī flourished at or about that time. But in a copper-plate inscription of Devapāla, discovered in Munghyr it is found that some Raṇṇadevī was the wife of Dharma-pāla and Raṇṇādevī was the daughter of Govinda III. According to Ghana-rām, however, the chief queen of Dharma-pāla was Ballabhā. To us the account given by Ghana-rām does not seem to be historically correct; he seems to have given rather a traditional account of his hero Lāusen, who must have been a tribal chief at the time of some Pāla king named Dharma-pāla. The association of Rāmāi Paṇḍit with the Dharma-worship by Rañjāvatī and by Lāusen in later time seems to be merely traditional. Whenever there was the worship of Dharma the help of a

[1] *Vide Supra* Ch. xiii.

[2] Many scholars have committed a great mistake by assuming that Rāmāi Paṇḍit was contemporaneous with king Dharma-pāla of Gauḍa, of whom Rañjāvatī, the mother of Lāusen was the sister-in-law. (See *Vaṅga-bhāṣā O Sāhitya* by Dr. D. C. Sen, D.Litt., chapter on *Baudha-yuga*; Introduction to the *Śūnya-purāṇa* by Mr. C. C. Banerjee, p. 89). Nowhere in the Dharma-maṅgalas do we find Rañjāvatī described as the sister-in-law of Dharma-pāla; she was the sister-in-law of the son of Dharma-pāla. *Cf. dharma-pāl nāme chila gauḍer ṭhākur* l *prasaṅge prasave puṇya pāp yāy dūr* || *pṛthivī pāliyā svarga bhuñje nṛpavar* l *bīryavanta putra tār rājā gauḍeśvar* || *Śrī-dharma-maṅgala* of Ghana-rām (Baṅgavāsī edition), p. 12. It was this last Gauḍeśvara, son of Dharma-pāla, of whom Rañjāvatī is said to have been the sister-in-law. The same account is also found in the *Anādi-maṅgala* of Rām-dās Ādak, see p. 13 (Sāhitya-pariṣat edition).

Paṇḍit (*i.e.*, a priest versed in Dharma-worship) was required, and Rāmāi being the most famous of the Paṇḍits, it is very likely that his name should be associated with the Dharma-worship of different times. On all occasions of Dharma-worship the priest or the Paṇḍit, who is generally said to be Rāmāi Paṇḍit himself, gave instruction consulting a scriptural text which is called *Dharma-purāṇa* or *Hākanda-purāṇa* or simply the Purāṇa.[1] Hanūmān, who has in many occasions given instruction of Dharma-worship, is described as well-versed in the *Hākanda-purāṇa* (which, we have seen, is another name for the text of *Śūnya-purāṇa*). This fact leads to the conclusion that among the poets of the later times there was the tradition of some liturgical text containing all the details of Dharma-worship and the text of the *Śūnya-purāṇa* in its modern form may represent some confusedly collected portions of the aforesaid text.

As for the other ritualistic text, *viz.*, the *Dharma-pūjā-vidhāna*, we are definitely of opinion that it is a compilation of much later times. The followers of the Dharma cult, however, speak of the *Śūnya-purāṇa* and the *Dharma-pūjā-vidhāna* as the fifth Veda embodying the new religion of Dharma, which was first revealed to Rāmāi Paṇḍit. The vernacular verses in the latter text are very few in comparison with the Sanskritic and the pseudo-Sanskritic Mantras and other injunctions regarding the worship not only of Dharma-ṭhākura, but of almost all the gods and goddesses of the popular Hindu pantheon, of esoteric Buddhism as well as of purely local deities of indigenous origin. Beginning with the worship of Gaṇeśa (as the custom in popular Hindu worship is) we find here injuctions and Mantras for the worship of the Sun, Brahmā, Viṣṇu, Śiva, Durgā, Lakṣmī, Viṣahari, Bhairava, Vāśulī, Sarasvatī, Kuvera, Saṣṭhī, Bhagavatī, Vasumatī, Viśālākṣī, Baṭuka-

[1] See, *Śrī-dharma-maṅgala* of Ghana-rām, p. 40; *Ibid.*, p. 41, p. 216.
dharma-purāṇer mata pūjā jathocita I
Dharmāyaṇa of Narasiṁha Vasu, Vol. 1.
MS. C.U. No. 3224, p. 68(B).
paṇḍit pustak hāte balān vacan I
Ibid., Vol. II., MS. C.U. No. 3226, p. 32(A).
Cf. also p. 18(B).
Śrī-dharma-maṅgala of Ghana-rām, p. 8.

nātha, Kṣetrapāla, Brahmāṇī, Māheśvarī, Vaiṣṇavī, Bārāhī, Nārasimhī, Indrāṇī, Cāmuṇḍā, Garuḍa, Viśvakarmā, Nandī, Kāmadeva, Vāṇeśvara, Paṇḍāsura, the ten Dik-pālas, the gate-keepers (Dvāra-pāla), and a host of others. In the colophon of the vernacular verses we find the name of Rāmāi Paṇḍit as the author, whereas the text as a whole is ascribed to Raghu-nandana. It is very easy to detect that many of the Bengali verses of the *Dharma-pūjā-vidhāna* are nothing but different version of the verses found in the *Śūnya-purāṇa*, and the Sanskrit Mantras regarding the meditation and the salutation of the Hindu gods and goddesses are nothing but the corrupted forms of them found in the Hindu texts on worship; the portions composed by our Raghu-nandana, are the peculiarly funny pseudo-Sanskritic portions introduced here and there in the text. Whoever the author of these pseudo-Sanskritic portions might have been, it is apparent that the text as a whole has been ascribed to Raghu-nandana only to bestow on it the dignity and importance of being composed by Raghu-nandana, the great authoirty on Smṛti.

Besides these liturgical texts there are the Dharma-maṅgalas which represent in many places a type of really good literature in the art of plot-construction as well as in characterisation. Though Rāmāi Paṇḍit appears to have flourished some time before the twelfth century, Dharma-maṅgala literature did not flourished before the seventeenth and the eighteenth centuries. Mayūra-bhaṭṭa has been unanimously credited by other poets of the cults to have been the first poet of the Dharma-maṅgala literature and all poets have saluted him (Mayūra-bhaṭṭa) as the pioneer in the field. But the work of Mayūra-bhaṭṭa has not yet been discovered and the *Śri-dharma-purāṇa* of Mayūra-bhaṭṭa discovered and edited by Mr. B. K. Chatterjee (and published by the Sāhitya Pariṣat) seems to us to be spurious for various reasons, and this had rightly been the opinion also of many other scholars after it was first published.[1] Moreover, even in its spurious form the text pub-

[1] *Vide* B.S.P.P., B.S. 1338, No. 2.
The reasons, why this text seems to us to be purely spurious may briefly be

lished is incomplete, the Lāusen-story being missing. After Mayūra-bhaṭṭa the poetical works of about twenty poets have been discovered, many in the complete form and some in parts. As we have already pointed out, almost all of these poets flourished during the period of a century from the last half of the seventeenth century to the last half of the eighteenth century.[1] Of these poets, however, Rūpa-rām, Khelā-rām, Māṇik Gāṅgulī, Sītā-rām, Rām-dās Ādak, Ghana-rām Cakravartī, Sahadev Cakravartī, Narasiṁha Vasu, Rām Candra Bandyopādhyāy seem to be more important.[2] Excepting the work of Sahadev Cakravartī, in whom we find a mixture of the legends of the Dharma literature and of the Nāth literature, all the other works are almost the same so far as the theme is concerned. The main theme of all the Dharma-maṅgalas is the story of Lāusen, and there is a striking unanimity among the poets not only in the description of the main story, but also in the minute description of the incidents.

The Dharma-maṅgala literature as a whole, like all other Maṅgala literatures of Bengal, represents, as we have already explained in the introduction,[3] the continuation of the spirit of the Purāṇic literature in the vernacular. It is some sort of a propaganda literature to glorify the god or the

noted below. In the first place the manuscript of the text, as the editior himself admits, is almost brand new (written in 1310 B.S., *i.e.*, 58 years old), and secondly the language is hopelessly modern. Thirdly, Mayūra-bhaṭṭa being the pioneer in the field, the later poets should have followed him in their works; but that has not been the case. Again, the later poets do not attach so much importance to the stone-image of Dharma (*i.e.*, Dharma-śilā) as the neo-Mayūra-bhaṭṭa does. Moreover, we find here innumerable legends of purely Purāṇic character very cleverly interwoven in the text to explain all the peculiar customs and factors found in connection with Dharma-worship. Again it is very curious to note that though Mayūra-bhaṭṭa is the earliest poet of the Dharma-maṅgala literature, flourishing in or about the fourteenth century A.D., the Dharma ṭhākura depicted in this work bears not even the faintest trace of any Buddhistic character whatsoever and has flatly identified himself with Lord Visnu !

1 Dr. D. C. Sen in his *Typical Selections from Bengali Literature*, Part 1, says that the manuscript of the *Dharma-maṅgala* of Govindarām Bandyopādhyāy is dated 1071 B.S. (*i.e.*, 1665 A.D.), and from this he assumes that Govindarām flourished in the seventeenth century. But Mr. B. K. Chatterjee holds that the date of the MS. is not of B.S., but of the Malla Era, (1071 Malla Era,—1766 A.D.) and thinks that the poet flourished in the first half of the eighteenth century. (*Vide* Introduction to the *Śri-dharma-maṅgala* of Mayūra-bhaṭṭa, p. 6).

2 For detailed information about these poets and their works *vide Bāṁlā-maṅgala-kāvyer Itihās* by Dr. Asutosh Bhattacharya, M.A., Ph.D., Calcutta, 1958.

3 *Supra*.

goddess in question with reference to innumerable incidents on which occasions he or she had the opportunity of displaying his or her sovereign power. The stories are introduced to popularise the worship of the deity pointing out the celestial benefit which the previous worshippers did obtain. The Dharma-maṅgalas relate the eventful life-sketch of the hero Lāusen, who owed his birth to the grace of Dharma and in all the adventures throughout his eventful life was saved from all sorts of calamities through the gracious intervention of Lord Dharma. We have already pointed out that in the delineation of the plot there is a general agreement among all the poets; let us therefore take the version of Ghana-rām Cakravartī to be the representative version of the story and give a summary of the whole story in the following pages.

After creating the universe Lord Dharma was in a fix as to how to introduce his worship in the world. Hanūmān, the sole agent and the main advisor of the Lord, advised him to make device to have Ambuvatī, a dancer-girl in the court of Indra, brought down on earth through some curse. The advice was promptly carried out and Ambuvatī took her human birth with Benu-rāy and Mantharā as her parents and wicked Mahāmad Pātra as her brother, she herself was named Rañjāvatī.

The son of Dharma-pāla (*i.e.*, Deva-pāla) was at that time the emperor of Gauḍa, and he married the elder daughter of Benu-rāy. Mahāmad Pātra (called by Ghana-rām generally as Pātra or Mahāpātra), who was the brother-in-law of the emperor, eventually became the minister. Once the emperor went a-hunting and chanced to meet Soma-ghoṣ who had been arrested on the order of the minister for non-payment of tax. The emperor took pity on him, ordered his release and placed him as a superintendent over Karṇa-sen, the chief of the fort of Triṣaṣṭi, situated on the bank of the river Ajaya. But ere long Ichāi-ghoṣ became very powerful, drove Karṇa-sen away, established a new fort for the name of Ḍhekur and defied the supremacy even of the emperor himself. The emperor went to subdue the rebellion with nine lacs of soldiers, but was sadly defeated. The six sons of Karṇa-sen were killed in the battle and his wife was shocked to death. The emperor then took pity on

Karṇa-sen and gave his sister-in-law, Rañjāvatī, in marriage to him. This, however, was strongly resented by Mahāpātra for various reasons. Unfortunately Rañjā proved barren and all rituals, ceremonies and worship of gods and goddesses came to be of no avail. Once, by chance, she came across a religious procession on the occasion of Dharma's *Gājana*,[1] and from among the processionists Rāmāi Paṇḍit explained to Rañjā and her husband the glory of Dharma and assured them that they also might have a son born to them by worshipping Dharma. With the instructions from Rāmāi Rañjāvatī laid herself on pikes before Dharma; and the lord was propitiated and granted her a son, whose name was Lāusen. When Mahāmad Pātra came to know of the birth of a son to Rañjā by Karṇa-sen he engaged a rogue, Indāmeṭe by name, to steal away the child, but the child was saved through the grace of Dharma. Dharma vouchsafed Lāusen a brother, Karpūra by name, as a playmate to him. When the two brothers grew in age Dharma sent Hanūmān from Vaikuṇṭha to teach them duel-fighting and archery. When his education was completed Lāusen, accompanied by his brother, started for Gauḍa to meet the emperor. They had thrilling encounters on the way,—Lāusen had to kill the pet tiger of Pārvatī, kill another crocodile, pass through the land of wicked women,—and Lāusen always came out victorious through the grace of Dharma, which was bestowed mainly through the agency of Hanūmān. After Lāusen reached Gauḍa his maternal uncle Mahāmad Pātra left no stone unturned to harass and insult Lāusen; but Lāusen got the upper hand through the grace of Dharma and returned home safe. Mahāmad Pātra then made another device against Lāusen; he instructed the emperor to send Lāusen to Kāmarūpa with some sturdy followers. This time also Lāusen had to encounter many difficulties; but the grace of Dharma through the agency of Hanūmān made him victorious throughout. He conqured Kāmarūpa very easily and married Kaliṅgā, the princess. When he was returning home in glory, he married on his

[1] *Gājana* (=skt. *garjana*=roaring) means the ceremonies that take place in honour of Dharma-ṭhākura. It is perhaps the tumultous nature of the ceremonies which are responsible for the name *Gājana*.

way Amalā, the daughter of Gajapati of Maṅgala-koṭa, and also Vimalā, daughter of the king of Burdwan.

After returning home Lāusen was passing his happy time in the company of his wives; but Dharma realised that if Lāusen were thus allowed to pass his time in peace the worship of Dharma would not be introduced in the world. He then held conference with Hanūmān and made another device. Through his magical power the emperor of Gauḍa became mad after Kānaḍā, the young beautiful daughter of Haripāla, king of Simulā. The emperor made proposal of marriage and it was sternly refused by Kānaḍā. The emperor got excited and attacked Simulā with nine lacs of soldiers. Kānaḍā then made a promise that, whoever would be able to break a particular iron rod, would be selected as her husband. The emperor failed ludicrously and the man who succeeded was Lāusen. After several other developments in the story, in which gods and goddesses played important parts, Kānaḍā was married by Lāusen.

Mahāmad Pātra was not the man to be cowed down. Lāusen must be crushed by hook or by crook. A fresh intrigue came to his mind and he proposed to the emperor that Lāusen should be sent to Ḍhekur to collect tax from Ichāi-ghoṣ. In spite of all remonstrance from his parents, who could not forget the death of their six sons at the hands of Ichāi-ghoṣ, Lāusen started for Ḍhekur and after a great fight killed Ichāi-ghoṣ, of course, through the grace and device of Dharma. Mahāmad Pātra was then convinced that Lāusen had the blessings of Dharma upon him,—and that to get the victory over Lāusen he should propitiate Dharma and obtain a boon from Him. Accordingly he advised the emperor of Gauḍa to worship Dharma, and his advice was followed. Dharma came to know of the evil intention of Mahāmad Pātra and through the agency of Hanūmān sent storm and rain below. The emperor got frightened and on the advice of the minister sent for Lāusen, who alone could save them from the direful wrath of the Lord. Lāusen came instantly but the Pātra made an absurd proposal. The Pātra said that the divinely decreed evil of the whole country could be remedied only if Lāusen could make the sun rise in the west at the dead of night on the new moon. Lāusen agreed and did make the sun rise in the west by his austere penances and thus the almighty power and the divine glory of Lord Dharma was finally established. Mahāmad Pātra was, however, punished with leprosy for his wickedness and afterwards relieved at the request of Lāusen; and Lāusen had heaven as his reward. Thus was the worship of Dharma introduced and popularised by Lāusen all over the world.

The struggle of Lāusen is virtually the struggle of Dharma himself to be introduced to the people of the world and to be recognised and worshipped by them as the Lord Supreme. It appears from the incidents of the Dharma-maṅgalas that Dharma-ṭhākura had to establish his supremacy against the Supremacy of the śakti (*i.e.*, the female deity) in the form of Durgā or Vāśulī or Kālī. The opponents of Lāusen were all worshippers of Śakti and were protected by her. Goddess Durgā even stooped so low as to assume the form of a charming damsel to allure Lāusen and to convert him to the Śakti cult; but all her attempts were frustrated by the strength of character of Lāusen and also by his sincere devotion towards Lord Dharma. The severest fight, virtually between Dharma and Śakti, in the person of Lāusen and Ichāi-ghoṣ respectively, took place in the battle of Ḍhekur. Ichāi was protected by the goddess herself and Lāusen with his backing in Lord Dharma could do no harm to him. As many times as Lāusen cut the head of Ichāi-ghoṣ, the head of Ichāi, separated from the body, muttered the name of Durgā and the separated head was joined with the body by the grace of the goddess. Lord Dharma found himself in a fix and Hanūmān was helpless there. Immediately, however, an assembly of the gods was invited and advice from them solicited. It was then finally decided that the sage Nārada must be sent forth to devise some means whereby the attention of the goddess might be diverted from Ichāi. Nārada, the reputed quarrel-monger, went to goddess Durgā and informed her that, taking advantage of her long absence from Kailāsa (she being long in Ḍhekur to protect her devotee Ichāi-ghoṣ), old Śiva had left home and was visiting the quarters of the Kotch (a hilly tribe) and having dalliances with Kotch-women; Kārttika and Gaṇeśa (the two sons of Durgā) had left home and went away, Jayā and Vijayā (the daughters) were starving to death, the condition of the whole family was topsy-turvy. Hearing these words from Nārada Durgā at once left Ḍhekur for Kailāsa and found all the informations, supplied by Nārada, to be totally false; but taking advantage of her absence from Ḍhekur Dharma, through the agency of Hanūmān, instructed Lāusen to attack and kill Ichai-ghoṣ which Lāusen easily succeeded in executing. By the time Durgā hurried up to Ḍhekur, Hanūmān carried the head of Ichāi to the netherland and she found, it was too late to give her devotee any help. Thus the honour of Lord Dharma was somehow saved through the cunning device of Nārada, against whom, we are not told, what step was taken by the enraged goddess.

APPENDIX (E)

ENIGMATIC LANGUAGE OF THE OLD AND MEDIEVAL POETS

WE have seen before that many of the religious movements, with which we have dealt, were esoteric in nature and it was quite in the fitness of things that the language in which the religious contents were given poetic expression was often extremely enigmatic. This enigmatic language of the old and medieval poetry is popularly styled as *Sandhyā-bhāṣā*, which, according to its conventional spelling, literally means 'the evening language',—and the word 'evening' here may be explained as pointing to the mystical nature of the language. In the Hindu as well as Buddhist Tantras, and in the Buddhist Dohās and songs, we find much use of this *Sandhyā-bhāṣā* and MM. H. P. Śāstrī has explained it as the 'twilight language', *i.e.*, half expressed and half-concealed (*ālo-āṁdhāri*). But MM. Vidhuśekhara Śāstrī in an enlightening article in the *Indian Historical Quarterly*[1] has demonstrated with sufficient evidences from authoritative texts that the language is not *Sandhyā-bhāṣā*, but is *Sandhā-bhāṣā* (*sam*$+\sqrt{}$*dhā*) or the 'intentional language'' *i.e.*, the language literally and apparently meaning one thing, but aiming at a deeper meaning hidden behind. Reference to this word *Sandhā-bhāṣā* is found in many texts of Pāli Buddhism as well as in Sanskrit Mahāyāna texts. Warning has often been given not to interpret the sayings of Buddha literally, but one should sink deep into them to catch at the right meaning aimed at by the Lord, and we find that the Buddhist preachers, particularly of the esoteric schools, would often use this intentional language to which the faithful adepts only had access. The same device was adopted by all the esoteric schools within the province of Hinduism.[2]

[1] 1928, Vol. IV, No. 2

[2] It may be incidentally noted here that Jesus Christ did also preach in a parabolic language (which also is nothing but a form of *Sandhā bhāṣā*) to cenceal the truth from the unbelievers like the scribes and the pharisees.

With regard to the spelling of the word *Sandhā-bhāṣā* or *Sandhā-vacana* as *Sandhyā-bhāṣā* or *Sandhyā-vacana* MM. V. Śāstrī is of opinion that it is a mistake of ignorant scribes. But it may be noticed in this connection that the word has consistently been spelt as *Sandhyā* and not as *Sandhā* in all the manuscripts of the Buddhist Tantras. May it therefore be postulated that it is not a mistake pure and simple of the scribes; but through the enigmatic and technical nature of the language and because of the mystical nature of its contents, it acquired in time a secondary meaning of 'twilight language' from its original meaning of 'intentional language' and hence it is that it is spelt as *Sandhyā* by the scribes ?

The tradition of the use of enigmas to conceal the real meaning from the ordinary people is as old as the Vedas. We often meet with riddles in the *Ṛg-veda* and the *Atharva-veda*,[1] which, when interpreted literally yield a meaning, which, as it is evident from the context, is not the real meaning. There are again statements in the ritualistic works known as the *Brāhmaṇas*, which give us no meaning literally; but the Pūrva-mīmāṁsakas discover important truth behind them with the help of metaphorical interpretation. But the use of technical *Sandhā-bhāṣā* became popular with the rise and development of the various Tāntric literature. The Sādhanā of the Tantras, be it Hindu or Buddhist, was generally a secret Sādhanā, and the best way to maintain the secrecy of the Sādhanā was to express the ideas and experiences of the Sādhakas with the help of technical and enigmatic language. The Tantras have, therefore, a language of their own which is accessible only to the initiated.

The Nature of the *Sandhā-bhāṣā* of the old Bengali Buddhist songs is not however exactly the same as that of the *Sandhā-bhāṣā* of the Tāntric literature. While the Tantras are full of technicalities, the songs are full of enigmas in addition to the technicalities.[2] *Sandhā-bhāṣā* of the Tantras generally means the infusion into some

[1] See *Ṛg-veda*, (1.164), (1.152.3), (10.55.5), (8.90.14), etc. *Atharva-veda*, (7.1), (11.8.10).

[2] But enigmas are also sometimes found in the Tāntric and Yogic texts. *Cf. go-māṁsaṁ bhakṣayen nityaṁ etc.*, *Supra*.

words of some technical meaning which is known only to the adept and to none else. It was the greatest sin on the part of a Tāntric to let the uninitiate into the secret of their cult, and this extreme technicality of the language, we have already pointed out, was taken as a device to prevent the public from making out anything of the secret of their cult. In the *Hevajra-tantra* there is a chapter on the *Sandhā-bhāṣā* where the Lord Vajra-sattva explains to Vajra-garbha the technical meaning of many such terms. In the eighteenth chapter of the *Śrī-guhya-samāja* also many such technical terms have been explained.[1]

The Caryā-songs of the Buddhist Siddhācāryas abound in technical terms; but more interesting are the enigmas. Couplets like—

māria śasu naṇanda ghare śālī |
māa māria kāhna bhaia kavāli ||[2]

are frequently to be met with in the Caryā-songs. The peculiarity of such imageries is that, when interpreted literally, they yield the most absurd meaning,—but when one obtains the key to them and learns to enter in, one gets at the true meaning hidden behind. Thus there is a poem of Kukkurī-pāda which runs as follows:—"When the *two* (teats) are milked (or when the tortoise is milked), it cannot be preserved in the pot; the tamarind of the tree is eaten by the crocodile. The front is near the house, harken lady of the nature of consciousness (*biāti*); the ear-ring (or the ornament of the ear) is stolen away at mid night (*adharāti*) The father-in-law falls asleep, the daughter-in-law awakes, —the thief has stolen away the ear-ring, where can it be searched? Even in the day-time the daughter-in-law shrieks in fear of the crow,—where does she go at night? Such a Caryā is sung by Kukkurī-pāda, and it has entered into the heart of only one among crores".[3]

Here the *two* refers to the two nerves on the right and the left; the substance milked is the *samvṛtti-bodhicitta* and the pot

[1] See *Hevajra-tantra*, MS. pp. 44(A)-44(B) and *Śrī-guhya-samāja*, edited by Dr. B. Bhaṭṭācāry (G.O.S.) See also the note on *Sandhā-bhāṣā* and *Sandhā-vacana* by Dr. P. C. Bagchi in the *Studies in the Tantras*, pp. 27-33.

[2] For the literal meaning and the esoteric significance of this couplet see *Supra* Ch. III.

[3] Song No. 2.

(*piṭa*=*pīṭha*) is the plexus named Maṇipura-cakra in the navel region. The tree (*rukha*=*vṛkṣa*) refers to the body, and the tamarind fruit is the semen in the form of Bodhicitta, and the crocodile (*kumbhīra*) is the yogic process of suspending the vital wind within (*kumbhaka*). *Biāti* and *Bahuḍī* refer to *Avadhutikā*, and the house is the centre of purified bliss; the ear-ornament (*kāneṭa*) is the principle of defilement, and the thief is *sahajānanda*, and the mid-night is the yoga-stage just before the state of complete absorption in supreme bliss. The father-in-law (*sasurā*) is the vital wind; day represents the active state (*pravṛtti*) of the mind, night the state of rest (*nivṛtti*) and *Kāmaru* may refer to Kāma-rūpa, or the Mahāsukha-cakra, Kāma-rūpa being the greatest centre of the Tāntrikas.

The most remarkable fact is that this use of the enigmatic style has its unbroken history in the modern Indian literatures from the time of the Caryā-padas down to the present time. Esoteric poets of all periods have used such extremely epigrammatic and enigmatic style in giving expression to their religious doctrines. There is a song of Ḍheṇḍhaṇa pāda,—

> *ṭālata mora ghara nāhī paḍiveśī* ।
> *hāḍita bhāta nāhi niti āveśī* ॥
> *beṅga saṁsāra baḍhila jāa* ।[1]
> *duhila dudhu ki beṇṭe samāa* ॥
> *balada biāala gaviā bāṁjhe* ।
> *piṭā duhiai e tinā sāṁjhe* ॥
> *jo so budhī sodha nibudhī* ।
> *jo so cora soi sādhī* ॥
> *niti niti siālā siha sama jujhaa* ।
> *ḍheṇḍhaṇa pāera gīta birale bujhaa* ॥

Literally the song means:—"On the height is situated my house, no neighbours have I; there is no rice in the pot, but they (guests) come every day. The frog-like world goes on increasing (or as Dr. Shahidullah and Dr. Bagchi reconstruct the line,—The serpent is being chased by the frog); does the milked milk enter into the teats again? The ox has given

[1] *beṇgasa sāpa baḍhila jāa*—Bagchi.

birth but barren is the cow; it is milked in the pot thrice a day. He who is wise is purely a fool, who is the thief is honest. The fox fights with the lion every day,—understand this song of Ḍheṇḍhaṇa-pā in secret."[1] With this poem we may compare a poem of Kabīr, which is not only substantially the same, but agrees with the above poem line by line.

kaisaiṁ nagari karauṁ kuṭavāri ।
cañcala puriṣa bicaṣana nārī ॥
bail biyā gāi bhai bāṁjh ।
bachrā duhai tīnyuṁ sāṁjh ॥
makaḍo dhari māṣī chachi hārī ।
mās pasārī cilha rakhavārī ॥
mūsā khevaṭ nāv bilaiyā ।
miṁḍhak sovai sāpa paharaiyā ॥
nita uṭhi syāl syaṁghasuṁ jhujhai ।
kahai kabīr koi biralā bujhāi ॥[2]

"How can I guard the city where fickle is the man and clever is the woman? The bull has given birth and barren is the cow; the calf is milked thrice a day. The spider has caught hold of the fly which struggles and is defeated; the kite has been kept guard for meat. The mouse is the boatman, the cat is the boat, and the frog is sleeping under the protection of the serpent. Everyday does the fox fight with the lion; says Kabīr, some understand it in secret."

Enigmatic poems of this nature are found abundantly in the works of Kabīr and these are generally known as the *Ulṭāwāṁsī*. These enigmas are generally employed by Kabīr to emphasise the absurdity that *Māyā* or the principle of illusion should so completely overpower the *Jīva*, who has his support in Brahman and who lives in Brahman in his ultimate nature; it is a pity that *Jīva* should become completely oblivious of his true nature and of his divine strength and act as a toy in the hands of *Māyā*. We are giving below a few more specimens of the enigmatic poems of Kabīr. In one of his poems Kabīr says,

[1] For the inner significance see *supra* Ch. II.
[2] *Kabīr-granthāvalī*, p. 113.

ek acaṁbbau sunahu tum bhāi ।
dekhata siṁha carāvata gāi ॥
jal kī machulī tarvar vyāī ।
dekhata kutrā lai gai bilāī ॥
talere vaisā ūpar sūlā ।
tiskai peḍ lāge phala phūlā ॥
ghorai cari bhais carāvan jāī ।
bāhar bail goni ghar āī ॥
kahata kabīr yo is pada bujhai ।
rām ramata tisu sav kichu sūjhai ॥[1]

"Hear of some thing strange, O my brother,—I have seen a lion tending a cow. The fish of water have given birth to the young ones upon the tree and while the dog was looking at, the cat took them away. There is something untoward beneath the tree and a trident on the top of it, and such a tree also bears fruits and flowers. Somebody rode on the horse and went to tend the buffalo; outside remained the bullock and the sack returned home. Says Kabīr, he who understands this poem, always dwells in Rāma and everything becomes clear to him".[2]

Again,—"Is there any wise Guru who can understand the Veda reversed? In water fire is burning and the blind is made to see. One frog makes a meal of five serpents and the cow has cut the lion into pieces and devoured it. The kid has devoured the tiger and the deer has eaten up the leopard; the crow has snared the fowler, the quail has triumphed over the hawk. The mouse has eaten up the cat, the jackal has eaten up the dog; this is the primal teaching, says wise Kabīr".[3]

Again it is said in another song,—

O knower of Brahma, swing on.
Heavily, heavily the rain was pouring out, but never a drop of water fell,
To the foot of an ant an elephant was tied: the goat devoured the wolf.

[1] *Kabīr-granthāvalī*, pp. 304-305.
[2] *Cf.* also *Ibid.*, *Padāvālī*, No. 11, pp. 91-92.
[3] *hai koī jagat guru gyāṁnīṁ ulaṭi beda bujhai* । etc.
Ibid., *Padāvalī*, 160, p. 141.

From the midst of the sea came a waterfowl, demanding a spacious house.
The frog and the snake dwell together, and the cat is wedded to the dog.
Ever the lion joins battle with the jackal: here is a wonder that cannot be told.
Doubt as a deer besets the forest of the body: the arrow aims at the archer.
The ocean is burning and consumes the forest: the fish is angling for its prey, etc.[1]

We need not multiply the examples,—for poems of this nature are numerous in Kabīr. This enigmatic style became very popular also among the later Hindi poets. Thus in Sundar-dās we find as many as three different sections devoted entirely to the treatment of these enigmas.[2] It is said there,—"The blind sees the three worlds and the deaf hears various sounds; the man without nose smells the lotus and the dumb supplies much news. The broken-handed man lifts the mountain, the lame dances and makes merry; whoever will be able to make out the meaning of these lines, will be able to enjoy (bliss). The ant has swallowed the elephant, the fox has eaten the lion; fish finds much comfort in fire—but becomes much perturbed in water. The lame man climbs upon the mountain, death is afraid at the sight of the dead; these reverse pranks, O Sundar, are known to those who have realisation. The sea merges itself in the bubble; the mountain merges itself in the mustard seed; it has become a fun in the three worlds that the sun has made every thing dark. It is only a fool, O Sundar, who will be able to bring out the significance of it—this is a puzzle of words. Fish has caught hold of the crane and made a meal of it,—and the mouse has eaten the serpent; the parrot has captured and devoured the cat and all affliction is pacified thereby. The daughter has eaten her mother, the son has eaten the father. Says Sundar, hear O saint, none of them commits sin thereby, etc.[3]

[1] *The Bijak of Kabir* by Ahmad Shah, p. 119.

[2] See *Sundar-granthāvalī* (Rajasthan Research Society edition) Vol. 1, *Atha Pūrabī Bhāṣā Barabai*, pp. 377 *et seq*. *Atha Biparyaya Śabda Ko Aṅg*, *Savaiyā*, Vol. II, pp. (504 *et seq*); *Sāṣī*, *Atha Biparyaya Kau Aṅg*, Vol. II, pp. 787 *et seq*.

[3] *Ibid.*, Vol. II, pp. 508-516. For an attempt at interpreting these lines see the commentary given in the said edition of the work.

Enigmas are found abundantly in the Nāth literature all over India. Gorakh-nāth, in making his Guru Mīna-nāth return to his senses, used this device of enigma and we came across many such enigmas in our previous discussion on the Nāth cult. These enigmas of Gorakh are still now popular as *Gorakh dhāṁdhāṁ* or the puzzles of Gorakh. It is said in the *Gorakṣa-vijaya*—"There is no water in the pond, yet why is it that the banks are over-flooded? There is no egg in the nest, how is it then that the young ones of the birds are flying above? There is no man in the city, but every house has its roof. The blind man is selling and the deaf man buys."[1] In the song of Gopī-candra we find, "Mind is the name of the tree, *Rasika* (he who is endowed with good taste) is the name of the fruit; the frut of the tree remains on the tree, but the stalk falls down. If cut down, the tree grows on, if not cut down it dies out; one fruit of the two trees is conceived by the mother."[2] In the same text we find old Śiva worshipping a boat with a *ulṭā mantra* or an enigmatic verse of a funny nature.[3] Peculiar songs of this nature, often rousing the sense of the ludicrous, in the form of an address of Gorakh-nāth to his Guru Mīna-nāth, are still prevalent in the rural areas of Bengal. The writer himself has heard many such stray songs in his native district of Bakergunj. The writer cannot check the temptation of presenting such a song collected by Maulavi Abdul Karim in the introduction to the *Gorakṣa-vijaya* edited by him.

[1] *Gorakṣa-vijaya*, pp. 137-38.
Cf. also:— *śrāvaṇ māsate nadī maiddhete ujāe* l
āuṭ hātera naukā bāhī chāli berāe ||
udur pāile śuā bilāi dhari khāe l
gagana maṇḍole bāsā korila suyāe || etc.
Ibid., p. 144.

[2] *Gopī-candrer Gān*, Vol. I, p. 78.

[3] *madha gaṅgā-jal dila naukāe chiṭiyā* l
naukā puje buḍā śiv ulṭā mantra kaiyā ||
āgun kyāman nāle brammā kyāman nāle l
brammā beṭā maila jāre pāni maila tiyāse ||
ḍheki ānlām dhān bānite seo pālāila āse l
kulā ānlām dhān jhāḍite pāḍiyā kilāy tuse ||
eluyā-bāḍi beluyā-bāḍi kāsiyā-bāḍi di ghāṭā l
śiyālak dekhi jānawyār pālāy hāsiyā maila pāṭhā ||
āge uwjila choṭa bhāi pāche uwajila dādā l
kemo bemo kariyā māo uwajila pācheta uwaja bābā || etc.
Ibid., Vol. I, p. 124.

"O my preceptor, all the laws do I find topsy-turvy; rice is dried in the bottom of the pond and is served beneath the granary. O my preceptor, on the mango-tree lie the young ones of the *Śaula* fish and they catch hold of the crane and devour it up, and at the sight of it small ants are marching forward with a machine of bamboo (to catch fish). O my preceptor, with five annas have I brought the boat, nine pice is the price of the nail; in the arum forest did I keep it,—but a frog has swallowed up the seat of the helmsman. O my preceptor, one thing have I heard in the ghat of *Tripini*—a dead man is cooking food in the womb of a living man. O my preceptor, in the forest of *Erali* live the young ones of the *Karali* and the tigress went for them; and a flat frog is waiting to prey upon the tigress."[1]

It is indeed very difficult to attempt a thorough interpretation of these lines; but the most important point is the assemblage of all sorts of absurd epigrams, which are all put together to emphasise the absurdity that even a great self-controlled yogin like Mīna-nāth should fall a prey in the hands of the women of Kadalī. Again there are lines in these enigmas, which, though shrouded in obscurity, point to a deeper significance behind. Thus there is the line in the above poem that a dead man is cooking food in the womb of a living man in the ghat of *Tripini*. *Tripini* here stands for *Tri-veṇī* or the place where the three important rivers *Gaṅgā*, *Yamunā* and *Sarasvatī*, and in Tāntricism the three nerves, *viz*., *Iḍā*, *Piṅgalā* and *Suṣumṇā*, meet together. When a yogin can control his nerves and can make the two side-nerves *Iḍā* and *Piṅgalā* function conjointly with the middle nerve, he becomes dead so far as the world of physical existence is concerned and that dead man within the physically living man matures from within all the virtues of the spiritual life.

Almost a similar song is found in the *Dharma-maṅgala* of Sahadev Cakravartī and here also the song is addressed by Gorakh-nāth to his Guru Mīna-nāth. We are giving here rather a free translation of the verse:—

O my Guru, I beg to submit to your lotus-feet this (strange) fact, the sea has overflown with the milk of worms

[1] *Guru mīna-nāth re ulṭā ulṭā dhārā*, etc.

and the mountains are floating away. O my Guru, try to understand it on your own merit,—dry was the tree, but it has shot forth foliages and stone has been pierced through by the worm. See here, the tigress is coming,—through the lids of his eyes man covers the tigress with (different) skin and then tames her in every house. Quarrel has broken out between the *Śila* and the *Noḍā*,[1] and the mustard seed is intervening as the mediator,—the pumpkin gourd on the thatched roof is rolling down, and the herb *Puṁi* dies of laughing. An absurd tale it is,—the completely barren one has given birth, and the child wants milk of the dove. With much care have I tied the boat and the crab held the rope; by the kick of the mosquito the mountain is broken and the ant goes on laughing. First the boat flies above, and then it burns and dust is raised every now and then; there is not a drop of water to wet the mustard seed, but the peaks of the temples are drowned. I have yoked the tiger and the bullock together and the monkey has become the plough-man; the crocodile of water has removed the weeds and the mouse has sown paddy-seed. The young ones of the *Śaula* fish are on the palm-tree, and they are catching hold of the hawks and devouring them; *Kai* fish revels in the water of the sea, and the lame one runs with a machine of bamboo (to catch them). I have placed sentinels in the mid-sea, *Sajaki* (?) are flocking in abundance; the buffalo and rhinoceros die of fear and hinds flee away in lacs. The lamp is extinguished when there is oil in it,—and the city becomes dark; Sahadev meditates on Kālu Rāy and sings this clever description of the body."[2]

[1] *Śila* is the slab of stone on which spice is rubbed and prepared and *Noḍā* is the rod-like stone with which spice is rubbed and prepared.

[2] *Vide*, B.S.P.P., B.S. 1304.

Cf. The German poem *I came A-riding* by Reinmar Von Eweter:—

I came a-riding in a far countrie
On a blue goose, and stragne, things I did see.
There was a crow and hawk that in a brook
Fished many a swine; a falcon by a hear
Was hunted in the upper realms of air;
Midges were playing chess; and I did look
Upon a stag that span the fine silk thread;
A wolf was shepherd of the lambs that fed
In the willow tops; a cock caught in a trap
Three giants; and a coney trained a hound;
A crab raced with a dove and won a pound.
If this is true, an ass can sew a cap.

Translated by Jethro Bithell.

Songs of the type, which are still now to be heard in the rural areas, particularly of Bengal, are generally known as the songs of the *Ulṭā Bāul*. Mr. Asutosh Chaudhuri of Chittagong collected some of these songs from the district of Tippera and published them in the journal *Pāñca-janya*.[1] We are giving below the translation of two of these songs as specimen:—"Under the depth of sixty cubits of water is burning the straw of *Āman* rice, and the bird *Pheccuyā* is picking it up with its beak and eating fried paddy; the tiger and the wild buffalo are yoked together to the plough and the ant has pressed the ladder. One day, O brother, I went to the bank of the river *Meghnā*, and found the cat breaking the mast of the ship by scratching. I went to the fields of the North and found the crane ploughing; and the *Tyāṁrā* fish has swallowed up a very big *Boyāl*. When the boys of this house go to that house, dead rats serve them with blows of fists in the path; etc."[2] Again,—"....In the marsh lives the kite and the dog lives in the tree; all the kites are devoured by the fish of the river *Rāma-dariyā*. In the northern marshes grass the hawks and the cows are flying in the air; the father was born on the day of the mother's marriage and the son was born two days after. The frog is dancing on the head of the serpent and the mongoose is laughing on; the buffalo is smoking the tobacco pipe, but small leeches are coughing. At the sight of the spade the black-smith flees away, the pond cuts the workman; the yoke has been placed on the shoulder of the ploughman and the cow is walking behind. Stone floats on the sea but the lightest of woods sinks down; water of the ebb-tide goes against the current,—and boats are steering men; etc."[3]

The enigmatic style was a popular technique also with the Vaiṣṇava Sahajiyās and the Bāuls of Bengal. The *rāgātmika padas* (the poems where the doctrines of the love-religion are preached) of Caṇḍī-dās are full of technicalities and riddles. Thus it is said,—"The flower is placed on the fruit and smell remains on it, and on smell are placed these

[1] B.S. 1343, Autumnal Number, pp. (94-96).
[2] *Ibid.*, p. 94.
[3] *Ibid.*, p. 95.

three letters, a riddle it is to understand. The fruit lives above the flower, and on that remains the wave; and on the wave remains the wave,—does any one know this secret?"[1] Again,—"Keep your secret love always secret and have your desire satisfied. You must make the frog dance before the serpent and then only are you true lovers. The skilful man, who can wreathe the peak of mount Sumeru with thread and can ensnare the elephant into the web of the spider, becomes eligible for such a secret love."[2]

From what is illustrated above it will be clear that the different modern Indian literatures grew not only under some common religious movements, but they show striking similarity even in form, technique and language. The enigmas of the Caryā songs, of Kabīr and Sudar-dās are substantially of the same nature as are found in the rural areas of Bengal even at the present day. The *Sandhyā-bhāṣā* or the *Sandhā-bhāṣā* thus becomes an all-Indian literary technique for giving expression to esoteric doctrines, and, as we have said, it has an unbroken history for centuries.

phaler upare phuler basati
tāhār upare gandha I *etc.*

Anthology of Caṇḍī-dās (Mr. N. Mukherjee's edition), Song No. 788.

Ibid., Song. No. 797.

Cf. also:— *kamal upare jaler basati*
tāhate basila tārā I
tāhāder tāhāder rasik mānuṣ
parāṇe hāniche hārā ||
sumeru upare bhramar pasila
bhramar dhari(che) phul I
tāhāder tāhāder rasik mānuṣ
harāyeche jāti kul ||
hariṇ dekhiyā beyādh palāy
kamal gela se bhṛṅga I
yamer bhitare ālaser basati
rāhute gilila candra ||
sumeru upare bhramar pasila
e-kathā bujhile ke I
caṇḍī-dās kahe rasik haile
bujhite pārive se ||

Ibid., Song No. 803.

It may be noticed that Vidyāpati also composed a number of *prahelikā* songs. See Songs of Vidyāpati, edited by Prof. K. N. Mitter, M.A., and Prof. Biman Behari Majumdar, M.A., Ph.D.

INDEX

The words are arranged in order of the English alphabet. English words are given in Roman with a capital. Non-English general names and words are given in Roman with a capital and diacritical marks. Names of books are in italics with a capital. Technical non-English words are in small italics.